THE PSYCHOLOGY OF PLANNING IN ORGANIZATIONS

This book examines planning as the critical influence on performance at work and in organizations. Bridging theory and practice, it unites cutting-edge research findings from cognitive science, social psychology, industrial and organizational psychology, strategic management, and entrepreneurship, and describes the practical applications of these research findings for practitioners interested in improving planning performance in organizations.

Michael D. Mumford is the George Lynn Cross Distinguished Research Professor and Program Director for the Department of Psychology at the University of Oklahoma, USA.

Michael Frese is Professor at the Business School of the National University of Singapore and jointly at Leuphana University of Lueneburg, Germany.

Organization and Management

Series Editors: Arthur P. Brief, *University of Utah*, Kimberly D. Elsbach, *University of California, Davis*, Michael Frese, *University of Lueneburg* and *National University of Singapore*

THE PSYCHOLOGY OF PLANNING IN ORGANIZATIONS

Research and Applications

Edited by Michael D. Mumford and Michael Frese

Routledge
Taylor & Francis Group

NEW YORK AND LONDON

First published 2015
by Routledge
711 Third Avenue, New York, NY 10017

and by Routledge
27 Church Road, Hove, East Sussex BN3 2FA

Routledge is an imprint of the Taylor & Francis Group, an informa business

© 2015 Taylor & Francis

Library of Congress Cataloging in Publication data
    The psychology of planning in organizations : research and applications / edited by Michael Frese and Michael D. Mumford.
        pages   cm. – (Series in organization and management)
    Includes bibliographical references and index.
    1. Business planning.   2. Organizational behavior. 3.   Management–Psychological aspects.   4. Organizational sociology.   I. Frese, Michael, 1949-   II. Mumford, Michael D.
    HD30.28.P795 2015
    658.4'012019–dc23
    2014047645

ISBN: 978-1-848-72604-8 (hbk)
ISBN: 978-1-138-80047-2 (pbk)
ISBN: 978-0-203-10589-4 (ebk)

Typeset in Bembo
by Out of House Publishing

Printed and bound in the United States of America by Publishers Graphics, LLC on sustainably sourced paper.

CONTENTS

ABOUT THE CONTRIBUTORS

Alana S. Arshoff is a doctoral student at the Centre for Industrial Relations and Human Resources at the University of Toronto. Her research interests include goal setting, leadership, and training and development. She completed her undergraduate degree in business at the University of Western Ontario and her Master's degree in IR and HR at the University of Toronto.

Roger Buehler is Professor of Psychology at Wilfrid Laurier University. He obtained his doctoral degree from the University of Waterloo in 1991 in the field of social psychology. His research focuses on the psychology of prediction, motivation, and goal pursuit. His work on the planning fallacy over the past two decades is widely cited in academic journals, textbooks, and media reports.

Laura B. Cardinal is Professor of Strategic Management at the C.T. Bauer College of Business at the University of Houston. She earned her Ph.D. from the University of Texas at Austin. Her expertise is principally in the area of implementation of innovation goals and strategies and includes the effects of organizational control and coordination on innovation, R&D, and new product development teams. Laura sits on the Board of Directors of the Strategic Management Society, is an Associate Editor of the *Academy of Management Annals*, and serves on the editorial boards of the *Academy of Management Journal, Organization Science, Strategic Management Journal, Academy of Management Discoveries*, and *Journal of Organization Design*. Prior service includes roles as Director of the Burkenroad Institute for the Study of Ethics and Leadership at Tulane University, Chair for the Competitive Strategy Interest Group of the Strategic Management Society, and Division Chair for the Technology and Innovation Management Division of the Academy of Management. She is a National Science Foundation grant recipient and has published in journals such as *Strategic Management Journal, Organization Science, Academy of Management Journal*, and *Journal of Accounting and Economics*. Her most recent published book is entitled *Organizational Control*.

Dorothy R. Carter is a Ph.D. student in the Organizational Psychology Program at the Georgia Institute of Technology and a research assistant in the Developing Effective Leaders, Teams, and Alliances (DELTA) laboratory. Her research focuses on understanding leadership and effective collaboration in complex, multidisciplinary, and virtually mediated collectives. She has served as a graduate student lead on several large-scale research projects funded through the National Science

Foundation and has multiple publications, conference proceedings, and book chapters on topics including leadership, social network analysis, teams, and multi-team systems. Dorothy holds a B.S. in Psychology with a minor in Business Management from Wright State University and an M.S. in Organizational Psychology from Georgia Tech.

Shane Connelly is a Professor in the Department of Psychology at the University of Oklahoma. She earned her Ph.D. in I/O Psychology from George Mason University. She has published numerous articles on leadership, emotions, and integrity and serves on the editorial boards of *Leadership Quarterly* and *Human Performance*. She is a member of the American Psychological Association (Divisions 5, and 14), the American Psychological Society, the Academy of Management, and the Society for Industrial and Organizational Psychology. Her research addresses issues such as how emotions and emotion processes influence the attitudes and performance of leaders and followers, skills contributing to leader performance over time, and how case-based training can be structured to develop leaders effectively. She is also interested in ethical decision making in organizations, particularly how to assess and train research ethics. Recently, she has examined the relationship of emotion and communication strategies to attitudes within ideologically driven discussions on the internet. Much of her research integrates novel and traditional approaches to assessing individual differences. She is a founding faculty member and serves on the governing board and executive committee of the Center for Applied Social Research.

Matthew P. Crayne is a doctoral student in the Industrial and Organizational Psychology area at Penn State University. He received a Bachelor's degree in Psychology from the University of Connecticut, where he also worked as a consultant for Leadership Research Institute, Inc. Mr Crayne's current research interests include ambition in the workplace, leadership, and selecting for executive positions.

Leslie A. DeChurch is Associate Professor of Organizational Psychology at the Georgia Institute of Technology. Her research interests include leadership and teamwork in organizations. Her research has appeared in top journals including the *Journal of Applied Psychology*, *Journal of Management*, *Leadership Quarterly*, *Journal of Applied Social Psychology*, *Group Dynamics: Theory, Research, & Practice*, *Small Group Research*, *Educational and Psychological Measurement*, and the *International Journal of Conflict Management*, and she serves on the editorial boards of the *Journal of Applied Psychology*, *Small Group Research*, *Journal of Occupational and Organizational Psychology*, and the *Journal of Business and Psychology*. Her research has been funded by the National Science Foundation and the Army Research on the Social and Behavioral Sciences. In 2011, DeChurch was awarded an NSF CAREER award to study leadership in virtual organizations, and in 2012 she was awarded an NSF Research Coordination Network project (co-PI with Noshir Contractor) to leverage big data for the advancement of computational social science. She is currently working in the areas of leadership networks and multi-team systems, and teaching Social Psychology and Social Networks. Professor DeChurch earned a B.S. in Environmental Science from the University of Miami, Coral Gables, and an M.S. and Ph.D. in Industrial and Organizational Psychology from Florida International University in Miami.

Wendelien van Eerde is an Associate Professor of Organizational Behavior at the University of Amsterdam (Amsterdam Business School). She received her Ph.D. in Organizational Psychology at the University of Amsterdam, and was an Assistant Professor at the Eindhoven University of Technology. Her research focuses on work motivation, with a specific focus on time-related issues such as planning, procrastination, and time management in work settings.

Anna M. Engel is a research associate at the Lower Saxony Institute for Early Education and Development in Osnabrück, Germany. She has a Master's degree in Psychology, with a focus on personal development, and is currently pursuing her doctoral degree in the Department of Work and Organizational Psychology, specializing in cross-cultural business psychology, with Dr Karsten Müller at Osnabrück University. She has managed the Intercultural Mentoring Program for international students at the university since 2011. In addition, she works at IMPART GmbH (www.impart.de), a start-up connected to the university that offers personality tests developed at the Department of Personality Psychology to counselors and coaches.

Dawn L. Eubanks is an Associate Professor at Warwick Business School at University of Warwick, UK. Dawn's research interests are primarily in the areas of leadership and innovation, with particular interest in destructive leadership. Dawn's current focus is on leader errors and follower reactions to errors. Innovation research includes a focus upon how to foster this characteristic across a range of contexts (e.g. teams, virtually). Dawn is a member of the editorial board for *Leadership Quarterly* and *Journal of Occupational and Organizational Psychology*. Dawn has been successful earning grants in excess of £100,000 from government funding bodies such as the Engineering and Physical Sciences Research Council (EPSRC).

Michael Frese has a joint appointment as full professor at NUS Business School and at University of Lueneburg. His research is on the psychology of entrepreneurship, including innovation, personal initiative, training entrepreneurs (often focused on transitional economies), and learning from errors and experience. Guiding concepts are evidence-based entrepreneurship, including randomized controlled experiments and action regulation theory. He has published more than 200 book chapters and more than 125 articles in journals such as *Academy of Management Journal*, *Journal of Applied Psychology*, *Personnel Psychology*, and *Journal of Business Venturing* as well as *Entrepreneurship: Theory and Practice* and is highly cited (more than 16,000 Google Scholar citations). He was an editor of *Applied Psychology: An International Review* and is an area editor of *Journal of Business Venturing*.

Carter Gibson is a doctoral student in the industrial and organizational psychology program at the University of Oklahoma. His research interests include creativity, ethics, and leadership.

Michael M. Gielnik currently works at the Institute of Strategic HR Management in the Leuphana University of Lueneburg, Germany. He studied psychology at the University of Giessen, Germany, and received his Ph.D. from the Leuphana University of Lueneburg. His research interests are entrepreneurship, particularly entrepreneurial learning and training, the entrepreneurial process, and aging in entrepreneurship. He has taken a special interest in entrepreneurship in the developing context. He has conducted several research and practice projects on entrepreneurship in different countries in sub-Saharan Africa and Asia.

Vincent Giorgini is a doctoral student in the industrial and organizational psychology program at the University of Oklahoma. His research interests include planning, leadership, and creativity.

Peter M. Gollwitzer is Professor of Psychology at the University of Konstanz and New York University. His research focuses on the willful pursuit of goals. He is a Fellow of the Association of Psychological Science, the American Psychological Association, and the Academia Europaea; he received the Max Planck Research Award (1990) and the TRANSCOOP Award (1994) for international collaboration. He has co-edited three volumes on action control: *The Psychology* *of Action: Linking Cognition and Motivation to Behavior* (Gollwitzer and Bargh, 1996), *Oxford Handbook of Human Action* (Morsella, Bargh, and Gollwitzer, 2009), and *Acting Intentionally and Its Limits: Individuals, Groups, Institutions. Interdisciplinary Approaches* (Seebaß, Schmitz, and Gollwitzer, 2013). He regularly publishes his work in high-ranking journals in social psychology and related fields such as education, health psychology, cognitive psychology and economics.

Dale Griffin is Professor of Marketing and Behavioral Sciences at the Sauder School of Business, University of British Columbia. He received his doctoral degree from Stanford University in 1988 in the fields of social and cognitive psychology. His research interests include decision making, forecasting, and risk perception in consumers, managers, and the financial markets. He is the co-editor of the book *Judgment Under Uncertainty: Heuristics and Biases*, which collects the second wave of research inspired by Kahneman and Tversky's pioneering study of judgment biases.

Yael Grushka-Cockayne is an Assistant Professor of Business Administration at the Darden School of Business at the University of Virginia. Yael's research and teaching activities focus on decision analysis, forecasting, project management, and behavioral decision making. Before starting her academic career, she worked in San Francisco as a marketing director of an Israeli enterprise resource planning company. As an expert in the areas of project management, she has served as a consultant to international firms in the aerospace and transportation industries. She is the secretary/Treasurer of INFORMS Decision Analysis Society, a UVA Excellence in Diversity fellow and a member of INFORMS and the Project Management Institute (PMI).

Melissa Gutworth is a Ph.D. student in the Industrial and Organizational Psychology program at Penn State University. She has presented research at conferences for both the Society for Industrial and Organizational Society (SIOP) and the Association for Psychological Science (APS). Additionally, she has co-authored a book chapter on the antecedents of workplace deviance. Her research interests include deviance, creativity, and identity threat.

Jenifer M. Hatcher is a graduate student at the University of Central Oklahoma in Public Administration. Jenifer's research focuses on planning and organizational communication. Jenifer also serves as the project manager for the Broncho Business Leadership Program and on the Academic Appeals Board. She received her Bachelor's degree in Business Administration with a minor in Marketing from the University of Central Oklahoma.

Samuel T. Hunter is an Associate Professor in the Industrial and Organizational Psychology area at Penn State University. He has two primary areas of research, innovation management and leadership. Within these areas, Dr Hunter has published more than 50 peer-reviewed articles, books, and book chapters and presented at more than 50 conferences and symposia. His work has appeared in outlets such as the *Journal of Applied Psychology*, *Leadership Quarterly*, and *Human Resource Management Review* and he also serves on multiple editorial boards, including the *Leadership Quarterly* and the *Journal of Creative Behavior*. Dr Hunter has received funding from the National Science Foundation and the Office of Naval Research. Sam has also worked with a number of industry partners, including Google, Lockheed Martin, Del Monte, Oakley, Epic Games, and NATO.

Bradley S. Jayne is a graduate student in the Industrial and Organizational Psychology area at Penn State University. His research areas include innovation and leadership, with a special focus on organizations overcoming the challenges of innovation. Before attending Penn State, Brad earned a B.S. and B.A. from James Madison University in Sociology and History.

Genevieve Johnson is a doctoral candidate in Industrial and Organizational Psychology at the University of Oklahoma, USA. Her current research interests include emotions in the workplace, ethical decision making, leadership, interpersonal and organizational communication, and performance feedback. She has been published in journals including *Human Relations*, *Leadership Quarterly*, and *Journal of Computer-Mediated Communication*.

Markus Kreutzer is Assistant Professor of Strategic Management at the Institute of Management at the University of St. Gallen, Switzerland. He serves as Executive Director of the Excellence Initiative on 'Responsible Corporate Competitiveness' (RoCC), a multidisciplinary initiative at the same university. He earned his Ph.D. from the University of St. Gallen. His research interests are in the area of organizational adaptation and change and the role of activity systems and their interdependency, as well as in the area of organizational control and coordination, focusing on their influence on teams, strategic initiatives, and strategic renewal.

Julius Kuhl is the head of the Department of Personality Psychology at Osnabrück University, Germany, where he has worked since 1986, and a group leader at the Lower Saxony Institute for Early Education and Development in Osnabrück. He was a research fellow at the Max-Planck-Institute for Psychological Research, Munich, from 1982 to 1986 and a visiting scientist at the University of Michigan, Stanford University and the Universidad Nacional Autónoma de México (UNAM). He has explored the functional basis of personality development, and created the widely used Personality Systems Interaction Theory (PSI), integrating modern scientific evidence into motivational, developmental, cognitive, and neuropsychological research. Using PSI and a comprehensive assessment system derived from it (EOS, Development-oriented system diagnostics), Dr Kuhl's research group at the Lower Saxony Institute for Early Education and Development (nifbe: www.nifbe.de) aims to bridge the gap between various abilities and scholastic performance of young children.

Gary P. Latham is the Secretary of State Professor of Organizational Effectiveness in the Rotman School of Management. He is a past president of the Canadian Psychological Association and the Society for Industrial-Organizational Psychology, and President Elect of Work and Organizational Psychology, Division I, of the International Association of Applied Psychological. In addition, he has been awarded the status of fellow in the Academy of Management, American Psychological Association, Association for Psychological Science, Canadian Psychological Association, International Association of Applied Psychology, Society for Industrial-Organizational Psychology, and the Royal Society of Canada. Gary has served on the board of governors for the Centre for Creative Leadership and currently serves on the board of directors for the Society of Human Resources Management.

Kenneth N. McKay is Professor of Management Sciences, University of Waterloo. For three decades, he has been pursuing an interdisciplinary research agenda on planning and scheduling. This has included extensive research on expertise in decision making for rapidly changing situations requiring human judgment, ethnographic field methods for studying positions involving cognitive skill such as planners and schedulers, and predictive risk management heuristics.

Shannon Marlow is a doctoral student in the Industrial/Organizational Psychology program at the University of Central Florida. Ms. Marlow earned a B.S. in Psychology with a minor in Statistics from the University of Central Florida in 2013. She is currently a graduate research assistant at the Institute for Simulation and Training. Her research interests include team training, virtual teams, and performance assessment. She is currently involved in projects investigating aspects of team dynamics, including projects funded by the Army Research Laboratory.

Jessie Martin is a Ph.D. student in Cognitive and Brain Sciences at the Georgia Institute of Technology. Jessie's research interests include memory, aging, and bilingualism and its impact on cognitive processes and perception. Jessie earned a B.A. in Psychology from Furman University in Greenville, SC. Jessie's contribution to this chapter was supported by National Institute of Health Training Grant #5T32AG000175-24.

Jensen T. Mecca is a doctoral student in the Industrial and Organizational Psychology program at the University of Oklahoma. Her research interests include leadership, planning, and creativity.

C. Chet Miller is the C.T. Bauer Professor of Organizational Studies at the University of Houston. He earned his Ph.D. from the University of Texas. His published research has been focused on cognitive diversity within executive teams, the design of strategic decision processes, and the design of management systems. His work has appeared in *Academy of Management Journal, Academy of Management Review, Academy of Management Executive, Organization Science, Strategic Management Journal, Journal of Organizational Behavior,* and *Journal of Behavioral Decision Making.* He is an active member of the Academy of Management and the Strategic Management Society. Over the years, he has served in a number of academic roles including guest editor, associate editor, best paper panelist, program track chair, and interest group representative. General academic honors include a number of research and teaching awards, such as the best paper award from Academy of Management Review and the Melcher Teaching Excellence Award from the University of Houston.

Alejandra C. Montoya is an undergraduate student majoring in Psychology at the Georgia Institute of Technology. Alejandra's interests include teams and cognition. Alejandra's contribution to Chapter 9 was supported by a National Science Foundation Research Experiences for Undergraduates Award (REU supplement to SES-1219469).

Michael D. Mumford is the George Lynn Cross Distinguished Research Professor of Psychology at the University of Oklahoma where he directs the Center for Applied Social Research. He received his doctoral degree from the University of Georgia in 1983 in the fields of industrial and organizational psychology and psychometrics. Dr Mumford is a fellow of the American Psychological Association (Divisions 3, 5, 10, 14), the Society for Industrial and Organizational Psychology, and the American Psychological Society. He has written more than 300 peer-reviewed articles on creativity, innovation, leadership, ethics, and planning. He has served as senior editor of *Leadership Quarterly,* and he sits on the editorial board of the *Creativity Research Journal,* the *Journal of Creative Behavior, IEEE Transactions on Engineering Management,* and *Ethics and Behavior.* Dr Mumford has served as principal investigator of grants totaling more than $30 million from the National Science Foundation, the National Institutes of Health, the Department of Defense, the Department of Labor, and the Department of State. He is recipient of the Society for Industrial and Organizational Psychology's M. Scott Myers Award for Applied Research in the Workplace.

Holly K. Osburn is an Assistant Professor of Management at the University of Central Oklahoma. She received both her M.S. and Ph.D. in Industrial and Organizational Psychology from the University of Oklahoma. Her primary areas of interest include leadership, planning, creativity, and business ethics. Her research can be found in the *Journal of Creative Behavior,* the *Journal of Applied Behavioral Science, Creativity Research Journal* and a recent chapter in *The Handbook of Organizational*

Creativity. In addition, she has presented numerous papers at national conferences, including the Society for Industrial and Organizational Psychology and the Association for Psychological Science. Dr Osburn teaches courses in Management, Organizational Behavior, and Leadership. In addition to her academic interests and pursuits, she has worked as a consultant in both the government and private sectors, doing job analysis, skills assessments, conflict management, and leadership coaching.

Daniel Read is a Professor of Behavioral Science at Warwick Business School, UK. Daniel has held positions at Carnegie Mellon University, University of Illinois: Urbana Champaign, University of Leeds, and London School of Economics, as well as visiting positions at Rotterdam University, INSEAD and Yale School of Management. Daniel's research focuses on a number of issues in behavioral economics. He has studied variety seeking (how consumers choose to diversify consumption), intertemporal choice (how people trade off current and future consumption), and decision making under risk. He has written many papers on theoretical issues in decision making. In addition to his academic work, he has been a consultant for many UK government bodies, including the Financial Services Authority, the Department for Constitutional Affairs and the Department for Food, Environment and Rural Affairs. Daniel's work has appeared in *Management Science*, *Psychological Review*, *Organizational Behavior & Human Decision Processes*, *Journal of Behavioral Decision Making*, *Journal of Risk and Uncertainty*, *Risk Analysis*, *Journal of Experimental Psychology*, and *Experimental Economics*.

Eduardo Salas is Pegasus & Trustee Chair Professor of Psychology at the University of Central Florida, where he also holds an appointment as Program Director for the Human Systems Integration Research Department at the Institute for Simulation and Training. Previously, he was the Director of UCF's Applied Experimental & Human Factors Ph.D. Program. Before joining IST, he was a senior research psychologist and Head of the Training Technology Development Branch of NAWC-TSD for 15 years. During this period, Dr Salas served as a principal investigator for numerous R&D programs, including TADMUS, that focused on teamwork, team training, decision making under stress and performance assessment. Dr Salas has co-authored over 450 journal articles and book chapters and has co-edited 25 books. His expertise includes assisting organizations in how to foster teamwork, design and implement team training strategies, facilitate training effectiveness, manage decision making under stress, and develop performance measurement tools. Dr Salas is a past president of the Society for Industrial/Organizational Psychology, Fellow of the American Psychological Association, Human Factors and Ergonomics Society, and a recipient of the Meritorious Civil Service Award from the Department of the Navy. He is also the recipient of the 2012 Society for Human Resource Management Losey Lifetime Achievement Award, and the 2012 Joseph E. McGrath Award for Lifetime Achievement.

Nastassia Savage is a Master's student in the Industrial/Organizational Psychology program at the University of Central Florida. Ms. Savage earned a B.A. in Psychology with a minor in Sociology from the University of Central Florida in 2011. She is currently a graduate research assistant at the Institute for Simulation and Training, where her research interests include team training, diversity, and organizational health. She is currently involved in projects investigating aspects of team dynamics, including projects funded by the National Science Foundation and Army Research Laboratory.

Miriam S. Stark is currently working on her Ph.D. at the Institute for Strategic HR Management and the Institute of Corporate Development at the Leuphana University of Lueneburg under the supervision of Prof. Frese. She studied business psychology at the Fresenius University of Applied Sciences in Cologne. Her research interests are entrepreneurship, particularly well-being and personal initiative, as well as sustainability in entrepreneurship. She has also taken a special interest in psychological research in the developing context. She has conducted several research and practice projects in East Africa and in Sri Lanka.

Logan Steele is a doctoral student in the Industrial and Organizational Psychology program at the University of Oklahoma. His research interests include leadership, creativity, and planning.

Candace TenBrink is a doctoral student at the C.T. Bauer College of Business at the University of Houston. Her research interests include crisis management and entrepreneurship.

J. Lukas Thürmer is a post-doctoral researcher at the University of Konstanz, where he received his Ph.D. in 2013. His research focuses on self-regulation in groups, and how individual and collective planning enhances performance. Moreover, he investigates the self-regulation of self-defensive behaviors (e.g. creating or claiming an obstacle to one's performance). With the support of the Excellence Initiative, he founded the International Doctorate Network of Collective Self-Regulation, is collaborating with researchers from various European countries and the United States, and organized a workshop on collective self-regulation in summer 2012. He has published articles in several academic journals, including the *Journal of Behavioral Decision Making*, the *American Journal of Psychology*, and *Motivation and Emotion*.

Toni Waefler is Professor of Work and Organizational Psychology, University of Applied Sciences and Arts Northwestern Switzerland. In his research he focuses on human factors and sociotechnical system design. Main research domains include industrial planning and scheduling as well as system safety. In both domains, humans are considered crucial resources for system resilience. This is required for coping with uncertainty and risks in order to make the system effective, efficient, and safe.

Logan L. Watts is a doctoral student in the Industrial and Organizational Psychology program at the University of Oklahoma. His research interests include leadership, creativity, and planning.

Wout van Wezel is Assistant Professor Operations Management, University of Groningen, the Netherlands. Through a behavioral operations lens, he employs various methodologies to investigate how planners think, work, coordinate, and cooperate. This includes field research, cognitive task analyses, laboratory experiments, development of decision-support systems, and design of interactive scheduling algorithms.

Frank Wieber is a Research Associate at the University of Konstanz in Germany. He received his Ph.D. in 2006 from the University of Jena, Germany. His research focuses on the question of how self-regulatory strategies impact on the goal attainment of individuals as well as social groups in challenging interpersonal, intra-, and intergroup contexts. He edited a special issue of *Social Psychology* on the limits of intentionality from an interdisciplinary perspective in 2011 and has published articles in high-ranking journals in the field (e.g. *Journal of Personality and Social Psychology*, *Journal of Experimental Social Psychology*, and the *European Journal of Social Psychology*).

Bianca M. Zongrone is a Ph.D. student in Industrial and Organizational Psychology at the University of Nebraska at Omaha. She is also a Research Associate at UNO's Center for Collaboration Science, where her research focuses on virtual teams, human and computer teams, creativity, social network analysis, and problem construction. She received a Master's degree in Human Resource Development at Villanova University and a Bachelor's degree at Rensselaer Polytechnic Institute.

1

ORGANIZATIONAL PLANNING

The Psychology of Performance Introduction

Michael Frese, Michael D. Mumford, and Carter Gibson

Planning is often considered a critical influence on performance at work and the performance of organizations. Beginning in the 1970s, interest in planning diminished among psychologists and students of organizational behavior. Moreover, with the advent of interest in emotions and their survival value and an increasing focus on intuition, planning was often contrasted with these approaches and found to be slow, inefficient, constraining, and wanting. Also, descriptive studies showed that managers plan much less than originally thought (Mintzberg, 1975) and business plans were often a useless endeavor (Honig & Karlsson, 2004), partly because, in the chaotic development of a firm, entrepreneurs needed to engage in a lot of bricolage and improvisation (Baker, Miner, & Eesley, 2003). Moreover, with the advent of the understanding that rationality is limited (bounded rationality) (March & Simon, 1958) and that people are unable to predict future or complex events in technology and economics, it became highly plausible that people make planning errors, leading to the conclusion that planning leads to failures. Indeed, since Kahneman and Tversky introduced the term planning fallacy, planning has often been combined with biases – thus, planning was often conceptualized as useless and biased. Practice has similarly weighed in and suggested that it is often best to make decisions through intuition rather than careful planning, so as not to waste time and other resources, and that strategic planning departments in large companies often just lead to an increase in bureaucracy (compare comments by prominent managers like Jack Welch). All of this has led to a certain degree of skepticism towards planning and less willingness to do research in this area.

While some researchers have discounted the value of planning to organizations, others see planning as highly valuable. Regarding the direct effects of planning, we know that planning structures activities, allows for timely action, and ensures that requisite resources will be available (e.g. Earley & Perry, 1987; Gaerling, 1994; Liberman & Trope, 1998; Smith, Locke, & Barry, 1990). There also exist several indirect effects of planning: it allows for the identification and evaluation of information, it allows people to recognize opportunities, and it allows people to adapt to change (e.g. Jaudas & Gollwitzer, 2004; Patalano & Seifert, 1997). Taken together, these direct and indirect effects suggest that planning can be of significant value to work and organizational performance.

What are plans? There are different definitions within the various research traditions, and we do not have a common definition throughout this volume. These are the most important concepts: (a) steps and sub-steps to achieve goals (Miller, Galanter, & Pribram, 1960); (b) if–then commands (Miller et al., 1960; Newell & Simon, 1975); (c) mental simulation of future actions to achieve a goal (Frese et al., 2007; Hacker, 1998; Mumford, Mecca, & Watts, 2015); (d) thinking through potential actions and operations and potential responses by the environment (Frese et al., 2007); (e) implementation intentions, which automatize cognitive response tendencies for action opportunities (Gollwitzer, 1999); (f) a strategy for accomplishing a task (Wood, Whelan, Sojo, & Wong, 2013); (g) case-based thoughts (Mumford et al., 2015).

We believe that it is time for a revival of research on planning. Because of the important functions of plans, both psychology and organizational behavior research should stop neglecting planning in research. If planning is not considered, there are intellectual and practical difficulties to understanding actions. We therefore thought that it was time to assemble the very disparate and interdisciplinary literature on planning in one book and bring together the knowledge that exists. We approached the best researchers on planning and asked them to contribute their knowledge for this definitive book on planning. This book describes the knowledge we have but also describes areas in which new research ideas and new research are needed.

The renewed interest in planning may be traced to three broader trends. The first of these trends is the development of new cognitive models examining the basic mechanisms underlying plan generation. Second is a new awareness of how planning influences the performance of individuals and teams at work. Third is an emerging concern with the impact of organizational planning processes in organizations. Although these three streams of research have proceeded relatively independently, they do paint a coherent picture of planning. Accordingly, our intent in this book is to present in one volume the key considerations emerging from these streams of research: (1) cognitive science, (2) social psychology, (3) industrial and organizational psychology, (4) strategic management, and (5) entrepreneurship. Each of the chapters examines critical aspects of the planning process, describing critical findings emerging from new research initiatives and delineating the practical implications of these findings from practitioners interested in improving planning performance in organizations.

This book is organized into four major sections. The first section is focused on the cognitive mechanisms and motivational variables that influence planning performance. The second section examines individual- and group-level variables that influence planning performance among people at work. The third section considers organizational-level planning studies on how plans are developed and executed by organizations. The fourth and final section looks at applications of planning research.

The section on the psychology of planning starts out with a chapter on the critical cognitive processes of planning (Mumford et al., 2015). Chapter 2 argues forcefully that planning requires case-based knowledge. This case-based knowledge is organized in a library of cases. Whenever we plan, we scan this library for diagnostic characteristics of the situation and the goals being pursued. These plans rely on forecasts, and Mumford et al. agree with the view that forecasts are usually wrong. However, two important processes help – forecasts become better with knowledge of situations, and backup plans become more frequent and better with expertise. Case-based knowledge is based on good causal models that understand the important parameters of the situation and how these affect potential outcomes. All of these processes are effortful, unstable, and fraught with errors. Indeed, planning is a highly complex endeavor – so it is not surprising that many things can go wrong; expertise helps to improve these processes, and shared mental models, information exchange, leadership, and networking provide resources to get the planning right. The authors also discuss the organizational level along these lines.

Chapter 3 closely shadows these types of argument, although it emphasizes the negative side of planning fallacies (Buehler & Griffin, 2015). Buehler has worked for roughly a quarter of a century on the issues of planning fallacies and provides a terse summary of his expertise in what can go wrong in planning, particularly as concerns the timing of plans. He is able to explain why most projects are not on time and not on budget. He differentiates between task performance time and task completion time. Even when task performance time is adequately forecast, task completion time needs to include both time spent on competing tasks and procrastination (as discussed in Chapter 16 by van Eerde, 2015). Uncertainty of task completion time is therefore higher and this is where most short-term experiments underestimate the effect of the planning fallacy. People tend to fall for the planning fallacy even when they are asked to think with a pessimistic bias. Unfortunately, most people take an inside view of planning – they envision how long it will take to do a certain task (and unfortunately, when groups are required to discuss their plans, this inside view seems to be subject to even greater planning fallacy). An outside view takes a historic view of how long it took to do similar tasks – this outside view seems to reduce the planning fallacy to some extent. Similarly, neutral observers seem to be more realistic in their estimates of time required. They focus less on how well people can fulfill their plans and more on the obstacles that need to be overcome. Buehler finishes his chapter with practical advice for better planning.

Personality influences planning. This is so on the most superficial level – the Big Five personality traits and conscientiousness should be positively related to planning. However, Chapter 4 (Engel & Kuhl, 2015) is less interested in the trait approach to learning but takes a process perspective based on Kuhl's PSI (Personality Systems Interactions) theory. Kuhl was the first to describe personality attributes as being state oriented (that is, slow to put an intention into action) and action oriented (meaning that an intention is put into action immediately) (Kuhl, 1992). In Chapter 4, Engel and Kuhl describe linear and non-linear components of planning. Emotions and motivations are included in their description. When something 'feels good,' a plan may be put into action more easily. However, if something 'does not feel good,' we may actually enhance our development and grow in this process. Engel and Kuhl maintain that planning involves both analytic processing and hierarchical planning as well as holistic processing and flexibility. They liken these processes to differences in the right and left hemisphere of the brain. Their theory then leads to the interesting suggestion that people should switch between analytical and holistic modes of planning, and affect regulation is central to this switching.

Chapter 5 looks at the basic processes of planning through the lens of goal setting (Latham & Arshoff, 2015). Goal setting is the most successful psychological theory of performance used in practice (Locke & Latham, 2002, 2013). Plans are studied as mediators in a goal-setting perspective: hard and specific goals lead to better plans, which in turn lead to higher performance (of course, other issues are also important, such as goal commitment, self-efficacy, and feedback processes). This point cannot be overstated: they are arguing that the effects of goal setting are mediated through planning. Without planning, there would be no effects for goal setting. Plans may also be moderators of goal-setting processes, however, such that those who are prepared with a good plan will profit more from a challenging and specific goal. This is particularly so if one is dealing with a complex task environment.

Chapter 6 addresses the understudied area of emotions and planning in organizations (Connelly & Johnson, 2015). In this chapter, the authors convincingly argue for the importance of the influence of emotions on motivating planning processes and behavior, an interesting point to make considering that planning research languished because planning was assumed to depend so heavily on rationality. Furthermore, Connelly and Johnson consider the topic of planning in a social context, that is, taking into account the social influences of emotions on planning that arise in organizations.

In the second section of this handbook, the focus will turn to the major variables shaping planning performance in the workplace; this emphasis is relative, as much of the research was also discussed on work-related planning in the first section. Work is done within organizations; therefore the focus now turns to include teams and organizations rather than primarily emphasizing the individual level.

Chapter 7, in a way, lies at the transition between the basic processes described in the first section and teamwork; it takes the general concept of implementation intentions and develops it for teams – a highly useful undertaking. Implementation intentions are those intentions that have a simple plan associated with the intention: I do not just know what I want to achieve (the goal intention), I am also thinking about when and where I can put that intention into action (implementation intention). However, in this case, it is not the individual who stands in the foreground but the team (Thürmer, Wiebera, & Gollwitzer, 2015). Thürmer et al. show in Chapter 7 that implementation intentions can be transferred to the team level and functions similarly to how it does at the individual level. In a highly sophisticated analysis, they discuss under which conditions the plan referent needs to be the group and under which conditions it should be the individual. Moreover, they argue that their analysis helps to produce add-on effects of the analysis in Chapter 2 – implementation intentions help to produce actions as a result of goals and plans. Moreover, implementation intentions may be the mechanism by which a specific goal leads to higher performance (compare Chapter 5) – since a specific goal is easily translatable into an if–then plan.

Chapter 8 examines the specific area of planning for innovation (Hunter, Gutworth, Crayne, & Jayne, 2015). This is a central chapter because scholars have often argued that planning does not help with creativity and innovation. However, Hunter et al. maintain that planning is often the starting point for organizational innovation. To deal with the issue of innovation, which always includes surprises because it ventures into the unknown and unpredictable, Hunter et al. introduce the notion of agility. They argue that to conceptualize planning as non-dynamic – as a sort of a checklist that is implemented without thought in a rote fashion – is wrong. Planning is dynamic, thoughtful, incremental, and adaptive to new information. Hunter et al. use the approach by Mumford and co-workers introduced in Chapter 2 and show how this approach can be useful for innovation. They connect the individual approach with an organizational approach, and the concept of agility is used to connect the individual model to an organizational process model of plan refinement and adjustment. Agility is conceptualized as an organizational concept that provides adaptation, adjustments to changing requirements and opportunities. To support their arguments on the importance of agility for organizational innovation, they provide a number of organizational cases.

Chapter 9 approaches some of the problems and remedies of planning in teams (Montoya, Carter, Martin, & DeChurch, 2015). As Montoya et al. so eloquently argue, the wisdom of relying on teams is based on the idea that team members have diverse perspectives on problems and solutions and that they can synthesize their knowledge. Unfortunately, teams tend to have problems sharing unique knowledge and solutions that deviate from the present consensus in the team, thus sometimes negating the potential benefits of teamwork. Montoya et al. discuss the five major team planning problems: the tendency for teams to discuss shared as opposed to unique information, a focus on pre-discussion preferences, participation in discussion is often unevenly distributed, excessive team cohesiveness leads to blind faith and escalation, and teams tend to avoid planning. The chapter then goes on to discuss potential remedies for each one of these team problems. All of these require planning processes.

Chapter 10 emphasizes the importance of a multi-level approach to planning (Savage, Marlow, & Salas, 2015). It ties the individual literature to the team and organizational approaches. It shows that organizational planning has an effect on all levels of the organization – the individual level and the team level – as well as on organizational performance.

The third section of this volume examines planning at the organizational level. This section will begin with Chapter 11 examining the impact of planning on expert performance, considering its effects on task execution, adaptation, learning, and memory (McKay, van Wezel, & Waefler, 2015).

McKay et al. describe what a good plan looks like, decomposing it into assumptions about the future, options based on strengths and weaknesses, feasibility, sub-activities, resources, and effective organizational governance processes. It then goes on to describe what expertise is and how it is related to different aspects of the planning process. For this, the authors develop an organizational planning expertise (OPE) model with four components (task level, planning activities, type of ability and knowledge, level of expertise) that can be thought of as being a contextual structure within which the psychological model of Chapter 2 is integrated.

Chapter 12 concerns itself with biases as constraints on planning performance (Eubanks, Read, & Grushka-Cockayne, 2015). The chapter discusses how individual-level biases play out in organizations and how they constrain organizational planning. They close their chapter by integrating the literature on biases with ideas about effective planning processes, such as case-based reasoning, reference-class forecasting, and wisdom of crowds.

Chapter 13 examines a highly neglected topic – the issue of planning as an important leadership task (Mumford, Giorgini, & Steele, 2015). This chapter starts out by showing how important plans are for leadership performance. Moreover, it presents studies demonstrating that goals (visions) are related to planning not just in the sense that a goal is needed first that is then put into action through a plan, but that visions themselves become better when there are better planning processes involved.

Chapter 14 is a qualitative sequel to the famous meta-analysis on the value of strategic planning and firm success (Miller & Cardinal, 1994). This chapter (Cardinal, Miller, Kreutzer, & TenBrink, 2015) examines conceptual and empirical issues that have appeared since the meta-analysis in 1994. The chapter then carries out a significance count of a much larger database including studies outside North America and Europe and with improved indicators of planning and firm performance. The results are quite clear – strategic planning is a success story, particularly when planning is not too formal but rather more inclusive and involving more organizational members.

While every chapter has talked about the application of planning, the next three chapters are more application oriented. Entrepreneurship is the area in which planning is most often critically discussed. Therefore, it was important to have a detailed discussion of planning in entrepreneurship. Chapter 15 (Gielnik, Frese, & Stark, 2015) discusses this literature. It develops a theory of planning in entrepreneurship by providing a taxonomy of positive and negative functions of planning. Gielnik et al. differentiate between formal and informal planning; informal planning is then differentiated into long-term vs. short-term planning, comprehensiveness of planning, planning for flexibility, and pre-planning vs. planning while acting (the latter being improvisation). In addition, they also discuss the development of milestones as one form of plan. They show that different functions of plans (such as learning, legitimacy, communication, implementation intention, escalation of commitment, stickiness, and predictability and knowledge as prerequisites of planning) all have different effects on these plans. They come to the conclusion that there is no escape from planning; therefore the question cannot be not to plan but rather to develop better adjusted and flexible plans as are needed in an entrepreneurial setting.

In Chapter 16, van Eerde (2015) applies knowledge of planning to the area of procrastination and time management. As she writes, most people believe that planning is often done too much by people who want to be perfect and who, therefore, procrastinate. But this may be a false lay theory – rather a plan would help such people to develop an implementation intention (as described in Chapter 7). Indeed, most people who procrastinate also talk about their fear of failure. Again, that may not be the case, because competence seems to affect the correlation between fear of failure and procrastination. Competent people do something when they are fearful of failure. Another fascinating issue is that the evidence for the efficacy of time management is thin and again is most likely affected by moderators.

Chapter 17 (Osburn, Hatcher, & Zongrone, 2015) provides an overview of how a basic model of planning can contribute to training and development of planning competence. The authors use the planning approach outlined in Chapter 2 as a starting point for their endeavor. Osburn et al. strongly advocate taking a cognitive approach to planning development based on the idea of plans being mental simulations, because a purely behavioral approach (e.g. in the sense of lists) falls short of understanding the important parameters of good planning. Good planning is then exemplified along the lines of environmental scanning, goal identification, case-based reasoning, identification of key causes, constraints, and resources, plan generation, forecasting, and plan refinement and implementation. Interestingly, they argue that planning often leads to better goal setting and not necessarily the other way around.

We think this book provides a fascinating introduction to the complexity of planning (Chapters 2, 3, 4, 17). It may be true that the result of planning (the plan) is often less important than the functionality of the planning process (Chapter 17). Through planning, people often learn more about their own goals and visions, about what information they need, what kind of problems they may encounter, and how they can prepare for them now, than they do from the end-product of the planning process (Chapters 15, 16). Moreover, planning leads to an implementation intention, which produces a higher motivation to persist in implementing one's goals (Chapter 7). One important implication of this is that the more people are involved in the planning process, the greater are the advantages of planning (Chapter 14).

The complexities are high enough on the individual level, but they become greater when higher levels of analysis are introduced (Chapter 10), such as the team or organizational level (Chapters 11, 14).

While pretty much every chapter talks about the inevitability of planning, it also clear that there are a number of biases and difficulties in planning (Chapters 12, 15, 16) – including the perennial planning fallacy (Chapter 2). Interestingly, the conclusion of learning through planning does not translate into the area of learning to provide the timing of plans. The time-estimation problem seems to be alleviated more by NOT being involved in the planning process (Chapter 2). This shows again the complexity of the planning process and, therefore, the necessity of a differentiated approach to the learning and expertise of planning (Chapters 11, 17).

We also believe that this book is eminently practical. As a matter of fact, we think that taking Chapters 2, 3, 7, 9, 15, 16, and 17 together can lead to the development of certain types of plans that can be contrasted with each other in field experiments to find the best planning approach. At the same time, we need to acknowledge that interventions do not always work well, for example, in time management (Chapter 16), which is probably due to the planning fallacy (Chapter 3).

These are, in our opinion, some of the big questions of planning:

- What is the relationship between goal setting and planning?
- What are effective mechanisms of planning and how do goals develop into actions through plans?
- Why is the timing of plans so much more difficult than the process of planning itself?
- What is an optimal plan in what kind of environment, given the many different ways of conceptualizing plans?
- What is the relationships between affect and plans?
- What are the signals, primes, and affective stimulants of plans? And how do subconscious and conscious planning interact?
- How should bottom-up planning and top-down planning interact – what are the models to make this work?
- How do we innovate through planning?

- Could it be that there is a trait of planning (Frese, Stewart, & Hannover, 1987)? And how do traits change planning (Escher et al., 2002)?
- What is the relationship between culture and performance, and is planning–performance affected by culture (Rauch, Frese, & Sonnentag, 2000; Rauch et al., 2013)?
- How do people manage constraints (e.g. time demands, scarce resources) on planning?
- What is the structure of mental models and the nature of expertise that contribute to planning performance?
- How do plans unfold over time, individual, and organizations?

References

Baker, T., Miner, A., & Eesley, D. (2003). Improvising firms: Bricolage, account giving, and improvisational competency in the founding process. *Research Policy*, 32, 255–276.

Buehler, R., & Griffin, D. (2015). The planning fallacy: When plans lead to optimistic forecasts. In M. D. Mumford & M. Frese (Eds.), *The psychology of planning in organizations: Research and applications.* New York: Routledge.

Cardinal, L. B., Miller, C. C., Kreutzer, M., & TenBrink, C. (2015). Strategic planning and firm performance: Towards a better understanding of a controversial relationship. In M. D. Mumford & M. Frese (Eds.), *The psychology of planning in organizations: Research and applications.* New York: Routledge.

Connelly, S., & Johnson, G. (2015). Emotions and planning in organizations. In M. D. Mumford & M. Frese (Eds.), *The psychology of planning in organizations: Research and applications.* New York: Routledge.

Earley, P. C., & Perry, B. C. (1987). Work plan availability and performance: An assessment of task strategy priming on subsequent task completion. *Organizational Behavior and Human Decision Processes*, 39, 279–302.

Engel, A., & Kuhl, J. (2015). Personality and planning: The interplay between linear and holistic processing. In M. D. Mumford & M. Frese (Eds.), *The psychology of planning in organizations: Research and applications.* New York: Routledge.

Escher, S., Grabarkiewicz, R., Frese, M., van Steekelenburg, G., Lauw, M., & Friedrich, C. (2002). The moderator effect of cognitive ability on the relation between planning strategies and business success of small scale business owners in South Africa: A longitudinal study. *Journal of Developmental Entrepreneurship*, 7, 305–318.

Eubanks, D. L., Read, D., & Grushka-Cockayne, Y. (2015). Biases as constraints on planning performance. In M. D. Mumford & M. Frese (Eds.), *The psychology of planning in organizations: Research and applications.* New York: Routledge.

Frese, M., Krauss, S., Keith, N., Escher, S., Grabarkiewicz, R., Luneng, S. T., et al. (2007). Business owners' action planning and its relationship to business success in three African countries. *Journal of Applied Psychology*, 92, 1481–1498.

Frese, M., Stewart, J., & Hannover, B. (1987). Goal-orientation and planfulness: Action styles as personality concepts. *Journal of Personality and Social Psychology*, 52, 1182–1194.

Gaerling, T. (1994). Processing of time constraints on sequence decisions in a planning task. *European Journal of Cognitive Psychology*, 6, 399–416.

Gielnik, M. M., Frese, M., & Stark, M. S. (2015). Planning and entrepreneurship. In M. D. Mumford & M. Frese (Eds.), *The psychology of planning in organizations: Research and applications.* New York: Routledge.

Gollwitzer, P. M. (1999). Implementation intentions: Strong effects of simple plans. *American Psychologist*, 54, 493–503.

Hacker, W. (1998). *Allgemeine Arbeitspsychologie [General work psychology].* Bern: Huber.

Honig, B., & Karlsson, T. (2004). Institutional forces and the written business plan. *Journal of Management*, 30, 29–48.

Hunter, S. T., Gutworth, M., Crayne, M. P., & Jayne, B. S. (2015). Planning for innovation: The critical role of agility. In M. D. Mumford & M. Frese (Eds.), *The psychology of planning in organizations: Research and applications.* New York: Routledge.

Jaudas, A., & Gollwitzer, P. M. (2004). Führen Vorsätze zu Rigidität im Zielstreben?[Do implementation intentions lead to rigidity in goal striving?]. In symposium "Recent developments in research on implementation intentions" at the 46th Meeting of Experimental Psychologists, Giessen, Germany.

Kuhl, J. (1992). A theory of self-regulation: Action vs. state orientation, self-discrimination, and some applications. *Applied Psychology: An International Review*, 41, 97–129.

Latham, G. P., & Arshoff, A. S. (2015). Planning: A mediator in goal setting theory. In M. D. Mumford & M. Frese (Eds.), *The psychology of planning in organizations: Research and applications*. New York: Routledge.

Liberman, N., & Trope, Y. (1998). The role of feasibility and desirability considerations in near and distant future decisions: A test of temporal construal theory. *Journal of Personality and Social Psychology*, 75, 5–18.

Locke, E. A., & Latham, G. P. (2002). Building a practically useful theory of goal setting and task motivation. *American Psychologist*, 57, 705–717.

Locke, E. A., & Latham, G. P. (Eds.). (2013). *New developments in goal setting and task performance.* New York.: Routledge.

McKay, K. N., van Wezel, W., & Waefler, T. (2015). Expertise in organizational planning: Impact on performance. In M. D. Mumford & M. Frese (Eds.), *The psychology of planning in organizations: Research and applications*. New York: Taylor and Francis: Routledge.

March, J., & Simon, H. A. (1958). *Organisations*. New York: Wiley.

Miller, C., Chet., & Cardinal, Laura, B. (1994). Strategic planning and firm performance: A synthesis of more than two decades of research. *Academy of Management Journal*, 37(6), 1649–1665.

Miller, G. A., Galanter, E., & Pribram, K. H. (1960). *Plans and the structure of behavior*. London: Holt.

Mintzberg, H. (1975). The manager's job: Folklore and fact. *Harvard Business Review*, 53, 49–61.

Montoya, A. C., Carter, D. R., Martin, J., & DeChurch, L. A. (2015). The five perils of team planning: Regularities and remedies. In M. D. Mumford & M. Frese (Eds.), *The psychology of planning in organizations: Research and applications*. New York: Routledge.

Mumford, M. D., Giorgini, V., & Steele, L. (2015). Planning by leaders: Factors influencing leader planning performance. In M. D. Mumford & M. Frese (Eds.), *The psychology of planning in organizations: Research and applications*. New York: Routledge.

Mumford, M. D., Mecca, J. T., & Watts, L. I. (2015). Planning processes: Relevant cognitive operations. In M. D. Mumford & M. Frese (Eds.), *The psychology of planning in organizations: Research and applications*. New York: Routledge.

Newell, A., & Simon, H. A. (1975). Computer science as empirical inquiry: symbols and search. *Communications of the ACM*, 19, 113–126.

Osburn, H. K., Hatcher, J. M., & Zongrone, B. M. (2015). Training and development in organizational planning skills. In M. D. Mumford & M. Frese (Eds.), *The psychology of planning in organizations: Research and applications*. New York: Routledge.

Patalano, A. L., & Seifert, C. M. (1997). Opportunistic planning: Being reminded of pending goals. *Cognitive Psychology*, 34, 1–36.

Rauch, A., Frese, M., & Sonnentag, S. (2000). Cultural differences in planning – success relationships: A comparison of small enterprises in Ireland, West Germany, and East Germany. *Journal of Small Business Management*, 38, 28–41.

Rauch, A., Frese, M., Wang, Z.-M., Unger, J., Lozada, M., Kupcha, V., et al. (2013). National culture and cultural orientations of owners affecting the innovation-growth relationship in five countries. *Entrepreneurship & Regional Development: An International Journal*, 25, 732–755.

Savage, N., Marlow, S., & Salas, E. (2015). Examining the multi-level effects of organizational planning on performance. In M. D. Mumford & M. Frese (Eds.), *The psychology of planning in organizations: Research and applications*. New York: Routledge.

Smith, K. G., Locke, E. A., & Barry, D. (1990). Goal setting, planning, and organizational performance: An experimental simulation. *Organizational Behavior and Human Decision Processes*, 46, 118–134.

Thürmer, J. L., Wiebera, F., & Gollwitzer, P. M. (2015). Planning high performance: Can groups and teams benefit from implementation intentions? In M. D. Mumford & M. Frese (Eds.), *The psychology of planning in organizations: Research and applications*. New York: Routledge.

Van Eerde, W. (2015). Time management and procrastination. In M. D. Mumford & M. Frese (Eds.), *The psychology of planning in organizations: Research and applications*. New York: Routledge.

Wood, R. E., Whelan, J., Sojo, V., & Wong, M. (2013). Goals, goal orientations, strategies and performance. In E. A. Locke and G. P. Latham (Eds.), *New developments in goal and task performance* (pp. 90–114). New York: Routledge.

2

PLANNING PROCESSES

Relevant Cognitive Operations

Michael D. Mumford, Jensen T. Mecca, and Logan L. Watts

In organizations, and in life outside work, planning is commonly held to be critical to performance. For example, team performance has been found to depend, in part, on planning (Weldon, Jehn, & Pradhan, 1991). Firms plan their investments and the work flowing from these investments in research and development, personnel, and supply chains (Cascio & Aguinis, 2005; Ettlie, 2008). Leaders plan how they will respond to crises (Mumford, Friedrich, Caughron, & Byrne, 2007). Professionals plan how they will conduct their work (Hershey, Walsh, Read, & Chulef, 1990; Xiao, Milgram, & Doyle, 1997). Although other examples of this sort might be provided, the foregoing seem sufficient to make our basic point. Planning is a powerful force shaping performance in organizations.

Scholars have long recognized the impact, the substantial impact, of planning on performance (Davies, 2003; Delaney, Ericsson, & Knowles, 2004). Accordingly, over the years a number of models of critical cognitive processes contributing to planning have been proposed. Initial models were focused on the structure of planning activities. These models saw planning as a method for mentally simulating the requirements for goal attainment, stressing the efficient organization of action sequences (Miller, Galanter, & Pribram, 1960; McDermott, 1978; Read, 1987). Although these models are plausible when goals and actions for goal attainment are known, they are not adequate when goals are emergent or poorly defined (Patalano & Seifert, 1997).

Accordingly, in recent years, an alternative model of planning processes has been proposed intended to describe the planning outcomes in more complex, ill-defined, settings where goals and actions for goal attainment are not fully known. In these models, planning is viewed as an activity requiring the mental simulation of future actions, where these simulations permit construction of viable goals and actions contributing to goal attainment (Mumford, Schultz, & Van Doorn, 2001). In fact, the evidence accrued in a variety of studies, using a variety of different methods (Hayes-Roth & Hayes-Roth, 1979; Kaller, Rahm, Spreer, Mader, & Unterrainer, 2008; Kiewiet, Jorna, & Wezel, 2005; Noice, 1991), indicates that this mental-simulation model of planning provides a more plausible, and more generalizable, conception of the cognitive processing activities underlying planning performance or the degree to which an individual is able to successfully develop plans. With this point in mind, our intent in the present effort is to examine the key cognitive processing operations that allow people to forecast, and act on, their mental simulations of future events. Subsequently, we will consider the variables shaping effective process execution at the individual, team, and firm levels.

Planning and Knowledge

Knowledge Content

Specification of processing operations must take into account the content, or knowledge, to which these processes are to be applied (Mumford, Medeiros, & Partlow, 2012). Accordingly, the nature of the knowledge employed in planning, or mental simulation, provides a framework for discussion of planning processes. In an initial study of the types of knowledge employed in planning, Nutt (1984) asked managers, a job role where planning is considered critical to performance, what planning techniques they were most likely to apply. He found that, in planning, managers tended to rely on cases reflecting prior experiences of addressing analogous problems. Thus, Nutt's (1984) findings suggest that case-based, or experiential, knowledge may be critical to planning and understanding planning processes.

Somewhat more direct evidence bearing on the use of case-based knowledge in planning has been provided by Berger and Jordan (1992). They asked undergraduates, some 70 in all, to generate plans for requesting a date, persuading someone to change their opinion, ingratiating oneself to a roommate, and becoming a millionaire. A think-aloud procedure was used to examine how people generated plans for each of these tasks. A subsequent content analysis indicated that the knowledge used most frequently in formulating these plans included specific prior episodes of performance, hypothetical episodes, ensemble episodes, and role models – all forms of the knowledge subsumed under the rubric of case-based, or experiential, knowledge (Kolodner, 1997).

Other studies pointing to the importance of case-based knowledge in planning have been con-ducted by Klein, Robertson, and Delton (2011) and Klein, Robertson, Delton, and Lax (2012). In these studies, participants were asked to formulate plans for common life tasks, for example, planning a dinner party, planning a picnic, or planning survival in an arctic expedition. Participants were presented with words (e.g. sugar, carrots, glue, kerosene) that were relevant to these planning tasks. Following an intervening anagram completion task, participants were asked to recall the words presented earlier. It was found that recall of the words was greater when personally famil-iar planning scenarios, a dinner versus arctic survival, were presented. Thus, recall of knowledge in planning appeared to depend on personal familiarity with the task or case-based knowledge.

Not only does case-based knowledge, or experience, contribute to information recall on plan-ning tasks, it appears that available case-based knowledge influences subsequent task perform-ance. Strange and Mumford (2005) asked undergraduates to formulate a vision for leading an experimental secondary school. Visions were evaluated for perceived utility and emotional impact. Notably, prior to preparing these vision statements, speeches to be given to students, parents, and teachers based on their plans, participants were presented with cases differing in effectiveness, and were asked to analyze these cases in different ways. It was found that case content and the strategies participants used in working with these cases influenced the quality of plans and the strength of the resulting vision statement.

Knowledge Structure

Taken as a whole, our foregoing observations indicate that plans are formulated using case-based, or experiential, knowledge when such knowledge is available (Kolodner, 1997). Case-based know-ledge structures, however, are held to be highly complex, with cases including information bear-ing on causes, resources, restrictions, contingencies, goals, actors, affect, and actions (Hammond, 1990). This material, abstracted from prior personal experiences or observational experiences, is held to be organized in a library system in which a case prototype is stored along with major, or common, exceptions to the case prototype. Cases stored in this "library" are indexed with respect to diagnostic characteristics of the situation and the goals being pursued through action (Conway, 1990). When applying cases in problem-solving or planning, diagnostic characteristics and activated goals lead to recall of the case prototype, unless diagnostics indicating the relevance of an exceptional case are evident and salient.

The available evidence indicates that prototype cases are activated and recalled relatively quickly when people encounter relevant cases and situational cues (Barsalou, 1988). However, due to the complexity of the information included in cases, people have difficulty in working with multiple cases in problem-solving and planning. Rather, it appears people employ the most strongly activated case and systematically modify this case in formulating problem solutions or plans (Scott, Lonergan, & Mumford, 2005). Indeed, at times, plans may be formulated simply by acting as if the most strongly activated case held, thereby minimizing investment in planning (Nutt, 1984).

Some support for the relevance of this description of the case-based knowledge structures to planning performance has been proposed in a series of studies by Barrett, Vessey, and Mumford (2011) and Vessey, Barrett, and Mumford (2011). In both of these studies, participants, undergraduates, were asked to formulate plans for addressing issues arising in a marketing firm or an educational institution. Prior to formulating these written plans, which were evaluated by judges for quality, originality, elegance, feasibility, efficiency, and reputation enhancement, participants were provided with instruction in strategies for working with the various types of information embedded in cases, for example, in work with causes that have large effects or work with contingencies that can be controlled. It was found that training in viable strategies for working with case-based knowledge resulted in the production of better plans in these two managerial roles – with the effects of the strategy training being the most pronounced when managers did not experience time pressure but did believe they personally had control of the situation at hand.

Planning Processes

Process Model

If it is granted that plans are formulated using case-based knowledge, a new question comes to the fore. How do people work with case-based knowledge in formulating plans? The ways in which people work with knowledge, or the mental operations employed in working with this knowledge, are what is meant by the term "processes." In recent years, a series of studies by Mumford and colleagues (Mumford, Bedell-Avers, & Hunter, 2008; Mumford et al., 2007; Mumford, Schultz, & Osburn, 2002; Mumford, Schultz, & Van Doorn, 2001) have begun to isolate the key cognitive processes contributing to planning performance. This model is illustrated in Figure 2.1.

The model presented in Figure 2.1 is based on a number of propositions. To begin, although this model presents a rather complex description of planning processes, execution of these processes can be simplified by simply employing activated, available, cases (Hogarth, 1981). More centrally, following the proposition that planning requires the mental simulation of future events, the model assumes the importance of forecasting, with forecasts being refined through evaluation of forecasted outcomes, as indicated in the lower third of the model (Lonergan, Scott, & Mumford, 2004). Commonly, we assume that people's forecasts are inaccurate (Pant & Starbuck, 1990). However, the evidence provided by Dailey and Mumford (2006) indicates that when people have requisite experience and intend to act on their forecasts, the accuracy of forecasts improves substantially. These forecasts, moreover, are used not only to formulate plans but also to identify monitoring markers for plan execution and to formulate backup plans (Xiao et al., 1997). In fact, the evidence accrued by Xiao et al. (1997) indicates that experts not only formulate more backup plans but their backup plans are better organized, and more flexible, and are tied to monitoring markers. The

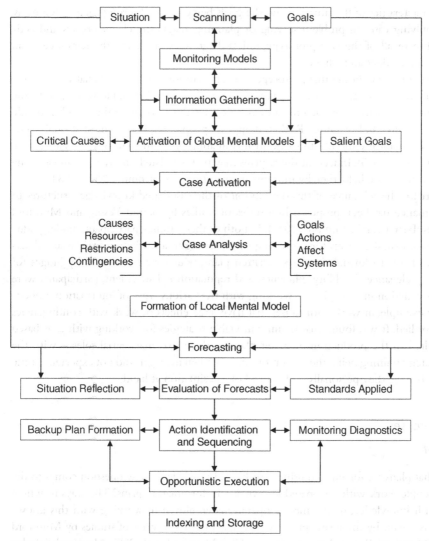

FIGURE 2.1 Planning process model

availability of plans, backup plans, and monitoring markers, in turn, points to a broader feature of this model. More specifically, the model of planning processes assumes that plans are executed in a conscious, opportunistic, fashion, as per the base of the model at hand (Patalano & Seifert, 1997). On the one hand, conscious opportunistic plan execution promotes adaptability through focused processing (Jaudas & Gollwitzer, 2004). On the other hand, focused, conscious processing may lead to the loss of plan-irrelevant information (Masicampo & Baumeister, 2012).

Influences on Forecasting

What should be recognized here, however, is that viable forecasts do not arise in a vacuum. It is typically held that forecasts people produce are based on the mental models they employ for understanding the situation at hand (Rouse & Morris, 1986). Mental models reflect a set of causes where changes in the status of causes, under certain conditions, lead to certain outcomes (Goldvarg &

Johnson-Laird, 2001). As a result, manipulations of causal operatives, or the conditions under which these causal operatives act, provide a basis for forecasting, as indicated by the steps directly preceding forecasting in the model in Figure 2.1. The question broached by these observations, however, pertains to how the local mental models, models which provide a basis for forecasting, are formulated. This model of planning processing holds, in keeping with earlier observations concerning the basis of planning in case-based knowledge (e.g. Berger & Jordan, 1992; Nutt, 1984; Vessey et al., 2011), that the analysis of activated cases to identify causes, resources, restrictions, contingencies, goals, actors, affect, and systems provides the basis for formulation of "local" mental models.

Case Indexing and Activation

As noted earlier, however, case-based knowledge structures are complex and people have difficulty working with multiple cases (Hammond, 1990; Scott et al., 2005). Accordingly, a key proposition underlying development of the planning model is that cases are indexed with respect to global mental models. With activation of a global mental model, prototype cases are activated. Activated case prototypes will also be influenced by situational appraisals and apparent goals operating in the situation, as well as by information gathered with regard to the situation at hand. Activated case prototypes, typically a relatively small number, will be used to identify critical causes and salient goals (Mumford, Schultz, & Van Doorn, 2001). Cross-indexing of cases with respect to causes and goals will give rise to the cases activated for further analysis. Analysis of cases will typically focus on critical case elements, causes, resources, goals, actors, with local mental models being built using this material (Marcy & Mumford, 2010).

In this model of planning processes, it is assumed that activation of general mental models depends on the situation, goals, and information gathering – with the mental model activated also serving as a guide for information gathering, as illustrated by the bidirectional arrows in the portion of the model surrounding the activation of global mental models (Weick, 1995). In fact, plans can often go awry because the wrong general mental model is activated, resulting in inappropriate information gathering – a point made by Weick (1995) in his study of the Mann Gulch disaster. The information gathered, however, will also be influenced by the monitoring models being applied – models that specify key diagnostics. Monitoring models, of course, direct attention to salient aspects of the situation indicating the need to initiate action either to enhance goal attainment or to prevent loss. These monitoring models are noteworthy, however, because they provide a basis for environmental scanning (Ford & Gioia, 2000; Koberg, Uhlenbruck, & Sarason, 1996; Souitaris, 2001). Environmental scanning, in turn, is used both to appraise the situation and to identify goals applying in this situation, with the extensiveness of scanning contributing to planning performance.

The model of planning processes presented above indicates that planning involves a complex, highly complex, set of operations. As a result, it is not surprising that planning skills develop rather slowly (Kliegel, Martin, McDaniel, & Phillips, 2007; Lidstone, Meins, & Fernyhough, 2010). Moreover, the processes specified in this model are held to operate in a dynamic, interactive fashion. Thus, activation of global mental models is held to "feed back" into information gathering, again indicated in Figure 2.1 by the use of bidirectional arrows. Although this model indicates that a complex set of processes underlie planning, planning operations can be readily simplified in this model: if cases are tightly bound to situational cues, only one case is used to build a local mental model, forecasting is limited, and backup plans are not generated (Nutt, 1984). Thus, this process model allows for both complexity and simplicity in planning. Finally, it should be recognized that different planning tasks, and different task domains, may stress and require effective execution of different processes. For example, scanning may be of great importance for research and development planning (Mumford et al., 2008), while forecasting may be of greater importance for leader planning (Marta, Leritz, & Mumford, 2005).

Evidence for Processes

Clearly, a model of the sort described above cannot be tested through any single study. Rather, different studies must be used to examine different processes and their impact on performance. In fact, the evidence accrued in a rather extensive series of studies provides substantial support for this model of planning processes. Accordingly, we will, in the following section, examine the findings emerging from each of these studies.

Forecasting

A critical proposition of this model is that forecasting is necessary for planning (Noice, 1991). Shipman, Byrne, and Mumford (2010) asked undergraduates to assume the role of principal of an experimental secondary school and write a speech based on their plan for leading this school. Speeches were evaluated by judges for quality, originality, elegance, perceived utility, and affective impact. Prior to preparing their speeches, as they worked on their plans, participants received a series of emails from a consulting firm, a nationally recognized firm hired to help them formulate a viable plan, which asked participants to forecast the outcomes of executing their plan in one year. Written responses to this email were evaluated by judges with respect to 21 attributes (e.g. identification of resource changes, forecasting negative outcomes, forecasting positive outcomes, anticipating errors) and judges' ratings of these attributes were factored. It was found that two dimensions, the extensiveness of forecasts and the timeframe over which forecasts occurred, were positively related, 0.20 to 0.40, to the quality, originality, elegance, perceived utility, and emotional impact of the speeches flowing from these leadership plans. Moreover, these forecasting skills proved to be better predictors of performance than variables such as intelligence and divergent thinking. Other studies by Byrne, Shipman, and Mumford (2010) and Dailey and Mumford (2006) have provided evidence confirming the substantial impact of forecasting on planning performance, especially the extensiveness of forecasting. Thus the Shipman et al. (2010) study provides support for one key proposition of this model of planning processes.

Another proposition of this model is that forecasted actions must be evaluated with respect to certain standards. The impact of standards on evaluation of forecasts has been examined in a study by Lonergan et al. (2004). In this study, undergraduates were asked to assume the role of a manager evaluating advertising campaigns of varying quality and originality. After evaluating these plans they were to produce their own advertising campaigns, and these advertising campaign plans were evaluated for quality, originality, and elegance. In evaluation of initial campaigns, however, the description of the advertising firm stressed the use of either innovation standards or operating efficiency standards. It was found that the highest quality, most original, and most elegant plans were obtained when efficiency standards were used to appraise original plans and when innovation standards were used to appraise high-quality plans. This finding is noteworthy not only because it points to the importance of evaluating forecasts but also because it underscores the point that forecast evaluation is an active process contributing to improvement of plans through compensation.

Mental Models

The model of planning processes also holds that local mental models provide a basis for forecasts and plan formation. To examine the impact of local mental models of planning, Mumford et al.

(2012) asked undergraduates to assume the role of manager in a marketing division or principal in an experimental secondary school. In both tasks, participants were asked to provide, following training, an illustration of their local mental models for understanding the task at hand. These local mental models were evaluated with respect to both their objective features (e.g. number of cross-goal linkages, number of moderators, number of contingencies) and their subjective features (e.g. coherence, novelty, structuring principles). Subsequently, evaluations of plans for addressing the marketing and educational problems were correlated with and regressed on the objective and subjective features of the local mental models underlying plan formation. It was found that both objective and subjective attributes of people's local mental models were effective ($r = 0.40$) predictors of the quality, originality, and elegance of the resulting solution plans.

Case-Based Knowledge

Formulation of local mental models, of course, is held to depend on the analysis of case-based knowledge. In fact, this model of the planning process stresses the analysis of causes both in identification of relevant cases and in the formation of local mental models. Marcy and Mumford (2007, 2010) examined the impact of causal analysis on the formation of plans for solving social innovation problems and mental models employed in solving university leadership problems. In both these studies, prior to working on the performance task, undergraduates were asked to complete a set of self-paced instructional modules intended to provide viable strategies for the analysis of causes – for example, think about causes that have large effects, think about causes that influence multiple outcomes, think about causes that have synergistic effects. The findings obtained in the Marcy and Mumford (2007) study indicated that this training in causal analysis strategies resulted in the acquisition of stronger local mental models. Other studies have confirmed these findings with regard to the need for causal analysis (Hester et al., 2012) and indicated that goal analysis might exert similar effects on plan formation (Earley & Perry, 1987).

Information Gathering and Reflection

Of course, analysis of causes and goals is contingent on information gathering. In a study of information gathering, Mumford, Baughman, Supinski, and Maher (1996) asked participants to provide plans for marketing a new product, the 3-D holographic television, which were appraised for quality and originality. Prior to preparing these plans, however, participants, university undergraduates, were asked to work on an information-gathering task. On this task, the time participants spent reviewing different types of information was recorded. It was found that those who spent time gathering information about key facts and anomalies provided stronger plans for marketing this new product. Thus information gathering also appears to contribute to planning performance.

Along somewhat different lines, the model of planning processes under consideration also holds that reflection on the situation at hand contributes to evaluation of forecasts and planning performance. Some evidence bearing on the importance of reflection in planning has been provided in a study by Strange and Mumford (2005). In this study, participants, undergraduates, were asked to formulate plans for leading an experimental secondary school and prepare speeches to be given to students, parents, and teachers describing their plans. These speeches were evaluated for perceived utility and emotional impact. Notably, a manipulation was induced to encourage participants to reflect on their prior personal experience in secondary school. It was found that reflection, specifically self-reflection, contributed to the production of plans of greater utility and emotional impact.

Backup Planning

In a final study, Giorgini and Mumford (in press) examined the impact of backup planning on planning performance. In this study, participants were asked to formulate a plan for solving a marketing problem, where plans were evaluated for quality, originality, and elegance. Prior to preparing these "final" plans, participants were asked to formulate an initial plan and a set of backup plans intended to address problems that might arise in plan execution. These backup plans were evaluated by judges with respect to various attributes that might reflect the viability of the backup plans formulated, such as the number, depth, and flexibility of these plans. It was found that the quality, originality, and elegance of "final" plans was positively related ($r = 0.35$) to these attributes of backup plans. When these findings are considered in light of the findings emerging from other investigations (Xiao et al., 1997), they indicate that backup planning is, in fact, one process involved in plan production.

Of course, the studies cited above have not examined every process specified in this model of planning processes. In this regard, however, it should be noted that other studies have provided some evidence for the relevance of other processes specified in the model. For example, Souitaris (2001) has provided evidence pertaining to the importance of scanning. Other work by Earley and Perry (1987) has provided evidence pertaining to the importance of goal analysis in planning. When these findings are considered in light of the findings noted above and the findings obtained in other studies of planning (Dörner & Schaub, 1994; Isenberg, 1986; Thomas & McDaniel, 1990), it seems reasonable to conclude that sufficient evidence is available to argue for the plausibility of the model of planning processes presented in Figure 2.1.

Performance in Process Execution

Having provided a model of the processing operations underlying plan formation, a new question arises. What variables contribute to more or less effective execution of these processes? One might answer this question with respect to either specific processing operations in plan formation or cross-process influences on planning performance. At this juncture, research has not, for the most part, focused on the requirements for effective execution of specific processes – however desirable such research might be. Rather, the focus has been on variables that influence planning performance in general. However, given that these processes underlie planning performance, this research does provide some clues about the variables influencing effective execution of these processes.

Errors

One key characteristic of the model of planning processes under consideration is that multiple, complex processing operations must be executed in plan performance. As a result, one would expect that errors would arise in process execution. In fact, Dörner and Schaub (1994), in a series of studies using a planning simulation task, found that a variety of errors might arise in execution of these processes including (1) failure to balance contradictory goals, (2) selective, self-confirming, information gathering, (3) oversimplification of causal relationships, (4) failure to take into account non-linear relationships, (5) discounting side effects and negative downstream consequences, (6) failure to monitor lagged outcomes, and (7) premature action when confronted with loss. Other work by Buehler, Griffin, and Ross (1994) and Forsyth and Burt (2008) indicates that errors may arise in planning due to over-optimistic assumptions about the workability or likely success of plans. Thus, a variety of errors may arise in execution of any given process, as well as in the assumptions made about the viability of process products (e.g.

over-optimism) – errors that will influence planning performance. The likely presence of errors in the planning process may have differential impact depending on the level of expertise of individuals engaging in planning, as indicated by Zapf, Brodbeck, Frese, Peters, and Prumper's (1992) finding that experts correct errors more quickly than do novices, indicating that errors may be more influential with regard to novice planning performance. Furthermore, errors may appear more frequently when individuals engaged in planning efforts are fatigued due to compromised executive control, the ability to regulate processes related to goal-directed behavior, and reduced task engagement (van der Linden, Frese, & Meijman, 2003; van der Linden, Frese, & Sonnentag, 2003).

Resources

The model of planning processes presented above, moreover, indicates that a number of resource-intensive processing operations must be executed in plan formation. Accordingly, one would expect that factors limiting resource availability would contribute to diminished planning performance. Thus Gaerling (1994), Hayes-Roth and Hayes-Roth (1979), and Liberman and Trope (1998) have provided evidence indicating that time pressure, both overt pressure and psychological pressure induced by temporal nearness, undermined the complexity and effectiveness of plans by leading people to focus on immediate practical difficulties. In contrast, conditions that lead to increases in available resources, for example motivation and challenging goals, appear to contribute to planning performance (Earley & Perry, 1987; Smith, Locke, & Barry, 1990). Moreover, people appear more likely to invest resources in planning when the environment displays turbulence, the availability of requisite resources is uncertain, and when multiple events must be managed simultaneously (Dean & Sharfman, 1996; Johanssen & Rouse, 1983).

Functional Fixedness

In addition to errors and resources, a third variable that influences planning processes might be referred to as functional fixedness. More specifically, as people invest resources in a plan, a planning process, or the outcomes of the planning process, this investment leads to commitment and unwillingness to consider alternatives. In keeping with this proposition, Masicampo and Baumeister (2011, 2012) found that engagement in a planning task allowed people to suppress the debilitating effects of other activated goals, but, by the same token, it led them to dismiss emergent goals. Accordingly, functional fixedness can be beneficial, leading people to focus on plan formation and execution. However, functional fixedness arising from resource investment in process execution may lead people to discount changing conditions or emergent opportunities. Indeed, this observation is consistent with the findings of Gollwitzer (1999) indicating that people are committed to plans they have formulated once action has been initiated following analysis. Equally, it may also at times act to limit planning performance.

Simplification Strategies

Along with functional fixedness, another key variable that appears to influence planning performance is use of simplification strategies. Thus, Nutt (1984) found that managers preferred to employ simple, accessible or available cases in planning. Similarly, Hershey et al. (1990), in a study of financial planners, found that errors in planning often arose from misapplication of frequently employed mental models, albeit mental models inappropriate to the planning task at hand. The simplification of the demands of planning processes through limited information gathering, restricted forecasting, use of familiar mental models, or reliance on a single available case may at times result in suboptimal plans. In this regard, however, a point made by Hogarth (1981) should be borne in mind. More specifically, simplification of planning processes may also allow for rapid, adaptive plan formation and plan execution.

Task Complexity

Still another variable that has been found to influence the effective execution of planning processes pertains to the difficulty or complexity of the planning task. For example, Berger, Karol, and Jordan (1989) found that as the complexity of planning tasks increased, the accessibility of key plan components, for example, critical causes, decreased along with the effectiveness of plan execution. Similarly, Davies (2003) examined the conditions under which people prepared problem solutions as opposed to organizing in "online" or "concurrent" planning during problem-solving. He found that on more complex problems with more moves, greater move latencies, and more parts, people preferred to engage in concurrent as opposed to pre-planning problem solutions. Thus, in planning on difficult tasks, planning may proceed from general models with opportunistic exploitation of these general models (Hayes-Roth & Hayes-Roth, 1979; Patalano & Seifert, 1997). Although the complexity or difficulty of the task may make planning more difficult, studies by Gardner and Rogoff (1990) and O'Hara and Payne (1998) indicate that investment in planning and effective execution of planning processes increase as the perceived difficulty of the planning task increases.

Instability

Along similar lines, instability also appears to increase people's willingness to invest in planning activities, with plans contributing more to performance on difficult tasks being executed in unstable environments where workload demands are high (Mumford, Schultz, & Van Doorn, 2001). By the same token, instability in the conditions under which planning processes are executed results in uncertainty with regard to the effects of any given action. One implication of this observation is that, under conditions of instability, planning will proceed from more general plans, with sub-plans being formulated to address potential emergent conditions (Løvendahl, 1995). Another implication of this observation, however, is that a greater investment must be made in the execution of many planning processes, for example, forecasting, monitoring, and backup plan formation, when plans must be formulated and executed under unstable conditions.

Our foregoing observations are noteworthy because they suggest that planning contributes to performance on difficult, unstable tasks, but that task difficulty and instability make effective execution of planning processes more difficult. However, under conditions of perceived difficulty and instability, people are more willing to invest in planning. This investment in planning is, of course, most likely to occur when other pressures do not diminish available resources – and, the individual has invested in process execution. At the same time, planning may be undermined by certain errors, for example, insufficient forecasting or routine application of available cases and mental models (Dörner & Schaub, 1994; Hershey et al., 1990). These observations with regard to the demands made on execution of relevant planning processes in turn bring forth a new set of questions bearing on the individual, group, and organizational conditions that make effective execution of planning processes possible.

Performance Conditions

Individual-Level Influences

Expertise

Perhaps the most important, and obvious, implication of this model of planning performance with regard to individual-level influences pertains to the role of expertise (Mumford, Friedrich, Caughron, & Antes, 2009). Not only will expertise provide people with the mental models and cases needed for planning, it should also provide a better-organized set of cases for analysis with respect to both initial appraisals of key causes and goals and analysis of activated cases with respect to case elements such as restrictions, contingencies, resource requirements, actors and actor goals. Moreover, among experts, these cases are likely to be better organized, or indexed, with exceptions to case prototypes being greater in number and more accessible. As a result, one would expect to see greater flexibility in the plans formulated by experts. In addition, there is some evidence to suggest that experts spend more time on local planning, or thinking about the next step in a process rather than considering long-term plans (Sonnentag, 1998).

Not only will expertise exert a pervasive influence on the execution of planning processes, it may also result in shifts in the strategies people employ when executing these processes. This point is illustrated in a study by Delaney, Ericsson, and Knowles (2004), in which undergraduates were asked, in a series of studies, to work on planning tasks where think-aloud data was collected to identify strategies employed as people acquired expertise. It was found that expertise acquisition resulted in better recall of plan-relevant information. More centrally, planning expertise led to the application of depth-first, or principle-based, search strategies, which resulted not only in better plans but also in more efficient planning activities in that the need for goal-based, means–ends analysis decreased. Thus, expertise may result in acquisition of better strategies for executing the various processing operations included in plan formation.

Process Execution

By reducing processing demands, expertise may, moreover, make possible another action by individuals likely to contribute to process execution. Each of the processes involved in planning represents a relatively complex operation. As a result, one might expect that the more extensive the execution of requisite processing operations, the better the processing execution will be. In fact, Shipman et al. (2010), in their study on forecasting, found that the extensiveness of forecasting emerged as a unique dimension of forecasting. More centrally, the extensiveness of forecasting activities was found to be the strongest predictor of planning performance. When these findings are considered in light of other findings by Koberg et al. (1996), examining the extensiveness of managerial scanning in plan formation, and Mumford et al. (1996), examining the extensiveness of information gathering in planning for social innovation, it seems reasonable to conclude that more extensive, and intensive, execution of the various processing operations involved in planning will contribute to production of stronger, more effective, plans.

Critical Element Identification

In execution of any given processing operation, however, a variety of elements exist that might be considered in process execution. Thus Isenberg (1986) and Thomas et al. (1993) found that in formulating plans managers focused on identification of critical causes and causes that were subject to their control. Similarly, Marcy and Mumford (2007, 2010) found that training interventions intended to encourage people to focus on critical causes resulted in better planning performance. In other studies, it has been found that planning performance improves when people focus on critical attributes of mental models in plan formation (Weick, 1995) or when they focus on critical change events in scanning (O'Connor, 1998). Thus, planning process execution can be expected to improve when people expressly seek to identify central, critical, elements involved in process execution. Thus, skilled planners will often focus on identification and management of critical constraints (Tushman & O'Reilly, 1997).

Evaluative Thinking

One implication of these observations pertains to the role of evaluation in planning. Identification of critical elements involved in process execution requires evaluative thinking (Cropley, 2006). Effective evaluation will, of course, be influenced by basic abilities such as intelligence. However, in planning process execution, the importance of an element must be appraised along with strategies for working with that element. For example, should the element be assumed to be fixed, or should an attempt be made to act on it (or acquire more resources)? Thus while process execution requires evaluation of critical elements, effective evaluation will require considering the feasibility of acting on, or exercising control with respect to each of these elements. Thus Mumford and Van Doorn (2001), in a study of social innovation by Benjamin Franklin, found that Franklin not only evaluated critical issues impinging on his plans but also expressly sought to identify those elements where his actions would induce expected change. Thus, in executing planning processes, performance is likely to improve to the extent that evaluative actions in process execution focus on aspects of the situation subject to control. Non-controllable elements, in turn, should be treated as a context in which action occurs. Also, there is some reason to suspect that skilled planners devote some attention to definition of these "fixed" attributes when identifying and acting on manipulable elements in process execution (Mumford et al., 2008).

Situational Awareness

As noted earlier, in real-world settings, the conditions under which plans are being formulated and executed are subject to change or instability (Løvendahl, 1995). One implication of this statement is that skilled planners will identify attributes of the situation subject to change and carefully monitor these attributes. More centrally, however, the significance of changes in conditions implies that scanning and monitoring activities will occur throughout execution of various planning operations, with changes in process execution occurring in response to the changes in setting. Thus execution of planning processes will occur in a "dual-process" model where changes in situational contingencies provide a basis for adjusting the content and outcomes sought in execution of any given process. Effective execution of requisite processing operations in planning will therefore depend on the attention given to situational nuances (Rouse & Morris, 1986).

Backup Planning

Not only will effective execution of planning processes depend on situational nuances, it will also require the availability of viable backup plans and monitoring of diagnostics indicative of the need to execute these backup plans (Xiao et al., 1997). However, backup plans are typically broad, template, plans. Thus, at an individual level, when backup plans must be executed, online plan elaboration and revision will be required. This online elaboration and revision of backup plans will typically prove demanding, focusing attention on elaboration and execution of the backup plan. By the same token, with execution of these backup plans, new opportunities may emerge that permit opportunistic exploitation of plans to promote pursuit of emergent goals (Patalano & Siefert, 1997). Thus, individual planning performance may depend on the availability of a number of well-organized backup plans within a broader planning structure (Hayes-Roth & Hayes-Roth, 1979).

Investment

Of course, our foregoing observations indicate that even in the later stages of plan formation, process execution is not passive. Rather, a substantial investment of cognitive resources will be required. Given this observation, the complexity of early-cycle planning processes, and the need for ongoing monitoring of the environment in which the plan is being formulated and executed, it seems clear that execution of relevant planning processes will be a demanding, resource-intensive activity. One implication of these observations is that motivation will prove critical to effective execution of planning processes (Earley & Perry, 1987). Another implication of this observation, however, is that environmental events that reduce resource investment (e.g. extraneous task demands) will undermine effective execution of requisite planning processes. Accordingly, skilled planners are likely to place substantial focus on execution of each planning process involved in plan formation.

Hence, with regard to individual-level planning performance, seven key characteristics are likely to be displayed by skilled planners: (1) expertise, (2) extensive process execution, (3) identification of critical elements, (4) evaluation of elements, (5) situational awareness, (6) backup planning, and (7) investment. Of course, many of these performance-shaping variables can be developed. For example, people can be given training to improve situational awareness and identification of critical plan elements (Marcy & Mumford, 2010). Moreover, some of these characteristics, or attributes, of effective planners, for example, expertise and motivation, can be used to develop viable selection systems. Thus interventions are available to improve planning performance given the processes underlying plan formation. Moreover, this model of planning processes suggests a number of other interventions, for example, assessment of mental model structures or appraisal of depth in case analysis, that might also prove of value.

Group-level Influences

In organizations, planning process may be executed by either an individual or a group. This straightforward observation, in turn, raises a new question: what attributes of groups or teams will influence the effectiveness with which people execute various planning processes? Although research examining the impact of group-level variables on planning processes is generally not available, the nature of these processing operations vis-à-vis research on team planning does point to some group- or team-level variables likely to prove of some importance in this regard.

Shared Mental Models

The model of planning processes presented earlier stresses the importance of mental models, specifically, monitoring models, global mental models, and mental models bearing on the plan being formulated. Although, in the team's literature, distinctions are not drawn among different types or forms of mental models, the available evidence indicates that the availability of shared mental models among team members contributes to both effective interpersonal exchange among team members and team performance (Day, Gronn, & Salas, 2004). More centrally, the availability of shared mental models apparently contributes to team planning performance (Orasanu and Salas, 1993; Rouse, Cannon-Bowers, & Salas, 1992). For example, Mumford, Feldman, Hein, and Nagao (2001) induced shared mental models through team training interventions. They found that teams produced stronger plans, as indicated by appraisals of plan quality, when they possessed shared mental models relevant to the planning task.

Information Exchange

The availability of shared mental models, however, is not the only team-level variable that might influence execution of the planning processes. The model of planning processes under consideration stresses processes involving the analysis of case-based knowledge. What should be recognized here, however, is that different team members possess different case-based knowledge, and effective exchange of this case-based knowledge should contribute to planning performance. In fact, studies by Waller (1999) and Zaccaro, Gualtieri, and Minionis (1995) have shown that performance on team planning tasks improves with exchange of information among team members – presumably information reflecting an exchange of case-based knowledge.

Networks

In teams, exchange of case-based knowledge is typically held to occur through networks of interpersonal exchange (Balkundi & Kilduff, 2005). This observation led Friedrich, Vessey, Schuelke, Ruark, and Mumford (2009) to argue that, in planning, leaders must be able to capitalize on these network structures to bring relevant case-base knowledge to bear on the planning task. Some support for this proposition has been provided in a historiometric study of George C. Marshall, United States Army Chief of Staff during World War Two, conducted by Vessey et al. (2014). They found that Marshall's exceptional performance as a planner was to a large extent based on his ability to create and exploit networks, ensuring the availability of requisite case-based knowledge.

Participation and Leadership

In teams, networks may be a source of requisite knowledge; however, the model of planning processes also stresses the need to analyze this knowledge and employ it in forecasting and plan formation. Accordingly, a variety of studies indicate that attributes of team interactional processes, for example, openness to alternative perspectives, minimization of interpersonal conflict, mission definition, and clarity of role definition (Menon, Bharadwaj, & Howell, 1996; West & Sacramento, 2012) will contribute to effective execution of these planning processes in team settings. Of these variables, however, active, and skilled, participation of team members in the planning activity is likely to prove of special significance with respect to team planning performance (Yukl, 2012). The significance of participation, of course, arises from the fact that unless people participate they cannot share knowledge or contribute to the analysis of this knowledge.

The need to *use* knowledge in planning, for example, in forecasting, backup plan formation, and identification of critical causes and goals, however, has another important implication with regard to team-level influence. More specifically, attributes of team process that encourage active analyses can be expected to contribute to effective execution of many of the planning processes when they are being executed in team settings. One key team-level influence in this regard is team leadership, and, in keeping with this proposition, transformational leadership, a leadership style that includes intellectual stimulation, has been shown to contribute to team planning performance (Mumford et al., 2002). Similarly, positive team affective climate, a climate that allows team members to invest cognitive resources in analysis, can be expected to contribute to the effectiveness of case analyses, model formation, forecasting, and backup plan formation (Pirola-Merlo, Härtel, Mann, & Hirst, 2002).

Organization-Level Influences

Resources

Although it may not be surprising that team-level variables influence the effective execution of various planning processes, it should also be recognized that various organizational-level influences are also of some importance. For example, organizations often set constraints on plans (Kidder, 1981). Inclusion of these organizational constraints on plans clearly will affect the execution of a number of planning processes. More centrally, the number and complexity of the cognitive processes involved in planning indicates that planning is a time-consuming, resource-intensive activity. Accordingly, if an organization does not provide adequate time, time free from distractions, it is unlikely that effective execution of many planning processes will prove possible.

Strategy and Structure

One variable influencing the organization's willingness to devote time and resources to planning may be found in strategy. As Miles and Snow (1978) have pointed out, organizations pursue different strategies – prospectors, analyzers, reactors, or defenders. As firms employing a prospector or analyzer strategy stress product development and effective use of resources in product development, it can be expected that these firms will stress the value of and need for planning. Moreover, firms which seek to take proactive action on their environment can also be expected to stress the need for, and value of, planning, along with firms of high capital intensity (Bluedorn, Johnson, Cartwright, & Barringer, 1994; Dean & Sharfman, 1996). The strategy being pursued by a firm, however, will have two other potentially noteworthy effects. First, a climate may be established where key planning processes, for example, scanning, cause analysis, forecasting, and backup planning, are encouraged and/or routinized. Thus prior to approving plans, firms may require forecasting and extensive analysis. Second, when planning is valued strategically, those who plan will be rewarded – rewards that motivate and encourage the investment of resources in planning.

Although strategy and climate represent potentially significant influences on planning, the structure of the firm and its basic operations will also influence people's investment in planning and requisite planning processes (Mumford et al., 2008). Typically, planning will prove of greater concern in operations where long-term challenges involving investment of firm resources are of concern. Thus planning will be viewed as critical to performance in research and development and manufacturing (Mumford, Scott, Gaddis, & Strange, 2002). However, in this regard, it should be recognized that the structure of firms also dictates certain likely forms of interaction. Accordingly, Damanpour and Aravind (2012) and Kazanjian and Drazin (2012) have argued that planning processes will be more intensive in firms that rely on a professional structure and stress ongoing learning. Indeed, an argument can be made that firms which stress ongoing learning will provide a richer store of case-based knowledge and thus provide a key foundation on which to base planning operations. Moreover, such firms may view effective execution of many planning processes, for example, forecasting or situational reflection, as critical to firm operations.

Not only will firm structure influence the investment of resources in execution of planning processes, the firm itself may provide a groundwork for execution of many processes. For example, at a firm level, integration and exchange of the information garnered in various scanning activities may provide a basis for individuals' effective execution of scanning processes. Similarly, firm reporting requirements may call organizational members' attention to key diagnostics, thereby contributing to effective execution of the monitoring process. These observations are noteworthy because they suggest ways in which an organization's structure of work processes may provide support systems that facilitate the execution of planning processes while encouraging people to invest in the effective execution of these processes.

Discussion

Before turning to the broader implications flowing from the present effort, certain limitations should be noted. To begin, we have assumed that planning contributes to performance. Although the available evidence (Delaney et al., 2004; Davies, 2003) indicates that planning does, in fact, contribute to performance when people are asked to work on difficult tasks under dynamic, unstable conditions, it is also true that planning may not prove valuable for all tasks at all times (Finkelstein, 2002). Moreover, planning processes are subject to error (Dörner & Schaub, 1994). Thus even when people need to, and do, plan, their plans may not always lead to the outcomes sought. Furthermore, Mintzberg (1993) suggests that planning may represent more of an obsession than an effective strategy. Even bearing these points in mind, the available evidence does indicate that planning contributes to individual, team, and firm performance (Mumford et al., 2002).

If it is granted that planning does contribute to performance, there is a need to understand how people go about planning. In other words, we need to understand the cognitive operations involved in the production of viable plans. In the present effort we have presented a general model of the processes involved in planning. This model of planning processes, however, is not tied to a particular task or a particular domain of planning activity (Baer, 2012). This point is of some importance because some processes may prove more important on some tasks, in some performance domains, than others. As a result, some caution is called for in extrapolating this general model of planning processes to planning performance in specific tasks domains. Moreover, based on their experience and the demands imposed by the planning task at hand, individuals may or may not execute all of these processes. For example, we do not, typically, forecast drive times to work when planning our daily trips, relying instead on simplified plans based on past experience.

Along related lines, it should be recognized that the model of planning processes presented in the present chapter was based on a key assumption. More specifically, we assumed that plans are formulated using case-based, or experiential, knowledge. Although the available evidence does suggest that plans are typically formulated using case-based knowledge (e.g. Berger & Jordan, 1992; Klein, Robertson, & Delton, 2010), the possibility does remain that other types of knowledge might be used in plan formation, and, if other types of knowledge are used, then a different model of planning processes than the model presented herein would be indicated.

Finally, we should note that we have in the present manuscript focused on planning *processes*. As a result, little has been said about how people might employ different elements of knowledge embodied in experiential cases in planning (Gaerling, 1994). For example, little has been said about how people trade off affective reactions vis-à-vis key causes in formulating plans. Similarly, little has been said about when, and how, constraints or restrictions shape the plans people formulate (Mumford & Van Doorn, 2001). Clearly, there is a need for future research along these lines.

Even bearing these limitations in mind, we believe we have, in the present chapter, provided a basis for understanding the cognitive processes contributing to plan formation. The model of planning processes presented here holds that planning requires "envisioning" the effects of action or mental simulation (Mumford, Schultz, & Van Doorn, 2001; Noice, 1991). To envision the effects of future actions, people must forecast. These forecasts, however, are based on mental models. The mental models used to formulate these forecasts, in turn, are based on the analyses of available case-based knowledge. The case-based knowledge analyzed, however, is selected based on general mental models and the inferences drawn from these models with respect to critical causes and critical goals. The critical causes, critical goals, and global mental model employed, however, are based on information gathering, monitoring models, and scanning. Moreover, effective execution of these planning processes is held to depend on various "support" processes, such as evaluation of forecasts, backup plan formation, and situational reflection (Mumford et al., 2007; Xiao et al., 1997).

Clearly, planning, the mental simulation of the effects of future actions, is an exceptionally complex cognitive activity. Consider the four or five critical processes involved in analogical reasoning (Sternberg, 1986) compared to the 15 to 20 processes involved in planning (Mumford et al., 2007). Moreover, execution of each process in itself, for example, forecasting, case analysis and scanning, is resource intensive (Scott et al., 2005). As a result, it seems clear that planning may be one of the most demanding, resource-intensive activities in which we engage as human beings. It is therefore no surprise that planning is fraught with error (Dörner & Schaub, 1994), and people use strategies, for example, applying a single case or forecasting only likely outcomes of acting on one or two critical causes (Isenberg, 1986; Nutt, 1984), as a means of making planning processes less demanding.

Of course, these observations bring to the fore a new question: what evidence is available indicating that these demanding, resource-intensive processes are actually used in planning? Broadly speaking, the available evidence indicates that these processes are, in fact, involved in planning, given that effective execution of the processes has been shown to influence the production of viable plans. For example, Shipman et al. (2010) have provided evidence for the impact of forecasting. Marcy and Mumford (2010) have provided evidence for the importance of causal analysis. Mumford et al. (2012) have provided evidence for the importance of employing viable mental models. Lonergan et al. (2004) have provided evidence for the importance of evaluating forecasts. When these studies are considered in light of the findings obtained in other investigations (e.g. Souitaris, 2001; Xiao et al., 1997), it seems reasonable to conclude that the model of planning processes presented in the present effort is, in fact, plausible.

Of course, these studies suffer from certain limitations – limitations that point to some promising direction for future research. For example, interactions among processes have not been examined in these studies, and it is in fact plausible that forecasts shape the nature of the backup plans people produce (Giorgini & Mumford, in press). Similarly, little research has examined the specific strategies contributing to effective execution of these processes (Lonergan et al., 2004). Finally, these studies have not sought to identify the content employed in process execution (Marcy & Mumford, 2010). Hopefully, future studies will examine these and other potential factors influencing process execution.

Research along these lines is not only of theoretical interest; it is also of interest because it might provide critical data needed to improve planning performance. In the present effort, we have examined some of the variables that might influence effective execution of these processes at the individual, group, and organizational levels. At the individual level, expertise and extensiveness of process execution, among other variables, were found to be of some importance. At the group level, shared mental models and team networks, among other variables, were found to be of some importance. At the organizational level, strategy and learning orientation, among other variables, were found to be of some importance. These individual-, group-, and organizational-level influences are noteworthy, in part, because they suggest how we might seek to improve the effectiveness of planning process execution in organizations. We hope the present effort will serve as an impetus for future research intended to illustrate the kinds of actions organizations might take to encourage effective execution of planning processes.

Acknowledgments

We would like to thank Carter Gibson, Vincent Giorgini, Tamara Friedrich, and Rosemary Schultz for their contributions to the present effort.

References

Baer, J. (2012). Domain specificity and the limits of creativity theory. *Journal of Creative Behavior*, 46, 16–29.

Balkundi, P., & Kilduff, M. (2005). The ties that lead: A social network approach to leadership. *The Leadership Quarterly*, 16, 941–961.

Barrett, J. D., Vessey, W. B., & Mumford, M. D. (2011). Getting leaders to think: Effects of training, threat, and pressure on performance. *The Leadership Quarterly*, 22, 729–750.

Barsalou, L. W. (1988). The content and organization of autobiographical memories. In U. Neisser & E. Winograd (Eds.), *Remembering reconsidered: Ecological and traditional approaches to the study of memory* (pp. 192–243). New York: Cambridge University Press.

Berger, C. R., & Jordan, J. M. (1992). Planning sources, planning difficulty, and verbal fluency. *Communication Monographs*, 59, 130–148.

Berger, C. R., Karol, S. H., & Jordan, J. M. (1989). When a lot of knowledge is a dangerous thing. *Human Communication Research*, 16, 91–119.

Bluedorn, A. C., Johnson, R. A., Cartwright, D. K., & Barringer, B. R. (1994). The interface and convergence of strategic management and the organization environment domain. *Journal of Management*, 20, 201–263.

Buehler, R., Griffin, D., & Ross, M. (1994). Exploring the "planning fallacy": Why people underestimate their task completion times. *Journal of Personality and Social Psychology*, 67, 366–381.

Byrne, C. L., Shipman, A. S., & Mumford, M. D. (2010). The effects of forecasting on creative problem-solving: An experimental study. *Creativity Research Journal*, 22, 199–138.

Cascio, W. F., & Aguinis, H. (2005). *Applied psychology in human resource management* (6th ed.). Upper Saddle River, NJ: Prentice Hall.

Conway, M. A. (1990). Associations between autobiographical memories and concepts. *Journal of Experimental Psychology: Learning, Memory, and Cognition*, 16, 799–812.

Cropley, A. (2006). Dimensions of creativity: Creativity: A social approach. *A Journal on Gifted Education*, 28, 125–130.

Dailey, L. R., & Mumford, M. D. (2006). Evaluative aspects of creative thought: Errors in appraising the implications of new ideas. *Creativity Research Journal*, 18, 367–384.

Damanpour, F., & Aravind, D. (2012). Organizational structure and innovation revisited: From organic to ambidextrous structure. In M. Mumford (Ed.), *Handbook of organizational creativity* (pp. 483–515). Oxford, UK: Elsevier.

Davies, S. P. (2003). Initial and concurrent planning in solutions to well-structured problems. *The Quarterly Journal of Experimental Psychology*, 56, 1147–1164.

Day, D., Gronn, P., & Salas, E. (2004). Leadership capacity in teams. *The Leadership Quarterly*, 15, 857–880.

Dean, J. W., & Sharfman, M. P. (1996). Does decision process matter? A study of strategic decision-making effectiveness. *Academy of Management Journal*, 39, 368–396.

Delaney, P. F., Ericsson, K. A., & Knowles, M. E. (2004). Immediate and sustained effects of planning in a problem-solving task. *Journal of Experimental Psychology*, 30, 1219–1234.

Dörner, D., & Schaub, H. (1994). Errors in planning and decision making and the nature of human information processing. *Applied Psychology: An International Review*, 43, 433–453.

Earley, P. C., & Perry, B. C. (1987). Work plan availability and performance: An assessment of task strategy priming on subsequent task completion. *Organizational Behavior and Human Decision Processes*, 39, 279–302.

Ettlie, J. E., (2008). Templates for innovation. In M. D. Mumford, S. T. Hunter, K. E. Bedell-Avers (Eds.), *Multi-Level Issues in Creativity and Innovation* (pp. 155–168). Oxford, UK: Elsevier.

Finkelstein, S. (2002). Planning in organizations: One vote for complexity. In F. J. Yammarino & F. Dansereau (Eds.), *Research in multi-level issues: The many faces of multi-level issues* (pp. 73–80). New York: Elsevier.

Ford, C. M., & Gioia, D. A. (2000). Factors influencing creativity in the domain of managerial decision making. *Journal of Management*, 26(4), 705–732.

Forsyth, D. K., & Burt, C. D. B. (2008). Allocating time to future tasks: The effect of task segmentation on planning fallacy bias. *Memory & Cognition*, 36(4), 791–798.

Friedrich, T. L., Vessey, W. B., Schuelke, M. J., Ruark, G. A., & Mumford, M. D. (2009). A framework for understanding collective leadership: The selective utilization of leader and team expertise within networks. *The Leadership Quarterly*, 20, 933–958.

Gaerling, T. (1994). Processing of time constraints on sequence decisions in a planning task. *European Journal of Cognitive Psychology*, 6, 399–416.

Gardner, W., & Rogoff, B. (1990). Children's deliberateness of planning according to task circumstances. *Developmental Psychology*, 26, 480–487.

Giorgini, V., & Mumford, M. D. (in press). Backup plans and creative problem solving: Effects of causal, error, and resource planning. *International Journal of Creative Problem Solving*.

Goldvarg, E., & Johnson-Laird, P. N. (2001). Naïve causality: A mental model theory of causal meaning and reasoning. *Cognitive Science*, 25, 565–610.

Gollwitzer, P. M. (1999). Implementation intentions: Strong effects of simple plans. *American Psychologist*, 54, 493–503.

Hammond, K. J. (1990). Case-based planning: A framework for planning from experience. *Cognitive Science*, 14, 385–443.

Hayes-Roth, B., & Hayes-Roth, F. (1979). A cognitive model of planning. *Cognitive Science*, 14, 275–310.

Hershey, D. A., Walsh, D. A., Read, S. J., & Chulef, A. S. (1990). The effects of expertise on financial problem-solving: Evidence for goal-directed problem-solving scripts. *Organizational Behavior and Human Decision Processes*, 46, 77–101.

Hester, K. S., Robledo, I. C., Varrett, J. D., Peterson, D. R., Hougen, D. P., Day, E. A., & Mumford, M. D. (2012). Causal analysis to enhance creative problem-solving: Performance and effects on mental models. *Creativity Research Journal*, 24, 115–133.

Hogarth, R. M. (1981). *Judgment and choice*. New York: Wiley.

Isenberg, D. J. (1986). Thinking and managing: A verbal protocol analysis of managerial problem solving. *Academy of Management Journal*, 29, 775–778.

Johanssen, G., & Rouse, W. B. (1983). Studies of planning behavior of aircraft pilots in normal, abnormal, and emergency situations. *IEEE Transactions on Systems, Man, and Cybernetics*, 13(3), 267–278.

Jaudas, A., & Gollwitzer, P. M. (2004). Führen Vorsätze zu Rigidität im Zielstreben?[Do implementation intentions lead to rigidity in goal striving?]. In symposium "Recent developments in research on implementation intentions" at the 46th Meeting of Experimental Psychologists, Giessen, Germany.

Kaller, C. P., Rahm, B., Spreer, J., Mader, I., & Unterrainer, J. M. (2008). Thinking around the corner: The development of planning abilities. *Brain and Cognition*, 67(3), 360–370.

Kazanjian, R. K., & Drazin, R. (2012). Organizational learning, knowledge management and creativity. In M. D. Mumford (Ed.), *Handbook of organizational creativity* (pp. 547–568). San Diego, CA: Academic Press.

Kiewiet, D. J., Jorna, R. J., & Wezel, W. (2005). Planners and their cognitive maps: An analysis of domain representations using multi-dimensional scaling. *Applied Ergonomics*, 36, 695–708.

Klein, S. B., Robertson, T. E., & Delton, A. W. (2010). Facing the future: Memory as an evolved system for planning future acts. *Memory & Cognition*, 38(1), 13–22.

Klein, S. B., Robertson, T. E., & Delton, A. W. (2011). The future-orientation of memory: Planning as a key component mediating the high levels of recall found with survival processing. *Memory*, 19, 121–129.

Klein, S. B., Robertson, T. E., Delton, A. W., & Lax, M. (2012). Familiarity and personal experience as mediators of recall when planning for future contingencies. *Journal of Experimental Psychology: Learning, Memory, and Cognition*, 38(1), 240–245.

Kidder, T. (1981). *The Soul of a New Machine*. New York: Avon.

Kliegel, M., Martin, M., McDaniel, M. A., & Phillips, L. H. (2007). Adult age differences in errand planning: The role of task familiarity and cognitive resources. *Experimental Aging Research*, 33(2), 145–161.

Koberg, C. S., Uhlenbruck, N., & Sarason, Y. (1996). Facilitators of organizational innovation: The role of life-cycle stage. *Journal of Business Venturing*, 11, 133–149.

Kolodner, J. L. (1997). Educational implications of analogy: A view from case-based reasoning. *American Psychologist*, 52, 57–66.

Liberman, N., & Trope, Y. (1998). The role of feasibility and desirability considerations in near and distant future decisions: A test of temporal construal theory. *Journal of Personality and Social Psychology*, 75, 5–18.

Lidstone, J. S. M., Meins, E., & Fernyhough, C. (2010). The roles of private speech and inner speech in planning during middle childhood: Evidence from a dual task paradigm. *Journal of Experimental Child Psychology*, 107, 438–451.

Lonergan, D. C., Scott, G. M., & Mumford, M. D. (2004). Evaluative aspects of creative thought: Effects of appraisal and revision standards. *Creativity Research Journal*, 16(2–3), 231–246.

Løvendahl, B. R. (1995). Organizing the Lillehammer Olympic winter games. *Scandinavian Journal of Management*, 11, 347–362.

McDermott, D. (1978). Planning and acting. *Cognitive Science*, 2, 71–109.

Marcy, R. T., & Mumford, M. D. (2007). Social innovation: Enhancing creative performance through causal analysis. *Creativity Research Journal*, 19, 123–140.

Marcy, R. T., & Mumford, M. D. (2010). Leader cognition: Improving leader performance through causal analysis. *The Leadership Quarterly*, 21, 1–19.

Marta, S., Leritz, L. E., & Mumford, M. D. (2005). Leadership skills and the group performance: Situational demands, behavioral requirements, and planning. *The Leadership Quarterly*, 16(1), 97–120.

Masicampo, E. J., & Baumeister, R. F. (2011). Consider it done! Plan making can eliminate the cognitive effects of unfulfilled goals. *Journal of Personality and Social Psychology*, 101, 667–683.

Masicampo, E. J., & Baumeister, R. F. (2012). Committed but closed-minded: When making a specific plan for a goal hinders success. *Social Cognition*, 30, 37–55.

Menon, A., Bharadwaj, S. G., & Howell, R. (1996). The quality and effectiveness of marketing strategy: Effects of functional and dysfunctional conflict in intraorganizational relationships. *Journal of the Academy of Marketing Science*, 24, 299–313.

Miles, R. E., & Snow, C. C. (1978). *Organizational strategy, structure and process*. New York: McGraw-Hill.

Miller, G. A., Galanter, E., & Pribram, K. H. (1960). *Plans and the structure of behavior*. New York: Holt.

Mintzberg, H. (1993). The pitfalls of strategic planning. *California Management Review*, 36, 32–47.

Mumford, M. D., & Van Doorn, J. R. (2001). The leadership of pragmatism: Reconsidering Franklin in the age of charisma. *The Leadership Quarterly*, 12, 279–309.

Mumford, M. D., Baughman, W. A., Supinski, E. P., & Maher, M. A. (1996). Process-based measures of creative problem-solving skills: II. Information encoding. *Creativity Research Journal*, 9, 77–88.

Mumford, M. D., Feldman, J. M., Hein, M. B., & Nagao, D. J. (2001). Tradeoffs between ideas and structure: Individual versus group performance in creative problem solving. *The Journal of Creative Behavior*, 35, 1–23.

Mumford, M. D., Schultz, R. A., & Van Doorn, J. R. (2001). Performance in planning: Processes, requirements, and errors. *Review of General Psychology*, 5, 213–240. doi:10.1037//1089-2680.5.3.213

Mumford, M. D., Schultz, R. A., & Osburn, H. K. (2002). Planning in organizations: Performance as a multi-level phenomenon. In F. J. Yammarino & F. Dansereau (Eds.), *Many faces of multi-level issues* (pp. 3–65). Oxford, UK: Elsevier.

Mumford, M. D., Scott, G. M., Gaddis, B., & Strange, J. M. (2002). Leading creative people: Orchestrating expertise and relationships. *The Leadership Quarterly*, 13, 705–750.

Mumford, M. D., Friedrich, T. L., Caughron, J. J., & Byrne, C. L. (2007). Leader cognition in real-world settings: How do leaders think about crises? *The Leadership Quarterly*, 18, 515–543. doi:10.1016/j.leaqua.2007.09.002

Mumford, M. D., Bedell-Avers, K. E., Hunter, S. T. (2008). Planning for innovation: A multi-level perspective. In M. D. Mumford, S. T. Hunter, & K. E. Bedell-Avers (Eds.), *Multi-Level Issues in Creativity and Innovation* (pp. 107–154). Oxford, UK: Elsevier.

Mumford, M. D., Friedrich, T. L., Caughron, J. J., & Antes, A. L. (2009). Leadership research: Traditions, developments, and current directions. In D. A. Buchanan & A. Bryman (Eds.), *The Sage handbook of organizational research methods* (pp. 111–127). Los Angeles, CA: Sage.

Mumford, M. D., Medeiros, K. E., & Partlow, P. J. (2012). Creative thinking: Processes, strategies, and knowledge. *The Journal of Creative Behavior*, 46, 30–47. doi:10.1002/jocb.003

Mumford, M. D., Hester, K. S., Robledo, I. C., Peterson, D. R., Day, E. A., Hougen, D. F., & Barrett, J. D. (2012). Mental models and creative problem-solving: The relationship of objective and subjective model attributes. *Creativity Research Journal*, 24, 311–330.

Noice, H. (1991). The role of explanations and plan recognition in the learning of theatrical scripts. *Cognitive Science*, 15, 425–460.

Nutt, P. C. (1984). Types of organizational decision processes. *Administrative Science Quarterly*, 29, 414–450.

O'Connor, G. C. (1998). Market learning and radical innovation: A cross case comparison of eight radical innovation projects. *Journal of Product Innovation and Management*, 15, 151–166.

O'Hara, K. P., & Payne, S. J. (1998). The effects of operator implementation cost on planfulness of problem-solving and learning. *Cognitive Psychology*, 35, 34–70.

Orasanu, J., & Salas, E. (1993). Team decision making in complex environments. In G. A. Klein, J. Orasanu, R. Calderwood, & C. E. Zsambok (Eds.), *Decision making in action: Models and methods* (pp. 327–345). Westport, CT: Ablex.

Pant, P. N., & Starbuck, W. H. (1990). Innocents in the forest: Forecasting and research methods. *Journal of Management*, 16, 433–460.

Patalano, A. L., & Seifert, C. M. (1997). Opportunistic planning: Being reminded of pending goals. *Cognitive Psychology*, 34, 1–36.

Pirola-Merlo, A., Härtel, C., Mann, L., & Hirst, G. (2002). How leaders influence the impact of affective events on team climate and performance in R&D teams. *The Leadership Quarterly*, 13, 561–581.

Read, S. J. (1987). Consulting causal scenarios: A knowledge approach to causal reasoning. *Journal of Personality and Social Psychology*, 52, 288–302.

Rouse, R. B., Cannon-Bowers, J. A., & Salas, E. (1992). The role of mental models in team performance in complex systems. *IEEE Transactions on Systems, Man, and Cybernetics*, 22, 1290–1308.

Rouse, W. B., & Morris, N. M. (1986). On looking into the black box: Prospects and limits in the search for mental models. *Psychological Bulletin*, 100, 349–363.

Scott, G. M., Lonergan, D. C., & Mumford, M. D. (2005). Conceptual combination: Alternative knowledge structures, alternative heuristics. *Creativity Research Journal*, 17, 79–98.

Shipman, A. S., Byrne, C. L., & Mumford, M. D. (2010). Leader vision formation and forecasting: The effects of forecasting extent, resources, and timeframe. *The Leadership Quarterly*, 21, 439–456.

Smith, K. G., Locke, E. A., & Barry, D. (1990). Goal setting, planning, and organizational performance: An experimental simulation. *Organizational Behavior and Human Decision Processes*, 46, 118–134.

Sonnentag, S. (1998). Expertise in professional software design: A process study. *Journal of Applied Psychology*, 83, 703–715.

Souitaris, V. (2001). Strategic influences of technological innovation in Greece. *British Journal of Management*, 12, 131–147.

Sternberg, R. J. (1986). Toward a unified theory of human reasoning. *Intelligence*, 10, 281–314.

Strange, J. M., & Mumford, M. D. (2005). The origins of vision: Effects of reflection, models, and analysis. *The Leadership Quarterly*, 16, 121–148.

Thomas, J. B., & McDaniel, R. R. (1990). Interpreting strategic issues: Effects of strategy and the information-processing structure of top management teams. *Academy of Management Journal*, 33, 286–306.

Thomas, J. B., Clark, S. M., & Gioia, D. A. (1993). Strategic sensemaking and organizational performance: Linkages among scanning, interpretation, action, and outcomes. *Academy of Management Journal*, 36, 239–70.

Tushman, M. L., & O'Reilly, C. A. (1997). *Winning through innovation: A practical guide to learning organizational change and renewal*. Boston, MA: Harvard Business School Press.

van der Linden, D., Frese, M., & Meijman, T. F. (2003). Mental fatigue and the control of cognitive processes: Effects on perseveration and planning. *Acta Psychologica*, 113, 45–65.

van der Linden, D., Frese, M., & Sonnentag, S. (2003). The impact of mental fatigue on exploration in a complex computer task: Rigidity and loss of systematic strategies. *Human Factors*, 45, 483–494.

Vessey, W. B., Barrett, J., & Mumford, M. D. (2011). Leader cognition under threat: "Just the Facts." *The Leadership Quarterly*, 22, 710–728.

Vessey, W. B., Friedrich, T. L., Schuelke, M. J., Mumford, M. D., Yammarino, F. J., & Ruark, G. A. (2014). Collective leadership and George C. Marshall: A historiometric analysis of career events. *The Leadership Quarterly*, 25(3), 449–467.

Waller, M. J. (1999). The timing of adaptive group responses to nonroutine events. *Academy of Management Journal*, 42, 127–137.

Weick, K. (1995). *Sensemaking in organizations*. Thousand Oaks, CA: Sage.

Weldon, E., Jehn, K. A., & Pradhan, P. (1991). Processes that mediate the relationship between a group goal and improved group performance. *Journal of Personality and Social Psychology*, 61, 555–569.

West, M., & Sacramento, C. A. (2012). Creativity and innovation: The role of team and organizational climate. In M. D. Mumford (Ed.), *Handbook of Organizational Creativity* (pp. 359–386). San Diego, CA: Academic Press.

Xiao, Y., Milgram, P., & Doyle, D. J. (1997). Planning behavior and its functional role in interactions with complex systems. *IEEE Transactions on Systems, Man, and Cybernetics*, 27, 313–325.

Yukl, G. (2012). *Leadership in organizations* (8th ed.). Upper Saddle River, NJ: Prentice Hall.

Zaccaro, S. J., Gualtieri, J., & Minionis, D. (1995). Task cohesion as a facilitator of team decision making under temporal urgency. *Military Psychology*, 7, 77–93.

Zapf, D., Brodbeck, F. C., Frese, M., Peters, H., & Prumper, J. (1992). Errors in working with computers: A first validation of a taxonomy for observed errors in a field setting. *International Journal of Human-Computer Interaction*, 4, 311–339.

3

THE PLANNING FALLACY

When Plans Lead to Optimistic Forecasts

Roger Buehler and Dale Griffin

Planning a project is a key and perhaps necessary stage in forecasting project completion. Planning for a task involves the predetermination of a course of action that will result in successful task completion (Mumford, Schultz, & Osburn, 2002), and prediction represents an attempt to foresee what is likely to transpire (Dunning, 2007). In the realm of project management and scheduling, planning and scheduling a timeline of activities is closely intertwined with making time completion predictions. Of course, events don't always unfold as planned, and thus forecasters concerned with accuracy might be wise to make predictions that diverge from plans. In this chapter, we examine the psychology of time predictions relevant to project planning and management. We focus on a phenomenon known as the "planning fallacy," where processes of planning and prediction are too closely aligned, resulting in unrealistically optimistic forecasts. We begin by defining and documenting the planning fallacy and identifying its underlying psychological mechanisms. We then examine empirical tests of strategies proposed to curb the planning fallacy.

Defining and Documenting the Planning Fallacy

The Planning Fallacy and Underestimation Bias

The planning fallacy refers to a prediction phenomenon, all too familiar in organizational settings, wherein people underestimate the time it will take to complete a future task, despite knowing that similar tasks have taken longer in the past. The term was first introduced to the psychological literature by Kahneman and Tversky (1979, 1982, p. 415) to describe people's tendency "to underestimate the time required to complete a project, even when they have considerable experience of past failures to live up to planned schedules." Although Kahneman and Tversky did not conduct empirical studies of the planning fallacy, they offered a single case study that still stands as the defining test case for theory and research on the phenomenon. In this case, a team of academics working on a curriculum development project predicted they could finish within a couple of years, though they shared the knowledge that similar projects had taken no less than seven years to finish and were often abandoned unfinished. As it turned out, the project took eight years to finish, by which time the Ministry of Education had lost interest and the curriculum was rarely used (Lovallo & Kahneman, 2003).

According to the original definition, then, the signature of the planning fallacy is not simply that planners are optimistic but that they maintain their optimism about a project in the face of historical evidence to the contrary. Accordingly, to identify examples of the planning fallacy requires two pieces of evidence. First, predictions of task completion times must be more optimistic than beliefs about the distribution of past completion times for similar projects; second, predictions of task completion times must be more optimistic than actual outcomes. Numerous studies of personal time predictions have revealed this dual pattern. For example, in one of the first assessments of the planning fallacy, we examined student predictions for completion of a computer-based tutorial session (Buehler, Griffin, & Ross, 1994). Although students reported that they usually completed similar academic tasks about a day before the deadline, they expected to complete the tutorial session, on average, about six days in advance of the deadline. In fact, only about 30 percent completed by their predicted date – most finished, as usual, considerably closer to deadline. Similarly, moving outside the academic domain, Canadian taxpayers predicted that they would file their tax returns about a week earlier than they had typically done in the past (three weeks before deadline rather than their usual two weeks), but instead, history repeated itself. On average, they completed the forms at their usual time, so that the predictions averaging three weeks before deadline were optimistically biased (Buehler, Griffin, & MacDonald, 1997).

These findings and others (see Buehler, Griffin, & Peetz, 2010) are consistent with the classic definition of the planning fallacy, revealing a paradoxical combination of optimism about the future with realism about the past. We note, however, that the term planning fallacy is now quite commonly used in a broader sense to describe the basic tendency to underestimate the time it takes to complete tasks. Although we maintain that such definitions miss much of the richness of the planning fallacy as a psychological phenomenon, clearly there is value in understanding the causes and consequences of this more general "optimistic bias" or "underestimation bias," and we include the relevant findings in our review. The basic tendency to underestimate completion times has been documented in the psychological literature for a wide range of personal, academic, and work-related tasks (e.g. Buehler et al., 1994; Buehler & Griffin, 2003; Byram, 1997; Griffin & Buehler, 1999; Kruger & Evans, 2004; Min & Arkes, 2012; Roy, Christenfeld, & McKenzie, 2005; Taylor, Pham, Rivkin, & Armor, 1998).

Furthermore, although most controlled studies focus on relatively short-term individual tasks and projects, there is also ample evidence of bias for large-scale projects in both the public and private sectors. The Standish Group publishes an annual survey of the success of information technology projects in the United States; in 2010, only 37 percent of surveyed projects were classified as successes, meaning they were delivered on time, on budget, and with required features and functions; 42 percent were challenged, which meant that they were delivered late, over budget, or with less than the required features; and 21 percent failed and were canceled or never used (The Standish Group, 2010). In a comprehensive study of private-sector planning and forecasting, Norris (1971) compiled forecasted and completed times and costs for close to 300 industrial R&D projects. The projects were, on average, about 250 percent over time budget and about 125 percent over cost budget. Furthermore, there is historical evidence that cost and time overruns have been characteristic of public works projects in both the US (Engerman & Sokoloff, 2004) and Europe (Flyvbjerg, Holm, & Buhl, 2005) for hundreds of years.

Intentional Deception vs. Unintentional Delusion

To better characterize the scope and nature of the underestimation bias we consider two further distinctions. First, for many project completion forecasts, the apparently optimistic time estimates may represent duplicitous attempts to manipulate an audience for political ends rather than true predictions about the future. Bent Flyvbjerg and his colleagues (e.g. Flyvbjerg, Bruzelius, & Rothengatter, 2003; Flyvbjerg Holm, & Buhl, 2004, 2005) have argued that large public works are plagued by estimates that are deliberately deceptive, either because politicians wish to develop major projects but know that their true cost will not be borne by the taxpayer, or because contractors low-ball the estimated cost or effort prediction to gain the contract, or because employees underestimate the cost and scope of projects to gain political favor and project approval from their managers. Flyvbjerg and colleagues provide anecdotal reports indicating that employees are sometimes implicitly or explicitly rewarded for deliberately underestimating project magnitude. Flyvbjerg also argues that because the history of project overruns is so well known, the continuing pattern of optimistic forecasts in large-scale public projects clearly suggests that fraud and deception are playing a role. Whatever the role of the "honest" planning fallacy in project overruns, then, there is undoubtedly a strong case for the role of deception and strategic misrepresentation in the underestimation of time and cost in public works and private industry projects.

Flyvbjerg and colleagues acknowledge that time and cost overruns do not always stem from strategic misrepresentation, and that even when planners attempt to predict as accurately as possible, there are a number of psychological mechanisms that leave them prone to optimistic "delusions" (Flyvbjerg, 2007; Flyvbjerg, Garbuio, & Lovallo, 2009). The goal of basic psychological research on the planning fallacy has been to capture and explore these processes that leave even honest, well-intentioned, planners prone to optimistic bias.

Task Performance Time vs. Completion Time

Second, as research on the planning fallacy has developed, it has become increasingly apparent that there is a need to distinguish between two types of temporal project predictions. Although various terms have been used previously to refer to this distinction, we adopt the terminology recommended recently by Halkjelsvik and Jørgensen (2012) for consistency across disciplines. Predictions of task *performance time* refer to the amount of actual working time required to carry out a task; that is, the time spent working at the task itself. In contrast, predictions of task *completion time* refer to when the task is finished, which might be expressed as a date, the number of days that will elapse before task completion, or how far before a deadline the task will be done. A scientist asked to review a journal article may estimate that the review will demand about six hours of actual working time (performance time prediction) and that the review will be submitted before the deadline in about three weeks (completion time prediction). Sometimes task completion times will be closely determined by performance times, and, in fact, they are identical when an individual starts a task right after making a prediction and works at it continuously until it is done. This is the case in many controlled laboratory studies of time estimation. But in real life, task completion times often diverge markedly from task performance times. This is because task completion time includes not only the performance time for the target task, but also time taken by factors external to the task, such as time spent on competing activities, interruptions, delays, and procrastination.

Theorists and researchers have differed in their approach to this distinction. Some have suggested that the same processes and outcomes characterize both types of prediction (Roy et al., 2005; Roy & Christenfeld, 2007), and that underestimation of performance time is the root cause of the planning fallacy. Others have argued that optimistic predictions of task completion time often reflect processes that differ from those underlying predictions of performance time (Buehler, Griffin, & Ross, 2002; Buehler, Griffin, & Peetz, 2010; Griffin & Buehler, 2005; Halkjelsvik & Jørgensen, 2012). In particular, we have proposed that predictions of performance time, where uncertainty is solely about the nature and difficulty of the target task, should be less prone to bias than are predictions of task completion time, where uncertainty is greater and comes not only from the nature of the task but also from a host of other complicating factors (e.g. competing tasks, difficulties in coordinating with others, unexpected interruptions, challenges in scheduling resources and self-control failure). Consistent with this reasoning, recent literature reviews reveal a much stronger tendency to underestimate task completion times than performance times. A review of basic psychological studies of task completion estimates (Buehler, Griffin, & Peetz, 2010) found that there was a consistent tendency to underestimate task completion times regardless of task type or length, whereas results for task performance time were mixed, with about as many studies showing overestimation as underestimation. Furthermore, for predictions of task performance time, the degree and direction of bias was dependent on the magnitude of the task: for very short laboratory tasks overestimation was typical, whereas for longer tasks underestimation was more common (a relationship documented previously, Roy & Christenfeld, 2008; Roy et al., 2005). Halkjelsvik and Jørgensen (2012) conducted an exhaustive meta-analysis of performance time studies across fields of psychology, software engineering, and management science and drew a similar conclusion: there was not a consistent tendency to underestimate performance times; instead there was a tendency to overestimate performance times for very short tasks and underestimate them for longer tasks.

Very few studies have compared the two types of predictions for the same target task. In an early study, we collected both performance time and completion time estimates for an academic project (Buehler et al., 1994, Study 2; results reported in Buehler 1991), and found that completion time estimates were optimistically biased even though estimates of performance time were not, and that the two predictions were uncorrelated. In another study that we supervised, participants were asked to perform a standard task that required the same amount of actual working time, but differed as to whether participants could complete the work in a single session or were required to spread it out across multiple sessions (Deslauriers, 2002). Even though task requirements were identical, there was greater optimistic bias when the task was spread out over multiple sessions (and thus more prone to delays from factors external to the task). Such findings suggest that task completion times are determined by factors other than the performance time of the target task itself, and that the underestimation bias for completion times is not driven primarily by a tendency to underestimate performance times.

A similar conclusion was drawn from a longitudinal study of product development projects in which engineers made time estimates over the course of projects for 835 separate "work packages" (van Oorschot, Bertrand, & Rutte, 2005). The engineers' estimates of task performance times were remarkably accurate and did not reveal an underestimation bias except for very large work packages (i.e. those requiring more than 40 hours of working time). However, analyses of "flow time" indicated that the work packages were nearly always finished later than the expected date, typically because new work packages were discovered that competed for the engineers' time. The authors concluded that performance time estimates were not a primary cause of lateness.

Psychological Mechanisms

The Inside and Outside View

Psychological explanations for the planning fallacy have been guided by the seminal theorizing of Kahneman and Tversky (1979), who distinguished between two approaches to prediction they labeled the "inside" and "outside" views (Kahneman & Lovallo, 1993). People who adopt an inside view of a task are looking forward and focusing on singular information relevant to only that one task: specific aspects of the target task that might lead to longer or shorter completion times. People who adopt an outside view are looking across other projects in the past and present and focusing on distributional information: how the current task fits into a set of related tasks. This approach requires the ability to identify a set of related task outcomes to use as a basis for prediction. Thus, the two general approaches differ primarily in whether individuals base their prediction only on their knowledge of the specific case at hand or also on their knowledge of historical patterns.

For a number of reasons, it seems that people typically prefer to adopt the inside view when developing plans and predictions (Kahneman & Lovallo, 1993; Kahneman & Tversky, 1979). That is, people are inclined to make predictions by planning ahead and trying to envision how the specific project will unfold. For example, when estimating the time needed for a home repair project, people might try to imagine when they will start the project, the resources that are required, and the specific steps they will need to take to carry it out. They are likely to consider their goals and wishes for the project, including when they hope to be done. They may consider other activities and events that will compete for their time, and try to schedule the work accordingly. They may even try to foresee potential obstacles and how these obstacles could be overcome. Essentially, then, the inside view involves sketching out a specific plan or scenario that leads from the beginning to the successful conclusion of the project.

People seem much less inclined to base predictions on historical outcomes. This may be partly because prediction, by its very nature, evokes a focus on the future rather than the past. However, a failure to use historical information does not always result from inattention to the past. People may sometimes consider the past, but fail to incorporate the information into their predictions because it doesn't seem applicable. People may have difficulty extracting an appropriate set of past experiences; the various instances seem so different from each other on a surface level that individuals cannot compare them meaningfully (Kahneman & Lovallo, 1993; Kahneman & Tversky, 1979). People may also make attributions that diminish the relevance of past experiences to the current prediction. To the extent that people perceive a previous episode to be caused by external, unstable, and specific factors – factors unlikely to generalize to other projects – they are unlikely to see it as relevant to prediction. Furthermore, people are probably most inclined to discount experiences when they dislike the implications (e.g. that a project will take longer than hoped), consistent with the self-serving bias in attribution documented in many domains (Miller & Ross, 1975; Taylor & Brown, 1988). Along similar lines, recent research suggests that the success or failure of imagined future events is attributed more to willpower than is the success level of the same events in the past (Helzer & Gilovich, 2012), and that this attributional asymmetry can lead people to remain confident about future performances despite a history of past failure. People believe future tasks will be more personally controllable than the same tasks were in the past, and thus do not see past lateness as diagnostic of future outcomes.

A problem with basing prediction on a plan-based, future scenario is that such scenarios typically do not provide a comprehensive and thorough representation of future events. Mental scenarios tend to be idealized, schematic, and oversimplified (Dunning, 2007). When individuals imagine the future, they often fail to entertain alternatives to their favored scenario and do not appreciate the uncertainty inherent in every detail of a constructed scenario (Griffin, Dunning, & Ross, 1990; Hoch, 1985). Furthermore, given that people plan for success rather than failure, the scenarios tend to focus on positive rather than negative information. When individuals are asked to predict based on "best-guess" scenarios, their forecasts are generally indistinguishable from those generated by "best-case" scenarios (Griffin et al., 1990; Newby-Clark, Ross, Buehler, Koehler, & Griffin, 2000). Finally, the very act of generating a scenario can cause people to exaggerate the likelihood of that scenario unfolding (for reviews see Gregory & Duran, 2001; Koehler, 1991). Focusing on a plan-based scenario, then, may lead predictors to ignore or underweight the chances that some other events will occur. This is a formula for over-optimism because even when a particular success scenario is relatively probable, a priori, chance will still usually favor the whole set of possible alternative events because there are so many (Dawes, 1988; Kahneman & Lovallo, 1993).

Empirical Support for the Inside-Outside Account

Studies that include "think aloud" procedures and written "thought listing" measures have shown that a focus on plan-based future scenarios – and a consequent neglect of past experience – is indeed characteristic of the prediction process. For example, in a typical study of academic and home projects (Buehler et al., 1994, Study 3), more than 70 percent of all thoughts reported by participants referred to their plans for the current project, for the most part describing scenarios in which they finished the task without problems arising; the verbal protocols revealed an almost total neglect of other kinds of information, including their own past experiences or others' experiences with similar projects.

Another experiment (Buehler et al., 1994, Study 4) examined whether the relative neglect of past experience was due to a lack of attention or the perceived irrelevance of the past. Participants predicted when they would finish a standard, one-hour computer assignment due in a week. Those in the Recall condition reported on their previous experiences with similar assignments (and recalled finishing them very close to deadlines) just before making their predictions. Nonetheless, they underestimated actual completion times to the same degree as participants in a control condition. This pattern, replicated in other studies (e.g. Buehler & Griffin, 2003), suggests that attention to and awareness of the past is not enough to make the past seem relevant to prediction. The relevance interpretation is further strengthened by a demonstration that forcing the past to become relevant eliminates the underestimation bias (Buehler et al., 1994, Study 4). In a Recall-Relevance condition, participants were required to actively link their past experiences with the upcoming computer assignment, by first determining when they would finish the assignment if they finished as far before deadline as usual, and then describing a plausible scenario that would result in this outcome. After this thought exercise, participants predicted their actual completion time for the assignment. The manipulation was designed to prevent participants from either ignoring past experiences with similar tasks or discounting their relevance, and for this task at least, it was effective in eliminating prediction bias.

To test the role of attribution processes in the planning fallacy, we have asked participants to recall and explain an occasion when they failed to complete a task by the predicted time, and a similar failure experienced by a close acquaintance (Buehler et al., 1994, Study 3). We coded the reasons using the dimensions of the Attributional Style Questionnaire (Peterson et al., 1982). The reasons participants reported for their own lateness were more external, transitory, and specific than the reasons they provided for similar tardiness by close acquaintances. Participants attributed their own lateness to such rare events as their computer crashing, whereas others' failures seemed to reflect enduring personal problems with time management. In a related study (Buehler et al., 1994, Study 4), participants who either succeeded or failed in meeting their time predictions provided reasons for the success or failure. Those who finished late offered reasons that were more transitory and specific than those who finished on time. These findings suggest that people interpret their own past tardiness in a manner that makes it seem unique and unlikely to recur (see also Helzer & Dunning, 2012).

We have further documented the perceived irrelevance of the past through interviews with software engineers engaged on major projects at a taxation software firm. Although this small sample does not provide a confirmatory test of the attributional hypothesis, it does provide vivid descriptions of the logic that drives the dissociation of past from future projects. Of the dozen software engineers interviewed, there was virtual unanimous agreement that past projects tended to be late and that the results of past projects could not be used to inform future predictions. Participants were first asked "When you made the prediction … did you think of past projects and their outcomes?" Typical answers included "No … because it's a unique working environment and I've never worked on anything like it"; "No, not relevant. It's not the same kind of project at all." Participants were also asked "When you made this prediction did you think about other people's projects here or within the field in general?" Answers included: "There didn't seem to be anything that was comparable. This is a bit unique. A lot of it relies on new technology, new software on which to build reports, etc. It's difficult to compare to other projects"; "No, not on this one. The nature of this project is a little strange; it's not like anything I've ever worked on"; "No comparison, because this type of thing hasn't been done before."

Overall, research evidence for the cognitive processes underlying the inside-outside account of the planning fallacy is highly consistent, whether in terms of thought-listing analysis, manipulations of attention to and perceived relevance of past experiences, or measures of attributional processes that diminish the relevance of the past to prediction.

Additional Psychological Mechanisms

Theorists have proposed that the planning fallacy could also be supported by processes of anchoring and adjustment (Jørgensen & Sjøberg, 2004; König, 2005; LeBoeuf & Shafir, 2009; Thomas & Handley, 2008; Thomas, Newstead, & Handley, 2003). In many domains, people arrive at judgments by first contemplating a salient value that serves as the starting point or anchor and then adjusting (insufficiently) from that value (Strack & Mussweiler, 1997; Tversky & Kahneman, 1974). LeBoeuf and Shafir (2009) proposed that a salient anchor for task completion predictions is the present. In particular, respondents asked to estimate completion times as a number of days might begin at the present (a natural, self-generated anchor) and then adjust incrementally in a forward direction by the proposed day-based units. However, as with other anchoring effects, their adjustments from the anchor are likely to be insufficient, resulting in systematic underestimation. Respondents asked to predict in terms of a calendar date should be less inclined to engage in this process. Supporting this anchoring account, participants predicted they would finish various tasks (e.g. reading a book, completing a self-nominated project, going shopping at the mall) sooner when asked to estimate in days rather than in dates. Furthermore, participants instructed to estimate the number of weeks rather than days they would need to complete a target task made longer estimates. This effect of unit sizes is consistent with an anchoring-adjustment process: if people focus on large units, then even a few adjustments from the anchor can greatly increase predicted time. Along similar lines, Buehler, Peetz, and Griffin (2010) demonstrated that predictors make earlier completion time estimates when provided with a "starting point" that is further before the deadline. For example, participants made earlier predictions when they used a timeline where the initial starting point was the current date (early anchor) rather than the deadline date (late anchor) and they were asked to adjust from this starting point to arrive at their prediction.

In many planning contexts there could be other salient anchors, besides the present, that could systematically influence prediction. Research on performance time predictions has demonstrated that predictions can be influenced by an ostensibly arbitrary starting point suggested by the researcher. König (2005) asked participants to first consider whether they would need more or less than 30 minutes (short anchor) or more or less than 90 minutes (long anchor) before estimating the time needed for a catalog search task. Participants made shorter, and more biased, time estimates after exposure to the short anchor than the long anchor. Related studies demonstrated that performance time predictions can be biased in the direction of anchors emanating from a variety of other sources, including the time it took a randomly selected person to carry out the task previously (Thomas & Handley, 2008) and clients' initial expectations about how long a software project should take (Aranda & Easterbrook, 2005; Jørgensen & Grimstad, 2008; Jørgensen & Sjøberg, 2004).

A second explanation proposed for the planning fallacy is the "memory bias account" (Roy & Christenfeld, 2007, 2008; Roy et al., 2005). According to this account, people tend to underestimate performance times because they misremember how long similar tasks have taken in the past, and then use these faulty estimates of performance time as input for predictions of completion time. The problem, then, is not that people disregard historical information, but rather that people's memories of previous performance times are systematically biased, resulting in a corresponding bias in prediction. In support of this account, researchers have documented that people tend to underestimate in retrospect how long tasks have taken, and that the same factors that influence these retrospective biases are also related to prediction biases. Related research has shown that people were able to make more accurate predictions of task performance time when they were provided with accurate records of previous performance times rather than relying on their memories (Roy, Mitten, & Christenfeld, 2008).

As we have previously noted (Buehler, Griffin, & Peetz, 2010; Griffin & Buehler, 2005), the memory bias account may be limited in its ability to explain the planning fallacy or the underestimation bias in prediction of task completion time. After all, studies of the planning fallacy find that predictions diverge markedly from people's reported memories and beliefs about previous completion times. Moreover, as noted above, the general tendency to underestimate task completion times does not appear to be driven primarily by performance time estimates. Thus although it has been argued that the memory-bias account could explain bias in both types of prediction (assuming that predictions of performance time are used as the basis for predictions of task completion times), this account seems to be most applicable to performance time predictions, and indeed the research testing the account has to date targeted performance time predictions.

There could also be individual differences (e.g. personality, cognitive style, cultural background) that contribute to the tendency to underestimate task completion time; however, surprisingly little research has examined such factors. An initial cross-cultural comparison (reported in Buehler et al., 2010) suggested that the tendency to underestimate the completion time of academic tasks was equally pronounced in Canadian and Japanese university students. Studies have also found that prediction bias is not associated with individual differences in dispositional optimism (Buehler et al., 2003; Weick & Guinote, 2010) or procrastination (Buehler et al., 2003; Pychyl, Morin, & Salmon, 2000). However, some traits do appear to moderate the underestimation bias. One study found that individuals scoring higher on "yuppie traits" (i.e. goal oriented, hardworking, and punctual) tended to complete unpleasant tasks sooner, and thus exhibit less prediction bias. In contrast, "hippie traits" (i.e. a laid-back, live-for-the-moment philosophy) were related to both earlier predictions and later actual completion times, resulting in greater prediction bias (Pezzo, Litman, & Pezzo, 2006). Other research has found that individuals with a greater tendency to engage in planning (i.e. propensity to plan, Lynch, Netemeyer, Spiller, & Zammit, 2010) are more inclined to underestimate task completion times. For example, Spiller and Lynch (2009) found that people higher in propensity to plan were more inclined to underestimate the time they would take to finish their holiday shopping. This finding provides further support for the view that a focus on planning can contribute to prediction bias.

We next review research examining several other factors that may amplify or inhibit the tendency to underestimate completion times, focusing in particular on those with potential application for debiasing in organizational contexts. We focus on studies examining task completion times, with some mention of relevant effects for performance times (for a comprehensive review

TABLE 3.1 Overview of research on factors proposed to reduce underestimation bias in task completion times

Factor	Support	Summary of effects
Short vs. long tasks	No★	Underestimation bias found for short and long tasks
		Bias not moderated by task length
Distributional information	Yes★	Drawing on past experience reduces bias
		Reference class forecasting reduces bias for major infrastructure projects
Focus on plans and implementation intentions	Mixed	Focus on plans increases bias
		Forming implementation intentions decreases bias
		Effects may depend on ease of generation
Focus on obstacles	Mixed	Sometimes reduces bias
		Sometimes increases bias
		Sometimes no effect
		Effects may depend on ease of generation
		Effects may depend on the importance of accuracy
Alternative scenarios	No★	No effect on bias
Decomposition	Mixed	Sometimes reduces bias
		Sometimes no effect
		Effects may depend on temporal distance
Speed incentives	No	Increases bias
Neutral observers	Yes★	Reduces bias
Observer perspective	Yes	Reduces bias
Collaborative prediction	No★	Increases bias
Temporal proximity	Mixed★	Sometimes reduces bias
		Sometimes increases bias
		Effects may depend on degree of focus on plans vs. obstacles
Subjective proximity	Yes	Reduces bias
Predictions influence behavior	Mixed	Sometimes predictions influence completion time
		Effects may depend on whether tasks are open to interruption

★ Indicates that studies of task performance time (i.e. time on task) have revealed a different pattern of effects than studies of task completion time (i.e. when task is finished) summarized here. Support column indicates whether there is evidence that the factor reduces prediction bias.

of performance time studies, see Halkjelsvik and Jørgensen, 2012). Table 3.1 presents an overview of the factors we discuss and the associated pattern of effects.

How to Minimize Bias

Distributional Information

A central implication of the inside–outside model of the planning fallacy is that people can reduce optimistic bias by adopting an outside view, wherein they use distributions of similar project outcomes as the basis for prediction, rather than relying on goal-based plans and scenarios. A direct application is seen in reference class forecasting, an approach to forecasting described by Kahneman and Tversky (1979), named by Lovallo and Kahneman (2003), and tested in the realm of major infrastructure projects (Flyvbjerg, 2008; Flyvbjerg et al., 2009). Reference class forecasting sidesteps the problems associated with an inside view, as well as people's disinclination to base predictions on past experience, by *requiring* forecasters to base their predictions on the outcomes of a distribution of comparable projects. The empirical tests of this approach support its effectiveness in reducing time and cost overruns in large-scale construction projects. Similarly, on a smaller scale, recall that our research on individual projects showed that an intervention designed to induce individuals to base predictions on past experience (by highlighting the relevance of their typical completion times to the target project) yielded unbiased predictions (Buehler et al., 1994). Of course, forecasts based on past experience may still be overly optimistic to the extent that people believe previous tasks took less time than they actually did (Roy et al., 2005, 2008). However, given that individuals often hold relatively pessimistic views of their own previous completion times, we believe interventions that induce people to base predictions on past experience (such as reference class forecasting) can often help to debias prediction.

There appears to be general agreement, then, that structured procedures such as reference class forecasting can help to attenuate optimistic prediction biases by comparing the current project to a class of similar projects. However, it is worth noting that this procedure is most applicable in those contexts where a class of comparable projects can be identified. And, as noted previously, forecasters do not seem naturally inclined to adopt this outside approach. What about those instances where forecasters adopt an inside approach to prediction? Are there still ways to avoid or minimize bias? Below we consider several processes that have been proposed and tested as potential debiasing strategies for the prediction of a subjectively "unique" project.

Potential Obstacles vs. Plans for Success

According to Kahneman and Tversky's (1979) initial theorizing, the inside view incorporates all case-specific content, including possible problems or obstacles to completion as well as plans for how to overcome them. Thus, an inside view can, at least in theory, vary in the balance of its content between plans for success and possible obstacles or interruptions. However, our research suggests that people naturally focus on positive plans for success, with relatively little attention to obstacles, and that the balance of content (between plans and obstacles) influences their predictions. Newby-Clark et al. (2000) found that people generate remarkably similar scenarios about future projects whether they are instructed to develop a "realistic" or a "best-case" scenario, suggesting that planning a task and estimating its completion may often be similar to "assuming the best and working from there."

Research has also examined the impact of prompting people to focus narrowly on a plan-based scenario. Given that scenarios can vary in the extent to which they are tightly focused on an optimistic future plan versus open to acknowledging the possibility of obstacles, it follows that a greater than normal focus on detailed planning could exacerbate the degree of optimistic bias. In two studies, we experimentally manipulated the degree of focus on plans by having some participants make detailed, step-by-step plans about an upcoming project, whereas other participants merely reported their completion time predictions (Buehler & Griffin, 2003). The enhanced focus on concrete plans exacerbated the optimistic bias in prediction because this focus, induced at the time of prediction, substantially affected predictions but did not carry through to affect actual completion times.

What happens if predictors are directly instructed to focus on potential obstacles as they generate predictions? Relevant research findings are mixed. Some studies of task completion time found that people predict longer completion times when they are prompted to focus on potential obstacles or problems (Peetz, Buehler, & Wilson, 2010). However, other studies that instructed participants to generate a worst-case scenario of task completion (which included myriad obstacles, interruptions, and delays) did not find an effect of generating these scenarios on prediction

(Newby-Clark et al., 2000). Similarly, studies of performance time prediction for brief laboratory tasks found that predictions were not influenced by instructions to consider potential problems or surprises (Byram, 1997; Hinds, 1999). Thus, to date, there is not conclusive evidence for the effectiveness of manipulating attention to potential obstacles and problems.

We have speculated that people confronted directly with potential obstacles and problems may be reluctant to incorporate this information into their predictions. Their desire for successful task completion may instead elicit a form of motivated reasoning (Kunda, 1990) or desirability bias (Krizan & Windschitl, 2007) wherein they discount negative possibilities. Furthermore, in some contexts, inducing a focus on obstacles can result in "counteractive optimism," when people generate optimistic predictions in order to overcome anticipated obstacles in goal pursuit (Zhang & Fishbach, 2010). When asked to give a rough estimate of when they would complete a take-home test, students predicted that they would finish earlier if they were warned that it might be difficult to complete the test in a timely fashion than if they were not given this warning. Although this pattern of counteractive optimism was not found for participants told that accurate prediction was important (in which case, warning about obstacles yielded longer predictions), the research highlights the intriguing possibility that focusing on obstacles can sometimes prompt early completion time estimates.

The effectiveness of focusing on obstacles versus plans for success can further depend on the ease of generating these cognitions (Min & Arkes, 2012; Sanna and Schwarz, 2004; Sanna, Parks, Chang, & Carter, 2005). Sanna and Schwarz (2004) manipulated the number and type of thoughts (plans for success vs. obstacles) that forecasters were required to list and found that forecasters made more optimistic predictions when success thoughts were experienced as easy to bring to mind (because participants were asked to list only a few) and potential problems were perceived as difficult to bring to mind (because participants were asked to list many). Conversely, forecasters made less optimistic predictions when success thoughts were difficult to bring to mind and potential obstacles were easy to bring to mind. This implies that drawing attention to obstacles may curb optimism only in contexts where obstacles can be readily identified, and that otherwise this strategy could backfire.

Alternative Scenarios

In many business and organizational contexts, where uncertain and uncontrollable events present serious difficulties for long-term planning, techniques involving multiple scenarios are commonly advocated (Bunn & Salo, 1993; Schoemaker, 1993; Wright & Cairns, 2011). However, experiments that applied this technique to the planning fallacy (Newby-Clark et al., 2000) found no evidence that generating alternative scenarios led to more realistic forecasts. Even when participants were instructed to generate pessimistic scenarios that were highly plausible, they continued to disregard the scenarios when arriving at their "best-guess" forecast. These findings highlight once again the problem with basing forecasts on the judged plausibility of an imagined scenario: the very scenarios that seemed most plausible to predictors (the most optimistic ones) were also the least accurate. It is also worth noting that additional research examining performance time predictions for laboratory-based tasks (Byram, 1997 Experiment 2) similarly found that asking people to generate a worst-case scenario prior to prediction did not result in longer time estimates. Thus, to date, there is no clear empirical support for the effectiveness of alternative scenario techniques in reducing the planning fallacy.

Decomposition

Another strategy that varies the content of the inside view is to require planners to break down a task into smaller segments (Byram, 1997; Connolly & Dean, 1997; Forsyth & Burt, 2008; Kruger

& Evans, 2004). The idea is that plans generated holistically tend to be incomplete and oversimplified, and thus breaking down the larger task into smaller sub-tasks can highlight steps that need to be completed but may have been overlooked (Kruger & Evans, 2004). Kruger and Evans found that asking people to unpack a task (i.e. identify all the necessary sub-tasks before generating an overall prediction) reduced the underestimation bias in performance time predictions for several lab tasks, and had a parallel effect on completion time predictions for holiday shopping. Similarly, Forsyth and Burt (2008) reported a "segmentation effect" on short performance time predictions: participants in the segmentation condition provided time estimates separately for each task sub-component and these were aggregated to produce the estimate for the task as a whole. The aggregated total of the decomposed estimates was longer than the overall estimates, and this served to reduce the underestimation bias for relatively 'long' tasks lasting 20–40 minutes, and actually produced an overestimation bias for shorter tasks.

It is worth noting that studies have not always found an effect of asking people to break down tasks into smaller steps (Byram, 1997; Connolly & Dean, 1997). Recent studies suggest that effects of unpacking on prediction may be limited to tasks occurring in the near future, as it appears more difficult to identify sub-components of distant future tasks (Moher, 2012). It is also noteworthy that nearly all of the studies examined predictions of performance time rather than completion time (with the exception of the holiday shopping study by Kruger & Evans, 2004). It would be informative to examine unpacking strategies for extensive tasks prone to external interruptions and delays. One intriguing possibility is that unpacking manipulations might help to identify more of the necessary steps in a task (thereby increasing performance time predictions) but, as a result, distract attention from complicating factors external to the task itself (thereby decreasing completion time predictions).

Why would unpacking manipulations result in longer time estimates and reduced bias (Kruger & Evans, 2004), whereas a focus on concrete step-by-step planning heightens bias (Buehler & Griffin, 2003)? Both manipulations focus the predictor on more specific details. Although speculative, we suggest that the effects of breaking down a task into concrete details may depend on the type of information that is highlighted. If people are induced to focus on otherwise ignored non-focal aspects of a task, as in the unpacking manipulation, this should lead to reduced optimism because these minor details are more likely to reveal unrealized distractions, obstacles, and inhibiting factors. If, however, people are induced to focus in greater detail on how they will carry out the central task components (without contemplating the otherwise ignored sub-components), this would increase optimism, because this enhanced task focus takes away any attention from obstacles or past experiences. Given that the planning focus instructions emphasized the creation of a flowing scenario for a unitary task (e.g. "Try to provide a complete picture, from beginning to end, of how this assignment will be completed"), they likely lead participants to focus on plans for carrying out central task components rather than to recognize previously ignored aspects of the task. In sum, strategies that involve decomposition of a task (unpacking, task segmentation) show strong potential to produce longer, and thus less optimistically biased forecasts. However, most of the research has focused on performance time predictions and more work is needed to clarify how these strategies will play out for completion time predictions. Planners should also be cognizant of the potential for concrete thinking to exacerbate optimistic bias.

Incentives for Speed

On the surface, it may seem that people who are more motivated to finish a task quickly should be less prone to the planning fallacy. However, consistent with theories of motivated reasoning (Kunda, 1990) and desirability bias (Krizan & Windschitl, 2007), we have proposed that incentives to finish a task quickly will lead to optimistic forecasts (through a greater focus on plans and a reduced focus on potential obstacles) and thus exacerbate the prediction bias – assuming that completion behavior is not equally influenced by the incentives. Our contention is that it is relatively easy to generate plans and predictions that correspond with one's current goal, but it is usually much more difficult to translate that goal into behavior. Studies have supported this reasoning by demonstrating that incentives for speedy completion of a task result in more optimistic predictions, both for task completion times (Buehler et al., 1997) and task performance times (Byram, 1997). In each case, the incentive for speed increased bias because it had a substantial impact on prediction but this impact did not carry through to influence actual behavior. Furthermore, there was evidence that motivation increased the optimism of prediction through a heightened focus on concrete future plans and a reduced focus on past experiences and possible obstacles (Buehler et al., 1997). In other words, the speed incentives appeared to strengthen the pattern of cognitive processes that support the planning fallacy.

The work on incentives has important implications, because planners and project managers often encounter a variety of organizational pressures as well as direct financial incentives that heighten the motivation for speedy project completion (Kahneman & Lovallo, 1993; Lovallo & Kahneman, 2003). The research suggests that such motivations can encourage planners to delude themselves by altering how they arrive at their predictions. When accurate predictions are crucial, organizations may be well advised to avoid financial incentives for speedy project completion, at least for those making the forecasts, and also to attempt to minimize the sorts of intangible organizational pressures that promote optimism.

Neutral Observers

A strategy to minimize the role of motivational processes solicits predictions from neutral observers with no stake in the outcome. Theorists have long noted that people appear to make more realistic estimates about completion times for others than for themselves, and that this actor–observer difference in prediction may reflect differences in the underlying cognitive and motivational processes that typically give rise to underestimation. Observers typically do not have access to the detailed information that actors possess about their plans and life circumstances, making it less likely they will focus narrowly on a plan for completing the task by a desired time. In addition, neutral observers do not generally share the same motivations as actors (e.g. the motivation to finish promptly) and thus their predictions are less likely to be colored by these motives.

Consistent with this theorizing, an early study (Buehler et al., 1994, Study 5) found that observers are generally less attentive than actors to the actors' reported plans and more attentive to potential obstacles, the actors' past experiences, and task deadlines – in other words, observers were more likely to adopt the outside view *and* to construct a more problem-focused inside view. Another study found that observers gave little weight to an actor's motivation for early completion. Actors who imagined themselves completing a school project predicted they would finish it much earlier in a scenario where they were offered incentive grades for early completion; however, knowing that the student had been offered this incentive did not affect the predictions generated by observer participants (Mulhern, 2006). Thus it appears that observers are more skeptical than actors about whether incentives that operate on the actor are enough to overcome past behavioral tendencies. Along similar lines, prompting actors to contemplate worst-case scenarios of task completion (which included myriad obstacles, interruptions, and delays) had no impact on the actors' own predictions but led observers to predict later completion times (Newby-Clark et al., 2000). Again this finding suggests that observers are guided less by the actors' desires, and they are more receptive to the possibility of obstacles than are actors.

To further examine the role of motivation in actor and observer predictions, a series of studies (reported in Buehler, Griffin, & Peetz, 2010), explored what would happen if observers were motivated to see an actor achieve an early completion time. Conceivably, for such observers, the same motivated reasoning processes that encourage optimism in actors would operate, so that they adopt an inside perspective dominated by plans for success. We tested this possibility by offering financial incentives to observers that were contingent on a target (actor) individual's timely task completion. Observers in this contingent incentive condition tended to underestimate the actor's task completion time to the same degree as actors did, whereas neutral observers did not exhibit this bias. Furthermore, measures of thought process indicated that the incentives affected observers' predictions, in part, because they prompted observers to rely more heavily on the target individual's future plans and to place less weight on reports of past experiences and potential obstacles.

Notably, studies examining predictions of task performance time, rather than completion time, have not found a general actor–observer difference in prediction (Byram, 1997; Hinds, 1999; Jørgensen, 2004; Roy, Christenfeld, & Jones, 2013). For example, Byram (1997) asked participants to build a computer stand in the lab and found that participants underestimated the time it would take to an equal degree regardless of whether their predictions concerned themselves or the average person. Hinds (1999) examined predictions of the time it would take new users of a cell phone to perform voicemail tasks. Estimates were obtained from a group of observers highly experienced with the tasks (expert observers), a group of observers with limited experience (intermediate observers), as well as from the novice users. All three groups underestimated task performance time, and, whereas this bias was lower for the intermediate observers than for the novice users, it was actually higher for the expert observers than for the novice users. Roy et al. (2013) found very similar patterns of bias (sometimes underestimation and sometimes overestimation depending on task characteristics) in actor and observer predictions for brief laboratory tasks, suggesting that prediction bias, at least for performance times, is not due to the predictors' level of involvement with the task.

The discrepancy in findings between studies of performance time and completion time is striking and again suggests that bias in these two types of predictions stems from different sources. From a practical perspective, the research suggests that planners seeking to estimate realistic task completion times may be well advised to seek input from neutral observers.

Observer Perspective

Recent research extends the work on observer prediction by testing whether people can be induced to take on an observer-like perspective for their own tasks, and whether this perspective curbs prediction bias (Buehler, Griffin, Lam, & Deslauriers, 2012). This approach was motivated by evidence in psychology that people can choose strategically to imagine future events from differing perspectives (Libby & Eibach, 2002, 2011; Pronin & Ross, 2006). People who adopt a *first-person* perspective would see a project unfolding as if they were actually carrying it out, whereas those who adopt a *third-person* perspective see events from an observer's vantage point. The third-person perspective could help to minimize optimistic bias because it elicits cognitive processes similar to those in neutral observers (e.g. Frank & Gilovich, 1989; Pronin & Ross, 2006) and reduces the salience and intensity of emotional engagement with imagined events (e.g. Kross, Ayduk, & Mischel, 2005; McIsaac & Eich, 2002). Thus third-person imagery may attenuate the cognitive and motivational processes that contribute to optimistic forecasts.

To test this theorizing, a series of experiments varied the imagery perspective people adopted as they contemplated an upcoming task (Buehler et al., 2012). Student participants identified a specific upcoming task, imagined it unfolding, and then predicted when they would complete it.

We measured (Study 1) or directly manipulated (Studies 2–4) the perspective participants adopted as they imagined themselves carrying out the task. The initial study revealed that approximately two-thirds of participants spontaneously adopted first-person imagery and one third adopted third-person imagery. The remaining studies demonstrated that encouraging predictors to adopt a third-person perspective curbed the planning fallacy. Individuals predicted longer completion times – and thus were less prone to bias – when they imagined the task from a third-person rather than a first-person perspective. This effect of perspective was partially mediated by people's cognitive focus on plans versus obstacles at the time of prediction: third-person imagery reduced people's inclination to focus narrowly on optimistic plans and increased their focus on potential obstacles. Taking a third-person perspective also altered the role of task-relevant motivation in prediction. The desire to finish a task promptly was reduced, and weighted less heavily, when individuals adopted a third-person rather than a first-person perspective. In essence, then, the third-person perspective elicited predictions and underlying psychological processes that mimic those found in neutral observers (Buehler et al., 1994; Newby-Clark et al., 2000), suggesting that planners could gain the benefits of observer-based prediction without actually needing to consult with others.

Collaborative Prediction

Most research on the planning fallacy has examined tasks and predictions of individuals, so it is conceivable that the optimistic biases found for individual tasks are reduced or eliminated for group-based tasks. An important feature of truly interactive group tasks is that people are interdependent – they must often wait for contributions of others before they can do their own part. In some ways, then, group participants' viewpoints are similar to those of observers of other people's activities, which can mitigate optimistic bias. However, membership in a collaborative group also creates important differences in perspective relative to neutral observers. Although a group member may be partially an observer (for the other members' contributions), he or she is also an active participant (for his or her own contribution) and has a stake in the task as a whole, which could override any tendency to think as an outside observer. Consistent with this reasoning, studies have found that the tendency to underestimate task completion times does indeed generalize to group tasks (e.g. Buehler, Messervey, & Griffin, 2005; Sanna et al., 2005).

A challenge unique to group-based projects is that forecasters must attempt to gauge not only the benefits of sharing the workload but also problems of coordination, redundancy, and inefficiency inherent in work teams. Because of such coordination costs, the total performance time (e.g. person-hours) is often much greater for large than for small work teams. Within the realm of software development projects, Brooks' Law famously states that "adding manpower to a late software project makes it later" (Brooks, 1975). However, recent findings (Staats, Milkman, & Fox, 2012) indicate that judges do not fully appreciate the costs of coordination and consequently underestimate performance times more for large work teams than for small work teams. This "team-scaling fallacy" is found for judges involved in the task as well as observers estimating the work of others.

Related research has explored the effects of generating predictions collaboratively versus individually. Given that group discussion prompts individuals to focus selectively on information that supports the initial inclination of individual group members (Hinsz, Tindale, & Vollrath, 1997; Kerr & Tindale, 2004), this could reinforce the tendency to focus narrowly on future success. To test this possibility, two studies examined predictions for group projects with a monetary incentive for speedy task completion, and compared individual predictions with group-based (consensus and consultation based) predictions (Buehler et al., 2005). Participants generally underestimated how long they would take to complete the target tasks, but predictions based on group discussion were significantly more optimistic (and hence more biased) than predictions generated by individual group members. Additional process measures indicated that group discussion prompted an increased focus on positive future scenarios (i.e. scenarios in which things go according to plan) and a decreased focus on negative future scenarios (i.e. scenarios that included possible obstacles or problems), and that this pattern of thought focus resulted in more optimistic forecasts.

Notably, the findings were consistent whether the studies examined completion time predictions for a take-home assignment (Study 3), or performance time predictions for a 100-piece jigsaw puzzle in the lab (Study 2). In contrast, research on performance time predictions in a software development context suggests that group discussion helps to reduce the underestimation bias seen in individual predictions (Moløkken-Østvold & Jørgensen, 2004; Moløkken-Østvold, Haugen, & Benesad, 2008). Group discussion helped work teams to identify a larger set of activities that would be required for completion of the project, resulting in longer and more realistic time estimates. As Halkjelsvik and Jørgensen (2012) note, a feature of the studies that could plausibly account for the different effects is the incentive for speed in the tasks studied by Buehler et al. (2005). Contextual factors such as this can determine whether group discussion attenuates or accentuates judgmental biases found in individuals (Kerr & Tindale, 2004).

Thus, findings to date do not yield consistent evidence for the effectiveness of group discussion as a prediction strategy. Indeed, the only study examining task completion time (Buehler et al., 2005 Study 3) suggests that group discussion exacerbates the tendency toward unrealistic prediction through a heightened tendency to "plan for success." This finding may be applicable to many collaborative work ventures that are similar in form to the projects examined here – that is, projects to be completed collaboratively by groups who are motivated to finish early. Under such circumstances, forecasters may be well advised to collect and aggregate individual forecasts instead of engaging in group discussion.

There are many additional forms of social pressure that could contribute to optimistic prediction bias. One study tested the possibility that self-presentation concerns may influence individuals' task completion predictions (Pezzo, Pezzo, & Stone, 2006). Participants generated more optimistic predictions when they reported them verbally to an experimenter than when the experimenter was absent and predictions were anonymous. Also people's social roles and positions may influence how they generate task completion predictions. Weick and Guinote (2010) proposed that people who occupy positions of power in a social hierarchy – and experience the sense of power associated with that role – may be particularly prone to optimistic bias. This hypothesis is based on previous evidence that power induces goal-directed attention and a tendency to disregard information that lies outside the focal goal (Guinote, 2007a, 2007b). Applied to the planning fallacy, then, powerful individuals should be particularly inclined to focus narrowly on planning for success. Consistent with this reasoning, a series of experiments demonstrated that individuals were more likely to underestimate task completion times when they were induced to experience feelings of power. Additional findings revealed that the effect of power on prediction was mediated by attentional focus: drawing participants' attention to relevant information outside the focal goal (i.e. relevant past completion times) eliminated the effect of power on prediction.

Temporal Distance

The temporal distance to future events (i.e. how far in the future the task will be performed) influences the level of optimism in many judgmental domains (Liberman, Trope, & Stephan, 2007; Eyal, Liberman, Trope, & Walther, 2004; Gilovich, Kerr, & Medvec, 1993; Savitsky, Medvec, Charlton, & Gilovich, 1998), and researchers have begun to examine how the distance to a future project may influence the planning fallacy. This research is guided primarily by Construal Level

Theory (CLT) (Liberman & Trope, 1998; Trope & Liberman, 2003). According to CLT, temporal proximity increases the tendency for forecasters to focus on concrete, specific representations of an event, whereas temporal distance increases the tendency for forecasters to focus on high-level, abstract representations. Accordingly, people should make more optimistic predictions when tasks are further in the future, because temporal distance should heighten the prevailing tendency to rely on oversimplified representations of the task that typically provide a clear roadmap to completion and to neglect non-focal considerations, which often provide reasons why the task may not be straightforward. In support of this reasoning, people predict they can accomplish more within a week in the distant future than a week in the near future, and are also less sensitive to time constraints and peripheral activities that will compete for their time in the distant future (Liberman & Trope, 1998). Similarly, Zauberman and Lynch (2005) demonstrated that people expect to have more time free to pursue their goals in the distant than in the immediate future. This work implies that people will generate more conservative and realistic forecasts for tasks occurring in the immediate future because they are more likely to contemplate concrete issues of feasibility.

Peetz and colleagues (Peetz et al., 2010), however, suggested that temporal proximity and concrete thinking won't always minimize optimism. When contemplating a future project, there are two very different types of concrete cognitions – plans for success and potential obstacles – that could be increasingly available as a task draws near, and these two cognitions have opposite implications for prediction. These researchers further proposed that temporal proximity is likely to have a greater impact on whichever type of concrete cognition is most salient at the time of prediction. Thus, contextual factors that alter the relative focus on plans vs. obstacles should determine how temporal proximity affects prediction. Experimental findings support this reasoning. In contexts that prompted concerns about potential obstacles (e.g. when the tasks were real, or when participants were primed to focus on obstacles), individuals made more conservative predictions for close than for distant tasks. In contexts where predictors were naturally inclined to develop optimistic plans, with relatively little concern about feasibility (e.g. when the tasks were hypothetical, or when participants were primed to focus on step-by-step plans), individuals made more optimistic predictions for close than for distant tasks. Thus, although the findings again indicate that temporal proximity heightens the role of concrete information in prediction, they also stress the importance of distinguishing the types of concrete thought that may be affected. The practical upshot is that forecasters and managers may be most likely to generate realistic, conservative estimates if they are required to make predictions close in time to project commencement, *and* to maintain a focus on potential obstacles.

Research has also examined effects of temporal distance for predictions of task performance time. For this type of prediction there was no evidence that distance resulted in more optimistic predictions; in fact, some evidence points the other way. Indeed, Byram (1997, Experiment 1) found that people made much longer predictions several months in advance of a furniture assembly task than immediately before carrying out the task. Similarly Kanten (2011) found that people predicted various hypothetical tasks (e.g. painting a barn, proofreading an article, writing a chapter summary) would take longer when they imagined themselves performing the tasks in the distant future, or when they were primed to adopt an abstract rather than concrete mindset. The research also tested a novel "time contraction" process to account for the effects: with greater distance and abstraction, time units are perceived as smaller and thus more units are needed to cover the same amount of work. For example, a year from now, one hour does not seem like much, and so it seems that many hours would be needed to paint a barn. Consistent with this account, the effect of temporal distance on prediction was mediated by a perceived shrinkage of time units.

Subjective Temporal Distance

Whereas the above studies examined the objective distance to an upcoming task, additional research has examined predictors' subjective perceptions of distance. Is it possible to make an upcoming task or deadline "feel closer" to the present, and how would this affect prediction? Sanna and colleagues (2005) manipulated perceived distance with instructions that implied a standard period of time was either short or long. Using class projects with a three-month deadline, a negative temporal frame was created by reminding some forecasters that "given the deadline … you only have 12 weeks remaining," and a positive temporal frame was created by reminding other forecasters that "beginning today … you still have 12 weeks remaining." Predictions made under the positive temporal frame were essentially identical to those made in a control condition, whereas the negative temporal frame led forecasters to rate the deadline as perceptually closer, to rate thoughts about success as more difficult to bring to mind, and to make later and less biased forecasts of completion time. The same pattern was replicated for performance time predictions for furniture assembly.

Boltz and Yum (2010) also proposed that the underestimation bias could be curbed by altering people's conceptualization of time. These researchers note that people can adopt different conceptualizations of time that vary in terms of whether the individual is moving through time (ego-motion perspective) or time is moving toward the individual (time-motion perspective). Student participants were induced to adopt either a time-motion or ego-motion perspective using visual scenes (e.g. clouds moving toward the viewer vs. the viewer moving toward clouds) or linguistic cues (e.g. "as the end of the hour approaches us" vs. "as we approach the end of the hour") and then to predict how long it would take to perform a journal sorting task. Adopting the time-motion perspective served to eliminate the underestimation bias for this task, and made the end of the session feel closer in time. Boltz and Yum suggest that the time-motion perspective attenuates the underestimation bias because it makes future deadlines feel more impending, reduces one's sense of control, and induces more concrete task representations, though these mechanisms were not directly tested. Related research suggests that tasks and task deadlines can be made to feel closer or further away by highlighting the amount of effort needed to carry out the task (Jiga-Boy, Clark, & Semin, 2010). When people face an explicit deadline, those anticipating a more arduous and demanding task perceive it as closer in time and believe they must start preparing earlier. As the authors note, such perceptions could potentially curb the tendency to make optimistic time estimates, though this effect was not tested.

Predictions that Influence Behavior

Of course, the degree of optimistic bias is determined not only by processes occurring at prediction, but also by what transpires after the prediction has been generated. Thus one way to increase the accuracy of prediction is to bring people's behavior in line with the predictions they have generated. For example, given that people's focus on their goals and plans (salient at the time of prediction) may diminish across time, one remedy would be to enhance the salience of goal-directed plans throughout the entire project period. In a relevant test of this idea (Taylor et al., 1998), students were trained to imagine themselves performing each of the steps needed to complete a school-related project by their predicted completion time. Participants rehearsed these simulations each day of the week during which they carried out the project. The exercise increased the proportion of students who finished by the predicted time from 14 percent (in a control condition) to 41 percent. Along similar lines, Koole and Van't Spijker (2000) found that students were more likely to finish a brief writing task by the expected time if they were instructed to form "implementation intentions" (Gollwitzer, 1999; Gollwitzer & Brandstätter, 1997; see also Thürmer, Wieber, & Gollwitzer, this volume) that specified the exact time and place they would do the task.

Additional research suggests that behavior-based approaches may vary in effectiveness depending on the nature of the task, and particularly the extent to which it is prone to unexpected interruptions, problems, and delays (Buehler, Peetz, & Griffin, 2010). This research tested the widely held notion that optimistic plans and predictions may influence when tasks are actually completed. It is commonly argued that ambitious plans and predictions can help people finish earlier than they would otherwise. In addition, several theoretical approaches – including goal-setting, motivational, and consistency theories – imply that optimistic predictions should facilitate task completion. However, note that, despite these potential facilitating processes, the research we have summarized in this chapter suggests that predictions themselves often have little or no influence on completion times: manipulations that indirectly affect predicted task completion times have typically failed to show corresponding behavioral effects.

To reconcile these ideas, we proposed that task completion predictions are more "translatable" (Koehler & Poon, 2006) into the one-time action of starting a project than into the continuing actions necessary to complete a project. This assumption has clear implications for identifying the type of tasks for which optimistic predictions will have beneficial effects. In particular, tasks that can be completed in a single continuous session, and thus are not usually prone to interruptions and delays once they have been started, are the type of tasks where we expect an effect of predictions on completion times. We term these "closed tasks" due to the fact that, once initiated, these tasks are relatively impervious to outside disruption. In contrast, "open tasks" require multiple steps to be completed at different times or locations. These are the kinds of tasks that typically require several work sessions to finish and thus are relatively prone to interruptions and delays even after they have been started; hence, for these tasks, differential plans, intentions, and starting times may not influence the ultimate completion times. Our reasoning, then, is that a task completion prediction will exert its greatest impact on the early stages of a project, but this impact will diminish across time. Consequently, optimistic predictions will have a greater impact on actual completion times for closed tasks than for open tasks. As one test of this logic, we performed a quantitative review of studies with manipulations that affected predicted completion times (Buehler, Peetz, & Griffin, 2010) and classified the target tasks as being either relatively closed (e.g. a one-hour computer tutorial, a short writing assignment) or relatively open (e.g. major school projects, income tax returns). Effects found on prediction were much more likely to carry through to behavior for closed tasks than for open tasks.

A related study assessed the impact of planning and prediction on completion behavior (Deslauriers, 2002). Some participants were instructed to think about (and describe) the specific details of when, where, and how they would complete the target writing assignment (plan focus condition), and others were not given this instruction (control condition). To manipulate the extent to which the assignment was open or closed, participants were told either that they could complete all three parts of the writing assignment in one sitting (closed task condition) or that they were required to let one day elapse between writing and submitting each part (open task condition). Consistent with our theorizing, for the open version of the task, focusing on plans increased the optimistic bias: participants predicted to finish the task in fewer days when they were induced to focus on plans than when they were not (Ms = 7.4 vs. 8.9 days), but their actual completion times did not differ (Ms = 10.4 vs. 10.3 days). In other words, in the open version of the task, the effect of plan focus did not carry through from prediction to affect actual completion times. For the closed version of the task, participants again predicted to finish in less time in the plan focus condition than in the control condition (Ms = 5.8 vs. 7.7 days); however, the actual completion times were also shorter in the plan focus than in the control condition (*Ms* = 7.9 vs. 10.2 days), and thus the bias was similar across the two conditions.

Another set of experiments (Buehler, Peetz, & Griffin, 2010) examined the impact of predictions more directly, by using anchoring procedures to manipulate the optimism of participants' task completion predictions (i.e. how far before deadline they expected to finish). The specific anchoring manipulations varied across studies, from drawing a card to sliding a pointer along a numbered time line, but in each case yielded a strong effect on prediction, allowing us to investigate whether the completion times would be influenced by these predictions. The type of task (open vs. closed) was varied across studies as well as experimentally manipulated within a study. Results supported the three guiding hypotheses. First, at least for tasks that were closed (e.g. a computer tutorial assignment, a simple writing assignment), the manipulated differences in prediction carried on to affect actual completion times. Second, predictions had a greater impact on the actual completion times of closed tasks than of open tasks: indeed, for each of the open tasks that we examined (e.g. major school projects, income tax returns), completion times were not affected significantly by the prediction manipulation. Third, even though predictions did not influence completion times for open tasks, the predictions did influence when these tasks were started. The findings again support the idea that completion predictions have their greatest impact on the beginning phases of a project, particularly the initiation time, but this effect diminishes over the course of an extensive, multi-stage project.

These studies begin to address the complex questions of whether, or when, it may be beneficial to predict an early task completion time. People hoping to finish a task early may be well advised to predict an early completion time if the task is relatively closed, because the predictions appear to facilitate early completion times without increasing proneness to underestimation (and any associated costs). When the task is relatively open, people may be advised to make more conservative forecasts, especially if there are serious costs associated with underestimation, because the predictions appear to have little benefit for actual completion times but have clear potential to exacerbate bias. When an earlier starting time has value in itself, then optimistic forecasts may be valuable regardless of the nature of the task. The findings also provide some guidance for inducing desired task completion times in others, at least when tasks are relatively closed. Techniques used in the early anchor condition of our studies could be adapted for use in a range of applied settings where practitioners (e.g. teachers, managers, co-workers) seek to encourage others to complete tasks promptly. A potential benefit of a suggested anchor, rather than simply imposing a goal on others, is that it may be less likely to jeopardize the individual's commitment to finish at the desired time (Hinsz, Kalnbach, & Lorentz, 1997).

To fully understand the behavioral effects, we believe it is also necessary to consider the role of deadlines in guiding task completion behavior. Note that the target tasks we studied had a firm deadline for completion, and previous research has shown that such deadlines exert a powerful impact on when people actually finish their tasks – even when people hope to finish well in advance of a deadline, their actual time ends up being driven largely by that deadline (Ariely & Wertenbroch, 2002; Buehler et al., 1994; Tversky & Shafir, 1992; Van Oorschot et al., 2005). We suspect that for open tasks, the salience of an early prediction (and perhaps the task itself) may fade until a looming deadline pulls it back into focus. That is, people's final task completion times may be a function of two psychological forces – people's plans to finish early and their deadlines. Optimistic plans to finish early may get tasks started, but then the effects of external factors take over and it is the force of deadlines that controls actual completion times.

Applications and Conclusions: Lessons from the Planning Fallacy

The planning fallacy is a phenomenon born out of the practice of forecasting. As such, its initial description carried clear lessons for application. But the ongoing research reviewed in this chapter, much of it inspired by the original inside-outside model originally formulated by Kahneman and Tversky (1979), has added considerably to the practical usefulness of the model. Applications vary according to whether the optimistic prediction comes from a failure of prediction or a failure of action.

Consider the first case, a failure of prediction. A manager at a major software company needs to forecast the shipping date of a new operating system, call it Doors 9. He knows that 80 percent of prior operating system roll-outs have gone out substantially later than predicted, causing substantial customer frustration and a reduced reputation for reliability. After reading a review of the original planning fallacy work in *Harvard Business Review*, our manager questions his stubborn intuition that past failures are irrelevant to the current product schedule because of the new – and currently untested – workflow system he has put in place. He realizes that the current shipping date forecast should be informed by the lessons of the past, despite the apparently unique situation he now faces. Moreover, he has learned that old unpredictable problems are likely to be replaced by new unpredictable problems. Based on subsequent research on debiasing, our manager himself can try to think like an outsider, couching his predictions in the language of the third person. If he successfully thinks of the company from an outside perspective, he may be more aware of the lessons from similar past projects at his own or at other companies or in other industries, and his specific forecasted planning stages are likely to be more open to consideration of possible barriers and less biased towards a pure path to success. Or he may accomplish this outside view by hiring an outside consultant, who does not know the inside story of the organization, and who – furnished with expert knowledge, past performance and generic current plans – should be able to "see" the current estimates as one of a set of equally salient (although not equally relevant) pieces of information.

Now consider the second case, a manager who interprets his forecasting challenges and cost overruns as a failure of execution: for some reason, plans do not roll out as expected. Here, the attributional underpinnings of the planning fallacy – the documented tendency to blame past failures on external and unstable causes – can be the source of the most useful applied lessons. In fact, executives who we meet in consulting and executive education roles often start with denial, stating that "we never exactly repeat a project and so it is very difficult to learn what to do differently." The insight that all projects can be roughly classified into reference classes, using more abstract analogies if necessary, is something that takes thought and practice to apply. The most important outcome of this learning process is the realization that it is worthwhile tracking and maintaining records about even the apparently unique, one-off projects carried out by a company.

On a smaller scale, most of us suffer from an occasional failure of action to carry out smaller commitments by the time we have promised, such as drafting an annual budget report, or providing a performance review – especially when such promises are given well before the due date. In such cases, the due date is not a variable, but a constant, and no useful lesson can be drawn about making predictions per se. The key is to learn from the past about the factors that lead to the current target task being "crowded out" by competing activities. Even in the case of personal projects, the structure required to overcome the planning fallacy is much the same as for large organizational projects: develop a reference class of experiences, draw the lessons of the past, and be aware of how the past will repeat itself unless deliberate and thoughtful attempts are made to change the task competition environment under which the project takes place.

We do not wish to imply that people should simply avoid planning for future tasks. Although several scholars argue against planning due to the uncertainty inherent in the future (e.g. Mintzberg, 1994; Sarasvathy, 2001), planning serves many important functions, including the initiation and regulation of actions that promote successful task completion (Gielnik, Frese, & Stark, this volume). We believe that plans can also provide valuable input into the prediction of task completion time and enhance accuracy when used appropriately. We suggest, however, that forecast accuracy may be best served if processes of planning and prediction are segregated, and an initial forecast is based solely and exclusively on the most relevant base rate. This is the basic logic of the UK Department of Transport, who, using the framework of reference class forecasting, assume that a new project will face the same time challenges and cost overruns that characterize its reference class *unless* the project contractor can "prove" otherwise (Flyvbjerg, 2008; Flyvbjerg et al., 2009). Note that this approach maintains the Bayesian logic with which Kahneman and Tversky began when they first structured their analysis of the planning fallacy: the success rate of the reference class of projects serves to define the prior probability distribution of success, and the diagnosticity of the forecast resulting from planning each unique current project defines the likelihood ratio. When the diagnosticity of the plans is near zero – that is, optimistic plans are just as likely to be associated with failing as with successful projects – Bayesian rationality tells us that we should rely on the prior distribution, or reference class, alone. However, as the plans and resulting forecasts become more diagnostic – that is, as extremely optimistic plans become more associated with successful outcomes and less associated with unsuccessful outcomes – Bayesian rationality allows us to let go of the lessons of the past and rely entirely on the case-specific forecasts for this project. Complete reliance on the plan-based forecast is appropriate only in the case of perfect diagnosticity – when all positive forecasts are associated with success and all negative forecasts are associated with failure.

Given that this state of forecast perfection is unattainable in practice, we are left with a balancing act – forecasts should be centered on the base rate (reference class mean) and then adjusted according to the informativeness of the specific plans. In our research on personal projects, we have consistently seen evidence of over-optimistic forecasts on average (which we interpret as evidence of base-rate neglect in this context), along with moderate between-subject correlations between forecasts and plan outcomes (which we interpret as evidence of moderate plan-based diagnosticity). Thus, it is not that plans need to be thrown out but that the lessons of the past need to be better integrated with the plan-based forecasts about the future. In this light, many of the debiasing manipulations we have explored can be classified as either (or most often, both) (1) focusing forecasters more on the reference class and less on the details of the unique plan-based forecast (e.g. relying on past experience, neutral observers, distanced perspectives) or (2) focusing forecasters more on the content of the plans so that content becomes more balanced in valence and hence more predictive or diagnostic of actual outcomes (e.g. focus on obstacles, decomposed plans, alternative scenarios). In our view, the simple advice to ignore planning when forecasting would be an unnecessary gesture of defeat in the face of many hopeful signs that forecasting can be improved through a better understanding of the planning fallacy.

In summary, although the sources of optimistic completion time predictions are relatively simple – the dominance of specific plans for success over distributional information about similar projects – the possible corrective strategies are many. We hope that the organizational framework presented here helps both managers and scholars to develop effective ways to reduce the underestimation bias in completion time predictions and to control the costs of this bias.

Acknowledgment

This program of research was supported by the Social Sciences and Humanities Research Council of Canada.

References

Aranda, J., & Easterbrook, S. (2005). Anchoring and adjustment in software estimation. *Software Engineering Notes*, 30, 346–355. doi:10.1145/1095430.1081761

Ariely, D., & Wertenbroch, K. (2002). Procrastination, deadlines, and performance: Self-control by precommitment. *Psychological Science*, 13, 219–224. doi:10.1111/1467-9280.00441

Boltz, M. G., & Yum, Y. N. (2010). Temporal concepts and predicted duration judgments. *Journal of Experimental Social Psychology*, 46(6), 895–904. doi:10.1016/j.jesp.2010.07.002

Brooks, F. P., Jr. (1975). *The mythical man-month: Essays on software engineering*. Reading, MA: Addison-Wesley.

Buehler, R., (1991). *Why individuals underestimate their own task completion times*. Doctoral dissertation, University of Waterloo, Ontario, Canada.

Buehler, R., & Griffin, D. (2003). Planning, personality, and prediction: The role of future focus in optimistic time predictions. *Organizational Behavior and Human Decision Processes*, 92, 80–90. doi:1016/S0749-5978(03)00089-X

Buehler, R., Griffin, D., & Ross, M. (1994). Exploring the "planning fallacy": Why people underestimate their task completion times. *Journal of Personality and Social Psychology*, 67, 366–381. doi: 10.1037/0022-3514.67.3.366

Buehler, R., Griffin, D., & MacDonald, H. (1997). The role of motivated reasoning in optimistic time predictions. *Personality and Social Psychology Bulletin*, 23, 238–247. doi, 10.1177/0146167297233003

Buehler, R., Griffin, D., & Ross, M. (2002). Inside the planning fallacy: The causes and consequences of optimistic time predictions. In T. Gilovich, D. Griffin, & D. Kahneman (Eds.), *Heuristics and biases: The psychology of intuitive judgment* (pp. 250–270). Cambridge, UK: Cambridge University Press.

Buehler, R., Messervey, D., & Griffin, D. (2005). Collaborative planning and prediction: Does group discussion affect optimistic biases in time estimation? *Organizational Behavior and Human Decision Processes*, 97, 47–63. doi:10.1016/j.obhdp.2005.02.004

Buehler, R., Griffin, D., & Peetz, J. (2010). The planning fallacy: Cognitive, motivational, and social origins. In M. P. Zanna & J. M. Olson (Eds.), *Advances in experimental social psychology* (Vol. 43, pp. 1–62). San Diego, CA: Academic Press. doi, 10.1016/S0065-2601(10)43001-4

Buehler, R., Peetz, J., & Griffin, D. (2010). Finishing on time: When do predictions influence actual completion times? *Organizational Behaviour and Human Decision Processes*, 111, 23–32. doi, 10.1016/S0065-2601(10)43001-4

Buehler, R., Griffin, D., Lam, K. C. H., & Deslauriers, J. (2012). Perspectives on prediction: Does third-person imagery improve task completion estimates? *Organizational Behavior and Human Decision Processes*, 117, 138–149. doi:10.1016/j.obhdp.2011.09.001

Bunn, D. W., & Salo, A. A. (1993). Forecasting with scenarios. *European Journal of Operational Research*, 68(3), 291–303. doi: http://dx.doi.org/10.1016/0377-2217(93)90186-Q

Byram, S. J. (1997). Cognitive and motivational factors influencing time predictions. *Journal of Experimental Psychology: Applied*, 3, 216–239. doi, 10.1037/1076-898X.3.3.216

Connolly, T., & Dean, D. (1997). Decomposed versus holistic estimates of effort required for software writing tasks. *Management Science*, 43, 1029–1045. doi, 10.1287/mnsc.43.7.1029

Dawes, R. M. (1988). *Rational choice in an uncertain world*. New York: Harcourt Brace Jovanovich.

Deslauriers, J. (2002). *Should we plan for upcoming tasks? Effects of planning on prediction accuracy for simple and difficult assignments*. Honors thesis, Wilfrid Laurier University, Ontario, Canada.

Dunning, D. (2007). Prediction: The inside view. In A. W. Kruglanski and E. T. Higgins (Eds.), *Social psychology: Handbook of basic principles* (2nd ed., pp. 69–90). New York: Guilford Press.

Engerman, S. L., & Sokoloff, K. L. (2004). Digging the dirt at public expense: Governance in the building of the Erie Canal and other public works. *NBER Working Paper No. w10965*.

Eyal, T., Liberman, N., Trope, Y., & Walther, E. (2004). The pros and cons of temporally near and distant action. *Journal of Personality and Social Psychology*, 86, 781–795. doi, 10.1037/0022-3514.86.6.781

Flyvbjerg, B. (2007). Policy and planning for large-infrastructure projects: problems, causes, cures. *Environment and Planning B: Planning and Design*, 34, 578–597. doi: 10.1068/b32111

Flyvbjerg, B. (2008). Curbing optimism bias and strategic misrepresentation in planning: Reference class forecasting in practice. *European Planning Studies*, 16, 3–21. doi:10.1080/09654310701747936

Flyvbjerg, B., Bruzelius, N., & Rothengatter, W. (2003). *Megaprojects and risk: An anatomy of ambition*. Cambridge, UK: Cambridge University Press.

Flyvbjerg, B., Holm, M. K. S., & Buhl, S. L. (2004). What causes cost overrun in transport infrastructure projects? *Transport Reviews*, 24, 3–18. doi, 10.1080/01944360508976688

Flyvbjerg, B., Holm, M. K. S., & Buhl, S. L. (2005). How (in)accurate are demand forecasts in public works projects? *Journal of the American Planning Association*, 71, 131–146. doi, 10.1080/01944360508976688

Flyvbjerg, B., Garbuio, M., & Lovallo, D. (2009). Delusion and deception in large infrastructure projects: Two models for explaining and preventing executive disaster. *California Management Review*, 51, 170–193.

Forsyth, D. K., & Burt, C. D. B. (2008). Allocating time to future tasks: The effect of task segmentation on planning fallacy bias. *Memory and Cognition*, 36, 791–798. doi, 10.3758/MC.36.4.791

Frank, M. G., & Gilovich, T. (1989). The effect of memory perspective on retrospective causal attributions. *Journal of Personality and Social Personality*, 57, 399–403.

Gielnik, M. M., Frese, M., & Stark, M. S. (this volume). Planning and entrpreneurship. In M. D. Mumford & M. Frese (Eds.), *The psychology of planning in organizations: Research and applications*. New York: Routledge.

Gilovich, T., Kerr, M., & Medvec, M. H. (1993). Effect of temporal perspective on subjective confidence. *Journal of Personality and Social Psychology*, 64, 552–560. doi, 10.1037/0022-3514.64.4.552

Gollwitzer, P. M. (1999). Implementation intentions: Strong effects of simple plans. *American Psychologist*, 54, 493–503.

Gollwitzer, P. M., & Brandstätter, V. (1997). Implementation intentions and effective goal pursuit. *Journal of Personality and Social Psychology*, 73, 186–199. doi, 10.1037//0022-3514.81.5.946

Gregory, W. L., & Duran, A. (2001). Scenarios and acceptance of forecasts. In J. S. Armstrong (Ed.), *Principles of forecasting: A handbook for researchers and practitioners* (pp. 519–540). Boston, MA: Kluwer Academic.

Griffin, D., & Buehler, R. (1999). Frequency, probability, and prediction: Easy solutions to cognitive illusions? *Cognitive Psychology*, 38, 48–78. doi:10.1006/cogp.1998.0707

Griffin, D., & Buehler, R. (2005). Biases and fallacies, memories and predictions: Comment on Roy, Christenfeld, and McKenzie (2005). *Psychological Bulletin*, 131, 757–760. doi, 10.1037/0033-2909.131.5.757

Griffin, D., Dunning, D., & Ross, L. (1990). The role of construal processes in overconfident predictions about the self and others. *Journal of Personality and Social Psychology*, 59, 1128–1139. doi, 10.1037//0022-3514.59.6.1128

Guinote, A. (2007a). Power and goal pursuit. *Personality and Social Psychology Bulletin*, 33, 1076–1087. doi:10.1177/0146167207301011

Guinote, A. (2007b). Power affects basic cognition: Increased attentional inhibition and flexibility. *Journal of Experimental Social Psychology*, 43, 685–697.

Halkjelsvik, T., & Jørgensen, M. (2012). From origami to software development: A review of studies on judgment-based predictions of performance time. *Psychological Bulletin*, 138(2), 238. doi, 10.1037/a0025996

Helzer, E. G., & Dunning, D. (2012). Why and when peer prediction is superior to self-prediction: The weight given to future aspiration versus past achievement. *Journal of Personality and Social Psychology*, 103(1), 38–53. doi: http://dx.doi.org/10.1037/a0028124

Helzer, E. G., & Gilovich, T. (2012). Whatever is willed will be: A temporal asymmetry in attributions to will. *Personality and Social Psychology Bulletin*, 38(10), 1235–1246. doi:10.1177/0146167212448403

Hinds, P. J. (1999). The curse of expertise: The effects of expertise and debiasing methods on predictions of novice performance. *Journal of Experimental Psychology: Applied*, 5, 205–221. doi, 10.1037//1076-898X.5.2.205

Hinsz, V. B., Kalnbach, L. R., & Lorentz, N. R. (1997). Using judgmental anchors to establish challenging self-set goals without jeopardizing commitment. *Organizational Behavior and Human Decision Processes*, 71, 287–308. doi, 10.1006/obhd.1997.2723

Hinsz, V. B., Tindale, R. S., & Vollrath, D. A. (1997). The emerging conceptualization of groups as information processors. *Psychological Bulletin*, 121, 43–64.

Hoch, S. J. (1985). Counterfactual reasoning and accuracy in predicting personal events. *Journal of Experimental Psychology: Learning, Memory, and Cognition*, 11, 719–731.

Jiga-Boy, G. M., Clark, A. E., & Semin, G. R. (2010). So much to do and so little time: Effort and perceived temporal distance. *Psychological Science*, 21(12), 1811–1817. doi:10.1177/0956797610388043

Jørgensen, M. (2004). A review of studies on expert estimation of software development effort. *Journal of Systems and Software*, 70, 37–60. doi:10.1016/S0164-1212(02)00156-5

Jørgensen, M., & Grimstad, S. (2008). Avoiding irrelevant and misleading information when estimating development effort. *Software, IEEE*, 25(3), 78-83.10.1109/MS.2008.57

Jørgensen, M., & Sjøberg, D. I. (2004). The impact of customer expectation on software development effort estimates. *International Journal of Project Management*, 22(4), 317–325. doi, 10.1016/S0263-7863(03)00085-1

Kahneman, D., & Lovallo, D. (1993). Timid choices and bold forecasts: A cognitive perspective on risk taking. *Management Science*, 39, 17–31. doi, 10.1287/mnsc.39.1.17

Kahneman, D., & Tversky, A. (1979). Intuitive prediction: Biases and corrective procedures. *TIMS Studies in Management Science*, 12, 313–327.

Kahneman, D., & Tversky, A. (1982). Intuitive prediction: Biases and corrective procedures. In D. Kahneman, P. Slovic, & A. Tversky (Eds.), *Judgment under uncertainty: Heuristics and biases* (pp. 414–421). Cambridge: Cambridge University Press.

Kanten, A. B. (2011). The effect of construal level on predictions of task duration. *Journal of Experimental Social Psychology*, 47(6), 1037–1047. doi:10.1016/j.jesp.2011.04.005

Kerr, N. L., & Tindale, R. S. (2004). Group performance and decision making. *Annual Review of Psychology*, 55, 623–55. doi, 10.1146/annurev.psych.55.090902.142009

Koehler, D. (1991). Explanation, imagination, and confidence in judgment. *Psychological Bulletin*, 110, 499–519. doi, 10.1037/0033-2909.110.3.499

Koehler, D., & Poon, C. S. K. (2006). Self-predictions overweight strength of current intentions. *Journal of Experimental Social Psychology*, 42, 517–524. doi, 10.1016/j.jesp.2005.08.003

König, C. J. (2005). Anchors distort estimates of expected duration. *Psychological Reports*, 96, 253–256. doi, 10.2466/pr0.96.2.253-256

Koole, S., & Van't Spijker, M. (2000). Overcoming the planning fallacy through willpower: Effects of implementation intentions on actual and predicted task-completion times. *European Journal of Social Psychology*, 30, 873–873. doi, 10.1002/1099-0992(200011/12)30:6<873::AID-EJSP22>3.0.CO;2-U

Krizan, Z., & Windschitl, P. D. (2007). The influence of outcome desirability on optimism. *Psychological Bulletin*, 133, 95–121. doi, 10.1037/0033-2909.133.1.95

Kross, E., Ayduk, O., & Mischel, W. (2005). When asking "why" doesn't hurt: Distinguishing rumination from reflective processing of negative emotions. *Psychological Science*, 16, 709–715. doi, 10.1111/j.1467-9280.2005.01600.x

Kruger, J., & Evans, M. (2004). If you don't want to be late, enumerate: Unpacking reduces the planning fallacy. *Journal of Experimental Social Psychology*, 40, 586–598. doi:10.1016/j.jesp.2003.11.001

Kunda, Z. (1990). The case for motivated reasoning. *Psychological Bulletin*, 108, 480–498.

LeBoeuf, R. A., & Shafir, E. (2009). Anchoring on the "here" and "now" in time and distance judgments. *Journal of Experimental Psychology. Learning, Memory, and Cognition*, 35(1), 81–93. doi, 10.1037/a0013665

Libby, L. K., & Eibach, R. P. (2002). Looking back in time: Self-concept change and visual perspective in autobiographical memory. *Journal of Personality and Social Psychology*, 82, 167–179. doi, 10.1037/0033-2909.108.3.480

Libby, L. K., & Eibach, R. P. (2011). Visual perspective in mental imagery: A representational tool that functions in judgment, emotion, and self-insight. *Advances in Experimental Social Psychology*, 44, 185–245. doi, 10.1016/B978-0-12-385522-0.00004-4

Liberman, N., & Trope, Y. (1998). The role of feasibility and desirability considerations in near and distant future decisions: A test of temporal construal theory. *Journal of Personality and Social Psychology*, 75, 5–18. doi, 10.1037/0022-3514.75.1.5

Liberman, N., Trope, Y., & Stephan, E. (2007). Psychological distance. In A. W. Kruglanski & E. T. Higgins (Eds.), *Social psychology: Handbook of basic principles*. Vol. 2, pp. 353–383. New York: Guilford Press.

Lovallo, D., & Kahneman, D. (2003). Delusions of success: How optimism undermines executives' decisions. *Harvard Business Review*, 81, 56–63.

Lynch, J. G., Netemeyer, R. G., Spiller, S. A., & Zammit, A. (2010). A generalizable scale of propensity to plan: the long and the short of planning for time and for money. *Journal of Consumer Research*, 37(1), 108–128. doi, 10.1086/649907

McIsaac, H. K., & Eich, E. (2002). Vantage point in episodic memory. *Psychonomic Bulletin and Review*, 9, 409–420. doi, 10.1111/j.0956-7976.2004.00660.x

Miller, D. T., & Ross, M. (1975). Self-serving biases in the attribution of causality: Fact or fiction? *Psychological Bulletin*, 82, 213–225. doi, 10.1037/h0076486

Min, K. S., & Arkes, H. R. (2012). When is difficult planning good planning? The effects of scenario-based planning on optimistic prediction bias. *Journal of Applied Social Psychology*, 42(11), 2701–2729. doi, 10.1111/j.1559-1816.2012.00958.x

Mintzberg, H. (1994). The fall and rise of strategic planning. *Harvard Business Review*, 72, 107–114.

Moher, E. (2012). *Tempering optimistic bias in temporal prediction: The role of psychological distance in the unpacking effect*. Ph.D. Thesis, University of Waterloo, Ontario, Canada.

Moløkken-Østvold, K., & Jørgensen, M. (2004). Group processes in software effort estimation. *Empirical Software Engineering*, 9, 315–334. doi:10.1023/B:EMSE.0000039882.39206.5a

Moløkken-Østvold, K., Haugen, N. C., & Benestad, H. C. (2008). Using planning poker for combining expert estimates in software projects. *Journal of Systems and Software*, 81, 2106–2117. doi:10.1016/j.jss.2008.03.058

Mulhern, K. (2006). *Self-other differences in task completion predictions: The impact of motivation.* Honors thesis, Wilfrid Laurier University, Ontario, Canada.

Mumford, M. D., Schultz, R. A., & Osburn, H. K. (2002). Planning in organizations: Performance as a multi-level phenomenon. In F. J. Yammarino & F. Dansereau (Eds.), *Research in multi level issues* (Vol. 1, pp. 3–65). Bingley: Emerald Group. doi, 10.1016/S1475-9144(02)01026-3

Newby-Clark, I. R., Ross, M., Buehler, R., Koehler, D., & Griffin, D. (2000). People focus on optimistic and disregard pessimistic scenarios while predicting task completion times. *Journal of Experimental Psychology: Applied*, 6, 171–182. doi, 10.1037//1076-898X.6.3.171

Norris, K. P. (1971). The accuracy of cost and duration estimates in industrial R&D. *R&D Management*, 2, 25–36. doi, 10.1111/j.1467-9310.1971.tb00091.x

Peetz, J., Buehler, R., & Wilson, A. (2010). Planning for the near and distant future: How does temporal distance affect task completion predictions? *Journal of Experimental Social Psychology*, 46(5), 709–720. doi:10.1016/j.jesp.2010.03.008

Peterson, C., Semmel, A., von Baeyer, C., Abramson, L. Y., Metalski, G. I., & Seligman, M. E. P. (1982). The attributional style questionnaire. *Cognitive Therapy and Research*, 6, 287–299.

Pezzo, M. V., Litman, J. A., & Pezzo, S. P. (2006). On the distinction between yuppies and hippies: Individual differences in prediction biases for planning future tasks. *Personality and Individual Differences*, 41, 1359–1359. doi:10.1016/j.paid.2006.03.029

Pezzo, S. P., Pezzo, M. V., & Stone, E. R. (2006). The social implications of planning: How public predictions bias future plans. *Journal of Experimental Social Psychology*, 42, 221–227. doi:10.1016/j.jesp.2005.03.001

PMI (2008). *A guide to the project management body of knowledge (PMBOK guide).* Newtown Square, PA: Project Management Institute.

Pronin, E., & Ross, L. (2006). Temporal differences in trait self-ascription: When the self is seen as another. *Journal of Personality and Social Psychology*, 90, 197–209. doi, 10.1037/0022-3514.90.2.197

Pychyl, T. A., Morin, R. W., & Salmon, B. R. (2000). Procrastination and the planning fallacy: An examination of the study habits of university students. *Journal of Social Behavior and Personality*, 15, 135–150.

Roy, M. M., & Christenfeld, N. J. S. (2007). Bias in memory predicts bias in estimation of future task duration. *Memory & Cognition*, 35, 557–564. doi, 10.3758/BF03193294

Roy, M. M., & Christenfeld, N. J. S. (2008). Effect of task length on remembered and predicted duration. *Psychonomic Bulletin and Review*, 15, 202–207.

Roy, M. M., Christenfeld, N. J. S., & Jones, M. (2013). Actors, observers, and the estimation of task duration. *The Quarterly Journal of Experimental Psychology*, 66(1), 121–137. doi, 10.1080/17470218.2012.699973

Roy, M. M., Christenfeld, N. J. S., & McKenzie, C. R. M. (2005). Underestimating the duration of future events: Memory incorrectly used or memory bias? *Psychological Bulletin*, 131, 738–756.

Roy, M. M., Mitten, S. T., & Christenfeld, N. J. S. (2008). Correcting memory improves accuracy of predicted task duration. *Journal of Experimental Social Psychology: Applied*, 14, 266–275.

Sanna, L. J., & Schwarz, N. (2004). Integrating temporal biases: The interplay of focal thoughts and accessibility experiences. *Psychological Science*, 15, 474–481. doi, 10.1111/j.0956-7976.2004.00704.x

Sanna, L. J., Parks, C. J., Chang, E. C., & Carter, S. E. (2005). The hourglass is half full or half empty: Temporal framing and the group planning fallacy. *Group Dynamics: Theory, Research, and Practice*, 9, 173–188.

Sarasvathy, S. D. (2001). Causation and effectuation: Toward a theoretical shift from economic inevitability to entrepreneurial contingency. *Academy of Management Review*, 26, 243–263.

Savitsky, K., Medvec, V. H., Charlton, A. E., & Gilovich, T. (1998). What, me worry?: Arousal, misattribution, and the effect of temporal distance on confidence. *Personality and Social Psychology Bulletin*, 24, 529–536. doi, 10.1177/0146167298245008

Schoemaker, P. J. H. (1993). Multiple scenario development: Its conceptual and behavioral foundation. *Strategic Management Journal*, 14, 193–213.

Spiller, S. A., & Lynch, J. G., Jr. (2009). *Individuals exhibit the planning fallacy for time but not for money.* Unpublished working paper. Available at SSRN: http://ssrn.com/abstract=1458380 (last accessed, January 27, 2015).

Staats, B. R., Milkman, K. L., & Fox, C. R. (2012). The team scaling fallacy: Underestimating the declining efficiency of larger teams. *Organizational Behavior and Human Decision Processes*, 118, 132–142. doi, 10.1016/j.obhdp.2012.03.002

Standish Group (2010). *CHAOS summary 2010*. Standish Group International Inc.

Strack, F., & Mussweiler, T. (1997). Explaining the enigmatic anchoring effect: Mechanisms of selective accessibility. *Journal of Personality and Social Psychology*, 73(3), 437–446.

Taylor, S. E., & Brown, J. D. (1988). Illusion and well-being: A social psychological perspective on mental-health. *Psychological Bulletin*, 103, 193–210. doi, 10.1037/0033-2909.103.2.193

Taylor, S. E., Pham, L. B., Rivkin, I. D., & Armor, D. A. (1998). Harnessing the imagination: Mental simulation, self-regulation, and coping. *American Psychologist*, 53, 429–439.

Thomas, K. E., & Handley, S. J. (2008). Anchoring in time estimation. *Acta Psychologica*, 127(1), 24–29. doi:10.1016/j.actpsy.2006.12.004

Thomas, K. E., Newstead, S. E., & Handley, S. J. (2003). Exploring the time prediction process: The effects of task experience and complexity on prediction accuracy. *Applied Cognitive Psychology*, 17(6), 655–673. doi, 10.1002/Acp.893

Thürmer, J. L., Wieber, F., & Gollwitzer, P. M. (this volume). Planning high performance: Can groups and teams benefit from implementation intentions? In M. D. Mumford & M. Frese (Eds.), *The psychology of planning in organizations: Research and applications*. New York: Routledge.

Trope, Y., & Liberman, N. (2003). Temporal construal. *Psychological Review*, 110, 403–421. doi, 10.1037/0033-295X.110.3.403

Tversky, A., & Kahneman, D. (1974). Judgment under uncertainty: Heuristics and biases. *Science*, 185, 1124–1131. doi:10.1126/science.185.4157.1124.

Tversky, A., & Shafir, E. (1992). Choice under conflict. The dynamics of deferred decision. *Psychological Science*, 3, 358–361. doi, 10.1111/j.1467-9280.1992.tb00047.x

Van Oorschot, K. E., Bertrand, J. W. M., & Rutte, C. G. (2005). Field studies into the dynamics of product development tasks. *International Journal of Operations & Production Management*, 25, 720–739. doi:10.1108/01443570510608574.

Weick, M., & Guinote, A. (2010). How long will it take? Power biases time predictions. *Journal of Experimental Social Psychology*, 46(4), 595–604. doi:10.1016/j.jesp.2010.03.005

Wright, G., & Cairns, G. (2011). *Scenario thinking: Practical approaches to the future*. New York: Palgrave Macmillan. doi:10.1037/a0018143

Zauberman, G., & Lynch, J. G., Jr. (2005). Resource slack and propensity to discount delayed investments of time versus money. *Journal of Experimental Psychology: General*, 134, 23–37.

Zhang, Y., & Fishbach. (2010). Counteracting obstacles with optimistic predictions. *Journal of Experimental Psychology: General*, 139, 16–31. doi, 10.1037/a0018143

4

PERSONALITY AND PLANNING

The Interplay Between Linear and Holistic Processing

Anna M. Engel and Julius Kuhl

> You need to have some intuition, some judgement about the issues you're in, and you need sometimes to pause to reflect on the decisions that you make on the basis of the information you've seen. But you can't be sort of so, you know, you can't analyse this to death. Reflection is fine to give you a bit of time to let your intuition understand the issues you're faced with, with a proper analysis of the facts, but you can't become so introverted about it that you don't make a decision at all. And you've got move quickly when you're dealing with many risk issues.

> Sir Michael Rake, 2011, Chairman BT Group
> http://www.open.edu/openlearn/money-management/management

What can personality contribute to our understanding of planning? To answer this question there are two possible starting points which are based on two different conceptions of personality. "Some research is interindividual ... Other work has an intra-individual focus" (Cervone, 2005, p. 445). The first conception, which defines personality in terms of individual differences, raises the question of which personality dispositions might affect planning. The second conception is based on a systems account of personality, looking at personality as a whole and the way its major constituent processes interact. How do motivation, emotion, cognition, and self-regulation mutually affect each other and how does this interaction determine experience and action? In this chapter, we examine planning from the perspective of the second conception of personality, which includes and transcends the notion of individual differences. Our approach is based on a dynamic theory of personality (Personality Systems Interactions Theory: PSI) which describes the interplay between cognitive, motivational, and dispositional sides of personality functioning (Kuhl, 2000, 2001; cf. Lewin, 1935). Here, a functional rather than phenomenological approach to personality is applied. From a functional perspective, the focus lies on the functions and features of processes underlying phenomenological experience and action.

Considering planning from this integrative perspective on personality, two things become visible. First, as our opening quote from Sir Michael Rake suggests, the analytical form of planning should be completed by addition of a more holistic form which integrates holistic intuition and emotional experience (cf. Epstein, Pacini, Denes-Raj, & Heier, 1996; Jung, 1936/2001; Kuhl, 1994b). Second, the motivational and emotional aspects of planning have an impact on facilitating the two forms of planning. Thus, the conventional linear conception of planning should be extended in at least two ways, one relating to another type of information processing (i.e. holistic processing) and the second referring to the impact of emotional and motivational states on either type of processing. From the perspective of a functional analysis of personality, we will argue that these two implications are closely connected. As it turns out, the creative potential of holistic planning derives from its close links to motivation and emotion, whereas the great potential of analytical processing is based on its capacity to process information independent of the current motivational and emotional state of the organism.

In the *first section*, we comment briefly on the current position of planning research from a personality perspective. The *second section* explains some cognitive differences between the two forms of planning by focusing on connectionistic modeling of holistic processing. The *third section* integrates the two forms of planning as well as the role of emotion, motivation, and self-regulation within a unifying theory.

1 Looking at Planning from a Personality Perspective

An important approach to individual differences in planning was proposed by Hacker (1985): "Differences in effectiveness between workers are largely due to differences in cognitive strategies. These strategy differences are, in particular, differences in ... planning of one's own activities" (p. 264). This statement is consistent with the common understanding that planning is mainly a cognitive phenomenon. "Planning is a complex form of symbolic action that consists of consciously preconceiving a sequence of actions that will be sufficient for achieving a goal" (Pea, 1982, p. 6, cf. Hoc, 1988). Following the nomenclature of Hayes-Roth and Hayes-Roth (1979), planning itemizes "the first stage of a two-stage problem-solving process" (p. 267), followed by control as some form of plan execution. Other models (e.g. Agre & Chapman 1987, 1990; Ambros-Ingerson & Steel, 1988; Chapman 1987, 1989), like ours, stress the "inexorable link between the planning process and the execution of plans" (Davies, 1991, p. 174).

1.1 A Neglected Part of Planning: The Holistic Self

Theories and research on planning do not typically refer to the self as an experiential knowledge base affecting planning. In this section, we will outline a modern conception of self that is well suited to specifying some of the processes underlying holistic planning. As illustrated in Table 4.1, the features of the self that can be derived from experimental research (Kuhl, 2000; Koole & Kuhl, 2003; Kuhl, 2010; Kuhl, Quirin & Koole, 2015) are consistent with the features of the fully functioning person described in Rogers' (1963) phenomenological approach to personality.

The self can be conceived of as an implicit and holistic cognitive-emotional network organizing personally relevant experiences in terms of personal (i.e. one's own and others') values, preferences, needs, and abilities. This happens in a way that integrates even seemingly contradictory experiences and makes them available for intuitive decision making and planning, taking account of many constraints without having to process each detail in a step-by-step manner (cf. Table 4.1). This notion differs from common-sense as well as scientific conceptions of planning as a conscious, focused, and systematic process of successive refinement across different levels of abstraction characterized in a hierarchical manner.

1.2 Limitations of Linear Planning

Certainly, linear planning seems to deliver a brilliant performance, with its orderly, systematic nature established through its top-down process and the simplicity of its hierarchical attempts, working

TABLE 4.1 Comparison of the fully functioning person and the features of the self

Fully functioning person (Rogers, 1963)	Empirically confirmed features of the self
Has confidence in one's own feelings	Interconnectedness with emotions and needs
Is willing to risk pain and suffering if necessary (rather than one-sided fight of negative feelings)	Integration of both positive and negative experiences
Is living a life filled with meaning, personal esteem, and responsibility	Total affirmation of one's existence (self-positivity)
Shows openness to experience	Vigilance (full attention to everything that is personally relevant): operating in the background of consciousness
Shows growth of consciousness: more and more parts of the self-awareness become aware and explicable	Only parts of the largely implicit self can become explicable because of its broad, parallel processing characteristics: that is why "growth" of consciousness is a lifelong process

from high-level goals (e.g. developing a new product) to more and more specific sub-goals (e.g. determining its unique selling position, optimizing production conditions; cf. Dahl, Dykstra, & Hoare, 1972; Hayes-Roth & Hayes-Roth, 1979). However, in recent years, several authors have regarded hierarchical plans as insufficient. "Nobody could doubt that people often make and follow plans. But the complexity, uncertainty, and immediacy of the real world require a central role for moment-to-moment improvisation." (Agre & Chapman, 1987, p. 268). Consequently, planning requires more than conscious linear processing. The next paragraphs list three examples for non-linear aspects of planning.

First, the hierarchical structure sometimes hampers disengagement from plans and goals, especially when a hierarchical plan is executed in a top-down manner with low sensitivity to situational changes (Brandstätter & Schüler, 2013; Carver & Scheier, 1990). Thus it impairs *flexibility* as a primary principle of planning (Pea, 1982; Stefik, 1981a, 1981b; cf. the least-commitment strategy). "A sophisticated control structure should provide flexibility for decision making – so that a problem solver can take advantage of new information, make guesses, and correct mistakes" (Stefik, 1981b, p. 272).

Second, planning and plan execution is frequently not a linear, consciously controlled phenomenon because in many settings it involves social interaction, which in turn includes intuitive interactions and spontaneous inputs from various sources (cf. Agre & Chapman, 1987). In short, planning has to be a *dialogical activity* (cf. Carver & Scheier, 1982; Hacker, 2000; Visser, 1994).

The *third* non-linear aspect of planning regards *multiple constraint satisfaction*. Models of linear, algorithmic decision making, like expectancy-value models (Feather, 1982), do not provide optimal solutions if many different constraints have to be taken into account within a short time window. Finding the best problem solution or the best fitting plan – especially if the result is not yet fixed – requires having representations of all possible solution patterns or all alternative steps integrated in the plan. Because of the limited capacity of conscious information processing, this is impossible in linear, consciously controlled planning (cf. Hacker, 1997; Visser, 1994).

2 Holistic Planning and Connectionistic Processing

One early attempt to overcome limitations of analytical and hierarchical plans is the *opportunistic model of planning* (Hayes-Roth & Hayes-Roth, 1979). Opportunistic planning means that "at each point in the process, the planner's current decisions and observations suggest various opportunities for plan development. The planner's subsequent decisions follow up on selected opportunities" (Hayes-Roth & Hayes-Roth, 1979, p. 276; cf. Pea, 1982; Stefik, 1981a, 1981b; Wilensky, 1981). Despite its merits, this seminal approach to a non-analytic form of planning is no longer satisfactory. For a deeper understanding of this "odd" type of planning we need to understand the underlying mechanisms.

At the highest level of personality functioning, the self as an implicit experiential network can be conceived of as a basis for non-linear planning (Kuhl, 2000). In order to understand the peculiarities of information processing associated with this level of personal knowledge integration, parallel processing has been proposed as a useful theoretical basis (cf. Table 4.1). Connectionist models of parallel (subsymbolic) processing in cognitive psychology provide a promising explanation of non-algorithmic processing, including holistic planning (e.g. McClelland, Rumelhart, & PDP Research Group, 1986). McClelland, Rumelhart, and Hinton start with questions, including:

> What makes people smarter than machines? … Yet people are far better at … making plans and carrying out appropriate actions … . What is the basis for these differences? … In our view, people are smarter than today's computers because the brain employs a basic computational architecture that is more suited to deal with a central aspect of natural information processing tasks people are so good at.
>
> *(2004, p. 75)*

The basic computational architecture is called *parallel distributed processing* (McClelland, Rumelhart, & PDP Research Group, 1986). In these networks, knowledge is not represented symbolically (i.e. there are no localizable symbol units) but by the distribution of the link-weights at the nodes ("synapses"). This distributed representation works in a parallel manner as was already stated as desirable by Newell and Simon (1972).[1] Why is this system so suitable for the process of holistic planning? The requirements stated in the first section above, namely flexibility, multiple constraint satisfaction, and dialogical activity, provide some interesting hints toward finding answers to this question.

Parallel distributed networks do not require *conscious awareness* or control. Conscious processing, with its relatively slow functioning and limited capacity (reducing information to whatever seems essential at the current moment), is not able to consider a lot of details at the same time. In contrast, parallel distributed processing is able to handle a wide range of information and conditions simultaneously.

> Solving a constraint-satisfaction problem with such a network involves multiple rounds of updating the activation of all the nodes in parallel by summing up the excitatory and inhibitory inputs they receive from all the connected nodes. Typically, this procedure yields a stable pattern of activation of some elements and inhibition of the others after a limited number of updates. This pattern then can be interpreted as a coherent mental representation at a given point in time.
>
> *(Schröder & Thagard, 2013, p. 257)*

Accordingly, this avoids the well-known "bottle-neck" in mental processing (cf. Hacker, 1985, 1989).

Because of its *integrative architecture*, parallel processing is better equipped than its analytical counterpart to ensure that planning satisfies many constraints simultaneously, for example, long-term and short-term goals, desirability and feasibility, my own and others' needs (cf. Dörner, 1996). With regard to planning, multiple constraint satisfaction may be the most important property in parallel distributed processing. The integration of multiple constraints does not incur the increased costs in time that are typical of sequential processing.

Furthermore, the activity of parallel distributed processing has a *spontaneous* and *intuitive* feature, because it does not depend on sequential processing of single and concrete (or even conscious) stimuli or conditions. Since a parallel network considers a variety of input information simultaneously, we often perceive no clear triggering stimulus on the conscious level. Parallel processing takes account of implicit "triggers" that cannot be specified as clear-cut single objects, but consist of many unconscious, only intuitively perceptible, items of information. This feature endows holistic plans with an in-built pop-up feature (that may be called "vigilance"): the environment is broadly monitored from the background of consciousness and any implicit change in the context pops up and becomes salient when it is relevant to a plan (cf. Table 4.1).

In order to fully appreciate its utility for the desired additional features of planning, it is useful to elaborate on some of the processing characteristics of parallel distributed processing. First, it compares specific situational information for its similarity with mentally represented prototypes. With imprecise, fast, and multitudinous information, parallel distributed processing shows greater robustness than analytical processing. This feature of parallel distributed processing is called *graceful degradation*: the system does not immediately collapse when confronted with incomplete or unexpected information, but reduces its precision gradually. At an intuitive level, this feature is easy to grasp: when a lot of information is considered simultaneously, the absence of a specific detail does not destroy overall performance. This is particularly evident when compared to sequential processing, where each successive step is based on the success of all previous steps. As a result, graceful degradation provides a *robustness* which includes flexibility.

Graceful degradation also accounts for the *impressionistic character* of parallel distributed processing, which may further increase flexibility. To be sure, parallel distributed processing is vague and less precise than symbolic syntactic thinking. However, "in this way, the model can fill in properties of individuals based on what it knows about other, similar instances. ... Of course, there is no reason why this should necessarily be the right answer, but generally speaking, the more similar two things are in respect to that we know about, the more likely they are to be similar in respects we do not, and the model implements this heuristic" (McClelland, Rumelhart & Hinton, 2004, p. 91). Due to its underlying process of *prototype detection*, parallel distributed processing is applicable to a variety of situations. Additionally, its greater power of integration enables its easy transfer to very complex situations, including interactive decision making. Parallel distributed networks could be a suitable model of collective decision making, thus remedying one of the limitations of linear processing mentioned earlier.

With parallel distributed processing, processing time does not depend on the number of input units, since processing is done in parallel for all units. Moreover, the processing of parallel distributed processing is not always syntactically explicable, thus it cannot fully be verbalized or represented by a logical algorithm. Likewise, parallel distributed processing has no explicit need for rules: "First, we do not assume that the goal of learning is the formulation of explicit rules. Rather, we assume it is the acquisition of connection strengths which allow a network of simple units to act as though it knew the rules" (McClelland, Rumelhart, & Hinton, 2004, p. 92). In sum, parallel distributed processing is robust, flexible, and able to integrate dialogical demands without necessitating fully conscious information processing and explicit rules.

3 PSI Theory: The Functional Significance of Emotion and Motivation for Systems Interactions

As mentioned before, multiple constraint satisfaction has the potential to be one of the most relevant properties of parallel distributed processing. Constraints may be any relevant determinants of successful planning and any desirable or undesirable consequences of plan execution, such as the needs and emotions of people involved, or the costs of making, postponing, or executing a plan. How can a parallel distributed processing system take these into account? Within an integrative personality approach to planning, needs and emotions are especially interesting determinants of planning, not only because they should provide the energy needed for generating or executing a plan, but also because they optimize the interaction among all cognitive and emotional systems relevant for making and executing plans. The theory of PSI mentioned earlier elaborates the role that emotions play in coordinating analytical and holistic modes of processing, including the two forms of planning related to them. As it turns out, the functional significance of emotion transcends the familiar specific effects of emotions, such as raising or reducing the level of stress or instigating emotion-specific behaviors.

While integrating theoretical and empirical work from the areas of personality, development, cognition, and neurobiology into a coherent architecture of interacting personality systems, PSI theory offers three elaborations to our analysis of planning. *First*, the two high-level systems described in PSI theory can explain and elaborate the distinction between the two types of planning mentioned in the introductory section (i.e. analytical vs. holistic planning). *Second*, PSI theory includes two low-level systems which help explain how planning is put into action and how planning benefits from experience. *Finally*, PSI theory explains how motivation and emotion affect the interaction among those four systems.

3.1 PSI: Preliminary Notes

Before summarizing the basic assumptions of PSI theory, two points deserve special attention: the use of neuro-anatomical evidence in the search for functional networks and the meaning of the term "system" when denoting such networks.

Being primarily based on behavioral rather than neurobiological evidence, PSI theory is a psychological theory. Nonetheless, the development of PSI theory has included *neurobiological evidence* as a heuristic to specify functional networks that justify the term "system" on a personality level of analysis. Specifically, the heuristic potential of *hemispheric lateralization* can be justified according to theoretical arguments, computer simulation, and empirical findings (Sporns, Chialvo, Kaiser, & Hilgetag, 2004). This work implies that the opportunity for functional networks to cooperate within one hemisphere is greater than between the two hemispheres. Because of their relatively low neuro-anatomical distance, ipsilateral compared to contralateral networks are more likely to cooperate effectively than neuro-anatomically more remote areas.

> Although they might be helpful to eliminate noise from irrelevant sources, too many intermediate transformations might interfere with the capacity of brain areas to cooperate on a specialized task … . In addition, failures of edges or nodes within clusters can be compensated for more easily, as nearby nodes share similar (matching) afferent and efferent connections.
>
> *(Sporns et al., 2004, p. 423)*

The two hemispheres seem not only to have substantially different processing characteristics (Rotenberg, 2013b; Rotenberg & Weinberg, 1999), but they also differ in their neuro-anatomical architecture: the right hemisphere appears much more suitable for the consideration of many constraints and conditions of planning as it involves larger networks (Beeman et al., 1994). The left hemisphere is neuro-anatomically better equipped for putting a multitude of highly specialized "expert systems" into action since it is characterized by a huge amount of small and isolated modules (neuron columns; Scheibel et al., 1985). These empirical findings on hemispheric differences underscore the importance of separating the two forms of planning.

The second preliminary note relating to PSI theory concerns the term *system*. According to an extended understanding of this term, a system is a network of a temporary or dispositional coalition of various functions. This concept of a mental system as a functional network of contributing modules has been argued to be more useful in psychology (Luria, 1973/1992) than the traditional concept of a system as a fixed hardware base for information processing (cf. Keren & Schul, 2009).

3.2 PSI: Overview

As mentioned before, PSI theory postulates four different systems. These are two high-level systems, Intention Memory and Extension Memory, and two low-level systems, Intuitive Behavior Control and Object Recognition. Presumably, Intention Memory and Object Recognition (primarily supported by the left hemisphere) are involved in hierarchical planning (see 3.3), whereas Extension Memory and Intuitive Behavior Control are primarily supported by the right hemisphere and play a crucial role in holistic planning (see 3.4). The postulated systems are activated by different affective states (see 3.5). Self-directed interactions among the four systems according to situational needs and individual preferences provide the key competencies of a fully functioning person (Rogers, 1963, cf. Table 4.1).

The core of PSI theory is described by two modulation assumptions:

1. Enactment of difficult intentions ("efficient will" or "volitional facilitation"), which requires an interaction between Intention Memory (representing and maintaining intentions) and Intuitive Behavior Control (behavioral enactment), is facilitated by a change from low positive affect (PA-) to high positive affect (PA+; see the diagonal arrow "efficient will" in Fig. 4.1).
2. Learning from mistakes (self-growth), which can be considered a crucial element of plan development (see 3.5.3), requires an interaction between Object Recognition (for identifying an error or its source) and Extension Memory or "self" (for integrating corrective information into a growing experiential knowledge base); this interaction is facilitated by a change from high negative affect NA+ (which facilitates "Object Recognition" and error detection) to low negative affect NA- (which facilitates integration of corrective information into Extension Memory; see the diagonal arrow "self-growth" in Fig. 4.1).

Direct empirical evidence for the *first modulation assumption* of PSI theory derives from results showing that efficient will can be considerably strengthened when the shift toward positive affect is experimentally alleviated, for example, through positive affective primes presented before a difficult self-regulatory task such as the Stroop task (Kuhl & Kazén, 1999; Kazén & Kuhl, 2005) or through having participants shift their attention between anticipation of the positive affect associated with goal attainment and the difficult sides of the immediate steps to be taken (Oettingen, Pak, & Schnetter, 2001). Presumably, plan enactment is mediated by this top-down influence from high-level Intention Memory to low-level Intuitive Behavior Control. Emotional support needed when difficult or unpleasant steps are to be taken can be generated from Extension Memory (see 3.5.1). Finally, when any step taken toward plan execution fails, alternative options for action can be retrieved from Extension Memory as well (see 3.5.2).

Empirical evidence directly supporting the *second modulation assumption* (i.e. facilitated self-access as a function of down-regulation of negative affect) stems from experiments on self-infiltration: impaired self-access as assessed by false self-ascription of assigned tasks is aggravated by negative affect unless it can be down-regulated (Baumann & Kuhl, 2003; Kuhl & Kazén,

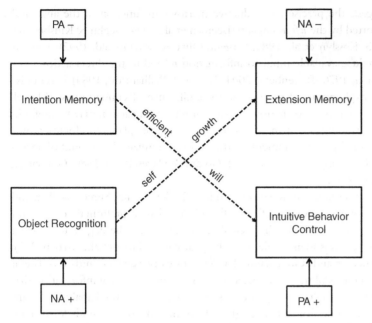

FIGURE 4.1   Affective modulation of personality systems interactions (PSI Theory)

1994; see 3.5.3). Moreover, a personality dimension associated with impaired down-regulation of negative affect (i.e. state orientation (see 3.6.1) moderates performance deficits in remote associates task (RAT), which presumably draws heavily on extended semantic networks provided by Extension Memory (Baumann & Kuhl, 2002).

People differ in their ability to self-regulate interactions among the four systems described above (see 3.6). In addition to the crucial role emotions play in the modulation of systems interactions, PSI theory claims that emotions are closely intertwined with Extension Memory and the self. Extension Memory and the self form the implicit experiential network underlying creativity and self-congruence, enabling decision makers to stay in touch with their own and others' emotions, needs, and values (see 3.7).

3.3 The Left Hemisphere: Analytic Processing and Hierarchical Planning

According to PSI theory, analytical processing is subdivided into analytical thinking (including Intention Memory) and Object Recognition. The main functions of low-level *Object Recognition* are recognition, categorization, and labeling of perceptual or semantic units. This involves the identification of individual objects and their abstraction from specific contexts in order to identify them across various contexts, for example, when the "reason" for repeated (i.e. across a variety of contexts) failures to meet deadlines is to be found in a team.

Within the analytical mode, the high-level system is called *Intention Memory*, and is responsible for the representation and maintenance of intentions. Intentions are understood as abstract, symbolic, and explicit representations of action plans, which do not necessarily specify the execution parameters of a sequence of actions (Kuhl, 1994b). Intention Memory is closely associated with analytical thinking, which has a sequential "if–then" structure (Anderson, 1983) and is thought to be a sequence of individual steps (operations), which is determined by logical links between those successive steps. Thus, Intention Memory seems to be the ideal system to schedule anticipated actions.

Empirical evidence suggests the precise and reductive (narrowing) function of the analytical mode to be primarily supported by the *left hemisphere* (Beeman et al., 1994; Deglin & Kinsbourne, 1996; Jager & Postma, 2003; Kosslyn et al., 1989; Sergent, Ohta, & MacDonald, 1992). The left hemisphere's tendency to reduce available input to information related to the direct action context only (Levy & Trevarthen, 1976; Rotenberg, 2004; Tucker & Williamson, 1984) is reminiscent of early experimental explorations of the functional significance of consciousness (Marcel, 1983). The left hemisphere's focus on information relevant for impending action may be useful in hierarchical planning and in planning as preparation of action. It assists the planner in focusing on a single area relevant in the hierarchy at any moment. To this end, it minimizes the amount of necessary cognitive capacities and working memory load (cf. Goldin & Hayes-Roth, 1980; Gollwitzer, 1999; Hayes-Roth and Hayes-Roth, 1979).

Using a well-known planning task (i.e. Tower of London), Kaller, Rahm, Spreer, Weiller, and Unterrainer (2010) found stronger activation of the left mid-dorsolateral prefrontal cortex with increasing demands on processing goal hierarchy: "Goal hierarchy reflects the degree to which a sequence for attaining several goals is identifiable from the goal state" (Kaller et al., 2010, p. 307). In a similar vein, Grafman, Spector, and Rattermann (2005) recently discussed left mid-dorsolateral prefrontal cortex functions in terms of the structural analysis of the propositional information that makes up a plan. They suggested that "planning processes requiring the structural analysis of plans may be more compromised by left prefrontal lesions" (p. 191). To this end, the left mid-dorsolateral prefrontal cortex may be more focused on specific features of individual events (Huey, Krueger, & Grafman, 2006).

Combining this evidence with findings suggesting that positive affect facilitates the left-hemispheric (prefrontal) processing involved in approach behavior (i.e. enactment of planned behavior, Harmon-Jones, 2006, 2007), the explanatory value of the left-hemispheric model of plan execution becomes apparent: both the maintenance of plans and their enactment seem to be mediated by a common (left-hemispheric) network (cf. the first modulation assumption of PSI theory described above).

3.4 The Right Hemisphere: Holistic Processing and Flexible Planning

According to PSI theory, holistic processing, just like its analytical counterpart, is supported both by a high-level and a low-level system. The low-level system of holistic processing called *Intuitive Behavior Control* is active in the context-sensitive execution of behavioral routines (Kuhl, 2001). Despite its receptivity to conscious plans and intentions, Intuitive Behavior Control itself largely operates independently of conscious planning and controls action steps that run automatically. Although the final execution of action steps requires serial processing, extensive parallel processing is necessary for online adaptation of ongoing behavior to changes in the environment (context-sensitivity).

Extension Memory is the high-level system within the holistic mode, representing its own (and others') internal states, goals, needs, and experiential knowledge. Hence, Extension Memory is supported by autobiographical memory. According to Rotenberg (2004, 2013b), the right prefrontal cortex, which provides networks supporting either holistic system, is associated with polysemantic information processing. This type of information processing simultaneously integrates a large number of elements, meanings, and interrelationships of a current perception in a multifaceted and complex (and thus polysemantic) context. The more potentially relevant situations and actions that plans can integrate, the more flexible they can be. In other words, an extended network of possible action alternatives across possible contexts provided by Extension Memory facilitates plan elaboration and plan modification when needed.

Compared to the left hemisphere, the *right hemisphere* appears to be better equipped for recognizing associative relationships (e.g. alternative options for action or plan-relevant context information). This is especially true for remote semantic features (Beeman et al., 1994; Bowden, Jung-Beeman, Fleck, & Kounios, 2005) or unusual action steps (Kaller et al., 2010). Kaller et al. report that right mid-dorsolateral prefrontal cortex activation increases with growing demands on search depth:

> Search depth refers to the actual mental generation and evaluation of sequences as it requires the integration of individual moves while taking into account their interdependencies ... That is, you have to take into account the interdependencies between the different alternative steps to achieve your goals. ... This interdependency thus clearly requires mentally looking ahead.
>
> *(2010, p. 307)*

The concept of search depth is reminiscent of Rotenberg's (2009, 2013a) theory of search activity which explains the contribution of the right hemisphere to creative problem-solving, cognitive flexibility, and coping with stress, even during sleep. Grafman, Spector, and Rattermann (2005) assume the right mid-dorsolateral prefrontal cortex to deal with the temporal and dynamic aspects of planning by mediating the integration of information into a coherent sequence (cf. Huey, Krueger, & Grafman, 2006). It is also expected that the larger involvement of the right mid-dorsolateral prefrontal cortex may be due to higher demands on monitoring and checking (Petrides, 2005; Shallice, 2002).

Bowden and Beeman (1998) investigated the involvement of the right hemisphere in the solution of *insight problems*. Insight problems display interesting similarities to the functional characteristics of parallel distributed processing and the information processing of Extension Memory as conceived of in PSI theory. Bowden and Beeman propose the following process to take place through the involvement of the right hemisphere:

> Insight problems contain ambiguous features that misdirect retrieval toward information that is strongly related to the typical interpretation of words in the problems, but does not lead to solution. Because of the LH's [left hemisphere] relatively fine semantic coding, the misdirection causes strongly focused activation of such information in the LH – to the exclusion of solution-relevant information. Because of the RH's [right hemisphere's] relatively coarse semantic coding, there is likely to be activation of solution-relevant information as well as misdirected information in the RH. However, problem solvers have difficulty using this weak activation.
>
> *(1998, p. 439)*

As we will discuss below in more detail, the right hemisphere's extended connectivity with emotional and other somatic markers provides an ideal basis for the motivational source supporting paying attention to those weakly activated remote associations that seem to form the basis of creative insight. All in all, the activation of the right hemisphere may serve to problem-solve and plan via its ability to propose, develop, and temporally maintain alternatives in the course of planning (cf. Goel & Grafman 2000; Goel & Vartanian 2005). This ability may account for the enhanced *flexibility* which we assume to be associated with holistic planning.

Over and above the association of the right hemisphere with negative mood (and left hemisphere with positive mood; Davidson, 1993), this hemisphere is more extensively and more directly related to body signals, including those related to both positive and negative feelings, which puts the right hemisphere in a better position to regulate affect, that is, to control the autonomic nervous system as the affect-generating system (Dawson & Schell, 1982; Luria, 1973/1992; Rotenberg, 2013b; Wittling, 1990). "From this point of view the ensemble of neural networks is sensitive not to logical, but to the 'emotional' content of information. Metaphorically speaking, we deal here with 'a feeling computer" (Artyushkin, Belyayev, Sandler, & Sergeyev, 1990, p.176). This connectedness of the right hemisphere with *emotion-generating structures* seems to be the basis of the ability to deal with emotions and needs (own and others'), even when they are not represented in an explicit symbolic or conceptual cognitive format, as mentioned above. Furthermore, emotional sensitivity may be one of the most important prerequisites to make people smarter at (holistic) planning than machines (cf. McClelland, Rumelhart, & Hinton, 2004): Right hemispheric processing combines parallel-holistic processing of experiential knowledge on a very high level of integration with "intellectual emotions" (Tichomirow, 1975; as cited in Mathäus, 1988) or "somatic markers" (Bechara & Damasio, 2005). This can be used for retrieving emotionally significant (helpful or problematic) information from that huge experiential network whose sheer vastness would render quick retrieval of relevant information almost impossible without those emotional markers.

In addition, the right hemisphere has also been found to be specialized in processing social "relationships" (cf. Kuhl & Kazén, 2008, Experiment 1–3; Schore, 2001) and empathy-related mentalization (Adolphs, Damasio, Tranel, Cooper, & Damasio, 2000; Shamay-Tsoory, Tomer, Berger, & Aharon-Peretz, 2003; Spinella, 2002).

> Empathy helps (a) to coordinate the actions of individuals in a rapid, automatic fashion …
> (b) to take each other's perspective, so that an individual is more likely to accurately perceive
> others' perceptions, intentions, and motivations, increasing the predictability of her or his
> behavior; and (c) to signal solidarity, providing the basis of interpersonal communication.
>
> *(Kuhl & Kazén, 2008, p. 457)*

The ability to be empathetic may account for planning as a *dialogical activity* (cf. Carver & Scheier, 1982; Hacker, 2000; Visser, 1994) and provides a social dimension to planning, especially in its holistic mode, which is needed for enhancing the social compatibility of plans or for resolving conflicts among various agents participating in the planning process.

Taking all the properties of the right hemisphere together, this hemisphere should be especially useful at an early stage of planning, for example, when planners generate the goals that are to guide the planning process, taking a variety of constraints into account (which would overtax explicit hierarchical planning) and when priorities among competing goals have to be evaluated (which is greatly facilitated when many constraints can be processed in a parallel rather than sequential way). In addition, holistic processing may enter at a later stage when plans have to be flexibly adapted to situational changes.

3.5 System Interactions are Modulated by Affective Change

Summing up the previous two sections, the left hemisphere is involved in hierarchical step-by-step planning through analytic processing, whereas the right hemisphere is more linked with flexible and integrative planning by parallel processing. How is it possible to explain that studies found *bilateral activation* during planning processes despite the just-mentioned hemisphere lateralization? A brief literature search reveals at least eleven studies showing bilateral activation during planning (e.g. Den Braber et al., 2008; De Ruiter et al., 2009; Kaller et al., 2010). The often observed bilateral patterns of mid-dorsolateral prefrontal cortex activation in complex tasks may reflect the concomitant and simultaneous operation of specific and separable cognitive processes "that to some degree may even involve a hemispheric specialization at the highest, most abstract, and flexible levels of information processing in the human brain" (Kaller et al., 2010, p. 315). It does not seem far-fetched to assume that analytical versus holistic planning can be identified as those two specialized forms of bilateral brain networks that would, ideally speaking, interact in a complementary way during planning.

In everyday life, as in most scientific approaches, planning is almost exclusively regarded as a cognitive achievement: once you have developed your plan, you can execute it. However, this cognitivist account ignores the typical risks associated with planning: difficult intentions are not always reliably enacted at the right moment and hierarchical plans are not always backed up by an extensive experiential network's ("holistic plans") that provide alternatives for action when a plan turns out to be inappropriate. These two examples illustrate challenges for effective planning that can be mastered through interaction among mental systems. How can the interaction between two profoundly different, if not incompatible, forms of information processing be brought about? How can one avoid conflict or dissociation between the two antagonistic systems? According to PSI theory, complex phenomena such as planning arise through the communication of the four systems relevant for personality functioning.

PSI theory integrates empirical findings, suggesting that this *communication among systems*, for instance, among analytical and holistic systems, is facilitated through affective change. It has been shown that some forms of positive affect promote creative thinking, whereas negative affect is conducive to analytical processing, in which the existing information needs to be processed more carefully and systematically (cf. Cohen & Andrade, 2004; Isen, 2010; Martin & Clore, 2001). The two modulation assumptions spell out similar effects for the interactions among the four personality systems involved: positive affect activates Intuitive Behavior Control and, indirectly, Extension Memory (especially when positive affect results from self-confrontational down-regulation of negative affect which is presumably mediated by Extension Memory), whereas negative affect intensifies Object Recognition and indirectly Intention Memory (especially when negative affect is associated with an inhibition of positive affect; cf. Kuhl, 2001). In a nutshell, the two right-hemispheric systems are associated with positive affect or down-regulation of negative affect, whereas activation of the two left-hemispheric systems is intensified by negative or low positive affect.

These *basic affect–cognition interaction assumptions* in PSI theory are corroborated by findings showing that people avoid opportunities that would increase positive mood (e.g. happy music) when confronted with an analytical task and avoid options associated with negative mood when anticipating a creative task (Cohen & Andrade, 2004). Apparently, people utilize some intuitive knowledge about emotions having an impact on the type of cognitive processing. Moreover, they use this information to modify their current affective states in the direction that appears most appropriate for the task at hand: "upward and downward affect regulation as well as positive and negative mood maintenance are all likely to be deliberately used to achieve instrumental goals" (Cohen & Andrade, 2004, p. 366).

According to PSI theory, the smooth interaction among systems can be disturbed by *affective fixations* that may be caused by any affective bias (i.e. over- or under-stimulation by positive or negative events, respectively). For example, optimism or any other kind of "positive orientation" can impair the maintenance of difficult plans and intentions (recall that Intention Memory requires some frustration tolerance). In a similar vein, a cool and relaxed mood (which relates to another attitude preferred in organizations) may impair risk sensitivity and learning from mistakes, which require a phase of "pain tolerance" (*self-confrontational* coping) for focusing on whatever new information is to be integrated into the experiential network (i.e. Extension Memory). Affective fixation is especially likely to interfere with smooth system interactions when a dispositional affective bias toward high or low sensitivity to emotional cues (positive or negative) cannot be counter-regulated by an intact ability to *self-regulate* emotional states. Research has shown, for example, that the self-motivational ability to up-regulate positive affect, when it is dampened after confronting a difficult or unpleasant task, facilitates volitional efficiency, for example when making a decision or enacting a plan (Beckmann & Kuhl, 1984; Harmon-Jones & Harmon-Jones, 2002). Likewise, Baumann, Kaschel, and Kuhl (2007) found that low sensitivity to positive affect and high sensitivity to negative affect become maladaptive only when self-motivation and self-relaxation are low. In contrast, when combined with intact emotion regulation, low positive or high negative affect even have a health-protecting and self-enhancing effect (Baumann et al., 2007). Presumably, *self-motivation* activates experience-based knowledge from Extension Memory to restore positive affect in difficult situations. According to this argument, the up-regulation of motivation occurs by scanning Extension Memory and finding self-relevant reasons and incentives for action (Kuhl, 2001). *Self-relaxation* refers to the ability to down-regulate negative emotions. This down-regulation occurs, again facilitated by scanning extension memory, either by acquiring new adequate alternatives for action by providing knowledge or experience to deal with the negative stimuli or by re-evaluating the negative stimuli (Kuhl, 2001).

In the following section we will focus on various interactions between the four systems. For example, the two high-level systems can affect the two low-level systems (top-down), which is relevant for plan enactment (see 3.5.1) or plan-monitoring (see 3.5.2), respectively. Furthermore, the low-level systems provide relevant information to the high-level systems, which is conducive to the development of planning knowledge (see 3.5.3). Finally, a horizontal interaction between the two high-level systems is essential (see 3.5.4).

3.5.1 Plan Execution: Self-Motivation Facilitates Enactment of Intentions

Execution of emotionally or cognitively difficult plans requires the interaction between Intention Memory and Intuitive Behavior Control (*IM-IBC interaction*[2]). This interaction can be either automatized through implementation intentions (Gollwitzer, 1999) or facilitated through negative affect (avoidance motivation: Elliot, 1999) or through positive affect, which in turn can be externally controlled or self-regulated (approach motivation: Elliot, 1999). The latter (positive) basis for plan execution is associated with a broader scope of attention and a more extended experiential network (i.e., extension memory) providing flexibility and creativity, especially when unexpected obstacles are encountered.

According to PSI theory, *self-regulation* of positive affect includes two facets: tolerance for low positive affect (*frustration tolerance*), which may be associated with maintenance of difficult intentions and delayed enactment, and, after a variable delay, the up-regulation of positive affect when an opportunity for enacting the intention is encountered (*self-motivation*). Beckmann and Kuhl (1984) found that students looking for an apartment gradually increased the value of the initially favored apartment during the course of decision making, despite the fact that they had been given no new information about the apartments that would justify such an upgrade (cf. "spread of alternatives" effect, Festinger, 1957).[3] Presumably, the emerging one-sided appreciation of a favored option can be regarded as an instance of self-motivation which enhances the stability of decision making and facilitates the implementation process.

The self-regulatory "dialectics" between low and high positive affect intensifies the interaction between plan-related intentions and the control of plan-relevant behavior. The *first modulation assumption* describes a self-regulated and fine-tuned mode of implementing intentions (Kazén & Kuhl, 2005; Kuhl & Kazén, 1999): whenever spontaneous (intuitive) enactment of an action is difficult or inappropriate, an explicit intention is formed and maintained in Intention Memory until it can be transacted. In contrast to implementation intentions, avoidance motivation and externally controlled approach motivation, *self-regulated* maintenance of an intention and the inhibition of premature behavior during a phase of dampened positive affect *(volitional inhibition)* is especially useful when a time window is needed for problem-solving, for waiting until an adequate opportunity arises for optimal plan execution, or when emotional and motivational resources have to be generated (from extension memory) for initiating and maintaining appropriate action. To this end, self-regulation of the intention–behavior link through self-initiated up-regulation of positive affect is not confined to the final stage of decision making or plan execution: it is also useful during motivationally difficult stages, for example when dealing with unpleasant duties.

In sum, only the *self-regulated* mode of implementing intentions on the basis of increasing positive affect according to the situational demands and affordances has the capacity to finely tune systems interactions according to the current context: the plan delivers possible actions or goals (with high-level goals and specific sub-goals) whenever there is a need (e.g. to go on to the next step or visualize an alternative because one step has failed). Alternative forms of facilitating enactment such as forming automatized implementation intentions (e.g. Gollwitzer, 1999; Gollwitzer & Sheeran, 2009) or increasing avoidance motivation through pressure (e.g. from impending deadlines) can be efficient for plan enactment, but they may be less useful for the fine-tuning of phases that require volitional inhibition to maintain a difficult intention and establish the time window mentioned above. They may also be less useful for flexibly and creatively changing parts of the plan whenever situational changes require transcending its original scope. By definition, implementation intentions facilitate the automatic execution (bypassing extension memory) upon encountering the trigger conditions (as spelled out by the if-part of the if–then-proposition: "if situation X is encountered plan Y is to be automatically implemented." Future research is needed to further delineate the personal, situational, and organizational conditions that call for self-regulated versus automatized forms of plan execution.

3.5.2 Plan Monitoring: Vigilance Enables Creative Flexibility of Plans

As pointed out in the preceding section, the interaction of Intuitive Behavior Control and Intention Memory is needed when emotionally or cognitively difficult intentions are to be executed. When enactment is possible without having to overcome such difficulties, another pathway into action can be chosen which involves the interaction of Extension Memory (including the self) and Intuitive Behavior Control (*EM-IBC interaction*). We assume that Extension Memory possesses an implicit pictorial network of the entire plan, similar to a mind map. As long as a plan can be executed on the basis of this implicit experiential network and all obstacles encountered can be smoothly overcome without switching to analytically controlled processing (not unlike the well-known flow experience (e.g. Nakamura & Csikszentmihalyi, 2009), there is no need to switch to Intention Memory with its demanding form of emotional dialectics (i.e. switching between frustration tolerance and subsequent self-motivation). Instead, wherever plan execution can be managed within the largely implicit flow-like state of mind, a relaxed and positive mood should facilitate implicit control of plan execution. Recall that relaxed mood facilitates Extension Memory and positive affect facilitates Intuitive Behavior Control, the two systems presumably involved in flow-like states (cf. *second modulation assumption*, Fig. 4.1).

Facilitation of holistic processing through relaxed and positive mood states has been demonstrated in studies showing that holistic processing involving intuitive judgments about remote semantic associations (e.g. "Do the words *mower, plant* and *play* have anything in common"[4]) are facilitated by a right-prefrontal network (Bowden & Beeman, 1998; Bowden et al., 2005) and by a positive and relaxed mood (Isen, Daubman, & Nowicki, 1987). In a similar vein, holistic person perception (recognizing patterns of attributes characterizing people one met before) is facilitated by positive and relaxed mood and impaired by negative mood (Baumann & Kuhl, 2002).

The capacity to intuitively detect even remote semantic associations (which has been regarded as one component of creativity: Mednick, 1962) can be regarded as an example for a particular form of broad and implicit attention. It is called *vigilance* (Posner & Rothbart, 1992; cf. Table 4.1) and operates from the background of consciousness (Posner & Petersen, 1990). In contrast to the Activation-Trigger-Schema System (Norman, 1981), whose operations are similar to Gollwitzer's if–then propositions because they are based on the activation and selection of schemas and use "a triggering mechanism that requires that appropriate conditions be satisfied for the operation of a schema" (Norman, 1981, p. 3), vigilance can be described as an attentional mechanism using an extended (global) filter for identifying information that matches any component of a holistic plan (Kuhl, 2001). It is a diffuse readiness to monitor all the information from the outside world and amplify those parts that match with any part of the currently active network of experiential knowledge, including the current implicit goal-network (i.e. the holistic plan including a variety of relevant contexts, possible actions, and acceptable outcomes). Vigilant congruence orientation can be illustrated by its inherent salience effect: any cue in the internal or external world automatically pops up when it is congruent with or relevant for any detail of the active plan. To this end, vigilance serves as an implicit "monitoring mechanism of behavior – a mechanism that is separate from that responsible for the selection and execution of the act" (Norman, 1981, p. 3).

Vigilance (and holistic planning in general) is especially useful when the concrete details of a plan cannot be specified yet (e.g. exactly what should be done to improve the personal climate within a team, and where and when relevant steps should be taken). In this case, the system must remain sensitive over time, for a relevant, possibly rare event that typically originates from a larger, unspecified set of events. Compared to a highly specified plan (e.g. spelling out which team member should be addressed at what time and in which way), a global plan[5] based on a few ideas such as encouraging team members to be more outspoken or being more friendly and personal in everyday interactions allows greater flexibility than a specific plan in terms of generating a variety of behaviors that seem adequate depending on the concrete situation encountered. Unlike concrete, explicit, and fully explicable plans, global plans can and should not be reduced to particular and specific ideas because they are based on an extended implicit network of possible sub-goals and goal-oriented actions that is open for a variety of situations and actions (Kuhl, 2010). It goes without saying that such a global network is especially useful when planning is to deal with underspecified challenges or dynamic situations involving fast and partly unpredictable changes.

Moreover, because of their implicit nature, global plans can affect behavior, even in situations in which they are not in the focus of conscious attention. This is even true for simple goals. In contrast to priming specific goals ("avoiding cookies"), experimental priming with implicit global goals ("being thin") helps restraint from unobtrusive temptation, for example, when the temptation to eat high-calorie food is disguised as a consumer test (Ferguson, 2007). To the extent that the scanning operates on an unconscious level of processing, it is more likely to detect *implicit* plan-jeopardizing distractors or temptations that would go undetected on the basis of the conscious and narrowly focused form of attention (i.e. target detection). Conscious efforts to try to think of a global plan at the right moment are likely to fail, because consciously focused attention, which is useful when a specific goal or target is to be detected, is not particularly useful in the long-term monitoring of global goals or plans. On the contrary, Posner et al. (1992) cited findings showing a negative correlation between the activation of the brain structures that are associated with implicit vigilance performance (right prefrontal cortex) and the activation of the structures that are associated with the detection of explicit targets. On the other hand, when a person becomes aware of a temptation, specific conscious goals (Gollwitzer, 1999) may be more effective than global goals.

The assumption that the implicit monitoring of global goals is facilitated by positive affect, as described above, was also confirmed in Ferguson's (2007) study: global goals prevented goal-incompatible behavior (e.g. eating high-calorie food when primed with the global goal "being thin") only when they were implicitly associated with positive affect (i.e. when primes reminding of a global goal were associated with reduced latencies in categorizing the emotional quality of positive words in an emotional priming task). These findings are consistent with research on avoidance motivation and prevention (in contrast to promotion) focus (Elliott, 2008), suggesting that negative affect has the potential to facilitate specific rather than global goals.

In sum, global planning supports implicit monitoring of plan-relevant cues and opportunities for plan execution. It is supported by down-regulation of negative mood (i.e. a relaxed state of mind) and by up-regulation of positive affect, because those emotional states activate Extension Memory, which is conceived of as the basis of flow-like execution of plan-relevant behavior. The question as to how emotional states facilitate or impair the formation of and guidance by global goals and holistic planning deserves more systematic future research.

3.5.3 Development of Planning Knowledge

So far we have described two forms of plan execution (or "action control") which involve one of the two high-level systems (i.e. Intention Memory with its specific plan or Extension Memory with its holistic plan). In either case, the relevant higher-order system has an (top-down) impact on the state of the low-level system relevant for performing plan-relevant behavior (i.e. Intuitive Behavior Control: see Fig. 4.1). In contrast to plan execution, the *development of planning knowledge* involves the reverse (bottom-up) direction of processing: the flow of information from low- to high-level systems helps to modify the latter and hence can be a powerful source of learning. Two types of interaction are of central importance in the development of planning knowledge. The first type, which supports the development of *holistic plans*, involves the interaction between low-level Object Recognition or Intuitive Behavior Control and high-level Extension Memory. The second form supports the development of *hierarchical plans* and involves the interaction between low-level Intuitive Behavior Control and Intention Memory. During either type of bottom-up interaction, an assimilative and an accommodative form of learning can be distinguished. We will describe this distinction in the remainder of this section.

In the context of developing *holistic* plans, *assimilative* learning (based on Extension Memory – Intuitive Behavior Control interactions) takes place by making minor adaptations of a plan to apply it to more and more situations. One result of assimilative plan development is the planner's increasing awareness of situations or opportunities that are relevant for the plan.

During the *accommodative* type of developing holistic planning knowledge (based on Extension Memory – Object Recognition interactions), learning is not easily grasped, since it takes place in "dialectic" manner. Assimilative learning does not require leaving the intuitive mode because it is based on the interaction of two intuitive systems (i.e. Extension Memory and Intuitive Behavior Control). In contrast to simple (assimilative) feedback-based forms of learning in parallel (connectionist) networks (e.g. backward propagation: Rumelhart et al., 1986), the dialectical (accommodative) form of learning entails the interaction between parallel-holistic and analytical processing. This interaction requires leaving the holistic mode (i.e. subsymbolic Extension Memory) once an error has been detected and focusing on it through activating the analytical (symbolic) Object Recognition System. Analytical processing of errors and their possible causes may yield a much more precise input for the feedback mechanism. Typically, any confrontation with unexpected errors or mistakes may be associated with negative affect, which, if it perseverates too long at an excessively high intensity, impairs self-access and creative, context-sensitive plan execution (Baumann & Kuhl, 2002, 2003; Cohen & Andrade, 2004; Isen, 1984). For this purpose, *self-relaxation* is needed, which can be considered as another form of self-regulation of affect (i.e. in addition to self-motivation described in section 3.5.1). According to PSI theory, self-relaxation facilitates the bottom-up type of *learning from mistakes* by self-initiated affective change. In a first phase, sensitivity to negative affect should be maintained, because negative affect facilitates Object Recognition, that is the detection of unexpected details and errors (Fig. 4.1). In a subsequent phase, negative affect should be down-regulated as a necessary condition for self-access and flexible plan execution as well as the integration of whatever can be learned from the mistake into Extension Memory (cf. section 3.2).

To this end, errors are valuable pieces of information, because they serve as feedback for one's actions and can point out what aspects of one's knowledge and skills need further correction and refinement (Frese & Zapf, 1994; Ivancic & Hesketh, 1995/1996). Furthermore, errors can be used retrospectively to evaluate the effectiveness of one's previous strategies (Neubert, 1998). All in all, under the precondition of an *error-tolerant attitude* (Ivancic & Hesketh, 1995/1996; cf. Keith & Frese, 2008; van Dyck, Frese, Baer, & Sonnentag, 2005), incorporating insights from former errors or otherwise unexpected events into a growing Extension Memory should gradually improve the initial plan and its execution through global plan monitoring.

Accommodative learning occurs in "qualitative jumps" rather than in a continuously growing quantitative learning curve: in accommodative learning, errors are detected, considered, analyzed, and integrated (i.e. fed back into the parallel experiential network) – if necessary with revision of the knowledge network.[6] The integration of new knowledge into the ever growing knowledge base of Extension Memory shows remarkable overlap with the concept of case-based planning described in the Chapter 2, "Planning processes: relevant cognitive operations," in this volume. Case-based or experiential knowledge includes specific prior episodes of performance, hypothetical episodes, ensemble episodes, and role models (Kolodner, 1997). Case-based knowledge structures are highly complex and take into account multiple constraints (Hammond, 1990), and are supposed to be organized in a library system of case prototypes (Mumford, Schultz, & Van Doorn, 2001), which are activated and recalled relatively quickly (cf. parallel distributed processing described earlier in this chapter).

In sum, according to the PSI account of plan development, the dialectical ("accommodative") interaction between Extension Memory (with its direct access to Intuitive Behavior Control) and Object Recognition, that is between plan application and error analysis drives a particularly strong form of developing *holistic plans*.

It can be assumed that both assimilative and accommodative plan development make a plan more robust through new constraints yielding an optimal balance between stability and flexibility. As a consequence, fewer revisions of decisions and less post-decision regret (Festinger & Walster, 1964) should be observed. It is important to examine empirically how planning knowledge is developed when implementation experiences are made, for example, when implicit work experience is implemented.

The *hierarchical* form of plan development is characterized by an exchange between the Intuitive Behavior Control system and Intention Memory (cf. section 3.3). This interaction provides feedback emanating from performed actions and indicating the contexts in which an action was successful or not. Through *assimilative* integration of more and more options for action, a growing network of actions for fulfilling the plan is created. Thus, by performing plan-relevant behavior, hierarchical plans are elaborated by assimilating more and more behavioral routines in the hierarchy of goals and action alternatives. In contrast, *accommodative* revisions of hierarchical plans adapt them more and more to reality (cf. the concept of meta-plans: Stefik, 1981b; Wilensky, 1981). Similar to accommodative revision of holistic plans, the accommodative revision of hierarchical plans involves a shift between intuitive processing (in this case: Intuitive Behavior Control) and analytical processing (e.g. analyzing why an attempt to enact a plan-related action failed). Exploring the differences between assimilative (intuitive) and accommodative (analytical) forms of hierarchical plan development constitutes a promising challenge for future research.

In sum, integrating corrective information into high-level systems (especially Extension Memory) is the basis for "self-development," which amounts to building an ever growing knowledge base for planning loaded with personally relevant, as well as system- and task-relevant experiences, and therefore constitute a "storehouse of useful methods for future goal-directed activities" (Pea, 1982, p. 14).

3.5.4 Interaction Between the Two High-Level Systems: Plan Integration

Since *Extension Memory* has access to a parallel-holistic network of experiential knowledge, it seems especially suited for *forming* flexible plans that are open to creative adjustments to unexpected conditions. In contrast, *Intention Memory* is optimally designed for actual plan *delivery* under concrete, specified conditions. In this context, the coordination of the two systems involved in plan formation or plan delivery comes into view.

For example, reflecting "about one's future and effectively planning it often requires answering self-evaluative questions" (Gervey, Igou, & Trope, 2005, p.1), which amounts to connecting a specific hierarchical plan with the personal part of Extension Memory. The combination of a concrete plan or goal with the personal part of Extension Memory (i.e. the self) facilitates enactment because it provides emotional and experiential support during the course of implementation. Moreover, integration of an explicit hierarchical plan with Extension Memory improves plan development because that integration combines the concrete (linear) plan with an extended network of relevant situations and a variety of possible action alternatives, thereby increasing its adaptability to changing situations.

According to PSI theory, the coordination of Extension Memory and Intention Memory can be optimized by the flexible modulation of affect relevant for the activation of those two systems. Specifically, the interaction between the two high-level systems depends on a particular type of *emotional dialectics* that can be derived from the model (Fig. 4.1).

How can emotional states promote this integration of a linear plan into the extended experiential network of Extension Memory? As shown in Fig. 4.1, in the first phase of this process, the reduction of positive affect associated with forming and maintaining a specific intention must be endured. Individuals who prefer to avoid frustration or difficult intentions tend to skip the difficult or unpleasant parts of plan development. However, people who are overly involved in analyzing possible problems can get stuck in planning difficult steps while missing opportunities to elaborate an implicit holistic network of alternative options for action, including the recruitment of emotional support at various stages of the planning process. This elaboration relates to the second phase of plan integration: the specific plan conceived needs to be evaluated within the broader context of all relevant constraints, values, competencies, and competing priorities involved (own and others'). To that end, Intention Memory needs to make contact with Extension Memory and its personal section (i.e. the self).

According to PSI theory, this flow of information from Intention Memory to Extension Memory necessitates a shift from low positive or "tense" mood to a more relaxed mood (Fig. 4.1). Presumably, tense mood, which should be associated more with low than with high positive affect, is assumed to facilitate the "objective" attitude necessary for clear thinking and keeping specific intentions in mind. Lewin (1951) described intentions as "tension systems" that are not released until their completion. Empirical findings confirm the close association between an uncompleted intention (e.g. induced by announcing a task coming up later in the experiment) and an increase in tense mood, unless it can be counter-regulated by increasing positive affect (Koole &

Jostmann, 2004). In contrast, relaxed mood should facilitate access to the holistic knowledge base (i.e. Extension Memory). Likewise, a similar "emotional shift" is necessary for targets that are not self-generated (i.e. not within Extension Memory) but suggested by other people and need to be integrated into the self-system.

3.6 Individual Differences in Self-Regulation

In what ways do people differ in their ability to self-regulate interactions among systems involved in planning, plan execution, and plan evaluation? To answer this question, it is important to consider states or traits affecting emotions as well as individual differences in cognitive style. For this purpose, we will take a brief look at some relevant personality variables: action orientation, personal initiative, impulsivity, and cognitive style.

3.6.1 Action Orientation

According to PSI theory, both the enactment of plan-related intentions (volitional facilitation) and feedback-based plan improvement or revision is facilitated by individual differences in the regulation of positive and negative emotions, respectively. The individual difference variable called "action orientation" captures the two major forms of emotion regulation, that is (1) the ability to up-regulate positive affect (called *prospective, demand-related, action orientation* facilitating *decisiveness* and *initiative*) and (2) the ability to down-regulate negative affect (*retrospective* or *threat-related action orientation*). The opposite pole, called *state orientation*, impedes efficient self-regulation through *hesitation* or *preoccupation* – "the preoccupation dimension is concerned with whether distracting thoughts interfere with initiating action, whereas the hesitation dimension emphasizes the behavioral capacity to initiate action" (Diefendorff, Hall, Lord, & Strean, 2000, p. 251; cf. Kuhl, 1994b).

Empirical research has shown that *prospective action orientation* promotes the ability of self-determined transition from plan to action (Dibbelt, 1997; Jostmann & Koole, 2007; Kazén, Kaschel, & Kuhl, 2008; Kuhl & Goschke, 1994). According to PSI theory, the action-oriented transition from intention to behavior is mediated by an implicit up-regulation of positive affect (self-motivation), which presumably requires self-access (because the self and its Extension Memory provide access to an extended network of positive emotions related to possible forms of action). Koole and Jostmann (2004) confirmed this hypothesis: when confronted with a demanding task (that had to be maintained in Intention Memory because it was announced as coming up later in the experiment), action-oriented participants faster detected positive information among an array of negative information. This selective (self-motivational) focus on positive affect was mediated by self-access (i.e. the positive bias disappeared when individual differences in the speed of self-evaluative decisions were statistically controlled).

In sum, *hesitation* – with opposing poles of hesitation versus initiative[7] – presumably modulates the dynamic interplay of the two psychological systems involved in plan execution, that is, Intention Memory and Intuitive Behavior Control (cf. Fig. 4.1). "Differences in individual initiative may explain why equally motivated people may nevertheless fail to attain the same level of performance" (Jaramillo, Locander, Spector, & Harris, 2007, p. 59; cf. Diefendorff et al., 2000; Diefendorff, Richard, & Gosserand, 2006), thus showing the inherent interconnectedness of "willing and able," which only together cover the full term of motivation (cf. Van Dijke, De Cremer, Brebels, & Van Quaquebeke, 2013). Professional activities often require dealing with demanding situations and taking initiative. The ability to initiate actions independently (i.e. without external sources of motivation) has become increasingly important, as more companies rely on employees who can independently manage their work-related tasks (Frese, 1997). Taking initiative in a timely manner plays a major role in western societies, where deadlines and time constraints are ubiquitous (Roxburgh, 2004). Accordingly, hesitation has been shown to predict job performance (Diefendorff et al., 2000[8]; Jaramillo et al., 2007; Van Dijke et al., 2013).

The second major form of emotion regulation, *threat-related action-orientation*, is related to efficient monitoring and revision of plans and intentions, including utilizing failure information for improving decision making and performance rather than for debilitating rumination about negative events (Jungermann, Pfister, & May, 1994; Kuhl, 1981; Kuhl & Beckmann, 1983; Kuhl & Weiss, 1994; Stiensmeier-Pelster, John, Stulik, & Schürmann, 1989; Stiensmeier-Pelster, Schürmann, John, & Stulik, 1991).

Although the vast majority of recent empirical studies focus on the examination of the hesitation dimension (i.e. prospective state vs. action orientation), there has been interesting research on the *preoccupation* scale as well. Preoccupation – with the opposing poles of preoccupation versus disengagement (e.g. from unrealistic goals) – refers to the inability to detach from thoughts about alternative goals or undesirable events that may interfere with progress on the task at hand. Diefendorff et al. (2000) found that the preoccupation subscale was generally negatively related to ratings of performance. However, the preoccupied form of state orientation might be beneficial in some cases, depending on the role and type of task (cf. Beckmann, 1994; Beckmann & Kazén, 1994; Koole, Kuhl, Jostmann & Vochs, 2005):

> State-oriented individuals may be more cautious, diligent, and thoughtful than action-oriented individuals. These behavioral attributes may facilitate work performance for jobs that require careful decision making and are rated by supervisors as requiring thoroughness. It is important for many jobs, however, that persons who are thoughtful in the planning stage then proceed to enact their plans (as assessed by the Initiative vs. Hesitation subscale).
>
> *(Diefendorff et al., 2000, p. 260)*

Thus, it seems quite important to consider both subscales, so that planning can be efficient before and during the actual implementation of an action. Even the combination of preoccupation and initiative can be useful. An inclination toward preoccupation can have the advantage of careful planning that can in turn be promptly implemented when combined with high initiative (i.e. low hesitation). This case seems to refer in particular to *hierarchical plans*. According to PSI theory, the motivational energy needed for implementation increases with a growing number of hierarchical steps planned. To this end, hierarchical plans need action-oriented initiative for enactment (as a function of plan size), despite the fact that they can benefit from state-oriented preoccupation for careful planning.

How do individual differences in action vs. state orientation affect *holistic planning*? Some tentative suggestions can be derived from research by Diefendorff and associates (2006). Individuals low in hesitation performed better than individuals high in hesitation when satisfaction or involvement was low, but no differences in performance were observed when satisfaction or involvement was high. Since action orientation (i.e. initiative as opposed to hesitation) is mediated by self-motivation (Koole & Jostmann, 2004), it is plausible that individual differences in this particular self-regulatory capacity come into play when a plan or some work content is not inherently associated with positive incentives. In contrast, when a task is attractive enough (arousing involvement and satisfaction), the self-motivational capacity associated with action orientation is not needed.

3.6.2 Personal Initiative

A trait construct conceptually similar to hesitation is *personal initiative*. Personal initiative is defined as "work behavior characterized by its self-starting nature, its proactive approach, and by being persistent in overcoming difficulties that arise in the pursuit of a goal" (Frese & Fay, 2001, p. 133). It is also grounded on action control theory. However, it is not yet clear how the constructs interact. Jaramillo et al. (2007) stated: "Although initiative [i.e. action orientation] and personal initiative have some conceptual overlap, they also function at two distinct levels of behavior – personal initiative mainly represents good planning, whereas [action-oriented] initiative denotes a high capacity of moving the plan forward" (p. 61, cf. Diefendorff et al., 2006; Frese, Fay, Hilburger, Leng, & Tag, 1997). An even more important conceptual difference between the two constructs refers to the self-regulatory component: personal initiative captures a dispositional *readiness* to initiate action, whereas prospective action orientation describes the self-regulatory *ability* to restore positive motivation for action once it is reduced (e.g. when confronting a difficult or unpleasant task). Most personality variables including the "Big Five" factors (e.g. McCrae & Costa, 1987) describe some *readiness* for a particular type of behavior as a primary response to any situation encountered (e.g. initiate action, respond with positive or with negative affect). In contrast, action orientation relates to the question whether individuals can change their primary response readiness if they consider this desirable (e.g. when the task at hand requires behavior that differs from the individuals' primary response readiness). The construct of action orientation implies that an individual can shift to a response needed in the situation encountered, irrespective of what his or her primary response might be. This theoretical argument may guide future research on the issue of conceptual separation and interaction of personal initiative versus self-regulated initiative, especially in the context of planning.

3.6.3 Impulsivity

Another construct having a possible overlap with hesitation is *impulsivity*, which can be regarded as a component of extraversion (Anderson & Revelle, 1994). Impulsivity as a high state of *readiness* to act might be positively associated with initiative or even with action orientation (i.e. it may reduce hesitation), but there are some conceptual differences. Actions of individuals high in (action-oriented) initiative are mediated by central executive functions, which regulate behavior on the basis of an integrated overview of all relevant internal (plan-related or need-based) and external constraints (Kuhl, 1994b). Impulsive people tend to act immediately on every impulse that has been activated by the context, regardless of whether this impulse fits the individual's other objectives, priorities, and plans. They may stick to an intention and implement it until they are distracted by a more attractive alternative and switch to something else. Aside from the temperament-based form of impulsivity, this term has also been used to describe a cognitive style with *reflexivity* as its opposing pole (Kagan, Rosman, Day, Albert, & Phillips, 1964; cf. Messer, 1976). Reflexivity is characterized by the rule "stop and think" (or "make a plan") rather than taking premature action. It is plausible that an individual's tendency toward reflexivity vs. impulsivity has a direct impact on the choice of the planning strategy. Presumably, impulsivity supports opportunistic planning, whereas reflexivity is more useful for hierarchical planning. These relationships may be verified in future research.

3.6.4 Cognitive Style

In addition to emotional states or traits facilitating analytic or holistic processing, individual differences in *cognitive style* may affect the preferred mode of planning. A cognitive style that is based on the distinction between holistic and analytical representations is field dependence vs. field independence (Witkin, 1950). Specifically, field independence implies the extraction of objects from their context (cf. Object Recognition in PSI theory), which we also consider to be useful in hierarchical planning. Future research concerning individual differences in the proclivity toward analytical versus holistic planning may benefit from the various ways of operationalizing individual differences in field dependence (e.g. Kühnen, Hannover, Roeder, Shah, Schubert, Upmeyer, & Zakaria, 2001; Kühnen, Hannover, & Schubert, 2001; Witkin, 1950; Witkin, Moore, Goodenough, & Cox, 1977).

3.7 Embodied Plans: Emotions Accomplish More than the Modulation of System Interactions

According to PSI theory, the functional significance of emotions is not confined to modulating system interactions. When a specific plan makes contact with the rich experiential knowledge base of Extension Memory, the broad integration of emotions inherent in this system (cf. Table 4.1) provides motivational power, which is especially useful when holistic planning explores the experiential network for creative and original ideas. Such ideas sometimes emerge as weak and remote associations (cf. Bowden et al., 2005) based on relatively faint signals. These faint signals will be lost and cannot be recovered by conscious awareness unless they receive some motivational enhancement. Empirical support for this hypothesis has been reported by Alice Isen's work on the creativity-enhancing effects of experimentally induced positive affect (Isen, 1984, 2010). Theoretically speaking, the close integration of emotional and somatic states into the broad associative network of right-hemispheric holistic processing (i.e. Extension Memory) explains both the cognitive and the motivational side of creativity. On the one hand, right hemispheric processing supports coarse rather than fine-grained processing of extended semantic networks, thereby increasing the likelihood of finding a possibly useful hint (i.e. the cognitive side of creativity: Beeman et al., 1994; Rotenberg, 2009; 2013a & b). At the same time, right hemispheric processing provides the emotional support needed to stick to those unusually weak signals detected in this network. This motivational side of creativity may be derived from the right hemisphere's extensive connectedness with the autonomic nervous system and somatic markers (Bechara & Damasio, 2005; Dawson & Schell, 1982; Wittling, 1990).

The integration of emotions within extended semantic networks (supporting holistic planning) has an additional advantage: it helps a plan to stay in touch with the needs and values of the people involved in or affected by it, because positive or negative emotions typically indicate whether a need (or value) is or will be satisfied or frustrated, respectively. Hierarchical plans that are decoupled from holistic processing may lead the planner to drift into an overly analytical form of planning, which increases the risk of neglecting the needs and values of the people involved. Because of the central importance of the emotions and somatic markers associated with holistic planning, we introduce the concept of an *embodied plan* to denote the emotional side of holistic planning. The German term *Leib* conveys the deep interconnection between holistic cognition and somatic feeling (Nietzsche, 2005). *Leib* is understood as the phenomenological side of the body – approximately describable with bodily sensations utilized by the self in decision making (Bechara & Damasio, 2005). It represents an interface between body and mind which is compatible with the deep interconnectedness of holistic cognition with emotions and somatic markers.

4 Practical Implications

In what ways can our functional analysis of the cognitive, emotional, and motivational processes underlying the two forms of planning be utilized in applied contexts? It should be clear that this cannot be achieved simply by selection strategies. From our systems-oriented personality perspective, it seems clear that one cannot always divide organizational and managerial tasks into two separate categories, one requiring analytic people and the other one drawing upon people specialized in holistic planning. Our personality approach to planning suggests at least two recommendations related to those questions.

4.1 Practice Switching among Analytical and Holistic Modes

In light of the dominant role of analytical planning in Western societies, switching among modes requires methods that facilitate the shift from analytical to holistic planning. It is beyond the scope of this chapter to elaborate on specific training tools. Suffice it to say that there are many methods that have the potential to activate the personality systems supporting holistic planning and its interaction with analytical processing (e.g. Alsleben & Kuhl, 2010; De Shazer, Dolan, & Korman, 2007; Erickson, 1958; Gendlin, 1962; Gilligan, 2013; Storch & Kuhl, 2011; Strehlau & Kuhl, in press). PSI theory explains why those methods work and when a particular method should be applied: both their functional basis and their indication can be derived from the functional profiles (Table 4.1) of the systems involved (e.g. Extension Memory and the integrative self as a parallel-holistic experiential knowledge base).

4.2 Develop Affect Regulation

The second target of intervention relates to the development of affect regulation. We have described this process earlier in this chapter (see 3.5). According to PSI theory, the most important point concerning affect regulation is the empirically confirmed assumption that the ability to self-regulate one's emotions supports switching among personality systems (cf. Fig. 4.1). But how can affect regulation be developed?

Based on the principle of classical conditioning, Kuhl (2001) developed the concept of system conditioning. In contrast to classical conditioning, this is about linking two systems rather than two stimuli or responses. Specifically, in order to learn how to self-regulate emotions, the self and the emotional system need to be connected. The self is always activated when a person expresses his or her feelings and needs or when he or she feels understood, appreciated, and addressed on a personal level. The emotion system can be activated, for instance, when a discouraged or nervous person is encouraged or comforted by another person. In this case, an externally controlled counter-regulation of emotions restores positive mood. According to systems conditioning, temporal contiguity between activation of the self and activation of the desired emotional change strengthens the connection between the self system and the affective system, with the effect that, on later occasions, an activation of the self would suffice to elicit encouragement or relaxation. This happens simply because affective change is now linked to activation of the self, for example, when the person becomes (self-) aware of his or her mood. Note that, according to this model, effective encouragement or comforting is not sufficient for acquiring self-competence in affect regulation: whenever the self is not activated, as for instance, when the recipient does not feel understood or accepted by the interaction partner, even an effective external mood regulation cannot be connected to or integrated into the self.

According to Greenberg and Paivio (1997), the development of affect regulation takes place throughout a person's whole life in a constant co-regulatory process between the individual and his or her social environment. Thus, encouragement and reassurance by a mentor in an accepting relationship can be internalized. These assumptions show remarkable overlap with the construct of team psychological safety (Edmondson, 1999) and the high-quality relationships that foster it

(Carmeli & Gittell, 2009) – both playing a central role in learning from errors mentioned above (cf. 3.5.3). By the same token, consulting and coaching concepts such as solution-focused brief therapy (e.g. De Shazer et al., 2007) or rational emotive therapy (Ellis, 1969) and its derivatives for stress management (Abrams & Ellis, 1994) can support the development of adaptive affect-regulative skills.

5 Conclusions and Outlook

In addition to explicit analytical (hierarchical) planning, a more implicit, *holistic mode of planning* deserves much more attention than it has received in the past. Since both plan enactment and plan development depend on the *interaction* among those two modes of processing, the interaction between analytical and holistic processing constitutes a further promising topic for future research. The *modulatory impact of emotions* on system interactions suggests affect regulation and its development as a third issue for scientific scrutiny. To the extent that the two hemispheres of the human brain are differentially related to analytical versus holistic planning, a potential avenue for future research may be to further examine the contribution of the two *hemispheres* at the different stages of planning.

More research is also needed to delineate the personal, situational, and organizational conditions that call for *self-regulated or automatized* forms of plan execution contrasted with the useful concept of implementation intentions (e.g. Gollwitzer, 1999). Furthermore, the involvement of *vigilance* and its beneficial role when dealing with underspecified challenges or dynamic situations may be a promising field of research.

Concerning the *development of planning knowledge*, it might be interesting to examine the cooperation of case-based knowledge (Kolodner, 1997) and parallel distributed processing (McClelland, Rumelhart, & PDP Research Group, 1986). Moreover, it is important to examine empirically how planning knowledge is developed when implementation experiences are made and how plans may change by the fact that parts of them are performed in new situations.

When considering *individual variables* that affect the individual planning process, it seems desirable to have a closer look at both subscales of action orientation (e.g. Kuhl, 1994a) and their interplay during different planning stages. In addition, it might be fruitful to further investigate the separation and interaction of the concepts of action orientation, personal initiative (Frese & Fay, 2001), and impulsivity (Anderson & Revelle, 1994). Finally, the correlation between the preferred cognitive style of an individual (e.g. reflexivity vs. impulsivity, Kagan et al., 1964; or field dependence, Witkin, 1950) and the choice between holistic and hierarchical planning strategies also needs further investigation.

Acknowledgments

The authors thank Michael Frese and Ruth Bonazza for their valuable comments on earlier versions of this chapter.

Notes

1   In describing the basic characteristics of the human information-processing system, Newell and Simon stated the following: "The system operates essentially serially, one-process-at-a-time, not in parallel fashion. ... These properties – serial processing, small short term memory, infinite long-term memory with fast retrieval but slow storage – impose strong constraints on the ways in which the system can seek solutions to problems in larger problem spaces. A system not sharing these properties – a parallel system, say,

or one capable of storing symbols in long term memory in milliseconds instead of seconds – might seek problem solutions in quite different ways from the system we are considering" (Newell & Simon, 1972, p. 149).

2   This connectivity is called action control (Kuhl, 1984) or volitional facilitation (Kuhl & Kazén, 1999).

3   The "spread of alternatives" effect was only observed among high-decisive individuals and not among low-decisive individuals (cf. 3.6.1).

4   An above-chance rate of correct answers can be found intuitively, even without explicitly knowing the solution word (in this example: *power* is a word that can be combined with each of the three words mentioned in the text).

5   A global plan is an associative network of possible outcomes and possible courses of action that might be relevant for the global picture of what is to be achieved. Meta-plans (Stefik, 1981b; Wilensky, 1981) in contrast, are seen as high-level hierarchical problem-solving and planning structures based on analytical and symbolic processing.

6   The difference between assimilative and accommodative forms of learning can be illustrated by Piaget's example of a baby developing her grasping schema by assimilating more and more objects into it (e.g. adapting the movements developed for grasping a ball to a movement pattern for grasping a bar) compared with accommodating the grasping schema when she discovers that her attempts to grasp the water in her bath tub repeatedly fail until the grasping schema is qualitatively restructured and becomes a scooping schema.

7   Investigation of the latent factor structure of the action control scale suggests that the "hesitation subscale" may further be subdivided into two related factors: discipline and planning (Kanfer, Dugdale, & McDonald, 1994). The planning dimension is concerned with the extent of constructive problem-solving and the discipline dimension investigates the ease of initiation of boring or unpleasant tasks. It might be interesting to follow up this subdivision in the context of planning.

8   Remarkably, hesitation scores (i.e. prospective state orientation) explained four to five times more variance in supervisor ratings than a conventional "Big Five" personality measure, which assessed individual differences in extraversion, agreeableness, conscientiousness, emotional stability, and intellect (Diefendorff et al., 2000).

References

Abrams, M., & Ellis, A. (1994). Rational emotive behaviour therapy in the treatment of stress. *British Journal of Guidance and Counselling*, 22(1), 39–50.

Adolphs, R., Damasio, H., Tranel, D., Cooper, G., & Damasio, A. R. (2000). A role for somatosensory cortices in the visual recognition of emotion as revealed by three-dimensional lesion mapping. *The Journal of Neuroscience*, 20(7), 2683–2690.

Agre, P. E., & Chapman, D. (1987). Pengi: An implementation of a theory of activity. In *Proceedings of the sixth National Conference on Artificial Intelligence* (pp. 268–272).

Agre, P. E., & Chapman, D. (1990). What are plans for? *Robotics and Autonomous Systems*, 6(1), 17–34.

Alsleben, Ph., & Kuhl, J. (2010). Touching a person's essence: Using implicit motives as personal resources in counseling. In W. M. Cox & E. Klinger (Eds.), *Handbook of motivational counseling: motivating people for change* (2nd ed., pp. 109–131). Sussex: Wiley.

Ambros-Ingerson, J., & Steel, S. (1988). Integrating planning, execution and monitoring. In *Proceedings of the Seventh National Conference on Artificial Intelligence* (pp. 83–88).

Anderson, J. R. (1983). *The architecture of cognition*: Cambridge, MA: Harvard University Press.

Anderson, K. J., & Revelle, W. (1994). Impulsivity and time of day: is rate of change in arousal a function of impulsivity?. *Journal of Personality and Social Psychology*, 67(2), 334–344.

Artyushkin, V. F., Belyayev, A. V., Sandler, Y. M., & Sergeyev, V. M. (1990). Neural network ensembles as models of interdependence in collective behavior. *Mathematical Social Sciences*, 19(2), 167–177.

Baumann, N., & Kuhl, J. (2002). Intuition, affect, and personality: Unconscious coherence judgments and self-regulation of negative affect. *Journal of Personality and Social Psychology*, 83(5), 1213–1223.

Baumann, N., & Kuhl, J. (2003). Self-infiltration: Confusing assigned tasks as self-selected in memory. *Personality and Social Psychology Bulletin*, 29, 487–497.

Baumann, N., Kaschel, R., & Kuhl, J. (2007). Affect sensitivity and affect regulation in dealing with positive and negative affect. *Journal of Research in Personality*, 41(1), 239–248.

Bechara, A., & Damasio, A. R. (2005). The somatic marker hypothesis: A neural theory of economic decision. *Games and Economic Behavior*, 52(2), 336–372.

Beckmann, J. (1994). Volitional correlates of action vs. state orientation. In J. Kuhl & J. Beckmann (Eds.), *Volition and personality: Action versus state orientation* (pp. 155–166). Seattle, WA: Hogrefe & Huber.

Beckmann, J., & Kazén, M. (1994). Action and state orientation and the performance of top athletes. In J. Kuhl & J. Beckmann (Eds.), *Volition and personality: Action versus state orientation* (pp. 439–451). Seattle, WA: Hogrefe & Huber.

Beckmann, J., & Kuhl, J. (1984). Altering information to gain action control: Functional aspects of human information processing in decision making. *Journal of Research in Personality*, 18(2), 224–237.

Beeman, M., Friedman, R. B., Grafman, J., Perez, E., Diamond, S., & Lindsay, M. B. (1994). Summation priming and coarse semantic coding in the right hemisphere. *Journal of Cognitive Neuroscience*, 6(1), 26–45.

Bowden, E. M., & Beeman, M. J. (1998). Getting the right idea: Semantic activation in the right hemisphere may help solve insight problems. *Psychological Science*, 9(6), 435–440.

Bowden, E. M., Jung-Beeman, M., Fleck, J., & Kounios, J. (2005). New approaches to demystifying insight. *Trends in Cognitive Sciences*, 9(7), 322–328.

Brandstätter, V., & Schüler, J. (2013). Action crisis and cost–benefit thinking: A cognitive analysis of a goal-disengagement phase. *Journal of Experimental Social Psychology*, 49(3), 543–553.

Carmeli, A., & Gittell, J. H. (2009). High-quality relationships, psychological safety, and learning from failures in work organizations. *Journal of Organizational Behavior*, 30(6), 709–729.

Carver, C. S., & Scheier, M. F. (1982). Control theory: A useful conceptual framework for personality–social, clinical, and health psychology. *Psychological Bulletin*, 92(1), 111.

Carver, C. S., & Scheier, M. F. (1990). Origins and functions of positive and negative affect: A control-process view. *Psychological Review*, 97(1), 19–35.

Cervone, D. (2005). Distinguishing among models and goals in personality science: Comment on Ashton and Lee (2005). *European Journal of Personality*, 19(5), 443–446.

Chapman, D. (1987). Planning for conjunctive goals. *Artificial Intelligence*, 32(3), 333–377.

Chapman, D. (1989). Penguins can make cake. *AI magazine*, 10(4), 45.

Cohen, J. B., & Andrade, E. B. (2004). Affective intuition and task-contingent affect regulation. *Journal of Consumer Research*, 31(2), 358–367.

Dahl, O. J., Dijkstra, E. W., & Hoare, C. A. R. (1972). *Structured programming*. London: Academic Press.

Davidson, R. J. (1993). Cerebral asymmetry and emotion: Conceptual and methodological conundrums. *Cognition & Emotion*, 7(1), 115–138.

Davies, S. P. (1991). Characterizing the program design activity: Neither strictly top-down nor globally opportunistic. *Behaviour & Information Technology*, 10(3), 173–190.

Dawson, M. E., & Schell, A. M. (1982). Electrodermal responses to attended and nonattended significant stimuli during dichotic listening. *Journal of Experimental Psychology: Human Perception and Performance*, 8(2), 315–324.

Deglin, V. L., & Kinsbourne, M. (1996). Divergent thinking styles of the hemispheres: How syllogisms are solved during transitory hemisphere suppression. *Brain and Cognition*, 31(3), 285–307.

Den Braber, A., Ent, D. V. T., Blokland, G. A., van Grootheest, D. S., Cath, D. C., Veltman, D. J., De Ruiter, M. B., & Boomsma, D. I. (2008). An fMRI study in monozygotic twins discordant for obsessive–compulsive symptoms. *Biological Psychology*, 79(1), 91–102.

De Ruiter, M. B., Veltman, D. J., Goudriaan, A. E., Oosterlaan, J., Sjoerds, Z., & Van den Brink, W. (2009). Response perseveration and ventral prefrontal sensitivity to reward and punishment in male problem gamblers and smokers. *Neuropsychopharmacology*, 34(4), 1027–1038.

De Shazer, S., Dolan, Y. M., & Korman, H. (2007). *More than miracles: The state of the art of solution-focused brief therapy*. New York: Haworth Press.

Dibbelt, S. (1997). *Wechseln und Beibehalten von Zielen als Subfunktionen der Handlungskontrolle* [Change and maintenance of goals as functional components of action control]. Unpublished doctoral dissertation, University of Osnabrück, Osnabrück, Germany.

Diefendorff, J. M., Hall, R. J., Lord, R. G., & Strean, M. L. (2000). Action-state orientation: Construct validity of a revised measure and its relationship to work-related variables. *Journal of Applied Psychology*, 85(2), 250–263.

Diefendorff, J. M., Richard, E. M., & Gosserand, R. H. (2006). Examination of situational and attitudinal moderators of the hesitation and performance relation. *Personnel Psychology*, 59(2), 365–393.

Dörner, D. (1996). Eine Systemtheorie der Motivation [A system theory of motivation]. In J. Kuhl & H. Heckhausen (Eds.), *Enzyklopädie der Psychologie: Motivation, Volition und Handlung* (pp.329–358). Göttingen: Hogrefe.

Edmondson, A. (1999). Psychological safety and learning behavior in work teams. *Administrative Science Quarterly*, 44, 350–383.

Elliot, A. J. (1999). Approach and avoidance motivation and achievement goals. *Educational Psychologist*, 34(3), 169–189.

Elliot, A. J. (Ed.) (2008). *Handbook of approach and avoidance motivation*. New York: Psychology Press.

Ellis, A. (1969). Rational-emotive therapy. *Journal of Contemporary Psychotherapy*, 1(2), 82–90.

Epstein, S., Pacini, R., Denes-Raj, V., & Heier, H. (1996). Individual differences in intuitive–experiential and analytical–rational thinking styles. *Journal of Personality and Social Psychology*, 71(2), 390–405.

Erickson, M. H. (1958). Naturalistic techniques of hypnosis. *American Journal of Clinical Hypnosis*, 1(1), 3–8.

Feather, N. T. (1982). *Expectations and actions: Expectancy-value models in psychology*. Hillsdale, NJ: Lawrence Erlbaum.

Ferguson, M. J. (2007). On the automatic evaluation of end-states. *Journal of Personality and Social Psychology*, 92(4), 596–611.

Festinger, L. (1957). *A theory of cognitive dissonance*. Stanford, CA: Stanford University Press.

Festinger, L., & Walster, E. (1964). Post–decision regret and decision reversal. In L. Festinger (Ed.), *Conflict, decision and dissonance* (pp. 112–127). Stanford, CA: Stanford University Press

Frese, M. (1997). Dynamic self-reliance: An important concept for work. In C. L. Cooper & S. E. Jackson (Eds.), *Creating tomorrow's organization* (pp. 399–416). Chichester, UK: Wiley.

Frese, M., & Fay, D. (2001). Personal initiative: An active performance concept for work in the 21st century. *Research in Organizational Behavior*, 23, 133–187.

Frese, M., & Zapf, D. (1994). Action as the core of work psychology: A German approach. In H. C. Triandis, M. D. Dunette, & L. M. Hough (Eds.), *Handbook of industrial and organizational psychology* (Vol. 4, pp. 271–340). Palo Alto, CA: Consulting Psychologists Press.

Frese, M., Fay, D., Hilburger, T., Leng, K., & Tag, A. (1997). The concept of personal initiative: Operationalization, reliability and validity in two German samples. *Journal of Occupational and Organizational Psychology*, 70(2), 139–161.

Gendlin, E. T. (1962). *Experiencing and the creation of meaning: A philosophical and psychological approach to the subjective*. Evanston, IL: Northwestern University Press.

Gervey, B., Igou, E. R., & Trope, Y. (2005). Positive mood and future-oriented self-evaluation. *Motivation and Emotion*, 29(4), 267–294.

Gilligan, S. G. (2013). *Therapeutic trances: The co-operation principle in Ericksonian hypnotherapy*. London: Routledge.

Goel, V., & Grafman, J. (2000). Role of the right prefrontal cortex in ill-structured planning. *Cognitive Neuropsychology*, 17(5), 415–436.

Goel, V., & Vartanian, O. (2005). Dissociating the roles of right ventral lateral and dorsal lateral prefrontal cortex in generation and maintenance of hypotheses in set-shift problems. *Cerebral Cortex*, 15(8), 1170–1177.

Goldin, S. E., & Hayes-Roth, B. (1980). *Individual differences in planning processes*. Santa Monica, CA: The Rand Corporation.

Gollwitzer, P. M. (1999). Implementation intentions: Strong effects of simple plans. *American Psychologist*, 54(7), 493–503.

Gollwitzer, P. M., & Sheeran, P. (2009). Self-regulation of consumer decision making and behavior: The role of implementation intentions. *Journal of Consumer Psychology*, 19(4), 593–607.

Grafman, J., Spector, L., & Rattermann, M. J. (2005). Planning and the brain. In R. Morris & G. Ward (Eds.), *The cognitive psychology of planning* (pp. 181–198). Hove: Psychology Press.

Greenberg, L. S., & Paivio, S. C. (1997). *Working with emotions in psychotherapy*. New York: The Guilford Press.

Hacker, W. (1985). Activity: A fruitful concept in industrial psychology. In M. Frese & J. Sabini (Eds.), *Goal directed behavior: The concept of action in psychology* (pp. 262–284). Hillsdale, NJ: Erlbaum Associates.

Hacker, W. (1989). On the utility of procedural rules: conditions of the use of rules in the production of operation sequences, *Ergonomics*, 32(7), 717–732.

Hacker, W. (1997). Improving engineering design-contributions of cognitive ergonomics. *Ergonomics*, 40(10), 1088–1096.

Hacker, W. (2000). Arbeit der Zukunft – Zukunft der Arbeitspsychologie [Work of the future – the future of work psychology]. *Zeitschrift für Psychologie*, 208, 190–206.

Hammond, K. J. (1990). Case-based planning: A framework for planning from experience. *Cognitive Science*, 14, 385–443.

Harmon-Jones, E. (2006). Unilateral right-hand contractions cause contralateral alpha-power suppression and approach motivational affective experience. *Psychophysiology*, 43, 598–603.

Harmon-Jones, E. (2007). Asymmetrical frontal cortical activity, affective valence, and motivational direction. In E. Harmon-Jones & P. Winkielman (Eds.), *Social neuroscience: Integrating biological and psychological explanations of social behavior* (pp. 137–156). New York: Guilford Press.

Harmon-Jones, E., & Harmon-Jones, C. (2002). Testing the action-based model of cognitive dissonance: The effect of action orientation on postdecisional attitudes. *Personality and Social Psychology Bulletin*, 28(6), 711–723.

Hayes-Roth, B., & Hayes-Roth, F. (1979). A cognitive model of planning. *Cognitive Science*, 3(4), 275–310.

Hoc, J. M. (1988). *Cognitive psychology of planning*. London: Academic Press.

Huey, E. D., Krueger, F., & Grafman, J. (2006). Representations in the human prefrontal cortex. *Current Directions in Psychological Science*, 15(4), 167–171.

Isen, A. M. (1984). Toward understanding the role of affect in cognition. In R. S. Wyer, Jr. & T. K. Srull (Eds.), *Handbook of social cognition* (Vol. 3, pp. 179–236). Hillsdale, NJ: Erlbaum Associates.

Isen, A. M. (2010). Some ways in which positive affect influences decision making and problem solving. In M. Lewis, J. M. Haviland-Jones, & L. F. Barrett (Eds.), *Handbook of emotions* (3rd ed., pp. 548–573). New York: Guilford Press.

Isen, A. M., Daubman, K. A., & Nowicki, G. P. (1987). Positive affect facilitates creative problem solving. *Journal of Personality and Social Psychology*, 52(6), 1122–1131.

Ivancic, K. and Hesketh, B. 1995/1996, Making the best of errors during training, *Training Research Journal*, 1, 103–125.

Jager, G., & Postma, A. (2003). On the hemispheric specialization for categorical and coordinate spatial relations: A review of the current evidence. *Neuropsychologia*, 41(4), 504–515.

Jaramillo, F., Locander, W. B., Spector, P. E., & Harris, E. G. (2007). Getting the job done: The moderating role of initiative on the relationship between intrinsic motivation and adaptive selling. *Journal of Personal Selling and Sales Management*, 27(1), 59–74.

Jostmann, N. B., & Koole, S. L. (2007). On the regulation of cognitive control: action orientation moderates the impact of high demands in Stroop interference tasks. *Journal of Experimental Psychology: General*, 136(4), 593–609.

Jung, C. G. (1936/2001). *Typologie* [Typology]. Munich: Deutscher Taschenbuch-Verlag.

Jungermann, H., Pfister, H. R., & May, R. S. (1994). Competing motivations or changing choices: Conjectures and some data on choice-action consistency. In J. Kuhl & J. Beckmann (Eds.), *Volition and personality: Action versus state orientation* (pp. 195–208). Seattle, WA: Hogrefe & Huber.

Kagan, J., Rosman, B. L., Day, D., Albert, J., & Phillips, W. (1964). Information processing in the child: Significance of analytic and reflective attitudes. *Psychological Monographs*, 78(1). 1–37.

Kaller, C. P., Rahm, B., Spreer, J., Weiller, C., & Unterrainer, J. M. (2010). Dissociable contributions of left and right dorsolateral prefrontal cortex in planning. *Cerebral Cortex*, 21(2), 307–317.

Kanfer, R., Dugdale, B., & McDonald, B. (1994). Empirical findings on the action control scale in the context of complex skill acquisition. In J. Kuhl & J. Beckmann (Eds.), *Volition and personality: Action versus state orientation* (pp. 61–77). Seattle, WA: Hogrefe & Huber.

Kazén, M., & Kuhl, J. (2005). Intention memory and achievement motivation: Volitional facilitation and inhibition as a function of affective contents of need-related stimuli. *Journal of Personality and Social Psychology*, 89(3), 426–448.

Kazén, M., Kaschel, R., & Kuhl, J. (2008). Individual differences in intention initiation under demanding conditions: Interactive effects of state vs. action orientation and enactment difficulty. *Journal of Research in Personality*, 42(3), 693–715.

Keith, N., & Frese, M. (2008). Effectiveness of error management training: a meta-analysis. *Journal of Applied Psychology*, 93(1), 59–69.

Keren, G., & Schul, Y. (2009). Two is not always better than one: A critical evaluation of two-system theories. *Perspectives on Psychological Science*, 4(6), 533–550.

Kolodner, J. L. (1997). Educational implications of analogy: A view from case-based reasoning. *American Psychologist*, 52, 57–66.

Koole, S. L., & Jostmann, N. B. (2004). Getting a grip on your feelings: Effects of action orientation and external demands on intuitive affect regulation. *Journal of Personality and Social Psychology*, 87(6), 974–990.

Koole, S. L., & Kuhl, J. (2003). In search of the real self: A functional perspective on optimal self-esteem and authenticity. *Psychological Inquiry*, 14, 43–48.

Koole, S. L., Kuhl. J., Jostmann, N., & Vohs, K. D. (2005). On the hidden benefits of state orientation: Can people prosper without efficient affect regulation skills? In A. Tesser, J. Wood, & D. A. Stapel (Eds.), *On building, defending, and regulating the self: A psychological perspective* (pp. 217–243). London: Taylor & Francis.

Kosslyn, S. M., Koenig, O., Barrett, A., Cave, C. B., Tang, J., & Gabrieli, J. D. (1989). Evidence for two types of spatial representations: Hemispheric specialization for categorical and coordinate relations. *Journal of Experimental Psychology: Human Perception and Performance*, 15(4), 723–735.

Kuhl, J. (1981). Motivational and functional helplessness. *Journal of Personality and Social Psychology*, 40(1), 155–170.

Kuhl, J. (1984). Volitional aspects of achievement motivation and learned helplessness: toward a comprehensive theory of action control. *Progress in Experimental Personality Research*, 13, 99–171.

Kuhl, J. (1994a). Action versus state orientation: Psychometric properties of the Action Control Scale (ACS-90). In J. Kuhl & J. Beckmann (Eds.), *Volition and personality: Action versus state orientation* (pp. 47–52). Seattle, WA: Hogrefe & Huber.

Kuhl, J. (1994b). Motivation and volition. In G. D'Ydevalle, P. Bertelson, & P. Eelen (Eds.), *International perspectives on psychological science* (pp. 311–349). Hillsdale, NJ: Erlbaum.

Kuhl, J. (2000). A functional-design approach to motivation and self-regulation: The dynamics of personality systems interactions. In M. Boekaerts, P. R. Pintrich, & M. Zeidner (Eds.), *Handbook of self-regulation* (pp. 111–169). San Diego, CA: Elsevier.

Kuhl, J. (2001). *Motivation und Persönlichkeit: Interaktionen psychischer Systeme* [Motivation and personality: Interactions of psychological systems]. Göttingen: Hogrefe.

Kuhl, J. (2010). *Lehrbuch der Persönlichkeitspsychologie: Motivation, Emotion und Selbststeuerung* [Textbook psychology of personality: motivation, emotion and self-control]. Göttingen: Hogrefe.

Kuhl, J., & Beckmann, J. (1983). Handlungskontrolle und Umfang der Informationsverarbeitung: Wahl einer einfachen (nicht optimalen) Entscheidungsregel zugunsten rascher Handlungsbereitschaft [Action control and extent of information processing: Choice of a simple (not optimal) decision rule for quick readiness for action]. *Zeitschrift Für Sozialpsychologie*, 14(3), 241–250.

Kuhl, J., & Goschke, T. (1994). A theory of action control: Mental subsystems, modes of control, and volitional conflict-resolution strategies. In J. Kuhl & J. Beckmann (Eds.), *Volition and personality: Action versus state orientation* (pp. 93–124). Seattle, WA: Hogrefe & Huber.

Kuhl, J., & Kazén, M. (1994). Self-discrimination and memory: State orientation and false self-ascription of assigned activities. *Journal of Personality and Social Psychology*, 66(6), 1103–1115.

Kuhl, J., & Kazén, M. (1999). Volitional facilitation of difficult intentions: Joint activation of intention memory and positive affect removes Stroop interference. *Journal of Experimental Psychology. General*, 128(3), 382–399.

Kuhl, J., & Kazén, M. (2008). Motivation, affect, and hemispheric asymmetry: Power versus affiliation. *Journal of Personality and Social Psychology*, 95(2), 456–469.

Kuhl, J., & Weiss, M. (1994). Performance deficits following uncontrollable failure: Impaired action control or global attributions and generalized expectancy deficits. In J. Kuhl & J. Beckmann (Eds.), *Volition and personality: Action versus state orientation* (pp. 317–328). Seattle, WA: Hogrefe & Huber.

Kuhl, J., Quirin, M., & Koole, S. L. (2015). Being someone: The integrated self as a neuropsychological system. *Social and Personality Psychology Compass*, 9(3), 115–132.

Kühnen, U., Hannover, B., & Schubert, B. (2001). The semantic-procedural interface model of the self: The role of self-knowledge for context-dependent versus context-independent modes of thinking. *Journal of Personality and Social Psychology*, 80(3), 397–409.

Kühnen, U., Hannover, B., Roeder, U., Shah, A. A., Schubert, B., Upmeyer, A., & Zakaria, S. (2001). Cross-cultural variations in identifying embedded figures: Comparisons from the United States, Germany, Russia, and Malaysia. *Journal of Cross-Cultural Psychology*, 32(3), 366–372.

Levy, J., & Trevarthen, C. (1976). Metacontrol of hemispheric function in human split-brain patients. *Journal of Experimental Psychology: Human Perception and Performance*, 2(3), 299–312.

Lewin, K. (1935). *A dynamic theory of personality: Selected papers*. New York: McGraw-Hill.

Lewin, K. (1951). *Field theory in social science*. New York: Harper & Row.

Luria, A. (1973/1992). *Das Gehirn in Aktion* [The brain in action]. Hamburg: Rowohlt.

McClelland, J. L., Rumelhart, D. E., & PDP Research Group (1986). *Parallel distributed processing: Explorations in the microstructure of cognition* (Vol. 2). Cambridge, MA: MIT Press.

McClelland, J. L., Rumelhart, D. E., & Hinton, G. E. (2004). The appeal of parallel distributed processing. In D. A. Balota & E. J. Marsh (Eds.), *Cognitive psychology: Key readings* (pp. 75–99). New York: Psychology Press.

McCrae, R. R., & Costa, P. T. (1987). Validation of the five-factor model of personality across instruments and observers. *Journal of Personality and Social Psychology*, 52(1), 81–90.

Marcel, A. J. (1983). Conscious and unconscious perception: Experiments on visual masking and word recognition. *Cognitive Psychology*, 15, 197–237.

Martin, L. L., & Clore, G. L. (2001). *Theories of mood and cognition: A user's guidebook*. Mahwah, NJ: Lawrence Erlbaum.

Mathäus, W. (1988). *Sowjetische Denkpsychologie* [Soviet psychology of thinking]. Göttingen: Hogrefe.

Mednick, S. (1962). The associative basis of the creative process. *Psychological Review*, 69(3), 220–232.

Messer, S. B. (1976). Reflection-impulsivity: A review. *Psychological Bulletin*, 83(6), 1026–1052.

Mumford, M. D., Schultz, R. A., & Van Doorn, J. R. (2001). Performance in planning: Processes, requirements and errors. *Review of General Psychology*, 5, 225–251.

Nakamura, J., & Csikszentmihalyi, M. (2009). Flow theory and research. In S. J. Lopez & C. R. Snyder (Eds.), *Oxford handbook of positive psychology* (pp. 195–206). Oxford: Oxford University Press.

Neubert, M. J. (1998). The value of feedback and goal setting over goal setting alone and potential moderators of this effect: A meta-analysis. *Human Performance*, 11, 321–335.

Newell, A., & Simon, H. A. (1972). *Human problem solving* (Vol. 14). Englewood Cliffs, NJ: Prentice Hall.

Nietzsche, F. (2005). *Sämtliche Werke. 4. Also sprach Zarathustra I-IV* [Thus spoke Zarathustra]. Munich: Deutscher Taschenbuch-Verlag.

Norman, D. A. (1981). Categorization of action slips. *Psychological Review*, 88(1), 1–15.

Oettingen, G., Pak, H. J., & Schnetter, K. (2001). Self-regulation of goal-setting: Turning free fantasies about the future into binding goals. *Journal of Personality and Social Psychology*, 80(5), 736–753.

Pea, R. (1982). What is planning development the development of? *New Directions for Child Development*, 18, 5–27.

Petrides, M. (2005). Lateral prefrontal cortex: architectonic and functional organization. *Philosophical Transactions of the Royal Society B: Biological Sciences*, 360(1456), 781–795.

Posner, M. L., & Petersen, S. E. (1990). The attention system of the human brain. *Annual Review of Neuroscience*, 13, 25–42.

Posner, M. I., & Rothbart, M. K. (1992). Attentional mechanisms and conscious experience. In A. D. Milner, & M. D. Rugg (Eds.), *The neuropsychology of consciousness. Foundations of neuropsychology* (pp. 91–111). San Diego, CA: Academic Press.

Rogers, C. R. (1963). The concept of the fully functioning person. *Psychotherapy: Theory, Research & Practice*, 1(1), 17–26.

Rotenberg, V. S. (2004). The peculiarity of the right-hemisphere function in depression: solving the paradoxes. *Progress in Neuro-Psychopharmacology and Biological Psychiatry*, 28(1), 1–13.

Rotenberg, V. S. (2009). Search activity concept: Relationship between behavior, health and brain functions. *ANS: The Journal for Neurocognitive Research*, 51(1), 12–44.

Rotenberg, V. S. (2013a). "Genes of happiness and well being" in the context of search activity concept. *ANS: The Journal for Neurocognitive Research*, 55(1–2), 1–14.

Rotenberg, V. S. (2013b). The two high levels of self-identification in relationships to consciousness, social motives and brain laterality. *ANS: The Journal for Neurocognitive Research*, 54(3–4), 77–83.

Rotenberg, V. S., & Weinberg, I. (1999). Human memory, cerebral hemispheres, and the limbic system: A new approach. *Genetic Social and General Psychology Monographs*, 125, 45–70.

Roxburgh, S. (2004). "There just aren't enough hours in the day": The mental health consequences of time pressure. *Journal of Health and Social Behavior*, 45(2), 115–131.

Scheibel, A. B., Paul, L. A., Fried, I., Forsythe, A. B., Tomiyasu, U., Wechsler, A., Kao, A., & Slotnick, J. (1985). Dendritic organization of the anterior speech area. *Experimental Neurology*, 87(1), 109–117.

Schore, A. N. (2001). Effects of a secure attachment relationship on right brain development, affect regulation, and infant mental health. *Infant Mental Health Journal*, 22(1–2), 7–66.

Schröder, T., & Thagard, P. (2013). The affective meanings of automatic social behaviors: Three mechanisms that explain priming. *Psychological Review*, 120(1), 255–280.

Sergent, J., Ohta, S., & MacDonald, B. (1992). Functional neuroanatomy of face and object processing: A positron emission tomography study. *Brain*, 115(1), 15–36.

Shallice, T. (2002). Fractionation of the supervisory system. In D. T. Stuss & R. T. Knight (Eds.), *Principles of frontal lobe function* (pp. 261–277). Oxford: Oxford University Press.

Shamay-Tsoory, S. G., Tomer, R., Berger, B. D., & Aharon-Peretz, J. (2003). Characterization of empathy deficits following prefrontal brain damage: the role of the right ventromedial prefrontal cortex. *Journal of Cognitive Neuroscience*, 15(3), 324–337.

Spinella, M. (2002). A relationship between smell identification and empathy. *International Journal of Neuroscience*, 112(6), 605–612.

Sporns, O., Chialvo, D. R., Kaiser, M., & Hilgetag, C. C. (2004). Organization, development and function of complex brain networks. *Trends in Cognitive Sciences*, 8(9), 418–425.

Stefik, M. (1981a). Planning with constraints (MOLGEN: Part 1). *Artificial Intelligence*, 16(2), 111–139.

Stefik, M. (1981b). Planning and meta-planning (MOLGEN: Part 2). *Artificial Intelligence*, 16(2), 141–169.

Stiensmeier-Pelster, J., John, M., Stulik, A., & Schürmann, M. (1989). Die Wahl von Entscheidungsstrategien: Der Einfluss von Handlungs- und Lageorientierung und die Bedeutung psychologischer Kosten [The choice of decision-making strategies: The effects of action vs state orientation and the role of psychological costs]. *Zeitschrift Für Experimentelle und Angewandte Psychologie*, 36(2), 292–310.

Stiensmeier-Pelster, J., Schürmann, M., John, M., & Stulik, A. (1991). Umfang der Informationsverarbeitung bei Entscheidungen: Der Einfluss von Handlungsorientierung bei unterschiedlich dringlichen und wichtigen Entscheidungen [Extent of information processing in decision making: The influence of action orientation in decisions of varying degrees of urgency and importance]. *Zeitschrift Für Experimentelle und Angewandte Psychologie*, 38(1), 94–112.

Storch, M., & Kuhl, J. (2011). *Die Kraft aus dem Selbst: Sieben PsychoGyms für das Unbewusste*. [The power of the self: Seven PsychoGyms for the unconscious]. Bern: Huber.

Strehlau, A., & Kuhl, J. (in press). Der innere Dialog: Selbststeuerungsfähigkeiten des Coachs [The internal dialogue: Self control skills of the coach]. In, A. Ryba, D. Pauw, D. Ginati, & S. Rietmann (Eds.), *Coaching im Dialog (working title)*. Weinheim: Beltz.

Tichomirow, D. K. (1975). Ein Ansatz zur Untersuchung des Denkens als Tätigkeit der Person [An approach to the study of the mind as an activity of the person]. In D. K. Tichomirow (Ed.), *Psychologische Untersuchungen der denkerischen Tätigkeit*. Moscow: Nauka.

Tucker, D. M., & Williamson, P. A. (1984). Asymmetric neural control systems in human self-regulation. *Psychological Review*, 91(2), 185–215.

Van Dijke, M., De Cremer, D., Brebels, L., & Van Quaquebeke, N. (2013). Willing and able: Action-state orientation and the relation between procedural justice and employee cooperation. *Journal of Management*, 1–22.

Van Dyck, C., Frese, M., Baer, M., & Sonnentag, S. (2005). Organizational error management culture and its impact on performance: a two-study replication. *Journal of Applied Psychology*, 90(6), 1228–1240.

Visser, W. (1994). Organisation of design activities: Opportunistic, with hierarchical episodes. *Interacting with Computers*, 6(3), 239–274.

Wilensky, R. (1981). Meta-planning: Representing and using knowledge about planning in problem solving and natural language understanding. *Cognitive Science*, 5(3), 197–233.

Witkin, H. A. (1950). Individual differences in ease of perception of embedded figures. *Journal of Personality*, 19(1), 1–15.

Witkin, H. A., Moore, C. A., Goodenough, D. R., & Cox, P. W. (1977). Field-dependent and field-independent cognitive styles and their educational implications. *Review of Educational Research*, 47(1), 1–64.

Wittling, W. (1990). Psychophysiological correlates of human brain asymmetry: Blood pressure changes during lateralized presentation of an emotionally laden film. *Neuropsychologia*, 28(5), 457–470.

5

PLANNING

A Mediator in Goal-Setting Theory

Gary P. Latham and Alana S. Arshoff

In the behavioral sciences, for a theory to be complete, it must enable scientists and practitioners to do five things, namely, to (1) predict, (2) explain, and (3) influence an individual's behavior. Furthermore, a theory must identify the (4) moderators or boundary conditions and the (5) mediators that explain causal relationships. An example of a theory that satisfies these five conditions is Locke and Latham's (1990, 2013) goal-setting theory, where planning is a mediating variable.

Goal-Setting Theory

A goal refers to pursuing and attaining a specific standard of proficiency on a given task, usually within a specified time limit (Locke & Latham, 1990). Goal-setting theory (Locke & Latham, 1990, 2002, 2013; Latham & Locke, 2007) states that individuals who set specific, difficult goals have significantly higher performance than those with specific, easy goals, or a vague goal such as to do their best. Further, there is a linear relationship between goal difficulty and performance. Finally, incentives, including performance feedback, participation in decision making, and competition only influence a person's behavior to the extent that they lead to the setting of a specific, challenging goal.

Goal-setting theory is based on more than a thousand studies conducted in eight countries, on more than 88 different tasks, in both laboratory and field settings, for time spans ranging from one minute to 25 years, where the goals were assigned, self-set or set participatively (Locke & Latham, 1990; Mitchell & Daniels, 2003). However, the theory is not applicable for everyone under all conditions. An individual must have the ability and resources to attain the goal. The person must receive feedback on goal pursuit, and, most importantly, be committed to attaining the goal. These four "musts" are the moderator variables specified by the theory.

Moderators

Moderator variables specify the boundary conditions within which a theory is valid or applicable. Goal-setting theory states that setting a specific, high goal significantly increases performance only if four conditions (moderators) are met. The absence of any one of these conditions weakens, if not vitiates, the goal–performance relationship.

The first moderator is *ability*. Laboratory experiments (e.g. Erez & Zidon, 1984; Locke 1982) have shown that goals are linearly related to performance when the goals range from easy to difficult. Performance drops when the goal is, or is perceived as, impossible to attain.

A second moderator is *situational resources/constraints*. A field study revealed that when supervisors perceived that they lacked the resources to attain goals that they viewed as excessively high, and hence beyond their ability to attain, they experienced anger and anxiety, which in turn were related to abusing their subordinates (Mawritz, Folger, & Latham, 2014).

Feedback is a third moderator. Feedback on goal pursuit allows one to discern what one needs to continue doing, start doing, stop doing, or be doing differently to attain the goal (Locke, Cartledge, & Koeppel, 1968).

Lastly, and arguably, the most important moderator is commitment to attaining the goal. Locke and Latham (1990) argued that *goal commitment* is the *sine qua non* of the goal–performance relationship because, without it, by definition, one does not have a goal. A field study revealed that leaders should not focus on goal setting alone, but should also focus on ways to ensure that employees are committed to goal attainment in order to increase their department's performance (Porter & Latham, 2013).

Mediators

Four mediators explain the goal–performance relationship. First, goal specificity focuses an individual's attention or *direction*, that is, the *choice* of desired behavior or outcome relevant to goal attainment. Locke and Bryan (1969), for example, found that scores on a driving simulation changed only on the dimension for which a specific, high goal was set. The goal singled out for action only the aspects of performance that were relevant to goal attainment.

A second mediator is *effort*. A goal regulates a person's effort so that it is proportionate to the difficulty level of the goal. Latham and Locke (1975) found that woods workers, paid on a piece-work basis, who had harder production goals as a consequence of shorter time limits due to company-imposed wood quotas, harvested as much wood in three days as they normally did in a five-day work week.

Related to effort is a third mediator, *persistence*. Numerous studies have shown that a specific, challenging goal results in people working longer on a task than is the case with easier or no goals (e.g. Bavelas & Lee, 1978, Kaplan & Rothkopf, 1974; Kirsch, 1978).

The fourth mediator in goal-setting theory that explains the beneficial effect of specific, high goals on subsequent performance is the subject of this chapter, *planning or strategizing* ways for goal attainment.

Goal-setting theory (Locke & Latham, 1990, 2002, 2013) distinguishes between two types of goals, performance and learning. When ability is not an issue, a specific, high performance goal should be set regarding a desired outcome (e.g. a score of 75 in golf). This is because, given goal commitment, the *choice* to exert *effort*, and to *persist* until the goal is attained occurs automatically. But, as Locke and Latham (1990) noted, sheer effort and persistence are not sufficient when an individual lacks the knowledge/ability to attain the goal. In such cases, the fourth mediator, the development of strategies, explain the goal–performance relationship.[1] An individual must plan ways of identifying processes, procedures, or systems that will provide answers as to how the goal is to be attained. Planning is inherent in setting a learning goal (e.g. developing a specific plan for improving your putting). An individual's focus of attention shifts from a specific, desired outcome to developing an effective plan. In short, as the name implies, a learning goal promotes the acquisition of knowledge through problem-solving and learning, leading to the development of new strategies. A learning goal is essential for the effective performance of departments that are operating in a dynamic or turbulent environment (Porter & Latham, 2013).

Goals Lead to Plans

When people commit to a goal, among the first questions they ask is, "How can this goal be attained?" A performance goal activates strategies on the same or analogous tasks already stored in long-term memory (Locke & Latham, 1990). For example, a forest products company was losing money because their logging trucks were running at less than full capacity. Consequently, the unionized truck drivers were given the goal to load each truck at the maximum legal net weight. None of them immediately knew how to do so. All of them knew that overloading their trucks would lead to legally imposed fines and ultimately job dismissal. Devising a specific plan for goal attainment led these drivers to raise the forward stakes in their respective trucks. Doing so enabled them to increase the accuracy of their judgments of their truck's weight. Performance improved dramatically. According to the company's accounting procedures, the same increase in performance, without goal setting, would have required an expenditure of a quarter of a million dollars for the purchase of additional trucks (Latham & Baldes, 1975).

A subsequent productivity problem involving unionized truck drivers occurred in another state in the United States. The lack of productivity was due to slow truck turnaround time at the loading station. Upon receiving a specific, high goal for driving time (i.e. time for loading logs at one terminal and unloading them at another), the truck drivers immediately began planning ways to attain their productivity goal. Specifically, the drivers used their CB-radios to coordinate their efforts so that one of them would always be at the logging site with a truck when timber was ready to be loaded. The truck drivers were constantly discussing this plan with one another. The result was a significant increase in productivity as measured by the increase in number of trips per truck per day. The average increase for the experimental group was 0.53 trips per truck. The overall increase in number of truck trips was approximately 1,800. This number, involving 39 drivers over an 18-week period, revealed a substantial performance improvement. The company reported that the monetary value of this steady increase in trips per truck was approximately 2.7 million dollars (Latham & Saari, 1982).

That planning that fails to include goal setting is ineffective was shown in an experiment by Bandura and Simon (1977) where dieters were randomly assigned to one of three conditions. In the first condition, people set a goal for weight-loss. They then developed plans for limiting their intake throughout the day, especially when they knew they would be subsequently experiencing an "eating occasion" such as a dinner party later that evening. They also planned their food choices carefully by choosing only the food they most enjoyed when they saw that they were close to reaching their caloric maximum. In the second condition, the dieters only monitored their eating behavior. No goals were set. In the third condition, neither goal setting nor self-monitoring occurred. Only those in the goal-setting condition lost a significant amount of weight. Self-monitoring alone was not effective. In short, a plan, no matter how brilliantly developed, has little or no influence on behavior unless a specific goal or goals are set to implement it.

Earley, Wojnaroski, and Prest (1987) conducted two studies on the effects of assigned goals and task information on effort, persistence, planning how to perform the task, and subsequent performance. The first study involved undergraduate students who worked on a business simulation. The goals and task information influenced planning activities. That is, the number of steps the participant engaged in, the extent to which planning was important to the participant, the extent to which the participant carefully planned how to attain the goal, and the extent to which accomplishing the goal was deliberate increased performance significantly. In addition, the researchers found that planning predicted an individual's performance. In the second study, employees in a service organization and a moving company completed a survey assessing their goal setting, job training, energy expended, and the planning they undertook prior to pursuing a specific, high goal. Planning, and the effort expended, mediated the relationship between the training an individual received and that person's subsequent performance. Both studies revealed that setting a specific, high goal led individuals to plan the steps necessary to attain it. Consequently, performance was significantly higher than those in the control group, who had a vague goal, namely, to "do your best."

In a subsequent study, Earley and Perry (1987, p. 282) examined the relationship between planning and performance using an obtrusive, unobtrusive, and a control prime. The directions in the obtrusive prime condition stated:

> I would like to give you some information that will help you work on three experimental tasks. One way to generate more uses for an object is to visualize a familiar room, such as your dorm room, and to mentally scan around the room looking at each object you encounter to see if it gives you ideas for uses. For instance, a door might give you the use of a book as a doorstop.

In the unobtrusive prime condition the experimenter stated:

> Before we continue with the experiment, I want you to rest a bit. Before you continue, I would like you to work on another task for a few minutes. My assistant will describe the new task.

The assistant asked the participants to play the role of an interior designer where it was stated that:

> To do this, designers often will visually scan around a room to determine a common theme from the various objects they encounter. For instance, if you saw a ship's clock and a picture of the ocean this might suggest a nautical theme. Please take a few minutes and then write down a decorating theme for your own room.

The researchers measured the amount of planning engaged in by the participants using four items: (1) Please describe in as much detail as possible how you went about listing uses; (2) How detailed was the scheme that you used to work on the task (where 1 = little or no planning and 5 = a great deal of planning)? (3) How much planning did you do before starting work on the listing uses task (where 1 = little or no planning and 5 = a great deal of planning)? and (4) Which of the following statements best describes how you went about working (where 1 = I just got started without a plan and 5 = I developed a general scheme to work and then set up sub-steps to achieve each general plan element)?

Participants who were given a specific, challenging goal in the first study engaged in more task planning, and developed more sophisticated plans than those in the control group. That is, they spent more time devising a plan or creating a more detailed plan. In the second experiment, goal setting increased strategic planning, and task performance was dependent on the type of plan (i.e. more detailed and sophisticated) developed by an individual.

Earley, Lee, and Hanson (1989) found that the quality of a plan mediated the relationship between goal setting and performance on complex jobs. The authors conducted a field study to assess the moderating role of job experience and task complexity. The results indicated that task complexity moderated the effect of goal setting on performance. In addition, experience moderated the relationship between goal setting and task strategy quality as well as performance on jobs having a great deal of task component complexity. Planning as a moderator variable is discussed in a subsequent section in this chapter.

Field research has shown that the first step in an organization's strategic planning process is to set goals (Steiner, 1979). For example, Smith, Locke, and Barry (1990) measured goal setting and two aspects of planning, namely, time and quality. The results indicated that setting specific organizational goals was positively related to planning quality and the organization's subsequent performance. The amount of time spent planning was associated with high performance when planning quality was high, but with low performance when planning quality was low.

Planning quality was assessed with a questionnaire based on five planning quality attributes identified by Lorange and Vancil (1977) and Steiner (1969), namely, (1) a future orientation, (2) extensive interaction among organizational members, (3) a systematic and comprehensive analysis of the organization's strengths, weakness, opportunities, and threats, (4) a clear definition of the roles and functions of all members and departments, and (5) the development and communication of action plans that include the allocation of resources to action plans.

Using a complex management simulation, Chesney and Locke (1991) examined the effect of goal difficulty and the use of business strategies in a computer simulation that required participants to make decisions in the role of a firm's president. In making these decisions, participants' plans were measured. Their strategies were measured using three approaches. Two were based on a questionnaire developed from business strategy typologies (Miles & Snow, 1978; Miles, Snow, Meyer, & Coleman, 1978; Kotler, 1976; Hofer & Schendel, 1978, Paine & Anderson, 1983; Porter, 1980). The third involved data from the simulation. Both goals and strategies were shown to have a significant effect on performance, but the effect of strategy was even stronger than goals. The participants developed marketing plans, such as ways to increase sales, in order to attain their goals. In summary, goals led to strategies, and strategies moderated the goal–performance relationship. The moderating, as opposed to the mediating, effects of strategy on goal setting, as previously noted, are discussed later in this chapter.

Learning Goals

As noted earlier, ability is one of the four moderators in goal-setting theory. In the studies cited in the previous section, the participants were able to draw on general experiences/strategies stored in long-term memory, and the environment was stable or relatively stable. When ability, that is, the requisite knowledge or skill for performing a given task is truly lacking, setting a specific, high goal for a desired level of performance decreases rather than increases performance. This is because a performance goal does not encourage individuals to take the opportunity to learn ways to attain it. A performance goal can lead to a level of arousal that interferes with cognitive processes involved in the selection and development of an effective plan (Locke & Latham, 1990).

Kanfer and Ackerman (1989), using a highly complex task, namely, an air traffic control simulation, found that when people lack the knowledge to perform a task effectively, assigning them a specific, high performance goal leads to a decrease rather than an increase in performance, relative to those who are urged to "do their best." Performance decreases because an individual's cognitive resources need to be allocated to learning the process required to perform well rather than focusing on performing at a specific, difficult level.

When ability is an issue, a plan for knowledge/skill acquisition is typically required for a goal to improve performance. But the plan for goal attainment must not be developed in a haphazard way. Mone and Shalley (1995), in a laboratory simulation conducted over a three-day period, found that setting a specific, high performance goal for a task where people lacked the ability to perform it resulted in them mindlessly switching strategies relative to those who were urged to "to do their best." The individuals in the latter group systematically planned ways to master the task.

Winters and Latham (1996) showed that the type of goal that is set explains the results obtained by both Kanfer and Ackerman (1989) and Mone and Shalley (1995). When a task is straightforward for people, setting a specific, high performance goal leads to higher performance than urging them to do their best because they can use their extant plans for goal attainment. As Wood and Locke (1990) noted, these are typically stored as task-specific plans that have been previously learned through modeling, practice, or instruction on analogous tasks. However, when a task requires the acquisition of knowledge, Winters and Latham too found that urging people to do their best leads to higher performance than the setting of a specific, challenging performance goal. But, when a specific, high learning goal is set, they found that performance is even higher than it is when people are urged to do their best. This is because when a learning goal is set, people take the time to plan ways to master the task. They search, develop, evaluate, and then choose a plan for goal attainment.

Changes in task demands typically require the search for and processing of information in order to develop a plan for goal attainment. Latham and Seijts (1999) conducted a study where young adults were paid on a piece-rate basis to make toys. Participants were randomly assigned to three conditions, namely, a "do your best" goal condition, a specific, difficult distal goal condition, and proximal goals in addition to a specific, difficult distal goal condition. What was true at one point in time for making money was not true at another. The researchers found that the proximal goals allowed the individual to focus attention on the identification of appropriate strategies to attain the distal goal. To the extent that ineffective or suboptimal strategies were being used, performance was altered through the feedback received from pursuit of the proximal goals.

Seijts and Latham (2001) examined the effects of learning versus performance goals in conjunction with proximal goals. The task was the same as that used by Winters and Latham (1996), namely, acquiring knowledge in order to form class schedules correctly. Once again, a "do your best" goal led to higher performance than the assignment of a specific, difficult performance goal. However, the assignment of a specific, difficult learning goal led to even higher performance than urging people to "do their best." Moreover, the correlation between the development of task-relevant plans and performance was positive and significant. The number of task-relevant plans implemented by participants who were assigned a distal learning goal in conjunction with proximal goals was higher than in any other goal condition. These plans included repeatedly scheduling the same subject, repeatedly scheduling the same class section, scheduling night classes and recording the classes and times in chronological order.

In short, a specific, challenging goal for a desired performance outcome does not have the same positive effect on task performance that requires the acquisition of knowledge as it does for tasks that are straightforward for an individual. On tasks requiring knowledge acquisition, a specific, high performance goal typically generates pressure for relatively immediate effective performance, and as a result leads to no planning, or leads to the development of an inappropriate plan for goal attainment. Setting a specific, high goal for performance is an effective technique for increasing performance only when the task is straightforward for people.

In contrast to a performance goal, a learning goal emphasizes the development of specific strategies, processes, or procedures for effective performance on a task rather than relying on extant knowledge and skill (Seijts & Latham, 2005). Developing a plan for goal attainment is the focus of attention when a learning goal is set (Winters & Latham, 1996). For example, a new assistant professor might set a specific learning goal to develop five strategies to attain high student evaluations of teaching in the classroom.

A meta-analysis by Seijts, Latham, and Woodwark (2013) revealed that the search for strategies as well as self-efficacy mediate the effect of learning goals on performance, and that the mediating relationship between strategy and self-efficacy on task performance is reciprocal. Self-efficacy is the belief that the plan or strategy can be implemented effectively to attain the goal.

Plans as Moderators of the Goal–Performance Relationship

As noted throughout this chapter, plans and strategies are a product of the goals that arc set. That is, they mediate the effects of goals on performance. When knowledge acquisition is required to perform effectively, a learning goal stimulates the development of a plan for goal attainment. Wood, Whelan, Sojo, and Wong (2013), however, have argued that strategies or plans can also be a moderator of the goal–performance relationship. That is, a specific, high goal has a greater effect on performance for those individuals who already have a plan to attain it than it does for those who have no plan or have one that is inappropriate. However, as those authors noted, this is only the case when the task, such as loading trucks to their legal net weight, or truck turnaround time, is relatively stable so that the application of extant knowledge on analogous tasks remains relevant.

Durham, Knight, and Locke (1997) found that there are goal–strategy interactions on tasks that are complex for people. This means that goal effects are strongest on such tasks when plans are developed to attain them. Strategic plans moderate the positive effect of a specific, difficult goal on work that is highly complex for people (Knight, Durham, & Locke, 2001).

A meta-analysis by Wood et al. (2013) revealed that the overall pattern of results "of the mediating and moderating models show that specific, challenging goals remain strong and general predictors of performance when strategies are taken into account" (p. 109). The mediating role of strategies and plans in goal-setting theory was strongly supported. Tests of the moderator variable also "provided positive support for the argument that specific, challenging goals combined with appropriate strategies produce stronger performance effects than either alone" (p. 107).

Application

Behavioral scientists are interested in practice, that is, the application of theoretical frameworks to field settings. This is particularly true for organizational psychologists regarding the application of research findings to the workplace.

Organizational Change

The influence of goal setting and planning on the transformation of IBM, Boeing, and Ford Motor Company has been described by Saari (2013). At IBM, an organizational transformation initially resulted in a great deal of confusion with regard to desired changes directed by senior management. However, by giving each employee clear goals related to their job and aligned with the superordinate goals of "Win, Execute, and Team," the employees focused in a systematic way on the most important things to be accomplished. Moreover, the employees developed and documented task-specific plans to attain their goals as part of IBM's new performance management process.

At Boeing, the specific, challenging goal set by Alan Mulally, CEO of Boeing Commercial Airplane, was to "design, build, and deliver the first 777 airplane in 24 months." This was communicated across the organization. Systematic, documented planning of all activities was then aligned to these three highly visible superordinate goals. A noteworthy fact is that Mulally's affectionate nickname among the employees was "Mr Goal-Plan-Team." His nickname reflected his emphasis on measuring performance and then providing feedback to employees on their goal progress. In the initial stages of the 777 project, he repeatedly asked employees, "Where's the plan?"

Mulally left Boeing in 2006 to become the CEO of Ford Motor Company. At the time that he joined Ford, the organization was struggling with regard to profitability, union relations, innovative products, and teamwork. Consequently, Mulally conducted in-depth interviews with employees, customers, dealers, and suppliers. He then developed and assigned three superordinate goals for Ford: One Team, One Goal, One Plan. The entire organization worked towards these goals through planning and executing their work.[2]

Goal Setting in Teams

Salas, Dickinson, Converse, and Tannenbaum (1992) defined a team "as a distinguishable set of two or more people who interact dynamically, interdependently, and adaptively toward a common and valued goal/objective/mission, which have been assigned specific roles or functions to perform and who have a limited lifespan of membership" (p.4). Kramer, Thayer, and Salas (2013) argued that without a purpose or goal, there is no marker to guide the definition of an individual's role on the team or to determine how to engage in team processes. When an individual's goal is in conflict with the team's, the team's performance suffers (Seijts & Latham, 2000). Hence it is critical for team members to participate in setting their team's goals in order to provide a shared understanding, through planning, as to each individual's responsibilities for goal attainment (Wegge, Bipp, & Kleinbeck, 2007).

Kramer et al. (2013) described a method for training teams in goal setting. The emphasis is on learning goals for planning team processes that affect team performance so that it may readily adapt to changing situations. Team process was defined by Marks, Mathieu, & Zaccaro (2001) as the members' interdependent acts that convert inputs to outputs. Team process is a mediator of the relationship between team goal setting and performance (e.g. Hackman, 1987; McGrath, 1964). Among the effective team processes are goal specification and planning activities (Marks et al., 2001).

A meta-analysis conducted by Kleingeld, van Mierlo, and Arends (2011) showed that specific, difficult goals yield higher group performance in comparison to vague goals. This is because a group's goal triggers cooperation, morale building, communication, and collective efficacy. In addition, DeShon, Kozlowski, Schmidt, Milner, and Wiechmann (2004) showed that team goals, goal commitment, and collective efficacy interact with one another to determine how much action will be taken by a team to develop plans for, and engage in effort towards, obtaining their goals. Mehta, Feild, Armenakis, and Mehta (2009) argued that the process of setting a specific course of action to attain a team's goal is an effective regulatory tactic for increasing a team's performance. This is because actively planning strategies and coordinating one another's efforts increases the chances of attaining a team's goals (Park, Spitzmuller, & DeShon, 2013)

Performance Appraisal

The purpose of a performance appraisal is at least two-fold. First, a supervisor assigns or jointly sets with an employee specific, challenging goals for that individual to attain. Second, performance appraisals provide feedback, a moderator variable in goal-setting theory, to individuals that enable them to plan ways to attain these goals. However, as Locke and Latham (1990) noted, on tasks that are not straightforward for an individual, providing feedback solely on performance outcomes may hinder rather than enhance an employee's planning of ways to attain the goals. This is because of the difficulty in interpreting the effects of random error in the data the employee is provided. The feedback must contribute to the employee's further understanding of the task (e.g. processes, behaviors).

Management by objectives (MBO), introduced by Drucker (1974), is a system of motivating and integrating the efforts of managers and their employees by setting specific, high goals for the organization as a whole and then cascading these goals down through each management level. Goal attainment at each level facilitates goal attainment at the next higher level, and ultimately the goals of the entire firm (Carroll & Tosi, 1973). MBO requires a manager and an employee not only to agree on the goals to be set, but also to agree on the specific plans for their attainment. With information and input from lower levels in an organization's hierarchy, knowledge from subordinates is made known to higher-level management so that they can take that information into account in their planning process.

Latham, Mitchell, and Dossett (1978) showed the importance of involving employees in setting goals and developing plans to attain them in the performance appraisal process. Engineers/scientists either participated in the setting of, or were assigned, specific goals. Participative goal setting resulted in more difficult goals being set than was the case when the goals were assigned. Consistent with goal-setting theory, the higher the goal, the higher an employee's performance.

Self-Management

Goal setting is a core variable in self-management. Self-management requires identifying problems, setting specific, high goals in relation to a specific problem, writing a behavioral contract with oneself outlining a plan for goal attainment, monitoring ways in which the environment facilitates or hinders goal attainment, and identifying and administering rewards for working toward the goal and punishers for failing to work towards them (Kanfer, 1970). Planning is key to this action sequence because the subsequent steps to goal setting cannot be implemented effectively without it.

Frayne and Latham (1987) gave state government unionized employees training in self-management of their job attendance for one hour a week for eight weeks. The employees were taught how to use charts and diaries to record their attendance and their reasons for missing work, as well as the necessity of developing a plan for coming to work. For each specific problem that prevented employees from coming to work, such as illness and family issues, the employees were tasked with developing a plan to deal with these issues. Moreover, the employees identified various rewards and punishers to self-administer contingent upon their job attendance. The employees wrote a behavioral contract with themselves that specified the weekly goal to be attained, the timeframe, the consequences of attaining or failing to attain the goal, and, most importantly, their plan for attaining their job attendance goal. A plan for mitigating relapses was also developed. Doing this raised their self-efficacy that they could exercise influence over their environment. In other words, the employees successfully planned strategies to overcome their specific obstacles to goal attainment. As a result of this training in self-management, employee attendance was significantly higher than that of the control group. This training was successfully replicated with the control group (Latham & Frayne, 1989).

Millman and Latham (2001) conducted a quasi-experimental field study that examined whether training in verbal self-guidance (VSG) regarding a job search led to reemployment and whether the subsequent changes in self-efficacy and outcome expectancies increased job search behavior. VSG is a methodology for training people to identify dysfunctional self-statements and translate them into functional "self-talk." The unemployed managers were assigned to a training or a control group. Managers in the training group participated in seven two-hour training sessions in VSG. Managers in the control group continued their job search as they had been doing before. The VSG training is based on training in functional self-talk developed by Meichenbaum (1971, 1977). As part of this training, the trainers asked the managers to plan when and how they would use self-talk in the context of networking and "cold calls." In addition, the managers were also asked to plan relapse-prevention procedures. For example, each manager identified obstacles to effective job search and developed a plan to cope with these specific obstacles. Data were then collected on the managers' subsequent job search and whether they found employment. The results showed that 45 percent of the managers in the training group obtained reemployment within six months and 50 percent obtained reemployment within nine months of the training. Only 12 percent of the managers in the control group obtained reemployment.

Gist, Bavetta, and Stevens (1990) investigated whether goal setting alone is as effective as teaching people self-management skills. The results of the study showed that those who received self-management training performed better on a negotiation task than the people who only set a goal. The difference in performance levels was due to the emphasis in self-management training on developing plans for goal attainment. The plans involved identifying obstacles to a successful negotiation, planning how to overcome these obstacles, monitoring the implementation of their plans with regard to the negotiation, and using rewards to motivate their behavior.

Latham and Budworth (2006) conducted a study on the application of training that involved VSG to increase Native North Americans' self-efficacy during a selection interview, and in obtaining a job offer from Caucasian managers. In the first day of training, they discussed how they planned to apply VSG to their job search. For example, they planned how to use VSG in the interview process (e.g. "I will enter the room in a confident manner."). At the end of the training program, the trainees who acquired skills in VSG had higher self-efficacy than those in a control group. They also performed better in the selection interview. Most important, they also secured employment after this training program.

Yanar, Budworth, and Latham (2009) conducted a study on VSG involving Muslim women over the age of 40 in Turkey who were unemployed. Those who received training in VSG that included planning had significantly higher self-efficacy with regard to reemployment than those in the control group. They also persisted in job search behavior significantly longer than the women in the training group. The women in the training condition were more likely to find a job in their field within six months to one year of the training program than were those in the control group.

Morin and Latham (2000) conducted a field study at a pulp and paper mill to investigate the impact of mental practice and goal setting as a post-training intervention to enhance the transfer of newly taught communication skills to the workplace. The supervisors in either the mental practice or in the goal setting plus mental practice conditions were observed to have improved their communication skills at work. No change was observed for the supervisors who did not engage in mental practice, did not set goals, or were assigned to the control group.

Oettingen, Wittchen, and Gollwitzer (2013) found that there are four challenges to goal implementation that frequently confront people, namely, people fail to get started with goal striving, do not stay on track, overextend themselves with one goal and lose sight of others, and fail to recognize and abandon an unattainable goal. The solution for overcoming these challenges is to plan in advance ways to overcome these challenges. As such, goals require plans. Effective planning leads to goal attainment.

Personal Initiative and Error Training

Action theory, developed by Frese and Zapf (1994), emphasizes the importance of both goal setting and planning. The theory states that high performance is not always the result of effort and persistence; it is also the result of understanding the task, as well as developing the strategy or plan necessary for completing it. The theory also states that an action sequence consists of five steps, namely, goal setting, information collection, planning, execution, and feedback. An action sequence involves the monitoring of one's environment in order to gather information to aid in planning a course of action. As a result of setting goals and collecting information, plans can be developed.

Frese (2005) has used action theory as a framework for developing a training program designed to increase an employee's personal initiative in the workplace. Personal initiative involves an employee changing the environment as opposed to only reacting to it, going beyond what one has been told to do, and finding improvements in work procedures. The key components of this training program, based on the five steps in the action sequence, consist of goal development, collecting information for making a prognosis, planning and monitoring action, and seeking feedback. After employees set a goal, they are taught to systemically seek information required to achieve it. Plans are then developed, executed, and monitored based on this information. Self-monitoring allows employees to use the feedback they obtain to adjust their plans.

The effectiveness of this training program has been demonstrated in at least three studies. First, Frese, Kring, Soose, and Zempel (1996), in a longitudinal study conducted in Germany, found that unemployed people with a high degree of personal initiative were able to find a job faster than those with low personal initiative. In that study, initiative was measured based on the plans people had formed. For example, in response to questions related to their plans for educational purposes, the respondents with personal initiative knew which courses they should take. Second, Frese (2000) found that the personal initiative taken by owners of small businesses in Africa was related to a firm's subsequent success. Third, Baer and Frese (2003), in a study of mid-sized German companies, found that the widespread use of training in personal initiative, including creating a climate that fostered initiative and planning, led to significant increases in company profitability.

When pursuing a difficult goal, individuals inevitably make mistakes. Frese (2005) and his colleagues have shown that people can be taught to embrace errors and negative feedback by framing errors as beneficial to the learning process, and to be resilient, subsequent to making an error, through systematic exploration. When faced with errors, individuals are taught to frame them positively (e.g. "the more errors you make the more you will learn."). Frese found that providing people with ample opportunities to make errors and explicit encouragement to learn from them improves their performance.

Planning and Subconscious Goals

Both goal-setting theory and action theory focus on the effect of consciously set goals on task performance. A limitation of these two theories is that they do not acknowledge the effect of goals in the subconscious on performance (Locke & Latham, 2004). However, research has shown that even when people consciously plan on what to do to attain their goals, subconscious processes play an additive role.

Gollwitzer (1993, 1999) found that people can enhance the likelihood of goal attainment by devising implementation intentions, that is, plans for goal attainment. When creating implementation intentions, individuals plan the "when, where, and how" of striving for a goal in an "if–then" format. By pre-planning how to act in response to a specific situation, implementation intentions allow people to control the initiation of goal-directed behavior in response to environmental cues, in the absence of their awareness of doing so (Gollwitzer, Kappes, & Oettingen, 2012).

In short, the formulation of an implementation intention or plan is done consciously, but consciousness is not required to trigger or implement the plan. The mere presence of a situational stimulus associated with a plan allows one to initiate the intended response in the absence of conscious choice.

Henderson, Gollwitzer, and Oettingen (2007) hypothesized that forming implementation intentions (i.e. plans) is especially helpful when an individual is faced with a failing course of action. To test this hypothesis, participants in a laboratory experiment were asked to select a strategy that they thought would maximize their performance on a knowledge test. One implementation intention specified reflection and thinking about what the individual would do. The other specified only the action that the individual would take. Participants in the control condition received no instructions; they were simply told to do their best. After ten trials on a general knowledge test, the participants were told that their performance was poor or moderate relative to others. The dependent variable was whether participants changed or maintained their initial strategies. Participants in both experimental conditions were more likely to develop effective plans compared to those in the control condition.

Bargh's (1990) "automotive model" states that routines, processes, and plans involved in the pursuit of a goal are implicitly associated with the goal as part of a mental representation. Furthermore, when a goal representation is activated, an individual's actions do not need to be consciously processed and selected (Custers, Eitam, & Bargh, 2012). For example, repeatedly pursuing a goal through a certain course of action creates a strong cognitive link between the goal representation and the representation of this behavior. The link is so strong that activation of a goal can automatically lead to the activation of habitual plans for goal pursuit. For instance, if an individual has a goal for going to work each day, the individual does not need to deliberately plan how to get there, as the job attendance goal automatically activates the idea of walking, taking a bus, or driving a car (Custers et al., 2012).

Similarly, Shantz and Latham (2009) found that there was a significant main effect for both the primed and the specific, high conscious goal on performance of call center employees measured by the number of donors. This result regarding the primed goal–performance relationship was replicated in three additional call centers (Shantz & Latham, 2011; Latham & Piccolo, 2012).

Chen and Latham (2014) showed that a primed goal (i.e. a photograph of Rodin's *The Thinker*) can lead individuals to set a learning goal. Plans were set in the absence of awareness for performing a task that required knowledge acquisition. A significant main effect for priming a learning goal on performance of the complex scheduling task used by Winters and Latham (1996) and Seijts and Latham (2001) was obtained.

Future Research

Both Locke and Latham (1990) and Wood et al. (2013) have made recommendations for future research on goal setting and the importance of planning to the goal–performance relationship. Because researchers have yet to respond to these suggestions they bear repeating here.

Research is needed on the effects of goal specificity as well as difficulty level on strategy development, particularly in regard to communication and comprehensiveness.

Research is also needed to determine whether the underlying processes by which a goal and a plan affect performance on complex, as opposed to straightforward, psychomotor tasks are the same as those for cognitive tasks.

Wood et al. (2013) noted that the strategies included in their meta-analysis assumed that there is a linear relationship between plans and performance. Are there tasks, they asked, where the relationship between knowledge acquisition and subsequent performance may be non-linear due to the synergistic effects of devising multiple plans? Furthermore, as people learn more strategies will they be able to make better use of their knowledge in a wider range of task situations? Wood et al. also called for research on how difficult goals interact with different levels of strategic expertise. Tests of the moderator model, they argued, should examine the benefits of different types of plans and difficult goals on different types of tasks. Strategy knowledge manipulations could include training in search and information processing skills, including hypothesis testing, and testing the goal effects on tasks that are straightforward for an individual versus tasks that require knowledge acquisition.

Field studies should examine the benefits of goal setting and planning across different job levels or role expertise in complex, dynamic workplaces. Finally, Wood et al. argued that future research on the moderator model should take into account the specific knowledge requirements for a specific task and then ensure that operationalization of strategies creates or captures that knowledge.

Summary

For a theory to be complete, it should specify the causal relationships, the moderator variables regarding the causal relationships, and the mediating variables that explain the causal relationships. Planning is a mediating variable that explains the goal–performance relationship specified in goal-setting theory. Planning is also a moderator of the beneficial effect of setting a goal on tasks that are relatively stable.

In practice, the importance of planning is paramount for ensuring that goals increase performance. In the context of organizational change, planning was essential to goal attainment during the large-scale organizational changes at IBM, Boeing, and Ford Motor Company. In the context of teamwork, planning is especially important on ways to coordinate roles and responsibilities for goal attainment. An effective performance appraisal requires managers and employees to engage in planning ways to attain specific, challenging goals. Self-management requires planning, in addition to the setting of specific, high goals, in writing a behavioral contract with oneself that includes ways of monitoring one's environment, and administering rewards and punishers during goal pursuit. Training on personal initiative emphasizes the importance of planning, as does error training. Emerging research on subconscious goals suggests that through priming, goal setting and planning can occur in the absence of awareness.

Notes

1   A strategy is a "plan or pattern of decision making or action designed or undertaken to achieve a goal" (Wood, Whelan, Sojo, & Wong, 2013, p. 94). Hence these two terms are used interchangeably throughout this chapter.
2   Is it correlation or causation that the on-time success of the Boeing 777 is in sharp contrast to Boeing's 787/Dreamliner, where multiple delays occurred following Mulally's departure from Boeing to Ford? We will never find an answer that satisfies scientific criteria. But many employees believe the answer lies in his departure.

References

Baer, M., & Frese, M. (2003). Innovation is not enough: Climates for initiative and psychological safety, process innovation and firm performance. *Journal of Organizational Behavior*, 24, 45–68.

Bandura, A., & Simon, K. M. (1977). The role of proximal intentions in self-regulation of refractory behavior. *Cognitive Therapy and Research*, 1, 177–193.

Bargh, J. A. (1990). Auto-motives: Preconscious determinants of thought and behavior. Multiple affects from multiple stages. In E. T. Higgins & R. M. Sorrentino (Eds.), *Handbook of motivation and cognition: Foundations of social behavior* (Vol. 2, pp. 93–130). New York: Guilford Press.

Bavelas, J., & Lee, E. S. (1978). Effect of goal level on performance: A trade-off of quantity and quality. *Canadian Journal of Psychology*, 32, 219–240.

Carroll, S. J., & Tosi, H. L. (1973). *Management by objectives: Applications and research.* New York: Macmillan.

Chen, X., & Latham, G. P. (2014). The effects of priming learning vs. performance goals on a complex task. *Organizational Behaviour and Human Decision Processes*, 125(2), 88–97.

Chesney, A. A., & Locke, E. A. (1991). An examination of the relationships among goal difficulty, business strategies, and performance on a complex management simulation task. *Academy of Management Journal*, 34, 400–424.

Custers, R., Eitam, B., & Bargh, J. A. (2012). Conscious and unconscious processes in goal pursuit. In H. Aarts & A. Elliot (Eds.), *Goal-directed behavior* (pp. 231–266). New York: Psychology Press.

DeShon, R. P., Kozlowski, S. W. J., Schmidt, A. M., Milner, K. R., & Wiechmann, D. (2004). Multiple goal feedback effects on the regulation of individual and team performance in training. *Journal of Applied Psychology*, 89, 1035–1056.

Drucker, P. F. (1974). *The practice of management.* New York: Harper & Row.

Durham, C. C., Knight, D., & Locke, E. A. (1997). Effects of leader role, team-set goal difficulty, efficacy, and tactics on team effectiveness. *Organizational Behavior and Human Decision Processes*, 72, 203–231.

Earley, P. C., & Perry, B. (1987). Work plan availability and performance: An assessment of prior training on subsequent task completion. *Organizational Behavior and Human Decision Processes*, 39, 279–302.

Earley, P. C., Wojnaroski, P., & Prest, W. (1987). Task planning and energy expended: An exploration of how goals influence performance. *Journal of Applied Psychology*, 72, 107–114.

Earley, P. C., Lee, C., & Hanson, L. A. (1989). Joint moderating effects of job experience and task component complexity: relations among goal setting, task strategies, and performance. *Journal of Organizational Behavior*, 11, 3–15.

Erez, M., & Zidon, I. (1984). Effect of goal acceptance on the relationship of goal difficulty to performance. *Journal of Applied Psychology*, 69, 69–78.

Frayne, C. A., & Latham, G. P. (1987). The application of social learning theory to employee self-management of attendance. *Journal of Applied Psychology*, 72, 387–392.

Frese, M. (2000). *Success and failure of micro business owners in Africa: A psychological approach.* Westport, CT: Quorum Books.

Frese, M. (2005). Grand theories and midrange theories. Cultural effects on theorizing and the attempt to understand active approaches to work. In K. G. Smith and M. Hitt (Eds.), *The Oxford handbook of management theory: The process of theory development.* New York: Oxford University Press.

Frese, M., & Zapf, D. (1994). Action as the core of work psychology: A German approach. In H. C. Triandis, M. D. Dunnette, & L. Hough (Eds.), *Handbook of industrial and organizational psychology* (Vol. 4, pp. 271–340). Palo Alto, CA: Consulting Psychologists Press.

Frese, M., Kring, W., Soose, A., & Zempel, J. (1996). Personal initiative at work: Differences between East and West Germany. *Academy of Management Journal*, 39, 37–63.

Gist, M. E., Bavetta, A. G., & Stevens, C. K. (1990). Transfer training method: Its influence on skill generalization, skill repetition, and performance level. *Personnel Psychology*, 43, 501–523.

Gollwitzer, P. M. (1993). Goal achievement: The role of intentions. In W. Stroebe & M. Hewstone (Eds.), *European review of social psychology* (Vol. 4, pp. 141–185). Chichester, UK: Wiley.

Gollwitzer, P. M. (1999). Implementation intentions and effective goal pursuit: Strong effects of simple plans. *American Psychologist*, 54, 493–503.

Gollwitzer, P. M., Kappes, H. P., & Oettingen, G. (2012). Needs and incentives as sources of goals. In H. Aarts & A. Elliot (Eds.), *Goal-directed behavior* (pp. 231–266). New York: Psychology Press.

Hackman, J. R. (1987). The design of work teams. In J. Lorsch (Ed.), *Handbook of organizational behavior.* Englewood Cliffs, NJ: Prentice Hall.

Henderson, M. D., Gollwitzer, P. M., & Oettingen, G. (2007). Implementation intentions and disengagement from a failing course of action. *Journal of Behavioral Decision Making*, 20, 81–102.

Hofer, C. W., & Schendel, D. E. (1978). *Strategy formulation: Analytical concepts.* St. Paul, MN: West Publishing.

Kanfer, F. H. (1970). Self-regulation: Research issues and speculations. In C. Neuringer & L. Michael (Eds.), *Behavior modification in clinical psychology.* New York: Appleton-Century-Crofts.

Kanfer, R., & Ackerman, P. L. (1989). Motivation and cognitive abilities: An integrative/aptitude-treatment interaction approach to skill acquisition. *Journal of Applied Psychology*, 74, 657–690.

Kaplan, R., & Rothkopf, E. Z. (1974). Instructional objectives as directions to learners: Effect of passage length and amount of objective-relevant content. *Journal of Educational Psychology*, 66, 448–456.

Kirsch, I. (1978). Tangible self-reinforcement in self directed behavior modification projects. *Psychological Reports*, 43, 455–461.

Kleingeld, A., Van Mierlo, H., & Arends, L. (2011). The effect of goal setting on group performance: A meta-analysis. *Journal of Applied Psychology*, 6, 1289–1304.

Knight, D., Durham, C. C., & Locke, E. A. (2001). The relationship of team goals, incentives, and efficacy to strategic risk, tactical implementation, and performance. *Academy of Management Journal*, 44, 326–338.

Kotler, P. (1976). *Marketing management: Analysis planning and control* (3d ed.). Englewood Cliffs, NJ: Prentice Hall.

Kramer, W. S., Thayer, A. L., & Salas, E. (2013). Goal setting in teams. In. E. A. Locke & G. P. Latham (Eds), *New developments in goal setting and task performance*. New York: Routledge Academic.

Latham, G. P., & Baldes, J. J. (1975). The "practical significance" of Locke's theory of goal setting. *Journal of Applied Psychology*, 60, 122–124.

Latham, G. P., & Budworth, M. (2006). The effect of training in verbal self guidance on self-efficacy and performance of Native North Americans in the selection interview. *Journal of Vocational Behavior*, 68, 516–523.

Latham, G. P., & Frayne, C. A. (1989). Self management training for increasing job attendance: A follow-up and a replication. *Journal of Applied Psychology*, 74, 411–416.

Latham, G. P., & Locke, E. A. (1975). Increasing productivity with decreasing time limits: A field replication of Parkinson's Law. *Journal of Applied Psychology*, 60, 524–526.

Latham, G. P., & Locke, E. A. (2007). New developments in and directions for goal setting research. *European Psychologist*, 12, 290–300.

Latham, G. P., & Piccolo, R. F. (2012). The effect of context specific versus non-specific subconscious goals on employee performance. *Human Resource Management*, 51, 535–538.

Latham, G. P., & Saari, L. M. (1982). The importance of union acceptance for productivity improvement through goal setting. *Personnel Psychology*, 35, 781–787.

Latham, G. P., & Seijts, G. H. (1999). The effects of proximal and distal goals on performance on a moderately complex task. *Journal of Organizational Behavior*, 20, 421–429.

Latham, G. P., Mitchell, T. R., & Dossett, D. L. (1978). The importance of participative goal setting and anticipated rewards on goal difficulty and job performance. *Journal of Applied Psychology*, 63, 163–171.

Locke, E. A. (1982). Relation of goal level to performance with a short work period and multiple goal levels. *Journal of Applied Psychology*, 67, 512–514.

Locke, E. A., & Bryan, J. F. (1969). The directing function of goals in task performance. *Organizational Behavior & Human Performance*, 4, 35–42.

Locke, E. A., & Latham, G. P. (1990). *A theory of goal setting and task performance*. Upper Saddle River, NJ: Prentice Hall.

Locke, E. A., & Latham, G. P. (2002). Building a practically useful theory of goal setting and work motivation: A 35-year odyssey. *American Psychologist*, 57, 705–717.

Locke, E. A., & Latham, G. P. (2004). What should we do about motivation theory? Six recommendations for the twenty-first century. *Academy of Management Review*, 29, 388–403.

Locke, E. A., & Latham, G. P. (2013). *New developments in goal setting and task performance*. New York: Routledge Academic.

Locke, E. A., Cartledge, N., & Koeppel, J. (1968). The motivational effects of knowledge of results: A goal-setting phenomenon? *Psychological Bulletin*, 70, 474–485.

Lorange, P., & Vancil, R. V. (1977). *Strategic planning systems*. Englewood Cliffs, NJ: Prentice Hall.

McGrath, J. E. (1964). *Social psychology: A brief introduction*. New York: Holt, Rinehart and Winston.

Marks, M. A., Mathieu, J. E., & Zaccaro, S. J. (2001). A temporally based framework and taxonomy of team processes. *Academy of Management Review*, 26, 356–376.

Mawritz, M., Folger, R., & Latham, G. P. (2014). Supervisors' exceedingly difficult goals and abusive supervision: The mediating effects of hindrance stress, anger, and anxiety. *Journal of Organizational Behavior*, 35(3), 358–372.

Mehta, A., Feild, H., Armenakis, A., & Mehta, N. (2009). Team goal orientation and team performance: The mediating role of team planning. *Journal of Management*, 35, 1026–1046.

Meichenbaum, D. H. (1971). Examination of model characteristics in reducing avoidance behavior. *Journal of Personality and Social Psychology*, 17, 298–307.

Meichenbaum, D. H. (1977). *Cognitive behavior modification. An integrative approach*. New York: Plenum Press.

Miles, R. E., & Snow, C. C. (1978). *Organizational strategy, structures and process*. New York: McGraw-Hill.

Miles, R. E., Snow, C. C., Meyer, A. D., & Coleman, H. J., Jr. (1978). Organizational strategy, structure, and process. *Academy of Management Review*, 3, 546–562.

Millman, Z., & Latham, G. P. (2001). Increasing re-employment through training in verbal self-guidance. In M. Erez, U. Kleinbeck, & H. K. Thierry (Eds.), *Work motivation in the context of a globalizing economy.* Mahwah, NJ: Lawrence Erlbaum.

Mitchell, T. R., & Daniels, D. (2003). Motivation. In W. C. Borman, D. R. Ilgen, & R. J. Klimoski (Eds.), *Comprehensive handbook of psychology: Industrial organizational psychology* (Vol. 12, pp. 225–254). New York: Wiley.

Mone, M. A., & Shalley, C. E. (1995). Effects of task complexity and goal specificity on change in strategy and performance over time. *Human Performance,* 8, 243–262.

Morin, L., & Latham, G. P. (2000). Effect of mental practice and goal setting as a transfer of training intervention on supervisors' self-efficacy and communication skills: An exploratory study. *Applied Psychology: An International Review,* 49, 566–578.

Oettingen, G., Wittchen, M., & Gollwitzer, P. M. (2013). Regulating goal pursuit through mental contrasting with implementation intentions. In E. A. Locke and G. P. Latham (Eds.), *New developments in goal setting and task performance.* New York, NY: Routledge, 523–548.

Paine, F. T., & Anderson, C. R. (1983). *Strategic management.* New York: Dryden Press.

Park, G., Spitzmuller, M., & DeShon, R. P. (2013). Advancing our understanding of team motivation: Integral conceptual approaches and content areas. *Journal of Management,* 39, 1339–1379.

Porter, M. E. (1980). *Competitive strategy, techniques for analyzing industries and competitors.* New York: Free Press.

Porter, R. L., & Latham, G. P. (2013). The effect of employee learning goals and goal commitment on departmental performance. *Journal of Leadership and Organizational Studies,* 20, 62–68.

Saari, L. M. (2013). Goal setting and organizational transformation. In E. A. Locke and G. P. Latham (Eds.), *New developments in goal setting and task performance* (pp. 262–269). New York: Routledge.

Salas, E., Dickinson, T. L., Converse, S. A., & Tannenbaum, S. I. (1992). Toward an understanding of team performance and training. In R. W. Swezey & E. Salas (Eds.), *Teams: Their training and performance* (pp. 3–29). Westport, CT: Ablex.

Seijts, G. H., & Latham, G. P. (2000). The effects of goal setting and group size on performance in a social dilemma. *Canadian Journal of Behavioural Science,* 32, 104–116.

Seijts, G. H., & Latham, G. P. (2001). The effect of learning, outcome, and proximal goals on a moderately complex task. *Journal of Organizational Behavior,* 22, 291–307.

Seijts, G. H., & Latham, G. P. (2005). Learning versus performance goals: When should each be used? *Academy of Management Executive,* 19, 124–131.

Seijts, G. H., Latham, G. P., & Woodwark, M. (2013). Learning goals: A qualitative and quantitative review. In E. A. Locke and G. P. Latham (Eds.), *New developments in goal and task performance* (pp. 195–212). New York: Routledge.

Shantz, A., & Latham, G. P. (2009). An exploratory field experiment on the effect of subconscious and conscious goals on employee performance. *Organizational Behavior and Human Decision Making Processes,* 109, 9–17.

Shantz, A., & Latham, G. P. (2011). The effect of primed goals on employee performance: Implications for human resource management. *Human Resource Management,* 50, 289–299.

Smith, K. G., Locke, E. A., & Barry, D. (1990). Goal setting, planning and organizational performance: An experimental simulation. *Organizational Behavior and Human Decision Processes,* 46, 118–134.

Steiner, G. A. (1969). *Top management planning.* New York: Macmillan.

Steiner, G. A. (1979). *Strategic planning: What every manager must know.* New York: Free Press.

Wegge, J., Bipp, T., & Kleinbeck, U. (2007). Goal setting via videoconferencing. *European Journal of Work and Organizational Psychology,* 16, 169–194.

Winters, D., & Latham, G. P. (1996). The effect of learning versus outcome goals on a simple versus a complex task. *Group and Organization Management,* 21, 236–250.

Wood, R. E., & Locke, E. A. (1990). Goal-setting and strategy effects on complex tasks. In B. Staw and L. Cummings (Eds.), *Research in organizational behavior* (Vol. 12, pp. 73–109). Greenwich, CT: JAI Press.

Wood, R. E., Whelan, J., Sojo, V., & Wong, M. (2013). Goals, goal orientations, strategies and performance. In E. A. Locke and G. P. Latham (Eds.), *New developments in goal and task performance* (pp. 90–114). New York: Routledge.

Yanar, B., Budworth, M. H., & Latham, G. P. (2009). The effect of verbal self-guidance training for overcoming employment barriers: A study of Turkish women. *Applied Psychology: An International Review,* 58, 586–601.

6

EMOTIONS AND PLANNING IN ORGANIZATIONS

Shane Connelly and Genevieve Johnson

Overview

Planning is an important organizational activity that creates the basic scaffolding that enables organizations to function. Performed by individuals and groups, planning is conducted for a wide variety of purposes such as business planning, marketing, risk mitigation, and project planning, among others. These efforts help individuals and organizations to identify and prioritize goals and key work activities, to assess the costs and benefits of these activities, and to obtain and coordinate the people and resources needed to do them (Mumford, Schultz, & Osburn, 2002). Broadly defined, planning is "the construction of future action sequences intended to direct action and optimize attainment of outcomes" (Mumford, Schultz, & Van Doorn, 2001, p. 214). Plans are more than to-do lists. They reflect the interplay of action sequences, time, resources, and contingencies, implying the need for cognitive activities as well as social processes related to communication, collaboration, and negotiation with co-workers, supervisors, and other groups or people. Taking these demands into account along with the research relating emotions to motivation, cognition, and social behavior, exploring the role of emotions in planning appears to be an important endeavor.

Generalized affect and discrete emotional states exert influence on cognitions and social behavior in a variety of ways. Accordingly, the first goal of this chapter is to highlight the relevance of emotion for directing and motivating planning processes and behavior. There is a broad literature on emotions and motivation (e.g. Buck 1985, 1988; Carver & Scheier, 1981; Damasio, 1994; Kanfer & Stubblebine, 2008; Lazarus, 1991; Seo, Barrett, & Jin, 2008) suggesting that emotions help people identify important and meaningful activities to pursue, provide feedback regarding goal process, and influence perceptions about the likelihood of success (Carver, 2006). A second objective is to identify influences of affect and emotion states on the execution of specific planning processes. Emotional states have been shown to influence various cognitive processes used in planning, including but not limited to memory (Kensinger & Schacter, 2008; Levine & Pizarro, 2004), information processing (Bodenhausen, Kramer, & Süsser, 1994; Forgas, 1998), creative thinking (Fredrickson, 2001; Isen, 2008; Isen, Daubman, & Nowicki, 1987; Mackie & Worth, 1989), and risk assessment (Lerner & Keltner, 2000, 2001; Rick & Loewenstein, 2008). Third, given the distinctly social nature of organizations, some or all aspects of planning may involve dyadic or group interaction. Therefore, it is important to consider some of the social influences of emotions on planning that occurs in dyads and work groups. Finally, we explore the role of emotion regulation in planning. Regulating emotional states is a complex process, and greater understanding is needed of how emotion regulation can be used to facilitate planning for individuals and groups.

Defining Affect and Emotional States

Prior research has suggested that mood, affect, and discrete emotions reflect emotional experiences that have different physiological underpinnings, experiential components, and impacts on thought and behavior. Moods are generalized positive or negative states that lack specific triggers, are short or long in duration, and are temporary (Frijda, 2009). Affect is generally understood to reflect an emotional experience characterized by the dimensions of valence (positive and negative) and arousal (low and high) (Feldman Barrett & Russell, 1998; Russell & Feldman Barrett, 1999), or positive affectivity-PA (positive valence and high activation) and negative affectivity-NA (negative valence and high activation) (Watson & Tellegen, 1985). Affect can be trait-based or situationally induced and can be either incidental to planning efforts (i.e. not directly related) or integral to planning activities in that it is directly associated with and stems from those activities. Research has also demonstrated distinct effects of more specific forms of emotional experience, often referred to as discrete emotions (e.g. Roseman, 1991; Tiedens & Linton, 2001).

Discrete emotions have also been widely studied. Discrete emotions such as anger and happiness are relatively short-lived, occur in response to people, events, and things, reflect basic combinations of valence and arousal, and are linked to appraisals of certainty, control, other-responsibility, and other appraisal dimensions (Smith & Ellsworth, 1985). Some scholars argue that emotions motivate goal-directed behavior and that specific emotions motivate people in different ways (Lazarus, 1991; Levine & Pizarro, 2004; Zeelenberg, Nelissen, Breugelmans, & Pieters, 2008; Zeelenberg & Pieters, 2006). Appraisal theories of emotion suggest that not only are arousal and valence important, but dimensions such as control, level of certainty, goal blockage, and other-responsibility also characterize the experience of discrete emotions (Roseman, Spindel, & Jose, 1990; Smith & Ellsworth, 1985). While most emotions have a positive or negative valence, this does not suggest that they are inherently good or bad. Emotions reflect adaptive states of action readiness (Frijda, 1988, 2007) and can have beneficial or destructive outcomes regardless of their valence (Fitness, 2008). While discrete emotion action tendencies like escape (often linked to fear) or attack (often linked to anger) do not always directly influence actions, they tend to narrow down potential courses of action (Fredrickson, 2001). As with affect, both incidental and integral discrete emotions can influence important outcomes. We include research on discrete emotions here because it offers additional insight into how emotional states might influence people's willingness and capacity to plan.

Emotional States and Motivation for Planning

Planning requires time and cognitive effort. These resources are already heavily taxed in organizational environments where social connectedness and information overload are ever-increasing (Hudson, Christensen, Kellogg, & Erickson, 2002). Consequently, people have to be motivated to plan, and emotions can influence this in a variety of ways. At a very basic level, people are typically motivated to maintain positive moods and to repair or reduce negative moods (Isen, 1993; Schaller & Cialdini, 1990; Wegener & Petty, 1994). It is also the case that sometimes affective regulation focuses on lessening positive emotions or increasing negative ones, but this occurs less often (Gross, 1998). It is interesting to consider how mood maintenance and mood repair as motivational tendencies might influence planning activity. One reason people may not be motivated to plan relates to the disruptive effect planning can have on positive mood states. Thinking about goals, resource shortages, potential problems, and the need to convince organizational skeptics to back a plan will almost certainly generate some degree of negative emotion. Avoiding such tasks preserves a more positive mood state in the short term. Alternatively, people who are in negative mood states, especially if these stem from problems within an organization, may be motivated to plan as a way of dealing with those problems. Planning in this case can be used to determine underlying causes of the problems, generate ideas for resolving problems, and identify and allocate resources to implement the plan. Thus, planning has the potential to reduce or repair negative mood states by reducing uncertainty and offering a defined path for resolving organizational issues.

Emotions can also be seen as a component of action tendencies or approach/avoid self-regulatory processes that motivate work behavior (Cacioppo, Gardner, & Berntson, 1999; Carver 2006; Gray, 1994a; 1994b). A promotion regulatory focus or striving for accomplishment and to meet aspirational self-standards is generally associated with positive emotional states when progress is being made towards goals, but negative emotional states when progress is frustrated or goals are not met (Baas, De Dreu, & Nijstad, 2011; Idson, Liberman, & Higgins, 2000). Emotional states differ for individuals with a prevention focus, who strive for security, to avoid loss, and to meet duty-based self-standards. When prevention-focused individuals are working towards these goals, negative emotions such as fear and worry are present, while more positive emotional states occur once goals have been met (Brockner & Higgins, 2001; Idson et al., 2000). Both of these regulatory states and their affective correlates may motivate planning behavior, but are likely to result in different expectancies of what types of efforts will positively influence outcomes as well as different valences or values placed on those outcomes. Thus, the nature of goals and action sequences resulting from these regulatory styles may look very different.

Consider the example of two small business owners planning in the midst of an economic downturn. The owner with a promotion-focused regulatory style sees diversification, growth, and expansion into new markets as the solution to surviving the current economic situation. The owner with a prevention-focused style sees cost cutting, securing the current customer base, and cutting inventory as essential. While these are viable strategies that might enable the companies to survive, the planning associated with each would be radically different. Planning in the diversify-and-expand scenario involves risk-seeking and potentially longer-term goals, continual scanning of the environment for opportunities, and a flexible approach that is open to ongoing revisions. Positive emotion states such as optimism and interest may have influenced the decision to proceed with this type of plan (Fredrickson, 2001; Higgins, 1998). Planning in the cost-cutting scenario involves risk-averse, shorter-term goals, ongoing evaluation of internal resources, inventory and expenditures, and a stay-the-course approach until the economy improves. Here, fear of loss and other negative emotion states may have influenced the approach taken. While somewhat of an oversimplification, this example illustrates the potential for negative and positive emotions to motivate planning in very different directions, either of which could be effective or ineffective in meeting the goal of surviving the economic downturn. We now turn to research on the relationships of affect and emotion states to specific cognitive processes involved in planning.

Emotions and Cognitive Planning Processes

The cognitive activities involved in planning suggest the utility of taking a process-oriented approach to examining emotions and planning. While a variety of cognitive processes have been identified in prior research (e.g. Berger, Guilford, & Christensen, 1957; Dörner & Schaub, 1994; Hammond, 1990; Hayes-Roth & Hayes-Roth, 1979; Kreitler & Kreitler, 1972; Xiao, Milgram, & Doyle, 1997), Mumford and colleagues provide one of the most comprehensive treatments and modeling of the cognitive processes involved in planning (Mumford et al., 2001). This model proposes that individuals scan the broader environment for opportunities and threats which shape the goals for a given planning process. Individuals draw on prior experience or cases of prior planning efforts related to and potentially useful for attaining the goals of the current planning effort. Using the case information helps planners to identify key causes and restrictions that must be kept mind when constructing both a template plan and a more fully developed plan. Once an elaborated plan exists, refinements are often necessary based on forecasts or estimates of how well the plan is likely to work in meeting the goals. This leads to the development of backup plans, progress markers, and eventual implementation of the plan. There are multiple feedback loops in this dynamic model such that information gleaned from one aspect of planning informs other aspects. General affective states and specific emotions have been shown to influence many of the processes outlined in this model. Accordingly, we highlight theories and research showing the relevance of emotional states to: (1) environmental scanning and goal identification, (2) information search and case selection, (3) information processing and identification of causes and restrictions, (4) initial template and plan generation, and (5) forecasting and idea evaluation.

Environmental Scanning and Goal Identification

Scanning the environment for opportunities and threats relevant to an organization shapes the goals that will guide planning and may well be influenced by emotional states. Returning to the example of the small business owners, the one with a promotion-oriented aspirational regulatory style is likely to attend to and seek out new opportunities and new directions, while the prevention-oriented owner may be more likely to attend to and avoid threats. What is the resulting impact on goals? Positive moods may increase the desirability of approach goals while negative moods may increase the desirability of avoid goals according to some planning theorists (Gollwitzer, 1993). However, the relationship of emotion states to goal setting is probably more complex.

Seo, Barrett, and Bartunek (2004) suggest that the self-regulatory aspect of core affect impacts what goals are initially set and people's judgments about those goals (expectancies regarding what will lead to goal attainment, how well one is progressing towards a goal, and commitment to a goal). Positive core affect will result in expectancies of positive outcomes, high utility judgments for those outcomes, and a promotion-focused regulatory style. In turn, this increases goal level, effort expended, and goal commitment. Despite this, less frequent and less thorough monitoring of goal progress is expected when core affect is positive. Affective reactions serve as signaling functions (Schwarz & Bless, 1991), with positive emotions indicating that things are going well and that there is little felt discrepancy between goals and goal progress. Alternatively, negative core affect is proposed to increase expectancies of negative outcomes with low utilities and a prevention focus. Negative emotions remind people of the potential for negative outcomes and discrepancies between one's current state and desired goals (Cron, Slocum, VandeWalle, & Fu, 2005; Kanfer & Stubblebine, 2008). This discrepancy can sometimes be useful when it increases the amount of time and effort spent on a task (George & Zhou, 2002; Sy, Côté, & Saavedra, 2005).

Recent research on the differential effects of same-valence discrete emotions on information processing indicates that specific feeling states such as happiness, fear, sadness, and anger are likely to have different effects on goal specification and goal-directed behavior (e.g. Lerner & Keltner, 2000, 2001). Levine and Pizarro (2004) highlight the different motivational or goal states associated with each of these emotions. Happiness motivates people to maintain their current state and to attain new goals, which likely results in the broad, heuristic information-processing characteristic of positive emotion states (Clore, Gasper, & Garvin, 2001). Fear motivates people to avoid threats and goal failure, focusing them on information relevant to perceived and actual sources of threats and strategies to prevent them from having an impact. Anger motivates people to remove obstacles to goal attainment, thereby narrowing information processing to goal- and obstacle-relevant information. Sadness motivates people to adapt to goal failure, focusing information processing on outcomes and consequences of goal failure. In a planning context, these emotional states and their associated information-processing styles will shape goal identification and goal setting in different ways.

Information Search and Case Selection

Accessing knowledge and experiences relevant to planning goals often relies on underlying memory processes such as information encoding, consolidation, and retrieval. People draw from past planning experiences in which they have been involved (or observed, learned about, etc.) to help guide the development of new plans (Mumford et al., 2001). Social psychological research as well as neuroimaging and neurophysiological studies have greatly informed our understanding of how emotion influences memory. Reviews by Kensinger and Schacter (2008) and Levine and Pizarro (2004) indicate that emotional events influence memory in at least three ways. First, emotional events are remembered better than non-emotional ones, with positive and negative events showing comparable encoding and retrieval advantages. Second, the vividness or details of memories for emotional events is also better than for emotionally neutral events. Interestingly, in laboratory studies, negative events are more vividly recalled than positive ones, while the picture is more mixed with autobiographical memory recall. Accuracy is a third dimension of memory influenced by emotion-specific processing. The central features of emotional events are remembered better than the central features of neutral events; however, this advantage is not realized with respect to how accurately context and other peripheral aspects of the event are remembered. These effects are not simply due to the fact that emotional events are more interesting or distinct (Kensinger & Schacter, 2008). Neuroimaging studies have shown that emotion-specific processing in the amygdala and orbito-frontal cortex interacts with the hippocampus (where non-emotional memories are processed) in ways that increase encoding, consolidation, and retrieval of emotional memories (e.g. Dolcos, LaBar, & Cabeza, 2004; Hamann, Ely, Grafton, & Kilts, 1999; Kensinger & Corkin, 2004; Richardson, Strange, & Dolan, 2004).

Levine and Pizarro (2004) suggest that the mixed findings on emotional valence and autobiographical memory may be due to different styles of information processing associated with positive and negative emotions. The general, heuristic processing often seen with positive emotions contributes to reconstructing details of happy memories (Bernsten, 2002). The systematic, focused information processing associated with negative emotions leads to selective remembering of information relevant to repairing the negative event or preventing future ones. Studies have shown that negative affect and sad moods are less susceptible to false memories than happy moods (Forgas, Laham, & Vargas, 2005; Storbeck & Clore, 2011).

Prior planning efforts, one's own or those vicariously observed, will lie somewhere on a continuum of epic failure to unparalleled success. Cases nearer to the ends of this continuum are arguably tagged with more negative or positive emotional states, and as such, are likely to be remembered better and more vividly in terms of their central features than those in the middle of the continuum. For better or worse, planning cases associated with emotions may be where we turn first in searching for relevant information and cases in formulating new plans. From one perspective, this is advantageous because these types of cases have the potential to alert us to failures to avoid, such as underestimates of project timeframes, insufficient resources, or lack of awareness of interdependencies among actions and people. Successful cases also provide valuable information for possible incorporation into new plans, such as appropriate goal type/level, effective action sequences, and contingencies that worked. The disadvantage of relying on emotional cases is that a number of effective but unremarkable or non-emotional cases may actually be more informative to the planning effort at hand. It may be important to tap into these cases as well, because the conditions, restrictions, and contexts may be more similar to the effort at hand than the emotionally tagged cases.

Emotional states have also been shown to influence not only the search for information in memory, but information search in the surrounding environment. In a series of experiments, Shani and Zeelenberg (2007, 2012) found that the experience of regret after making a bad decision, or fear and other emotions associated with uncertainty about the future, prompted information search. However, people appear to weigh the costs and benefits of having versus not having certain information, such as negative work evaluations or a diagnosis of a serious medical condition. Additional studies in this area have revealed that people are inclined to temporarily delay information search and uncertainty reduction if they think having the information will interfere with positive mood states, enjoyable events, or future plans (Shani, van de Ven, & Zeelenberg, 2012). Shani et al. (2012) suggest this may be a form of emotion regulation based on how well a person thinks he or she can handle the negative information. While this delay in searching for information may effectively regulate negative emotions, it can be costly when the information is needed at a specific point in a planning process. This may be particularly true early in planning when it is important to identify key causes and restrictions in the organization or broader environment. Along related lines, positive emotional states may influence selective information acquisition. Acquiring confirmatory information for a preferred approach is a common planning error (Dörner & Schaub, 1994) that could be exacerbated by the unwillingness to disrupt a positive mood.

Information Processing and Identification of Causes and Restrictions

Goldin and Hayes-Roth (1980) and Mumford et al. (2001) note that plans are more successful when potential opportunities and restrictions are considered during planning. This involves carefully considering the relevance and value of information about key causal factors as well as limitations or constraints in the environment that a plan must take into account. Causes and restrictions are often identified during information search and case selection, although estimating the extent to which these are important to a new plan relies on additional information processing.

There are numerous studies examining the influence of positive affect on information processing (see Isen, 2000, 2008 for reviews). People experiencing positive affect tend to rely on less-effortful information processing, drawing on general knowledge and heuristics, more so than people experiencing negative affect (Bodenhausen et al., 1994; Forgas, 1998; Mackie & Worth, 1989). However, these impairments occur when task engagement is low, when the task does not seem personally relevant, or when accountability for task outcomes is low (Isen, 2008). Positive affect also facilitates flexible categorization of information through its effect on the ability to make more connections among similar items and see more differences in dissimilar items compared to people in neutral moods (Isen et al., 1987; Isen, Rosenzweig, & Young, 1991; Murray, Sujan, Hirt, & Sujan, 1990). This is essential for understanding the relevance of the causes and restrictions operating in planning case exemplars to new plans. The broaden-and-build theory of positive emotions reinterprets and extends this data by proposing that positive emotions broaden the range of thoughts and action tendencies, building intellectual, social, and other resources (Fredrickson, 2001). Positive emotional states and their associated types of broadening may be temporary, however, while the resources acquired during those states are more lasting. In terms of planning, the intellectual resources (e.g. willingness to explore new ideas and think creatively) and social resources (e.g. establishing effective relationships and workplace collaborations) are most applicable.

Negative emotional states also have advantages and disadvantages when it comes to information processing. General negative affect has been shown to result in effortful information processing that is careful and systematic (Bless & Schwarz, 1999). However, research on discrete negative emotions such as fear, anger, and sadness reveals different styles of information processing that are consistent with the motivations and appraisals associated with each emotion. For example, DeSteno, Petty, Rucker, Wegener, and Braverman (2004) found that different negative emotional states (sadness, anger) made people more sensitive to information matching that emotion.

Anger is a highly arousing negative emotion arising from perceived offense to oneself (or a person one cares about) that motivates people to remove obstacles to goal attainment (Lazarus, 1991). Appraisal patterns associated with anger include high certainty regarding the obstacle, high control (over outcomes), and other-responsibility (someone else caused the event) (Smith & Ellsworth, 1985). Lerner and Tiedens's (2006) review showed that anger activates heuristic processing (more stereotypic judgments, use of common scripts from memory, reliance on superficial cues vs. argument quality), results in overly optimistic risk assessments, and results in attributions of blame to individuals rather than the situation. Thiel, Connelly, and Griffith (2012) found that leader displays of anger led subordinates to feel angry and subsequently identify fewer opportunities and restrictions on a planning task compared to leaders who displayed pessimism. This kind of angry state may be deleterious to accurately identifying key causes and restrictions for planning purposes.

Alternatively, sadness is a negative, moderately arousing emotion with appraisals of high situational control and moderate uncertainty. This emotion has shown a number of effects that could facilitate the depth and accuracy of information processing, such as increased attention to new information, resistance to fundamental attribution errors when making assessments of people, and persisting longer on cognitive tasks (Forgas, 2013).

Fear, like anger, is a high-arousal, negative emotion but shows different patterns on other appraisal dimensions. High uncertainty and low control tends to result in more careful, systematic processing to lessen the uncertainty, higher perceptions of risk, and pessimistic judgments (Lerner & Keltner, 2001). Depending on the planning situation, this information processing style could be helpful (e.g. when an organization needs to have a relatively safe, risk-averse plan) because many relevant causes and restrictions are likely to be identified. Fear could also be detrimental if an organization wants to diversify, change, or otherwise pursue new directions.

Initial Template and Plan Generation

Constructing a plan template provides a starting point for developing a more elaborate plan. The goals, case exemplars, and other information gathered so far feed into the specification of a plan or future action sequences that will be used to direct organizational activity. This is an inherently creative activity requiring divergent thinking and idea generation, both of which have been shown to be influenced by affective states. As mentioned previously, when the task is motivating, positive affect contributes to flexible thinking, cognitive variation, openness to new information, and novel associations that facilitate divergent thinking and creative problem-solving (Amabile, Barsade, Mueller, & Staw, 2005; Fredrickson, 2001; Isen & Baron, 1991; Isen et al., 1987). Being in a positive mood may be particularly helpful when developing an initial plan template, where making connections across cases and coming up with new ideas is essential. Meta-analytic findings by Baas, De Dreu, and Nijstad (2008) further showed that positive moods resulted in more creativity than neutral moods and about the same level as negative moods.

Indeed, a number of studies have shown benefits of negative mood and specific emotions to creative thought. For example, Kaufmann and Vosburg (2002) demonstrated that while positive affect contributed to idea generation in the early phase of a timed idea-production task, negative affect was more beneficial later on, when task constraints were greater. Another study conducted in an organizational setting found that naturally occurring negative moods at work were associated with greater effort and the generation of more novel, useful ideas than positive moods when two boundary conditions were present: (1) when people were clear about their mood state and (2) when they thought the organization rewarded and supported creative efforts (George & Zhou, 2002). Some scholars have suggested that more research is needed into the role of discrete emotions and creativity, given their distinctive motivational properties, appraisal tendencies, and implications for regulatory focus (Baas, De Dreu, & Nijstad, 2008; Lench, Flores, & Bench, 2011; Rank & Frese, 2008).

Forecasting and Idea Evaluation

Once a plan has been generated, Mumford et al. (2001) suggest that projecting the likely success of the plan or forecasting is an important part of planning. This involves mentally simulating the implementation of a plan, thinking about the ways in which it might go right or wrong and the likelihood of each. Forecasting may lead to anticipating goal blockages and associated emotional reactions. Given their informational value with respect to goals, emotional reactions can bring a greater awareness and salience to the need to change or revise plans, identify contingencies, and create backup plans. While emotions have not been directly studied in relation to forecasting, judgment and decision-making literature has linked emotions to idea evaluation and risk assessment. Plan forecasts involve assessing the viability of ideas and their likelihood of success as well as the risks associated with the proposed sequence of activities.

Research on economic decision making suggests that decisions or choices about future actions are influenced not only by the assessment of positive/negative consequences and their likelihood of occurring but by the emotions we expect to feel in response to the consequences. Isen and Patrick (1983) demonstrated that positive affect (vs. neutral) generated more optimism about the likelihood of good outcomes, but less willingness to take risks to achieve those outcomes. The risk-as-feelings hypothesis suggests that emotional and cognitive reactions to anticipated consequences may result in different choices and that preferences regarding risky choices may be more influenced by emotions than cognitive evaluations (Loewenstein, Weber, Hsee, & Welch, 2001). Emotions are sensitive to the vividness of potential outcomes and how soon those outcomes will occur, so short-term forecasts and plans may be more susceptible to emotion influences than longer-term ones. Lerner and Keltner (2001) demonstrated differential influences of fear and anger on optimism about future risks and risk-seeking choices. People experiencing anger engaged in more optimistic assessments about the likelihood of negative future events occurring and made more risky choices than people experiencing fear. Additionally, anger triggers a desire to evaluate others' ideas, but those evaluations are more negative than warranted, especially for lower quality ideas (Wiltermuth & Tiedens, 2011). Given the heuristic nature of processing that is associated with anger, evaluating one's own ideas while angry may not be beneficial either.

Anticipated regret about future outcomes may also influence the forecasting process. Regret is the feeling that things might have been better if we had taken a different course of action or made a different decision (Zeelenberg, 1999). Anticipated regret during forecasting has the potential to make risk-taking more likely or less likely, depending on which option elicits the most anticipated regret. Anticipated regret has more influence when there are a number of possible good options, when the negative consequences for a decision will occur quickly, and when the decision is irreversible (Zeelenberg, 1999).

When forecasts indicate that a plan or parts of a plan are unlikely to work out, they can lead to disappointment. Van Dijk and Van Harreveld (2008) identified different responses to disappointment and reducing the dissonance it causes. Response-focused regulation of disappointment involves identifying the lessons learned regarding the shortcomings of the potential outcomes and changing the plan. Mumford and colleagues' (2002) planning model assumes that planners will attend to projected negative consequences and will refine the plan accordingly. However, cognitive reappraisals to reduce disappointment may also occur, leading to discounting the negative aspects of the forecast as unimportant, or comparing the negative outcome to worse outcomes not likely to occur. As a result, the plan might not be appropriately altered. Dörner and Schaub (1994) noted that discounting negative consequences was a common planning error. Thus, reappraising forecasting information to curb the feelings associated with a disappointing forecast may only justify a low quality plan.

Awareness of one's own emotions and the impact they have on thought processes as well as interactions with those around us must also be considered in ascertaining emotional influences on planning. We turn now to a discussion of the social side of planning.

Emotions and Social Aspects of Planning

Work in organizations is often completed by groups or teams of people (Kozlowski & Bell, 2003). This may be especially true for complex, multifaceted projects where expertise from different areas within the organization is required. While plans for small projects can be completed by individuals, plans for large-scope efforts are likely to be developed by one or more groups of people. In additional to considering the individual-level effects that emotion states can have, groups and teams must also take into account group processes susceptible to affective influences, processes that ultimately could impact planning performance.

There has been much research on the social effects of emotions in dyadic and group settings (e.g. Barsade & Gibson, 2007, 2012; Keltner & Haidt, 1999). Emotions convey information about people's emotions, beliefs, and intentions, and about the surrounding environment to those experiencing the emotion and those observing it (Keltner & Haidt, 1999; Schwarz, 2011). Group affective states can arise from top-down influences such as the affective context or overall affective culture of the group, and also from bottom-up influences or the sum of the individual affective states of group members (Ashkanasy & Humphrey, 2011; Kelly & Barsade, 2001). Affective context comprises group and organizational norms about appropriate emotional displays, as well as the prior emotional history of the group. Emotional displays by individuals generate affective responses in other group members by triggering reciprocal emotions (e.g. sympathy in response to sadness) or through mood contagion (Hatfield, Cacioppo, & Rapson, 1993), where positive or negative emotions "spread" from one person to another through unconscious mimicry of facial expressions, posture, vocal cues, and other emotional displays. Explicit affective processes also operate in work-group contexts when emotional displays are deliberate and aimed at managing impressions or achieving specific purposes (Barsade & Gibson, 2007; Liu, Liu, & Wu, 2012). Positive emotions have been shown to increase liking and cooperation, lessen conflict, and increase perceptions of task performance, while the opposite is true of negative emotions (Fredrickson, 2001; Kelly & Barsade 2001). However, negative emotional displays may be helpful in groups engaged in planning activities when groupthink is occurring or there is a need to challenge current thinking (Schwenk, 1990). Additionally, authentic negative emotional displays by group members can serve signaling functions when one or more group members is dissatisfied with the content or quality of a plan or the pace at which it is being developed.

Extending Schwarz's (1990) mood-as-information theory, Van Kleef (2008, 2009) proposed the emotions as social information (EASI) model, which suggests that emotional displays provide information to observers and can influence their behavior through two routes: inferential and affective. Observers make inferences about emotional displays which provide information on the current state of events. The nature of those inferences will impact later behavior. For example, if a member of a planning group gives low quality work to group members for review and they convey disappointment after reading it, the member may infer that the work does not meet group standards, prompting him or her to redo it or work harder on the next part of the project. However, a second route through which emotional displays can influence behavior is through affective reactions. The member who submitted the shoddy work could feel embarrassed or ashamed that she or he let the group members down and may withdraw from the group to avoid the situation. Alternatively, the group member could feel guilty and respond by apologizing to the group and correcting the work. Van Kleef (2009) makes the point that the inferential and affective routes of influence sometimes motivate similar behavioral responses, but often motivate different behavioral responses. The reactions, affective experiences, and behavior occurring in response to emotional displays in dyads and groups have implications for group processes (e.g. cohesion and conflict) and activities (e.g. feedback and negotiation) likely to be important when planning occurs in groups.

Emotions, Group Cohesion, and Conflict

Group cohesion, or member attraction to the group (Evans & Jarvis, 1980), has been conceptualized and studied as a multi-dimensional construct encompassing task cohesion (shared commitment to the group's task) and interpersonal cohesion (liking of the group), with both types being positively associated with group performance (Kozlowski & Bell, 2003). When groups experience disagreements and conflict, these can be categorized as task-based or relationship-based (De Dreu & Weingart, 2003) as well as process-based conflicts (Jehn, Greer, Levine, & Szulanski, 2008). Findings regarding the influence of different types of conflict on performance have been mixed. Prior research suggested that task conflict is beneficial because it highlights problems with the work that need to be addressed, whereas relational conflict is detrimental because it interferes with group interpersonal communication and coordination (Jehn, 1995, 1997). However, a meta-analysis by De Dreu and Weingart (2003) showed that both task and relational conflict had negative impacts on performance, although the relationship was smaller when task and relational conflict were minimally correlated and the task was simple. Given the complexity of planning tasks, it appears that both types of conflict could be harmful for planning performance in group settings. More recently, Jehn et al. (2008) found that task, relationship, and process conflict decreased positive group states such as cohesion and that the negative emotions associated with relationship conflict made this effect much worse. Lower cohesion was also related to lower perceptions of group viability. Other research has shown that relationship conflict led to lower perceptions of group cohesion and higher levels of group anger compared to task conflict (Griffith, Connelly, & Thiel, 2014).

Considering others' reactions to a plan has been proposed as an important part of urban planning (Hoch, 2006). Hoch notes the importance of emotions in the attention, perception, and reflective aspects of planning, suggesting that people need to anticipate others' emotional responses to various phases of planning. How will particular individuals within and outside of the planning group react to the plan? Will they feel challenged or threatened by the plan? How can those reactions be mitigated, either through changes to the plan design, or through arguments and justifications as to why this is a good way to proceed?

Emotions and Feedback

Another social aspect of planning occurs when feedback is provided to individuals and groups as they progress with planning activities. Many factors influence the effectiveness of feedback, including emotional states (Kluger & DeNisi, 1996). Some research has suggested that it is important for affective states to match the valence of the feedback in order to be perceived as useful (Newcombe & Ashkanasy, 2002). Providing negative feedback with positive emotion was not well received in that study. In line with the motivational states associated with different discrete emotions discussed earlier, there is also some evidence suggesting that negative emotions are generated by negative feedback, but the effectiveness of the response to feedback depends on the specific negative emotion triggered. A study by Gaddis, Connelly, and Mumford (2004) indicated that leader displays of anger during negative feedback to groups led the groups to perform worse after the feedback, potentially because group resources were used to cope with the emotional arousal or to retaliate rather than to improve task work. More recently, Johnson and Connelly (2014) found that when negative feedback was accompanied by anger, recipients felt angry in return and engaged in less social reparative behavior with co-workers and the leader. However, when negative feedback was conveyed with disappointment, this evoked feelings of guilt in recipients, who sought to make amends. Guilt mediated the relationship of disappointment displays to quality of post-feedback performance.

Emotions can also influence the likelihood of feedback occurring at all. Kiefer (2002) found that human resource managers experiencing fear in response to a merger were more reluctant to criticize or give feedback that might help to improve organizational plans for change. While fear and the associated appraisal mindset may be conducive to evaluating solutions at an individual level, it can hamper the willingness to communicate evaluative information to others.

Emotions and Negotiation

Negotiation is commonly thought of with respect to formal bargaining settings. However, more informal kinds of negotiation occur regularly in work-group settings over group member roles and responsibilities, different approaches to projects and tasks, assigning credit for contributions to the work, and others. Findings in the literature on emotions and negotiation suggests that fewer concessions are made to opponents displaying happiness (compared to angry and even neutral opponents), while more concessions are made to an opponent displaying anger, although this is moderated by the recipient's low level of power and few alternative courses of action (Van Kleef, De Dreu, & Manstead, 2004; Van Kleef, De Dreu, Pietroni, & Manstead, 2006). More concessions are also made to negotiators who display negative emotions such as disappointment and anger compared to guilt or regret, but these effects are moderated by the conceder's level of trust and competitiveness (there were no differences in concessions when trust was low and competitiveness was high) (Van Kleef, De Dreu, & Manstead, 2004, 2006). These authors highlight that while some negative emotions produce greater gains in the short term, these emotional displays may have longer-term negative consequences on the ability to maintain relationships and willingness to negotiate in the future.

Emotion Regulation and Planning

The variety of influences that affective and emotional states have on motivational, cognitive, and social aspects of planning gives rise to an important question about emotion regulation. When and how should individuals and groups regulate their emotions? While there is no straightforward answer to this question, a variety of regulation strategies have been identified and researched.

Emotion regulation involves "the set of processes whereby people seek to redirect the spontaneous flow of emotions" (Koole, 2009, p. 6). This could involve increasing, decreasing, or keeping stable positive and negative emotional states. Extensive research and theorizing on emotion regulation suggests that people are capable of influencing what emotions they have, when those emotions occur, how emotional experiences unfold, and how emotions are expressed (Gross, 1999). Regulation processes may be deliberate and conscious, but can also be implicit and automatic (Mauss, Bunge, & Gross, 2007), and have varying degrees of success. One well-established model of emotion regulation identifies a number of regulation strategies related to response tendencies at different points during the emotional experience (Gross, 1998, 1999). This response-tendency model specifies antecedent-focused strategies, used before an emotional reaction has fully unfolded, and response-focused strategies, used after an emotion has been elicited. Multiple emotion regulation strategies are sometimes operating at the same time, and regulation can start and stop at any point during the emotional experience. Antecedent strategies include situation selection (entering or avoiding situations to manage emotional states), situation modification (changing the situation in specific ways to manage emotions), attentional deployment (shifting one's focus away from the emotional aspects of the situation), and cognitive construal (reappraising the situation in a different way to alter one's emotional response). Response-focused strategies (breathing, suppressing emotional behavior) influence physiological, experiential, or behavioral responses once an emotion has unfolded. Regulation strategies can also be categorized by the functions they serve, for example, to achieve ideal hedonic states (usually more positive and less negative due to the resource demands of negative states), to achieve specific goals, and to facilitate both stability and flexibility in personality functioning (Koole, 2009).

Empirical work has revealed the efficacy and consequences of various regulation strategies, with particular emphasis on cognitive reappraisal and suppression. Suppressing emotional reactions effectively decreases their expression but not the emotional experience or feelings. Additionally, suppression has negative effects on stress and cortisol levels, which can be detrimental to well-being over time (Thiruchselvam, Blechert, Sheppes, Rydstrom, & Gross, 2011; Levenson, 1994), and can impair memory for emotional events (Gross, 2002). Reappraising the meaning of the situation, or one's emotional response to it, effectively regulates emotional experience and expression and does not impact memory (Gross, 2002). Gross and John (2003) demonstrated that suppression but not reappraisal is negatively related with interpersonal functioning. More extensive reviews of available empirical evidence suggest that strategies involving attentional deployment and person-focused response strategies such as breathing and mindfulness have positive regulatory and well-being outcomes (Koole, 2009).

In the context of planning, several key considerations are important with respect to regulating emotions. First, because different affective and discrete emotional states can facilitate or inhibit different cognitive and social processes involved in planning, gaining a better understanding of these relationships is important for knowing when to regulate emotions. Relatedly, awareness of specific emotional states in oneself and others also informs decisions about which ones to regulate and when. Third, regulation of emotional states when working autonomously on planning activities should consider affective influences on cognitive processes more heavily, while working in groups should consider affective influences on interpersonal and group processes. Finally, in selecting explicit regulation strategies, ease of use, costs to memory and cognitive resources, and longer-term well-being are important to bear in mind.

Conclusions and Future Directions

Emotions appear to have substantial relevance to planning activities in terms of their motivational, cognitive, and social implications. From a motivational perspective, emotional states are tied up with self-regulatory focus and have the potential to initiate planning activities or to urge people to avoid them. Positive and negative emotional states can result in different types of planning goals, leading to alternative pathways for developing effective plans. More research is needed on the nature and size of effects that discrete emotional states might have on the choice to engage in planning or not and how much effort to put forth.

The research on emotions and cognition suggests that general affect as well as discrete emotions are likely to influence cognitive processes at the very heart of individual planning efforts. Whether these emotional states will be beneficial depends in large part on what cognitive processes are relied on most heavily at a particular point in planning. One thing is certain: a variety of positive and negative emotional states have the potential to improve planning processes. Given some of the subconscious ways in which emotions influence decisions, an interesting area for extending the research here is to identify emotional influences on decisions and processes involved in generating backup plans or revising existing plans.

In considering the social side of organizational planning, we identified mechanisms through which affect and discrete emotions can influence general group processes such as mood contagion and the affective culture of the group. Positive emotional states are more likely than negative ones to foster positive interpersonal interactions and build interpersonal cohesion. Interpersonal conflict, and the negative emotions that accompany it, has few if any benefits for group cohesion and performance. However, negative emotions accompanying task conflict could be beneficial for solving problems with planning tasks. Feedback and negotiation are discussed as two examples of group activities likely to accompany group planning efforts, and different discrete emotions have different effects on the goals these activities serve (i.e. providing information to improve the work and negotiating planning approaches, project roles, resource use, and other aspects of the work). Group processes beyond those discussed here, such as shared mental models and transactive memory, may be influenced by emotions and emotion processes and could be fruitful areas for further study. We hope this review stimulates further thinking and research into emotion-based influences on organizational planning.

References

Amabile, T. M., Barsade, S. G., Mueller, J. S., & Staw, B. M. (2005). Affect and creativity at work. *Administrative Science Quarterly*, 50(3), 367–403. doi:10.2189/asqu.2005.50.3.367

Ashkanasy, N. M., & Humphrey, R. H. (2011). Current emotion research in organizational behavior. *Emotion Review*, 3(2), 214–224.

Baas, M., De Dreu, C. W., & Nijstad, B. A. (2008). A meta-analysis of 25 years of mood-creativity research: Hedonic tone, activation, or regulatory focus? *Psychological Bulletin*, 134(6), 779–806. doi:10.1037/a0012815

Baas, M., De Dreu, C. W., & Nijstad, B. A. (2011). When prevention promotes creativity: The role of mood, regulatory focus, and regulatory closure. *Journal of Personality and Social Psychology*, 100(5), 794–809. doi:10.1037/a0022981

Barsade, S. G., & Gibson, D. E. (2007). Why does affect matter in organizations? *The Academy of Management Perspectives*, 21(1), 36–59. doi:10.5465/AMP.2007.24286163

Barsade, S. G., & Gibson, D. E. (2012). Group affect: Its influence on individual and group outcomes. *Current Directions in Psychological Science*, 21(2), 119–123. doi:10.1177/0963721412438352

Berger, R. M., Guilford, J. P., & Christensen, P. R. (1957). A factor-analytic study of planning abilities. *Psychological Monographs: General and Applied*, 71(6), 1–31. doi:10.1037/h0093704

Berntsen, D. (2002). Tunnel memories for autobiographical events: Central details are remembered more frequently from shocking than from happy experiences. *Memory and Cognition*, 30, 1010–1020. doi.org/10.3758/BF03194319

Bless, H., & Schwarz, N. (1999). Sufficient and necessary conditions in dual-mode models: The case of mood and information processing. In S. Chaiken, Y. Trope (Eds.), *Dual-process theories in social psychology* (pp. 423–440). New York: Guilford Press.

Bodenhausen, G. V., Kramer, G. P., & Süsser, K. (1994). Happiness and stereotypic thinking in social judgment. *Journal of Personality and Social Psychology*, 66(4), 621–632. doi:10.1037/0022-3514.66.4.621

Brockner, J., & Higgins, E. (2001). Regulatory focus theory: Implications for the study of emotions at work. *Organizational Behavior and Human Decision Processes*, 86(1), 35–66. doi:10.1006/obhd.2001.2972

Buck, R. (1985). Prime theory: An integrated view of motivation and emotion. *Psychological Review*, 92(3), 389–413. doi:10.1037/0033-295X.92.3.389

Buck, R. (1988). *Human motivation and emotion* (2nd ed.). Oxford, UK: John Wiley & Sons.

Cacioppo, J. T., Gardner, W. L., & Berntson, G. G. (1999). The affect system has parallel and integrative processing components: Form follows function. *Journal of Personality and Social Psychology*, 76(5), 839–855. doi:10.1037/0022-3514.76.5.839

Carver, C. S. (2006). Approach, avoidance, and the self-regulation of affect and action. *Motivation and Emotion*, 30(2), 105–110. doi:10.1007/s11031-006-9044-7

Carver, C. S., & Scheier, M. F. (1981). *Attention and self-regulation: A control theory approach to human behavior.* New York: Springer-Verlag.

Clore, G. L., Gasper, K., & Garvin, E. (2001). Affect as information. In J. P. Forgas (Ed.), *Handbook of affect and social cognition* (pp. 121–144). Mahwah, NJ: Erlbaum.

Cron, W. L., Slocum, J. W., Vande Walle, D., & Fu, F. Q. (2005). The role of goal orientation on negative emotions and goal setting when initial performance falls short of one's performance goal. *Human Performance*, 18(1), 55–80. doi:10.1207/s15327043hup1801_3

Damasio, A. R. (1994). *Descartes' error: Emotion, reason, and the human brain.* New York: Avon Books.

De Dreu, C. W., & Weingart, L. R. (2003). Task versus relationship conflict, team performance, and team member satisfaction: A meta-analysis. *Journal of Applied Psychology*, 88(4), 741–749. doi:10.1037/0021-9010.88.4.741

DeSteno, D., Petty, R. E., Rucker, D. D., Wegener, D. T., & Braverman, J. (2004). Discrete emotions and persuasion: The role of emotion-induced expectancies. *Journal of Personality and Social Psychology*, 86(1), 43–56. doi:10.1037/0022-3514.86.1.43

Dolcos, F., LaBar, K. S., & Cabeza, R. (2004). Interaction between the amygdala and the medial temporal lobe memory system predicts better memory for emotional events. *Neuron*, 42, 855–863.

Dörner, D., & Schaub, H. (1994). Errors in planning and decision-making and the nature of human information processing. *Applied Psychology: An International Review*, 43(4), 433–453. doi:10.1111/j.1464-0597.1994.tb00839.x

Evans, C. R., & Jarvis, P. A. (1980). Group cohesion: A review and re-evaluation. *Small Group Behavior*, 11, 359–370.

Feldman Barrett, L., & Russell, J. A. (1998). Independence and bipolarity in the structure of current affect. *Journal of Personality and Social Psychology*, 74(4), 967–984. doi, 10.1037/0022-3514.76.5.805

Fitness, J. (2008). Fear and loathing in the workplace. In N. M. Ashkanasy & C. L. Cooper (Eds.), *Research companion to emotion in organizations* (pp. 61–72). Northampton, MA: Edward Elgar.

Forgas, J. P. (1998). On being happy and mistaken: Mood effects on the fundamental attribution error. *Journal of Personality and Social Psychology*, 75(2), 318–331. doi:10.1037/0022-3514.75.2.318

Forgas, J. P. (2013). Don't worry, be sad! On the cognitive, motivational, and interpersonal benefits of negative mood. *Current Directions in Psychological Science*, 22(3), 225–232.12

Forgas, J. P., Laham, S. M., & Vargas, P. T. (2005). Mood effects on eyewitness memory: Affective influences on susceptibility to misinformation. *Journal of Experimental Social Psychology*, 41(6), 574–588. doi:10.1016/j.jesp.2004.11.005

Fredrickson, B. L. (2001). The role of positive emotions in positive psychology: The broaden-and-build theory of positive emotions. *American Psychologist*, 56(3), 218–226. doi:10.1037/0003-066X.56.3.218

Frijda, N. H. (1988). The laws of emotion. *American Psychologist*, 43(5), 349–358. doi:10.1037/0003-066X.43.5.349

Frijda, N. H. (2007). *The laws of emotion.* Mahwah, NJ: Lawrence Erlbaum.

Frijda, N. H. (2009). Emotion experience and its varieties. *Emotion Review*, 1(3), 264–271. doi:10.1177/1754073909103595

Gaddis, B., Connelly, S., & Mumford, M. D. (2004). Failure feedback as an affective event: Influences of leader affect on subordinate attitudes and performance. *The Leadership Quarterly*, 15(5), 663–686. doi:10.1016/j.leaqua.2004.05.011

George, J. M., & Zhou, J. (2002). Understanding when bad moods foster creativity and good ones don't: The role of context and clarity of feelings. *Journal of Applied Psychology*, 87(4), 687–697. doi:10.1037/0021-9010.87.4.687

Goldin, S. E., & Hayes-Roth, B. (1980). *Individual differences in planning processes*. Santa Monica, CA: Rand Corp.

Gollwitzer, P. M. (1993). Goal achievement: The role of intentions. In W. Stroebe & M. Hewstone (Eds.), *European review of social psychology* (Vol. 4, pp. 141–185). Chichester, UK: Wiley.

Gray, J. A. (1994a). Personality dimensions and emotion systems. In P. Ekman & R. J. Davidson (Eds.), *The nature of emotion: Fundamental questions* (pp. 329–331). New York: Oxford University Press.

Gray, J. A. (1994b). Three fundamental emotion systems. In P. Ekman & R. J. Davidson (Eds.), *The nature of emotion: Fundamental questions* (pp. 243–247). New York: Oxford University Press.

Griffith, J. A., Connelly, S., & Thiel, C. E. (2014). Emotion regulation and intragroup conflict: When more distracted minds prevail. *International Journal of Conflict Management*, 25(2), 148–170. doi:10.1108/IJCMA-04-2012-0036

Gross, J. J. (1998). The emerging field of emotion regulation: An integrative review. *Review of General Psychology*, 2(3), 271–299. doi:10.1037/1089-2680.2.3.271

Gross, J. J. (1999). Emotion regulation: Past, present, future. *Cognition and Emotion*, 13(5), 551–573. doi:10.1080/026999399379186

Gross, J. J. (2002). Emotion regulation: Affective, cognitive, and social consequences. *Psychophysiology*, 39(3), 281–291. doi:10.1017/S0048577201393198

Gross, J. J., & John, O. P. (2003). Individual differences in two emotion regulation processes: Implications for affect, relationships, and well-being. *Journal of Personality and Social Psychology*, 85(2), 348–362. doi:10.1037/0022-3514.85.2.348

Hamann, S. B., Ely, T. D., Grafton, S. T., & Kilts, C. D. (1999). Amygdala activity related to enhanced memory for pleasant and aversive stimuli. *Nature Neuroscience*, 2(3), 289–293. doi:10.1038/6404

Hammond, K. J. (1990). Case-based planning: A framework for planning from experience. *Cognitive Science*, 14(3), 385–443. doi:10.1207/s15516709cog1403_3

Hatfield, E., Cacioppo, J. T., & Rapson, R. L. (1993). Emotional contagion. *Current Directions in Psychological Science*, 2(3), 96–99. doi:10.1111/1467-8721.ep10770953

Hayes-Roth, B., & Hayes-Roth, F. (1979). A cognitive model of planning. *Cognitive Science*, 3(4), 275–310. doi:10.1207/s15516709cog0304_1

Higgins, E. T. (1998). Promotion and prevention: Regulatory focus as a motivational principle. *Advances in Experimental Social Psychology*, 30, 1–46. doi.org/10.1016/S0065-2601(08)60381-0

Hoch, C. (2006). Emotions and planning. *Planning Theory & Practice*, 7(4), 367–382. doi.org/10.1080/14649350600984436

Hudson, J. M., Christensen, J., Kellogg, W. A., & Erickson, T. (2002). I'd be overwhelmed, but it's just one more thing to do: Availability and interruption in research management. In *Proceedings of the SIGCHI Conference on Human factors in computing systems* (pp. 97–104). ACM.

Idson, L., Liberman, N., & Higgins, E. (2000). Distinguishing gains from nonlosses and losses from non-gains: A regulatory focus perspective on hedonic intensity. *Journal of Experimental Social Psychology*, 36(3), 252–274. doi:10.1006/jesp.1999.1402

Isen, A. (1993). Positive affect and decision making. In M. Lewis & J. Haviland (Eds.), *Handbook of Emotion* (pp. 261–277). New York: Guilford Press.

Isen, A. M. (2000). Positive affect and decision making. In M. Lewis & J. M. Haviland-Jones (Eds.), *Handbook of emotions* (2nd ed., pp. 417–435). New York: Guilford Press.

Isen, A. M. (2008). Some ways in which positive affect influences decision making and problem solving. In M. Lewis, J. M. Haviland-Jones, & L. Barrett (Eds.), *Handbook of emotions* (3rd ed., pp. 548–573). New York: Guilford Press.

Isen, A. M., & Baron, R. A. (1991). Positive affect as a factor in organizational behavior. In L. L. Cummings & B. M. Staw (Eds.), *Research in organizational behavior* (Vol. 13, pp. 1–53). Greenwich, CT: JAI Press.

Isen, A. M., & Patrick, R. (1983). The effect of positive feelings on risk taking: When the chips are down. *Organizational Behavior & Human Performance*, 31(2), 194–202. doi:10.1016/0030-5073(83)90120-4

Isen, A. M., Daubman, K. A., & Nowicki, G. P. (1987). Positive affect facilitates creative problem solving. *Journal of Personality and Social Psychology*, 52(6), 1122–1131. doi:10.1037/0022-3514.52.6.1122

Isen, A. M., Rosenzweig, A. S., & Young, M. J. (1991). The influence of positive affect on clinical problem solving. *Medical Decision Making*, 11, 221–227.

Jehn, K. A. (1995). A multimethod examination of the benefits and detriments of intragroup conflict. *Administrative Science Quarterly*, 40(2), 256–282. doi:10.2307/2393638

Jehn, K. A. (1997). Affective and cognitive conflict in work groups: Increasing performance through value-based intragroup conflict. In C. W. De Dreu, & E. Van de Vliert (Eds.), *Using conflict in organizations* (pp. 87–100). Thousand Oaks, CA: Sage.

Jehn, K. A., Greer, L., Levine, S., & Szulanski, G. (2008). The effects of conflict types, dimensions, and emergent states on group outcomes. *Group Decision and Negotiation*, 17(6), 465–495. doi:10.1007/s10726-008-9107-0

Johnson, G., & Connelly, S. (2014). Negative emotions in informal feedback: The benefits of disappointment and drawbacks of anger. *Human Relations*, 67(10), 1265–1290.

Kanfer, R., & Stubblebine, P. C. (2008). Affect and work motivation. In N. M. Ashkanasy & C. L. Cooper (Eds.), *Research companion to emotion in organizations* (pp. 170–182). Northampton, MA: Edward Elgar.

Kaufmann, G., & Vosburg, S. K. (2002). The effects of mood on early and late idea production. *Creativity Research Journal*, 14(3–4), 317–330. doi:10.1207/S15326934CRJ1434_3

Kelly, J. R., & Barsade, S. G. (2001). Mood and emotions in small groups and work teams. *Organizational Behavior and Human Decision Processes*, 86(1), 99–130. doi:10.1006/obhd.2001.2974

Keltner, D., & Haidt, J. (1999). Social functions of emotions at four levels of analysis. *Cognition & Emotion*, 13(5), 505–521.

Kensinger, E. A., & Corkin, S. (2004). Two routes to emotional memory: Distinct neural processes for valence and arousal. *Proceedings of the National Academy of Sciences of the USA*, 101, 3310–3315. doi.org/10.1073/pnas.0306408101

Kensinger, E. A., & Schacter, D. L. (2008). Memory and emotion. In M. Lewis, J. M. Haviland-Jones, & L. Barrett (Eds.), *Handbook of emotions* (3rd ed., pp. 601–617). New York: Guilford Press.

Kiefer, T. (2002). Analyzing emotions for a better understanding of organizational change: Fear, joy, and anger during a merger. In N. M. Ashkanasy, W. J. Zerbe, & C. E. J. Härtel (Eds.), *Managing emotions in the workplace* (pp. 45–69). London: M. E. Sharpe.

Kluger, A. N., & DeNisi, A. (1996). The effects of feedback interventions on performance: A historical review, a meta-analysis, and a preliminary feedback intervention theory. *Psychological Bulletin*, 119(2), 254–284. doi:10.1037/0033-2909.119.2.254

Koole, S. L. (2009). The psychology of emotion regulation: An integrative review. *Cognition & Emotion*, 23(1), 4–41. doi:10.1080/02699930802619031

Kozlowski, S. J., & Bell, B. S. (2003). Work groups and teams in organizations. In W. C. Borman, D. R. Ilgen, & R. J. Klimoski (Eds.), *Handbook of psychology: Industrial and organizational psychology* (Vol. 12, pp. 333–375). Hoboken, NJ: John Wiley & Sons.

Kreitler, H., & Kreitler, S. (1972). The model of cognitive orientation: Towards a theory of human behaviour. *British Journal of Psychology*, 63(1), 9–30. doi.org/10.1111/j.2044-8295.1972.tb02079.x

Lazarus, R. S. (1991). Cognition and motivation in emotion. *American Psychologist*, 46(4), 352–367. doi:10.10 37/0003-066X.46.4.352

Lench, H. C., Flores, S. A., & Bench, S. W. (2011). Discrete emotions predict changes in cognition, judgment, experience, behavior, and physiology: A meta-analysis of experimental emotion elicitations. *Psychological Bulletin*, 137(5), 834–855.

Lerner, J. S., & Keltner, D. (2000). Beyond valence: Toward a model of emotion-specific influences on judgment and choice. *Cognition and Emotion*, 14(4), 473–493. doi:10.1080/026999300402763

Lerner, J. S., & Keltner, D. (2001). Fear, anger, and risk. *Journal of Personality and Social Psychology*, 81(1), 146–159. doi:10.1037/0022-3514.81.1.146

Lerner, J. S., & Tiedens, L. Z. (2006). Portrait of the angry decision maker: How appraisal tendencies shape anger's influence on cognition. *Journal of Behavioral Decision Making*, 19(2), 115–137. doi:10.1002/bdm.515

Levenson, R. W. (1994). Emotional control: Variation and consequences. In P. Ekman & R. J. Davidson (Eds.), *The nature of emotion: Fundamental questions* (pp. 273–279). New York: Oxford University Press.

Levine, L. J., & Pizarro, D. A. (2004). Emotion and memory research: A grumpy overview. *Social Cognition*, 22(5), 530–554. doi:10.1521/soco.22.5.530.50767

Liu, Y., Liu, J., & Wu, L. (2012). Strategic emotional display: an examination of its interpersonal and career outcomes. *Career Development International*, 17(6), 518–536. doi.org/10.1108/13620431211280114

Loewenstein, G. F., Weber, E. U., Hsee, C. K., & Welch, N. (2001). Risk as feelings. *Psychological Bulletin*, 127(2), 267–286. doi:10.1037/0033-2909.127.2.267

Mackie, D. M., & Worth, L. T. (1989). Processing deficits and the mediation of positive affect in persuasion. *Journal of Personality and Social Psychology*, 57(1), 27–40. doi:10.1037/0022-3514.57.1.27

Mauss, I. B., Bunge, S. A., & Gross, J. J. (2007). Automatic emotion regulation. *Social and Personality Psychology Compass*, 1(1), 146–167. doi:10.1111/j.1751-9004.2007.00005.

Mumford, M. D., Schultz, R. A., & Osburn, H. K. (2002). Planning in organizations: Performance as a multi-level phenomenon. In F. J. Yammarino & F. Dansereau (Eds.), *The many faces of multi-level issues* (pp. 3–65). New York: Elsevier Science/JAI Press. doi:10.1016/S1475-9144(02)01026-3

Mumford, M. D., Schultz, R. A., & Van Doorn, J. R. (2001). Performance in planning: Processes, requirements, and errors. *Review of General Psychology*, 5(3), 213–240. doi:10.1037/1089-2680.5.3.213

Murray, N., Sujan, H., Hirt, E. R., & Sujan, M. (1990). The influence of mood on categorization: A cognitive flexibility interpretation. *Journal of Personality and Social Psychology*, 59(3), 411–425. doi:10.1037/0022-3514.59.3.411

Newcombe, M. J., & Ashkanasy, N. M. (2002). The role of affect and affective congruence in perceptions of leaders: An experimental study. *The Leadership Quarterly*, 13(5), 601–614. doi:10.1016/S1048-9843(02)00146-7

Rank, J., & Frese, M. (2008). The impact of emotions, moods and other affect-related variables on creativity, innovation and initiative. In N. M. Ashkanasy, & C. L. Cooper (Eds.), *Research companion to emotion in organizations* (pp. 103–119). Northampton, MA: Edward Elgar.

Richardson, M. P., Strange, B. A., & Dolan, R. J. (2004). Encoding of emotional memories depends on amygdala and hippocampus and their interactions. *Nature Neuroscience*, 7, 278–285.

Rick, S., & Loewenstein, G. (2008). The role of emotion in economic behavior. In M. Lewis, J. M. Haviland-Jones, L. Barrett (Eds.), *Handbook of emotions* (3rd ed., pp. 138–156). New York: Guilford Press.

Roseman, I. J. (1991). Appraisal determinants of discrete emotions. *Cognition and Emotion*, 5(3), 161–200. doi:10.1080/02699939108411034

Roseman, I. J., Spindel, M. S., & Jose, P. E. (1990). Appraisals of emotion-eliciting events: Testing a theory of discrete emotions. *Journal of Personality and Social Psychology*, 59(5), 899–915. doi:10.1037/0022-3514.59.5.899

Russell, J. A., & Feldman Barrett, L. (1999). Core affect, prototypical emotional episodes, and other things called emotion: Dissecting the elephant. *Journal of Personality and Social Psychology*, 76(5), 805–819. doi:10.1037/0022-3514.76.5.805

Schaller, M., & Cialdini, R. B. (1990). Happiness, sadness, and helping: A motivational integration. In E. Higgins & R. M. Sorrentino (Eds.), *Handbook of motivation and cognition: Foundations of social behavior* (Vol. 2, pp. 265–296). New York: Guilford Press.

Schwarz, N. (1990). Feelings as information: Informational and motivational functions of affective states. In E. T. Higgins & R. Sorrentino (Eds.), *Handbook of motivation and cognition: Foundations of social behavior* (Vol. 2, pp. 527–561). New York: Guilford Press.

Schwarz, N. (2011). Feelings-as-information theory. *Handbook of theories of social psychology*, 1, 289–308.

Schwarz, N., & Bless, H. (1991). Happy and mindless, but sad and smart? The impact of affective states on analytic reasoning. In J. P. Forgas (Ed.), *Emotion and social judgments* (pp. 55–71). Elmsford, NY: Pergamon Press.

Schwenk, C. R. (1990). Effects of devil's advocacy and dialectical inquiry on decision making: A meta-analysis. *Organizational Behavior and Human Decision Processes*, 47(1), 161–176. doi:10.1016/0749-5978(90)90051-A

Seo, M. G., Barrett, L. F., & Bartunek, J. M. (2004). The role of affective experience in work motivation. *Academy of Management Review*, 29, 423–439.

Seo, M., Barrett, L., & Jin, S. (2008). The structure of affect: History, theory, and implications for emotion research in organizations. In N. M. Ashkanasy, C. L. Cooper (Eds.), *Research companion to emotion in organizations* (pp. 17–44). Northampton, MA: Edward Elgar.

Shani, Y., & Zeelenberg, M. (2007). When and why do we want to know? How experienced regret promotes post-decision information search. *Journal of Behavioral Decision Making*, 20(3), 207–222. doi:10.1002/bdm.550

Shani, Y., & Zeelenberg, M. (2012). Post-decisional information search: Balancing the pains of suspecting the worst with the comforts of knowing the worst. *Social Influence*, 7(3), 193–210. doi:10.1080/15534510.2012.679219

Shani, Y., van de Ven, N., & Zeelenberg, M. (2012). Delaying information search. *Judgment and Decision Making*, 7(6), 750–760.

Smith, C. A., & Ellsworth, P. C. (1985). Patterns of cognitive appraisal in emotion. *Journal of Personality and Social Psychology*, 48(4), 813–838. doi:10.1037/0022-3514.48.4.813

Storbeck, J., & Clore, G. L. (2011). Affect influences false memories at encoding: Evidence from recognition data. *Emotion*, 11(4), 981–989. doi:10.1037/a0022754

Sy, T., Côté, S., & Saavedra, R. (2005). The contagious leader: Impact of the leader's mood on the mood of group members, group affective tone, and group processes. *Journal of Applied Psychology*, 90(2), 295–305. doi:10.1037/0021-9010.90.2.295

Thiel, C. E., Connelly, S., & Griffith, J. A. (2012). Leadership and emotion management for complex tasks: Different emotions, different strategies. *The Leadership Quarterly*, 23(3), 517–533. doi:10.1016/j.leaqua.2011.12.005

Thiruchselvam, R., Blechert, J., Sheppes, G., Rydstrom, A., & Gross, J. J. (2011). The temporal dynamics of emotion regulation: An EEG study of distraction and reappraisal. *Biological Psychology*, 87(1), 84–92. doi:10.1016/j.biopsycho.2011.02.009

Tiedens, L. Z., & Linton, S. (2001). Judgment under emotional certainty and uncertainty: The effects of specific emotions on information processing. *Journal of Personality and Social Psychology*, 81(6), 973–988. doi:10.1037/0022-3514.81.6.973

Van Dijk, W., & Van Harreveld, F. (2008). Disappointment and regret. In N. M. Ashkanasy, & C. L. Cooper (Eds.), *Research companion to emotion in organizations* (pp. 90–102). Northampton, MA, US: Edward Elgar Publishing.

Van Kleef, G. A. (2008). Emotion in conflict and negotiation: Introducing the emotions as social information (EASI) model. In N. M. Ashkanasy, & C. L. Cooper (Eds.), *Research companion to emotion in organizations* (pp. 392–404). Northampton, MA: Edward Elgar.

Van Kleef, G. A. (2009). How emotions regulate social life: The emotions as social information (EASI) model. *Current Directions in Psychological Science*, 18(3), 184–188.

Van Kleef, G. A., De Dreu, C. W., & Manstead, A. R. (2004). The interpersonal effects of anger and happiness in negotiations. *Journal of Personality and Social Psychology*, 86(1), 57–76. doi:10.1037/0022-3514.86.1.57

Van Kleef, G. A., De Dreu, C. W., & Manstead, A. R. (2006). Supplication and appeasement in conflict and negotiation: The interpersonal effects of disappointment, worry, guilt, and regret. *Journal of Personality and Social Psychology*, 91(1), 124–142. doi:10.1037/0022-3514.91.1.124

Van Kleef, G. A., De Dreu, C. W., Pietroni, D., & Manstead, A. R. (2006). Power and emotion in negotiation: Power moderates the interpersonal effects of anger and happiness on concession making. *European Journal of Social Psychology*, 36(4), 557–581. doi:10.1002/ejsp.320

Watson, D., & Tellegen, A. (1985). Toward a consensual structure of mood. *Psychological Bulletin*, 98(2), 219–235. doi:10.1037/0033-2909.98.2.219

Wegener, D. T., & Petty, R. E. (1994). Mood management across affective states: The hedonic contingency hypothesis. *Journal of Personality and Social Psychology*, 66(6), 1034–1048. doi:10.1037/0022-3514.66.6.1034

Wiltermuth, S. S., & Tiedens, L. Z. (2011). Incidental anger and the desire to evaluate. *Organizational Behavior and Human Decision Processes*, 116(1), 55–65. doi:10.1016/j.obhdp.2011.03.007

Xiao, Y., Milgram, P., & Doyle, D. J. (1997). Planning behavior and its functional role in interactions with complex systems. *IEEE Transactions on Systems, Man, and Cybernetics*, 27, 313–325.

Zeelenberg, M. (1999). Anticipated regret, expected feedback and behavioral decision making. *Journal of Behavioral Decision Making*, 12(2), 93–106. doi:10.1002/(SICI)1099-0771(199906)12:2<93::AID-BDM311>3.0.CO;2-S

Zeelenberg, M., & Pieters, R. (2006). Feeling is for doing: A pragmatic approach to the study of emotions in economic behavior. In D. De Cremer, M. Zeelenberg, & J. Murnighan (Eds.), *Social psychology and economics* (pp. 117–137). Mahwah, NJ: Lawrence Erlbaum.

Zeelenberg, M., Nelissen, R. A., Breugelmans, S. M., & Pieters, R. (2008). On emotion specificity in decision making: Why feeling is for doing. *Judgment and Decision Making*, 3(1), 18–27.

7

PLANNING HIGH PERFORMANCE

Can Groups and Teams Benefit from Implementation Intentions?

J. Lukas Thürmer, Frank Wieber, and Peter M. Gollwitzer

> Es ist nicht genug zu wissen, man muss auch anwenden; es ist nicht genug zu wollen, man muss auch tun.
> (Knowing does not suffice, one has to apply it; willing does not suffice, one has to act.)
> *J. W. von Goethe,* Wilhelm Meisters Wanderjahre

Challenging organizational goals such as meeting high sales targets, becoming highly consumer-friendly, or "going green" can only be attained if employees change their behavior successfully. Unfortunately, even when employees readily adopt organizational goals, they frequently fail to act on them. Holland, Aarts, and Langendam (2006) observed employees' recycling behavior after their company had introduced a convincing "go green" initiative, including appeals to recycle plastic cups and paper waste. Despite the company's persuasive appeals, employees did not increase their recycling behavior one week, two weeks, and one month after the baseline measure. However, participants in an experimental condition who had been asked to additionally plan out when, where, and how they wanted to recycle paper waste and plastic cups (i.e. had formed an *implementation intention*, Gollwitzer, 1993, 1999), increased their recycling behavior and recycled almost all of their waste. Implementation-intention participants even maintained their high levels of recycling behavior one week, two weeks, and one month later.

At the level of the individual, implementation intention effects have been observed for numerous types of goals (e.g. health goals, Adriaanse, Vinkers, De Ridder, Hox, & De Wit, 2011; profit goals, Kirk, Gollwitzer, & Carnevale, 2011; emotion regulation goals, Webb, Schweiger Gallo, Miles, Gollwitzer, & Sheeran, 2012) and with various populations (e.g. company employees, Holland et al., 2006; undergraduate students, Hagger et al., 2012; and even drug addicts under withdrawal, Brandstätter, Lengfelder, & Gollwitzer, 2001), and the processes underlying their effectiveness are quite well understood (see Gollwitzer & Oettingen, 2011; Gollwitzer & Sheeran, 2006, for review and meta-analysis). In the present chapter, we therefore ask whether organizations can effectively use implementation intentions to attain their goals. As teams nowadays commonly perform work in organizations (West, 2012), we will focus on the use of implementation intentions in groups and organizational teams. Although performance groups are sometimes distinguished from organizational teams, this distinction can be blurry at times and they seem to have much in common (Kerr & Tindale, 2004). We therefore use the terms interchangeably throughout the chapter but will consider potential differences in the discussion. We will first connect the concepts of planning and goal pursuit, then introduce implementation intentions, and discuss how groups and teams can use this highly effective type of plan with special regard to the level of planning within groups (i.e. group plans vs. individual plans). We will then report our most recent research on these questions. Lastly, we will discuss how our approach relates to other planning research, how teams in organizational settings might profit from our findings, and why we are confident that they will.

The Role of Planning in Goal Pursuit

McGrath (1984) defines planning as the activity "to lay out a course of action by which it can attain an *already chosen* objective" (p. 127, emphasis added). Planning is therefore concerned with the implementation of a set goal (i.e. that one is already committed to attaining). Why is planning important with respect to goal attainment? Lewin's psychology of action (Lewin, Dembo, Festinger, & Sears, 1944; see Frese & Zapf, 1994; Hacker, 2003, for the action approach in organizations) assumes that one has to master two subsequent tasks in order to attain one's goals: strongly committing to goals and successfully implementing them. In line with the assumption that committing strongly to goals is not sufficient to actually attain them, setting goals accounts for no more than 28 percent of the variance in goal-directed behavior (Sheeran, 2002).

More recent research suggests that four hindrances most commonly prevent people from implementing their goals (Gollwitzer & Sheeran, 2006): people may fail to get started with acting, fail to stay on track once goal striving has been started, overly deplete their resources during goal striving, thereby making the pursuit of equally important current goals impossible, and lastly, people may fail to disengage from futile means or unattainable goals. Unsatisfactory intention-behavior relations point to the fact that mere goals are not sufficient to deal with these hindrances but that planning out how to strive for one's goal might be necessary. Indeed, one type of plan has been shown to be highly effective in improving goal attainment and performance by helping people to overcome the aforementioned hindrances: implementation intentions.

Planning with Implementation Intentions

Gollwitzer (1999, 2014) highlighted the importance of furnishing goals (also referred to as goal intentions) with implementation intentions. Goal intentions specify a desired endstate or response one is committed to attaining or performing (e.g. "*I want to attain endstate Z!*" or "*I want to perform response Z!*"); in contrast, implementation intentions specify when, where, and how one wants to act towards an already set goal in an if (situation)–then (response) format (e.g. *And if situation Y occurs, then I will show response Z!*). To form an implementation intention, one therefore has to identify a goal-relevant situational cue (such as a good opportunity or a critical obstacle) and link it to an instrumental response (such as a goal-directed response in an opportune situation or a coping response to an obstacle). Implementation intentions are always formed in addition to goals and are therefore considered to be subordinate plans. Research over the past 20 years has consistently supported the assumption that forming implementation intentions improves goal attainment (see Adriaanse et al., 2011; Bélanger-Gravel, Godin, & Amireault, 2013; Gollwitzer & Oettingen, 2011; Gollwitzer & Sheeran, 2006, for review and meta-analyses).

How do the beneficial effects of implementation intentions come about? Action control by mere goals relies on effortfully initiating goal-directed responses in appropriate situations (Gollwitzer, 1993). As this is a deliberative process, it is prone to disruption by external factors (e.g. distractions). Action control by implementation intentions, on the other hand, facilitates goal attainment on the basis of *psychological mechanisms* related to the if-part and the then-part of the plan: first, the situation specified in the if-part becomes cognitively activated and is thus easily accessible from memory (e.g. Achtziger, Bayer, & Gollwitzer, 2012; Parks-Stamm, Gollwitzer, & Oettingen, 2007; Webb & Sheeran, 2007; Wieber & Sassenberg, 2006). Second, the response specified in the then-part is linked to the situation specified in the if-part (Webb & Sheeran, 2007). This situation–response link allows for swift response initiation once the specified situation is encountered (e.g. Parks-Stamm et al., 2007; Webb & Sheeran, 2007) without requiring another conscious intent (Bayer, Achtziger, Gollwitzer, & Moskowitz, 2009). Some studies have even demonstrated that the accessibility of the situational cue in the if-part and the strength of the if (situation)–then (response) link mediate the performance increases caused by implementation intentions (Webb & Sheeran, 2007, 2008). In effect, if–then planners immediately recognize the specified situational cue (accessibility of the if-part) and respond swiftly with the specified response (if–then link).

Action control by implementation intentions is assumed to possess features of automaticity (e.g. immediacy, efficiency, redundancy of conscious intent; cf. Bargh & Chartrand, 2000). Indeed, numerous studies indicate that if–then planners respond more swiftly (Gollwitzer & Brandstätter, 1997, Study 3), deal more effectively with high cognitive demands (e.g. act on their goals even when under cognitive load; Brandstätter et al., 2001; Cohen & Gollwitzer, 2008), and do not require a conscious intent to initiate the pre-planned response when encountering the specified situational cue (e.g. respond even if the situational cue is presented subliminally, Bayer et al., 2009; or the superordinate goal has been activated outside of their awareness, Sheeran, Webb, & Gollwitzer, 2005, Study 2). Importantly, the automaticity created by implementation intentions is strategic in the sense that it is based on an act of will: if–then planners intentionally form an implementation intention and thereby allow the situational cue (if-part) to trigger the goal-directed response (then-part). In other words, if–then planners delegate their action control to an external situational cue. Furthermore, implementation intentions do not run off if one abandons one's goal or the plan itself. In line with this claim, implementation intention effects require sufficient commitment to their superordinate goal (Sheeran et al., 2005, Study 1) and to the execution of the implementation intention (Achtziger et al., 2012). Overall, action control by implementation intentions possesses features of automaticity (i.e. is efficient and immediate, and does not require a conscious intent to respond), and is strategic, since willful decisions (i.e. the selection of an opportune situation and an instrumental response, commitment to the plan and the goal) put their automatic effects into place.

Implementation intentions help deal with all four of the aforementioned hindrances to goal striving (i.e. getting started, staying on track, not overextending oneself, and abandoning futile goals). Implementation intentions help to get started with goal striving because they help seize good opportunities before they pass (e.g. obtaining mammography, Rutter, Steadman, & Quine, 2006), help remember to act (e.g. taking vitamin pills regularly, Sheeran & Orbell, 1999), and help initiate actions despite initial reluctance (e.g. to perform unpleasant testicular self-examination, Sheeran, Milne, Webb, & Gollwitzer, 2005). Many important goals cannot be achieved with a single response or action, however. Therefore, even successfully initiated goal striving is jeopardized if staying on track fails. Fortunately, implementation intentions can help to stay on track with goal striving as well. In line with this claim, implementation intentions have been shown to protect ongoing goal striving against inferences from inside (e.g. Achtziger, Gollwitzer, & Sheeran, 2008) and outside the person (e.g. Wieber, von Suchodoletz, Heikamp, Trommsdorff, & Gollwitzer, 2011). Importantly, even when inferences cannot be anticipated, furnishing goals with implementation intentions specifying a goal-directed action can stabilize ongoing goal striving and thereby make it less prone to disruptions (Bayer, Gollwitzer, & Achtziger, 2010). Implementation intentions further allow for automated goal striving that does not require high levels of deliberation and the self should therefore not become depleted (Muraven & Baumeister, 2000). Indeed, participants with an implementation intention performing taxing tasks in classic ego-depletion paradigms did not show reduced self-regulation capacity in subsequent tasks (Webb & Sheeran, 2003) and performed well even when in a state of depletion (Bayer et al., 2010, Study 2). Lastly, implementation intentions help disengage from futile goals (Wieber, Thürmer, & Gollwitzer, in press) or means (Henderson, Gollwitzer, & Oettingen, 2007). All in all, implementation intentions help overcome the most common hindrances to goal attainment. Given these well-established, beneficial effects of implementation intentions for individuals, one might wonder whether if–then planning can promote group performance.

Implementation Intentions in Groups and Teams

Why would groups need implementation intentions? Group performance is commonly defined as "the process and outcome of members' joint efforts to attain a collective goal" (Levine & Moreland, 1990, p. 612). Improving group performance is therefore synonymous with improving a task group's goal attainment. As we have argued elsewhere (Wieber, Thürmer, & Gollwitzer, 2012, 2013), groups also face hindrances during goal striving that implementation intentions should help overcome. Whenever groups face such hindrances, having planned out goal striving in advance with respective implementation intentions should thus help to improve group performance.

But how can groups and teams form implementation intentions? In order to address this question, we will now briefly introduce our perspective on what groups are and how they perform tasks. Groups have no *bodily existence* beyond their members. That is, one can shake hands with a group member but not with a group per se. In order to explain the reality of the group, small group theories and team theories (e.g. Arrow, McGrath, & Berdahl, 2000; DeShon, Kozlowski, Schmidt, Milner, & Wiechmann, 2004) commonly draw on the interdependence of group members. Through their members' relation to and interaction with each other, groups produce outcomes and attain properties that are not easily attributed to any individual alone within the given group (e.g. cognitive products, Levine, Resnick, & Higgins, 1993). On the other hand, individuals within groups still maintain a certain degree of independence, which allows the group to be distinguished from the individual member. One can therefore distinguish between the individual level (group members) and the group level (group); groups are therefore said to be multi-level systems (Arrow et al., 2000; DeShon et al., 2004).

The fact that groups have no bodily existence raises the question of how groups can perform tasks. The combination of contributions framework (Hinsz & Ladbury, 2012; Steiner, 1972) assumes that individuals contribute by performing actions required for the task at hand, and the group then combines these contributions into the group's performance. In line with this perspective, collective actions can be conceptualized as individuals' (group members') intentional contributions to a group performance that the group combines into its performance. However, a group-as-system perspective assumes that individuals are embedded within groups (Arrow et al., 2000). This suggests that group members maintain a certain degree of independence and that they do not have to act collectively (e.g. with respect to contributing to a group performance) but can also act independently (e.g. with respect to their individual performance which may or might not aid group performance; cf. Crown & Rosse, 1995).

Assuming that individuals in groups can act individually and collectively, they should also be capable of planning these actions individually or collectively. This distinction raises the question of how individual and collective planning can be distinguished. Groups and teams allow for a variety of planning techniques that individuals alone do not have, such as developing plans conjointly (Burkert, Scholz, Gralla, Roigas, & Knoll, 2011), using skilled leaders to plan group performance (Marta, Leritz, & Mumford, 2005), and planning for actions that are performed conjointly (Prestwich et al., 2012). However, including such techniques into the definition of collective planning risks confounding planning with other constructs. For instance, defining collective planning as a joint process necessitates group interaction and sharedness, which are both known to improve performance (e.g. Marks, Zaccaro, & Mathieu, 2000; Mathieu, Heffner, Goodwin, Salas, & Cannon-Bowers, 2000). Similarly, if collective planning can only include actions that are performed conjointly, its effectiveness might be limited simply because some actions are better performed individually. From a basic research approach that seeks to isolate the sole effect of a variable (in this case: collective planning), these shortcomings are quite unsatisfactory. Consequently, we do not make assumptions about the source of the plan or how widely it is shared, but define collective planning parsimoniously as *a plan referring to the group*. Thus, collective plans refer to the group (e.g. we, us, ours; a "we-plan") and individual plans refer to the individual (e.g. I, me, mine; an "I-plan").

As implementation intentions traditionally refer to the individual (e.g. "*And if* I *encounter situation* Y, *then* I *will show response* Z!"), this individual–collective distinction suggests a new type of plan that refers to the group: *collective implementation intentions* (cIIs; e.g. "*And if* we *encounter situation* Y, *then* we *will show response* Z!"). Such "we-plans" or cIIs refer to the group and specify when, where, and how the group wants to act towards their collective goal. Because group members can pursue collective goals (e.g. Weldon & Weingart, 1993) and implementation intentions were also observed to improve goal striving in groups and in social contexts (Wieber et al., 2012, 2013), forming cIIs should create a situation–response link that aids collective goal striving. When group members have the goal to perform well and pre-plan when, where, and how to act or respond towards this goal collectively (i.e. form a cII), this should help them master the challenges of collective goal striving. When groups successfully integrate these contributions, this improves performance.

Teamwork and Taskwork

In order to ask how IIs and cIIs can help groups and teams perform well, it is helpful to understand what constitutes high performance. A common distinction is that between teamwork and taskwork (Marks, Mathieu, & Zaccaro, 2001). Taskwork is commonly defined as "a team's interactions with tasks, tools, machines, and systems" (Bowers, Braun, & Morgan, 1997, p. 90). Taskwork thus constitutes group members' actions that are directly related to task performance. But working side by side without interacting with one another is seldom enough to attain high team performance – in other words, teamwork is needed. Teamwork entails effective team interaction processes (Marks et al., 2001), that is, "members' interdependent acts that convert inputs to outcomes through cognitive, verbal, and behavioral activities directed toward organizing taskwork to attain collective goals" (Marks et al., 2001, p. 357). High performance therefore needs both taskwork and teamwork (Crawford & Lepine, 2013). If implementation intentions were to aid high performance, they would therefore prove effective for improving both taskwork and teamwork.

Empirical Evidence: Planning Teamwork with Implementation Intentions

What can implementation intentions do for teamwork? Interactions between team members are crucial for high performance (e.g. Marks et al., 2000; Mathieu et al., 2000) but are resource-intense as they require listening carefully, controlling one's emotions, and developing social interaction scripts. In line with the idea that teamwork is a resource-intense process that is difficult to master, Crawford and Lepine (2013) recently noted that "inherent in each of the teamwork processes is a communication requirement of additional time, attention, and energy from each team member, beyond attention that must be dedicated to taskwork" (p. 37). As discussed earlier, the benefits of planning with implementation intentions include a perceptual readiness for the specified situation and a situation response-link that leads to swift response initiation (Parks-Stamm et al., 2007; Webb

& Sheeran, 2007; Wieber & Sassenberg, 2006). Implementation intentions thereby strategically automate goal striving, which makes it efficient (e.g. one shows the pre-planned response when preoccupied with something else; Cohen & Gollwitzer, 2008). We consequently hypothesized that forming implementation intentions can support interaction and teamwork, thereby leading to group performance improvements.

Teamwork and Cooperative IIs

Cooperation crucially depends on the individual group member and therefore IIs geared towards cooperative teamwork should improve group performance. Even when cooperation is beneficial in terms of superior work results and performance, it is still more laborious than acting individually (Crawford & Lepine, 2013). This is because cooperation requires acting with other team members and therefore is more difficult to initiate than individual work. Implementation intentions are known to help initiate time-sensitive actions, such as going to vote on election day (Nickerson & Rogers, 2010), or easily forgotten actions, such as recycling disposable cups and paper waste (Holland et al., 2006). Moreover, implementation intentions also help to deal with disruptions, as they spell out how to act towards one's goal (Bayer et al., 2010). Both initiating responses at the right time (e.g. when a teammate is available) and shielding these actions against disruptions (e.g. talking about the task at hand instead of the game last night) should promote teamwork. Planning out how to cooperate in advance with IIs should therefore support group performance.

In order to test this hypothesis, Wieber and colleagues (Wieber, Gollwitzer, Fäsche, Heikamp, & Trommsdorff, 2015) conducted an experiment with ten-year-old schoolchildren who had been in one class for about three years. They invited groups of four to perform a cooperative puzzle task. Each participant received a number of puzzle pieces, some of which he or she was allowed to add to the puzzle (individual pieces, 1 point), but others which had to be handed over to a teammate before being added to the puzzle (cooperative pieces, 3 points). All groups learned the rules that cooperative pieces had to be handed to the respective teammate but that these pieces were also worth more points. Before performing the task, all groups formed the goal, "I want to score as many points with my group as possible!", but only experimental groups added the II: "And if I see a cooperative part, then I will give it to the appropriate child immediately!" In line with the prediction that this if (situation)-then (response) link improves teamwork, II groups scored more points overall and more cooperative points in particular. IIs geared towards handing over respective pieces thus indeed improved the cooperative behavior of group members; as handing over a puzzle piece cannot be performed independently (i.e. the respective teammate has to accept and add the piece), these findings support the idea that IIs can increase cooperation.

Teamwork and Cooperative cIIs

Cooperation is a group-based process and therefore should also be supported by collective planning with cIIs. Although little research has examined collective planning with cIIs to date, we assume that cIIs – just as IIs – create a situation–response link that aids goal striving. If this is true, cIIs that specify a cooperative behavior should also support effective teamwork. Effective teamwork is difficult when common practice or a routine cannot be applied to a problem at hand. Indeed, although group decisions are highly informed when group members capitalize on their unique knowledge (*unshared information*; Lu, Yuan, & McLeod, 2012; Mesmer-Magnus & DeChurch, 2009), groups routinely disregard such information – even if it comes up during discussions (Gigone & Hastie, 1993, 1997; Mojzisch, Grouneva, & Schulz-Hardt, 2010; Mojzisch & Schulz-Hardt, 2010) – and instead rely on their common knowledge (i.e. shared information; Wittenbaum & Park, 2001).

When unshared information is crucial to identifying the best decision alternative (i.e. in *hidden profile* situations; review by Stasser & Titus, 2003), this routine of ignoring unshared information leads groups to make suboptimal decisions and squander their performance potential. IIs are known to help break routines (Aarts, Dijksterhuis, & Midden, 1999) and can trigger deliberation about a certain issue when needed (Henderson et al., 2007). Since we assume that cIIs rely on similar processes to IIs, we predicted that cIIs to jointly reflect on available information should promote the consideration of crucial, unshared information during group discussions and improve group decisions in hidden profile situations.

We (Thürmer, Wieber, & Gollwitzer, 2015b, Study 2) tested this prediction in a laboratory experiment. Groups of three students formed the goal to make the best decision possible in several consecutive decision cases and we incentivized this goal by promising a monetary reward for each correct decision. Groups randomly assigned to a cII condition added the collective if (situation)-then (response) plan: "And when we finally take the decision sheet to note our preferred alternative, then we will go over the advantages of the non-preferred alternatives again." To ensure that the expected differences in decision quality were not due to different knowledge of the task, control participants added the same response strategies but without the situation–response link: "We will go over the advantages of the non-preferred alternatives again." Groups then worked on three hidden profile decision tasks. For each task, group members first received individual information pointing to a suboptimal decision alternative. After studying their material, groups gathered and discussed which alternative to choose. At the end of their discussion, groups marked their preferred alternative on a decision sheet. To analyze the discussion content, we recorded the group discussions. In line with prior research, solving the hidden profile decision cases was very difficult: Only about 6 percent of the cases were solved. However, comparing both experimental conditions showed that none of the control groups solved any of the hidden profiles, but about a third of the cII groups solved at least one case. Thus, the cII did indeed improve group decisions. Since only the entire group can identify the best alternative in hidden profile situations, this finding supports the assumption that cIIs can support teamwork. Indeed, when looking at the discussion content, cII groups jointly recapitulated more crucial information as they had pre-planned. In sum, this study demonstrates that cIIs geared toward improving group interaction indeed improve teamwork and lead to better group decisions.

Teamwork and Non-Cooperative cIIs

One might wonder whether an implementation intention always has to spell out how to cooperate in order to improve group interaction and teamwork. As discussed earlier, groups perform tasks through their members' contributions and we therefore conceptualized collective goal striving as one's willful contribution to a group performance. Collective goal striving should consequently be a cooperative process by nature. Indeed, with respect to goal setting, research (van Mierlo & Kleingeld, 2010) has found that group members with collective goals use more cooperative task strategies than group members with individual goals. If cIIs indeed support collective goal striving, they should therefore support cooperation such as verbal interaction between group members, even if they do not specify these behaviors explicitly.

To test this assumption, interdependent physical persistence tasks (e.g. lifting a weight together, Köhler, 1926; see Kerr & Hertel, 2011, for a review) are well suited. Such tasks can be performed cooperatively (e.g. with more verbal interaction) but also more individually (e.g. with less verbal interaction). Therefore, the difference between individual and collective goal striving should become apparent in naturally occurring verbal interaction. We (Thürmer, Wieber, & Gollwitzer, submitted-b, Studies 1 & 2) tested this hypothesis in two small group laboratory experiments with a well-established persistence task (adapted from Bray, 2004) that allowed for but did not necessitate verbal interaction. Groups all formed the goal to perform well and performed a baseline persistence round. Before the second, experimental, round, all groups received a plan with strategies that are known to help deal with detrimental states (Thürmer, McCrea, & Gollwitzer, 2013; Wieber et al., 2011) such as muscle pain. II groups received the individual if–then plan "And if my muscles hurt, then I will ignore the pain and tell myself: I can do it"; cII groups received the same if–then plan but with collective phrasing: "And if our muscles hurt, then we will ignore the pain and tell ourselves: We can do it"; and control groups received the same information in an individual or collective phrasing but not in an if–then format. Besides performance (task persistence), we analyzed verbal group interaction. As expected, both the II and the cII improved performance in comparison to the respective control group without an if–then plan. This supports the assumption that individual and collective goal striving are possible in groups, and that both types of goal striving can be supported by respective if–then plans. However, groups which had formed a cII communicated more than II groups, as indicated by the number of words spoken during task performance. Moreover, cII groups referred more to the group (first-person plural pronouns used, cf. Pennebaker, Mehl, & Niederhoffer, 2003) but II group members referred more to themselves (first-person singular pronouns used). This pattern of results suggests that both IIs and cIIs can support performance in interdependent persistence tasks but that they do so in different ways: while IIs support individual goal striving with little and self-referred interaction, cIIs support collective goal striving with more and group-referred interaction.

However, in this first experiment verbal interaction was only measured, which makes causal inferences difficult. To clarify the causal direction of our findings, we ran another experiment in which we manipulated the task communication. Our reasoning was as follows: if cIIs support collective goal striving, they should lead to better performance when the task is better suited to collective goal striving (e.g. encourages verbal interaction). On the other hand, if IIs indeed support individual goal striving, they should lead to better performance when the task is better suited to individual goal striving (e.g. prevents verbal interaction). In a replication of the first persistence study, we therefore manipulated whether group members were encouraged to communicate or were prevented from communicating. As predicted, the cII led to better performance when participants were encouraged to communicate (e.g. faced each other and wore a headset around their neck) and the II led to better performance when participants were prevented from communicating (e.g. looked away from each other and wore a headset on their ears). Both experiments are therefore in line with the assumption that IIs support individual goal striving, that cIIs support collective goal striving, and that both types of implementation intentions can support group performance. These findings moreover suggest that cIIs support teamwork even when they do not address cooperative behavior directly.

In sum, implementation intentions proved to be quite effective in improving teamwork behaviors. Both IIs and cIIs tailored towards cooperative behaviors were effective in promoting teamwork. Moreover, even when cIIs did not specify cooperative behaviors, they led to more teamwork, as indicated by increased interaction. This suggests that one should plan for tasks that require teamwork with respect to one's group – either by planning collectively or by specifying cooperative behaviors. Implementation intentions thus offer a variety of possibilities to support teamwork.

Empirical Evidence: Planning Taskwork with Implementation Intentions

High performance not only requires teamwork but also taskwork. Whereas teamwork is about how teams interact with each other in order to coordinate their actions, taskwork concerns what teams are doing or producing (Marks et al., 2001). Taskwork thus comprises "a team's interactions with tasks, tools, machines, and systems" (Bowers et al., 1997, p. 90). At times, teamwork and taskwork can be difficult to distinguish (Marks et al, 2001): when does task-related action end, and where does coordinating interaction begin? However, given the definition of teamwork as interdependent acts, it should be less likely to occur when interaction between group members is limited. Therefore, in addition to measuring task variables, we limited interaction during performance for this second set of studies concerned with taskwork.

While the effectiveness of IIs without interaction is well known, no studies have tested this in cIIs yet. This raises the question whether cIIs are also effective when group interaction is limited. One of the observed benefits of cIIs concerning teamwork is that they support group interaction. One might therefore argue that cIIs specifying performance-enhancing responses will only be enacted with the group members. However, we hypothesized that cIIs still draw on intra-individual processes (i.e. group members' ability to regulate their behavior willfully). Therefore, cIIs should improve performance even when interaction is limited during task performance.

Taskwork without Interaction

We first sought to test whether cIIs work in interacting groups when interaction is limited during planning and task performance. If the formation and execution of cIIs solely rely on group interaction, no effect is to be expected. On the other hand, if cIIs do indeed rely on intra-individual processes (i.e. the heightened availability of the if-situation and the formation of an if–then link), we should observe cII effects despite such limited interaction. To test this assumption, we used an idea-generation task. In idea generation, a collectivist norm is detrimental (Goncalo & Staw, 2006) because it entails viewing oneself as interdependently connected with others (Bechtoldt, Choi, & Nijstad, 2012). As argued earlier, we also assume that collective goal striving entails acting interdependently and we therefore hypothesized that collective goals would be detrimental to idea generation. A cII to come up with new ideas immediately, on the other hand, should automate goal striving and therefore improve idea-generation performance. This should be the case even when interaction is limited during task performance.

We (Thürmer, Wieber, & Gollwitzer, 2015a, Study 1) tested this prediction in a laboratory experiment. We first created strong and meaningful group memberships by having group members interact and leading them to believe that they had a common future. Multiple student participants talked to each other (e.g. came up with a common group name related to their goal to be creative) and learned that they would perform an interesting and creative task (develop a movie script) or a boring and less creative task (develop a financial plan for a movie) depending on their group performance in a creativity test. However, the following creativity test containing the independent measures and dependent measures was performed fully independently, that is, without interaction (see Weingart & Weldon, 1991, for a similar approach). Participants were then asked to form a plan for the following creativity test. This is where we manipulated the referent and the implementation intention factors. Plans either referred to the individual (I) or to the group (we); implementation intention participants received the if–then plan: "And when I (we) press ENTER, then I (we) will immediately start thinking about a new idea!" (cII phrasing in parentheses). Control participants received similar instructions, but without the if–then link. All participants then generated uses for a common object (a knife). In line with earlier findings showing that it is difficult to perform creativity tasks collectively (e.g. Goncalo & Staw, 2006), collective goal striving was less successful than individual goal striving. Participants who set goals and plans with a collective referent (we) generated fewer ideas from fewer semantic categories than participants who set goals and plans with an individual referent (I). However, the cII increased performance and led to the generation of as many ideas from as many semantic categories as individual goals and plans. Since group members were not allowed to interact during task performance, this finding is in line with our assumption that cIIs also rely on intra-individual processes. The II did not increase performance further, which might indicate that generating ideas individually was a fun and easy task (Stroebe, Nijstad, & Rietzschel, 2010) that did not require if–then planning to be performed successfully.

Taskwork without Interaction in Representation of the Group

One might wonder whether cIIs can also improve goal striving when no group interaction occurs during goal striving. It might be, for instance, that cIIs require group members to interact just before plan formation in order to commit to the plan successfully. Similarly, one might argue that group members all have to execute the plan, even if they do not interact with each other, because a single group member will not be committed to execute the necessary responses independently. On the other hand, we predict that cIIs rely on intra-individual processes that run even if group members are not present during any of these stages and do not perform the same task. Therefore, cIIs should be effective even when a group member acts in representation of his or her group (e.g. in *disjunctive tasks*, Steiner, 1972) without the other group members. A task that is commonly performed by a single individual for his or her group is grocery shopping (e.g. for the family, Polegato & Zaichkowsky, 1994). Unplanned purchases (impulse shopping) are very common in this setting (Park, Iyer, & Smith, 1989) and impulse purchases are likely when group norms favor impulse shopping (Luo, 2005). However, even when impulse shopping norms favor unplanned purchases, cIIs to take only what one needs should automate goal striving and help one stick to one's shopping list.

To test this prediction, we (Thürmer, Wieber, & Gollwitzer, submitted-a, Study 2) established two different group memberships – one with a detrimental norm and one with a supportive norm. Qualitative and quantitative pretesting showed that students belong to their peer group (i.e. friends from home) and their fellow student group (i.e. friends from university), that both groups are important, but that they have different norms when it comes to shopping: while peers have an indulgence norm and support impulse shopping (see also Luo, 2005), fellow students do not have such a norm and instead prefer being frugal. In the first part of the main experiment, student participants read a text describing either typical student activities (e.g. meeting at a friend's house to study together) or typical peer activities (e.g. meeting at a friend's house to hang out together). In the second part of the experiment, participants first formed one of three plans before performing an impulse shopping task. The cII participants formed a collective if–then plan constituting a useful strategy ("And if we want to put something in our basket, then we will only take what we really need"). Participants in one control condition received the same strategy but without the if–then link ("We will only take in our basket what we really need"), and those in a second control condition received an if–then plan with all relevant words that did not constitute a helpful strategy ("And if we want something that we really need, then we will put it in our basket!"). By doing this, we sought to determine whether the if–then format contributes to cII effects. Participants' task was to shop for dinner for their respective group (peers vs. fellow students) to prepare pasta and tomato sauce. Analyzing the content of their shopping baskets revealed that the cII did indeed reduce impulse purchases in groups with and without detrimental norms. Moreover, the if–then format further improved the effectiveness of the helpful strategy to take only what one needs. This finding suggests that the if–then format indeed contributes to cII effects. In sum, cIIs can support performance, even without any interaction with the group and in the presence of detrimental norms.

Taskwork without Interaction that Requires Sacrifices for the Group

A remaining question is whether cIIs even support taskwork that benefits the group but is costly for the individual. Group interests and individual interests are often in conflict, and behaving in one's group's best interests in such situations requires individual sacrifices (Hardin, 1968). These *social dilemmas* are difficult to resolve and can lead group members to behave detrimentally for their group (Komorita & Parks, 1995; Weber, Kopelman, & Messick, 2004). This is because temptations trigger selfish goals that are in conflict with cooperative group goals (see Shuhua & Frese, 2013, for a discussion of goal conflicts). Such selfish goals are strong when other group members' interaction is limited (i.e. in *one-shot games* where decisions are not disclosed until all relevant decisions have been made). This is because cooperation strategies such as reciprocity (*tit-for-tat*) are impossible to pursue without knowledge of past decisions. If-then planning is not only able to support concrete goal-directed responses but can also trigger the representation of a superordinate goal and thereby prioritize it over conflicting goals (Kirk et al., 2011; Stroebe, van Koningsbruggen, Papies, & Aarts, 2013). This reasoning is in line with research showing that a crucial role of plans is to prioritize goals (Shuhua & Frese, 2013). Furnishing a cooperative group goal with a cII that specifies a reminder of one's focal goal should help prioritize this goal over conflicting selfish goals.

To test this prediction, we (Thürmer, Wieber, & Gollwitzer, submitted-b, Study 3) used a mixed-motive social dilemma task that evoked an implicit cooperative group goal (i.e. to make cooperative pricing decisions). However, as cooperative decisions were costly for the individual (i.e. there was a monetary incentive for the individual to defect) the task also evoked a selfish goal to defect. After learning about their group and the task, participants received "decision training." The training either contained the cII "When we are about to make our pricing decision, then we will consider the group's revenue," the II "When I am about to make our pricing decision, then I will consider my revenue," or a neutral control plan, referring neither to the group nor to the individual: "When the decision screen appears, then a decision has to be made." Participants then played eight rounds of a pricing game (adapted from Sheldon & Fishbach, 2011) against purported group members without receiving feedback about the decisions of the other players (i.e. we used iterated games without feedback). We expected that the cII would help participants attain their group goal and make more cooperative pricing decisions. To test whether this expected cII-effect would generalize to situations where the group goal cannot be attained, eight rounds against purported non-group members followed. Moreover, we added a structurally similar investment game (adapted from Fischbacher, Gächter, & Fehr, 2001) at the end of the experiment to test whether the cII would generally increase cooperation within the group. Participants only learned about the other participants' decisions at the end of the experiment, thereby making it impossible for them to react to their fellow group members' decisions. As predicted, when playing against a group member, participants with the cII cooperated more than II participants or control participants. This demonstrates that cIIs even increase group performance when interaction is temporally distributed and cooperation is costly for the individual. However, cIIs specifically supported their superordinate group goal and did not generalize to other collectives (i.e. non-group members) or situations (i.e. an unrelated but structurally equivalent trust game). These findings are in line with the assumption that cIIs allow for goal-dependent automaticity in collective goal striving and rely on individuals' capability to regulate their behavior.

In sum, cIIs that specify a goal-directed response were also quite effective in supporting taskwork without interaction. This supports our assumption that the effectiveness of collective if–then plans also relies on intra-individual processes (the heightened activation of the situation and the creation of an if–then link). Indeed, cIIs were more effective in the if–then format, which has been established with regard to IIs. Moreover, cII effects were observed to be specific to their superordinate goal. This is an important finding as it suggests that our observed planning effects are indeed goal-dependent. To add to this finding, we observed that cII effects were specific to the group they were set for. This finding supports our assumption that cIIs support collective goal striving. In short, cIIs are an applicable and effective means to support taskwork.

Conclusion and Outlook

We have organized the review of our planning research along the distinction between teamwork and taskwork. In support of our assumption that IIs and cIIs can promote teamwork, individual and collective if–then planning promoted cooperative behaviors such as sharing task resources (Wieber, Gollwitzer, et al., 2015) or revising crucial information together (Thürmer et al., 2015b, Study 2). Moreover, cIIs promoted cooperation even if they did not explicitly specify cooperative behaviors (Thürmer et al., submitted-b, Studies 1 & 2), suggesting that cIIs indeed support collective goal striving. In line with the assumption that cIIs support taskwork, collective if–then plans improved performance when interaction between group members was limited, such as during idea generation without interaction or in one-shot dilemma games (Thürmer, Wieber, & Gollwitzer, 2015a, Study 1; submitted-b, Study 3). These findings also support the assumption that collective if–then planning still relies on intra-individual processes (i.e. the willful formation of the plan which leads to the heightened mental accessibility of the situation specified in the if-part and creates a link between this situation and the response specified in the then-part). In sum, if–then plans improved both teamwork and taskwork in the face of hindrances. Since high team performance requires teamwork as well as taskwork, these findings suggest that if–then planning can help groups and teams perform well.

Why we are Confident that Implementation Intentions will Help Teams in Organizations

We conduct our experiments (included those summarized above) in the laboratory in order to ensure maximal internal validity. Therefore we mainly use *ad hoc* student groups. Therefore, the question arises: do the current findings generalize to teams in organizational settings? Whether an empirical finding generalizes to the field is a case-to-case question. While most laboratory findings generalize well (Anderson, Lindsay, & Bushman, 1999; Mitchell, 2012), there is an enormous amount of variation. It seems that medium-to-large effects replicate well (Mitchell, 2012), and therefore the magnitude of a laboratory effect can provide a first clue as to whether it will also show in the field. Gollwitzer and Sheeran (2006) found that implementation intentions had a medium-to-large effect ($d = 0.65$) across 94 independent tests and the effects in the research reported here are of a similar magnitude. This suggests that cII-effects might generalize.

However, generalizability to the field needs to be tested empirically and implementation intentions should prove effective in the field. Support for this assumption comes from recent meta-analyses testing implementation intention effects in field settings (Adriaanse et al., 2011; Bélanger-Gravel et al., 2013). Across 23 studies investigating dieting (Adriaanse et al., 2011) as well as 26 studies investigating physical activity (Bélanger-Gravel et al., 2013), implementation intentions promoted goal achievement (i.e. eating a healthier diet and increasing levels of physical activity). Further support for the notion that implementation intentions are effective in applied settings comes from a large field study ($N = 287,228$) which demonstrated that pre-planning when and where to vote by forming respective implementation intentions increased voter turnout at the 2008 presidential election in the United States (Nickerson & Rogers, 2010). A first study has even tested implementation intentions in an organizational context: the study on complying with a company's recycling policy discussed at the outset of this chapter (Holland et al., 2006) demonstrates that implementation intentions help change employee behavior and achieve organizational goals (see Machin & Fogarty, 2003, for a correlational approach). In sum, field research supports the assumption that if–then planning has a considerable impact in organizational settings and helps attain high performance.

With respect to groups and teams, the question arises whether findings from group research will generalize to organizational teams. Organizational teams have usually been working together for quite some time, are responsible for an important organizational outcome, and have experience working on their task (Sundstrom, de Meuse, & Futrell, 1990). Although we have mainly used *ad hoc* student groups in the laboratory, some of our studies have incorporated characteristics typical of organizational teams. First, Wieber and colleagues (Wieber, Gollwitzer, et al., 2015) used groups of schoolchildren who had about three years' experience together in one class. Since group work is common in schools, it is highly likely that they have worked together as a team before. Despite this experience together, planning out their cooperation with an II improved their performance. Second, Thürmer and colleagues (Thürmer et al., 2015b, Study 2) incentivized group decisions and thereby made groups responsible for an important outcome: their payment in the experiment. Despite this monetary incentive, a cII led to improved decisions compared to a control group. Lastly, Thürmer and colleagues (Thürmer, Wieber, & Gollwitzer, submitted-b, Study 2) used an impulse shopping task that participants can be expected to be highly familiar with. Indeed, their shopping task was closely modeled to a supermarket that students frequently go to. Despite this task experience, planning with a cII successfully reduced impulse shopping. In sum, the present studies support the assumption that established teams which are responsible for an important organizational outcome and who have experience with the task at hand can benefit from if–then planning.

Responses that Implementation Intentions can Trigger: How If–then Planning can Help Teams in Organizations

If–then planning can support various different goal-directed responses. In the research reported here, these responses include goal-directed actions (e.g. cooperative behaviors; Wieber, Gollwitzer, et al., 2013), reflecting on different decision alternatives (Thürmer et al., 2015b, Study 2), and suppressing detrimental states (Thürmer, Wieber, & Gollwitzer, submitted-b, Studies 1 & 2). Even complex responses such as prioritizing one's focal goal over conflicting goals were supported by if–then planning (Thürmer, Wieber, & Gollwitzer, submitted-b, Study 3). If–then planning can thus support a host of goal-directed responses in groups. How can promoting such responses help organizational teams?

First, implementation intentions that specify a goal-directed action help respond swiftly when the specified situation presents itself. This is an advantage when good opportunities are easy to miss or necessary actions are somewhat uncomfortable. In organizational settings, this might be the case when new taskwork behaviors or concrete cooperation behaviors are necessary. Even though employees might realize the importance of performing these behaviors, they may fail to act at the right time. In line with the idea that new behaviors are difficult to implement in the workplace, new behaviors acquired through training are not always applied successfully on the job (Arthur, Bennett, Edens, & Bell, 2003; Baldwin & Ford, 1988). Importantly, this is even true for those highly motivated to apply those new behaviors, as demonstrated by moderate relations between motivation-to-transfer and actual transfer (e.g. Locht, Dam, & Chiaburu, 2013), and this should also be true for teams (Salas et al., 2008). Team training interventions could therefore be improved by including action implementation intention components (see Machin & Fogarty, 2003, for a correlational account of transfer implementation intentions).

Second, reflection implementation intentions that specify a reflective response before making a decision can help integrate crucial information. In an increasingly complex world, information overload is commonplace (Eppler & Mengis, 2004) and considering all the available information is difficult. Nevertheless, making informed decisions is crucial for team performance (Mesmer-Magnus & DeChurch, 2009) and improving decisions is a key interest of researchers and practitioners (Milkman, Chugh, & Bazerman, 2009). The present research suggests that if–then planning can help reflect on information available and improve decisions (Thürmer et al., 2015b). Importantly, the manipulations used only required participants to work on a paper-and-pencil form for five to ten minutes. This suggests that if–then planning is not only effective but also time- and cost-efficient.

Third, suppression implementation intentions that specify a detrimental state and link it to a suppression response help deal with detrimental states and stimuli. Detrimental states can also hinder organizational performance, such as when relationship conflict hinders team performance (de Wit, Greer, & Jehn, 2012). Although relationship conflict is ideally solved through conflict management strategies, this takes time and is not a viable option in the short term. A readily available option is to form a suppression implementation intention (e.g. "When I get angry at my co-worker, then I will ignore that and tell myself: 'let's get back to work'"). Given the consistently negative impact of relationship conflict on team performance (de Wit et al., 2012), and the repeatedly demonstrated positive effect of suppression implementation intentions (Schweiger Gallo, Keil, McCulloch, Rockstroh, & Gollwitzer, 2009; Thürmer et al., 2013; Wieber et al., 2011), this should help teams experiencing relationship conflict maintain high performance.

Lastly, prioritization implementation intentions activate the representation of one's focal goal in goal-conflict situations. This helps prioritize the focal goal and thereby attain it. Specifically, the dilemma study summarized in the present chapter shows that teams can profit from a prioritization cII that supports a collective goal when it is in conflict with an individual goal. Goal conflict between individual and group interests is common in organizations and can have a substantial impact on performance (Locke, Smith, Erez, Chah, & Schaffer, 1994). For instance, an employee might prefer to leave early on a Friday afternoon although a team member might need his or her support to finish an important presentation. Prioritizing the cooperative company goal over the personal leisure goal is difficult but important for the team's success. In line with this reasoning, voluntary contributions to organizational outcomes (*organizational citizenship behaviors*, OCB, Podsakoff, Whiting, Podsakoff, & Blume, 2009) have been shown to predict organizational performance. The present research suggests that prioritization implementation intentions can help employees prioritize their company goals and show more OCB.

In sum, implementation intentions can support a host of responses that can increase team performance. In line with the idea that implementation intentions can promote organizational performance, *action plans* ("steps toward important goals," Frese, 2010, p. 101) have been shown to be a powerful predictor of entrepreneurs' performance (Frese et al., 2007). Implementation intentions are very powerful action plans as they create situation–response links that help automate goal striving. This automaticity should help teams perform tasks efficiently and minimize errors. In other words, implementation intentions create instant routines (Gollwitzer, 1999) that may give organizations the competitive edge.

Goal Striving in Groups with Implementation Intentions and Existing Accounts of Planning

Implementation intention theory can complement existing planning accounts and research. Mumford, Schultz, and Van Doorn (2001) developed a model that describes the planning process from setting a goal that one wants to plan for to the final execution of the plan. Plan generation includes a series of steps, such as creating an initial template, generating a first plan and its refinement, and developing backup plans. The model therefore focuses on how plans are generated and refined. Plan execution is the last step after refining the plan, but the model does not explicate how exactly a plan is executed. Implementation intention theory complements Mumford and colleagues' model in that it details how if–then plans are executed (Gollwitzer, 1999; Gollwitzer & Oettingen, 2011; Gollwitzer & Sheeran, 2006): If-then planners recognize the specified situation immediately and respond swiftly in the pre-planned manner. Implementation intention research thereby treats planning as an independent variable (i.e. some participants or groups receive an implementation intention while others do not). Since this conceptualization allows subjects to be assigned to planning conditions randomly, it helps understand the causal effect of implementation intentions on performance (cf. Rubin, 1974). Connecting Mumford and colleagues' model of planning with implementation intention theory, future applied research could explore how teams come up with effective implementation intentions independently. High-performing teams might develop routines in which they identify when, where, and how they can attain their performance goals. In line with this idea, high-performance teams have been shown to evaluate their tasks and actions critically on a regular basis (i.e. have high *reflexivity*, West, 1996), which might already lead them to plan when, where, and how to act on their goals in the future. Further support for the idea that these conceptualizations of planning complement each other comes from implementation intention research that has compared self-generated and prescribed implementation intentions. Armitage (2009) had participants generate their own implementation intention or provided one. Results showed that both provided and self-generated implementation intentions had a positive effect of similar magnitude compared to control conditions without if–then plans. The model of planning processes (Mumford et al., 2001) can thus help us understand how people come up with helpful implementation intentions themselves.

Another line of research emphasizes that the quality of planning contributes to the positive effects of planning on performance. For instance, Smith, Locke, and Barry (1990) suggested that high-quality planning can be characterized by:

> (1) a future orientation, (2) extensive interaction between organizational members, (3) a systematic and comprehensive analysis of the organization's strengths, weakness, opportunities, and threats, (4) a clear definition of the roles and functions of all members and departments, and finally, (5) the development and communication of action plans and the allocation of resources to action plans.
>
> *(p. 124)*

Moreover, only plans suitable for the task at hand lead to performance enhancement, while unsuitable plans decrease performance (Earley & Perry, 1987). These findings are in line with implementation intention theory, which suggests that a very specific type of plan promotes goal achievement in the face of hindrances. Indeed, the if–then format has been found to be highly effective (Chapman, Armitage, & Norman, 2009) and implementation intention effects are stronger for difficult goals (Dewitte, Verguts, & Lens, 2003; Gollwitzer & Sheeran, 2006; Hall, Zehr, Ng, & Zanna, 2012).

Mumford, Schultz, and Osburn (2002) further suggest that planning can take place at multiple levels, such as the individual, the group or team, or the entire organization. In our research, we have so far looked at planning at the individual and the group level. Mumford and colleagues' research suggests that extending our framework to the organizational level can enhance its utility for applied settings. Furthermore, Mumford and colleagues' research points to the importance of interactions between multiple levels in an organization. Our research discussed in the present chapter is in line with this: plans referring to the group had effects both at the group and at the individual level. On the organization level, planning has been observed to promote performance when culturally appropriate (e.g. in Germany) but to hamper performance when it is not culturally appropriate (e.g. in Ireland; Rauch, Frese, & Sonnentag, 2000). This might also be true for implementation intentions: if an organization sets implementation intentions that are not accepted by the teams and employees within the company, they will likely have no effect. In sum, we have touched on the complexities of planning between the different organizational levels, which might provide a fruitful basis for future research.

Goal Striving in Groups with Implementation Intentions and Motivation

II- and cII-effects are based on strong goal commitment (Sheeran, Webb, & Gollwitzer, 2005; Thürmer, Wieber, & Gollwitzer, submitted-b, Study 3), and if–then planning can thus be expected to have a beneficial effect only when teams actually want to attain their goals. In turn, when the issue is to ensure sufficient worker motivation to comply with company goals, mere IIs and cIIs cannot be expected to have strong effects. In such cases, implementation intentions need to be supplemented with an intervention that ensures high goal commitment. A highly effective intervention in this regard is *mental contrasting* (Oettingen, 2000, 2012; Oettingen, Pak, & Schnetter, 2001). During mental contrasting, one contrasts the desired future with the reality that impedes the attainment of this future (e.g. obstacles). By doing so, one selectively and strongly commits to those goals that are feasible and desirable (Oettingen et al., 2001). Recent research supports the assumption that mental contrasting and implementation intentions complement each other: mental contrasting with implementation intentions (see review by Oettingen, Wittchen, & Gollwitzer, 2013) ensures strong goal commitment and action initiation and thereby improves goal attainment. When employee motivation is at stake, the combination of mental contrasting with implementation intentions should therefore be particularly effective. This might also be the case with regard to teams, an assumption that should be tested in future research.

Another well-established way to increase employee and team motivation is goal setting. Goal-setting theory (reviews by Locke & Latham, 1990, 2006, 2013) maintains that challenging and specific goals lead to better performance than easy or unspecific goals. Arguably, forming implementation intentions also adds specificity to one's goal. However, this specificity differs in kind: in goal setting, one quantifies the desired outcome (goal), which makes discrepancies easier to detect. In contrast, by forming implementation intentions one plans out how to achieve an already set goal by specifying actions and responses. The research reported in this chapter shows that groups can use implementation intentions, and goal setting has also been applied to groups successfully (review and meta-analysis by Kleingeld, van Mierlo, & Arends, 2011; O'Leary-Kelly, Martocchio, & Frink, 1994). Importantly, the individual–collective distinction discussed in the present chapter has also been shown to be crucial for goal setting. It has been argued that "groups offer the potential for setting goals at multiple levels of performance" (van Mierlo & Kleingeld, 2010, p. 525) as challenging-specific goals in groups can refer either to the individual (individual goals) or to the entire group (collective goals; Crown, 2007; Crown & Rosse, 1995; Locke & Latham, 1990). A recent meta-analysis on goal setting in groups (Kleingeld et al., 2011) showed that while collective goals had a positive effect on group performance on average, individual goals had, on average, no effect. When it comes to goal setting, referring to the group (setting collective goals) thus improves performance but referring to the individual is not always beneficial (Crown & Rosse, 1995; van Mierlo & Kleingeld, 2010). In the present chapter, we show that this individual–collective distinction also makes a difference for implementation intentions. This is quite remarkable since goal-setting effects rely on increased motivation and implementation intention effects on automating goal striving – the finding that the individual–collective distinction plays a role in both phenomena suggests that it is quite ubiquitous in goal pursuit in groups.

In closing, we return to challenging organizational goals and changing employee behavior. The research summarized here demonstrates the effectiveness of if–then planning in improving important performance behaviors related to teamwork and taskwork. By forming simple if–then plans, participants were able to overcome hindrances in goal striving and thereby improve their group performance. Further, we hope that we have made a compelling case as to why we are confident that our basic research lab findings could have an impact in field settings and for organizational scientists and practitioners. Future research will show whether this optimism is justified – we look forward to it!

Acknowledgments

We thank Michael Frese and the members of the Social Psychology and Motivation Lab at the University of Konstanz for their helpful comments on earlier versions of this manuscript and Srdjan Perko for language editing.

References

Aarts, H., Dijksterhuis, A. P., & Midden, C. (1999). To plan or not to plan? Goal achievement or interrupting the performance of mundane behaviors. *European Journal of Social Psychology*, 29, 971–979. doi, 10.1002/(SICI)1099-0992(199912)29:8<971::AID-EJSP963>3.0.CO;2-A

Achtziger, A., Gollwitzer, P. M., & Sheeran, P. (2008). Implementation intentions and shielding goal striving from unwanted thoughts and feelings. *Personality and Social Psychology Bulletin*, 34, 381–393. doi, 10.1177/0146167207311201

Achtziger, A., Bayer, U. C., & Gollwitzer, P. M. (2012). Committing to implementation intentions: Attention and memory effects for selected situational cues. *Motivation and Emotion*, 36, 287–300. doi, 10.1007/s11031-011-9261-6

Adriaanse, M. A., Vinkers, C. D. W., De Ridder, D. T. D., Hox, J. J., & De Wit, J. B. F. (2011). Do implementation intentions help to eat a healthy diet? A systematic review and meta-analysis of the empirical evidence. *Appetite*, 56, 183–193. doi, 10.1016/j.appet.2010.10.012

Anderson, C. A., Lindsay, J. J., & Bushman, B. J. (1999). Research in the psychological laboratory. *Current Directions in Psychological Science*, 8, 3–9. doi, 10.1111/1467-8721.00002

Armitage, C. J. (2009). Effectiveness of experimenter-provided and self-generated implementation intentions to reduce alcohol consumption in a sample of the general population: A randomized exploratory trial. *Health Psychology*, 28, 545–553. doi, 10.1037/a0015984

Arrow, H., McGrath, J. E., & Berdahl, J. L. (2000). *Small groups as complex systems: Formation, coordination, development, and adaptation.* Thousand Oaks, CA: Sage.

Arthur, W., Jr., Bennett, W., Jr., Edens, P. S., & Bell, S. T. (2003). Effectiveness of training in organizations: A meta-analysis of design and evaluation features. *Journal of Applied Psychology*, 88, 234–245. doi, 10.1037/0021-9010.88.2.234

Baldwin, T. T., & Ford, J. K. (1988). Transfer of training: A review and directions for future research. *Personnel Psychology*, 41, 63–105. doi, 10.1111/j.1744-6570.1988.tb00632.x

Bargh, J. A., & Chartrand, T. L. (2000). The mind in the middle: A practical guide to priming and automaticity research. In H. T. Reis & C. M. Judd (Eds.), *Handbook of research methods in social and personality psychology* (pp. 253–285). New York: Cambridge University Press.

Bayer, U. C., Achtziger, A., Gollwitzer, P. M., & Moskowitz, G. B. (2009). Responding to subliminal cues: Do if-then plans facilitate action preparation and initiation without conscious intent? *Social Cognition*, 27, 183–201. doi, 10.1521/soco.2009.27.2.183

Bayer, U. C., Gollwitzer, P. M., & Achtziger, A. (2010). Staying on track: Planned goal striving is protected from disruptive internal states. *Journal of Experimental Social Psychology*, 46, 505–514. doi, 10.1016/j.jesp.2010.01.002

Bechtoldt, M. N., Choi, H.-S., & Nijstad, B. A. (2012). Individuals in mind, mates by heart: Individualistic self-construal and collective value orientation as predictors of group creativity. *Journal of Experimental Social Psychology*, 48, 838–844. doi, 10.1016/j.jesp.2012.02.014

Bélanger-Gravel, A., Godin, G., & Amireault, S. (2013). A meta-analytic review of the effect of implementation intentions on physical activity. *Health Psychology Review*, 7, 23–54. doi, 10.1080/17437199.2011.560095

Bowers, C. A., Braun, C. C., & Morgan, B. B. (1997). Team workload: Its meaning and measurement. In M. T. Brannick, E. Salas, & C. Prince (Eds.), *Team performance assessment and measurement: Theory, methods, and applications* (pp. 85–108). Mahwah, NJ: Lawrence Erlbaum.

Brandstätter, V., Lengfelder, A., & Gollwitzer, P. M. (2001). Implementation intentions and efficient action initiation. *Journal of Personality and Social Psychology*, 81, 946–960. doi, 10.1037/0022-3514.81.5.946

Bray, S. R. (2004). Collective efficacy, group goals, and group performance of a muscular endurance task. *Small Group Research*, 35, 230–238. doi: 10.1177/1046496403260531

Burkert, S., Scholz, U., Gralla, O., Roigas, J., & Knoll, N. (2011). Dyadic planning of health-behavior change after prostatectomy: A randomized-controlled planning intervention. *Social Science & Medicine*, 73, 783–792. doi, 10.1016/j.socscimed.2011.06.016

Chapman, J., Armitage, C. J., & Norman, P. (2009). Comparing implementation intention interventions in relation to young adults' intake of fruit and vegetables. *Psychology & Health*, 24, 317–332. doi, 10.1080/08870440701864538

Cohen, A.-L., & Gollwitzer, P. M. (2008). The cost of remembering to remember: Cognitive load and implementation intentions influence ongoing task performance. In M. Kliegel, M. A. McDaniel & G. O. Einstein (Eds.), *Prospective memory: Cognitive, neuroscience, developmental, and applied perspectives* (pp. 367–390). New York: Lawrence Erlbaum.

Crawford, E. R., & Lepine, J. A. (2013). A configural theory of team processes: Accounting for the structure of taskwork and teamwork. *Academy of Management Review*, 38, 32–48. doi, 10.5465/amr.2011.0206

Crown, D. F. (2007). The use of group and groupcentric individual goals for culturally heterogeneous and homogeneous task groups. *Small Group Research*, 38, 489–508. doi, 10.1177/1046496407300486

Crown, D. F., & Rosse, J. G. (1995). Yours, mine, and ours: Facilitating group productivity through the integration of individual and group goals. *Organizational Behavior and Human Decision Processes*, 64, 138–150. doi, 10.1006/obhd.1995.1096

DeShon, R. P., Kozlowski, S. W. J., Schmidt, A. M., Milner, K. R., & Wiechmann, D. (2004). A multiple-goal, multilevel model of feedback effects on the regulation of individual and team performance. *Journal of Applied Psychology*, 89, 1035–1056. doi, 10.1037/0021-9010.89.6.1035

de Wit, F. R. C., Greer, L. L., & Jehn, K. A. (2012). The paradox of intragroup conflict: A meta-analysis. *Journal of Applied Psychology*, 97, 360–390. doi, 10.1037/a0024844

Dewitte, S., Verguts, T., & Lens, W. (2003). Implementation intentions do not enhance all types of goals: The moderating role of goal difficulty. *Current Psychology*, 22, 73–89. doi, 10.1007/s12144-003-1014-6

Earley, P. C., & Perry, B. C. (1987). Work plan availability and performance: An assessment of task strategy priming on subsequent task completion. *Organizational Behavior and Human Decision Processes*, 39, 279–302. doi, 10.1016/0749-5978(87)90025-2

Eppler, M., & Mengis, J. (2004). The concept of information overload: A review of literature from organization science, accounting, marketing, MIS, and related disciplines. *Information Society*, 20, 325–344. doi, 10.1080/01972240490507974

Fischbacher, U., Gächter, S., & Fehr, E. (2001). Are people conditionally cooperative? Evidence from a public goods experiment. *Economics Letters*, 71, 397–404. doi, 10.1016/S0165-1765(01)00394-9

Frese, M. (2010). Entrepreneurial actions: An action theory approach. In D. De Cremer, R. van Dick & J. K. Murnighan (Eds.), *Social psychology and organizations* (pp. 87–120). New York: Routledge.

Frese, M., & Zapf, D. (1994). Action as the core of work psychology: A German approach. In H. C. Triandis, M. D. Dunnette & L. M. Hough (Eds.), *Handbook of industrial and organizational psychology* (2nd ed., Vol. 4, pp. 271–340). Palo Alto, CA: Consulting Psychologists Press.

Frese, M., Krauss, S. I., Keith, N., Escher, S., Grabarkiewicz, R., Luneng, S. T., et al. (2007). Business owners' action planning and its relationship to business success in three African countries. *Journal of Applied Psychology*, 92, 1481–1498. doi, 10.1037/0021-9010.92.6.1481

Gigone, D., & Hastie, R. (1993). The common knowledge effect: Information sharing and group judgment. *Journal of Personality and Social Psychology*, 65, 959–974. doi: 10.1037/0022-3514.65.5.959

Gigone, D., & Hastie, R. (1997). The impact of information on small group choice. *Journal of Personality and Social Psychology, 72*, 132–140. doi: 10.1037/0022-3514.72.1.132

Gollwitzer, P. M. (1993). Goal achievement: The role of intentions. *European Review of Social Psychology, 4*, 141–185. doi, 10.1080/14792779343000059

Gollwitzer, P. M. (1999). Implementation intentions: Strong effects of simple plans. *American Psychologist, 54*, 493–503. doi, 10.1037/0003-066X.54.7.493

Gollwitzer, P. M. (2014). Weakness of the will: Is a quick fix possible? *Motivation & Emotion, 38*, 305–322. doi, 10.1007/s11031-014-9416-3

Gollwitzer, P. M., & Brandstätter, V. (1997). Implementation intentions and effective goal pursuit. *Journal of Personality and Social Psychology, 73*, 186–199. doi, 10.1037/0022-3514.73.1.186

Gollwitzer, P. M., & Oettingen, G. (2011). Planning promotes goal striving. In K. D. Vohs & R. F. Baumeister (Eds.), *Handbook of self-regulation: Research, theory, and applications* (2nd ed., pp. 162–185). New York: Guilford Press.

Gollwitzer, P. M., & Sheeran, P. (2006). Implementation intentions and goal achievement: A meta-analysis of effects and processes. In M. P. Zanna (Ed.), *Advances in experimental social psychology* (Vol. 38, pp. 69–119). San Diego, CA: Elsevier Academic Press.

Goncalo, J. A., & Staw, B. M. (2006). Individualism–collectivism and group creativity. *Organizational Behavior and Human Decision Processes, 100*, 96–109. doi, 10.1016/j.obhdp.2005.11.003

Hacker, W. (2003). Action Regulation Theory: A practical tool for the design of modern work processes? *European Journal of Work and Organizational Psychology, 12*, 105–130. doi, 10.1080/13594320344000075

Hagger, M. S., Lonsdale, A., Koka, A., Hein, V., Pasi, H., Lintunen, T., et al. (2012). An intervention to reduce alcohol consumption in undergraduate students using implementation intentions and mental simulations: A cross-national study. *International Journal of Behavioral Medicine, 19*, 82–96. doi, 10.1007/s12529-011-9163-8

Hall, P. A., Zehr, C. E., Ng, M., & Zanna, M. P. (2012). Implementation intentions for physical activity in supportive and unsupportive environmental conditions: An experimental examination of intention–behavior consistency. *Journal of Experimental Social Psychology, 48*, 432–436. doi, 10.1016/j.jesp.2011.09.004

Hardin, G. (1968). The tragedy of the commons. *Science, 162*, 1243–1248. doi, 10.1126/science.162.3859.1243

Henderson, M. D., Gollwitzer, P. M., & Oettingen, G. (2007). Implementation intentions and disengagement from a failing course of action. *Journal of Behavioral Decision Making, 20*, 81–102. doi, 10.1002/bdm.553

Hinsz, V. B., & Ladbury, J. L. (2012). Combinations of contributions for sharing cognitions in teams. In E. Salas, S. M. Fiore, & M. P. Letsky (Eds.), *Theories of team cognition: Cross-disciplinary perspectives* (pp. 245–270). New York: Routledge.

Holland, R. W., Aarts, H., & Langendam, D. (2006). Breaking and creating habits on the working floor: A field-experiment on the power of implementation intentions. *Journal of Experimental Social Psychology, 42*, 776–783. doi, 10.1016/j.jesp.2005.11.006

Kerr, N. L., & Hertel, G. (2011). The Köhler group motivation gain: How to motivate the "weak links" in a group. *Social and Personality Psychology Compass, 5*, 43–55. doi, 10.1111/j.1751-9004.2010.00333.x

Kerr, N. L., & Tindale, R. S. (2004). Group performance and decision making. *Annual Review of Psychology, 55*, 623–655. doi, 10.1146/annurev.psych.55.090902.142009

Kirk, D., Gollwitzer, P. M., & Carnevale, P. J. (2011). Self-regulation in ultimatum bargaining: Goals and plans help accepting unfair but profitable offers. *Social Cognition, 29*, 528–546. doi, 10.1521/soco.2011.29.5.528

Kleingeld, A., van Mierlo, H., & Arends, L. (2011). The effect of goal setting on group performance: A meta-analysis. *Journal of Applied Psychology, 96*, 1289–1304. doi, 10.1037/a0024315

Köhler, O. (1926). Kraftleistungen bei Einzel- und Gruppenarbeit. [Physical performance in individual and group situations]. *Industrielle Psychotechnik, 3*, 274–282.

Komorita, S. S., & Parks, C. D. (1995). Interpersonal relations: Mixed-motive interaction. *Annual Review of Psychology, 46*, 183–207. doi, 10.1146/annurev.ps.46.020195.001151

Levine, J. M., & Moreland, R. L. (1990). Progress in small group research. *Annual Review of Psychology, 41*, 585–634. doi, 10.1146/annurev.ps.41.020190.003101

Levine, J. M., Resnick, L. B., & Higgins, E. T. (1993). Social foundations of cognition. *Annual Review of Psychology, 44*, 585–612. doi, 10.1146/annurev.ps.44.020193.003101

Lewin, K., Dembo, T., Festinger, L., & Sears, P. S. (1944). Level of aspiration. In J. M. Hunt (Ed.), *Personality and the behavior disorders* (pp. 333–378). Oxford: Ronald Press.

Locht, M. v. d., Dam, K. v., & Chiaburu, D. S. (2013). Getting the most of management training: The role of identical elements for training transfer. *Personnel Review*, 42, 422–439. doi, 10.1108/PR-05-2011-0072

Locke, E. A., & Latham, G. P. (1990). *A theory of goal setting and task performance.* Englewood Cliffs, NJ: Prentice Hall.

Locke, E. A., & Latham, G. P. (2006). New directions in goal-setting theory. *Current Directions in Psychological Science*, 15, 265–268. doi, 10.1111/j.1467-8721.2006.00449.x

Locke, E. A., & Latham, G. P. (Eds.) (2013). *New developments in goal setting and task performance.* New York: Routledge Academic.

Locke, E. A., Smith, K. G., Erez, M., Chah, D.-O., & Schaffer, A. (1994). The effects of intra-individual goal conflict on performance. *Journal of Management*, 20, 67–91. doi, 10.1177/014920639402000104

Lu, L., Yuan, Y. C., & McLeod, P. L. (2012). Twenty-five years of hidden profiles in group decision making. *Personality and Social Psychology Review*, 16, 54–75. doi, 10.1177/1088868311417243

Luo, X. (2005). How does shopping with others influence impulsive purchasing? *Journal of Consumer Psychology*, 15, 288–294. doi, 10.1207/s15327663jcp1504_3

McGrath, J. E. (1984). *Groups: Interaction and performance.* Englewood Cliffs, NJ: Prentice Hall.

Machin, M. A., & Fogarty, G. J. (2003). Perceptions of training-related factors and personal variables as predictors of transfer implementation intentions. *Journal of Business and Psychology*, 18, 51–71. doi, 10.2307/25092846

Marks, M. A., Zaccaro, S. J., & Mathieu, J. E. (2000). Performance implications of leader briefings and team-interaction training for team adaptation to novel environments. *Journal of Applied Psychology*, 85, 971–986. doi, 10.1037/0021-9010.85.6.971

Marks, M. A., Mathieu, J. E., & Zaccaro, S. J. (2001). A temporally based framework and taxonomy of team processes. *The Academy of Management Review*, 26, 356–376. doi, 10.5465/AMR.2001.4845785

Marta, S., Leritz, L. E., & Mumford, M. D. (2005). Leadership skills and the group performance: Situational demands, behavioral requirements, and planning. *The Leadership Quarterly*, 16, 97–120. doi, 10.1016/j.leaqua.2004.04.004

Mathieu, J. E., Heffner, T. S., Goodwin, G. F., Salas, E., & Cannon-Bowers, J. A. (2000). The influence of shared mental models on team process and performance. *Journal of Applied Psychology*, 85, 273–283. doi, 10.1037/0021-9010.85.2.273

Mesmer-Magnus, J. R., & DeChurch, L. A. (2009). Information sharing and team performance: A meta-analysis. *Journal of Applied Psychology*, 94, 535–546. doi, 10.1037/a0013773

Milkman, K. L., Chugh, D., & Bazerman, M. H. (2009). How can decision making be improved? *Perspectives on Psychological Science*, 4, 379–383. doi, 10.1111/j.1745-6924.2009.01142.x

Mitchell, G. (2012). Revisiting truth or triviality. *Perspectives on Psychological Science*, 7, 109–117. doi, 10.1177/1745691611432343

Mojzisch, A., & Schulz-Hardt, S. (2010). Knowing others' preferences degrades the quality of group decisions. *Journal of Personality and Social Psychology*, 98, 794–808. doi: 10.1037/a0017627

Mojzisch, A., Grouneva, L., & Schulz-Hardt, S. (2010). Biased evaluation of information during discussion: Disentangling the effects of preference consistency, social validation, and ownership of information. *European Journal of Social Psychology*, 40, 946–956. doi: 10.1002/ejsp.660

Mumford, M. D., Schultz, R. A., & Van Doorn, J. R. (2001). Performance in planning: Processes, requirements, and errors. *Review of General Psychology*, 5, 213–240. doi, 10.1037/1089-2680.5.3.213

Mumford, M. D., Schultz, R. A., & Osburn, H. K. (2002). Planning in organizations: Performance as a multi-level phenomenon. In F. Dansereau & F. J. Yammarino (Eds.), *The many faces of multi-level issues* (pp. 3–65). Bingley: Emerald.

Muraven, M., & Baumeister, R. F. (2000). Self-regulation and depletion of limited resources: Does self-control resemble a muscle? *Psychological Bulletin*, 126, 247–259. doi, 10.1037/0033-2909.126.2.247

Nickerson, D. W., & Rogers, T. (2010). Do you have a voting plan? *Psychological Science*, 21, 194–199. doi, 10.1177/0956797609359326

O'Leary-Kelly, A. M., Martocchio, J. J., & Frink, D. D. (1994). A review of the influence of group goals on group performance. *The Academy of Management Journal*, 37, 1285–1301. doi, 10.2307/256673

Oettingen, G. (2000). Expectancy effects on behavior depend on self-regulatory thought. *Social Cognition*, 18, 101–129. doi, 10.1521/soco.2000.18.2.101

Oettingen, G. (2012). Future thought and behaviour change. *European Review of Social Psychology*, 23, 1–63. doi, 10.1080/10463283.2011.643698

Oettingen, G., Pak, H. J., & Schnetter, K. (2001). Self-regulation of goal-setting: Turning free fantasies about the future into binding goals. *Journal of Personality and Social Psychology*, 80, 736–753. doi, 10.1037/0022-3514.80.5.736

Oettingen, G., Wittchen, M., & Gollwitzer, P. M. (2013). Regulating goal pursuit through mental contrasting with implementation intentions. In E. A. Locke & G. P. Latham (Eds.), *New developments in goal setting and task performance* (pp. 523–548). New York: Routledge.

Park, C. W., Iyer, E. S., & Smith, D. C. (1989). The effects of situational factors on in-store grocery shopping behavior: The role of store environment and time available for shopping. *Journal of Consumer Research*, 15, 422–433. doi, 10.1086/209182

Parks-Stamm, E. J., Gollwitzer, P. M., & Oettingen, G. (2007). Action control by implementation intentions: Effective cue detection and efficient response initiation. *Social Cognition*, 25, 248–266. doi, 10.1521/soco.2007.25.2.248

Pennebaker, J. W., Mehl, M. R., & Niederhoffer, K. G. (2003). Psychological aspects of natural language use: Our words, our selves. *Annual Review of Psychology*, 54, 547–577. doi, 10.1146/annurev.psych.54.101601.145041

Podsakoff, N. P., Whiting, S. W., Podsakoff, P. M., & Blume, B. D. (2009). Individual- and organizational-level consequences of organizational citizenship behaviors: A meta-analysis. *Journal of Applied Psychology*, 94, 122–141. doi, 10.1037/a0013079

Polegato, R., & Zaichkowsky, J. L. (1994). Family food shopping: Strategies used by husbands and wives. *Journal of Consumer Affairs*, 28, 278–299. doi, 10.1111/j.1745-6606.1994.tb00852.x

Prestwich, A., Conner, M. T., Lawton, R. J., Ward, J. K., Ayres, K., & McEachan, R. R. C. (2012). Randomized controlled trial of collaborative implementation intentions targeting working adults' physical activity. *Health Psychology*. doi, 10.1037/a0027672

Rauch, A., Frese, M., & Sonnentag, S. (2000). Cultural differences in planning/success relationships: A comparison of small enterprises in Ireland, West Germany, and East Germany. *Journal of Small Business Management*, 38, 28–41.

Rubin, D. B. (1974). Estimating causal effects of treatments in randomized and nonrandomized studies. *Journal of Educational Psychology*, 66, 688–701. doi, 10.1037/h0037350

Rutter, D. R., Steadman, L., & Quine, L. (2006). An implementation intentions intervention to increase uptake of mammography. *Annals of Behavioral Medicine*, 32, 127–134. doi, 10.1207/s15324796abm3202_10

Salas, E., DiazGranados, D., Klein, C., Burke, C. S., Stagl, K. C., Goodwin, G. F., et al. (2008). Does team training improve team performance? A meta-analysis. *Human Factors*, 50, 903–933. doi, 10.1518/001872008x375009

Schweiger Gallo, I., Keil, A., McCulloch, K. C., Rockstroh, B., & Gollwitzer, P. M. (2009). Strategic automation of emotion regulation. *Journal of Personality and Social Psychology*, 96, 11–31. doi, 10.1037/a0013460

Sheeran, P. (2002). Intention-behavior relations: A conceptual and empirical review. *European Review of Social Psychology*, 12, 1–36. doi, 10.1080/14792772143000003

Sheeran, P., & Orbell, S. (1999). Implementation intentions and repeated behaviour: Augmenting the predictive validity of the theory of planned behaviour. *European Journal of Social Psychology*, 29, 349–369. doi, 10.1002/(SICI)1099-0992(199903/05)29:2/3<349::AID-EJSP931>3.0.CO;2-Y

Sheeran, P., Milne, S., Webb, T. L., & Gollwitzer, P. M. (2005). Implementation intentions. In M. Conner & P. Norman (Eds.), *Predicting health behavior* (2nd ed., pp. 276–323). Buckingham: Open University Press.

Sheeran, P., Webb, T. L., & Gollwitzer, P. M. (2005). The interplay between goal intentions and implementation intentions. *Personality and Social Psychology Bulletin*, 31, 87–98. doi, 10.1177/0146167204271308

Sheldon, O. J., & Fishbach, A. (2011). Resisting the temptation to compete: Self-control promotes cooperation in mixed-motive interactions. *Journal of Experimental Social Psychology*, 47, 403–410. doi, 10.1016/j.jesp.2010.11.003

Shuhua, S., & Frese, M. (2013). Multiple goal pursuit. In E. A. Locke & G. P. Latham (Eds.), *New developments in goal setting and task performance* (pp. 177–194). New York: Routledge.

Smith, K. G., Locke, E. A., & Barry, D. (1990). Goal setting, planning, and organizational performance: An experimental simulation. *Organizational Behavior and Human Decision Processes*, 46, 118–134. doi, 10.1016/0749-5978(90)90025-5

Stasser, G., & Titus, W. (2003). Hidden profiles: A brief history. *Psychological Inquiry*, 14, 304–313. doi: 10.108 0/1047840X.2003.9682897

Steiner, I. D. (1972). *Group process and productivity.* New York: Academic Press.

Stroebe, W., Nijstad, B. A., & Rietzschel, E. F. (2010). Beyond productivity loss in brainstorming groups: The evolution of a question. In M. P. Zanna & J. M. Olson (Eds.), *Advances in experimental social psychology* (Vol. 43, pp. 157–203). Waltham, MA: Academic Press.

Stroebe, W., van Koningsbruggen, G. M., Papies, E. K., & Aarts, H. (2013). Why most dieters fail but some succeed: A goal conflict model of eating behavior. *Psychological Review*, 120, 110–138. doi, 10.1037/a0030849

Sundstrom, E., de Meuse, K. P., & Futrell, D. (1990). Work teams: Applications and effectiveness. *American Psychologist*, 45, 120–133. doi, 10.1037/0003-066X.45.2.120

Thürmer, J. L., McCrea, S. M., & Gollwitzer, P. M. (2013). Regulating self-defensiveness: If-then plans prevent claiming and creating performance handicaps. *Motivation and Emotion*, 37, 712–725. doi, 10.1007/s11031-013-9352-7

Thürmer, J. L., Wieber, F., & Gollwitzer, P. M. (submitted-a). *Peer influence on unintended purchases: Can implementation intentions curb impulse buying?*

Thürmer, J. L., Wieber, F., & Gollwitzer, P. M. (2015a). *The role of implementation intentions in small group creativity: If-then planning enhances idea generation.* Unpublished manuscript, University of Konstanz.

Thürmer, J. L., Wieber, F., & Gollwitzer, P. M. (2015b). A self-regulation perspective on hidden profile problems: If-then planning to review information improves group decisions. *Journal of Behavioral Decision Making*, 28, 101–113. doi, 10.1002/bdm.1832

Thürmer, J. L., Wieber, F., & Gollwitzer, P. M. (submitted-b). Planning and performance in small groups: The role of collective implementation intentions.

van Mierlo, H., & Kleingeld, A. (2010). Goals, strategies, and group performance: Some limits of goal setting in groups. *Small Group Research*, 41, 524–555. doi, 10.1177/1046496410373628

Webb, T. L., & Sheeran, P. (2003). Can implementation intentions help to overcome ego-depletion? *Journal of Experimental Social Psychology*, 39, 279–286.

Webb, T. L., & Sheeran, P. (2007). How do implementation intentions promote goal attainment? A test of component processes. *Journal of Experimental Social Psychology*, 43, 295–302. doi, 10.1016/j.jesp.2006.02.001

Webb, T. L., & Sheeran, P. (2008). Mechanisms of implementation intention effects: The role of goal intentions, self-efficacy, and accessibility of plan components. *British Journal of Social Psychology*, 47, 373–395. doi, 10.1348/014466607X267010

Webb, T. L., Schweiger Gallo, I., Miles, E., Gollwitzer, P. M., & Sheeran, P. (2012). Effective regulation of affect: An action control perspective on emotion regulation. *European Review of Social Psychology*, 23, 143–186. doi, 10.1080/10463283.2012.718134

Weber, J. M., Kopelman, S., & Messick, D. M. (2004). A conceptual review of decision making in social dilemmas: Applying a logic of appropriateness. *Personality and Social Psychology Review*, 8, 281–307. doi, 10.1207/s15327957pspr0803_4

Weingart, L. R., & Weldon, E. (1991). Processes that mediate the relationship between a group goal and group member performance. *Human Performance*, 4, 33. doi, 10.1207/s15327043hup0401_2

Weldon, E., & Weingart, L. R. (1993). Group goals and group performance. *British Journal of Social Psychology*, 32, 307–334. doi, 10.1111/j.2044-8309.1993.tb01003.x

West, M. A. (1996). Reflexivity and work group effectiveness: A conceptual integration. In M. West (Ed.), *The handbook of work group psychology* (pp. 555–579). Chichester: John Wiley & Sons.

West, M. A. (2012). *Effective teamwork: Practical lessons from organizational research.* Malden: Blackwell.

Wieber, F., & Sassenberg, K. (2006). I can't take my eyes off of it – attention attraction effects of implementation intentions. *Social Cognition*, 24, 723–752. doi, 10.1521/soco.2006.24.6.723

Wieber, F., von Suchodoletz, A., Heikamp, T., Trommsdorff, G., & Gollwitzer, P. M. (2011). If-then planning helps school-aged children to ignore attractive distractions. *Social Psychology*, 42, 39–47. doi, 10.1027/1864-9335/a000041

Wieber, F., Thürmer, J. L., & Gollwitzer, P. M. (2012). Collective action control by goals and plans: Applying a self-regulation perspective to group performance. *American Journal of Psychology*, 125, 275–290. doi, 10.5406/amerjpsyc.125.3.0275

Wieber, F., Thürmer, J. L., & Gollwitzer, P. M. (2013). Intentional action control in individuals and groups. In G. Seebaß, M. Schmitz & P. M. Gollwitzer (Eds.), *Acting intentionally and its limits: Individuals, groups, institutions. Interdisciplinary approaches* (pp. 133–162). Berlin: De Gruyter.

Wieber, F., Thürmer, J. L., & Gollwitzer, P. M. (in press). Attenuating the escalation of commitment to a faltering project in decision-making groups by implementation intentions: An implementation intention approach. *Social Psychological and Personality Science*. doi: 10.1177/1948550614568158

Wieber, F., Gollwitzer, P. M., Fäsche, A., Heikamp, T., & Trommsdorff, G. (2015). *Improving children's cooperation at school by if–then planning*. Unpublished manuscript. University of Konstanz.

Wittenbaum, G. M., & Park, E. S. (2001). The collective preference for shared information. *Current Directions in Psychological Science*, 10, 70–73. doi: 10.1111/1467-8721.00118

8

PLANNING FOR INNOVATION

The Critical Role of Agility

Samuel T. Hunter, Melissa Gutworth, Matthew P. Crayne, and Bradley S. Jayne

A recent survey conducted by Boatman and Wellins (2011) asked more than 12,000 upper-level executives across more than 2,500 organizations and 70 countries what they believed their organizations needed to succeed in the business world, both now and into the future. The answer, quite overwhelmingly, was to produce more creative and innovative output. This observation is echoed by several other recent surveys, such as those conducted by the Boston Consulting Group (2010) and IBM's *Capitalizing on Complexity* report (2010), which also found that the ability to drive and facilitate innovation was listed as the single most desired leadership quality.

Such aspirations appear justified given that successfully bringing new products and processes to market has been associated with organizational performance across multiple studies, timeframes, and in various domains (Bullinger, Auernhammer, & Gomeringer, 2004; Crawford & di Benedetto, 2007; Dess & Pickens, 2000; Estrin, 2009; Janssen, van de Vliert, & West, 2004). Perhaps the most important observation from the aforementioned surveys (Andrew, Manget, Taylor, & Zablet, 2010; Boatman & Wellins, 2011; IBM, 2010), however, was that these managers felt that they were not well prepared to accomplish this task. That is, despite wanting to consistently produce high-quality, original output, managers felt that they lacked the capacities to innovate on a sustained basis. Thus, a critical message emerges: *Innovation, while strongly desired, is very difficult to do well* (Mumford & Hunter, 2005).

One reason for this disparity between desire and achievement is the challenge in knowing, precisely, how to put a team, division, or organization on the path to generating and instantiating new products and processes (Mumford, Bedell-Avers, & Hunter, 2008; Song, Im, van der Bij, & Song, 2011). By their very nature, creativity and innovation are difficult phenomena to plan for – new ideas lack templates for both generation and execution (Honig, 2004; Hutt, Reingen, & Ronchetto, 1988; Moorman & Miner, 1998). As will be discussed in detail later in this chapter, a strong debate exists as to whether planning is even possible for complex, dynamic phenomena such as innovation (Mintzberg, 1991, Mintzberg & Waters, 1985). As suggested in other venues (e.g. Hunter, Cassidy, & Ligon, 2012; Mumford, et al., 2008), however, we contend that, while difficult, planning makes sustained innovation *possible*. The key to resolving the debate on the utility of planning is in the ability to adjust, modify, and re-define plans in dynamic fashion. Thus, a central thesis for this chapter is that planning is necessary to succeed in innovation activities (Robinson &

Pearce, 1988), yet it is unique in its reliance on agility to do well (Honig, 2004; Song et al., 2011; Moorman & Miner, 1998).

In accordance with this thesis, the outline for the chapter is as follows. Our discussion begins with a definition of planning, building largely on the work of Mumford and colleagues (Mumford, Schultz, & Osburn, 2002, Mumford, Shultz, & Van Doorn, 2001). We will then move to models proposed by Mumford and colleagues (2008) and Hunter, Cushenbery, and Freidrich (2012) that outline approaches to planning for innovation specifically, addressing the debate on whether planning is indeed helpful or harmful to sustained creative output. Finally, we spend the remainder of the chapter discussing the role of agility in planning, with particular emphasis on the requirements and antecedents of agile plan development in the task of innovation.

A Process View of Planning

Mumford and his colleagues (2001, 2002) have laid a strong foundation for viewing and conceptualizing planning not as a rote set of activities or instructions to follow, but rather as a dynamic and largely cognitive set of processes (Anzai, 1984, Hayes-Roth & Hayes-Roth, 1979; Patalano & Seifert, 1997; Xiao, Milgram, & Doyle, 1997). According to Mumford et al. (2008), these processes are "based on the mental simulation of future activities – simulations that provide the basis for script assembly and organization" (p. 112). Key here is the differential emphasis placed on seeking a plan as an end goal (i.e. the plan itself as the desired outcome) and viewing primary utility in activities comprising the planning process. More precisely, the model put forth by Mumford and colleagues places greater evaluative weight on the *act* of planning than it does on the plan generated. Namely, the activities comprising planning (e.g. mental simulation, identification of key causes and antecedents) are *most* valuable to an organization. The plan itself, while a useful and indeed necessary outcome, serves only as a starting point. The information gathered from the planning process will prove essential as plans necessarily shift and are adjusted to suit the emergent needs and opportunities.

Turning to the specific framework of the model, Mumford and colleagues (2001, 2002) have grounded their approach in the proposition that, once relevant goals are identified, key causes and mechanisms for achieving those goals can be determined. It is with these key causes that restrictions, challenges, and requirements may be used to develop an initial plan – a starting point for final plan development. Also central to the model developed by Mumford and colleagues is that information about key causes often comes in the form of cases based on previous experience (i.e. case-based knowledge; Hunter, Bedell-Avers, Hunsicker, & Mumford, 2008). With this case-based information in hand, planners are able to move forward on generating initial template plans (e.g. Hammond, 1990; Hershey, Walsh, Read, & Chulef, 1990).

As alluded to above, the second key element of the model put forward by Mumford and colleagues is that initial templates serve as *starting* points for plan refinement. Further information is gathered, plans are revised, tested, and revised again before they are ultimately instantiated. Implementation, however, serves only as an additional stage in the planning process. That is, using relevant progress markers and key sources of information, plans are further revised and edited on an ongoing basis.

Linking the Process Model of Planning to Innovation

Two elements of the Mumford et al. (2008) model warrant explicit discussion given their relevance to the present chapter. First, a process model of planning places emphasis on the identification of key causes rather than the specific goals themselves (Mumford et al., 2001, 2002). This broader perspective permits greater flexibility and dynamism in plan refinement. Although goals are starting points, key causes, contingencies, and restrictions ultimately drive plan development. Although not discussed directly in the early work on planning, this approach is critical in innovation, where goals are often necessarily loosely defined; explicit goals are simply not available when novelty is the primary aim (Honig, 2004).

Second, this process perspective is grounded in iteration. That is, rather than focusing on developing a single plan that is to be executed precisely and without deviation, planning is instead viewed as a dynamic, ongoing activity. As such, successful planning efforts are sustained and continuous. This point will be of particular importance when we discuss the role of agility in planning for innovation.

Third and finally, the model put forward by Mumford and colleagues (2001, 2002) encourages the development of contingency plans based on possible changes and shifts in the environment and organizational capabilities. This activity is critical, in that when plans change, as they must, options have been considered and the planning process does not begin from nothing. Contingency plans ensure that shifts and adjustments can occur with minimal to moderate disruption to ongoing activities (Honig, 2004). Moreover, the act of contingency planning itself is useful in identifying relevant sources of information and actors in networks that may be of use during plan refinement.

Before turning our attention to the application of the process perspective to innovation, it is useful to consider whether such an application is appropriate. That is, a number of scholars have debated whether innovation is an activity that benefits from or is harmed by planning activities. This debate is summarized below.

The Debate on Planning for Innovation: Harmful or Helpful?

There is healthy debate centering on whether an activity as complex, dynamic, and iterative as innovation benefits from planning activities (see Ansoff, 1991 and Mintzberg, 1991). Those on the anti-planning side offer several arguments against planning that cluster around three main propositions. First, innovation simply does not follow a linear path and, as such, planning lacks utility when attempting to aid the execution of novel idea production (e.g. Mintzberg & Walters, 1985). Along similar lines is the second proposition, that planning – as an end goal or product – creates constraints that ultimately harm the organic nature of creative idea generation and novel thinking (e.g. Eisenhardt & Tabrizi, 1995; Miller & Osburn, 2008). Restricting autonomy and freedom through the implementation of strict plans is theorized to serve as a barrier, rather than an aid, to innovation. Finally, there is a reasonable argument that intrinsic motivation is a necessary component of creativity and innovation. Plans may serve as extrinsic drivers, deterring from the ownership and passion that defines self-directed creative efforts (Collins & Amabile, 1999).

Acknowledging the wisdom in the collective arguments outlined above, we (Hunter et al., 2012; Mumford et al., 2008) have suggested that the very nature of innovation necessitates some form of planning – albeit in a form not traditionally thought of in the planning literature. That is, because innovation is complex and challenging, it is rare for it to occur *without* guidance (Hunter, Cassidy, & Ligon, 2011; Mumford, Hunter, Eubanks, Bedell, & Murphy, 2007). Rather, organizational factors are necessary to help elicit creative thought and execution for sustained innovation. Planning, then, serves as a starting point to begin a very difficult task; plans "get the ball rolling," even if the path changes significantly in the project cycle. Moreover, plans help to identify resources that may be necessary to move forward, ensuring that once projects begin, those components needed to make progress are on hand or, at the very least, accessible. Successful acquisition of resources, however, requires significant contingency planning – identifying possible courses and routes that might be taken and ensuring broad acquisitions of resources, talent, and expertise are made (Honig, 2004).

Finally, the above speaks to an assumption about planning that is central to the thesis of this chapter. Namely, that plans do not have to be "to-do" lists aimed at being executed in rote fashion. Instead, we argue that they can serve as dynamic guideposts – activities that, themselves, are dynamic and iterative. It is only thorough embracing planning as a malleable activity that it can match the increasingly high demands of innovation. Indeed, a study of 227 firms revealed that dynamic, agile planning was significantly predictive of new products (Song et al., 2011). If viewed and approached in this way, we contend that planning is an essential part of the innovation process. We turn now to two planning models built upon this key proposition.

Models of Planning for Innovation

Process Model of Innovation

Utilizing the framework put forth by Mumford and colleagues (2001, 2002), two additional models of planning for innovation have been proposed, with the second building squarely on the work of the first. The first model, also developed at the University of Oklahoma by Mumford and colleagues (2008), modified the original planning model in several key ways. The researchers observed that, although cases were critical for planning in non-innovative efforts, they could be harmful to creative endeavors if applied indiscriminately. The nature of novel idea production means that previous efforts (i.e. cases) have reduced utility – there simply cannot be a template for how to do something original or it would lack the very element that defines it (Hutt et al., 1988; Moorman & Miner, 1998; Scott, Lonergan, & Mumford, 2005). Thus blindly applying previous cases would likely reduce the novel components of the product or process, hampering overall innovation but probably increasing efficiency and expediency.

The researchers also noted that, due to the complexity comprising innovation and creativity, the activities take time – more time than non-innovative endeavors (Amabile, Hadley, & Kramer, 2002; Honig, 2004, Mumford & Hunter, 2005). The implication here is two-fold. First, as initial plans are being developed, new environmental, competitor-based, and organization shifts may emerge during that extended timeframe. As such, initial plans must be adapted to meet the new requirements and opportunities. This also means that planners must continually seek and acquire information relevant to planning endeavors – they must learn what changes are occurring in order to be able to adjust and capitalize on them. The second key implication is that metrics often used to assess traditional forms of performance may not apply directly to planning for innovation. As plans shift and change, so will the markers for success. This, in turn, makes overall tracking of progress quite challenging for innovative efforts.

Along these lines, it must be noted that Mumford and colleagues stress the importance of developing novel and adaptive feedback markers through the use of fundamentals, forecasting, and forecasting adjustments. Thus, while the application of traditional rote metrics is of lessened utility in a planning context, adaptive feedback metrics are critical to ongoing planning success.

These difficulties and challenges in planning for innovation led Mumford and colleagues to propose their revised model, an approach that places at its core an *incremental* approach to planning. That is, the researchers suggested that to successfully plan for creative efforts, activities must be broken into components and increments as a means to account for the requisite shifts in planning activities. A summary version of this model is presented in Figure 8.1.

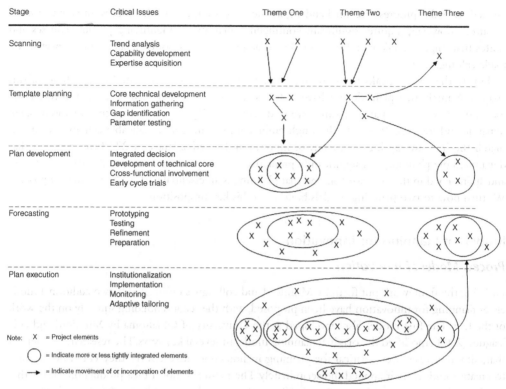

Stage	Critical Issues	Theme One	Theme Two	Theme Three
Scanning	Trend analysis Capability development Expertise acquisition			
Template planning	Core technical development Information gathering Gap identification Parameter testing			
Plan development	Integrated decision Development of technical core Cross-functional involvement Early cycle trials			
Forecasting	Prototyping Testing Refinement Preparation			
Plan execution	Institutionalization Implementation Monitoring Adaptive tailoring			

Note: X = Project elements

◯ = Indicate more or less tightly integrated elements

→ = Indicate movement of or incorporation of elements

FIGURE 8.1 Incremental model of process innovation

As may be seen Figure 8.1, there are five proposed phases of the model: (1) scanning, (2) template planning, (3) plan development, (4) forecasting, and (5) plan execution; each is described in greater detail below.

During the initial phase, scanning, the aim of planners is to search for and identify both push and pull factors that might shape innovation opportunities (Pelz, 1983; Verhaeghe & Kfir, 2002). These factors should be broad in scope so as not to limit the information obtained – data that might seem less relevant early on may prove valuable as the plan shifts and changes over time. This information serves as a critical foundation for guiding knowledge acquisition, permitting greater learning capacity in the organization.

In the second phase, template planning, the focus shifts to using results from scanning to acquire relevant expertise, develop competencies, and evaluate ongoing work in key areas identified in scanning efforts. It should be noted that the aim of template planning is not to develop formal plans, but rather to identify missing components or establish parameters that will be utilized in later planning stages. As is the case with the scanning phase, a key goal of this phase is to develop capacities that serve as the foundation for future projects through early exploratory efforts.

In the third phase, plan development, planners can begin the complex and time-intensive process of putting in place a more formal plan for innovation. This plan is not static and should evolve over time – data from early product and process cycles of innovations must be fed back to planners, allowing for necessary shifts and adjustments. After early testing and learning, parameters can be established and clearer agendas will emerge. These parameters can focus on the acquisition of requisite expertise (Cooper & Kleinschmidt, 2000), for example, or, more critically, on the development of performance metrics that are fluid enough to permit changes in assessment and goals but also rigid enough to provide guidance as to progress toward product fielding.

These early plans provide for the fourth stage, forecasting, where prototypes can be taken to a range of relevant focus and testing groups. This information provides insight into what is working, and what must be refined. Put another way, core to this stage is the central role of learning and feedback creation through the development and testing of prototypes. Organizational learning has been shown to be critical to the success of innovative efforts (Stata, 1989) in large part because learning permits greater flexibility on future challenges and opportunities. Organizational units and leaders who make a concerted effort to learn from failure and success help build capacity through more informed decision-making processes (van Dyck, Frese, Baer, & Sonnentag, 2005).

Assuming success in forecasting activities, work can begin on plan execution. In the final phase, information gathered from all stages is combined into bringing a product or process into final implementation (e.g. bringing a product to market). As noted by the researchers, this final phase may seem rather straightforward for activities other than innovation. For novel products, however, iterations and revisions still abound. In accordance with such demands, during initial activities comprising plan execution, it will be necessary to gather as much information as possible and focus substantively on monitoring activities to enhance organizational learning.

The staged, incremental approach to planning for innovation brings to fore two key points that are most directly relevant to our present effort. The first is that the slow, iterative nature of the planning process means that organizations must keep a balanced portfolio of projects moving through the innovation pipeline. Multiple ongoing projects ensure that testing can occur on a small level at multiple stages and employ multiple methods of testing and assessment. These projects comprising the portfolio, however, must be bound by some level of common scaffolding, but also be diverse enough that the lessons learned across projects can enhance divergent ideas and novel production. A guiding principle for building common scaffolding is to base project choice and selection on key fundamentals most central to the organization's or unit's strategy (Mumford et al., 2002). Fundamentals are defined as "broad conceptual infrastructure problems relevant to a number of current organizational operations" (p. 125). The second key point is that a staged approach requires the ability – significantly so – to be agile and adapt to changes in the environment, competition, and organization.

The Sub-Plan Process Model of Innovation

We recently put forth a revised version of the process model of innovation, dubbing it the sub-plan approach. The model was intended to be an extension of the work by Mumford and colleagues (2008), sharing many components from their original framework. For example, as the researchers (Mumford et al., 2008) originally suggested, we proposed that planning for innovation should be based around building a diverse project portfolio and grounded in use of fundamentals rather than explicit goals. Similarly, the sub-plan approach is also grounded in a staged, incremental approach. That is, we proposed that successful planning for innovation requires engaging in a *series* of highly related activities, all of which comprise the planning process as a whole. Also central to both models is that all stages build upon each other as a means to enhance learning capacity – leaders, units, and organizations must acquire knowledge about what works and what does not to successfully revise and adapt planning efforts.

Where the sub-plan approach differs slightly from the work by Mumford and colleagues (2008) is in its explicit emphasis on the creative process itself. Although this was implicit in previous work, we made this central in our approach to planning. More specifically, we began the chapter by asking what activities were necessary to succeed in creative and innovative endeavors. Akin to the stage approach utilized by Mumford and colleagues (2008), we used creative process models as

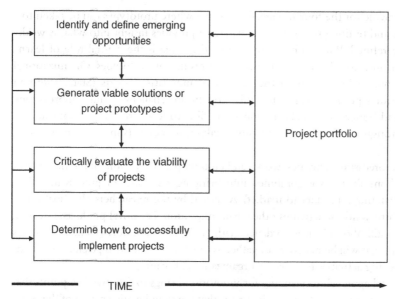

FIGURE 8.2   Sub-plan model of innovation

a foundation (Baughman & Mumford 1995; Dewey, 1910; Lubart, 2001; Wallas, 1926), suggesting that there were four primary innovation activities that should be focused on in the planning process: (1) identifying and defining emerging opportunities, (2) generating viable solutions or project prototypes, (3) critically evaluating viability of projects, and (4) determining how to successfully implement projects (see Figure 8.2).

The sub-plan approach to innovation planning proposes that planning for innovation requires organizations to develop unique plans for *each* of these activities. Given the unique needs for each activity, sub-plans are proposed to vary in multiple demands, including: their foundations for goal instantiation; behaviors and processes; specificity; and plan requirements. We proposed, for example, that to succeed in early stages, leadership plays a central role – shaping direction through vision and mission formation. In later stages such as implementation, however, relationship with networks and alliances with key stakeholders (e.g. suppliers and customers) will prove more critical. We also suggested that as sub-plans move from identifying opportunities to implementing projects, they become more specific in their requirements for successful planning.

As proposed by Mumford and colleagues (2008), by breaking processes into discrete activities, planning for innovation becomes more manageable and useful to organizations. In discussions of our model (Hunter et al., 2012), however, we stressed the importance of integrating *across* sub-plans with a particular focus on learning and feedback across plans. It is only at the intersection of these planning activities, where knowledge across all stages is combined, that innovation can occur. Integration across such activities, however, is predicated on having the knowledge and flexibility to adjust to requirements across processes as well as the emerging opportunities as project portfolios are refined and developed. That is, agility is a key requirement of planning success.

Agility: The Keystone to Successfully Planning for Innovation

Although process models put forth by Mumford and colleagues (2008) and Hunter and colleagues (2012) laid the foundation for planning innovative efforts, both chapters lacked explicit discussion on the role of plan adjustment and refinement. As alluded to when summarizing each model, both approaches mentioned the importance of planning forecasting and flexibility with comments such as: "ongoing environmental scanning and a willingness to revise and reconfigure initial plans may be integral to success in innovation planning" (Mumford et al., 2008; p. 114) and "innovation is not a static phenomenon and successfully planning for innovation will require a substantial degree of flexibility" (Hunter et al., 2012, p. 519). Other scholars have made similar statements such as "activities should be developed that interrelate in an open-ended dialectic manner, supporting the development of tacit knowledge and the ability to adapt and modify a plan, rather than the ability to preconceive and detail one" (Honig, 2004, p. 266).

Despite consistent commenting across endeavors, each has discussed agility only on the periphery, failing to expressly comment on the precise nature of plan adjustment and realignment. More critically, previous efforts have not provided specific guidance as to what is required for successful planning agility. Thus, in the second half of this chapter we move our discussion to the keystone requirement of planning for innovation: agility. Let us begin, however, with case illustrations of planning agility in an attempt to highlight the importance of this organizational capacity and ground our discussion on real-world examples.

Kodak: A Case of Planning Failure

Beginning as far back as the late 1890s, Kodak was not only successful in the world of photography, it was the clear and defined leader of the industry (Carroll & Mui, 2008). In fact, at its peak in the 1970s, Kodak captured nearly 90 percent of the market share in film. Its strategy during that era was simple and effective: focus on film and ensure they were doing it well.

In the early days, Kodak was a known innovator in the camera and film space. Notably, founder George Eastman proved very agile in his ability to move from early film development practices called "dry-plating" in the early 1900s to the focus on developing cheaper forms of film for amateur film aficionados. Where the organization proved less agile, however, was in the transition to digital photography after Mr Eastman's departure. In a form of irony, Kodak spent sizable amounts of capital on researching digital photography as a potential future avenue for camera application as well as photo sharing, only to dismiss the format when key technology was successfully developed within the organization. To be more precise, it was an engineer at Kodak named Steven Sasson who invented the first digital camera in the mid 1970s – the very technology that ultimately led to the company's downfall and recent bankruptcy.

Leadership within the organization was aware of its new invention and realized, superficially, the potential for digital photography. They righty feared, however, that if introduced too early it would cannibalize their film and camera business. Because they were the early inventors of digital technology, they knew they had some time to adjust their strategy – their innovation plan – to adapt to digital formats. Although correct in assuming it had time (technology was very expensive in early digital days), Kodak ultimately failed to adapt its approach. It let competitors drive the market in the digital space and, although the organization attempted to keep up, there was still a hope that a large-scale return to film would ultimately occur.

The lessons from the Kodak failures are clear. As an organization, it was unwilling to adapt, adjust, and modify its strategic approach to innovation. When presented with new information (i.e. the emergence of digital technology) and even new technology developed within the organization (i.e. the digital camera), it continued on an initial path defined decades earlier. Had Kodak been more agile in its planning process, seeking to adjust and modify within the constraints of the organization, it would likely be the leader it once was when George Eastman founded the company and embraced agility as a keystone to management.

Google and Amazon: Illustrations of Planning Agility and Success

Google

While still in its infancy, Google developed a core mission that it relies on even today: become the best search engine in the world while, as the founders stated, "doing no evil." Created and led by two software engineers, Sergey Brin and Larry Page, the search engine developed within the organization was one of the first to be profitable, doing so through innovative algorithms and a simple approach to design and pricing (Estrin, 2009; Vise & Malseed, 2006).

What makes Google particularly relevant to the discussion on planning is its embracing of broad goals and themes as well as its ability to adapt, improvise, and seek out new opportunities from its partners and employees. Although the organization could easily have focused its efforts on the search engine alone, it realized that it was acquiring the best and brightest talent in the software space. As such, it followed a model established by 3M, where a portion of the time was given to employees to engage in autonomous activities (Vise & Malseed, 2006). Strategic planning efforts such as these led to the highly popular email service, Gmail. Moreover, Google recently acquired video powerhouse YouTube, resulting in the ability to integrate web searches with video output. Finally, Google has embraced a number of collaborative suites such as Google Chat and Google Docs, which allow for collaboration in ways not possible prior to their instantiation. Thus, although the lessons on leading for innovation derived from Google are numerous, what is highlighted is its ability to seek new forms of input, be open to shifting opportunities and competition, and, most importantly, adjust its innovation plan to address these changes. Despite its size and influence, Google remains a highly agile organization, capable of sustained and impactful innovation.

Amazon

Demonstrating planning agility that may rival even Google is current web-superstore, Amazon. com (Johnson, 2010). Led by known innovative CEO, Jeff Bezos, Amazon had humble beginnings on the World Wide Web, focusing primarily on selling books ordered online which were efficiently shipped to customers. To the surprise of many, Mr Bezos took the company in an astute direction, extending their offering beyond simply hardcovers and paperbacks. The organization and its leaders recognized the value of serving as a storefront for a range of third-party vendors. Such an approach had never been undertaken on such a grand and creative scale. It was also wildly successful, seeing revenues jump from four million dollars to twenty million dollars over six years (Johnson, 2010).

Never resting on its laurels, Amazon once again noticed a trend in the marketplace around 2007, shifting to digital offerings of books, selling the wildly popular Kindle e-reader. With a digital reader in hand, Amazon also began to move into the periodical and newspaper market, disrupting heavily well-established and somewhat complacent business environments. More recently, Amazon has taken on video-hosting giant, Netflix, through its Amazon-Prime service by offering web-streaming movies and television shows. Given its success in other innovative endeavors, competitors would be justified in their concern over Amazon entering their market.

As can be surmised from the range of activities described above, Amazon's approach to planning and strategy is grounded squarely on agility. The philosophy is also nicely summarized by a few quotes given in an organization webcast. Bezos commented on the organization's willingness to respond to new opportunities, stating, "That doesn't mean that these things are guaranteed to work, but we have a lot of expertise and a lot of knowledge." Moreover, when discussing his strategic choices, Bezos noted that "All of these things based on our operating history are things we can analyze quantitatively rather than have to make intuitive judgments." On the whole, Google and Amazon highlight the importance of responding to change in the market, competition, customers, and their own organizational capacities. Put another way, both organizations place agility as a keystone in their approach to innovation.

Planning Agility: Definition and Requirements

What can hopefully be observed in the illustrations above is that organizational strategy and innovation plans, in particular, must be capable of meeting the dynamic shifts in requirements comprising the innovation process. *Thus, we define planning agility as the organizational capacity to adapt, adjust, and respond to emerging requirements and opportunities that allow for greater innovative achievement.*

In what is perhaps the best illustration of the criticality of agility in planning, Song et al. (2011) examined 227 firms, focusing on new product development as the primary criterion for innovative performance. The researchers found that formal planning activities actually hampered new product development, but those that were more improvised (i.e. agile) were associated with a greater number of new products. Song and colleagues note "Therefore, more flexible strategic plans that accommodate potential improvisations may be needed in new product development [NPD] management since innovation-related activities cannot be planned precisely due to the unexpected jolts and contingencies in the NPD process" (p. 503). Given similar messages provided coming from other studies and scholars (e.g. Honig, 2004; Hunter et al., 2012; Moorman & Miner, 1998; Mumford et al., 2008), we turn to those capacities that permit requisite planning flexibility.

Commitment to Frequent Forecasting

Foundational to both the Mumford and colleagues (2008) and Hunter and colleagues (2012) models of planning is the use of forecasting to develop successful plans. Forecasting involves consideration of how implemented plans may ultimately "play out" and is essential in revising, editing, and extending planning activities. With regard to planning agility specifically, forecasting is essential in identifying possible problems and challenges (e.g. timing difficulties), further guiding additional requisition of expertise or other additional resources.

The use of forecasting as a critical component of planning for innovation also underscores the importance of learning and feedback as a means to develop improved forecasts throughout ongoing planning activities (Berger, Guilford, & Christensen, 1957; Dörner & Schaub, 1994; Noice, 1991). Knowledge acquisition is contingent upon a number of factors discussed earlier in the chapter, most notably a commitment to continual and frequent scanning as well as the development and deployment of viable metrics to track progress in planning and project execution. Moreover, forecasting is essential in developing and refining contingency plans, suggesting that forecasting is particularly critical during later stages of the innovation and planning process, when enough knowledge is present to support fruitful forecasting activities.

Emphasis on Contingency Planning

In models outlined by Mumford and colleagues (2001, 2002), contingency planning played a critical role in successful planning efforts. Contingency planning involves the generation of viable alternative plans that may be applied if certain conditions (i.e. contingencies) arise. They are, colloquially speaking, "plans B and C" of the planning process – the backups to "plan A" should it fail.

Contingency plans aid in developing planning agility in two primary ways. First, they provide guidance regarding what the relevant change variables might be. That is, to develop a "plan B," planners must consider what might alter the utility of "plan A" and create a need for implementing a contingency plan. The identification of these key change variables helps to provide greater context and richness to the key causes approach to planning (Mumford et al., 2001, 2002). Contingency planning, in essence, provides input as to possible moderators and boundary conditions to the antecedents driving the planning process (e.g. key causes). Planners are then able to put in place markers and performance metrics around these key change variables that can provide important guidance as to when a plan may need to be adjusted. Thus, as is the case with planning as a process, the act of contingency planning becomes equally, or perhaps even more so, valuable as the actual product (i.e. a secondary plan) of the process.

The second, more pragmatic way contingency planning helps in promoting planning agility is in simply instantiating backup plans should the need arise. Effective contingency plans ensure that when changes are needed, planners need not necessarily begin from "zero." They have a place to start in evaluating necessary adjustments and, if the contingency plans suit the needs well, can make adjustments fairly quickly, providing an important advantage over those organizations that fail to put contingency plans in place. It should be borne in mind, however, that caution is warranted when applying contingency plans without carefully considering whether the new plan is appropriate for the emergent context. At times it may be necessary to develop entirely new approaches to innovation if contingency plans are not applicable – albeit new plans that are grounded in the fundamentals of the organization. Finally, contingency planning as a means to improve agility will be most beneficial in the middle and later stages of the innovation process, where enough information has been gathered that useful contingency plans can be created, but early enough to allow the development of contingencies to guide early-stage activities such as scanning.

Feedback and Learning

Whereas contingency plans provide guidance prior to initial plan instantiation, feedback provides guidance as the planning process continues and projects begin their innovation cycles. To make plan adjustments, it is critical that planners have, at the ready, information to guide plan refinement. Thus frequent feedback from a range of sources is essential to the innovation process, though it will be most useful to planning in later-stage activities where adjustments, rather than initial templates, are being made (Amabile, 1996; Amabile & Conti, 1999; Basu & Green, 1997; Choi, 2004; Frese, Teng, & Wijnen, 1999; Janssen, 2005; Lim & Choi, 2009; Madjar, Oldham, & Pratt, 2002; Oldham & Cummings, 1996; Rice, 2006; Tierney & Farmer, 2002, 2004; Unsworth, Wall, & Carter, 2005).

Diversity in information is one of two factors most essential for feedback to have the greatest utility in aiding planning agility. Due to the challenges in quantifying and measuring creative and innovative performance, no one single source of information will be sufficient to provide guidance on success (Mumford et al., 2008). Rather, it will be necessary to gather input from a range of sources, each with unique insight and data (Basset-Jones, 2005). Feedback may come from customers via sales figures or more intimately in focus group testing. Input from employees will be critical, given their knowledge of how a plan may be operating outside of the boardroom. Upper and mid-level management also bring with them their own insight into plan operation. Finally, other stakeholders such as suppliers, retailers, and manufacturers have a unique perspective on how a plan may be functioning. It is through the aggregate lens of these data that effective planning adjustments may be made.

An additional element of feedback that is critical to making effective modifications is frequency of information gathering. Given the resources necessary to acquire data from the wide range of individuals and groups described above, frequency becomes a critical factor – gathering input too often results in significant resources being wasted. Data gathered too infrequently, in contrast, means that planners lack the dynamic input necessary to be agile. Thus, the recommendation is to acquire as much feedback as possible, as frequently as possible, with one caveat: emphasize frequent data collection efforts (Alvero, Bucklin, & Austin, 2001) on those sources where frequency requires fewer resources, and make concerted efforts to acquire richer data from those sources where heavy resources are required.

One final comment regarding active learning is that leaders must make a clear effort to connect efforts from all planning activities into a cohesive planning approach (Hunter et al., 2012). Agility is grounded in knowledge and to the extent that leaders make active learning across various planning events a priority, the entire planning process will benefit.

Climate

Given the importance of feedback to developing agile plans, it is essential that sources of input feel comfortable *sharing* input on planning and innovation efforts (Sitkin, 1996). This can be somewhat challenging in organizations where feedback can be seen as undesirable, particularly if it indicates low performance (Baer & Frese, 2003). As such, researchers have begun to examine the role of climate in facilitating learning environments. In one such form of climate, termed error management, Van Dyck et al. (2005) examined 65 Dutch organizations and found that a positive error management environment was correlated with both organizational goal achievement and organizational performance. In a second study, the researchers found that across 47 German organizations, performance was also correlated with a positive approach to error management. On the whole, these studies suggest that a proactive approach to learning, even if learning means facing poor performance, is helpful for improving information sharing and overall organizational success. Moreover, a climate for learning will be most useful when early plans are being developed and a wide range of ideas are being considered, but also during evaluative activities where lessons from failure must be shared as a means to refine plans.

Along lines related to those above, a growing body of research suggests that high psychological safety is critical for innovative performance (e.g. Baer & Frese, 2003; Edmondson, 2004). A recent meta-analysis, for example, revealed that psychological safety produced some of the largest effect sizes for creative and innovative achievement (Hunter et al., 2007). One possible mechanism for the importance of this dimension of climate is the increased learning and feedback received from employees.

Although other examples exist, the above should suffice to make the basic point: organizations with environments characterized by appropriate error management and high psychological safety are most likely to facilitate appropriate channels of communication necessary for gathering data to be used in planning adjustment and refinement.

Opportunity for Realignment

Although it seems intuitive, it is critical for planners to set aside time specifically for examining current plans and determining if changes are necessary. Meetings designed expressly for strategic and planning development are critical for innovative planning agility for two reasons. First, they send the message to stakeholders, employees, and even leaders that planning is an ongoing, iterative process. Such role-modeling behavior is critical for establishing psychologically safe and learning-oriented climates such as those described above (Lovelace & Hunter, 2013). More pragmatic is the second reason, which is simply the opportunity to evaluate and assess the information planners will have worked so hard to obtain. With time set aside to evaluate and process these data, planners have the requisite opportunity to develop contingency plans or simply revise ongoing efforts. Given the focus on revision, opportunities for realignment are most useful during later-stage planning activities, where plans have been developed to the point that they benefit from evaluation.

Despite the intuitive importance of such meetings, several barriers stand in the way of establishing them as routine. The most substantial is that organizational demands limit the time and opportunities for key stakeholders to get together. Organizational life is busy, and regular meetings that may result in few if any changes are, not surprisingly, difficult to schedule. These challenges underscore the importance of making a *concerted* effort to establish regular meeting times where plans can be evaluated and assessed. Failure to do so means inertia takes over and monthly meetings become annual events.

Awareness of Capabilities

Should information gathered from the various sources reveal that a change should be made, it is critical that those attending the meeting have an awareness of organizational resources and knowledge available (Mumford et al., 2007). Research is clear in demonstrating that multi-functional teams are critical to innovation (Cooper & Kleinschmidt, 2000; Eisenhardt & Tabrizi, 1995; Thamhain, 2003), underscoring the importance of the range of resources needed for innovation. Plan adjustments, then, are contingent upon having this range of awareness across multiple divisions and departments, with particular emphasis on possessing knowledge regarding culture, structure, ongoing divisional, departmental, and team strategies, and the controls utilized in allocating resources (Cardinal, 2001; Howell & Boies, 2004). Organizations that lack such awareness may either miss an opportunity that they were capable of embracing or, perhaps more harmful, embrace endeavors they believed were within the capability of the organization. As such, awareness is particularly critical to innovation during mid- and later-stage innovation activities, where evaluations of planning success through forecasting are most beneficial to guiding plan adjustments and progress.

Leadership with Requisite Authority

As discussed throughout the chapter, it is necessary for organizations to have relevant information with which to decide potential plan adjustments and they must similarly have knowledge of what the organization is capable of – both limitations and strengths alike (Cardinal, 2001; Howell & Boies, 2004). Yet agility specifically requires the capacity to make the requisite changes quickly. That is, it is pointless to schedule planning meetings if those with the necessary authority to instantiate changes do not attend (Yukl & Falbe, 1991). If representatives for a given leader must go back to that leader to gain approval for plan changes, key opportunities to react and respond may be lost. Instead, those at the meeting should be able to make decisions and provide approval about shifts in plans. Along these lines, having requisite authority is most critical to later-stage innovation activities where plans have been developed to the point that they are more evaluative than generative.

Networks

Planning agility is predicated on having information about shifting demands and emerging opportunities. As such, ties, connections, and networks are critical to providing both linkages to emerging trends and guidance on capacities to capitalize on new opportunities (Mitra, 2000). Not surprisingly, strong networks have been tied to successful innovation endeavors across multiple studies (Mumford et al., 2007). Gemunden, Heydenbreck, and Herden (1992), for example, found that alliance formation was positively related to performance in new product development efforts.

Similarly, Allen and Cohen (1969) found that high-performing R&D team members had a greater number of ties outside of the organization. Thus, congruent with our discussion on expertise, alliance formation or network development helps provide necessary input for planning and innovation (Adams & Day, 1998; Nellore & Balachandra, 2001).

In addition to external alliances, it is critical to have strong networks within the organization (Abra, 1994; Gassman & van Zedwitz, 2003). Consider the example from Nissan's design team led by Jerry Hirschberg during a peak period of innovation for the organization. While leading the development of a new line of trucks at Nissan, Hirschberg (1999) lamented that discussing design options with sales or marketing groups was disallowed at the time. As head of design, he realized that such communication was necessary and, discretely, crossed departmental boundaries to engage in conversations with individuals within sales and marketing. Exchanges with individuals in these departments revealed that, although truck owners were very knowledgeable about truck-specific capabilities (e.g. towing capacity, bed-size), most trucks were used primarily for transportation and "not as trucks" (Hirschberg, 1999; p. 198) – owners actually used their vehicles as "trucks" only 25 percent of the time. This informal feedback from individuals in sales drove the *design* priorities for the truck and resulted in a highly innovative, and financially successful, outcome. Thus, by crossing organizational borders, planners can develop a much better picture of emerging opportunities and the design solutions for them.

One final point regarding networks should be borne in mind. Namely that, consistent with the planning model by Hunter and colleagues (2012), networks will play a greater or lesser role throughout various stages of the innovation process. Although connections will be useful throughout, professional networks are most useful in early-stage activities, while more extensive networks drive planning success at later stages of the process.

Resources

Given the lengthy discussion on requirements for planning agility, it is not surprising that effectively developing planning agility is a resource-intensive activity. Innovation, itself, is a costly endeavor that entails a substantial degree of risk. The vast majority of creative projects will fail and with them, substantial capital may be lost – particularly for those ideas that have reached later stages of production. Thus having capital is critical to the innovation process and particularly important to the capacity for agility as well.

Resources play three critical roles in supporting planning agility (Hunt & Morgan, 1995). The first is that resources in an organization allow planners to obtain and gather rich sources of data (Koberg, Uhlenbruck, & Sarason, 1996). This information is needed from a diverse audience and is needed with substantial frequency. Emerging technologies can aid in the gathering of such data, but the management of these data and technologies also requires significant financial investment. The second way resources contribute to planning agility is through allowing organizations to acquire and retain a diverse set of expertise within and outside of their organization (Cardinal, 2001; Li & Atuahene-Gima, 2001; Mitra, 2000; Sivadas & Dwyer, 2000). Google, for example, will seek out emerging talent without explicit knowledge of how they might contribute, knowing only that their expertise is likely to be helpful to the broader project portfolio. Resources allow for this type of talent acquisition in the workforce, but also permit organizations to bring in experts for short projects or even simple seminars. A growing number of highly innovative organizations make a concerted effort to have experts brought in weekly or monthly to give talks on highly diverse topics. This diversity in content allows employees and planners to make connections not readily apparent in their ongoing development efforts (Estrin, 2009) – connections particularly useful in early-stage planning and innovation activities.

Finally, resources allow for the extra time necessary to make adjustments to projects. Smaller organizations, those that are relying on one or two projects to survive, are unable to "shelve" a project and push it to another planning cycle. Large organizations with greater capital, however, have the capacity to both push and pull projects through cycles according to how they fit within the broader organizational strategy. In this role, resources are most helpful in later stages of the innovation process where execution activities often run into challenges not accounted for in initial plans.

Bounded Planning

One final point in the case for planning agility is that while planning for innovation should be flexible, such flexibility must necessarily be tempered by the pragmatic realities of organizational life. Put another way, if plans change so greatly that long-term progress is hampered, planning loses its primary functions, which is to guide and shepherd efforts toward innovative ends. Thus, planning must intentionally be bounded and limited for agility. The question brought to fore becomes, "In what way should planning efforts be bounded?"

Although organizations must assess and weigh their own unique organizational constraints, two factors warrant specific mention in guiding and limiting planning efforts. The first is through careful and explicit consideration of the core fundamentals that define project portfolios and overarching organizational strategies (Mumford et al., 2008). Extending too far beyond core strategies and fundamentals can limit the long-term effectiveness of planning and virtually ensures that successful, sustained innovation will not occur. The second key bounding factor is organizational expertise. Successful planning is contingent upon having requisite expertise to weigh, consider, and forecast scenarios – using an ongoing set of learning and feedback avenues to support experts' base of knowledge. Although successful planning efforts can provide indications as to what type of additional expertise is required, the fact remains that organizations have practical limitations on who they can hire and consult with (i.e. the experts they have access to). These practical limitations are often necessarily driven by fundamentals which dictate where and how resources are spent. As such, organizations must seek agility and flexibility within the confines of what can be accomplished. For innovation, these bounds are admittedly stretched, but cannot be wholly open ended. In more pointed terms, ignoring practical constraints is a recipe for fatal and frequent error, not successful innovation.

Conclusions and Future Directions

Before turning to the broader conclusions emerging from the present effort, at least three limitations must be borne in mind. First, although an attempt was made to summarize the literature on planning, we focused largely on our work (Hunter et al., 2012) as well as that of Mumford and colleagues (2001, 2002, 2008). Thus, our lens is largely a cognitive one and should be viewed as one of several perspectives on planning (Hayes-Roth & Hayes-Roth, 1979). Second, our summary and recommendations on planning were aimed at planners and leaders at upper levels of an organization. Thus, those leaders seeking to improve innovative output at a more micro level may find the chapter less applicable (see Hunter et al., 2011 for a more direct discussion). Third and finally, although we attempted to be as comprehensive as space permitted, our discussion on the requirements for planning agility remains a sample of those requirements. As such, our discussion should be viewed as a prioritized collection rather than a complete representation of requirements.

Conclusions

With these limitations noted, we turn now to the broader conclusions flowing from the present effort. The first, echoed throughout the chapter, is that planning must be viewed as a process – an ongoing activity that is continually shaped, defined, and redefined. This perspective resolves the debate surrounding the applicability of planning to innovation. Plans that are developed to be executed without deviation will not serve to aid in creativity and innovation. However, plans that are developed to help in guiding a complex activity yet which are responsive to the changing needs and demands of the project and external environment are essential tools for increasing innovative performance.

The second point, similar to the first, is that a staged or incremental approach to innovation is also critical to successfully applying planning to novel idea production and instantiation. The complexity surrounding creativity and innovation means that tackling the task of planning is nearly impossible as a broad activity. By breaking this task into more manageable components, effective plans can be developed. Moreover, planners can identify the key requirements, restrictions, and causes of each sub-plan, allowing for the obtainment of key resources and expertise. Using an incremental approach allows planners to tackle a large-scale, complex task in a reasonable manner.

Third, the primary contribution of the chapter was in proposing that the key to planning for innovation was in developing the capacity for agility. Given the increased timeframes required for innovative endeavors, planners will be faced with a changing landscape of demands. An inability to respond to these demands means that they will be bringing products and processes to market that may be unnecessary or outdated. In contrast, by taking a flexible approach to planning, organizations are able to respond to the changing demands and opportunities, turning planning into an asset rather than an anchor.

Finally, the aggregate of the above illustrates quite well the difficulty and challenges surrounding effective planning for innovation. Clearly, successfully engaging in planning requires substantial resources at both the organizational and the individual, cognitive level. This difficulty is likely where those organizations willing to engage in the activity will gain a competitive advantage over those lacking resources or fortitude to do so on an ongoing and sustained basis.

Future Directions and Parting Comments

Despite its importance, planning for innovation remains a relatively understudied topic. As more research is conducted, at least three areas seem particularly ripe for investigation. The first is a critical examination of the role of technology in the planning process (Fairchild, Cassidy, Cushenbery, & Hunter, 2011). In particular, new forms of technology are emerging that are helpful in gathering information about trends in customer bases, product use, and preferences for activities, among others. Given the resource demands for successful planning, these new forms of technology may limit the demands and allow access to data that was unavailable in the past.

Second, along the lines of the above, there is some indication that organizational size affects planning utility. Song and colleagues (2011), for example, found that planning was most useful in larger organizations attempting to develop new products. Those in smaller organizations saw less utility in the activities, likely due to their inherent ability to be agile. Thus, future research should examine the nature of organization size and bureaucratic structure on planning utility and implementation.

In closing, we attempted to summarize the many perspectives on planning for innovation, ultimately proposing that – as a process – planning represents a critical component of successful innovation. Being a bit metaphorical, plans should not be viewed as grocery lists dictating, without question, what must be purchased at the supermarket for dinner that night. Instead, plans are better viewed as themes that push us toward the local farmer's market. When we arrive, we will have considered a number of options we will look for, but we will be open and willing to adjust based on the availability of ingredients. Having smelled and tasted the offerings, we can also talk with local farmers about which vegetables may be available next week, what form of produce is particularly good this year, or which butcher we should trust. With this new information, we could adjust our dinner plan, inviting new guests or paring down the event to only a select few. Thus our desire to prepare a meal can bring us to the market, but we must be open to what is available that day and others in the future. In the end, a meal developed through an iterative, agile approach is one we would much prefer attending. It would simply be more creative.

References

Abra, J. (1994). Collaboration in creative work: An initiative for investigation. *Creativity Research Journal*, 8, 205–218.

Adams, J. E., & Day, G. S. (1998). Enhancing new product development performance: An organizational learning perspective. *Journal of Product Innovation Management*, 15, 403–422.

Allen, T. J., & Cohen, S. I. (1969). Information flow in research and development laboratories. *Administrative Science Quarterly*, 14, 12–19.

Alvero, A. M., Bucklin, B. R., & Austin, J. (2001). An objective review of the effectiveness and essential characteristics of performance feedback in organizational settings (1985–1998). *Journal of Organizational Behavior Management*, 21, 4–29.

Amabile, T. M. (1996). *Creativity in context: Update to "The social psychology of creativity."* Boulder, CO: Westview Press.

Amabile, T. M., & Conti, R. (1999). Changes in the work environment for creativity during downsizing. *Academy of Management Journal*, 42, 630–640.

Amabile, T. M., Hadley, C. N., & Kramer, S. J. (2002). Creativity under the gun. *Harvard Business Review*, 80, 52–61.

Andrew, J. P., Manget, J., Michael, D. C. Taylor, A., & Zablit, H. (2010, April). *Innovation 2010: A return to prominence – and the emergence of a new world order.* Boston, MA: The Boston Consulting Group.

Ansoff, H. I. (1991). Critique of Henry Mintzberg's "the Design School: Reconsidering the basic premises of strategic management." *Strategic Management Journal*, 12, 449–461.

Anzai, Y. (1984). Cognitive control of real-time event-driven systems. *Cognitive Science*, 8, 221–254.

Baer, M., & Frese, M. (2003). Innovation is not enough: Climates for initiative and psychological safety, process innovations, and firm performance. *Journal of Organizational Behavior*, 24, 45–69.

Bassett-Jones, N. (2005). The paradox of diversity management, creativity and innovation. *Creativity and Innovation Management*, 14, 169–175.

Basu, R., & Green, S. G. (1997). Leader-member exchange and transformational leadership: An empirical examination of innovative behaviors in leader-member dyads. *Journal of Applied Psychology*, 27, 477–499.

Baughman, W. A., & Mumford, M. D. (1995). Process analytic models of creative capacities: Operations involved in the combination and reorganization process. *Creativity Research Journal*, 8, 37–62.

Berger, R. M., Guilford, J. P., & Christensen, P. R. (1957). A factor-analytic study of planning abilities. *Psychological Monographs: General and Applied*, 71(6), 1–31.

Boatman, J. E., & Wellins, R. S. 2011. *Global leadership forecast 2011.* Pittsburgh, PA: Development Dimensions International.

Bullinger, H. J., Auernhammer, K., & Gomeringer, A. (2004). Managing innovation networks in the knowledge-driven economy. *International Journal of Production Research*, 42, 3337–3353.

Cardinal, L. B. (2001). Technological innovation in the pharmaceutical industry: the use of organizational control in managing research and development. *Organization Science*, 12, 19–37.

Carroll, P. B., & Mui, C. (2008). 7 ways to fail big. *Harvard Business Review*, 86, 82–91.

Choi, J. N. (2004). Individual and contextual predictors of creative performance: The mediating role of psychological processes. *Creativity Research Journal*, 16, 187–199.

Collins, M. A., & Amabile, T. M. (1999). Motivation and creativity. In R. J. Sternberg (Ed.), *Handbook of creativity* (pp. 297–312). New York: Cambridge University Press.

Cooper, R. G., & Kleinschmidt, E. J. (2000). New product performance: What distinguishes the star products. *Australian Journal of Management*, 25, 17–46.

Crawford, C. M., & Di Benedetto, C. A. (2007). *New products management* (7th ed). New York: McGraw-Hill Irwin.

Dess, G. G., & Pickens, J. C. (2000). Changing roles: Leadership in the 21st century. *Organizational Dynamics,* 28, 18–34.

Dewey, J. (1910). *How we think.* Lexington, MA: D.C. Heath.

Dörner, D., & Schaub, H. (1994). Errors in planning and decision making and the nature of human information processing. *Applied Psychology: An International Review,* 43, 433–453.

Edmonson, E. C. (2004). Learning from mistakes is easier said than done: Group and organizational influences on the detection and connection of human error. *Journal of Applied Psychology,* 40, 66–90.

Eisenhardt, K. M., & Tabrizi, B. N. (1995). Accelerating adaptive processes: Product innovation in the global computer industry. *Administrative Science Quarterly,* 40, 84–110.

Estrin, J. (2009). *Closing the innovation gap.* New York: McGraw-Hill.

Fairchild, J., Cassidy, S., Cushenbery, L., & Hunter, S. (2011). Integrating technology with the creative design process. In A. Mesquita (Ed.), *Technology for creativity and innovation: Tools, techniques and applications* (pp. 26–51). Hershey, PA: IGI Global.

Frese, M., Teng. E., & Wijnen, C. J. D. (1999). Helping to improve suggestion systems: Predictors of giving suggestions in companies. *Journal of Organizational Behavior,* 20, 1139–1155.

Gassman, O., & van Zedwitz, M. (2003). Trends and determinants of managing virtual R&D teams. *R&D Management,* 33, 243–263.

Gemunden, H. G., Heydebreck, P., & Herden, R. (1992). Technological interweavement: A means of achieving innovation success. *R&D Management,* 22, 359–376.

Hammond, K. J. (1990). Case-based planning: A framework for planning from experience. *Cognitive Science,* 14, 385–443.

Hayes-Roth, B., & Hayes-Roth, F. (1979). A cognitive model of planning. *Cognitive Science,* 3, 275–310.

Hershey, D. A., Walsh, D. A., Read, S. J., & Chulef, A. S. (1990). The effects of expertise on financial problem-solving: Evidence for goal-directed problem-solving scripts. *Organizational Behavior and Human Decision Processes,* 46, 77–101.

Hirschberg, J. (1999). *The creative priority.* New York: HarperBusiness.

Honig, B. (2004). Entrepreneurship education: Toward a model of contingency based business planning. *Academy of Management Learning and Education,* 3, 258–273.

Howell, J. M., & Boies, K. (2004). Champions of technological innovation: The influence of contextual knowledge, role orientation, idea generation, and idea promotion on champion emergence. *Leadership Quarterly,* 15, 130–149.

Hunt, S. D., & Morgan, R. M. (1995). The comparative advantage theory of competition. *Journal of Marketing,* 59, 1–15.

Hunter, S. T., Bedell-Avers, K. E., & Mumford, M. D. (2007). Climate for creativity: A quantitative review. *Creativity Research Journal,* 19, 69–90.

Hunter, S. T., Bedell-Avers, K. E., Ligon, G. S., Hunsicker, C. M., & Mumford, M. D. (2008). Applying multiple knowledge structures in creative thought: Effects on idea generation and problem-solving. *Creativity Research Journal,* 20, 137–154.

Hunter, S. T., Cassidy, S. E., & Ligon, G. S. (2012). Planning for innovation: A process-oriented perspective. In M. D. Mumford (Ed.), *Handbook of organizational creativity* (pp. 515–545). Oxford, UK: Elsevier.

Hunter, S. T., Cushenbery, L., & Freidrich, T. M. (2012). Hiring an innovative workforce: A necessary yet uniquely challenging endeavor. *Human Resource Management Review,* 22, 303–322.

Hutt, M. D., Reingen, P. H., & Ronchetto, J. R. (1988). Tracing emergent processes in marketing strategy formation. *Journal of Marketing,* 52, 4–19.

IBM Global Business Services (2010). *Capitalizing on complexity: Insights from the global chief executive officer study.* Somers, NY: IBM Corporation.

Janssen, O. (2005). The joint impact of perceived influence and supervisor supportiveness on employee innovative behavior. *Journal of Occupational and Organizational Psychology,* 78, 573–579.

Janssen, O., van de Vliert, E., & West, M. (2004). The bright and dark sides of individual and group innovation: A special issue introduction. *Journal of Organizational Behavior,* 25, 129–146.

Johnson, M. W. (2010). *Seizing the white space: Business model innovation for growth and renewal.* Boston, MA: Harvard Business School Publishing.

Koberg, C. S., Uhlenbruck, N., & Sarason, Y. (1996). Facilitators of organizational innovation: The role of life-cycle stage. *Journal of Business Venturing,* 11, 133–149.

Li, H., & Atuahene-Gima, K. (2001). Product innovation strategy and the performance of technology ventures in China. *Academy of Management Journal*, 44, 1123–1134.

Lim, H. S., & Choi, J. N. (2009). Testing an alternative relationship between individual and contextual predictors of creative performance. *Social Behavior and Personality*, 37, 117–136.

Lovelace, J. B., & Hunter, S. T. (2013). Charismatic, ideological, and pragmatic leaders' influence on subordinate creative performance along the creative process. *Creativity Research Journal*, 25, 59–74.

Lubart, T. I. (2001). Models of the creative process: Past, present, and future. *Creativity Research Journal*, 13, 295–308.

Madjar, N., Oldham, G. R., & Pratt, M. G. (2002). There's no place like home? The contributions of work and nonwork creativity support to employees' creative performance. *Academy of Management Journal*, 45, 757–787.

Miller, C., & Osburn, R. N. (2008). Innovation as contested terrain: Planned creativity and innovation versus emergent creativity and innovation. In M. D. Mumford, S. T. Hunter, & K. E. Bedell Avers (Eds.), *Multi-level issues in creativity and innovation* (pp.169–187). Oxford, UK: Elsevier.

Mintzberg, H. (1991). Learning-1, planning-0- reply. *Strategic Management Journal*, 12, 463–466.

Mintzberg, H., & Waters, J. (1985). Of strategies, deliberate and emergent. *Strategic Management Journal*, 6, 257–272.

Mitra, J. (2000). Making corrections: Innovation and collective learning in small businesses. *Education and Training*, 42, 228–237.

Moorman, C., & Miner, A. S. (1998). The convergence of planning and execution: improvisation in new product development. *The Journal of Marketing*, 62, 1–20.

Mumford, M. D. (Ed.) (2012). *Handbook of organizational creativity*. Waltham, MA: Academic Press.

Mumford, M. D., & Hunter, S. T. (2005). Innovation in organizations: A multi-level perspective on creativity. In F. J. Yammarino & F. Dansereau (Eds.), *Research in multi-level issues* (Vol. IV, pp. 11–74). Oxford, UK: Elsevier.

Mumford, M. D., Schultz, R. A., & Van Doorn, J. R. (2001). Performance in planning: Processes, requirements, and errors. *Review of General Psychology*, 5, 213–240.

Mumford, M. D., Schultz, R. A., & Osburn, H. K. (2002). Planning in organizations: Performance as a multi-level phenomenon. In F. J. Yammarino & F. Dansereau (Eds.), *Research in multi-level issues* (Vol. 1: The many faces of multi-level issues, pp. 3–36). Oxford, UK: Elsevier.

Mumford, M. D., Hunter, S. T., Eubanks, D. L., Bedell, K. E., & Murphy, S. T. (2007). Developing leaders for creative efforts: A domain-based approach to leadership development. *Human Resource Management Review*, 17, 402–417.

Mumford, M. D., Bedell-Avers, K. E., & Hunter, S. T. (2008). Planning for innovation: A multi-level perspective. In M. D. Mumford, S. T. Hunter, & K. E. Bedell-Avers (Eds.), *Research in Multi-level Issues* (Vol. VII, pp. 17–34). Oxford, UK: Elsevier.

Nellore, R., & Balachandra, R. (2001). Factors influencing success in integrated product development (IPD) projects. *IEEE Transactions on Engineering Management*, 48, 164–173.

Noice, H. (1991). The role of explanations and plan recognition in the learning of theatrical scripts. *Cognitive Science*, 15, 425–460.

Oldham, G. R., & Cummings, A. (1996). Employee creativity: Personal and contextual factors at work. *Academy of Management Journal*, 39, 607–634.

Patalano, A. L., & Seifert, C. M. (1997). Opportunistic planning: Being reminded of pending goals. *Cognitive Psychology*, 34, 1–36.

Pelz, D. C. (1983). Quantitative case histories of urban innovation: Are there innovating stages? *IEEE Transactions on Engineering Management*, 30, 60–67.

Rice, G. (2006). Individual values, organizational context, and self-perceptions of employee creativity. Evidence from Egyptian organizations. *Journal of Business Research*, 59, 233–241.

Robinson, R. B., & Pearce, J. A. (1988). Planned patterns of strategic behavior and their relationship to business-unit performance. *Strategic Management Journal*, 9, 43–60.

Scott, G. M., Lonergan, D. C., & Mumford, M. D. (2005). Conceptual combination: Alternative knowledge structures, alternative heuristics. *Creativity Research Journal*, 17, 79–98.

Sitkin, S. B. (1996). Learning through failure: The strategy of small losses. In M. D. Cohen & L. S. Sproull (Eds.), *Organizational learning* (pp. 541–578). Thousand Oaks, CA: Sage.

Sivadas, E., & Dwyer, F. R. (2000). An examination of organizational factors influencing new product success in internal and alliance-based processes. *Journal of Marketing*, 64, 31–49.

Song, M., Im, S., van der Bij, J. D., & Song, L. Z. (2011). Does strategic planning enhance or impede innovation and firm performance? *Journal of Product Innovation Management*, 28, 503–520.

Stata, R. (1989). Organizational learning – they key to management innovation. *Sloan Management Review*, 30, 63–74.

Thamhain, H. J. (2003). Managing innovative R&D teams. *R&D Management*, 33, 297–311.

Tierney, P., & Farmer, S. M. (2002). Creative self-efficacy: Potential antecedents and relationship to creative performance. *Academy of Management Journal*, 45, 1137–1148.

Tierney, P., & Farmer, S. M. (2004). The Pygmalion process and employee creativity. *Journal of Management*, 30, 413–432.

Unsworth, K. L., Wall, T. D., & Carter, A. (2005). Creative requirement: A neglected construct in the study of employee creativity? *Group & Organization Management*, 30, 541–560.

Van Dyck, C., Frese, M., Baer, M., & Sonnentag, S. (2005). Organizational error management culture and its impact on performance: A two-study replication. *Journal of Applied Psychology*, 90, 1228–1240.

Verhaeghe, A. and Kfir, R. (2002). Managing innovation in a knowledge intensive technology organization (KITO). *R&D Management*, 32, 409–418.

Vise, D. A., & Malseed, M. (2006). *The Google story: Inside the hottest business, media and technology success of our time*. London: Pan Macmillan.

Wallas, G. (1926). *The art of thought*. New York: Harcourt Brace.

Xiao, Y., Milgram, P., & Doyle, D. J. (1997). Capturing and modeling planning expertise in anesthesiology: Results of a field study. In C. Zsambok & G. Klein (Eds.), *Naturalistic decision making* (pp. 197–205). Hillsdale, NJ: Lawrence Erlbaum.

Yukl, G., & Falbe, C. M. (1991). Importance of different power sources in downward and lateral relations. *Journal of Applied Psychology*, 76, 416–42.

9

THE FIVE PERILS OF TEAM PLANNING

Regularities and Remedies

*Alejandra C. Montoya, Dorothy R. Carter, Jessie Martin,
and Leslie A. DeChurch*

Many modern forms of organizing focus on small teams as the basic task unit (Cash, Earl, & Morison, 2008; Edmondson, 2012; Hackman, 2012). Structuring work around teams allows organizations to bring diverse knowledge sets to bear on complex problems (Gardner, Gino, & Staats, 2012). However, the wisdom of relying heavily on teams for important decisions rests on the assumption that teams are able to synthesize their members' diverse informational sets. This chapter explores the duality between how teams plan and how they should plan. We review the research on team planning, focusing on regularities and remedies. The regularities are five natural tendencies of teams that limit their planning capabilities. The remedies are evidence-based strategies for mitigating these harmful tendencies in order to optimize team-based planning.

The plans made in teams are often highly consequential. For example, when a patient is diagnosed with cancer, health-care teams composed of general physicians, specialists, and nurses jointly develop detailed treatment plans. These teams have the challenge of generating plans that are specific to each specialty; every patient presents different conditions and requires a customized treatment plan that optimizes both the patient's quality of life and the destruction of the cancer – often competing goals. In large corporations, corporate governance is typically enacted collectively by a multi-member group (e.g. strategic planning CEO teams; Hambrick & Mason, 1984) rather than through a strict hierarchy (Bainbridge, 2002). The quality of plans developed by these types of teams can have repercussions throughout organizations. Importantly, team planning is not limited to the discussion that occurs prior to action. Consider, for example, the teams involved in the seventh manned mission in the American Apollo space program – Apollo 13. Despite a terrible disaster in which an oxygen tank exploded leaving the crew on Apollo 13 lacking sufficient water and carbon dioxide and without a clear plan for return to safety, the crew landed safely on Earth on April 17, 1970. With the stakes that high, failure to plan effectively was certainly not an option. Not only did the crew and ground control develop plans prior to launch, when disaster struck, they were able to quickly identify the problem, integrate their expertise, and creatively generate new reactive plans to bring the crew back to safety (Dumoulin, 2001).

Certainly, not all team planning occurs under life-or-death circumstances. In fact, for all teams – from those directing the strategy of entire organizations to those operating at lower organizational levels – planning is often an essential element of success (Weingart, 1992; Stout, Cannon-Bowers,

Salas, & Milanovich, 1999; Patrick, James, & Ahmed, 2006). Yet there are substantial challenges involved in collaboration, many of which are likely to surface when teams make group decisions. Unfortunately, groups often choose the wrong path due to breakdowns in teamwork and biases in decision making (Janis, 1971; Smith, Tindale, & Steiner, 1998). A long history of group research exposes the potential pitfalls of decision making in groups (Brodbeck, Kerschreiter, Mojzisch, Frey, & Schulz-Hardt, 2002; Hill, 1982; Hinsz, 1990; Asch, 1951; Janis, 1971). Thus, it is important for teams and their leaders to be aware of the potential biases teams face during planning so these pitfalls might be avoided.

The current chapter provides a framework for understanding typical pitfalls in team planning and how these might be mitigated. We begin by providing an overview of team planning processes. Team planning is divisible into three broad categories, each of which is vital to team success: (a) deliberate planning, (b) contingency planning, and (c) reactive strategy adjustment (Marks, Mathieu, & Zaccaro, 2001). The quality of these planning processes can be severely affected by group decision-making/planning biases or tendencies. We elaborate on five of these biases, each of which has the potential to greatly reduce a team's ability to plan effectively: (1) a tendency to discuss shared information, (2) a tendency to view the planning process in light of pre-discussion preferences, (3) a tendency toward uneven participation, (4) a tendency for group decisions to escalate, and (5) a tendency to ignore the planning process altogether. We discuss these biases in light of prior research on teams and offer specific remedies for how teams might overcome these regularities to reap the benefits of team-based planning.

Team Planning

Decades of research suggest that team success is due, in large part, to the quality of the *processes* (i.e. behavioral interactions) that occur among team members. This notion is central to models of team performance, which argue that team processes are a key mechanism through which inputs (e.g. team member knowledge and skills, available resources, organizational climate) are translated into important outcomes (e.g. team performance; Gist, Locke, & Taylor, 1987; Hackman, 1983; Guzzo & Shea, 1992; Ilgen, Hollenbeck, Johnson, & Jundt, 2005). In particular, *planning* is especially vital to team success (Marks et al., 2001; Stout et al., 1999).

In a broad sense, planning is the process of determining a course of action in order to reach a desired goal (Sitzmann & Johnson, 2012; Rousseau & Aubé, 2010; Weingart, 1992; Weldon, Jehn, & Pradhan, 1991). This process involves specifying several aspects of future actions. For example, planning may include specification of tasks that are relevant and necessary for goal achievement, the best course of action for executing critical tasks, and the resources needed to accomplish these tasks. Planning may also involve specification of how progress toward the goal will be monitored, and how surprises and distractions will be handled along the way (Rousseau & Aubé, 2010; Claessens, van Eerde, Rutte, & Roe, 2004; Weingart, 1992; Weldon et al., 1991).

In teams, planning is a dynamic process through which teams develop goals, share information related to task requirements, and clarify members' roles and responsibilities (Stout et al., 1999). Specifically, high-quality team planning is characterized by:

> (1) a future orientation, (2) extensive interaction between [team] members, (3) a systematic and comprehensive analysis of the [or team's] strengths, weakness, opportunities, and threats, (4) a clear definition of the roles and functions of all members and departments, and finally, (5) the development and communication of action plans and the allocation of resources to action plans.
>
> *(Smith, Locke, & Barry, 1990, p. 124)*

The quality of team planning plays an important role in setting a team's ability to meet future objectives (Mehta, Feild, Armenakis, & Mehta, 2009). For example, Smith and colleagues (1990) demonstrated that whereas the amount of time teams spent planning was associated with high team performance when the quality of planning was high, this relationship was reversed when planning quality was low, with more time spent planning yielding lower team performance.

High-quality planning is also important for team performance because it can enhance other critical teamwork processes. For example, creating shared task knowledge and common workflow expectations among team members through high-quality planning helps teams handle what may not or could not have been expected when originally developing their plans (Bechky & Okhuysen, 2011). Stout and colleagues (1999) showed that teams who engaged in high-quality planning were able to form accurate cognitions about the team task and other members. In turn, these teams were better able to provide information in advance of explicit requests, which facilitated subsequent group performance (Stout et al., 1999). In sum, research has demonstrated repeatedly that high-quality team planning is important for future success, underscoring the need for a clear understanding of the team planning process.

Team Planning Processes

The process of team planning can be understood through a temporal model of team performance developed by Marks and her colleagues in 2001. Marks et al. (2001) argue that as teams work to achieve their goals, they cycle repeatedly through two types of performance "phases" or "episodes," both of which are defined by the nature of the fundamental interaction processes occurring among team members. Specifically, teams cycle through multiple *transition* and *action* phases throughout task performance. Whereas action phases are the periods of time when teams engage in actions directly related to goal accomplishment, transition phases refer to those times when teams evaluate or re-evaluate environmental contingencies and plan for subsequent actions. Because of the focus on evaluating current conditions and deciding on future actions during team transition phases, team planning is considered a hallmark transition phase process.

Figure 9.1 displays how the processes of planning fit into dominant models of team performance (Ilgen et al., 2005; Kozlowski & Ilgen, 2006). These models imply that inputs such as team composition, resources, training, or leadership impact outputs such as team performance or viability through various mechanisms or mediators. These mediators might be observable behavioral processes such as planning, or they might be emergent psychological properties of the team such as trust, cohesion, or shared cognition. Importantly, as indicated by the directional arrows in Figure 9.1, relationships among all of these variables are cyclical such that team inputs, mediators, and outputs can shape subsequent inputs, mediators, and outputs. For example, Stout et al. (1999) found effective planning processes increased shared mental models among team members (an emergent state), which resulted in the use of more efficient communication strategies and improved coordination processes during subsequent action phases. Patrick et al. (2006) showed that effective planning processes improve team members' team situational awareness, which enables effective team performance.

According to Marks and her colleagues (2001), *strategy formulation and planning processes* are those behaviors and interactions that involve development of possible courses of action for task accomplishment. These activities include decision making regarding the behaviors that team members should engage in to reach their objectives, the timing of actions, and member roles and responsibilities (Hackman & Oldham, 1980; Stout et al., 1999). Additionally, Marks and colleagues (2001) note that effective strategy development involves consideration and incorporation into

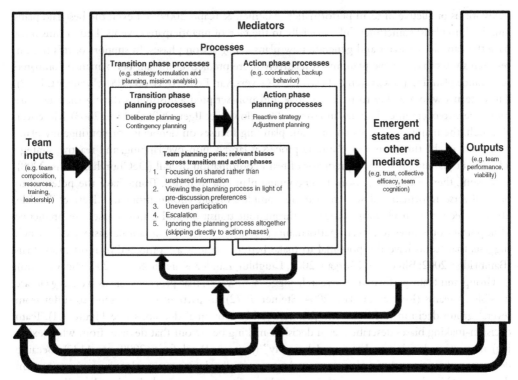

FIGURE 9.1 Planning processes and biases in dominant models of team effectiveness (Hackman, 1983; Ilgen et al., 2005; Kozlowski & Ilgen, 2006; McGrath, 1964)

plans of various environmental contingencies (e.g. time constraints, resources, team member abilities, potential changes).

Although team planning is central to team transition phases, scholars have noted that planning is critical both prior to working on a task as well as during task execution (e.g. Weingart, 1992). In alignment with this view, Marks et al. (2001) further categorized the planning and strategy formulation process into three sub-dimensions: (a) deliberate planning; (b) contingency planning; and (c) reactive strategy adjustment. Deliberate planning and contingency planning constitute what many might consider to be the primary focus of the team planning process and are the primary focus of initial transition phases. *Deliberate planning* refers to the specification of a principal course of action for task completion. *Contingency planning* refers to development of alternative plans and strategy adjustments to prepare for anticipated environmental changes. On the other hand, as shown in Figure 9.1, the third type of planning/strategic activity, *reactive strategy adjustment*, refers to plans developed *during* action phases. These are strategy or plan adjustments that occur throughout team performance cycles in response to unanticipated environmental changes.

Each of the three categories of team planning processes is important for team success. By clearly specifying how teams will interact and accomplish tasks, deliberate planning enables more effective processes (e.g. coordination, backup behavior) during subsequent action phases (Janicik & Bartel, 2003; Mathieu & Schulze, 2006). Similarly, developing backup (i.e. contingency) plans that delineate alternative teamwork and taskwork strategies that can be enacted should primary plans fail should enable more streamlined and coordinated actions in subsequent performance phases (DeChurch & Haas, 2008). Especially in early stages of team performance, generating explicit plans for how members will interact with one another (i.e. teamwork) and how they will accomplish goals (i.e.

taskwork) is predictive of team performance (Mathieu & Rapp, 2009). Yet even the best-laid plans (and backup plans) sometimes fail, especially in the face of unanticipated events. Thus, teams must have the capacity to adapt and generate new plans *during* action phases. In support of this notion, research shows that reactive planning is relatively more predictive of team performance compared to advance planning (DeChurch & Haas, 2008; Gevers, van Eerde, & Rutte, 2001; Weingart, 1992). Those teams who are able to make reactive and non-scripted adjustments during their task are more likely to overcome obstacles and succeed (Kozlowski & Ilgen, 2006; LePine, 2003). Moreover, although, the majority of research on team planning focuses on deliberate or contingency planning, each of the three types of planning process is largely non-overlapping, and reactive strategy adjustment planning is the best predictor of team coordination overall (DeChurch & Haas, 2008).

In sum, there are many reasons to encourage planning in teams. Teams have the potential to bring diverse informational sets to bear on complex organizational problems (Kerr & Tindale, 2004). Effective team planning processes throughout transition and action phases are predictive of important outcomes (e.g. team performance; Stout et al., 1999), and a long history of research suggests that teams have the potential to make better decisions as compared to most individuals (Bainbridge, 2002; Blinder & Morgan, 2000; Laughlin, Zander, Knievel, & Tan, 2003; Shaw, 1936).

Group and team performance research suggests, however, that process *losses* as well as *gains* are possible in teams (Kerr & Tindale, 2004; Steiner, 1972). In particular, teams tend to suffer from several group decision-making *biases* that can yield suboptimal decisions (see Figure 9.1). Team decision-making biases describe "team decision-making behaviour that deviates from what (existing) normative decision-making models imply" (Jones & Roelofsma, 2000, pp. 1132). Because decision making is embedded in team tasks – especially during team planning – certain team decision-making biases can negate the potential benefits of team-based planning throughout transition and action phases. Thus, we focus the remainder of this chapter on the team decision-making biases that might surface during deliberate, contingency, and reactive strategy adjustment planning.

Team Planning Perils: Five Biases that Hinder Team Planning and How to Remedy Them

Here we highlight several team biases that, if ignored, might greatly reduce a team's ability to effectively plan for future action: (1) a tendency to discuss shared as opposed to unshared information, (2) a tendency to view the planning process in light of pre-discussion preferences, (3) a tendency to engage in uneven participation, (4) a tendency toward escalation, and (5) a tendency to ignore the planning process altogether (see Figure 9.1). The following sections elaborate these five biases, discussing the conditions under which these biases are most likely, the possible detriments to team performance if they are ignored, and potential remedies to help overcome these regularities (see Table 9.1).

Bias 1: Ignoring Unshared Information

Knowledge is distributed in teams such that some information is shared (known to all or most members) and some is unique to one or a few members (Mojzisch, Grouneva, & Schulz-Hardt, 2010; Mesmer-Magnus & DeChurch, 2009). The underlying assumption of assigning planning or decision-making tasks to teams is that the members will be able to integrate their unique (unshared) information such that they collectively generate more superior decisions than any single member could have made individually. However, even when teams have all of the information needed to make an optimal decision, they do not always succeed in integrating their knowledge. This is, in part, because teams tend to spend the majority of their planning time reviewing shared, rather than

TABLE 9.1 Five common team planning perils and associated remedies

Team planning perils	Description	Potential solutions
1. Common information	Teams tend to discuss shared as opposed to unique information	• Structure team discussions • Frame tasks as intellective, problem-solving • Promote a cooperative climate • Train teams on common barriers to effective group decision making and strategies to combat these barriers • Define members' roles • Use task-oriented, goal-focused, and depersonalized communication technology • Compose teams of members high in psychological collectivism and cognitive ability
2. Pre-discussion preferences	Teams tend to focus on and argue for pre-discussion preferences	• Designate a time for discussing alternative plans • Promote diversity – include members with conflicting pre-discussion preferences • Develop accurate team cognition about the task at hand (e.g. employ direct leader-to-member communication about the embedding environment)
3. Uneven participation	Discussion participation is often unevenly distributed among team members, particularly in larger groups	• Limit group size for decision making • Use virtual communication platforms that enable asynchronous contributions to group discussion • Limit participation of more vocal members during discussions • Increase group cohesion • Ensure punishment for poor individual contributions for group performance • Increase members' interest in the task • Increase task interdependence • Increase individual identifiability

TABLE 9.1 (cont.)

Team planning perils	Description	Potential solutions
4. Escalation	Excessive team cohesiveness can lead to blind faith and escalation of team decisions	• Ensure team diversity • Train self-monitoring practices • Monitor team progress • Assign a devil's advocate • Break up into sub-groups • Allow anonymous opinion sharing • Require discussion of alternative plans • Establish a safe climate
5. Planning aversion	Teams tend to skip planning altogether	• Designate time for planning • Train team on importance of planning • Use tangible tools to plan such as a team charter or outline • Utilize low-workload periods to plan • Encourage team cohesion

unique, information (Mojzisch et al., 2010; Mesmer-Magnus & DeChurch, 2009; Greitemeyer & Schulz-Hardt, 2003). In other words, teams tend not to focus their time and energy understanding and integrating the information that only a few members hold – information that may be crucial for making the best decision. This bias can affect planning processes during the transition phase: teams need access to sufficient informational resources in order to generate deliberate and contingency plans. However, this bias might be particularly detrimental to reactive strategy adjustment planning during action phases when teams must quickly share newly acquired information in order to accurately revamp existing plans in the face of changing circumstances.

Several explanations have been offered for the shared information bias. First, the tendency to focus overly on shared information can be a consequence of the unequal distribution of shared vs. unshared information among members. Quite simply, as a team, shared information is more likely to be brought up in discussion because more members are able to possess it and remember it (Stasser & Stewart, 1992; Stasser, Taylor, & Hanna, 1989; Stasser & Titus, 1985). Second, certain social psychological processes, such as mutual enhancement (Wittenbaum, Hubbell, & Zukerman, 1999) or social validation, with members mutually accepting and validating shared information (Parks & Cowlin, 1996), are thought to underlie this tendency.

Unfortunately, the lack of discussion of unique information, and/or the dismissal of unique information as unimportant decreases a team's ability to develop and evaluate potential plans (Bonito, DeCamp, Coffman, & Fleming, 2006). Because shared information tends to be discussed by the group and repeated more often than unshared information (Greitemeyer & Schulz-Hardt, 2003), group members may wrongfully trust shared information to a greater extent than unique information. Through a social validation process, with members validating the correctness and adequacy of shared information, members begin to assign more weight and importance to shared information, viewing it as more accurate and reliable than unshared information and potentially undermining the quality of the group's plans (Boos, Schauenburg, Strack, & Belz, 2013; Mojzisch et al., 2010). The tendency to focus on shared information can also create a "law of small numbers bias" in decision making (Tversky & Kahneman, 1974). The law of small numbers bias occurs when an individual makes a decision based on a relatively small sample of information that he or she assumes is representative of the whole population of information (Tversky & Kahneman, 1974). In teams, members become more susceptible to the law of small numbers bias when the team focuses processing resources only on the information that is commonly held by the majority of members (Houghton, Simon, Aquino, & Goldberg, 2000).

Teams are most likely to share information "when (a) all members already know the information (biased information sampling), (b) members are capable of making accurate decisions independently (informational independence), and (c) members are highly similar to one another (member similarity)" (Mesmer-Magnus & DeChurch, 2009, p. 543). The dilemma for team planning is that these conditions typify teams whose members may not need to share unique information – because they already possess all of the information, are able to make the decision independently, and/or are so similar to one another that the amount of unique information among members is low. Meanwhile, those teams with diverse members who must integrate diverse knowledge sets in order to generate team decisions are less likely to share information, hindering their ability to plan effectively.

Potential Remedies

Several potential remedies are available to encourage unique information sharing. A recent meta-analysis identifies three conditions that mitigate the common information effect in teams, and that are important enablers of effective team planning: problem framing, structured discussions, and cooperative climate. All three are leverage points for team planning.

The first leverage point for team planning is to frame the planning situation as a problem to be solved rather than a judgment. Teams who frame their planning as a problem will share more unique information than will teams who view their task as one of making a judgment (Mesmer-Magnus & DeChurch, 2009). A judgment frame seems to prime individuals to hold tightly to their individual preferences and forgo an open exchange of information. To plan effectively, teams need to process information as a team, and not as an additive combination of individuals. The problem-solving frame is one key way to accomplish this.

The second leverage point for team information sharing is to use a structured discussion process. Teams who design a process of fact-finding, and who separate the "discovery of information" from the "evaluation of information" are more likely to discuss unique information than are teams who engage in unstructured discussions. This process suggestion is similar to one made in the creativity literature where teams are urged to separate the generation of ideas from the evaluation of ideas. The same advice, using a structured and segmented discussion process, benefits team planning.

The third leverage point is the cooperative tone of the team. Teams whose members have cooperative relationships with one another are more willing to share unique information than are teams with competitive relations. Team leaders play an important role in setting a positive and supportive climate where divergent viewpoints are encouraged (Gebert, Boerner, & Kearney, 2010; Hunter & Cushenbery, 2011), and seemingly irrelevant information is valued by the team during the fact-finding phase of the discussion. In hidden profile tasks, unique information will seem contradictory to the team's gut instinct, and so it is critical that teams set norms to value such information.

Three other interventions have received some support: team instruction, technology, and composition. Research provides some evidence that instructing teams on effective information-sharing procedures increases unique information sharing (Larson, Foster-Fishman, & Keys, 1994). Larson and his colleagues (1994) found that training teams on common barriers to effective group decision making (e.g. ignoring important information) as well as strategies that can be used to avoid these barriers (e.g. discussing with one another their doubts about proposed decisions, structuring group decisions) increased the amount of both shared and unshared information these teams discussed. A similar intervention is to make each member's specific role explicit. Clarifying members' roles can help draw the team's attention to the fact that only certain members have access to certain information (Stout et al., 1999). It may not always be possible to compose teams whose members have worked together previously or are high in psychological collectivism. In fact, many planning/decision-making tasks are specifically assigned to cross-functional teams, those whose members have different areas of expertise. However, teams or leaders of teams may see an improvement in decision making when strategies to improve familiarity are employed. Thus, teams may benefit from cross-training that enables better awareness of members' expertise (e.g. transactive memory systems; Lewis, 2003).

Boos and colleagues (2013) suggest a second intervention, utilizing task-oriented, goal-focused, and depersonalized information-technology-mediated communication settings to help teams overcome the shared information bias during planning and decision making. These scholars argue that relying on computer-mediated communication tools reduces members' need for social validation, thus limiting the tendency to downplay unshared information.

Lastly, there is some evidence that teams can be staffed to plan well. Team composition can also play a role in the degree to which shared vs. unshared information is discussed. For example, Randall and colleagues (2011) found that teams higher in psychological collectivism and cognitive ability tend to share information more readily, leading to better reactive planning in the face of disruptions. Other work suggests that teams are better able to integrate unshared knowledge when members have prior experience with one another (Gruenfeld, Mannix, Williams, & Neale, 1996).

Bias 2: Pre-Discussion Preferences

When a team begins a new task, each member starts by assessing their own knowledge base in order to come up with plans and possible courses of action to accomplish the task. Thus, members enter into team discussions with their own beliefs about how the task should be completed, expecting to complete the task in accordance with these individual beliefs (Hackman, Brousseau, & Weiss, 1976). Consequently, the group discussion becomes a place for members to exchange their pre-discussion preferences and negotiate the team's decisions based on those preferences (Greitemeyer & Schulz-Hardt, 2003).

Unfortunately, by entering the discussion focused on pre-discussion preferences, individuals are more likely to ignore new information and cues from their team members – cues that could lead to plans that are better suited to the unique situation. Instead, individuals typically tend to seek out and focus on pre-discussion preference-consistent information (i.e. "information that supports the group members' initial preferences"; Mojzisch et al., 2010). Often, the most convincing individual's plan is chosen rather than the plan that is most logical, preventing the team from reaching its fullest potential. Again, this bias can impact planning across all phases of team performance (i.e. transition, action). However, it may be particularly relevant during early phases, when members' initial plans are strongly influenced by pre-discussion experiences and preferences.

Scholars have offered pre-discussion preferences as an alternative explanation for the shared information bias (Bias 1 above). Gigone and Hastie (1993) argue that the pre-discussion distribution of information affects participants' pre-discussion preferences, thus determining the positions they hold when entering into initial discussion. These authors found that the pattern of pre-discussion preferences was the driving force in subsequent group discussion – pre-discussion preferences mediated the relationship between information distribution and group decision making. Gigone and Hastie (1993) noted that members tended to exchange and combine their initial opinions, but paid little attention to new (e.g. conflicting) information.

Potential Remedies

Overcoming the pre-discussion preference bias can be an extremely difficult task for teams. Individuals are typically reluctant to alter their choices and beliefs, especially if they have resulted in positive outcomes in the past or if the individual feels committed to their initial choices (Greitemeyer & Schulz-Hardt, 2003).

To help prevent teams from focusing solely on pre-discussion preferences, it may be beneficial for the team to allocate a proportion of planning time for members to focus solely on discussing alternative strategies. Although discussing alternative strategies does not guarantee an effective strategy will be identified, requiring such a discussion increases the degree to which the group may identify and select a strategy that is more effective relative to those that seemed 'obvious' to team members initially (Hackman et al., 1976).

Another course of action that may help weaken or eliminate pre-discussion preferences is to encourage the team to exchange unique, unshared information by including members with conflicting pre-discussion preferences (Greitemeyer & Schulz-Hardt, 2003). In particular, research suggests that better team decisions are made (and more unshared information is discussed) when teams have at least a minority of members with different pre-discussion preferences as compared to the majority (Brodbeck et al., 2002). Minorities can exert influence on groups by establishing and maintaining conflict (Moscovici, 1980). Whereas majorities encourage convergent thinking (i.e. alignment) and a focus toward the issue at hand, minority dissent can encourage divergent thinking (i.e. thinking about a problem in multiple ways), open-mindedness, and critical thinking (De Dreu & De Vries, 1996; Nemeth & Rogers, 1996; Nemeth & Kwan, 1987). Thus, providing opportunities for minority dissenters to give voice to their opinions can help counteract the pre-discussion bias by forcing a more in-depth discussion of alternative solutions and preventing the team from agreeing on a single course of action too quickly.

Finally, ensuring that members develop an accurate cognitive architecture regarding the task and the team can help mitigate the negative impact of members' pre-discussion preferences. When teams become more aware of the actual situation at stake (as opposed to the situations members have encountered in the past) they may be better able to develop plans that are aligned with the current task demands. With regard to reactive strategy adjustment planning, in particular, accurate team cognition (e.g. mental models; Cannon-Bowers & Salas, 1990; Cannon-Bowers, Salas, & Converse, 1993; Mohammed, Ferzandi, & Hamilton, 2010) plays a pivotal role in enabling team adaptive capacity (Burke, Stagl, Salas, Pierce, & Kendall, 2006). In fact, Burke et al. (2006) argue that team adaptation in the face of unexpected events is not possible when teams hold disparate interpretations of their environment. Here, leadership can be a critical leverage point. Leaders' communication to team members regarding the embedding environment helps facilitate the formation of more similar and accurate team mental models, which enables subsequent reactive strategy adjustment planning (Randall, Resick, & DeChurch, 2011).

Bias 3: Uneven Participation

Even participation in team decision making can help ensure available knowledge is accessed and utilized. A fairly even distribution of discussion participation may be likely in smaller groups, in part because individuals may feel more obligation to participate and confidence in their ability to contribute (Kooloos et al., 2011). However, as a team's size increases, the percentage of members participating in the group discussions shifts and uneven participation is more likely (Thomas & Fink, 1963). The tendency toward uneven participation can limit a team's ability to effectively plan by reducing the pool of knowledge made available to the team. Again, this bias might be observed throughout transition and action phases of team performance.

Uneven participation is likely in teams for several reasons. First, people vary in personal characteristics that make it more or less likely they will contribute to groups. For example, traits such as extraversion (Salgado, 1998; Judge, Bono, Ilies, & Gerhardt, 2002), narcissism (Brunell et al., 2008; Humphreys, Zhao, Ingram, Gladstone, & Basham, 2010), gender (Riggio, Riggio, Salinas, & Cole, 2003; Kent & Moss, 1994; Eagly & Karau, 1991), and cognitive ability (Smith & Foti, 1998; Zaccaro et al., 1997) have been shown to predict the likelihood that individuals will emerge as leaders or influential group members. In larger groups, these effects may be even more apparent. On the other hand, in smaller groups, even the quieter, more introverted individuals will see more opportunity and feel more pressure to participate.

Furthermore, a long history of research documents a tendency for individuals to show reduced motivation and contribution when in groups. Termed motivation losses (Steiner, 1972) or social loafing (Latané, Williams, & Harkins, 1979), this tendency to reduce effort in the presence of others is thought to be due to various factors, such as reduced risks of evaluation or more opportunities to free-ride. Moreover, as group size increases, although the total number of individuals who participate increases, the proportion of members who do so decreases.

Potential Remedies

The obvious solution in this case is to keep the group small. However, this is not always an option. Therefore, teams and leaders of teams must consider how best to encourage participation even when group size is large.

First, because group members' levels of participation within the team may be affected by personal characteristics (e.g. shyness, anxiety, status), it may be beneficial to utilize asynchronous (i.e. not immediate) virtual means of communicating rather than to have discussions face-to-face, especially when working in larger teams. For several reasons, when teams use virtual communication platforms such as message boards or chat rooms, there is a more equal participation as compared to face-to-face discussion (Böhlke, 2003). Virtual communication platforms can allow less-aggressive individuals to participate in team discussion. For highly diverse teams, relying on asynchronous tools such as email can serve to mitigate intercultural miscommunications and improve language accuracy (Shachaf, 2005). These platforms might encourage more thoughtful exchanges and extrapolations and reduce the natural dominance of others (Böhlke, 2003). Further, research suggests information technology positively impacts the number of alternative solutions generated during brainstorming, and improves subsequent performance on a brainstorming task (Valacich & Schwenk, 1995). Particularly for larger groups (n > 9), groups using computerized brainstorming tools tend to outperform nominal groups (Dennis & Valacich, 1993, 1994).

However, the use of virtual communication tools for planning activities should be approached with caution. For example, scholars have suggested that geographically distributed teams perform better when intense planning sessions are held face-to-face rather than across virtual communication tools (Maznevski & Chudoba, 2000). Other work shows a negative effect of information technology use on planning and coordination (e.g. Hollingshead, McGrath, & O'Connor, 1993), suggesting these tools may be inappropriate for planning that needs to occur "on the fly" (i.e. reactive strategy adjustment). Moreover, although virtual communication tools provide a greater opportunity for equal participation, this may not lead to information integration, because virtual communication platforms can reduce the exchange of social cues and implicit knowledge (Curşeu, 2006; Hollingshead, 1996).

Finally, to counteract the effects of social loafing, scholars have suggested increasing group cohesion (Worchel, Rothgerber, Day, Hart, & Butemeyer, 1998) and ensuring punishment for poor individual contributions to group performance (Miles & Greenberg, 1993). Other solutions include increasing members' interest and the importance placed on the task, team interdependence, and individual identifiability (Williams & Karau, 1991; Kerr & Stanfel, 1993; Kerr & Tindale, 2004).

Bias 4: Group Escalation

One of the most publicized biases in teams or groups is termed *groupthink* (Janis, 1971). Groupthink is a "mode of thinking that persons engage in when concurrence seeking becomes so dominant in a cohesive in-group that it tends to override realistic appraisal of alternative courses of action" (Janis, 1971, p. 9). According to Janis (1971), the "symptoms" of groupthink are: (1) an illusion of invulnerability, (2) a rationale to avoid negative feedback, (3) a belief of morality of the group, (4) the stereotyping of others not in the group, (5) pressure on dissenters, (6) self-censorship of doubts, (7) the illusion of unanimity, and (8) the mind-guarding of adverse information from the rest of the group. These conditions interact to increase the cohesiveness of the team members by inflating the sense of righteousness of the group and rejecting everything that would indicate otherwise, whether it is an outsider voicing an alternative opinion or an adverse thought.

The initial theory of groupthink argues that excessive team cohesiveness can lead teams to be too concerned with preserving that sense of cohesiveness and hesitant to criticize others' opinions and decisions, even when it would be in the team's best interest to do so. Thus, the groupthink symptoms are even more likely to appear in teams when there is closed leadership and an external threat, especially when the team is pressured on time (Choi & Kim, 1999). Groupthink is danger-ous to the extent that individuals begin to believe in the validity of the group's decisions without examining the consequences of the decision or considering alternatives (Janis, 1971). In this way, as symptoms of groupthink surface, the team may have more difficulty planning effectively.

However, critics have argued that the groupthink theory is deficient in several respects. For example, the initial theory was developed to explain reasons behind examples of disastrous deci-sions made by highly cohesive teams (e.g. the Bay of Pigs fiasco in 1961). The theory neglects sev-eral important characteristics of groups that might affect decision processes, such as group norms (Postmes, Spears, & Cihangir, 2001), leader power (Fodor & Smith, 1982), task characteristics (Shanteau, 1992), or the amount of time or experience the group has had together (Gruenfeld et al., 1996). Further, empirical support is limited for the link between group cohesiveness and groupthink (Park, 1990), and the theory ignores the social processes of group polarization in group-decision making.

Group polarization refers to the tendency for an initial group opinion or position to become more intensified after group discussion (Lamm, 1988). For example, groups might become more risk seeking than the average group member was before group discussion (i.e. risky shift) or they might become more risk averse than the average group member was before discussion (i.e. cau-tious shift). The drivers of group polarization overlap with many of the so-called symptoms of groupthink. For instance, scholars have argued that group polarization can occur through a process of social comparison: members want to be perceived in a way that is favorable to the group but more so than the average group member, so they express opinions that are more extreme than the average but in the direction of the majority (Jones & Roelofsma, 2000). In groups high in cohe-sion, with members who believe in the superiority or morality of the group, the drive for positive social perceptions may be much stronger. However, both the groupthink and the group polariza-tion literature support the notion that groups and teams tend to escalate (Bazerman, Giuliano, & Appelman, 1984; Jones & Roelofsma, 2000; Whyte, 1993), thus suggesting that teams and leaders of teams should not discount this work when attempting to improve team planning. Escalation might be especially likely when a team decision needs to be made quickly (i.e. reactive strategy adjustment), and it may severely limit the likelihood that teams will generate sufficient contingency plans because of the tendency to believe the team cannot fail.

Potential Remedies

One way to reduce the likelihood of team escalation is to ensure team member diversity (Harter, 2012). As mentioned above, team diversity can lead to teams composed of members with diverse pre-discussion preferences, leading to greater depth of discussion during team decision making. Alternatively, organizations can have teams take part in training to help recognize the symptoms of groupthink and to teach individuals how to self-monitor their progress by asking themselves questions such as "Are we still on target?" (Harter, 2012). Team leaders or organizations could potentially require team members to do this on a regular basis, perhaps by a paper or online survey or worksheet.

Another suggestion for preventing the negative implications of groupthink is to assign one member of the team to the dissenting "devil's advocate" role during planning to ensure the discussion of the pros and cons of each decision and to promote the consideration of alternative plans (Schweiger, Sandberg, & Ragan, 1986). However, more recent work suggests that genuine dissent due to group heterogeneity in initial opinions is much more likely to elicit critical analysis of information as compared to the contrived dissent of a devil's advocate, underscoring the benefits of team diversity.

Depending on the size of the team, it may also be beneficial to break teams up into sub-groups, each of which develop plans individually, and then joins together to work out the differences (Janis, 1971). Another suggestion to help alleviate the social pressures of conformity is to allow members to state their opinions anonymously, perhaps by paper. Having each member's opinions written down before planning aloud could prevent any single individual (e.g. the team leader) from influencing the thoughts of the other team members before everyone has had a chance to consider their initial opinions. Further, prior to planning, team leaders might facilitate the voicing of dissenting opinions by requiring all members to submit at least one or two alternatives to the main plan, explaining the pros and cons of each (Kahneman, Lovallo, & Sibony, 2011). Moreover, teams and team leaders should strive to create a climate wherein disagreements regarding plans and decisions are viewed as "a productive part of the decision process (and resolved objectively) rather than as a sign of conflict between individuals (and suppressed)" (Kahneman et al., 2011, p. 55).

Bias 5: Planning Aversion

A final team planning bias is the tendency for teams not to plan at all but instead to enter directly into action phases. Regrettably, without planning, the team is more likely to be unprepared and unable to handle a situation if an unexpected event were to occur. Further, by dismissing an opportunity to plan, the team is more inclined to miss vital details about the task that should be considered and integrated into the team's course of action.

This tendency is likely to emerge under several circumstances. First, planning aversion may be particularly likely when demands on the team are high and separate planning sessions are not available (Weldon et al., 1991). Weingart (1992) argues that planning may not occur when teams are working toward difficult goals requiring quick results. Teams may be reinforced for ignoring planning in favor of action, because immediate actions can result in tangible outcomes that immediately affect performance (Weingart, 1992). Second, planning aversion may be more likely to occur if the resources needed to plan are the same as those needed to accomplish the task at hand. This is because in order to engage in planning, the team must slow or stop their current work in order to redistribute the limited resources (Weldon et al., 1991). Finally, the likelihood of planning and developing performance strategies may be inhibited when the team's task is familiar or well structured and members do not believe planning is necessary (Hackman et al., 1976).

An additional tendency related both to planning aversion and groupthink biases is what Buehler, Messervey, and Griffin (2005) term the "group accentuation" effect or the group optimism bias (p. 47). Research on individual decision making has repeatedly demonstrated an optimism bias in decision making. Individuals often predict that they will be able to accomplish their tasks sooner and more easily than they eventually do (Buehler, Griffin, & Ross, 2002; Flyvbjerg, Holme, & Soren, 2002; Hall, 1980). Interestingly, Buehler and colleagues showed that this bias is even more extreme when groups make decisions. To demonstrate loyalty to the project and team, members may tend to exaggerate optimistic views and suppress pessimism (Buehler et al., 2005; Kahneman & Lovallo, 1993). This is assumed to be due, in part, to the tendency for group members to focus even more selectively on task-relevant information when in groups, ignoring information that conflicts with the desired plan.

Potential Remedies

In order to help counteract the planning aversion bias, organizations or team leaders should allocate time periods solely for team planning. Past studies have found that teams did little planning if they were not provided with separate planning periods or if they were not specifically instructed to do so (Weingart, 1992). By having a specified time available for planning, teams are encouraged to engage in planning and do not feel pressured to act too soon. Training interventions (Larson et al., 1994) directed toward teaching teams about the importance of planning and the tendency for teams to ignore planning phases has been shown to improve this bias. When groups are persuaded to plan explicitly how a task should be accomplished, performance improvements are often observed (Hackman, Weiss, & Brousseau, 1974; Orasanu & Salas, 1993).

Team leaders and organizations can use formalized forms to encourage the group members to engage in planning. For example, teams could complete a team charter or some other form of structured strategy-development outline (Mathieu & Rapp, 2009). These tangible planning tools may help remind teams to focus at least a portion of their energy toward planning.

For teams that have high performance demands and, consequently, do not have much additional time to spend planning, an efficient solution is to utilize low-workload periods for making additional plans (Stout et al., 1999). This way, the team is not forced to stop working completely in order to plan, which may be especially important in crucial situations where the team cannot afford to lose additional work time.

Finally, encouraging a positive, cohesive climate and setting challenging goals are two other potential steps suggested in team literature that may mitigate the tendency to avoid planning. For example, Zaccaro, Gualtieri, and Minionis (1995) found teams with higher levels of task cohesiveness tend to spend more time planning and exchanging information during planning periods and more time exchanging task-relevant information during performance periods. Research suggests more challenging team goals can lead to higher performance through their impact on planning, tactics, and effort (e.g. Durham, Knight, & Locke, 1997; Weingart, 1992). Thus, it follows that team leaders may help encourage more team planning by setting more challenging goals for their teams.

Conclusion

In conclusion, teams offer the opportunity to seed organizational plans with diverse knowledge, expertise, and skills. Designing functional team planning processes is of ongoing importance – effective teams continually develop and redevelop plans throughout their life cycle. Yet the benefits of team plans are often offset by the biases teams experience when making group decisions. Thus, teams and leaders of teams must learn to take an active role in overcoming these biases and effectively shaping their own futures.

Acknowledgments

This material is based upon work supported by the National Science Foundation under Grant Nos. SES-1219469 and SES-1063901. Any opinions, findings, and conclusions or recommendations expressed in this material are those of the author(s) and do not necessarily reflect the views of the National Science Foundation. This material is also based upon work supported by the National Institutes of Health Training Grant #5T32AG000175-24. Any opinions, findings, and conclusions or recommendations expressed in this material are those of the author(s) and do not necessarily reflect the views of the National Institutes of Health.

References

Asch, S. E. (1951). Effects of group pressure upon the modification and distortion of judgments. In H. Guetzkow (Ed.), *Groups, leadership and men* (pp. 177–190). Pittsburgh, PA: Carnegie Press.

Bainbridge, S. M. (2002). Why a board? Group decision-making in corporate governance. *Vanderbilt Law Review*, 55(1), 1–55.

Bazerman, M. H., Giuliano, T., & Appelman, A. (1984). Escalation of commitment in individual and group decision making. *Organizational Behavior and Human Performance*, 33(2), 141–152.

Bechky, B. A., & Okhuysen, G. A. (2011). Expecting the unexpected? How SWAT officers and film crews handle surprises. *Academy of Management Journal*, 54(2), 239–261.

Blinder, A. S., & Morgan, J. (2000). *Are two heads better than one?: An experimental analysis of group vs. individual decisionmaking* (Working Paper 7909). Cambridge, MA: National Bureau of Economic Research.

Böhlke, O. (2003). A comparison of student participation levels by group size and language stages during chatroom and face-to-face discussions in German. *CALICO Journal*, 21(1), 67–87.

Bonito, J. A., DeCamp, M. H., Coffman, M., & Fleming, S. (2006). Participation, information, and control in small groups: An actor-partner interdependence model. *Group Dynamics: Theory, Research, and Practice*, 10(1), 16–28.

Boos, M., Schauenburg, B., Strack, M., & Belz, M. (2013). Social validation of shared and nonvalidation of unshared information in group discussions. *Small Group Research*, 44(3), 257–271.

Brodbeck, F. C., Kerschreiter, R., Mojzisch, A., Frey, D., & Schulz-Hardt, S. (2002). The dissemination of critical, unshared information in decision-making groups: The effects of pre-discussion dissent. *European Journal of Social Psychology*, 32, 35–56.

Brunell, A. B., Gentry, W. A., Campbell, W. K., Hoffman, B. J., Kuhnert, K. W., & DeMarree, K. G. (2008). Leader emergence: The case of the narcissistic leader. *Personality and Social Psychology Bulletin*, 34(12), 1663–1676.

Buehler, R., Griffin, D., & Ross, M. (2002). Inside the planning fallacy: The causes and consequences of optimistic time predictions. In T. Gilovich, D. Griffin, & D. Kahneman (Eds.), *Heuristics and biases: The psychology of intuitive judgment* (pp. 250–270). New York: Cambridge University Press.

Buehler, R., Messervey, D., & Griffin, D. (2005). Collaborative planning and prediction: Does group discussion affect optimistic biases in time estimation? *Organizational Behavior and Human Decision Processes*, 97(1), 47–63.

Burke, C. S., Stagl, K. C., Salas, E., Pierce, L., & Kendall, D. (2006). Understanding team adaptation: A conceptual analysis and model. *Journal of Applied Psychology*, 91(6), 1189–1207.

Cannon-Bowers, J. A., & Salas, E. (1990). Cognitive psychology and team training: Shared mental models and team training. In *Fifth annual meeting of the Society for Industrial and Organizational Psychology*, Miami, FL.

Cannon-Bowers, J. A., Salas, E., & Converse, S. A. (1993). Shared mental models in expert team decision making. In N. J. Castellan, Jr. (Ed.), *Current issues in individual and group decision making* (pp. 221–246). Hillsdale, NJ: Erlbaum.

Cash, J. I., Earl, M. J., & Morrison, R. (2008). Teaming up to crack innovation and enterprise integration. *Harvard Business Review*, 86(11), 90–100.

Choi, J. N., & Kim, M. U. (1999). The organizational application of groupthink and its limitations in organizations. *Journal of Applied Psychology*, 84(2), 297–306.

Claessens, B. J. C., van Eerde, W., Rutte, C. G., & Roe, R. A. (2004). Planning behavior and perceived control of time at work. *Journal of Organizational Behavior*, 25, 937–950.

Curşeu, P. L. (2006). Emergent states in virtual teams: A complex adaptive systems perspective. *Journal of Information Technology*, 21, 249–261.

DeChurch, L. A., & Haas, C. D. (2008). Examining team planning through an episodic lens: Effects of deliberate, contingency, and reactive planning on team effectiveness. *Small Group Research*, 39(5), 542–568.

De Dreu, C. K. W., & De Vries, N. K. (1996). Differential processing and attitude change following majority versus minority arguments. *British Journal of Social Psychology*, 35(1), 77–90.

Dennis, A. R., & Valacich, J. S. (1993). Computer brainstorms: More heads are better than one. *Journal of Applied Psychology*, 78(4), 531–537.

Dennis, A. R., & Valacich, J. S. (1994). Group, sub-group, and nominal group idea generation: New rules for a new media? *Journal of Management*, 20(4), 723–736.

Dumoulin, J. (2001, June 29). *Apollo-13*. Retrieved from: http://science.ksc.nasa.gov/history/apollo/apollo-13/apollo-13.html (last accessed February 14, 2015).

Durham, C. C., Knight, D., & Locke, E. A. (1997). Effects of leader role, team-set goal difficulty, efficacy, and tactics on team effectiveness. *Organizational Behavior and Human Decision Processes*, 72(2), 203–231.

Eagly, A. H., & Karau, S. J. (1991). Gender and the emergence of leaders: A meta-analysis. *Journal of Personality and Social Psychology*, 60(5), 685–710.

Edmondson, A. C. (2012). *Teaming: How organizations learn, innovate, and compete in the knowledge economy*. San Francisco, CA: Jossey-Bass.

Flyvbjerg, B., Holme, M. S., & Soren, B. (2002). Underestimating costs in public works projects: Error or lie? *Journal of the American Planning Association*, 68, 279–295.

Fodor, E. M., & Smith, T. (1982). The power motive as an influence on group decision making. *Journal of Personality and Social Psychology*, 42(1), 178–185.

Gardner, H. K., Gino, F., & Staats, B. (2012). Dynamically integrating knowledge in teams: Transforming resources into performance. *Academy of Management Journal*, 55(4), 998–1022.

Gebert, D., Boerner, S., & Kearney, E. (2010). Fostering team innovation: Why is it important to combine opposing action strategies? *Organization Science*, 21(3), 593–608.

Gevers, J. M. P., van Eerde, W., & Rutte, C. G. (2001). Time pressure, potency, and progress in project groups. *European Journal of Work and Organizational Psychology*, 10(2), 205–221.

Gigone, D., & Hastie, R. (1993). The common knowledge effect: Information sharing and group judgment. *Journal of Personality and Social Psychology*, 65(5), 959–974.

Gist, M. E., Locke, E. A., & Taylor, M. S. (1987). Organizational behavior: Group structure, process, and effectiveness. *Journal of Management*, 13(2), 237–257.

Greitemeyer, T., & Schulz-Hardt, S. (2003). Preference-consistent evaluation of information in the hidden profile paradigm: Beyond group-level explanations for the dominance of shared information in group decisions. *Journal of Personality and Social Psychology*, 84(2), 322–339.

Gruenfeld, D. H., Mannix, E. A., Williams, K. Y., & Neale, M. A. (1996). Group composition and decision making: How member familiarity and information distribution affect process and performance. *Organizational Behavior and Human Decision Processes*, 67(1), 1–15.

Guzzo, R. A., & Shea, G. P. (1992). Group performance and intergroup relations in organizations. *Handbook of Industrial and Organizational Psychology*, 3, 269–313.

Hackman, J. R. (1983). *A normative model of work team effectiveness (No. TR-2)*. Arlington, VA: Office of Naval Research.

Hackman, J. R. (2012). From causes to conditions in group research. *Journal of Organizational Behavior*, 33, 428–444.

Hackman, J. R., & Oldham, G. R. (1980). *Work redesign*. Reading, MA: Addison-Wesley.

Hackman, J. R., Weiss, J. A., & Brousseau, K. R. (1974). *Effects of task performance strategies on group performance effectiveness (No. TR-5)*. New Haven, CT: Yale University New Haven, Connecticut Department of Administrative Sciences.

Hackman, J. R., Brousseau, K. R., Weiss, J. A. (1976). The interaction of task design and group performance strategies in determining group effectiveness. *Organizational Behavior and Human Performance*, 16, 350–365.

Hall, P. (1980). *Great planning disasters*. London: Weidenfeld & Nicolson.

Hambrick, D. C., & Mason, P. A. (1984). Upper echelons: The organization as a reflection of its top managers. *Academy of Management Review*, 9(2), 193–206.

Harter, N. W. (2012). Point of view: Using modalities of veridiction to prevent groupthink. *International Journal of Innovation Science*, 4(4), 269–272.

Hill, G. W. (1982). Group versus individual performance: Are $N + 1$ heads better than one? *Psychological Bulletin*, 91(3), 517–539.

Hinsz, V. B. (1990). Cognitive and consensus processes in group recognition memory performance. *Journal of Personality and Social Psychology*, 59(4), 705.

Hollingshead, A. B. (1996). Information suppression and status persistence in group decision making the effects of communication media. *Human Communication Research*, 23(2), 193–219.

Hollingshead, A. B., McGrath, J. E., & O'Connor, K. M. (1993). Group task performance and communication technology: A longitudinal study of computer-mediated versus face-to-face work groups. *Small Group Research*, 24(3), 307–333.

Houghton, S. M., Simon, M., Aquino, K., & Goldberg, C. B. (2000). No safety in numbers: Persistence of biases and their effects on team risk perception and team decision making. *Group & Organization Management*, 25(4), 325–353.

Humphreys, J., Zhao, D., Ingram, K., Gladstone, J., & Basham, L. (2010). Situational narcissism and charismatic leadership: A conceptual framework. *Journal of Behavioral and Applied Management*, 11(2), 118–136.

Hunter, S. T., & Cushenbery, L. (2011). Leading for innovation: Direct and indirect influences. *Advances in Developing Human Resources*, 13, 248–265.

Ilgen, D. R., Hollenbeck, J. R., Johnson, M., & Jundt, D. (2005). Teams in organizations: From input-process-output models to IMOI models. *Annual Review of Psychology*, 56(1), 517–543.

Janicik, G. A., & Bartel, C. A. (2003). Talking about time: Effects of temporal planning and time awareness norms on group coordination and performance. *Group Dynamics: Theory, Research, and Practice*, 7(2), 122–134.

Janis, I. L. (1971). Groupthink. *Psychology Today*, 5(6), 43–46.

Jones, P. E., & Roelofsma, P. H. M. P. (2000). The potential for social contextual and group biases in team decision-making: Biases, conditions and psychological mechanisms. *Ergonomics*, 43(8), 1129–1152.

Judge, T. A., Bono, J. E., Ilies, R., & Gerhardt, M. W. (2002). Personality and leadership: A qualitative and quantitative review. *Journal of Applied Psychology*, 87(4), 765.

Kahneman, D., & Lovallo, D. (1993). Timid choices and bold forecasts: A cognitive perspective on risk taking. *Management Science*, 39(1), 17–31.

Kahneman, D., Lovallo, D., & Sibony, O. (2011). The big idea: Before you make that big decision. *Harvard Business Review*, 50–60.

Kent, R. L., & Moss, S. E. (1994). Effects of sex and gender role on leader emergence. *Academy of Management Journal*, 37(5), 1335–1346.

Kerr, N. L., & Stanfel, J. A. (1993). Role schemata and member motivation in task groups. *Personality and Social Psychology Bulletin*, 19(4), 432–442.

Kerr, N. L., & Tindale, R. S. (2004). Group performance and decision making. *Annual Review of Psychology*, 55, 623–655.

Kooloos, J. G. M., Klaassen, T., Vereijken, M., van Kuppeveld, S., Bolhuis, S., & Vorstenbosch, M. (2011). Collaborative group work: Effects of group size and assignment structure on learning gain, student satisfaction and perceived participation. *Medical Teacher*, 33(12), 983–988.

Kozlowski, S. W. J., & Ilgen, D. R. (2006). Enhancing the effectiveness of work groups and teams. *Psychological Science in the Public Interest*, 7(3), 77–124.

Lamm, H. (1988). A review of our research on group polarization: Eleven experiments on the effects of group discussion on risk acceptance, probability estimation, and negotiation positions. *Psychological Reports*, 62(3), 807–813.

Larson, J. R., Jr., Foster-Fishman, P. G., & Keys, C. B. (1994). Discussion of shared and unshared information in decision-making groups. *Journal of Personality and Social Psychology*, 67(3), 446–461.

Latané, B., Williams, K., & Harkins, S. (1979). Many hands make light the work: The causes and consequences of social loafing. *Journal of Personality and Social Psychology*, 37, 822–832.

Laughlin, P. R., Zander, M. L., Knievel, E. M., & Tan, T. K. (2003). Groups perform better than the best individuals on letters-to-numbers problems: Informative equations and effective strategies. *Journal of Personality and Social Psychology*, 85(4), 684–694.

LePine, J. A. (2003). Team adaptation and postchange performance: Effects of team composition in terms of members' cognitive ability and personality. *Journal of Applied Psychology*, 88(1), 27–39.

Lewis, K. (2003). Measuring transactive memory systems in the field: scale development and validation. *Journal of Applied Psychology*, 88, 587.

McGrath, J. E. (1964). *Social psychology: A brief introduction*. New York: Holt, Rinehart & Winston.

Marks, M. A., Mathieu, J. E., & Zaccaro, S. J. (2001). A temporally based framework and taxonomy of team processes. *The Academy of Management Review*, 26(3), 356–376.

Mathieu, J. E., & Rapp, T. L. (2009). Laying the foundation for successful team performance trajectories: The roles of team charters and performance strategies. *Journal of Applied Psychology*, 94, 90–103.

Mathieu, J. E., & Schulze, W. (2006). The influence of team knowledge and formal plans on episodic team process-performance relationships. *Academy of Management Journal*, 49(3), 605–619.

Maznevski, M. L., & Chudoba, K. M. (2000). Bridging space over time: Global virtual team dynamics and effectiveness. *Organization Science*, 11(5), 473–492.

Mehta, A., Feild, H., Armenakis, A., & Mehta, N. (2009). Team goal orientation and team performance: The mediating role of team planning. *Journal of Management*, 35(4), 1026–1046.

Mesmer-Magnus, J. R., & DeChurch, L. A. (2009). Information sharing and team performance: A meta-analysis. *Journal of Applied Psychology*, 94(2), 535–546.

Miles, J. A., & Greenberg, J. (1993). Using punishment threats to attenuate social loafing effects among swimmers. *Organizational Behavior and Human Decision Processes*, 56(2), 246–265.

Mohammed, S., Ferzandi, L., & Hamilton, K. (2010). Metaphor no more: A 15-year review of the team mental model construct. *Journal of Management*, 36(4), 876–910.

Mojzisch, A., Grouneva, L., & Schulz-Hardt, S. (2010). Biased evaluation of information during discussion: Disentangling the effects of preference consistency, social validation, and ownership of information. *European Journal of Social Psychology*, 40, 946–956.

Moscovici, S. (1980). Toward a theory of conversion behavior. In L. Berkowitz (Ed.), *Advances in experimental social psychology* (Vol. 13, pp. 209–239). New York: Academic Press.

Nemeth, C. J., & Kwan, J. L. (1987). Minority influence, divergent thinking and detection of correct solutions. *British Journal of Applied Social Psychology*, 17(9), 788–799.

Nemeth, C. J., & Rogers, J. (1996). Dissent and the search for information. *British Journal of Social Psychology*, 35(1), 67–76.

Orasanu, J., & Salas, E. (1993). Team decision making in complex environments. In G. A. Klein, J. Orasanu, R. Calderwood, & C. E. Zsambok (Eds.), *Decision making in action: Models and methods* (pp. 327–345). Westport, CT: Ablex.

Park, W. (1990). A review of research on groupthink, *Journal of Behavioural Decision Making*, 3, 229–245.

Parks, C. D., & Cowlin, R. A. (1996). Acceptance of uncommon information into group discussion when that information is or is not demonstrable. *Organizational Behavior and Human Decision Processes*, 66(3), 307–315.

Patrick, J., James, N., & Ahmed, A. (2006). Human processes of control: Tracing the goals and strategies of control room teams. *Ergonomics*, 49(12–13), 1395–1414.

Postmes, T., Spears, R., & Cihangir, S. (2001). Quality of decision making and group norms. *Journal of Personality and Social Psychology*, 80(6), 918–930.

Randall, K. R., Resick, C. J., & DeChurch, L. A. (2011). Building team adaptive capacity: The roles of sensegiving and team composition. *Journal of Applied Psychology*, 96(3), 525–540.

Riggio, R. E., Riggio, H. R., Salinas, C., & Cole, E. J. (2003). The role of social and emotional communication skills in leader emergence and effectiveness. *Group Dynamics: Theory, Research, and Practice*, 7(2), 83–103.

Rousseau, V., Aubé, C. (2010). Team self-managing behaviors and team effectiveness: The moderating effect of task routineness. *Group and Organization Management*, 35(6), 751–781.

Salgado, J. F. (1998). Big Five personality dimensions and job performance in army and civil occupations: A European perspective. *Human Performance*, 11, 271–288.

Schweiger, D. M., Sandberg, W. R., & Ragan, J. W. (1986). Group approaches for improving strategic decision-making: A comparative analysis of dialectical inquiry, devil's advocacy, and consensus. *Academy of Management Journal*, 29(1), 51–71.

Shachaf, P. (2005). Bridging cultural diversity through e-mail. *Journal of Global Information Technology Management*, 8(2), 46–60.

Shanteau, J. (1992). Competence in experts: The role of task characteristics. *Organizational Behavior and Human Decision Processes*, 53(2), 252–266.

Shaw, M. (1936). *Group dynamics* (3rd ed). New York: Harper.

Sitzmann, T., & Johnson, S. K. (2012). The best laid plans: Examining the conditions under which a planning intervention improves learning and reduces attrition. *Journal of Applied Psychology*, 97(5), 967–981.

Smith, C. M., Tindale, R. S., & Steiner, L. (1998). Investment decisions by individuals and groups in sunk cost situations: The potential impact of shared representations. *Group Processes & Intergroup Relations*, 1(2), 175–189.

Smith, J. A., & Foti, R. J. (1998). A pattern approach to the study of leader emergence. *Leadership Quarterly*, 9(2), 147–160.

Smith, K. G., Locke, E. A., & Barry, D. (1990). Goal setting, planning, and organizational performance: An experimental simulation. *Organizational Behavior and Human Decision Processes*, 46(1), 118–134.

Stasser, G., & Stewart, D. (1992). Discovery of hidden profiles by decision-making groups: Solving a problem versus making a judgment. *Journal of Personality and Social Psychology*, 63(3), 426–434.

Stasser, G., & Titus, W. (1985). Pooling of unshared information in group decision making: Biased information sampling during discussion. *Journal of Personality and Social Psychology*, 48(6), 1467–1478.

Stasser, G., Taylor, L. A., & Hanna, C. (1989). Information sampling in structured and unstructured discussions of three- and six-person groups. *Journal of Personality and Social Psychology*, 57(1), 67–78.

Steiner, I. D. (1972). *Group process and productivity*. New York: Academic Press.

Stout, R. J., Cannon-Bowers, J. A., Salas, E., & Milanovich, D. M. (1999). Planning, shared mental models, and coordinated performance: An empirical link is established. *Human Factors*, 41(1), 61–71.

Thomas, E. J., & Fink, C. F. (1963). Effects of group size. *Psychological Bulletin*, 60(4), 371–384.

Tversky, A., & Kahneman, D. (1974). Judgment under uncertainty: Heuristics and biases. *Science*, 185(4157), 1124–1131.

Valacich, J. S., & Schwenk, C. (1995). Devil's advocacy and dialectical inquiry effects on face-to-face and computer-mediated group-decision making. *Organizational Behavior and Human Decision Processes*, 63(2), 158–173.

Weingart, L. R. (1992). Impact of group goals, task component complexity, effort, and planning on group performance. *Journal of Applied Psychology*, 77(5), 682–693.

Weldon, E., Jehn, K. A., & Pradhan, P. (1991). Processes that mediate the relationship between a group goal and improved group performance. *Journal of Personality and Social Psychology*, 61(4), 555–569.

Whyte, G. (1993). Escalating commitment in individual and group decision making: A prospect theory approach. *Organizational Behavior and Human Decision Processes*, 54(3), 430–455.

Williams, K. D., & Karau, S. J. (1991). Social loafing and social compensation: The effects of expectations of co-worker performance. *Journal of Personality and Social Psychology*, 61(4), 570–581.

Wittenbaum, G. M., Hubbell, A. P., & Zuckerman, C. (1999). Mutual enhancement: Toward an understanding of the collective preference for shared information. *Journal of Personality and Social Psychology*, 77(5), 967–978.

Worchel, S., Rothgerber, H., Day, E. A., Hart, D., & Butemeyer, J. (1998). Social identity and individual productivity within groups. *British Journal of Social Psychology*, 37(4), 389–413.

Zaccaro, S. J., Gualtieri, J., & Minionis, D. (1995). Task cohesion as a facilitator of team decision making under temporal urgency. *Military Psychology*, 7(2), 77–93.

Zaccaro, S. J., White, L., Kilcullen, R., Parker, C., Williams, D., & O'Connor-Boes, J. (1997). *Cognitive and temperament predictors of Army civilian leadership (No. TR-97-1)*. Bethesda, MD: Management Research Institute.

10

EXAMINING THE MULTI-LEVEL EFFECTS OF ORGANIZATIONAL PLANNING ON PERFORMANCE

Nastassia Savage, Shannon Marlow, and Eduardo Salas

There are a number of companies which have demonstrated extraordinary success in the business domain, but perhaps the most iconic example in recent memory is Google. Even in the current economic environment, Google continues to generate a profit while simultaneously shaping present technology with its innovation. Recent events also offer equally rich, detailed instances of failure. There are cases like Kodak, the company responsible for the birth of snapshot photography, which failed to adapt to the market's new taste for digital photography, despite being responsible for its original development, and ended up filing for Chapter 11 bankruptcy.

What leads to success for some corporations and what leads to failure for others? Obviously, the answer to this question is not a simple one. It's also obvious that a variety of factors, ranging from consumer taste to funding issues, are working collectively to produce results that may never be exactly as predicted.

Yet one distinct difference between success and failure in the case of Kodak and Google is the quality of their plans. Google has used strategic planning to initiate market changes that have benefited the company (Berry, Shankar, Parish, Cadwallader, & Dotzel, 2006; Iyer & Davenport, 2008). In contrast, Kodak was unable to exploit or even adjust to the market changes that resulted from its invention of the digital camera due to an inability to create and apply successful strategies (Lucas & Goh, 2009).

The lack of an effective plan designed to keep Kodak afloat while its target market underwent rapid changes may not have been the ultimate reason for its failure. Companies may have only a very small measure of control over the final outcome in these situations, but research suggests that this small degree of control, maybe only an infinitesimal piece of the whole, can make a difference (Miller & Cardinal, 1994). Specifically, research indicates that organizational planning, when designed and implemented in an appropriate manner, can lead to enhanced performance (Schwenk & Shrader, 1993).

Over the past few decades, the body of research addressing organizational planning has grown. Most of this research has focused on confirming that a positive correlation exists between planning and performance. Researchers have defined planning in a variety of ways as this relationship has received increased attention and as the volume of empirical evidence has increased (Boyne & Gould-Williams, 2003).

Across studies, there has been no clear or obvious way to approach planning as a construct. Original studies assessing planning based its definition on behavioral models and painted it as a predefined activity that, once implemented, was inflexible and incapable of change (Wilensky, 1983). One of the common arguments against the utility of planning is that planning can limit an organization's ability to adapt. Mintzberg (1987) likened planning to a "straitjacket" (p. 26) and claimed that a plan can be so rigid as to impede an organization's ability to make necessary adjustments to an environment that can, and most likely will, change.

Mumford, Schultz, and Van Doorn (2001) argued against defining planning in a manner that suggests rigidity or basing its conception on behavioral models. They claimed that defining planning as a predefined, inflexible sequence and attempting to study it accordingly would not lead to the most accurate results. Instead, they defined it as "the mental simulation of actions and their outcomes in a dynamic environment," suggesting (p. 214) a more flexible and adaptive force that is capable of changing and keeping pace with an evolving environment.

As the definition has changed across studies, the context in which planning's relationship to performance has been studied has also varied. It has been examined in a number of different industries at several levels of the organization. Although there are multiple ways to examine how planning shapes performance, we believe it is important to assess this relationship within the context of a multi-level framework including the individual, team, and organizational levels, because organizational planning affects performance on each of these levels in different ways (Mumford, Schultz, and Osburn, 2002).

The effect of planning on each related component of the organization must be examined in order to understand how performance is influenced. By assessing the way in which planning affects performance on each level, useful information will subsequently be available for companies to shape the way that they plan. Using empirical evidence to understand the planning process gives companies a better chance of effectively utilizing plans to increase performance.

To understand how planning influences performance on each level, we propose the following key question: how does organizational planning affect performance at the individual, team, and organizational levels? In addition to answering this question and discussing the intricacies of the planning–performance relationship relevant to each level, it is important to address how to measure performance. Each level of the organization requires a different measure of performance. Without an adequate understanding of how to assess performance, an accurate representation of the relationship between planning and performance cannot be obtained.

Individual Level

The effects of organizational planning are pervasive, impacting every aspect of an institution. Given that individual employees are the basis of an organization, it is integral to evaluate how an organizational plan affects their performance. For example, if the turnover rate increases, the company's expenditures increase as a result of having to hire and train new employees. Consequently, if implementing an organizational plan has a negative impact on the individuals within it, it is worth examining the situation to determine how and why.

The general consensus of the literature supports the notion that planning in any form increases performance (Locke & Latham, 1990; Ryan, 2008; Lanaj, Hollenbeck, Ilgen, Barnes, & Harmon, 2013; Akça, Esen, & Özer, 2013). Plans help employees to focus on a particular goal and develop a strategy for achieving that goal. However, plans should not be followed strictly if circumstances change but should allow some room for adaptation. Overarching plans also encourage increased adaptability from employees while still maintaining overall organizational goals. The benefit of information gathered at the individual level is that it is unique and can give a more detailed breakdown of how individual employees and their productivity are affected by an organizational plan.

However, there are a number of variables that influence the relationship between planning and performance, such as the cognitive capacity of individuals and their level of planning skills. Cognitive capacity is most commonly assessed by means of intelligence testing. While intelligence, or general mental ability, has been determined to be a significant predictor of performance (Devine & Philips, 2001), its link to planning and the impact of planning on individual performance has been less clear. Recent research has shown a significant relationship between elaborate and pro-active planning in small business owners and their cognitive ability across three different samples (Frese et al., 2007). The level of intelligence associated with the development or execution of a plan becomes a factor in an individual's performance for a number of reasons. Level of intelligence affects the quality of the plan being developed, resulting in the planning process being a proxy for determining intelligence in the individuals involved, as shown in the PASS (planning, attention, simultaneous, successive) framework for intelligence (Naglieri & Das, 1990). When it comes to the execution of a plan, a more intelligent individual is capable of adapting it when circumstances change and is more likely to accurately understand the overall intent of the plan (Novicevic, Harvey, Autry, & Bond, 2004).

Another variable to consider is the level of planning that comes from leaders within the organization. Planning on their part, while dependent upon the task characteristics, has a significant impact on group and team performance (Marta, Leritz, & Mumford, 2005). Planning skills have been shown to be a factor in effective leadership (Marta et al., 2005) and leadership emergence (Suriyamurthi, Velavan, & Radhiga, 2013), positively influencing individuals' performance (Wang, Oh, Courtright, & Colbert, 2011). It is therefore also important to evaluate the leader's planning skills as this has been shown to influence the quality of the plan produced (Marta et al., 2005).

Given that there is some evidence that planning has a direct impact on performance (Ryan, 2008), it is important to note that other variables also affect this relationship. For example, the level of commitment to the plan mediates the relationship of individual-level planning to performance. Commitment to a particular plan or strategy leads to better task performance, though it does depend on the quality of the plan (Diefendorff & Lord, 2003). It was also found that those individuals with a planning mindset perform better with a plan even when the quality of the plan is poor. This emphasizes the point that rigid or "straitjacket" plans (Mintzberg, 1987, p. 26) are not conducive to success, while simultaneously supporting Mumford et al.'s (2001) conclusion that plans need to be adaptable.

One of the common ways to evaluate the extent that organizational planning influences the company is to look at performance levels within the organization. The most efficient way to determine if planning has had an effect on individual performance is to evaluate it in some way. While the most common method of data collection is survey based, other methods include observations and using objective information such as sales figures and profits. When analyzing performance, it is important to determine which type of data collection will provide information that is most relevant to the goals of the company.

Surveys are most frequently used, particularly in field settings, because they allow for quick and, often, cheap data collection as they can be administered without a researcher present through paper-and-pencil forms or online, which also allows participants to complete the survey when most convenient for them. Another advantage is that surveys are easily validated. However, it is much easier for participants to "fool" the test and be insincere when filling out the survey, or respond carelessly, making its content invalid and skewing the final results.

Other data collection methods may be more expensive and time-consuming but they can lead to more accurate results. If the performance data of interest is an observable behavior, researchers can collect observations of participants. Examples of such data include communication styles with teammates or co-workers, a behavior that is difficult for individuals to recognize in themselves, or a behavior that people may not want to admit to, such as discriminatory behaviors. This requires the observers to undergo training in order to ensure that they all have the same mental model for the construct being evaluated. All of this requires researchers to be present and actively engaged in the data-collection process, which can take a few months to years, depending on the type of research being conducted and the research questions being asked.

A third type of data collection, and one which does not require participants, is assessing changes in objective information such as turnover rates and overall sales. When making a change in an organization, such as implementing an organizational plan, determining how that change impacts profits or the turnover rate can be a suitable indicator of whether the plan is effective or well received by the employees. For example, if a plan is implemented that suggests to employees that the organization is more committed to them than before, there will likely be an increase in profits and productivity as well as a lower turnover rate (Donald et al., 2005).

Team Level

Another layer of an organization that planning affects is the team level. Teams can consist of varying numbers of individuals with potentially different functional or educational backgrounds and various levels of demographic diversity. We define a team as "a distinguishable set of two or more people who interact dynamically, interdependently, and adaptively toward a common and valued goal/object/mission, who have each been assigned specific roles or functions to perform, and who have a limited life span of membership" (Salas, Dickinson, Converse, & Tannenbaum, 1992, p. 4). Team-level performance is important to examine when considering the effects of organizational planning as it demonstrates how groups within the organization are working together and is an indicator of the teamwork within those groups. An effective organizational plan will give teams a goal to work towards and help develop a clearer focus for their work (O'Leary-Kelly, Martocchio, & Fink, 1994).

Because organizations often utilize teams to work on particular tasks or projects, it is important to recognize not just how planning at the organizational level impacts the individuals in that organization, but how the teams composed of those individuals are influenced. Organizational planning, as mentioned earlier, is when an organization creates an outline to follow, emphasizing how the company wants to change while, ideally, including enough flexibility to allow for changes in the plan based on outside information and incidents (Mumford et al., 2001). While the organization's plan clearly impacts the plans individuals have within that organization, it also structures how the teams interact and what their goals are. As outlined by Montoya, Carter, Martin, and DeChurch (Chapter 9, this volume), there are five typical traps teams fall into when it comes to planning: ignoring unshared information, discussion based on pre-discussion preferences, uneven participation, group escalation, and an aversion to planning. Another important factor relating to whether teams plan is whether they have dedicated time to plan, as research has shown that teams do not dedicate adequate time to planning when not directly instructed to do so (Weingart, 1992).

As an example, a company like Google creates and adjusts its organizational plans to reflect the successes and failures of its products, such as their tablets, phones, or their new attempt at branching out into television. These plans should also reflect Google's goals for the future. When organizations create plans, they tend to dictate the allocation of resources, including who should work on what.

One area in which this is most easily observed is in product development teams. Teams such as these need to ensure their focus matches the organizational plan, be it to improve existing products, create new technology for future products, or determine why a product didn't do well and how to adjust their approach to future products.

As discussed earlier, planning at the organizational level clearly has an impact on individuals and their performance. However, this is both affected by and simultaneously affects team performance. Should a company have an organizational plan that is too rigid, vague, or contradictory, it is likely to cause more interpersonal conflict within teams and more time spent planning, reducing productivity and performance within the team. However, if an organization has a clear, specific, and adaptable plan in place, this enables teams to focus more on completing their tasks and delivering far better products that are more consistent with the company's plan.

Given that organizational planning impacts teams, not just individuals, it is possible to see effects of successful organizational planning at the team level. Appropriate planning manifests itself in increased performance (Woolley, Gerbasi, Chabris, Kosslyn, & Hackman, 2008), which can be demonstrated through changes in team processes such as communication and conflict from the Marks, Mathieu, and Zaccaro (2001) framework. Communication is an integral part of both planning and teams, and it increases in frequency and effectiveness when planning is utilized (Padmo Putri, 2013). Increased communication also enhances performance, as evidenced in numerous studies, in both the lab and the field (Padmo Putri, 2013; Espevik, Johnsen, & Eid, 2011; Neves & Eisenberger, 2012; Gulbrandsen, Jensen, Finset, & Blanch-Hartigan, 2013), emphasizing its importance as a link between organizational planning and its impact on teams.

When an organization creates and promotes clear, adaptable plans, there is less team-level conflict within the organization, as Schnake and Cochran (1985) demonstrated. As many people recognize, increased conflict has a negative impact on team performance, while aspects of conflict management (compromising and cohesiveness, for example) have significant positive relationships with performance (Chou & Yeh, 2007). As such, it is important to keep in mind how organizational planning affects teams, both from a practical perspective, that is, determining how to make teams more productive, and from a theoretical perspective, such as determining what analyses to run on data and how to generalize results.

While a direct connection between planning and team performance has been found in the literature, as supported by a meta-analysis by O'Leary-Kelly, Martocchio, and Fink (1994), they also found indicators of moderators of that relationship. One of the probable variables that may influence the planning–performance relationship is teamwork processes. Several teamwork processes are identified by Marks et al. (2001) and include, among others, goal specification, team monitoring and backup behavior, and conflict management. Studies have shown that these team processes are a central part of successful teams, affecting numerous other processes, not least of which is performance (Brannick, Prince, Prince, & Salas, 1995; Brannick, Roach, & Salas, 1993; Gladstein, 1984; Smolek, Hoffman, & Moran, 1999; Saavedra, Earley, & Dyne, 1993). While these processes are exhibited through individuals, it is only within a team context that they exist. As such, it is important to assess how planning at the organizational level impacts performance at the team level.

Analyzing the effects of organizational planning at the team level yields unique information beyond that found examining effects at the individual level, in that it shows how organizational planning influences how the team interacts, which directly impacts performance. This includes changing team processes, such as goal specification, team monitoring and backup behavior, and conflict management (Marks et al., 2001), which subsequently alters team outcomes like productivity and performance. When an effective organizational plan is developed, it reduces the need for teams to spend additional time during their transition phase specifying what their goals are. While teams still need to develop specific goals relevant to their task, having an organizational plan helps to provide a particular direction for teams to work towards.

Another important team process that is affected by organizational planning is that of conflict management. There are generally two forms of conflict in two specific areas: relationship or interpersonal conflict and task-related conflict. Relationship or interpersonal conflict refers to disagreements or problems among team members, usually stemming from problems of personal taste or differing values (Quigley, Tekleab, & Tesluk, 2007). Task conflict, however, is associated with issues resulting from the team's tasks. When a team has a clearly defined goal, it is less likely for conflict to occur, and the less conflict, the higher the performance (Locke & Latham, 2002).

Another distinction between the individual level and the team level is how measurement occurs, as variables evaluated at the individual level can also be evaluated at the team level using different methods of analysis. For example, it is common to measure personality traits in conjunction with any number of other variables. However, when conducting an individual-level analysis, researchers can correlate, for example, an individual's level of extraversion with other variables. Individual-level measures are generally direct, whereas team-level data is usually aggregated in some manner before any analyses can occur. To examine extraversion at the team level, researchers frequently use the mean, minimum, or maximum level of extraversion across team members, or standard deviations may be used as a proxy for the variance within the team. An example of a method that has been widely used to look at how diverse a team is in a particular variable, such as sex, is Blau's (1977) index.

There are also interaction effects between different team members as well as the effects of being in a team itself, which can be analyzed using processes such as hierarchical linear modeling. Another issue is how to measure the aforementioned team processes and other, more theoretical, team interactions (Dickinson & McIntyre, 1997). When analyzing data, it is also important to recognize the limitations that stem from inappropriately generalizing results from individual-level analyses. For example, determining that length of service is important to organizational commitment (Suman & Srivastava, 2012) does not take into account other factors, such as leadership behaviors, team diversity, or team cohesion and conflict. While there are clearly conceptual differences between individual-level and team-level data, there are significant practical implications for determining which level of analysis should be used and how the data should be interpreted.

Organizational Level

Some effects of organizational planning can be understood by examining its impact on the team and individual levels. However, to understand the full impact of planning, its influence at the organizational level must be assessed. Companies are utilizing planning techniques in pursuit of improved organizational performance, although planning can be a time-consuming and demanding process (Mumford et al., 2001). It is thus important to consider how planning affects organizational performance.

Researchers have suggested that planning may contribute to organizational success because it allows leaders to clarify objectives and thus clearly communicate these goals to employees, providing them with a comprehensive idea about what their central goals are and what they should be doing to accomplish these objectives (Boyne & Gould-Williams, 2003). Furthermore, in defining goals through the planning process, leaders understand exactly what resources are necessary for success and can create a system of organization to allocate the resources that will be most needed. This clarification also provides a more global view, allowing for considerations about precise objectives and knowledge about resources to guide decisions (Boyne & Gould-Williams, 2003). Despite this proposed rationale as to why planning may improve performance, the literature has offered conflicting evidence about the relationship between organizational planning and organizational performance. To understand these inconsistencies and to determine if planning is truly effective at the organizational level, a more thorough examination of the research is necessary.

Several studies seem to indicate that planning is not related to organizational performance. In one study, which used data gathered from interviews conducted with executives from 21 United Kingdom companies, no significant relationship was found between formal planning and financial performance (Grinyer & Norburn, 1975). Similarly, in assessing 328 of the largest Fortune 500 companies, no conclusive evidence was found to support the hypothesis that planning contributes to organizational success (Kudla, 1980). Yet another study, conducted by Robinson and Pearce (1983), obtained similar results, finding no significant difference in the performance of banks that placed an emphasis on planning and those that did not.

When examining these results, if not using a more critical eye, one might be tempted to conclude that planning is not an effective method of improving organizational performance. However, there are other studies that contradict these findings and paint an entirely different picture. Three meta-analytic studies have found evidence for a positive relationship between planning and organizational success (Schwenk & Shrader, 1993; Boyd, 1991; Miller & Cardinal, 1994).

Obviously, results have been inconsistent across studies and there is an apparent divide in the literature. Some studies seem to indicate that planning is a wasted, often costly, endeavor, while other research offers support for the use of organizational planning. It is important to examine the cause of this discrepancy. Several researchers have suggested that the answer to this contradiction lies in the methodology (Miller & Cardinal, 1994; Boyd, 1991; Beard & Dess, 1981; Pearce, Freeman, & Robinson, 1987; Cardinal, Miller, Kreutzer, & TenBrink, 2015, this volume). They have noted methodological differences across studies and propose that this is the ultimate reason why results have varied. There are several issues to consider when examining this association which, if not addressed, can interfere with the obtained strength of the relationship.

One of the largest inconsistencies researchers have noted is that not all research studying the relationship between planning and performance has properly or consistently controlled for extraneous variables (Miller & Cardinal, 1994; Boyd, 1991). These researchers have argued that not controlling for these influences will distort results. A number of factors have been proposed as having an influence on this association, but the variables that have received the most attention include turbulence, firm size, industry type, and capital intensity.

Like most aspects of the relationship between planning and performance, the influence of turbulence on the association has been debated. One common argument is that companies facing changing environments need pre-determined strategies in order to manage the related difficulties of operating in such an environment (Mumford et al., 2002; Ansoff, 1991). The other most frequent argument, suggesting that companies encountering high turbulence will actually perform better without planning, contends that planning will interfere with the company's ability to adjust to changes (Mintzberg, 1987). However, more conclusive evidence has been found in favor of the first claim, with the results of a meta-analysis suggesting that the higher the level of turbulence, the stronger the relationship between planning and performance (Miller & Cardinal, 1994).

Firm size has also been suggested by many researchers to have an influence (Beard & Dess, 1981; Wood & LaForge, 1979; Robinson & Pearce, 1983). The basis of this argument is that firm size has been demonstrated to be related to profit (Gooding & Wagner, 1985). Smaller firms may also plan in a different manner than larger firms, with differences reflected in both the duration and manner in which the planning is conducted (Cardinal et al., 2015). Results have been inconclusive regarding the influence of firm size. One study suggested that size has no effect on the planning–performance relationship (Miller & Cardinal 1994), while another demonstrated that there was a stronger relationship in larger firms (Robinson & Pearce, 1983). It is clear that further research is needed to clarify the precise nature of the influence of firm size on the planning–performance relationship.

Another factor which has been suggested to have some impact on this association is industry type (Dess, Ireland, & Hitt, 1990; Beard & Dess, 1981). Like firm size, researchers have argued that industry type will have an effect because a relationship with size and firm profitability has been supported by empirical evidence (Beard & Dess, 1981). Boyd (1991) noted that few studies in this area of research had controlled for industry effects. There has been some evidence that, when industry effects are controlled for, a stronger relationship between planning and performance can be obtained (Miller & Cardinal, 1994).

Capital intensity has also been emphasized as a potential confounding variable. The rationale behind this is that more capital-intensive organizations require more coordination to be successful and that planning will be more helpful in orchestrating that coordination, subsequently positively influencing performance (Miller & Cardinal, 1994; Mumford et al., 2002). A meta-analysis provided evidence for this assertion, demonstrating that companies with higher capital intensity benefited more from planning (Miller & Cardinal, 1994).

Given these results, it is probable that some of these extraneous variables may explain some of the contradictory outcomes in prior research. Some other variables, such as organizational culture, organizational climate, and goals (Mumford et al., 2002) have also been suggested as potentially having an effect, but more evidence is needed to authenticate these claims. However, the evidence presented by current research does illuminate to some degree what factors have an impact on the relationship between planning and performance.

Another issue creating inconsistencies in past research is the way that planning has been conceptualized (Boyd, 1991; Cardinal et al., 2015). Many past studies have merely placed companies into two categories, either planning or non-planning, to evaluate organizational planning. In using such a simple classification system, the quality of the plans being executed receives no consideration. It has been suggested that measuring planning on an interval or ordinal scale may lead to more accurate and informative results (Wood & LaForge, 1981). Also, how planning itself is defined, whether as a more standardized process or as a more general process incorporating both formal and informal components, may cause further disparity among findings (Cardinal et al., 2015). According to Miller and Cardinal (1994), describing planning in more general terms led to a more accurate idea of the planning process.

Yet another potential methodological issue is in the way that performance is measured (Cardinal et al., 2015). Cardinal et al. (2015) noted that performance has been assessed in a variety of ways, including both self-report and archival measures. This causes difficulties when researchers attempt to generalize findings. In research conducted at the organizational level, researchers have generally regarded performance as being synonymous with profit, with profit therefore being the most common way of measuring performance (Boyne & Gould-Williams, 2003). Miller and Cardinal (1994) found that the most popular and common ways of assessing performance at the organizational level fell into seven categories: sales growth, earnings growth, deposit growth, return on assets, return on equity, return on sales, and return on total invested capital. As financial measures are the simplest and easiest to use, those are the measures utilized most frequently.

However, using a financial measure to assess overall performance may not always be appropriate (Boyne & Gould-Williams, 2003). In organizations where increased profit is the most significant goal, financial measures are clearly suitable. But in industries where enhanced profit is not the most desired outcome, a measure of financial success may not reflect all aspects of performance. It is crucial that the goals of the company being targeted are established and understood so that performance can be measured in a corresponding manner.

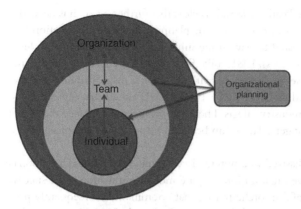

FIGURE 10.1 The impact of organizational planning on individual, team, and organization

Another potential difficulty in measuring performance is the timeframe in which the data is collected. Many studies take a cross-sectional approach, which some researchers argue will not lead to as accurate results as those provided by longitudinal studies (Boyd, 1991; Boyne & Gould-Williams, 2003). They claim that performance as a result of planning may take years to appear and a longitudinal approach would thus be the most accurate method for measuring performance resulting from planning (Boyne & Gould-Williams, 2003).

Clearly, there are various methodological problems that may influence the data and lead to ambiguous results. This is, most likely, the cause of the split in the literature. Overall, research (when potential methodological issues are thoroughly addressed) has indicated that planning is associated with increased organizational performance (Andrews, Boyne, Law, & Walker, 2009; Schwenk & Shrader, 1993; Miller & Cardinal, 1994).

There have obviously been multiple difficulties in confirming that a relationship between planning and performance exists. Therefore it is not unexpected that there is limited evidence to signify precisely how this relationship is manifested. However, the available findings offer a hazy sketch of the process and provide some indication as to what elements may potentially contribute to this association, including turbulence, firm size, industry type, and capital intensity. Beyond those variables, further research is needed to understand what other factors shape this complex relationship. However, when examining the planning–performance relationship in future studies, researchers must be careful to keep in mind the methodological issues that have plagued prior research.

Conclusion

While assessing how organizational planning affects the components of an organization (i.e. the individual, team, and organization as a whole) reveals some of its effects, this examination does not encompass how these components interact with one another. As is often quoted, "the sum of the parts does not equal the whole" and, accordingly, conducting research that emphasizes not just each level of the organization but also the longitudinal interactions of each level as a result of organizational planning is integral to understanding the various impacts of planning on the organization. Throughout this chapter, we have looked at how organizational planning impacts the individual, team, and organizational level separately, focusing on how planning influences performance at each of those levels.

When interested in evaluating organizational planning at the individual level, it is important to consider the potential moderators of the relationship between the variables, such as commitment

TABLE 10.1 Summary of the multi-level effects of organization planning

How does organizational planning affect individual performance?	• Moderated by individual's commitment to the plan and personality traits
	• Consider different methods of data collection and use what is most appropriate
	    • surveys
	    • observations
	    • objective data

How does organizational planning affect team performance?	• Diversity within teams
	• Significant moderator is team processes
	• Determine method of analysis
	    • mean
	    • minimum/maximum
	    • variance
	    • hierarchical linear modeling
	    • Blau's index

How does organizational planning affect organizational performance?	• Impact has been debated • Methodological issues explain inconsistencies in past research • Capital intensity, turbulence, firm size, and industry type proposed to influence relationship • Improves performance

to the plan and personality traits. These can emphasize or negate the effects of organizational planning, making them important variables to consider. It is also important to consider the types of data collection to be used, as this also determines the type of information to be gathered. Surveys are helpful in that they are cheap, easy to use, don't require researchers to be present, and can be relatively quick to distribute and collect. Observations are beneficial in that they can provide information that is either difficult for the participant to recognize or may reveal a behavior that people are hesitant to admit to, such as discriminatory behaviors. The third method of data collection discussed earlier is to collect objective information, such as turnover rates, productivity or the quality of work, and profits.

An important aspect to consider when looking at organizational planning and how it affects team performance involves the interactions among the team members, who will have varying levels of diversity. The most significant moderator of the effects of an organizational plan on team-level performance is team processes such as communication and conflict management. If data are collected from the individuals within the team, it is therefore essential to determine how analyses will be conducted at the team level. Using means, minimums, maximums, standard deviations, and other such methods are all common methodologies to evaluate a variable at the team level. Another method of analysis to consider is hierarchical linear modeling, which accounts for the differences in individuals given that they are in the same team and in the same organization. There are also methods of evaluating the diversity of a team on a specific variable, such as Blau's index. The method used to aggregate individual-level data to team-level data should reflect the questions the researcher is most interested in addressing.

There has been a lot of argument regarding the effect of organizational planning on organizational performance. Although its impact on the organizational level has been debated, ultimately researchers have found evidence that planning is associated with increased organizational performance (Miller & Cardinal, 1994, Schwenk & Shrader, 1993, Boyd, 1991). Researchers have concluded that methodological issues are to blame for the different outcomes across studies (Boyd,

1991; Beard & Dess, 1981; Pearce et al., 1987). One such problem is that not all researchers have properly controlled for extraneous variables. Variables like turbulence, firm size, industry type, and capital intensity have all been proposed to play a role in shaping the relationship between planning and performance (Mumford et al., 2002; Miller & Cardinal, 1994; Beard & Dess, 1981). Future research is needed to advance knowledge of this association and it is imperative that researchers address any potential methodological problems before proceeding.

Future Research

Given what the literature says about the impact of organizational planning on the different levels of performance, it is clear that planning has a significant influence on the organization at the individual, team, and organizational levels. It is therefore essential to ensure that the plans being developed are flexible and capable of adapting to a frequently changing environment, both internally and externally. As such, it is increasingly important to evaluate plans at all levels of the organization. While there has been some multi-level research, more is necessary for the full effects of organizational plans or subsequent changes to the plan to be accurately evaluated. This is both for research and practical purposes so that information is available for organizations to utilize in applied areas. As each level of the organization (individual, team, and organizational) reveals unique information about how planning affects performance, focusing on only one or two levels will not yield comprehensive information about interactions across the levels, as each level impacts the others in various ways.

Research should evaluate the effects of planning at each level and whether planning at multiple levels increases performance. When assessing performance, researchers should also be cautious regarding the types of criteria used, as they can give differing types of information. For example, if a field study with individual employees working on a product is undertaken, performance can be measured by either the number of units produced or the quality of the units via the percentage of defective units.

However, future research should endeavor to include multiple performance criteria. Some examples include the quantity and quality of products at the individual level, the level of teamwork and leadership effectiveness at the team level, and an evaluation of the profits and bottom line at the organizational level. It is also important to examine planning criteria, whether through self-report measures of perceived effectiveness or through more objective measures such as observations. Choosing the best criteria will depend upon the goal of the researcher, but the ideal would be to include multiple criteria from different sources to measure the impact of planning on performance within organizations.

References

Akça, Y., Esen, Ş., & Özer, G. (2013). The effects of education on enterprise resource planning implementation success and perceived organizational performance. *International Business Research*, 6(5), 168–179. doi:10.5539/ibr.v6n5p168

Andrews, R., Boyne, G. A., Law, J., & Walker, R. M. (2009). Strategy formulation, strategy content and performance. *Public Management Review*, 11(1), 1–22.

Ansoff, I. (1991). Critique of Henry Mintzberg's "The design school: Reconsidering the basic premises of strategic management." *Strategic Management Journal*, 12, 449–461.

Beard, D. W., & Dess, G. G. (1981). Corporate-level strategy, business-level strategy, and firm performance. *Academy of Management Journal*, 24(4), 663–688.

Berry, L. L., Shankar, V., Parish, J. T., Cadwallader, S., & Dotzel, T. (2006). Creating new markets through service innovation. *MIT Sloan Management Review*, 47(2), 56–63.

Blau, P. M. (1977). *Inequality and heterogeneity: A primitive theory of social structure.* New York: Free Press.

Boyd, B. K. (1991). Strategic planning and financial performance: A meta-analytic review. *Journal of Management Studies,* 28(4), 353–374.

Boyne, G., & Gould-Williams, J. (2003). Planning and performance in public organizations: An empirical analysis. *Public Management Review,* 5(1), 115–132.

Brannick, M. T., Roach, R. M., & Salas, E. (1993). Understanding team performance: A multimethod study. *Human Performance,* 6(4), 287–308. doi:10.1207/s15327043hup0604_1

Brannick, M. T., Prince, A., Prince, C., & Salas, E. (1995). The measurement of team process. *Human Factors,* 37(3), 641–651. doi:10.1518/001872095779049372

Cardinal, L. B., Miller, C. C., Kreutzer, M., & TenBrink, C. (2015). Strategic planning and firm performance: Towards a better understanding of a controversial relationship. In M. D. Mumford & M. Frese (Eds.), *The psychology of planning in organizations: Research and applications.* New York: Routledge.

Chou, H., & Yeh, Y. (2007). Conflict, conflict management, and performance in ERP teams. *Social Behavior and Personality,* 35(8), 1035–1048. doi:10.2224/sbp.2007.35.8.1035

Dess, G. G., Ireland, D., & Hitt, M. A. (1990). Industry effects and strategic management research. *Journal of Management,* 16(1), 7–27.

Devine, D. J., & Philips, J. L. (2001). Do smarter teams do better? A meta-analysis of cognitive ability and team performance. *Small Group Research,* 32(5), 507–532.

Dickinson, T. L., & McIntyre, R. M. (1997). A conceptual framework for teamwork measurement. In M. T. Brannick, E. Salas, C. Prince (Eds.), *Team performance assessment and measurement: Theory, methods, and applications* (pp. 19–43). Mahwah, NJ: Lawrence Erlbaum.

Diefendorff, J. M., & Lord, R. G. (2003). The volitional and strategic effects of planning on task performance and goal commitment. *Human Performance,* 16(4), 365–387. doi:10.1207/S15327043HUP1604_3

Donald, I., Taylor, P., Johnson, S., Cooper, C., Cartwright, S., & Robertson, S. (2005). Work environments, stress, and productivity: An examination using ASSET. *International Journal of Stress Management,* 12(4), 409–423. doi:10.1037/1072-5245.12.4.409

Espevik, R., Johnsen, B., & Eid, J. (2011). Communication and performance in co-located and distributed teams: An issue of shared mental models of team members? *Military Psychology,* 23(6), 616–638. doi:10.1080/08995605.2011.616792

Frese, M., Krauss, S. I., Keith, N., Escher, S., Grabarkiewicz, R., Luneng, S. T., Heers, C., Unger, J., & Friedrich, C. (2007). Business owners' action planning and its relationship to business success in three African countries. *Journal of Applied Psychology,* 92(6), 1481.

Gladstein, D. L. (1984). Groups in context: A model of task group effectiveness. *Administrative Science Quarterly,* 29(4), 499–517. doi:10.2307/2392936

Gooding, R. Z., & Wagner, J. A. (1985). A meta-analytic review of the relationship between size and performance: The productivity and efficiency of organizations and their subunits. *Administrative Science Quarterly,* 30(4), 462–482.

Grinyer, P. H., & Norburn, D. (1975). Planning for existing markets: Perceptions of executives and financial performance. *Journal of the Royal Statistical Society,* 138(1), 70–97.

Gulbrandsen, P., Jensen, B., Finset, A., & Blanch-Hartigan, D. (2013). Long-term effect of communication training on the relationship between physicians' self-efficacy and performance. *Patient Education And Counseling,* 91(2), 180–185. doi:10.1016/j.pec.2012.11.015

Iyer, B. & Davenport, T. H. (2008). Reverse Engineering Google's innovation machine. *Harvard Business Review,* 86(4), 58–69.

Kudla, R. J. (1980). The effects of strategic planning on common stock returns. *Academy of Management Journal,* 23(1), 5–20.

Lanaj, K., Hollenbeck, J. R., Ilgen, D. R., Barnes, C. M., & Harmon, S. J. (2013). The double-edged sword of decentralized planning in multiteam systems. *Academy Of Management Journal,* 56(3), 735–757. doi:10.5465/amj.2011.0350

Locke, E. A., & Latham, G. P. 1990. *A theory of goal setting and task performance.* Englewood Cliffs, NJ: Prentice Hall.

Locke, E. A., & Latham, G. P. (2002). Building a practically useful theory of goal setting and task motivation: A 35-year odyssey. *American Psychologist,* 57, 705–717.

Lucas, H. C., & Goh, J. M. (2009). Disruptive technology: How Kodak missed the digital photography revolution. *Journal of Strategic Information Systems*, 18, 46–55.

Marks, M. A., Mathieu, J. E., & Zaccaro, S. J. (2001). A temporally based framework and taxonomy of team processes. *Academy of Management Review*, 26, 356–376.

Marta, S., Leritz, L. E., & Mumford, M. D. (2005). Leadership skills and the group performance: Situational demands, behavioral requirements, and planning. *The Leadership Quarterly*, 16(1), 97–120.

Miller, C. C., & Cardinal, L. B. (1994). Strategic planning and firm performance: A synthesis of more than two decades of research. *Academy of Management Journal*, 37(6), 1649–1665.

Mintzberg, H. (1987). The strategy concept II: Another look at why organizations need strategies. *California Management Review*, 30(1), 25–32.

Montoya, A. C., Carter, D. R., Martin, J., & DeChurch, L. A. (2015). The five perils of team planning: Regularities and remedies. In M. D. Mumford & M. Frese (Eds.), *The psychology of planning in organizations: Research and applications*. New York: Routledge.

Mumford, M. D., Schultz, R. A., & Van Doorn, J. R. (2001). Performance in planning: Processes, requirements, and errors. *Review of General Psychology*, 5(3), 213–240.

Mumford, M. D., Schultz, R. A., & Osburn, H. K. (2002). Planning in organizations: Performance as a multi-level phenomenon. *Annual Review of Research in Multi-Level Issues*, 1, 3–65.

Naglieri, J. A., & Das, J. P. (1990). Planning, attention, simultaneous, and successive (PASS) cognitive processes as a model for intelligence. *Journal Of Psychoeducational Assessment*, 8(3), 303–337. doi:10.1177/073428299000800308

Neves, P., & Eisenberger, R. (2012). Management communication and employee performance: The contribution of perceived organizational support. *Human Performance*, 25(5), 452–464. doi:10.1080/08959285.2012.721834

Novicevic, M. M., Harvey, M., Autry, C. W., & Bond, E. (2004). Dual-perspective SWOT: A synthesis of marketing intelligence and planning. *Marketing Intelligence & Planning*, 22(1), 84–94. doi:10.1108/02634500410516931

O'Leary-Kelly, A. M., Martocchio, J. J., & Frink, D. D. (1994). A review of the influence of group goals on group performance. *The Academy of Management Journal*, 37, 1285–1301. doi: 10.2307/256673

Padmo Putri, D. A. (2013). The effect of communication strategy and planning intervention on the processes and performance of course material development teams. *Dissertation Abstracts International Section A*, 7.

Pearce, J. A., Freeman, E. B., & Robinson, R. B. (1987). The tenuous link between formal strategic planning and financial performance. *Academy of Management Review*, 12(4), 658–675.

Quigley, N. R., Tekleab, A. G., & Tesluk, P. E. (2007). Comparing consensus-and aggregation-based methods of measuring team-level variables: The role of relationship conflict and conflict management processes. *Organizational Research Methods*, 10(4), 589–608.

Robinson, Richard, B., & Pearce, John, A. (1983). The impact of formalized strategic planning on financial performance in small organizations. *Strategic Management Journal*, 4(3), 197–207.

Ryan, J. J. (2008). Examining the relationship between behaviors and outcomes: An investigation of the impact of behavior-based feedback and development action planning on individual outcome measures. *Dissertation Abstracts International*, 69.

Saavedra, R., Earley, P. C., & Dyne, L. V. (1993). Complex interdependence in task-performing groups. *Journal of Applied Psychology*, 78(1), 61–72.

Salas, E., Dickinson, T. L., Converse, S. A., & Tannenbaum, S. I. (1992). Toward an understanding of team performance and training. In R. W. Swezey & E. Salas (Eds.), *Teams: Their training and performance* (pp. 3–29). Norwood, NJ: Ablex.

Schnake, M. E., & Cochran, D. S. (1985). Effect of two goal-setting dimensions on perceived intraorganizational conflict. *Group & Organization Studies*, 10(2), 168–183. doi:10.1177/105960118501000205

Schwenk, C. R. & Shrader, C. B. (1993). Effects of formal strategic planning on financial performance in small firms: A meta-analysis. *Entrepreneurship: Theory and Practice*, 17(3), 53–64.

Smolek, J., Hoffman, D., & Moran, L. (1999). Organizing teams for success. *Supporting Work Team Effectiveness*, 24, 62.

Suman, S., & Srivastava, A. K. (2012). Antecedents of organisational commitment across hierarchical levels. *Psychology And Developing Societies*, 24(1), 61–83. doi:10.1177/097133361102400103

Suriyamurthi, S., Velavan, M., & Radhiga, T. D. (2013). Importance of leadership in innovations of HR practices. *Advances in Management*, 6(11), 47.

Wang, G., Oh, I. S., Courtright, S. H., & Colbert, A. E. (2011). Transformational leadership and performance across criteria and levels: A meta-analytic review of 25 years of research. *Group & Organization Management*, 36(2), 223–270.

Weingart, L. R. (1992). Impact of group goals, task component complexity, effort, and planning on group performance. Journal of Applied Psychology, 77(5), 682–693.

Wilensky, R. (1983). *Planning and understanding: A computational approach to human reasoning.* Reading, MA: Addison-Wesley.

Wood, D. R., & LaForge, R. L. (1979). The impact of comprehensive planning on financial performance. *Academy of Management Journal*, 22(3), 516–526.

Wood, D. R., & LaForge, R. L. (1981). Toward the development of a planning scale: An example from the banking industry. *Strategic Management Journal*, 2, 209–216.

Woolley, A., Gerbasi, M., Chabris, C., Kosslyn, S., & Hackman, J. (2008). Bringing in the experts: how team composition and collaborative planning jointly shape analytic effectiveness (English). *Small Group Research*, 39(3), 352–371.

11

EXPERTISE IN ORGANIZATIONAL PLANNING

Impact on Performance

Kenneth N. McKay, Wout van Wezel, and Toni Waefler

Introduction

In this chapter, we explore the contribution of group and individual expertise to the quality and effectiveness of organizational planning. We focus on the overall expertise of the planner as planning involves multiple skills or abilities, and individuals possess different levels of expertise in each of these. Planning can be viewed as a two-stage process, with the first stage involving thinking and decisions about the plan, and the second, optional, stage when the plan might be attempted or implemented and decision making is required as the planned activities evolve. As with the rest of this volume, we concentrate on decisions and plans that individuals or groups make for others to follow or to work together on. We will also touch upon the planning that occurs during plan execution and how expertise impacts this activity.

Organizational planning is a complex tableau. There is a wide range of decisions and plans made in an organization and the people doing the planning face a continuum from low-frequency, intermittent types of planning decisions and situations to high-frequency, continuous planning tasks. Some of these tasks may be carried out perhaps once a year or even less frequently, while others involve multiple replications of the same basic planning scenario each and every day, perhaps every few minutes or hours throughout the day. To complicate matters further, many plans are made, but only a fraction of them are actually implemented, creating a challenge for the feedback loop associated with learning. All of the planning might also be done by an individual, or in a group collaborative process with much interaction. The overall complexity creates a challenge when discussing the potential effect of expertise on planning performance.

We caution the reader in advance: there are no definitive models or proven causal relationships to be presented which predict or robustly explain how improvements or levels of expertise contribute to planning performance. There are, however, many indirect concepts and theories which in time might better explain and capture this aspect of organizational planning, and recent research into the task of planning also provides substantive insights.

The first task is to clearly define what we mean by *planning*, *organizational planning*, and *expertise*. At a conceptual level, we will partially adopt the definition of planning stated by Marta, Leritz, and Mumford (2005): "planning can be understood as a form of situated cognition where the mental simulation of future actions is used to generate action strategies likely to optimize goal attainment." We extend this to express a more holistic view of organizational planning, capturing not just the cognitive component but the realistic *in situ* nature of planning and the environment within which the planner(s) is situated (e.g. the situated context of execution; Suchman, 1987). We also recognize that planning is not always a slow, reasoned process with extensive mental simulation, but can also be characterized by quick, intuitive judgments that affect what is planned, how risks might be assessed, and what order planned tasks should take. For organizational planning, we refer to the types of planning to be found in organizational settings that affect the actions and activities of others, not individual types of planning such as planning one's own trip to the grocery store or planning a vacation. We also do not address the type of planning associated with urban or public planning (e.g. Kaufman & Escuin, 2000).

Expertise is a slippery word. In every field setting we have studied, some person is introduced as the organization's planning expert. It has never been clear what this really meant and what should be inferred from it. For example, "the expert" might have been doing the planning tasks the longest of anyone in the organization. Or, "the expert" might have the title of Master or Senior Planner. Or, "the expert" is just better at planning than another "expert" in the organization. We have never encountered pre-existing quantitative definitions, tests, or demonstrated evidence in any field setting for defending the phrase *person X is a planning expert*. In this chapter, use of *expertise* is strictly restricted to traits associated with characteristics of certain cognitive processes as researched in cognitive psychology (e.g. Feltovich, Prietula, & Ericsson, 2006), and is not a casual observation that one individual is considered to be an expert compared to another person.

As stated above, the theme of this chapter is how expertise relates to plan performance and this leads to a discussion about plan quality and how planning performance can be measured. Hence, the chapter starts off with a discussion on plan quality and two topics are highlighted that impact planning performance: the contextual structure of the task being planned (distinguishing, for example, repetitive planning tasks from unique planning tasks), and the nature of the planning expertise needed for the task being planned (e.g. different sub-tasks within planning and the various kinds of knowledge needed to make plans). The two highlighted topics yield two preliminary tools: a framework for the contextual planning structure and a model for planning expertise. Following the development of these tools, a literature review provides research linkages bringing the two tools together. The chapter concludes with discussions, issues, and challenges for empirical research on organizational planning expertise, and possible directions for future research.

Plan Quality

Unfortunately there is no existing universal test or objective definition for what defines *quality planning*. The very nature of planning makes it almost impossible to robustly measure the quality of a planner and hence the varying levels of possible expertise: planning is foreseeing future events and plotting a journey. How does one measure avoiding a potential risk? How many accidents did not occur at an intersection? Even if a plan was executed on time and on budget, it is not possible to thoroughly measure what did not occur. Many plans are created, but few are accepted and put into play; what makes one plan better than another and accepted, especially when potential results are speculated about?

Thus, it is difficult to ascertain and attribute different levels of planning expertise. When should some person or group be recognized for doing an excellent job of planning? When should they get a failing grade? When is the planning good enough? How does one recognize that planning is improving? How does one reconcile the differences between experts? The difficulty of assessing the quality of plans and strategies has been discussed for many years. An early empirical research effort on auditor judgment (Joyce, 1976) pointed out many challenges and issues associated with these types of discussions and, to the best of our knowledge, all of the challenges and issues remain valid today.

There are many possible attributes of plan quality which are rather slippery. For example, we have heard "he is a good planner, he is fair" – but how does one define fairness? This is not a minor attribute to be quickly dismissed and assumed away. A plan is full of compromises, and one of the attributes observed in practice is how fair the plan is with respect to compromises. In operational settings there are many plans and many opportunities for balance and long-term fairness. In these cases, simply using "on time," "on budget," "resource utilization," and "fitness for purpose" are too narrow in their scope. Of course, these are not the only performance metrics associated with plans (e.g. de Snoo, van Wezel, & Jorna, 2011). Was the plan comprehensive enough? Thorough enough? Was there sufficient risk included? Were the right tasks included? Not too many? Not too few? Was the right sequence laid out? Only time will answer these questions and only if the plan is implemented and followed, and only if there are no external forces at work that allow a poor plan to succeed and a good plan to fail.

Within an organization, the goals might be excessively generous and easy to achieve. For example, consider the difference in quality objectives between the North American automotive firms in the 1980s and their counterparts in Japan and Germany. All parties had goals for what they considered acceptable quality and all parties were apparently meeting their goals. Unfortunately, the Japanese and German goals were decidedly different and required different plans and strategies to achieve. There were marked differences in strategies and execution at the country level when quality improvement initiatives were carried out (e.g. Ittner & Larcker, 1997). There were also different expectations for production efficiency and effectiveness, and different goals for bringing new production designs to market. Thus, in any discussion about plan quality, the quality of the goals against which the plan will be measured becomes an integral component.

Were the goals appropriate? Too easy? Too difficult? To determine what might be considered reasonable goals, some companies utilize best-in-class comparisons to measure themselves; how close, equaling, or perhaps creating a new best-in-class benchmark. This approach can be used for almost any planning or decision situation, but it is difficult to ensure that the comparisons are valid and that the same sets of assumptions hold. The benchmarking can also be biased, as who is to say which organization is going to be used as the base case? For example, it is easy to compare oneself to local competitors when foreign firms have yet to enter your market and create a threat, your best-in-class being picked from the firms you consider your peers.

Benchmarking at the operational and tactical levels has been done since the early 1900s (Emerson, 1911) and, while faulty in several aspects, it does provide some basis for comparison. For example, the number of days of inventory on hand, first-pass yield, scrap rates, and order lead time are metrics often looked at for benchmarking operational planning and execution. There are maturity models and metrics to determine the level of sophistication, governance, and processes used in planning, but the actual outcomes of the plans are not part of the models. The practice of benchmarking at the strategic level of planning does not appear to be done to the same degree, with the exception of comparing one firm against another in the metrics studied by stock market analysts and investors. For example, the percentage of funds spent on research and development, the ability to increase market share, and various asset and profit ratios are in this category of surrogate measures for strategic planning quality.

There have been a number of debates and discussions about how to consider when a plan is a "good plan" (e.g. Rasmussen, Sieck, & Smart, 2009). Milestones and quantitative goals may be set that can be targeted for optimization, but these are only the stated and explicit goals. There are usually additional, implicit goals associated with cultural norms when compromising between constraints (e.g. fairness, risks which occur when allowing someone the opportunity to grow professionally, balancing work and home life, how much to weigh opinions versus facts) and it is difficult to include these types of goals in any definition of "good." Being iterative, there is also the issue of initial or potential plan quality versus interim plan quality, which is the realized quality as the plan is monitored and modified during the journey towards goal attainment, versus final plan quality when the journey is complete.

There are a number of general characteristics attributed to "good" plans found in the literature:

- resource utilization – cost-effective use of the organization's resources and assets in achieving the goal(s)
- goal attainment – meeting the stated goals (e.g. timing, costs, quality, quantity, waste)
- milestones – appropriate timing for governance, being clear and measureable
- risk management – matching the risks inherent in the journey, contingency options and capability matching the uncertainties and challenges.

To go beyond these general characteristics, it is necessary to discuss the specific type of planning being critiqued. For example, detailed resource scheduling is one of the lowest levels of operational planning found within a firm and is one of the areas that has been studied empirically. De Snoo et al. (2011) discuss 21 performance measures that were noted as part of their research agenda and present a model of scheduling performance.

A number of factors have been identified in the literature as being necessary for achieving a good plan:

- At its core, planning is always based on a multitude of interdependent assumptions about the future and the current state of the organization's abilities to execute, which are the outcomes of previous planning. Thus, the quality of the assumptions about the present and future are key factors which affect the quality of the plan.
- It is important to address the right problem or issue, to understand the various solution options, and to evaluate the strengths and weaknesses of each option that is being considered.
- It is necessary to know when a plan is operationally feasible and has a reasonable chance of actually being followed without being excessively optimistic or conservative.
- It must be possible to decompose the journey into the appropriate sub-activities (sequencing, scope, granularity, degree of autonomy, responsibility, duration, magnitude, complexity, task allocation or assignment).
- It is important that the current or future resource availability and capability matches the plan, either within the organization itself or through associated bodies (e.g. consultants, outsourcing).
- It must take into account resource ability and willingness to follow the plan and to work within the governance mechanisms. The teams and organizational units should not go rogue and say one thing but do another.
- There must be effective governance processes and mechanisms for plan adaptation during the journey.

These factors define the quality of the mental simulation(s) of future actions and strategies performed by the planner(s). If the organization has high standards for what "good" means, the realization or manifestation of the above will be different from an organization with lower expectations. The standards will dictate how closely a plan has to be followed during the journey to be considered a good plan, and how close to achieving the goals the journey must reach to be considered a good journey.

In some cases, the organizational standards also dictate how the real goals are translated or interpreted. For example, some organizations always set goals significantly higher than expected to provide incentive or energy to the project. Other organizations may set the promised goals lower and aim higher during the journey; promise low, deliver high. Unless the real goals are known and used, measuring and auditing plan performance for goodness is difficult and almost meaningless.

The above focuses on the initial plan-creation tasks. If a plan is chosen and is implemented, planning usually continues in some fashion. There might be a form of continuous planning, or planning might be revisited at milestones. This type of planning is somewhat different from the initial planning. The basic tasks such as forecasting and creating work breakdown structures are the same, leading to goal attainment via efficient and effective resource utilization. However, there is the history of the journey thus far, with all that implies, the current status, immediate future, and the remaining journey given that some of the uncertainties in the beginning are no longer uncertain and that new uncertainties have possibly developed. That is, planning is no longer 100 percent speculation and abstraction. The larger, initial plan might have also been decomposed, with multiple sub-units deployed, each with dedicated or unique planners. All of this suggests that additional types of expertise might be required in ongoing planning versus initial plan creation. For example, some additional skill might be needed in: the ability to work under demanding time pressures, the ability to track and understand the current situation via different information sources, the ability to problem-solve and negotiate concrete solutions in real time, the ability to understand the details of the activities being executed, the ability to perform coordination with peer planners, and the ability to carry out detailed risk management assessments. Quality planning during plan execution would suggest that expertise in these areas would also be required. Since the core planning tasks are largely the same, the nuances of planning during execution will be dealt with separately, later in the chapter.

In thinking about the quality of planning, four thoughts surface. First, there are many possible, independent variables that may (or may not) contribute to plan performance, some of which relate to expertise and some of which do not. Expertise is only part of the puzzle. Second, a theme is emerging that the context or type of planning being performed might be significant to a discussion of how expertise relates to plan performance, as frequency and feedback are known to be key factors in developing expertise. Third, there is a theme that the expertise and ability of the planners to perform the myriad of cognitive planning tasks (initial and ongoing) might also be significant, even if it is one of many possible factors in any situation. Fourth, there might be a dependency between the two themes: the contextual situation of planning and expertise in the cognitive planning tasks. The next two sections present concepts based on these two themes for possibly structuring a cognitive analysis of plan performance: (i) a framework for situating planning context, and (ii) a model for understanding organizational planning expertise. A literature review and discussion then follows.

Planning Context Framework

Clearly, organizational planning is quite varied and Anthony's (1965, 1988) view of strategic, tactical, and operational control layers has often been used to describe a hierarchy of planning tasks, granularity of detail, scope of planning tasks, and the frequency of the planning tasks. Although Anthony's initial view was focused on management control, he discusses how activities such as strategic planning are integral to the control process (Anthony, 1988). This three-layer structure will assist us in discussing the frequency of certain types of planning tasks. At the strategic level, the scope of the planning is usually broad and the time horizon long, with specific planning tasks at this level being relatively infrequent. As one proceeds to tactical and then operational planning, the scope narrows, the time horizon shortens, attention to detail increases, and the probability that a specific planning task will be more frequently encountered increases. However, there is a subtle complication associated with planning task frequency. A planning task may be infrequent, but it might be very structured and lend itself to a recipe. Another planning task might also infrequent, but it may be very ambiguous, unstructured, and cannot be left to rote processes. A similar point can be made for tasks which are frequently performed and are structured or unstructured. Frequency by itself is insufficient for understanding how expertise applies to planning performance.

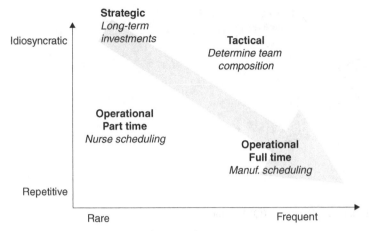

FIGURE 11.1   Task structure framework

Anthony's taxonomy raises a number of questions. Is it possible to have expertise when the planning tasks might be rare, or when not all plans are implemented? How is expertise in different planning situations acquired and developed? What types of expertise are needed to create a plan versus the execution? Are there different types of expertise in low-frequency versus high-frequency situations? What is the contribution of different types of expertise in a high-frequency situation? What does the ideal combination of expertise in a high-frequency situation imply? What might lower expertise and lower frequency mean? Where in the organization do we, or can we, find situations along these dimensions?

One possible approach to this problem is to consider two dimensions of the planning tasks. How frequently a planning task is performed is clearly important for any discussion about learning the skills required for planning and developing expertise. Frequency can range from rare to frequent. A second dimension relates to the repetitiveness or standardization of the task versus how unique the components or structures of the problem are. Repetition refers to the overall task structure and implies that almost all of the key factors repeat in known ways. In contrast, unique or idiosyncratic planning suggests the need for flexibility in the planning process and the ability to formalize or use profound knowledge about the situation that is likely to be different and behave differently in each instance. Figure 11.1 illustrates this tableau of planning.

The interplay between the dimensions can provide insight about how to view and discuss the planning tasks. For example, tasks that are rare but repetitive can still be standardized and subject to protocols and processes with little uncertainty. For example, a winter marketing campaign may be run only once a year, but it is the same every winter. Rare and unique tasks are the most problematic as there will be little history and knowledge about causal relationships, key dynamics, and quality of data. For example, planning a hostile takeover of a competitor is not an everyday task and is far from a guaranteed success. Tasks that are repetitive in all of the key aspects and frequent (e.g. daily build planning for assembly lines) can be formalized and possibly even automated. It is likely that many tasks in an organization are aligned along the diagonal, with few at the extremes.

Organizational Planning Expertise Model

In order to link the results of cognitive psychology and other research on planners to organizational planning, a four-part model is suggested. The planning tasks are assumed to occur in different roles to serve different functions as per the Anthony (1988) hierarchical taxonomy. This leads us to

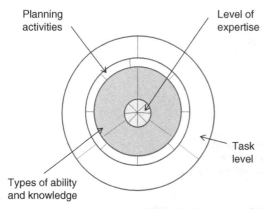

Planning activities

Level of expertise

Task level

Types of ability and knowledge

FIGURE 11.2 Organizational Planning Expertise (OPE) model

propose a multi-level, multi-functional model of planning that provides a contextual foundation. Previous models such as Mumford, Shultz, and Van Doorn (2001) provide a general planning process model that is task oriented and does not explicitly acknowledge the task scope, skill, knowledge, and contextual elements. Our Organizational Planning Expertise (OPE) model and its four components can be thought of as being a contextual structure within which the Mumford et al. model exists.

The four components of the OPE model are:

1   task level
2   planning activities
3   types of ability and knowledge
4   level of expertise.

This is illustrated in Figure 11.2.

Task Level

Each level in Anthony's planning hierarchy (strategic, tactical, operational) implies varying degrees of detail, specificity, and ambiguity, with each level guiding or constraining the next, lower, level of planning tasks. As one proceeds down the planning hierarchy, the frequency of certain types of planning activities will increase. For example, the planning and decision processes associated with entering a new market, acquiring existing players, or creating a presence in a certain country or geographic zone are not done with the same frequency as planning shifts in a factory or seasonal marketing campaigns. As the frequency increases and scope decreases, it is likely that the task of planning can be relegated to a reusable script, standard operating procedure, process, or guideline that has been designed to use the organization's resources in an efficient and effective fashion to achieve the organization's goals. For example, planning and developing a strategy for how orders should be taken, filled, and shipped is done relatively infrequently, but an "instance" of the plan is implicitly done for every order taken, production sequence, and final shipment to the customer. Each and every order might in fact have the general strategy interpreted and a unique version of the plan created.

Planning Activities

As noted in Mumford, Shultz, and Osburn (2002) and Finkelstein (2002), a common view in the literature constrains the definition of planning to part of what real planners have been observed to do: the subset being how a planner deals with a situation, creating a plan for moving forward. When planning is so restricted, the discussion and research will not usually include the factors we see as being crucial for developing a planner's abilities: learning what was well planned, what was not, which assumptions were valid, which were not, learning what and how to anticipate, learning how to construct plans suitable for adaptation, learning what can be quantified and measured, and what cannot, to name just a few post-plan generation activities and learning moments. The post-plan aspects of planning can be implicitly present in the thinking that goes into the initial plan generation. For example, an experienced planner will anticipate the need for replanning and can structure a plan so that suitable milestones and mechanisms exist. Without experiencing the post-plan generation activities associated with planning, a planner would have difficulty understanding what is needed in a plan beyond simple task completion.

For a cradle-to-grave perspective, a planning scenario at each task level can be decomposed into a set of cognitive tasks or activities. Seven major activities are:

1 Problem formulation, opportunity identification and isolation
  - Why are we planning? An issue, demand, or opportunity to address? (Skills in this activity, and the process involved, are discussed in Volkema, 1983.)
2 Outcome definition
  - What are we planning? A company reorganization, a new product launch, or a production run in the factory (e.g. Caves, 1980)?
3 Quality of outcome "goal" specification
  - What are the factors that will define success? Will it be cost, improved time to market, delivery targets, market share, shareholder value, or quality goals?
  - Will the expected outcomes include nebulous concepts such as innovation (e.g. Mumford, Bedell-Avers, & Hunter, 2008)?
4 Generation of the plan
  - The most effective and efficient sequence of actions and activities for organizational resources to follow which will achieve the desired goals taking risks and uncertainty into account.
5 Plan evaluation, approval, and project launch
  - A particular plan is agreed upon and activities launched.
6 Implementing, monitoring, and maintenance of the plan
  - As time proceeds, how good is the plan? Does the plan need altering, and, if so, what are the alterations?
  - What are the links between plan evaluation and implementation (e.g. Nutt, 2007)?
7 Closure of the plan
  - Knowing when the outcomes are achieved (or will not be) and understanding the quality of the planning and execution. Knowing what to do next, if there is a next.

There are many more sub-tasks associated with planning, as noted in the Mumford et al. (2001) planning process model, and the seven larger activity sets above provide a meta-level for discussion. Each of these meta-planning activities involves problem analysis and diagnosis, mental simulations of potential action plans, and the use of different abilities and knowledge bases. Empirical research such as Pettersen (1991) has shown that the importance of any specific ability may increase and decrease at different times during a management process. These activities can be done by individuals or with multiple parties contributing in either a distributed or collaborative fashion. An individual may participate in one or more of the activities, and in some cases, at the tactical and operational levels there can be multiple instances of the same type of planning decision to be made, with each instance being independent of the others (e.g. distributed decision making allowing freedom of choice within general constructs and constraints). Depending on an individual's role, the planning may be for a single project or task, or there might be multiple planning activities at the same time, which implies additional skills (Patanakul & Milosevic, 2008). When there is more than one party involved, we can discuss the organization of planning and the distribution of planning activities (de Snoo & van Wezel, 2011). Both of these topics will be explored in due course.

In one extreme case, each activity is done in the most optimal fashion, the outcomes are achieved to everyone's satisfaction, and success can be attributed to everyone's ability to plan and execute. In the other extreme case, all of the above phases can be done incorrectly or poorly, and the organization can still be "successful" in spite of itself because of external factors, such as being in a monopoly situation, operating in a seller's market, or because the competition did worse than you. Planning is one of those special situations where offsetting mistakes can also be made and two wrongs can make a right. While ability undoubtedly places a role in successful planning, appropriate attribution can be a daunting task. How often has it been said "they succeeded in spite of themselves"?

Types of Ability and Knowledge

Assuming that various abilities are vital for repeated success when performing planning tasks, there are three sets of abilities and knowledge associated with each activity and decision. This is the third, inner circle of the OPE model. Vested in either the individual or the group, the following must be present for a quality outcome:

- general planning knowledge and competencies related to making efficient and effective use of resources, while including appropriate risk management (Kerzner, 2013; PMBOK, 2004)
- domain-specific knowledge about the problem or issue being addressed – problem domain (e.g. Kautz & Selman, 1998)
- knowledge about the nature of the resources, capacities, politics, culture, and capabilities of the organization – solution domain (e.g. McKay & Wiers, 2006; MacCarthy, Wilson, & Crawford, 2001; McKay, 1987, 1992).

The knowledge of a *sole* expert planner must bridge all of these areas and allow for the creation of an effective cognitive map (Kiewiet, Jorna, & van Wezel, 2005), or the planning process must allow for the sharing and piecing together of the individual cognitive maps or models held by each of the plan's contributors and collaborators (Stout, Cannon-Bowers, Salas, & Milanovich, 1999). In either case, there is general schematic knowledge that the individuals know about the generic case or situation (e.g. that the width of steel will make a difference in the process sequence) and specific case knowledge (e.g. the widths of steel in the current work queue). Both specific and general types of knowledge in all three knowledge sets are important for knowing the types of things to consider and what they imply, and what they do not.

Level of Expertise

The final element in the taxonomy is the individual's or group's level of expertise in each of the knowledge sets, for each of the planning activities, and for each of the types of tasks associated with each of the hierarchy levels. It is generally agreed that expertise is a continuum and there is some debate over the levels. However, some general grouping of demonstrated expertise can be performed:

- unexposed
  - absolutely no ability or knowledge
- novice / beginner
  - needs guidance, oversight, training for almost all tasks
- advanced beginner / junior
  - can do many tasks, but not majority of them without oversight, instruction
- intermediate / proficient
  - can do most tasks competently in an independent fashion
- senior / journeyman
  - terminal career level for most individuals, able to guide and teach others
- expert / consultant
  - advanced counsel, advisor, deep knowledge of relationships and domain
- master / researcher
  - developer of organized knowledge and training, creator of new science and knowledge.

As noted in the introduction, cognitive psychology research has provided various characteristics associated with experts and novices (Feltovich et al., 2006). In the field, the casual use of the word *expert* can lead to individuals who are operating at the lower levels of ability being considered experts, and this might be true when comparing individuals in a specific setting or in a domain for which high levels of expertise might not be realistic to expect.

In situations with high-frequency, repetitive, structured planning tasks at the tactical or operational levels of Anthony's taxonomy, such as factory settings with planners and schedulers, we have often been introduced to someone as our expert planner. Compared to others in the plant, this is undoubtedly so. Compared to undergraduates and developing graduate students or theoretical researchers, this is also likely. But, when we have compared this individual planner to others studied over a 25-year research agenda, this adjective has not usually been justified. Most of the locally acclaimed experts encountered over the research agenda would have been considered to be of intermediate ability or at the lower end of competent. It is possible to develop production planning abilities to the master level, but these individuals are not found in every factory (McKay, Safayeni, & Buzacott, 1995). Yet they can be found.

By way of contrast, at the strategic level with many infrequent, non-repetitive, and ill-structured planning tasks, consider the planning and decisions involved in corporate mergers. It can be argued that, after many years of orchestrating mergers, an individual widely recognized as an expert in the popular press or trade may perhaps be only competent and proficient, if that. It would be almost impossible for the cognitive processes used in strategic and infrequent tactical thinking to exhibit the skills associated with higher levels of expertise. We will explain this reasoning and expand on this line of thought when we discuss expert and novice characteristics in the following sections.

Framework and Model Summary

The previous two sections have presented complementary concepts that help structure part of the puzzle relating to plan performance. The framework and model help position a situation and the planning tasks in a context that can guide a discussion as to how expertise relates to efficient and effective planning. The planning context framework assists in understanding how planning expertise might develop with respect to task frequency and the planning structure. The organizational planning expertise model then explores the knowledge, skills, and levels of expertise needed in the planning task. The following literature review links the research on expertise to these concepts.

Literature Review

The cognitive psychology perspective of expertise (e.g. Rikers & Paas, 2005; Ericsson, Charness, Feltovich, & Hoffman, 2006; Feltovich et al., 2006; Farrington-Darby & Wilson, 2006) will be used to anchor the discussion regarding individual expertise development and behavior. Since planning is also often a group or collaborative activity imposed on top of individual judgment (Bazerman, 1998), we will augment the discussion with research on sociotechnical networks in the area of group work and decision making. In any collaborative activity, different individuals may participate in different phases of the planning task and contribute different capabilities, either as the sole planner for that phase or by working together to create a greater ability than any individual may possess (e.g. Tan & Gallupe, 2006). Planning is also seen as an iterative, non-linear process which is confounded by onion-like layers of granularity and specificity, as illustrated by the operational tasks associated with planning and scheduling in factories (e.g. MacCarthy, 2006; McKay, 1992).

To address these and other types of complexities associated with organizational planning and provide a foundation for the proposed framework and model, a number of different research areas need to be reviewed and integrated. The review addresses the following seven sub-topics:

1 task frequency and expertise
2 institutional planning
3 natural decision making
4 general planning ability
5 collaboration in organizational planning
6 clinical and *in situ* research on planning
7 cognitive skill in planning performance.

Task Frequency and Expertise

Any cognitive skill such as planning can exhibit a continuum of expertise development, but there are fundamental conditions necessary for a cognitive skill to improve. It is possible for people to attain a particular level of expertise (e.g. intermediate or journeyman) and not develop further. One of the key factors is frequency of training and practice combined with suitable feedback and reflection. In Figure 11.1, we introduced a rough continuum of planning tasks, one dimension of which is frequency. At one end of the spectrum, we consider the people typically involved in strategic and tactical planning largely occupied with infrequently encountered tasks (repetitive or unique in nature). On the other hand, there are planners who frequently work with tasks which are more similar than they are different. Almost everyone in an organization is involved in some sort of planning. One key difference is how often the same type of task is encountered and how stable or deterministic the task components are. Examples of individuals who routinely deal with similar types of tasks are those who determine the approach of a vessel to a harbor (Hutchins, 1995), set out train-shunting schedules (van Wezel, Cegarra, & Hoc, 2011), develop a course of action on the battlefield (Serfaty, MacMillan, Entin, & Entin, 1997), plan, schedule, and dispatch work within a factory (Gasser, Fischer, & Waefler, 2011).

This second group of individuals can be considered focused planners and they exist in the lower right quadrant of Figure 11.1. Focused planners are not usually individuals with the title of project manager – assigned to one or more long-term projects to oversee. The focused planners have limited scope, decision-making power, and variety, concentrate on one type of planning, and create and interact with many planning instances in parallel; that is their primary role within the organization. They are involved in frequent and numerous planning tasks about the what, where, when, and who, in addition to annotating, documenting, reviewing, and tracking. They are continually involved in their planning tasks throughout the day, every day: not just when a problem occurs, when a new business initiative is decided upon, or during the yearly planning exercise.

The focused planners exist in an environment where there are repeated tasks of roughly the same nature (but with enough variety to create a breadth and depth of knowledge) and there is timely and regular feedback on the outcomes. This matches the general criteria for cognitive skill improvement: "The crucial factor leading to continued improvement and attainment of expert performance is the engagement in special practice activities that allow performers to improve specific aspects of their performance with problem solving and through repetitions with feedback" (Ericsson, 2005). Ericsson has referred to this activity as deliberate practice and learning. This deliberate and reflective activity is what helps to separate those doing the same cognitive job for a number of years or decades and hitting a performance ceiling from those who will continue to improve and develop mastery in tasks involving "monitoring, planning, reasoning, and anticipating" (Ericsson & Lehmann, 1996).

All planning tasks, be they frequent or infrequent, require the planner(s) to have generic competencies and the ability to abstract and structure a situation and to develop a schema for proceeding. Although a particular task may be infrequent, a strategic or tactical planner might make sufficient decisions and plans in the aggregate to develop specific abilities and expertise in approaching problems and developing plans. The types of tasks may also be repetitive, even if infrequent, and over time it is possible to learn and improve. These types of higher-level planning challenges would likely be aggregate strategies without granular personnel assignments, tasks, and daily details. In these cases, the expertise is found in the generic competencies related to the planning process, general strategies, and meta-organizational dynamics (e.g. two sister plants working together to satisfy a larger demand).

As long as the planner has the opportunity to perform frequent tasks in a domain of similar structure so that relationships can be learned about and results studied, some form of expertise development in both process and domain can and should be expected. If the repetition and training opportunities with feedback are absent in the situational context, high levels of expertise cannot be expected. For example, a senior or middle management individual does not make dozens of the same type of plan each and every day or every week. These are not the types of tasks they are involved in. For example, the number of new product plans a division might consider in any calendar year is relatively few, as are department reorganizations, hiring and training plans, or new information systems.

Institutional Planning

In the past decades, there has been considerable scientific debate about strategic planning. Authors point out an inherent problem of strategic planning. During the 1970s and 1980s, planning became increasingly associated with formalized procedures, which, due to environmental turbulence, does not work well with the formation of corporate strategies. This was excellently expressed by Mintzberg (1994), who discerns strategic thinking from strategic planning. He even proposed to "drop the label 'strategic planning' altogether" (ibid., p. 112). Although his call was not followed to the letter, it stirred the community to reconsider strategic planning, and follow-up articles show more consideration for the idiosyncratic nature of strategic planning.

Perhaps Mintzberg's disposition regarding the demise of strategic planning can be described in our model of Figure 11.1; there is consensus in the literature that planning tools and techniques that presume repetition should not be used for problems that call for a unique approach each time. Strategic thinking is synthesis, involving intuition and creativity. It should lead to an integrated perspective of the company, without scheduling when and where creative insights should occur. According to Mintzberg, attempts to formalize strategic planning lead to strategic planners being unable to transcend the current structure and goals of the organization, discourages out-of-the-box thinking, and obstructs organizational innovation. These ideas were not new, however. They can be traced back to the work of Anthony (1965), who argues that strategic planning is a process that is both creative and analytical, without much structure, which is driven by exceptions rather than fixed points in time, and which is primarily concerned with the external environment rather than the internal organization.

What, then, characterizes expertise in strategic planning? Mintzberg (1994) provides us with a starting point by describing what strategic planning should *not* be, based on the premise that "systems have never been able to reproduce the synthesis created by the genius entrepreneur or even the ordinary competent strategist, and they likely never will" (p. 110). Formal procedures that are often associated with planning will never be able to forecast discontinuities or create new strategies. Activities that are meant to implement a strategic plan need (or even should) not be part of the expertise of strategic planners. These activities involve codification, elaboration, and conversion of strategies into concrete activities. We agree with Mintzberg on this. Implementation activities are not idiosyncratic but repetitive, and need different tools and techniques than the generation of the strategy itself.

According to de Geus (1988), the goal of planning is institutional learning: "the real purpose of effective planning is not to make plans but to change the mental models that decision makers carry in their heads" (de Geus, 1988). Interestingly, this also is mentioned as an important aspect of strategic planning by Grant (2003): "Increased emphasis on planning as a process of communication and knowledge sharing was intended not only to influence and improve strategic decisions, but also to provide a basis for coordinating decentralized decision making." In itself, this does not differ from the frequent repetitive planning tasks. Results of, for example, McKay et al. (1995) and de Snoo et al. (2011), indeed indicate that an important role of planning is in processes of communication, negotiation, and persuasion.

All in all, strategic planning has both similarities and differences when compared to more operational repetitive/frequent planning tasks:

- Strategic planning involves management by exception rather than management by repetition.
- Strategic plans are often expressed as scenarios; the main task of strategic planning is to change the mental models that decision makers carry in their heads, rather than providing them with a list of actions to take.
- There is discontinuity in forecasting. Strategic planning questions key variables rather than trying to forecast values on these variables (Grant, 2003).
- Cause and effect are separated in time and place. Strategic planning typically (but not necessarily) relates to a long-time horizon at a level that does not lead to specific resource commitments.
- Grant (2003) reports that the typical time between signal and reaction is 12 to 18 months. This future orientation (far) of strategic planning coincides with the preferred planning horizon (long) of decision makers at the strategic level (Das, 1991).
- Strategic planning is done by a department rather than individuals. Typically, strategic planners only perform the task for a few years (Grant, 2003). In combination with the implementation horizon of strategic planners, this means that individual decision makers will not fulfill a full

plan, do, check, act (PDCA) cycle. Furthermore, "unlike certain other corporate functions (finance, law, and information systems), none of the companies recognized strategic planning as a career track" (Grant, 2003, p. 501).

In sum, strategic planning seems to be an organizational process, more so than many repetitive planning tasks where individual tasks are more easily identifiable. This is not strange, given the timeframe of strategy formulation and implementation. Few individuals will go through the full PDCA cycle and be able to learn and fine-tune their planning activities. Required expertise is related to out-of-the-box thinking, being able to sense coming changes in the external environment, considering the threats and opportunities these changes will have for the organization, and being able to challenge managers' view of the role of the organization.

If the person participates in sufficient planning exercises, is reflective, and learns from the process, true expertise in the higher-level plans and the planning process might develop and the person might be considered a planning expert within the organization. However, it will be harder for an individual to develop expertise about the actual subject or situation being planned, what might actually transpire, and what form the actual plan should take with respect to who does what when. Unfortunately, there are few (if any) extensive studies on infrequent decision making within the organization that focus on expertise and repeated results. As a result, most of the discussion in this chapter focuses on the lower right quadrant of Figure 11.1 – high-frequency decision making where high levels of expertise can be expected to be created through repetition.

Focused planners are not everything they may seem and it is not safe to assume that someone who has developed a high degree of expertise as a focused planner is a general-purpose planner. Many of the domain and organizational capabilities developed by expert planners are not directly transferable to other domains, nor to other environments. Ericsson (2005) provides a brief history of research on expertise and discusses the body of work that has developed since the 1960s. While Ericsson notes many differences between novices and experts, one important aspect about expertise he comments on is especially important when considering planners in the organizational setting: limited transfer of expertise. Two of the three knowledge sets we include in the OPE model are generally transferable – basic planning, and knowledge about the product and processes. The third knowledge set relates to understanding the culture and organizational setting and is not easily transferable. For example, we have often observed planners from one factory start with another company, working with similar products and processes. There is an extended learning curve as the planners discover how the new organization works and how they have to work with the culture, politics, non-verbal goals, and agendas. During this learning curve, which has been observed to last six to nine months, the new experienced planner makes many errors in creating feasible and executable plans. All three knowledge sets must be considered when planners move from one domain to another. A further complication can arise at the cultural level, which can influence how planning is done, and this can add another challenge to the transfer of expertise (e.g. Zwikael, Shimizu, & Globerson, 2005).

Natural Decision Making

The ability to research planning in the live situation is a key characteristic of the natural decision making (NDM) approach to studying people who plan (e.g. Gasser et al., 2011). The NDM perspective has been one of the key methodologies which has permitted the better understanding of planning expertise. Tasks may or may not include explicit decision making as part of the process. For example, a milestone decision or choosing path A versus path B are clear, explicit decisions. There are many other minor decisions subconsciously made or implicit as part of the planning process. For example, deciding which work breakdown unit to consider next is itself a decision, but would rarely merit consideration in a planning analysis. Klein (1998) studied explicit decision making of professionals in live situations featuring time pressure, high stakes, experienced decision makers, inadequate information, unclear goals, poorly defined procedures, context, dynamic conditions, and working in teams. He found that decision making in such situations is not largely based on analytical cognitive processes. Analytic decision making, which includes the explicit development of different scenarios as well as selective comparison of these scenarios on the basis of a set of decision criteria, was found rather seldom with highly experienced decision makers.

What he found instead was that decision making of highly experienced experts is based on recognition rather than on analysis. In contrast to traditional, laboratory-based research on decision making, Klein found that highly experienced decision makers develop the ability to "read" a situation on the basis of their experience with the domain, without any explicit sequence of rational sub-analyses and decisions. As they know the relevant cues of the situation, they can "see" plausible goals as well as what actions are required to achieve them. Furthermore, they develop expectations regarding the situation and its further development, which helps them to correct their perception of plausible goals and required actions when anomalies occur. That is, they arrive at the outcome of an aggregate decision-making process without explicitly performing all of the sub-tasks.

The ability to read the situation and hence to perceive the right task outcome is not based on analytic reasoning but on pattern recognition. The profound experience with the situation enables the planner to compare the actual situation with situations from the past and to recognize patterns, even if the similarity is not obvious to an inexperienced person and if there is a lot of noise. This recognition does not necessarily need to be a conscious process. However, what is very important for recognition-primed thinking is familiarity and feedback.

Klein's insights align with the general results of cognitive skill acquisition and reinforce the concept that organizational planners gain high expertise by developing the ability to recognize patterns in their planning situation. When planning with high frequency and getting feedback regarding the plans' quality, they can learn what the relevant cues of a situation are. This allows them in familiar contexts to read the situation and to immediately see what the right decision is, without analytic reasoning. Some of the expertise is transferrable between organizational settings (e.g. knowledge about the product), some is not (e.g. knowledge about the organizational culture). However, this kind of expertise can be fostered by a task design that allows the planner to learn the relevant cues and it is hampered by a high task fragmentation were the planners lose touch with reality.

In addition to the general NDM research on decision makers, specific situational research into the operational level of planning has yielded a number of insights into the planning task and what a planner does. For example, focused planners at the operational level will likely have multiple plans in play, have a base of organizational knowledge about the past and present, and a network of sources used to constantly acquire and distribute key information about the present and possible future states (MacCarthy et al., 2001; McKay, 1992). Not only do the focused planners know the current product and processes but they have developed the organizational memory about what has been done, what has worked well in the past, and what has not worked. They know the strengths and weaknesses of both the physical reality and the organizational environment. Memory plays a key role in developing expertise, as discussed by Seifert, Patalano, Hammond, and Converse (1997). As with all fields, not all planners who are engaged in a focused capacity are equally competent in the various abilities.

One key potential difference between focused and unfocused planning is the organizational structure in play. During operational planning, the planner is not necessarily a leader or someone with any significant decision-making ability, nor any other leadership trait or ability. It is their job to plan and sequence the work and possibly identify issues with satisfying the demand and the ability to supply. In a rare and unique situation, the planning might be guided by the most senior manager in the room or a decision maker with appropriate ownership of the problem. The planning might also be led by a leader surfacing from within the group, taking the lead in structuring the group and guiding the group's planning, contributing to a higher degree of planning quality (e.g. the type of situation studied by Marta et al., 2005).

General Planning Ability

There are different activities associated with "planning" and each type of activity has its own set of abilities and knowledge associated with it. The breadth and depth of the abilities and knowledge needed for high performance in a task will depend on at least two factors: the multi-dimensional complexity associated with the actual planning task or activity required to be performed, and the attributes associated with the outcome or goal of the task. For example, assigning a business case to students for a 1–2-hour "identify the key problems and develop a plan to address them" exercise has the same core activities in the planning task component of the OPE model, but the problem domain and organizational knowledge implications are substantially different from those encountered in a several-day planning marathon associated with a major business initiative, or even those planning activities of the factory floor scheduler (e.g. MacCarthy et al., 2001; McKay, 1987, 1992).

Any plan exists for a reason, with some kind of desired outcome or goal. The plan is guided by hard and soft constraints and is composed of a sequence of sub-activities which incrementally move towards the outcome. The sub-activities are ordered according to some form of thinking and reasoning. Osherson and Smith (1990) present an overview of the general thinking process from remembering, categorization, choice, judgment, rationality, memory, problem-solving, cognitive development, and the evolution of cognition. All of these factors impact on the quality of one's thinking and are related to the System 1 and System 2 analogies described by Kahneman (2011). Deciding what sub-activities are to be included, the task sequences, possible contingency options, and potential risks are the main components of the mental simulations involved in planning. For example, the quality of the mental models at the individual and group levels can influence performance (Langan-Fox, Anglim, & Wilson, 2004). It has been speculated that the basic abilities associated with this process also influence and contribute to the overall leader's expertise. Marta et al. (2005) note the leader's expertise in the following for structuring behavior during a planning activity: (i) identification of key causes, (ii) identification of restrictions, (iii) identification of downstream consequences, (iv) use of opportunistic implementation strategies, and (v) effective environmental scanning. It can be argued that being able to think in a systematic, structured way about planning is itself a key ability for certain types of planning and that this ability implies the knowledge about when to use structured and unstructured strategies (a non-structure is itself a form of structure) to develop the "best" plan. Researchers such as van Woerkum, Aarts, and de Grip (2007) discuss the role of creativity and loose forms of planning structures for certain types of situations. When taken together, an experienced and proficient planner's abilities would need to include the use of both structured and unstructured (creative) methodologies and approaches. Rigid thinking where the methodology becomes mythology and is blindly followed is not likely to identify novel or innovative solutions to problems, and the problems will be forced into pre-existing solution schemes.

As noted, in this chapter, planning is viewed holistically and we look at the skill and expertise elements from cradle to grave. During this journey, there are many tasks that an effective and efficient planner must be able to do, ranging from the initial problem and analysis and planning to communication, governance, and negotiating. Sources such as the *Guide to the Project Management Body of Knowledge* (PMBOK, 2004) provide a starting point for understanding the mechanics and structure for generic planning situations resembling projects. However, such resources do not provide insights and guidance on how to actually plan and how to create a good plan.

The need to improve management's ability to plan in the organizational context (e.g. the casual planner) has been often stated (Dill, 1975), as have specific types of management, such as planning in human resources (Ramlall, 2003). Dill discussed the challenges in improving planning and pointed out four topics for improving managers' expertise in planning: (i) self-selection of the things they will undertake and learn (an integrated view of training and developing management skills), (ii) skill in exploring, testing, and learning by asking questions, (iii) enthusiasm for testing assumptions and predictions, and (iv) enthusiasm for distant rather than local search (e.g. reaching outside of the immediate domain for solutions). The body of Dill's article describes the environmental context within which the manager as planner functions and the challenges this environment creates for developing planning skills. Another approach advocated for improving aspects of the planning task is that of case-based reasoning. This is a method that is common in medical studies for learning diagnostic skills and developing the appropriate pathway for the patient (e.g. Norman et al., 2006) and has also found application in disaster planning (e.g. Leake, 1995).

Collaboration in Organizational Planning

As we have noted, not all planning is individualistic. Distributed or group expertise is a way to address situations when individual abilities are not sufficient or desired. We note that organizations are based on division of labor and so is organizational planning. No single individual does all of the planning in an organization. As a consequence, planning is often not the task of an individual but is distributed to many human planners that can be part of the same organization or be distributed throughout different organization (e.g. Waefler, 2001). Planning therefore needs to be designed as a collaborative task in many situations. Planning can be considered as a form of situated cognition with objectives to be achieved and mental simulation of the future (Marta et al., 2005), and this puts some requirements on the collaboration.

The collaboration needs to provide cognitions adequate to the task on a social–system level (e.g. Hutchins, 1995; Patterson & Miller, 2010; Salas, Fiore, & Letsky, 2012). There is some debate whether this requires shared (Smith & Hancock, 1995) or distributed (Stanton et al., 2006) situation awareness. Whereas the concept of shared situation awareness claims that the planners concerned do need a shared comprehension of relevant information, the concept of distributed situation awareness rather claims a need for different, but compatible information tailored to the individual task. We support the latter view, as it implies that the individual human planner who is part of the distributed planning process does not need to have an all-embracing situated cognition, but just needs one that is relevant for his or her task. However, it also implies that the tasks of the individuals need to be compatible in order to provide the system as a whole with a comprehensive situated cognition.

This has some implications for task design when planning is the main agenda. On the level of dyadic collaboration (i.e. two planners), Windischer, Grote, Mathier, Meunier Martins, & Glardon (2009) elaborated requirements for collaboration. These include, among other things, communication of anticipated events, goal agreements, mutual knowledge of reference field characteristics, negotiation of alternatives, coordination of opportunistic planning, and common decision for plan cancelation. It can be seen from this list that such collaboration is quite demanding and requires trustful relations. Planners optimizing their task rather than the collaboration will most probably not involve requirements for collaboration, which will lead to local optimization at the cost of overall optimization. The task design must also include opportunities to develop the necessary expertise for each piece of the collaboration: what each contributor brings to the table.

On the sociotechnical system level, organizational planning is a task that resembles a sociotechnical network (Waefler, 2001). The social part of this network consists of human planners but also of other individuals who do not have a formal role in planning but have an impact on it (e.g. shop floor supervisors or warehouse clerks). The technical part of the network consists of IT systems (e.g. enterprise resource planning and advanced planning systems). Within the network, distributed situation awareness as described above needs to be provided. However, the network design does not normally aim at this objective. It rather aims at optimizing automated plan generation by algorithmic information processing. Whether or not this provides the human decision makers involved with an adequate distributed situation awareness is normally not in the scope of system design. Respective system design requires an adequate allocation of responsibilities and control opportunities as well as role design that allows for situated action and local control of variances and disturbances (Grote, 2009; Waefler, 2001; Waefler et al., 2011).

Clinical and In Situ Research on Planning

A common component of the planning context framework and OPE model is the contextual setting. There has been relatively little *in situ* longitudinal, holistic research performed on intermittent organizational planning tasks at the strategic and tactical levels beyond case-study descriptions (e.g. Young & Norris, 1988), and many clinical and controlled experiments in an academic setting use subjects such as undergraduate students as proxies or surrogates for real planners (Finkelstein, 2002). These two factors have created a conceptual gap between research efforts and results and the harsh and messy world of reality. This is not to say that we have not learned valuable lessons from research, but the research results must be interpreted in the appropriate context. For example, the clinical studies performed in Marta et al. (2005) are extremely well executed, and although the experiments involved undergraduates, we can (i) review the results as peer separation within an expertise level (all subjects likely to be considered novices), (ii) restrict the interpretation to relatively short, *ad hoc* planning meetings which do occur in business (versus more formal or extended planning) and populated largely by novice, unskilled, and inexperienced planners, and (iii) possibly gain insights about what the planning process and issues might be in start-up ventures dominated by recent undergraduates hitting the workforce.

The status of research on operational planning is substantially different from that at the strategic and tactical levels. There is a body of research based on clinical studies, numerous short- and long-term case studies, and more rigorous field-based studies on the planners and planning situation (e.g. see review in MacCarthy, 2006). Although this research can still be considered early and not yet fully mature, the body of work is growing, with substantial work being recently conducted in a collaborative fashion (e.g. results from EU COST project: Fransoo, Waefler, & Wilson, 2011). Not all of the results can be extended because of the casual and professional nature of the roles, frequency and structure of what is being planned, etc. However, there are some key results from the operational level that can provide insight into expectations about and a better understanding of higher-level planning. One observation from this body of research is that there are planners who might be consumed by a single task, and there are planners who are constantly planning new tasks, and have multiple plans in play at the same time.

Cognitive Skill in Planning Performance

A number of classic studies and discussions about expertise have been formative in the thinking about expertise. For example, the work of Anderson (1981), Sternberg (1985) and Dreyfus and Dreyfus (1986) demonstrate the broad base of views and perspectives about what expertise is, how it is exhibited, the value of expertise, and how it is acquired. The decades of research up to 2006 are thoroughly summarized in the seminal work of Ericsson et al. (2006) and this volume remains the main repository for an overview. A brief overview of the nature of expertise which outlines a number of psychological characteristics and strategies associated with expertise can be found in Farrington-Darby and Wilson (2006) and Feltovich et al. (2006). More in-depth discussions about earlier research on expertise can be found in such works as Ericsson and Smith (1991) and Chi, Glaser, and Farr (1988).

The list of possible differences between the novice level and the expert is rather long and will not be exhaustively explored in this chapter. A high-level list (from Feltovich et al., 2006) includes: (i) expertise is limited in its scope and elite performance does not transfer; (ii) knowledge and content matter are important to expertise; (iii) expertise involves larger and more integrated cognitive units; (iv) expertise involves functional, abstracted representations of presented information; (v) expertise involves automated basic strokes; (vi) expertise involves selective access of relevant information; (vii) expertise involves reflection; (viii) expertise is an adaptation; and (ix) simple experience is not sufficient for the development of expertise.

What do these attributes imply for expertise in planning? The attributes in the literature usually associated with expertise in problem-solving were pared down by Bjorklund and Eloranta (2008) in their work on expertise and creative problem-solving, and if *planning* is considered a creative problem-solving task, their summary of what expertise implies is relevant as a basis for discussion purposes:

- Better overall picture implies better recognition of problems, better options created.
- Broader interests implies better options created, better collaboration.
- Better and faster at knowing what is relevant implies better targeting of resources.
- Better knowledge of promisingness implies better targeting of resources, better options created.
- Better metaknowledge implies better collaboration, better targeting of resources.
- Better goal direction implies better targeting of resources.
- Better combinations of information from different fields implies better options created.
- Increased tacit knowledge implies challenges for sharing expertise and teaching.

Bjorklund and Eloranta conclude that expertise aids in at least four phases of creative problem-solving: (i) identifying the problem; (ii) operationalizing the problem (relevancy and promisingness judgments); (iii) generating good options; and (iv) developing the options in the most promising direction (or choosing the most promising option). Promisingness in this context refers to the expert's knowledge of what is relevant and which option or path shows the most promise.

Kahneman and Klein (2009) also provide a summary list of observations about expertise which are applicable to this chapter's discussion. Their summary includes:

- Intuitive judgments can be based on skill, but they can also arise from inappropriate application of heuristic processes.
- Those skilled are often unaware of the cues that guide them, those non-skilled are even less likely to know how the judgment was arrived at.
- A common view is that true experts know what they do not know, while non-experts do not and subjective confidence is not a reliable indicator of judgment quality.
- The quality of the intuitive judgment depends on the situational environment and the opportunity the individual has to learn the environment.

- An environment suitable for intuition must exhibit high validity: stable relationships between cues and subsequent events (they note that validity and uncertainty are not incompatible – e.g. poker and warfare).
- An environment must exhibit high validity for the development of skilled intuition along with rapid feedback and opportunity for prolonged practice.
- Lucky individuals may have an illusion of skill and exhibit overconfidence.
- Skill has boundaries and the boundaries may not clear to the individual or to others.

Expertise in the early stages of planning (e.g. Volkema, 1983) affects problem formulation, and without a strong and appropriately accurate understanding of the problem, the remaining elements of planning might represent an excellent solution to the wrong problem. Unfortunately, there are no existing instruments or tools to assess the quality of this first set of activities. Assessments are often left to those who are considered more *expert* than the parties performing the planning, which also raises the question of the assessors' real level of expertise versus a relative level.

As we move through the planning cycle after problem identification, isolation, and formulation, different abilities are required to solve or address the problem. In our context, this is creating the plan. In creating a plan, there are many activities to consider and multiple choices for the manifestation of each activity. It could be speculated that an expert planner would demonstrate wisdom in making these plans, knowing what options to consider, weighing options, and striking the best possible compromise. Planning wisdom would be an aggregate skill possibly capturing the knowledge and experience about many domain and environmental constraints and influencing factors. But what is wisdom and how does one develop it (e.g. Barbuto & Millard, 2012)? How does one know if one is wise (e.g. Redzanowski & Gluck, 2012)? Alas, wisdom is one of those facets that is easy to talk about, but the actual traits and development process are hard to define and measure (Baltes & Smith, 2008; Greene & Brown, 2009). Wisdom is generally agreed to be an ability that takes time and a process to develop: "It takes a complex coalition of enhancing factors from a variety of domains (psychological, social, professional, historical) to achieve peak levels of wisdom" (Baltes & Smith, 2008). Wisdom appears to capture the subtle level in planning that is beyond pure fact and rational thought.

The planning activities then move onto tasks relying on foresight, anticipation, mitigation, and ongoing plan adaptation. Planning is a mixture of proactive and reactive decision making. If an organization rewards firefighting and not fire avoidance, little foresight and preemptive planning will be valued or observed (McKay, 1987, 1992). A plan is launched and until a pothole is actually fallen into or a wall hit, nothing is done to avoid the pothole or wall. Alternatively, if the planners and organization do not have the skills, knowledge, or experience necessary to do proactive planning, proactive planning will not happen. The first case is a social or cultural problem and the latter one is cognitive. In some cases, such as that noted in McKay (1987, 1992), the individuals knew what should and could be done to avoid the firefighting, but the organizational culture did not encourage it. Poor planning execution in either case, but the causes are different.

During these activities, personal traits are also important for effective planning. For example, a planner must be able to engage, persuade, collaborate, and negotiate with others in a trustworthy bilateral arrangement. When we say that so-and-so can work with others, we are placing this type of characteristic in the trait category, although there are skills developed around this trait that allow the individual to leverage and exploit this ability.

Planning obviously involves many decisions and one aspect of decision making by planners that affects performance relates to the sub-task decisions. Kahneman and Klein (2009) delve into how NDM and heuristic biases (HB) deal with expertise and intuition. Decisions made quickly based on intuition can happen often during the planning process and this in itself is an important topic for future study. We do not know when or how often quick, gut-felt decisions are made based on intuition and when slower, more rational processes are used. It is probably safe to say that almost all decisions in the planning process have some degree of uncertainty in them. Intuition-based decisions in uncertain situations are directly related to expertise, and the Kahneman and Klein (2009) paper concludes with an excellent list of shared NDM and HB beliefs about expert and non-expert intuition.

Kahneman (2011) provides additional discussion linking true expertise, not pseudo-expertise, and its relationship with the quality of intuition-based decisions. Taleb (2007) discusses the human thought processes related to generalities and specifics which also underlie people's judgment and assessment of situations. The seminal text by Kahneman, Slovic, and Tversky (1982) provides the foundation for anyone wishing to understand the fundamental concepts behind HB. The NDM and HB research supports the general assumptions brought forward in this section: that certain domains are not likely to be friendly to the development of high performers in decision making (hence making discussing "experts" an oxymoron when in these domains); that while true experts are not always right, they are right more often than non-experts in both fast and slow thinking; and that non-experts will not be aware of what they do not know or their possible failures. It is also possible that a pseudo or faux expert will make correct decisions through a combination of luck or because the precise subsets of ability and knowledge happen to align in a narrow fashion, that is, a person may have a very narrow range of ability and knowledge that happens to help in one case. The slightest change in problem parameters might render all of that person's apparent expertise useless. In laboratory situations, it might be possible to explore this matter further, but in the field, it is difficult to know if the decision was indeed correct or not, as the desired goal might be reached (or not) independent of the actual decision quality.

Review Summary

Seven related topics have been briefly summarized in the preceding sub-sections. Individually and together, these topics provide the underpinnings of the contextual framework and OPE model. The *frequency of the task* combined with reflection is one of the key factors allowing expertise to be developed. *Institutional planning* helps decompose the structure of the task in terms of scope, frequency, and level of detailed knowledge, as frequency and reflection do not fully capture idiosyncratic types of situations versus recipe and repetitive types. *Natural decision making* research provides insights into the value of the cultural and *in situ* knowledge that planners use to recognize clues and to build mental models of the planning task. Research results regarding *general planning ability* and the structure of planning provide a roadmap for considering the sequencing and relationships associated with the planning tasks. Organizational planning is often a group activity conducted over relatively long time horizons, and *collaboration* research assists with understanding the processes and expertise factors when more than a single individual is involved. The *clinical and in situ* research overview illustrates how the cultural and contextual factors are problematic to identify or replicate in a clinical setting, where well-controlled experimentation is possible, and suggests that interdisciplinary research of a hybrid nature is necessary for truly understanding organizational planning. The review finished with a general review of the research results associated with the *cognitive skills used in planning* and how these skills impact plan performance. It is suggested that most, but admittedly not all, key factors can be found in the preliminary framework and OPE model.

The next sections discuss two remaining issues. First, what can we say about expertise and infrequent and unstructured planning? Second, what additional expertise is required during plan execution?

Infrequent and Unstructured Organizational Planning Tasks

If used alone, cognitive skill research would suggest that it is possible, but rare, for someone to develop true expertise at the strategic levels for many types of planning tasks. As noted in Perry (2001), there is a lack of robust evidence linking business failure with poor planning. There are many anecdotal expositions, but nothing that can be called a solid empirical study. Typical of the literature are comments similar to: "about 90 percent of all failures can be traced to lack of adequate management" (e.g. Sharma & Mahajan, 1980 referring to a number of other papers). Not all businesses fail, though, and this suggests that some skill and expertise in some forms of planning might be present.

The OPE model does not rely on cognitive psychology alone and suggests that it is not necessary to have complete, integrated expertise in all areas in order to plan effectively. The model supports both inductive and deductive approaches to the task of planning. It is suggested that for infrequent and unstructured planning tasks, successful planning likely uses a bottom-up or inductive approach to the task. This implies that the planner(s) have knowledge and expertise in various planning aspects and then integrate them to address a planning task not yet encountered. For frequent or structured tasks, a top-down or deductive planning style is possible and is effective. There are different thought processes in each approach and it is not clear whether all planners can effectively function in both styles. Furthermore, this perspective suggests that an inductive planner needs sufficient knowledge and expertise in the basic OPE elements to support a scaffolding approach. If an individual or group has limited expertise in some elements, it is unlikely that planning success will result, as not all of the tools are available for a bottom-up approach to the problem. The bottom-up methodology is potentially more transferable when all of the basic elements exist. A bottom-up planner in one situation might need a start-up or learning phase to address any element shortfall when faced by a new and different planning challenge.

The literature suggests some possible strategies to improve infrequent and unstructured planning:

- The decision-making mechanisms should be cautious of any intuition and rapid decision-making process. The processes should consciously utilize slow thinking (Kahneman, 2011).
- Individual planners should employ wise counsel on any key decisions and not rely on their sole judgment and gut feelings. The counsel team will likely not be static and involve the same people for all planning tasks unless the individuals actually have the necessary skill and expertise at the required breadth and depth. While an individual might not have all of the key elements for bottom-up planning, the group collaboration approach might.
- Self-awareness and conscious reflection are needed to consciously apply inductive approaches appropriately. It is suggested that part of the initial activity in infrequent planning tasks is to identify the most appropriate approach for the task and not assume that one approach is applicable to all situations.
- Since planning involves mental simulations of the future, it is possible to document the planner's view of the future and track the predictions. This will provide a feedback loop that will potentially help transform an unstructured planning task into a more structured one. It is also possible to document some of the inductive elements and reasoning to assist others in the future.
- The inductive planning process should be explicitly understood and steps taken to ensure the appropriate time is taken and that the basic elements are in place for bottom-up planning when the planning situation is not a direct transfer.

Planning During Plan Execution

The body of this chapter has concentrated on initial planning tasks. Planning and plan performance during plan execution has many of the same requirements and implications with respect to expertise. That being said, additional types of knowledge and skills are required for effective planning during execution, and the preliminary framework and model presented earlier still apply. Appropriate knowledge about the situation and what needs to be planned is still one of the main requirements. However, during execution, the knowledge is likely to be more detailed than in the initial planning. Contributing to the knowledge base is the history of the plan thus far. This contributes realized knowledge about many things that were possibly only speculated upon earlier. Different mental models are necessary and it is possible that someone capable of developing an excellent initial plan is incapable of effective planning midstream, or vice versa. The real-time planning possibly requires great expertise in information gathering, dissemination, and collaboration. It might also require greater skill with facts and details, keeping everything straight and maintaining a reasonably accurate model of the present and future. Skill in appropriate information acquisition is part of the OPE model, and this needs to be interpreted differently based on the planning phase – initial or midstream. The basic planning abilities also shift slightly with the increased emphasis on communication, negotiation, and so forth.

Unless the planners have the right abilities at the right time, it is unlikely that quality planning will result. An implication of this observation is that explicit skills and abilities of planners should be considered when assigning planning tasks to ensure that the planning capability matches the demand for initial and ongoing planning tasks.

Developing Organizational Planning Expertise

From what we know from the various research fields that touch upon organizational planning, it is not likely that everyone can be trained and developed into highly effective, expert planners. Not everyone has the same ability to develop mental simulations, networking, and communication skills, nor the opportunity to experience sufficient planning tasks to identify patterns and schemas. However, there are some practices that are likely to enhance or contribute to developing planning expertise in addition to the traditional planning methods:

- assessment of ability or skill gaps for particular planning tasks (e.g. repetitive) and the development of learning processes to create a balance in the OPE model
- participation of junior planners in more advanced planning tasks with conscious learning and debriefing activities
- explicit recognition of group or collaborative planning requirements and the fostering of codependent planning for larger planning tasks
- mentoring of junior planners by experienced planners (individually and in groups), with discussions and explorations of past and current planning activities
- strengthening the organizational planning knowledge about facets such as risk management clues, planning constraints, codependencies, and constraint elasticity
- development of processes for inductive or bottom-up planning with possible case-study analysis and debriefing sessions on how the planning task was approached.

Discussion

Starting from a discussion of planning performance and what quality planning might imply, preliminary ideas for how to decompose and better understand the complex world of organizational planning have been developed. The topic is complex because of the wide range of planning tasks that occur within an organization and what this variance entails. The contextual structure framework attempts to provide a way to discuss frequently performed tasks versus those less frequent, at the same time acknowledging that the structure of the problem is a key determinant of a planning strategy (inductive or deductive). This relates to the basic planning process. The *right* process itself will not guarantee high performance. It is necessary, but not sufficient.

What happens during the process is also important for quality planning. This is the subject of the OPE model. The model attempts to align several important knowledge and skill domains that provide the necessary totality for effective planning. This involves knowledge and skill about general planning, the type of domain, and the specific organization or culture. All three knowledge sets are necessary for the planner (or planning group), but are also not sufficient by themselves for quality planning. The planning process will dictate how the knowledge is applied.

As preliminary concepts, the framework and model are acknowledged to be speculative and in their current form possibly limited to describing organizational planning situations, or providing a structure for post-analyzing an executed plan. The concepts might also be useful as reflection tools when planning. They are not developed and supported to the point of explaining with strong causal relationships what has happened or what might happen. The concepts arose when initially trying to write this chapter about the role of expertise in plan performance. The topic was so complex that we had to step back and create concepts that helped decompose and structure the chapter, leading to the OPE relationships becoming clear and the realization that the frequency and structure of the planning task were interrelated with each other, and with expertise.

It is possible in the future that these concepts, or similar, might be useful in classifying organizational planning tasks and any associated research activity. For example, it is important to compare similar tasks and situations and to be clear about what is being researched.

Future Research

In reflecting upon the current state of knowledge pertaining to the role of expertise in organizational planning performance, several opportunities present themselves for future research both on what could be studied and on how to study it:

- What methods are appropriate to isolate and identify the level of expertise in each of the key knowledge sets? For example, are think-aloud protocols suitable? Ethnographic studies?
- What levels of expertise in each knowledge set are necessary for adequate and competent planning versus superior planning? Do all areas need to be of the same level? What if one area is weak, but others are strong?
- How can inductive and deductive planning expertise be developed and measured?
- How can planning performance be better defined? There is a need to develop measures and methods that allow comparison and quantitative assessments.
- How can we track and link expertise to the specific planning tasks while the tasks are being performed?
- What can be learned from studying what are considered planning failures versus successes? If the planning failure resulted in business failure, how can expertise be adequately studied when the business no longer exists?
- What methods are suitable to support collaborative planning under the condition of distributed expertise?
- What skills and knowledge are transferrable?
- What skills and knowledge are pertinent for initial planning versus replanning, and when does replanning resemble initial planning?

Conclusion

As we promised, we have provided no definitive causal models or theories that create a foundation for explaining the contribution of expertise to plan performance. We have tried to explain why this is the case and the difficulties surrounding any such discourse. This discourse led to the creation of the task structure framework and the OPE model.

In Figure 11.1, we provided a view of decision making associated with organizational planning with two dimensions related to frequency and plan structure. This view helps identify potential areas for well-developed expertise, as well as issues to be aware of in other areas. This is the starting point for understanding the relationship between expertise and organizational planning and helps identify the type of planning process that might be appropriate.

The OPE model in Figure 11.2 decomposes the knowledge space into three domains which align with planning situations and the types of expertise associated with each. We believe that planning contexts should be thought about using these views as they help clarify the role of generic competencies, specific abilities, and sole versus collaborative planning. There are multiple dimensions to the problem and a one-size-fits-all solution or schema is unlikely.

The expertise perspective forces us to think more deeply about what is actually being studied in the field and in controlled experiments. For example, what levels of performance are possible with a type of planning situation, what behaviors should be looked for, and what tools or mechanisms are needed to assess the behaviors? Experiments in the field are difficult because there are rarely two identical, controlled situations that can be observed and studied – to evaluate two planners solving the same problem within the same organization for execution. Controlled experiments in academic settings are not likely to have the ability, knowledge, and contextual elements representative of non-novice planning situations. This suggests that the research results of controlled studies using students or a contrived context-free situation must be carefully interpreted as to scope and generality. Given the challenges of developing planning expertise, the potential exists for exploring group planning processes which are structured to address possible gaps in ability and knowledge. This will likely be easier to do at the operational levels where niche or vertical areas of ability and knowledge can be brought to the process. At these levels, the group process has the potential for leveling out the planning process at the same degree of expertise, so that although the resulting plan might not surpass the intermediate level or basic competence, there are no parts of the plan at the novice or junior level.

There is also potential for the exploration of information technology to complement and augment the human decision maker, especially in the areas of low volume, unfocused plan making. In these unfocused planning situations, the technology platform might do a better job of identifying weak relationships and reduce the reliance on luck. In addition, much of the research in planning/scheduling is related to computer support, and this is probably the major change driver in many planning/scheduling departments. The dynamic relation between expertise and computer support (e.g. the paradox of task support: if you develop support for a task, the task changes and the support no longer fits) is considered by the authors as a potentially fruitful area for research.

In conclusion, the study of planner expertise and its role in organizational planning is still developing. As illustrated by the research noted in this chapter, the challenge of planner expertise is multidisciplinary and any agenda should be encouraged to be collaborative and bring together the cognitive, social, and decision sciences. As researchers, we have invested over 50 years on this topic and have over the last 15 years contemplated, discussed, argued, and debated with each other how individuals and groups plan and schedule organizational tasks. Our backgrounds represent three different disciplines and we have learned many things from each other. Within the research community looking at humans, planning, scheduling, and systems, we also routinely engage in interdisciplinary research with others. We strongly encourage others to travel the same path, as we believe that a single perspective on this problem will be severely limited in its ability to understand the dynamic relationships.

Acknowledgments

We would like to explicitly acknowledge the suggestions and advice we received from this book's editors during the process of writing. The suggestions were insightful and provided substantial assistance dealing with a difficult topic.

References

Anderson, J. R. (Ed.) (1981). *Cognitive skills and their acquisition*. Mahwah, NJ: Lawrence Erlbaum.

Anthony, R. N. (1965). *Planning and control systems*. Boston, MA: Harvard Business School Press.

Anthony, R. N. (1988). *The management control function*. Boston, MA: Harvard Business School Press.

Baltes, P. B., & Smith, J. (2008). The fascination of wisdom, its nature, ontogeny, and function. *Perspectives on Psychological Science*, 3, 56–64.

Barbuto, J. E., Jr., & Millard, M. L. (2012). Wisdom development of leaders: a constructive development perspective. *International Journal of Leadership Studies*, 5, 233–245.

Bazerman, M. (1998). *Judgment in managerial decision making* (4th ed.). New York: Wiley.

Bjorklund, T. A., & Eloranta, M. M. (2008). Fostering innovation: what we can learn from experts and expertise, *SEFI 36th Annual Conference*, July 2008, Aalborg, Denmark.

Caves, R. E. (1980). Industrial organization, corporate strategy and structure. *Journal of Economic Literature*, 18, 64–92.

Chi, M. T. H., Glaser, R., & Farr, M. J. (1988). *The nature of expertise*. Mahwah, NJ: Lawrence Erlbaum.

de Geus, A. P. (1988). Planning as learning. *Harvard Business Review*, 66(2), 70–74.

de Snoo, C., & van Wezel, W. (2011). Coordination and task interdependence during schedule adaptation. *Human Factors and Ergonomics in Manufacturing & Service Industries*, 24(2), 139–151. doi, 10.1002/hfm.20363

de Snoo, C., van Wezel, W., & Jorna, R. (2011). An empirical investigation of scheduling performance criteria. *Journal of Operations Management*, 29, 181–193.

Das, T. K. (1991). Time: the hidden dimension in strategic planning. *Long Range Planning*, 24(3), 49–57.

Dill, W. R. (1975). Integrating planning and management development. *Long Range Planning*, 8(5), 8–12.

Dreyfus, H. L., & Dreyfus, S. E. (1986). *Mind over machine*. New York: Free Press.

Emerson, H. (1911). *Twelve principles of efficiency*. New York: The Engineering Magazine.

Ericsson, K. A. (2005). Recent advances in expertise research: a commentary on the contributions to the special issue. *Applied. Cognitive Psychology*, 19, 233–241.

Ericsson, K. A., & Lehmann, A. C. (1996). Expert and exceptional performance: evidence of maximal adaptation to task constraints. *Annual Review of Psychology*, 47, 273–305.

Ericsson, K. A., & Smith, J. (Eds.) (1991). *Towards a general theory of expertise*. Cambridge, UK: Cambridge University Press.

Ericsson, K. A., Charness, N., Feltovich, P., & Hoffman, R. R. (2006). *Cambridge handbook of expertise and expert performance*. Cambridge, UK: Cambridge University Press.

Farrington-Darby, T., & Wilson, J. R. (2006). The nature of expertise: a review. *Applied Ergonomics*, 37, 17–32.

Feltovich, P. J., Prietula, M., & Ericsson, K. A. (2006). Studies of expertise from psychological perspectives. In K. A. Ericsson et al. (Eds.), *Cambridge handbook of expertise and expert performance* (pp. 41–68). Cambridge, UK: Cambridge University Press.

Finkelstein, S. (2002). Planning in organizations: one vote for complexity. In F. J. Yammarion & F. Dansereau (Eds.), *The many faces of multi-level issues* (Research in multi-level issues, Vol. 1, pp. 73–80). Bingley: Emerald.

Fransoo, J. C., Waefler, T., & Wilson, J. R. (Eds.) (2011). *Behavioral operations in planning and scheduling*. Berlin: Springer-Verlag.

Gasser, R., Fischer, K., & Waefler, T. (2011). Decision making in planning and scheduling: a field study of planning behaviour in manufacturing. In J. C. Fransoo, T. Waefler, & J. R. Wilson (Eds.), *Behavioral operations in planning and scheduling* (pp. 11–30). Berlin: Springer-Verlag.

Grant, R. M. (2003). Strategic planning in a turbulent environment: evidence from the oil majors. *Strategic Management Journal*, 24, 491–517.

Greene, J. A., & Brown, S. C. (2009). The wisdom development scale: further validity investigations. *International Journal of Aging and Human Development*, 68, 289–320.

Grote, G. (2009). *Management of uncertainty*. London: Springer.

Hutchins, E. (1995). *Cognition in the wild*. Cambridge, MA: MIT Press.

Ittner, C. D., & Larcker, D. F. (1997). Quality strategy, strategic control systems, and organizational performance. *Accounting, Organizations and Society*, 22, 293–314.

Joyce, E. J. (1976). Expert judgment in audit program planning. *Journal of Accounting Research*, 14, 29–60.

Kahneman, D. (2011). *Thinking, fast and slow*. New York: Farrar, Straus and Giroux.

Kahneman, D., & Klein, G. (2009). Conditions for intuitive expertise. *American Psychologist*, 64, 515–526.

Kahneman, D., Slovic, P., & Tversky, A. (Eds.) (1982). *Judgment under uncertainty: Heuristics and biases*. Cambridge, UK: Cambridge University Press.

Kaufman, J. L., & Escuin, M. (2000). Thinking alike. *Journal of the American Planning Association*, 66, 34–45.

Kautz, H., & Selman, B. (1998). The role of domain-specific knowledge in the planning as a satisfiability framework. *AIPS 1998 Proceedings*, 181–189.

Kerzner, H. (2013). *Project management: A systems approach to planning, scheduling, and controlling* (11th ed.). Hoboken, NJ: Wiley.

Kiewiet, D. J., Jorna, R. J., & van Wezel, W. (2005). Planners and their cognitive maps: an analysis of domain representations using multi dimensional scaling. *Applied Ergonomics*, 36, 695–708.

Klein, G. (1998). *Sources of power*. Cambridge, MA: MIT Press.

Langan-Fox, J., Anglim, J., & Wilson, J. R. (2004). Mental models, team mental models, and performance: process, development, and future directions. *Human Factors and Ergonomics in Manufacturing*, 14, 331–352.

Leake, D. B. (1995). Becoming an expert case-based reasoned: learning to adapt prior cases. *Proc. 8th Annual Florida Artificial Intelligence Research Symposium* (pp. 112–116). Melbourne, FL.

MacCarthy, B. L. (2006). Organizational, systems and human issues in production planning, scheduling and control. In J. Hermann (Ed.), *Handbook of production scheduling* (Intl Series in Operations Research and Management Science, pp. 59–90). New York: Springer.

MacCarthy, B. L., Wilson, J. R., & Crawford, S. (2001). Human performance in industrial scheduling: a framework for understanding. *Human Factors and Ergonomics in Manufacturing*, 11, 299–320.

McKay, K. N. (1987). *Conceptual framework for job shop scheduling*. Master's thesis, University of Waterloo, Ontario.

McKay, K. N. (1992). *A model for manufacturing decisions requiring judgement*. Doctoral thesis, University of Waterloo, Ontario.

McKay, K. N., & Wiers, V. C. S. (2006). The organizational interconnectivity of planning and scheduling. In W. van Wezel et al. (Eds.), *Planning in Intelligent Systems* (pp. 177–201). Hoboken, NJ: Wiley.

McKay, K. N., Safayeni, F. R., & Buzacott, J. A. (1995). Schedulers & planners: What and how can we learn from them. In D. E. Brown & W. T. Scherer (Eds.), *Intelligent Scheduling Systems* (pp. 41–62). Boston, MA: Kluwer.

Marta, S., Leritz, L. E., & Mumford, M. D. (2005). Leadership skills and the group performance: Situational demands, behavioral requirements, and planning. *The Leadership Quarterly*, 16, 97–120.

Mintzberg, H. (1994). The fall and rise of strategic planning. *Harvard Business Review*, 72, 107–114.

Mumford, M. D., Schultz, R. A., & Van Doorn, J. R. (2001). Performance in planning: processes, requirements, and errors. *Review of General Psychology*, 5, 213–240.

Mumford, M. D., Schultz, R. A., & Osburn, H. K. (2002). Planning in organizations: performance as a multi-level phenomenon. In F. J. Yammarion & F. Dansereau (Eds.), *The many faces of multi-level issues* (Research in multi-level issues, Vol. 1, pp. 3–65), Bingley: Emerald.

Mumford, M. D., Bedell-Avers, K. E., & Hunter, S. T. (2008). Planning for innovation: a multi-level perspective. In M. D. Mumford, S. T. Hunter, & K. E. Bedell-Avers (Eds.), *Multi-level issues in creativity and innovation* (Research in multi-level issues, Vol. 7, pp. 107–154). Bingley: Emerald.

Norman, G., Eva, K., Brooks, L., & Hamstra, S. (2006). Expertise in medicine and surgery. In K. A. Ericsson et al. (Eds.), *Cambridge handbook of expertise and expert performance* (pp. 41–68). Cambridge, UK: Cambridge University Press.

Nutt, P. C. (2007). Examining the link between plan evaluation and implementation. *Technological Forecasting & Social Change*, 74, 1252–1271.

Osherson, D. N., & Smith, E. E. (1990). *Thinking: An invitation to cognitive science* (Vol. 3). Cambridge, MA: MIT Press.

Patanakul, P., & Milosevic, D. (2008). A competency model for effectiveness in managing multiple projects. *Journal of High Technology Management Research*, 18, 118–131.

Patterson, E. S., & Miller, J. E. (Eds.) (2010). *Macrocognition metrics and scenarios*. Surrey UK: Ashgate.

Perry, S. C. (2001). The relationship between written business plans and the failure of small businesses in the *Journal of Small Business Management*, 39, 201–208.

Pettersen, N. (1991). What do we know about the effective project manager? *Project Management*, 9(2), 99–104.

PMBOK (2004). *A Guide to the Project Management Body of Knowledge* (3rd ed.), Pennsylvania: Project Management Institute.

Ramlall, S. J. (2003). Measuring human resource management's effectiveness in improving performance. *Human Resource Planning*, 26, 51–62.

Rasmussen, L. J., Sieck, W. R., & Smart, P. (2009). What is a good plan? Cultural variations in expert planners' concepts of plan quality. *Journal of Cognitive Engineering and Decision Making*, 3, 228–249.

Redzanowski, U., & Gluck, J. (2012). Who knows who is wise? Self and peer ratings of wisdom. *The Journals of Gerontology, Series B: Psychological Sciences and Social Sciences*, 68(3), 391–394. doi:10.1093/geronb/gbs079

Rikers, R. M. J. P., & Paas, F. (2005). Recent advances in expertise research. *Applied Cognitive Psychology*, 19, 145–149.

Salas, E., Fiore, S. M., & Letsky, M. P. (Eds.) (2012). *Theories of team cognition*. New York: Routledge.

Seifert, C. M., Patalano, A. L., Hammond, K. J., & Converse, T. M. (1997). Experience and expertise: The role of memory in planning for opportunities. In P. J. Feltovich, K. M. Ford, & R. R. Hoffman (Eds.), *Expertise in context* (pp. 101–123). Menlo Park, CA: AAAI Press/MIT Press.

Serfaty, D., MacMillan, J., Entin, E. E., & Entin, E. B. (1997). The decision-making expertise of battle commanders. In C. Zsambok & G. Klein (Eds.), *Naturalistic Decision Making* (pp. 233–246). Hillsdale, NJ: Lawrence Erlbaum Associates.

Sharma, S., & Mahajan, V. (1980). Early warning indicators of business failure. *Journal of Marketing*, 44, 80–89.

Smith, K., & Hancock, P. A. (1995). Situation awareness is adaptive, externally directed consciousness. *Human Factors*, 37, 137–148.

Stanton, N. A., Stewart, R., Harris, D., Houghton, R. J., Baber, C., McMaster, … & Green, D. (2006). Distributed situation awareness in dynamic systems: theoretical development and application of an ergonomics methodology. *Ergonomics*, 49, 1288–1311.

Sternberg, R. (1985). Implicit theories of intelligence, creativity, and wisdom. *Journal of Personality and Social Psychology*, 49, 607–627.

Stout, R. J., Cannon-Bowers, J. A., Salas, E., & Milanovich, D. M. (1999). Planning, shared mental models, and coordinated performance: an empirical link is established. *Human Factors*, 41, 61–71.

Suchman, L. A. (1987). *Plans and situated action: the problem of human-machine communications*. Cambridge, UK: Cambridge University Press.

Taleb, N. N. (2007). *The black swan*. New York: Random House.

Tan, F. B., & Gallupe, R. B. (2006). Aligning business and information systems thinking: a cognitive approach. *IEEE Transactions on Engineering Management*, 53, 223–237.

van Wezel, W., Cegarra, J., & Hoc, J. C. (2011). Allocating functions to human and algorithm in scheduling. In J. C. Fransoo, T. Waefler, & J. R. Wilson (Eds.), *Behavioral Operations in Planning and Scheduling* (pp. 339–370). Berlin: Springer-Verlag.

van Woerkum, C. M. J., Aarts, M. N. C., & de Grip, K. (2007). Creativity, planning and organizational change. *Journal of Organizational Change Management*, 20, 847–865.

Volkema, R. J. (1983). Problem formulation in planning and design. *Management Sciences*, 29, 639–652.

Waefler, T. (2001). Planning and scheduling in secondary work systems. In B. MacCarthy & J. Wilson (Eds.), *Human performance in planning and scheduling* (pp. 411–447). London: Taylor & Francis.

Waefler, T. von der Weth, R., Karltun, J. Starker, U., Gärtner, K., Gasser, R., & Bruch, J. (2011). Human control capabilities. In J. C. Fransoo, T. Waefler, & J. R. Wilson (Eds.), *Behavioral operations in planning and scheduling*. London: Springer.

Windischer, A., Grote, G., Mathier, F., Meunier Martins, S., & Glardon, R. (2009). Characteristics and organizational constraints of collaborative planning. *Cognition, Technology & Work*, 11, 87–101.

Young, F. E., & Norris, J. A. (1988). Leadership change and action planning: a case study. *Public Administration Review*, 48, 564–570.

Zwikael, O., Shimizu, K., & Globerson, S. (2005). Cultural differences in project management capabilities: a field study. *International Journal of Project Management*, 23, 454–462.

12

BIASES AS CONSTRAINTS ON PLANNING PERFORMANCE

Dawn L. Eubanks, Daniel Read, and Yael Grushka-Cockayne

Introduction

Organizations plan to anticipate resource needs, set direction, and establish goals to move forward. Plans give us a sense of security that we have a degree of control over the unknowns of the future. However, as we know, "the best laid schemes o' mice an' men / Gang aft agley." The limits of rationality vary by person and situation. Most important of all, consciousness of the limits may in itself alter them (Simon, 1947).

Planning is a broad term that can embrace all future-oriented, goal-directed decision making and decision implementation. There are difficulties associated with planning because it is a complex cognitive activity involving high-stake outcomes. As a result of this complexity, biases may arise. These biases in turn influence the success of organizational planning activities. Following the definition of Hogarth and Makridakis (1981), all plans require that the agent (either the group or individual) considers alternative courses of action (sometimes only one). These are assessed with respect to the degree to which they achieve the agent's objectives and their realism. Realism requires a sufficient implementation procedure and accurate forecasting.

Organizational leaders would like to believe that they are rational decision makers. But, as famously proposed by Herbert Simon (1947), it is unrealistic to treat agents (organizations as well as individuals) as fully rational optimizers (and planners). He proposed that there are restrictions on the capacity of agents to be rational, and that we should treat them as *intendedly* rational, but only *boundedly* so. For Simon, the bounds on rationality are cognitive limitations on knowledge, memory, and imagination. In a famous passage, he made the following contrasts between rationality and the actual capacity of agents (Simon, 1947, pp. 93–94):

1   Rationality requires a complete knowledge and anticipation of the consequences that will follow on each choice. In fact, knowledge of consequences is always fragmentary.
2   Since these consequences lie in the future, imagination must supply the lack of experienced feeling in attaching value to them. But values can be only imperfectly anticipated.
3   Rationality requires a choice among all possible alternative behaviors. In actual behavior, only a few of these possible alternatives ever come to mind.

The relevance of these limitations to organizational planning is very clear. We see these limitations played out again and again as organizations fail to plan accurately, leading to missed deadlines or poorly launched products.

There has been much research showing that the information available to the boundedly rational decision maker is not just a random draw from all relevant information but is likely to be biased in predictable ways. One example of this is the confirmation bias. Information search (and evaluation) is likely to favor the agent's preferred perspective. When evaluating a pet plan, for instance, agents are likely to seek information that favors their plan, and give relatively little weight to information discrediting it (Gavetti & Rivkin, 2005). This is not merely an individual bias, likely to be corrected when the agent is an organization rather than a group, but one that can even be aggravated when organizations are made of team players who value cohesiveness (for instance, in the case of an entire country submitting a bid to host the Olympics).

In this chapter, we consider biases as constraints in the context of organizational planning. Because organizational planning begins with individuals it is important to consider planning constraints at the individual level and in turn how they influence planning at the organizational level. At an individual level, someone concerned about their health, for instance, will plan a diet by considering options such as the grapefruit diet, or the Atkins diet, and then consider how likely they are to be able to stick with them and how quickly they will bring them to the desired waist size or scale measurement. The dieter will then undertake to apply the diet to themselves.

An organization planning to launch a new product will engage in environmental scanning to assess the market and in prototyping to facilitate the comparison of alternative product designs. The organization is likely then to develop a marketing and rollout plan. This plan will be based on assumptions that may or may not be correct because of the complexity of the process. Nonetheless, these plans need to be developed to have a starting point from which to work, to estimate budget and necessary resources, etc.

Although individuals and organizations realize that planning is necessary to anticipate needed resources, organize timeframes, and be prepared for roadblocks, it does not change the fact that planning is difficult and plans often fail. One reason is that the future is uncertain and plans must be enacted in an environment that may be strikingly different from the one in which they were made. This uncertainty, however, is not an a priori barrier to optimal planning, since it is theoretically possible to make plans that are optimal given the distribution of all possible futures. To illustrate, if I know my future will depend on the toss of a fair coin, then I can make a plan that constitutes the best attainable gamble involving the consequences if heads comes up or if tails comes up. Of course, uncertainty about the coin toss means that the outcome of the plan can only be described as a distribution, albeit the best distribution possible ex ante (i.e. before the plan is carried out). The degree of uncertainty and the multitude of decisions made throughout the planning process, make planning subject to the problem of combinatorial explosions, in which the number of possible plans will typically be much greater than is manageable, and likely greater than is even computable. Because people lack the cognitive capacity to juggle so many possibilities, biases may occur when we try to simplify by using heuristics.

An apparently ubiquitous problem is what Kahneman and Tversky called the "planning fallacy" or the tendency for plans to overpromise and under-deliver (Kahneman & Tversky, 1979). Douglas Hofstadter (1979) famously proposed "Hofstadter's law" which is "It always takes longer than you expect, even when you take into account Hofstadter's Law." This is true for everyday individual plans, such as those made to "get all the paperwork done today," and extends to major organizational projects, such as developing a long-range, superefficient and highly innovative aircraft that "responds to the overwhelming preferences of airlines around the world" (Boeing, 2013), and to warfare such as the Afghan conflict (CNN, 2003). Although there are many reasons for the planning fallacy to occur, including motivational biases and even outright deception, we will focus on the role played by cognitive biases.

Bounds to Rational Planning

Limitations on planning are limitations on planners and the institutions in which the planning takes place. Many of these limitations are therefore found throughout human activity and not just in planning. We start by considering the four cognitive biases we suggest have the greatest impact on planning: (1) anchoring, (2) overconfidence, (3) optimism bias, and (4) neglect of others. We next discuss how the initial information presented can influence how we perceive subsequent information and how this in turn influences our plans. We also highlight the cultural values of the organization that can influence what information that is selected and attended to when engaging in planning activities.

Anchoring

Plans involve making judgments about unknown quantities, most notably about the future. These judgments are made in the context of information about the current state of the world (such as macroeconomic indicators and sales figures), and in the context of pre-existing judgments about the future. "Anchoring" is the general principle that this context is a starting point for new judgments, and that these new judgments will tend to gravitate around the old ones. More generally, once an idea is aired, no matter how preliminary it is, it becomes the starting point for subsequent thinking. Organizational planning is therefore prone to path dependence, in that the order in which information is considered can influence the ultimate plan. This is likely to be aggravated if the initial judgments come with some authority, such as when a strong leader states he expects sales to increase by 10 percent next year – in such a situation, it is very likely that once all the data are in, and the "proper" analysis of those data is undertaken, it will turn out that sales will be forecast at around 10 percent over the coming year.

Tversky and Kahneman (1974) provided the first description of this phenomenon, linking it to a judgment rule they called the "anchoring and adjustment" heuristic. When people make point estimates of quantities, they start with existing values, no matter how arbitrary, and then adjust this value based on differentiating knowledge. In one famous study, Ariely, Loewenstein, and Prelec (2003) asked a group of MBA students to state their willingness to pay for six goods, including computer accessories and books. Before giving their willingness to pay, however, the students stated the last two digits of their social security number, and indicated whether they would pay more or less than that amount in dollars. A respondent whose social security number ended with 97, for instance, would first state whether or not they would pay $97 for a bottle of wine, and afterwards state precisely how much they would pay. There was an extremely strong correlation between the social security numbers of the respondents and their willingness to pay for all the goods on offer.

To illustrate the potential effects of anchoring and planning, imagine an organizational planning meeting in which the time to obtain permissions for a new building project are being estimated. One team member hazards a guess that the permissions will be obtained within three months. The whole team recognizes that it will be more than three months, so they immediately start thinking about how much more. Perhaps two months more, perhaps three … Because they have started with the almost arbitrary three-month estimate, however, that value will be heavily weighted in their final estimates. This problem can be exacerbated if the organization is fairly new and has little experience answering the question, or has no specific data that it can point to about past decisions and outcomes.

Anchoring is potentially one of the major causes of planning failures in organizations. Many project planning methods, such as critical path analysis, develop an initial plan that typically becomes the anchor for project expectations, regardless of updates that might surface later. Estimates of, for instance, the time to complete a building may start out optimistic (as we will discuss below) and this optimistic starting point becomes an anchor that is insufficiently adjusted as new information comes in. The initial optimism therefore cascades through the entire planning process even when no further optimism is injected into it.

Anchoring may also be the basis for primacy effects, in which first impressions are overweighed. A job candidate might suffer from a primacy effect if they show up late for an interview but perform exceptionally after that. The view formed by the candidate's lateness can act as an anchor that remains relatively unchanged even as new information is coming in (Highhouse & Gallor, 1997). First impressions can influence the adoption of a plan. If it is first presented by a highly respected (or dubious) person in the organization, then the initial positive (or negative) reaction is likely to influence the evaluation of all subsequent evaluation. This aspect of anchoring is often called a halo effect (e.g. Cooper, 1981; Rosenzweig, 2007).

Closely related to anchoring is what we call *the incumbency effect*, which has further consequences, including status quo bias and strategic inertia. The incumbency effect emerges from the operation of two well-established psychological processes, framing and loss aversion (Tversky & Kahneman, 1991). By loss aversion we mean the tendency to put more weight on advantages relative to disadvantages in decision making. By framing we mean that if two options are compared, with one option designated as the reference point, then changes relative to that reference point are treated as advantages (gains) or disadvantages (losses). Because of loss aversion, the losses are given more weight than the gains, so there is an automatic bias in favor of the reference point option. Typically, the first plan considered, or an initially preferred plan, will start as an incumbent. Alternatives will be considered based on how much better they are than the initial plan (on dimensions where they are better) and how much worse (on dimensions where they are worse). To illustrate, imagine two designs for a new tablet. Design A is more durable, design B has longer battery life. When comparing the two designs, which one is adopted might depend on which is considered first. If A, then the longer battery life of B will be treated as an advantage relative to A, but its reduced durability will be treated as a disadvantage. Design A will be favored in the comparison, in that its durability will receive more weight than if the situation was reversed and B was considered first. This has clear implications in organizational planning because a particular leader may have a vested interest in one characteristic over another and make sure that it is presented first to become the anchoring point. This may then encourage organizations to discount or dismiss external information such as what competitors are doing or what consumers may demand. This is a further example of how the order that something is presented in may influence future decisions and plans that are made by organizations.

Essential for plans to succeed is for them to differ from the status quo and avoid simple strategic inertia. They need to be customized based on skills within organizations. In organizations it is important to be flexible to adjust to changes in the environment and incorporate new innovations. If organizations are aware of some of the pitfalls that can occur because of anchoring, they can think more carefully about how plans are discussed and presented. While it is perhaps over-optimistic to believe that these biases can be eliminated, organizations can at least be mindful of them. Being aware of these biases may allow an organization to realize this limitation and engage in a discussion about anchoring bias that may be occurring and whether the person presenting an initial plan may be exerting an unbalanced influence on future planning.

Overconfidence

Overconfidence is a broad term that has been used in many ways, all of which are relevant to planners. Moore and Healy (2008) distinguish between overestimation, overplacement, and overprecision. Overestimation refers to people's tendency to overestimate their ability, how well they are doing a task, the amount of control they have over the outcome of that task, and the chance of succeeding at it. In situations where the organization is seen as a leader and has experienced few setbacks, there may be an increased likelihood that they experience the overconfidence bias during planning. If organizations have experienced success in the past, they may be more likely to be overconfident in the next instance. Indeed, this is the basis for Roll's (1986) influential account of why mergers and acquisitions so often underperform.

Overplacement means that people typically evaluate themselves as better than they are relative to others, and overprecision is that people are more certain about their beliefs than is warranted. As Moore and Healy point out, these three phenomena are not the same thing, and may not even be closely related empirically, in that the correlation between them is marginal or even quite low. Nonetheless, they are reliable in that the majority of people can be relied upon to overestimate, to overplace themselves and to be overprecise.

Barnes (1984) writes about overconfidence in terms of heuristics. He states that people typically have high levels of confidence about judgments that they make based on heuristics. In experiments conducted by Lichtenstein, Fischhoff, and Phillips (1982) related to individual ability to make accurate judgments, participants were asked to set upper and lower bounds so that there was a 98 percent chance that a true value fell between them. Rather than only 2 percent of the true value falling outside the range, it was between 20 and 50 percent. In the situation of managers making judgments about plans, this overconfidence could cause the planner to misjudge information. When organizational leaders rely on heuristics to make judgments, overconfidence may be increased. While heuristics are necessary when there are vast quantities of information to sift through, being aware of the overconfidence bias that can occur in these instances may help one to consider making different planning decisions.

Perhaps the most troubling aspect of (over)confidence for planners is that confidence is often weakly related to accuracy. That is, confidence in tasks is relatively stable, even when performance varies widely (Kruger & Dunning (1999) give some vivid demonstrations). This leads to the hard/easy effect, which is that overconfidence is greatest the more difficult the task at hand is. Because organizational planning is invariably complex, it is likely that it often falls on the difficult end of the spectrum where overconfidence is highest.

Optimism Bias

A further contributor to the planning fallacy is a general tendency toward optimism, or having unwarranted high expectations about how things will turn out. A vast literature shows it is typical for planners and forecasters to be optimistic, and, of course, plans are chosen and implemented based on these optimistic expectations.

Fildes, Goodwin, Lawrence, and Nikolopoulos (2009) provided an important demonstration of optimism in planning. They were interested in what people will do when given the opportunity to modify statistical forecasts. They analyzed a dataset containing more than 60,000 forecasts and outcomes from supply chain companies. The forecasts were first made by a computerized system and then adjusted by the manager if he or she believed they were inaccurate. The judgmentally adjusted forecasts were, on average, better than the unadjusted forecasts. But this advantage was partly undermined because the average judge's mental adjustment was optimistic, so that upward adjustments in forecasted demand added much less to accuracy than did downward adjustments. In short, while planners and forecasters were quite good at knowing which forecasts should be adjusted, they made excessively optimistic predictions.

Krizan and Windschitl (2007) proposed four reasons for optimism bias. The first is *strategic* optimism, the deliberate choice of an optimistic outlook as a motivational tool and coping mechanism. Strategic optimism is not, strictly speaking, a bias, since it is a kind of "nudge" deployed to achieve a larger goal. The second reason, already mentioned, is confirmation bias. Planners are more likely to generate positive hypotheses about the future, and then search for confirmatory information supporting those hypotheses. The third reason is differential scrutiny of information. Planners overweight evidence that supports optimistic forecasts. The fourth reason is valence priming. By their nature, optimistic hypotheses are likely to lead to the recall of optimistic information. If an organization or leader has experienced many successes, then the quantity of optimistic information will be greater and easier to identify in a search. This may be particularly problematic if a previously successful leader is in a new organization and he/ she recalls many past successes, making decisions and planning based on those rather than fully considering the new context.

Further optimistic biases relate to time estimation. Buehler, Messervey, and Griffin (2005) found that participants underestimated the time it would take them to complete both short laboratory experiments and longer real-world projects. These findings held for both individuals and groups, although groups were even more optimistic. This seemed to be because discussion often revolved around factors promoting successful task completion.

Optimism bias can be enhanced if an organization is trying to promote a positive image. There may be several reasons for this, including desire to appear at the forefront of the market, to attract top employees and investors, to boost sales by inspiring confidence through this positive image. Making planning decisions with the idea of a positive organizational image in mind can lead the organization to become excessively optimistic as they make decisions about the time and resources needed to execute a plan.

Neglect of Others

At every level, the success of a plan depends on other people doing what the plan expects them to do. A plan is likely to rely on at least some of: employees implementing it, regulators accepting it, competitors being unable to respond to it, and customers appreciating it. The behaviors on which the plan is contingent have therefore to be realistic. If it requires employees to accept split shifts, sleepless nights, open-plan offices, or loss of resources then it may be doomed from the very start. Even if employees are on board with the plan, regulators may or may not accept it. It is therefore important to understand protocols and precedence. Not considering how customers or competitors will respond to an action can carry consequences.

Consider, for instance, the case of Pfizer's Exubera (Johnson, 2007), a needle-free inhalable insulin product. The initial idea was that inhaled insulin would be preferred by patients afraid of sticking themselves with needles multiple times a day. The product was predicted to reach $2 billion a year in sales and serve as a game changer for the firm. Pfizer, however, neglected to consider the patients' experience. Exubera proved to be cumbersome and less discreet than needles. It was larger and clumsy to walk around with. Its dosage could not be adjusted as easily as the injected insulin and it carried the risk of lung problems. The failure of the drug, based on misunderstanding patients' reactions, cost Pfizer $2.8 billion.

Competitor neglect can have similarly striking consequences. As an illustration, Simonsohn (2010) examined data from 11,796 eBay auctions for DVDs. He found that the supply of DVDs peaked at a time when the demand for DVDs was relatively low. It appears that sellers launch their auctions without considering when other auctions for identical products are likely to end. When they all end at around the same time, competition is increased and prices depressed. A similar example is the simultaneous launch of multiple, similar gadgets at the same time of year (such as around Christmas), or the release of several films catering to the same audience on the same week-end. Such cases are always accompanied by the recognition, in hindsight, that more consideration of others in the market was required.

Neglect of others can be due to several organizational-level problems, such as a lack of feedback between consumers and organization or a failure to conduct research to identify how elements of the plan may affect consumers or competitors. While larger organizations presumably have research teams in place, such as in the case of Pfizer, they may become blinded to the needs of the consumer. Entrepreneurial organizations may not have the infrastructure in place to have a dedicated research team so the workforce may not be able to conduct a thorough investigation of consumer needs and competitor products. Instead, they may focus attention on regulations and, in turn, neglect others that may be worthy of consideration.

Towards More Effective Plans

Although awareness of cognitive biases may help organizations improve their planning, a great deal of research on debiasing suggests that awareness is not enough (Fischoff, 1981; Larrick, 2004). There are, however, more formal methods that can be used to remove or reduce biases from the planning process. In this section, we discuss three of these methods: case-based planning, reference-class forecasting, and aggregation of diverse opinion (wisdom of crowds). Each method can be used at different levels of formality to support the development of unbiased and robust plans. Case-based planning is a memory-based approach to generating more accurate plans, reference-class forecasting relies on statistical references to past planning instances in order to generate awareness of past accuracy, and aggregating diverse opinions can be utilized for capturing more of the collective wisdom that may exist within a firm.

Case-Based Planning

Case-based planning involves calling on past plans as a basis for current planning. Individuals who encounter a novel situation will reflect back on a familiar case and extract key elements to assist in determining a course of action in the current situation. Analogical reasoning is often needed when matching cases are not available. Many planning biases and errors are due to focusing on the details of the current situation and missing out on the big picture. Case-based planning calls on memory retrieval, which can weaken initial anchors, remind one of the influence of competition, and reduce overconfidence.

An example of case-based planning can be illustrated in the case of moving house. Say you have moved houses before but only within the same town. Because of this, the knowledge struc-ture you have for moving will include elements such as: finding a moving company, forwarding mail, changing address, canceling services and setting them up at new location. Next, imagine that you are relocating to another country. You may refer back to when you moved houses within the same town, but that schema will be incomplete. Not only will memory have faded some of the details that should be considered, you may make assumptions for missing information. For example, timeframes will be different for organizing an international move. Also costs and items allowed to be transported will be different. Relying on this past case can therefore result in inaccuracies in future planning. Individuals with greater expertise in this domain (having moved to many different countries) will have an advantage when engaging in this task again because of the richness of their mental model and superior analogical reasoning.

Hammond (1990) outlined three areas where case-based planning could improve planning: failure avoidance, plan repair, and plan reuse. Experts are important contributors to the planning process because they can reuse the hard reasoning they have used in the past (Kolodner, 1991). This is due to their richer experiences that allow them to select the important parts of a situation to focus on and identify the best cases to work with. Thus they are superior in case-based and analogical reasoning (Kolodner, 1991). Klein, Whitaker, and King (1988) report that using a case-based method is effective when there are many unknowns. This is often the case when engaging in planning activities. Thus, having high levels of expertise will help engage in analogical reasoning when using the case-based method.

It is not only an imperfect memory that can pose a problem for relying on mental models derived from cases during decision making. It could be that a misunderstanding of the business environment has led to incorrect use of a mental model. When considering the use of analogical reasoning processes in decision making, it appears that many individuals have great difficulty in drawing appropriate analogies (Gick & Holyoak, 1983; Markman & Gentner, 1993). Rather than focusing on the deep structural relations, individuals tend to focus on superficial surface features when selecting analogies (Gary, Wood, & Pillinger, 2012). It may be that in more complex situations, individuals are more likely to simply focus on superficial surface features.

Gary and Wood (2011) asked MBA students to use a computer simulation of a product launch that was either low complexity or high complexity. Respondents in the low-complexity condition used more accurate mental models. In addition, complexity was found to impair the development of these mental models. It is noteworthy that their findings demonstrate the importance of accurate mental models of key principles of the deep structure. In sum, this means that participants' stronger performance levels were positively influenced by having more accurate mental models of the relevant causal relationships in the environment. This has implications for organizational leaders trying to engage in planning because there is generally a high degree of complexity and they would therefore likely fall into the trap of using an inaccurate mental model. Experts, however, are more likely than novices to select the "right" model. Thus, identifying ways to improve planners' understanding of the causal relationships in the environment would potentially improve the quality of plans produced.

Decoupling or the ability to manipulate internal representations when there are distractions present is important for hypothetical thinking (Stanovich, 2006). Hypothetical thinking is in turn important for the planning process. One can see that in order for decoupling to occur effectively, one must have a degree of cognitive capacity available. When cognitive overload is present, these manipulations become difficult. Kokis et al. (2002) and Stanovich and West (2000) assert that, over time, these processes can become automatized. This would most certainly be the case with high-level leaders involved in organizational planning.

A successful example of appropriately using the deep structure of case-based knowledge is the incorporation of Botox at the dentist. Some argue that dentists are the perfect group of people to perform Botox injections. Not only are they working in a sterile environment, they have expert knowledge of facial structures and administering injections. In addition, many individuals feel more comfortable having this procedure at a trusted dentist rather than a beauty salon or a dermatologist. This is a clear example of manipulation of internal representations to clearly identify a problem – better dental care leading to fewer dental procedures and diminished treatment of teeth and gums – and generate a solution to broaden offerings at the dentist that complements their skills and expertise.

Reference-Class Forecasting

Planning is often considered a unique affair. It is typically task oriented, aimed at a one-off, distinct set of goals. It is done in a *singular* mode, where assessments are done on the basis of the individual properties of the specific case. Whether planning to write a new research paper or planning the IPO of a new venture, planners typically focus on the specific objectives of an upcoming project, such as its scope or timeline. The planners themselves, however, are common across many planning scenarios and their tendencies (or biases) are likely to determine the effectiveness of the planning in many instances. Reference-class forecasting, or planning using an "outside view" method (Kahneman & Tversky, 1979, Kahneman & Lovallo, 1993) offers an opportunity to reflect on past accuracy and to adjust.

Reference-class forecasting aims to dampen overconfidence and over-optimism, and at the same time provide planners with more comprehensive information concerning past project goal distribution. The approach relies on statistical inference and calls for developing a reference class, or benchmark, of related projects. For the reference group of projects, the distribution of the objectives is then assessed as well as the reliability of the past forecasts. It is at this stage that the forecaster's or planner's track record is examined. Finally, the current project's position within the distribution is determined and the forecasts are adjusted to reflect past over- or underestimation tendencies. The approach builds on lab studies showing that forecasts become significantly more accurate when individuals are asked questions requiring them to take an outside view and to think of past accuracy (Buehler, Griffin, & Preeze, 2010).

Reference-class forecasting has successfully been applied to large public projects in Denmark and the UK. Using predefined templates, organizations are guided to apply an "optimism bias uplift" that adjusts projected costs based on some characteristics of the project (Department for Transport, 2006; Flyvbjerg, 2013). For instance, when estimating the costs associated with building a new train station, the UK Network Rail determines the percentage of uplift (or the size of a cost contingency) based on the length of track, location, contractors, technology, etc.

Lovallo, Clarke, and Camerer (2012) propose a modification to the reference-class forecasting method that combines the benefits of reference-class forecasting and case-based reasoning. They suggest that using a distribution-based reference class, along with similarity-based weighting of each analogous case, can be more accurate than either method separately. They demonstrated the improved accuracy of their hybrid method, which they label similarity-based forecasting, in two domains: judgment of investments by private equity managers and forecasting of movie box-office success.

Wisdom of Crowds

Both case-based planning and reference-class forecasting guide planners to consider past planning instances to improve planning. In addition, organizations can draw on the "wisdom of crowds" (Surowiecki, 2005) and combine the opinions of multiple individuals or experts. It has been shown that aggregating the opinions of independent actors can yield superior results, with such "crowds" often outperforming even the best individuals within the crowd. While individual estimates, even when produced by experts, might include a component of error or bias, averaging those individual estimates yields higher accuracy as errors cancel out (Larrick & Soll, 2006; Lichtendahl, Grushka-Cockayne, & Winkler, 2013; O'Hagan et al., 2006)

The gains to be had from averaging opinions depend on the existence of two factors: diversity and expertise. Experts are better at identifying key constraints than novices, which allows for better plan formulation (Caughron & Mumford, 2008). In software development, the idea of relying on a team of diverse expert developers to produce project goal estimates has been formalized with methods such as Planning Poker, a technique used in agile project environments (Mahnic & Hovelja, 2012; Moløkken-Østvold, Haugen, & Benestad, 2008).

Certain conditions, however, must be present to reap the benefits from group aggregation. One of these is independence of opinion: once individuals start to share information and to discuss it among themselves, new biases emerge. Buehler et al. (2005) find a consistent optimistic bias in predictions based on group input and that group discussions resulted in more optimistic predictions than individual predictions. Plous (1995) found that only pooling techniques (in which the predictions are performed by individuals independently and then averaged to create the pooled prediction) reduced overprecision. Plous (1995) found that neither explicit warnings, providing instructions to expand interval widths, nor extended group discussions, were useful debiasing tools.

Herzog and Hertwig (2009) have suggested that diversity can exist, and be exposed, within a single mind. They propose that planners can enhance their forecasting by averaging their initial estimate with a second one. Asking a group of subjects in the lab to generate a second estimate to a set of date-estimation tasks, they show that there are accuracy gains from obtaining the second estimates. In a follow-up study, Herzog and Hertwig (2013) show that a further nudge to actively contradict an initial estimate yields even further accuracy benefits.

Larrick and Soll (2006) use lab experiments to show, however, that people often prefer to rely on experts, or to "chase the expert," instead of relying on the average of multiple opinions. They suggest that this is due to overconfidence in one's ability to identify experts. Indeed, expertise is sometimes difficult to identify and can be wrongly inferred in cases of extreme luck (Denrell & Fang, 2010). Budescu and Chen (2014) propose a method for identifying a subset of experts in a crowd. Averaging the forecasts of this subset of experts (5–7 experts) is likely to offer the most gains (Budescu & Chen, 2013; Mannes, Soll, & Larrick, 2014).

Conclusion

In summary, we have outlined constraints to planning in organizations that fall within the realm of cognitive biases. These bounds to our rational thinking include biases related to anchoring, overconfidence, optimism, and neglect of others. While this is certainly not an exhaustive list of biases that can place constraints on organizational planning, we focused on these elements as ones that may have the most detrimental impact on the planning processes. Along with identifying planning constraints related to cognitive biases that can hinder accurate planning, we have identified case-based planning, reference-class forecasting, and wisdom of crowds as possible solutions to help to mitigate these constraints. While these three strategies will certainly not eliminate bias, we hope that these possible remedies can help to improve the quality of plans developed in organizations.

Studying biases in planning research is important because decisions must be made all along the way as a plan is developed. If there is a limited understanding of biases, the relevance or value of these decisions made during the planning process should possibly be called into question. While biases are clearly difficult to eliminate, increasing our awareness of them can at a minimum allow us to question whether we have appropriately considered the information presented to us.

While great progress has been made in our understanding of biases that can act as constraints to planning effectiveness, we should note some limitations with this line of research. First, bias studies typically examine a single bias in isolation. While doing so allows us to understand that specific type of bias, it is not how bias occurs in a real business setting. Second, the results of lab research are highly correlated, in the sense that if one of the biases exists, it is more likely that the other biases are in operation too. More studies of both laboratory and field need to be conducted in order to tease apart what may be relevant for a real business planning situation.

These limitations offer ideas for future research in the lab and field to increase our understanding of biases and planning. First, a series of laboratory studies could be conducted to understand how planning biases operate in a multi-level capacity. In essence, it is not simply one individual that is falling culprit to bias. There are group and organizational variables that can either enhance or diminish these biases. Studying how planning works in a class project or lab study where people are formed into groups to develop a plan could help us begin to answer some of these questions. Along these same lines, it is important to consider what domains might be more prone to which types of biases. These results also need to be tested in combination in order to understand the interactive effect. For example, it might be that optimism bias and anchoring bias have an interactive effect. While the majority of research in this area has been conducted in the lab, there is a clear need for research in the field to understand these biases in a more contextualized way. Field studies could encourage companies to engage in case-based planning, reference-class forecasting, or wisdom of crowds in order to identify how these strategies affect planning accuracy. We can also learn from companies that have successfully or unsuccessfully planned by observing and interviewing various individuals in the organization.

From this chapter it is quite apparent that constraints can cause negative outcomes when engaging in planning activities. However, Gigerenzer and Brighton (2009) found that constraints can aid rationality in that they enable decisions to be made and can efficiently eliminate dead ends. In sum, limiting analysis can help us to move forward and progress our plans. While "the best laid schemes … ," with no plan in place, it is difficult to make progress at all.

References

Ariely, D., Loewenstein, G. F., & Prelec, D. (2003). Coherent arbitrariness: Stable demand curves without stable preferences. *Quarterly Journal of Economics*, 118, 73–105.

Barnes, J. H. (1984). Cognitive biases and their impact on strategic planning. *Strategic Management Journal*, 5, 129–137.

Boeing (2013). http://www.boeing.com/boeing/commercial/787family (last accessed January 30, 2015).

Budescu, D. V., & Chen, E. (2014). Identifying expertise and using it to extract the wisdom of crowds. Management Science, published online May 24, http://dx.doi.org/10.1287/mnsc.2014.1909 (last accessed January 30, 2015).

Buehler, R., Messervey, D., & Griffin, D. (2005). Collaborative planning and prediction: Does group discussion affect optimistic biases in time estimation? *Organizational Behavior and Human Decision Processes*, 97, 47–63.

Buehler, R., Griffin, D., & Peetz, P. (2010). Chapter one-the planning fallacy: Cognitive, motivational, and social origins. *Advances in Experimental Social Psychology*, 4, 1–62.

Caughron, J. J., & Mumford, M. D. (2008). Project planning: The effects of using formal planning techniques on creative problem-solving. *Creativity and Innovation Management*, 17, 204–215.

CNN (2003). Rumsfeld: Major combat over in Afghanistan. CNN.com, May, 1. http://edition.cnn.com/2003/WORLD/asiapcf/central/05/01/afghan.combat/ (last accessed January 30, 2015).

Cooper, W. H. (1981). Ubiquitous halo. *Psychological Bulletin*, 90(2), 218–244.

Denrell, J., & Fang, C. (2010). Predicting the next big thing: Success as a signal of poor judgment. *Management Science*, 56(10) 1653–1667.

Department for Transport (2006). *Transport Analysis Guidance (TAG), Unit 3.5.9, The Estimation and Treatment of Scheme Costs*. London: Department for Transport.

Fildes, R., Goodwin, P., Lawrence, M., & Nikolopoulos, K. (2009). Effective forecasting and judgmental adjustments: an empirical evaluation and strategies for improvement in supply-chain planning. *International Journal of Forecasting*, 25, 3–23.

Fischoff, B. (1981). *Debiasing* (No. PTR-1092-81-3). Eugene, OR: Decision Research.

Flyvbjerg, B. (2013). Quality control and due diligence in project management: Getting decisions right by taking the outside view, *International Journal of Project Management*, 31(5), 760–774.

Gary, M. S., & Wood, R. E. (2011). Mental models, decision rules, and performance heterogeneity. *Strategic Management Journal*, 32(6) 569–594.

Gary, M. S., Wood, R. E., & Pillinger, T. (2012). Enhancing mental models, analogical transfer, and performance in strategic decision making. *Strategic Management Journal*, 33, 1229–1246.

Gavetti, G., & Rivkin, J. W. (2005). How strategists really think: tapping the power of analogy. *Harvard Business Review*, 83(4) 54–63.

Gick, M. L., & Holyoak, K. J. (1983). Schema induction and analogical transfer. *Cognitive Psychology*, 15(1) 1–38.

Gigerenzer, G., & Brighton, H. (2009). Homo heuristicus: Why biased minds make better inferences. *Topics in Cognitive Science*, 1, 107–143.

Hammond, K. J. (1990). Case-based planning: A framework for planning from experience. *Cognitive Science*, 14, 385–443.

Herzog, S. M., & Hertwig, R. (2009). The wisdom of many in one mind, improving individual judgments with dialectical bootstrapping. *Psychological Science*, 20(2) 231–237.

Herzog, S. M., & Hertwig, R. (2013). *Think twice, and then: combining or choosing in dialectical bootstrapping?* Max Planck Institute for Human Development, Working paper.

Highhouse, S., & Gallor, A. (1997). Order effects in personal decision making. *Human Performance*, 10(1) 31–46.

Hofstadter, D. R. (1979). *Gödel, Escher, Bach: An eternal golden braid*. New York: Basic Books.

Hogarth, R. M., & Makridakis, S. (1981). Forecasting and planning: An evaluation. *Management Science*, 27(2) 115–138.

Johnson, A. (2007). Insulin flop costs Pfizer $2.8 billion. WSJ.com, October 19, http://online.wsj.com/article/SB119269071993163273.html (last accessed January 30, 2015).

Kahneman, D., & Lovallo, D. (1993). Timid choices and bold forecasts: A cognitive perspective on risk taking. *Management Science*, 39(1) 17–31.

Kahneman, D., & Tversky, A. (1979). Intuitive prediction: biases and corrective procedures. In S. Makridakis and S. C. Wheelwright (Eds.), *TIMS: Studies in management science*, 12, 313–327.

Klein, G., Whitaker, L., & King, J. (1988). Using analogues to predict and plan. In *Proceedings of the DARPA Workshop on Case-Based Reasoning*, volume 1, Ed. J. Kolodner, 224–232. San Mateo, CA: Morgan Kaufmann.

Kokis, J., Macpherson, R., Toplak, M. E., West, R. F., & Stanovich, K. E. (2002). Heuristic and analytic processing: Age trends and associations with cognitive ability and cognitive styles. *Journal of Experimental Child Psychology*, 83, 26–52.

Kolodner, J. L. (1991). Improving human decision making through case-based decision aiding. *AI Magazine*, 12(2) 52–68.

Krizan, Z., & Windschitl, P. D. (2007). The influence of outcome desirability on optimism. *Psychological Bulletin*, 133(1) 95–121.

Kruger, J., & Dunning, D. (1999). Unskilled and unaware of it: how difficulties in recognizing one's own incompetence lead to inflated self-assessments. *Journal of Personality and Social Psychology*, 77(6), 1121–1134.

Larrick, R. P., & Soll, J. B. (2006). Intuitions about combining opinions: misappreciation of the averaging principle. *Management Science*, 52, 111–127.

Larrick, R. P. (2004). Debiasing. In D. J. Koehler & N. Harvey (Eds), *The Blackwell handbook of decision making*. London: Blackwell.

Lichtendahl, K. C., Grushka-Cockayne, Y., & Winkler, R. L. (2013). Is it better to average probabilities or quantiles? *Management Science*, 59(7), 1594–1611.

Lichtenstein, S., Fischhoff, B., & Phillips, L. D. (1982). Evidential impact of base rates. In D. Kahneman, P. Slovic, & A. Tversky (Eds.), *Judgment under uncertainty: Heuristics and biases* (pp. 306–334). New York: Cambridge University Press.

Lovallo, D., Clarke, C., & Camerer, C. (2012). Robust analogizing and the outside view: Two empirical tests of case-based decision making. *Strategic Management Journal*, 33(5) 496–512.

Mahnic, V., & Hovelja, T. (2012). On using planning poker for estimating user stories. *Journal of Systems and Software*, 85(9), 2086–2095.

Mannes, A. E., Soll, J. B., & Larrick, R. P. (2014). The wisdom of select crowds. *Journal of Personality and Social Psychology*, 107(2), 276–200.

Markman, A. B., & Gentner, D. (1993). Structural alignment during similarity comparisons. *Cognitive Psychology*, 25, 431–467.

Moløkken-Østvold, K., Haugen, N. C., & Benestad, H. C. (2008). Using planning poker for combining expert estimates in software projects. *Journal of Systems and Software*, 81(12) 2106–2117.

Moore, D. A., & Healy, P. J. (2008). The trouble with overconfidence. *Psychological Review*, 115, 502–517.

O'Hagan, A. O., Buck, C. E., Daneshkhah, A., Eiser, J. R., Garthwaite, P. H., Jenkinson, D. J., Oakley, J. E., & Rakow, T. (2006). *Uncertain judgements: Eliciting experts' probabilities*. Chichester, UK: John Wiley & Sons.

Plous, S. (1995). A comparison of strategies for reducing interval overconfidence in group judgments. *Journal of Applied Psychology*, 80(4) 443–454.

Roll, R. (1986). The hubris hypothesis of corporate takeovers. *Journal of Business*, 59(2 Part 1), 197–216.

Rosenzweig, P. (2007). Misunderstanding the nature of company performance: The halo effect and other business delusions. *California Management Review*, 49(4) 6–20.

Simon, H. A. (1947). *Administrative behavior*. New York: Macmillan.

Simonsohn, U. (2010). eBay's crowded evenings: Competition neglect in market entry decisions. *Management Science*, 56(7) 1060–1073.

Stanovich, K. E. (2006). Fluid intelligence as cognitive decoupling. *Behavioral and Brain Sciences*, 29, 139–140.

Stanovich, K. E., & West, R. F. (2000). Individual differences in reasoning: Implications for the rationality debate? *Behavioral and Brain Sciences*, 23, 645–665.

Surowiecki, J. (2005). *The wisdom of crowds*. New York: Doubleday.

Tversky, A., & Kahneman, D. (1974). Judgment under uncertainty: Heuristics and biases. *Science*, 185, 1124–1131.

Tversky, A., & Kahneman, D. (1991). Loss aversion in riskless choice. *Quarterly Journal of Economics*, 107, 1039–1061.

13

PLANNING BY LEADERS

Factors Influencing Leader Planning Performance

Michael D. Mumford, Vincent Giorgini, and Logan Steele

Leadership represents a complex form of social performance requiring the timely, and appropriate, exercise of influence over others (Yukl, 2012). As a result of its complexity and interactional nature, a number of models of leadership emergence and leader performance have been proposed (Bass & Bass, 2008). For example, Graen and colleagues (Graen, Novak, & Sommerkamp, 1982; Graen & Uhl-Bien, 1995) have argued that leader performance depends on positive interpersonal exchanges between a leader and his or her followers. Avolio and Gardner (Avolio & Gardner, 2005; Gardner, Avolio, Luthans, May, & Walumbawa, 2005) have argued that leader performance depends on sincerity or authenticity. Bass and colleagues (Bass, 1985; Bass & Avolio, 1990; Bass & Steidlmeir, 1999) have argued that leader performance depends on transformational leadership – idealized influence, inspirational motivation, individualized consideration, and intellectual stimulation.

These and other theories (e.g. House, 1996; Sternberg, 2007; Yukl & Tracey, 1992) of leader performance all have value. By the same token, little is said in these theories about planning. In part, the tendency of leadership scholars to discount the importance of planning may be traced to the nature of the measures commonly used in leadership studies – typically behavioral observation measures. Because leader planning is often not observed by others (Marta, Leritz, & Mumford, 2005), students of leadership tend to discount the importance of planning. In part, however, planning has been seen as a managerial, as opposed to a leadership, phenomenon, resulting in a tendency to discount the importance of planning. As Yukl (2012) points out, however, in organizations, management is a critical aspect of leadership (Fleishman et al., 1992).

As a result of limitations in theory and method, the impact of planning on leader performance has been neglected. In the present effort, however, we will argue that planning is a critical, if not the most critical, influence on leader performance. Subsequently, we will present a model of leader performance (Shipman, Byrne, & Mumford, 2010; Strange & Mumford, 2005) which stresses the importance of planning in leadership performance. We will then consider some of the critical planning operations that contribute to leader performance, along with some of the situational attributes that influence planning performance.

Planning and Leadership

As noted above, leadership involves the effective exercise of interpersonal influence. In organizations, however, the exercise of influence, at least when the exercise of influence is effective, is not purely discretionary. Rather, the exercise of influence is intended to facilitate the attainment of organizational goals (Katz & Kahn, 1978). For leaders, moreover, the exercise of influence requires coordinating, directing, and motivating others to attain these goals (Yukl, 2012). And, the available evidence indicates that planning by leaders is critical to the coordination, direction, and motivation of others when they are asked to work in teams.

In one study along these lines, Weingart (1992) examined group performance in building tinker toy structures under conditions in which task complexity and goal difficulty were manipulated. She found that task complexity and goal difficulty lead to more planning and higher quality planning among group members. In another study along these lines, Weldon, Jehn, and Pradhan (1991) analyzed the content of group discussions. They found that planning mediated the impact of goal setting and goal difficulty on group performance, with planning contributing to the attainment of difficult goals. In still another study along these lines, Mehta, Feild, Armenakis, and Mehta (2009) asked teams to work on a business simulation exercise where team planning was measured through team members' self-reports of planning activities. They found that team planning was positively related ($r = 0.34$) to subsequent team performance.

Although teams can plan on their own, in organizations, leaders are typically charged with ensuring that teams have plans that allow coordination of team members' actions in achieving difficult goals. In the seminal work of Fleishman (1953), leadership behaviors were observed as groups worked on various tasks. A subsequent factoring of these behaviors revealed two key dimensions: consideration and initiating structure. Initiating structure, of course, implies planning on the part of leaders. And, in keeping with the findings of the value of planning for team performance, in a meta-analytic study, Piccolo et al. (2012) found that follower perceptions of leader effectiveness were positively related ($r = 0.30$) to initiating structure by leaders.

Somewhat more direct evidence pointing to the impact of planning on leader performance has been provided in a study by Marta, Leritz, and Mumford (2005). In this study, 55 teams of undergraduates were asked to work on a business restructuring task calling for formation of a plan to turn around a failing automotive company. Prior to starting work on this task, the planning skills of participants were assessed – identification of key causes, identification of restrictions, identification of downstream consequences, opportunistic implementation, and environmental scanning as measured through performance on a set of business planning cases. The restructuring plans produced by teams were appraised for quality and originality. It was found that the teams producing the highest quality and most original restructuring plans were directed by leaders, leaders identified through peer nomination, who evidenced substantial planning skills. These planning skills, moreover, were found to be particularly important to group performance as task complexity, turbulence (manipulated through change events), and diversity of ideas increased, with these planning skills influencing the effectiveness of leader structuring behavior. Thus, leader planning skills appear critical to good performance, especially when groups are working on complex tasks in turbulent environments where multiple approaches are available.

If leader planning is critical to effective structuring behavior and team performance, one would expect leaders not to delegate planning, but, instead, to view planning activities as important. In fact, in interviews with leaders of research and development teams, Hemlin (2009) found that leaders viewed planning as a critical activity and were unlikely to delegate key planning activities. Similarly, Globerson and Zwikael (2002) surveyed 282 project managers who were asked to rate the intensity with which they engaged in various job activities – for example, project plan development, cost budgeting, and risk analysis. It was found that planning activities required greater intensity of involvement for leaders than virtually all other activities. Thus, leaders appear to see planning as a critical aspect of their jobs in organizations.

Vision

Vision and Leadership

Our foregoing observations indicate that team performance depends on planning, and, in organizations, leaders influence team planning through structuring behavior – the effect of which depends on leader planning skills. Indeed, leaders recognize the importance of these planning activities, investing effort and, at times, refusing to delegate planning responsibilities. To students of leadership, however, these activities are held to reflect routine leader behavior (Bass, 1985). As a result, the question arises as to how plans are involved in exceptional incidences of leader performance. Broadly speaking, the answer to this key question may be found in the concept of vision.

Theories of charismatic (Conger & Kanungo, 1998; House, 1977) and transformational (Bass, 1985; Bennis & Nanus, 1985) leadership hold that leaders exert influence over followers through articulation of an image of an idealized future or a vision. This image of an idealized future proves to be a powerful influence on followers as a result of five mechanisms. First, the vision articulated by a leader results in followers personally identifying with that vision (Shamir, House, & Arthur, 1993). Personal identification with the vision being articulated by a leader gives rise to intrinsic motivation to act on this vision and results in appraisal of self-efficacy and self-esteem being based on these vision-relevant actions. That is, the vision influences the affective reactions of others. Second, the investment of the individual in a leader's vision results in followers modeling their behavior on the leader (Conger & Kanungo, 1998). Third, with personal investment in the leader's vision and modeling, followers actively seek rewards from and recognition by the leader (Yukl, 2012). Fourth, the leader's vision provides direction and structure for the behavior of followers (Mumford, 2006). Fifth, the structuring and investment of multiple followers in the leader's vision results in social reinforcement and contagion of affect, which serves to reinforce the leader's vision through social exchange (Bono & Illies, 2006).

As one might expect based on these multiple mechanisms of influence, the vision articulated by leaders has been found to be a powerful influence on follower performance. For example, Kirkpatrick and Locke (1996), in an experimental study, used actors to simulate behaviors linked to two key aspects of charisma – visioning and an expressive communication style. They found that both visioning and an expressive communication style had a strong impact on follower performance. Moreover, the impact of vision on follower performance appeared to result from followers setting more difficult goals and acquiring greater self-confidence with respect to the attainment of these goals. In another study along these lines, Sosik, Kahai, and Avolio (1999) manipulated statements made by confederate leaders as business students worked on an electronic brainstorming task. They found that visionary statements evidenced by confederate leaders resulted in greater follower motivation.

Other research, using measures of charismatic and transformational leadership, has examined the impact of visioning on performance in field settings. For example, Lowe, Kroeck, and Sivasubramaniam (1996) conducted a meta-analysis of 39 studies examining the impact of transformational leadership, a leadership style where vision is considered a critical component. They found that visioning was related, strongly related ($r = 0.40$), to various aspects of leader performance such as follower appraisals, team processes, and team production. In still another study along these lines, Rosing, Frese, and Bausch (2011) conducted a meta-analysis of various studies examining the impact of transformational leadership, and thus vision articulation, on follower innovation. They found that when senior leaders evidenced stronger visions, as reflected in appraisals of transformational behavior, greater innovation was observed among followers – with relationships on the order of 0.35 being obtained.

Not only have experimental and field studies provided evidence of the impact of vision on leader performance, studies using historiometric and qualitative methods have also provided support for the significance of leaders' visions. For example, Bennis and Nanus (1985) conducted interviews with 60 senior corporate leaders and 30 senior public sector leaders. They found that although senior leaders did not often make emotional appeals, all leaders articulated a vision for their organization. Moreover, in decision making, decisions were made with respect to the vision being articulated by the leader. Similarly, Roberts (1985) conducted a qualitative study of a successful educational leader. Analysis of news articles, participant observation, and interviews indicated that the success of this educational leader was to a large extent based on formation of a strategic vision for the organization.

Analysis of historically notable leaders has also pointed to the importance of vision. For example, Ellis (2001), in his historical analysis of George Washington, found that a vision he formulated during the Revolutionary War influenced not only his leadership as president of the United States but also the guiding structure he left to the United States after his two terms as president. Similarly, Mumford (2006) conducted a historiometric analysis of 120 historically notable leaders – Franklin Roosevelt, Winston Churchill, Dwight Eisenhower. He found that leaders' vision influenced the style and success of their leadership activities. Other work by Hunter, Cushenbery, Thoroughgood, Johnson, and Ligon (2011) has produced similar findings for a more routine form of leadership – football coaches.

Vision and Planning

Taken as a whole, the studies reviewed above, studies employing experimental, field, qualitative, and historic methods, all indicate that vision is, in fact, a critical, if not *the* critical component of effective leadership. Although these studies have provided ample evidence for the impact of vision on leader performance, they have not addressed a crucial issue. Where do visions come from? This issue has been addressed in a series of studies by Mumford and his colleagues (Ligon, Hunter, & Mumford, 2008; Mumford, Friedrich, Caughron, & Byrne, 2007; Mumford & Mecca, in press; Strange & Mumford, 2002, 2005) – all studies that suggest planning underlies vision formation. This is thus the focal point of this chapter.

The model of leader vision formation proposed by Mumford (Mumford, 2006; Mumford, Friedrich, Caughron, & Byrne, 2007) assumes that to envision a future for a team or organization, leaders must be able to engage in mental simulation. In other words, leaders must mentally simulate a desired future and paths to attaining this future. The need for leaders to engage in mental simulation of a projected future and paths to attaining this future, in turn, implies that planning underlies vision formation. In fact, prior studies by Anzai (1984), Noice (1991), and Xiao, Milgram, and Doyle (1997) all indicate that plans, like vision, are based on mental simulations of the future.

Visions, however, are not necessarily equivalent to plans as they are typically understood. Typically, it is assumed that plans are formulated with the attainment of specific goals in given, known, situations (Scholnick & Friedman, 1993). In vision formation, however, the vision, or plan, formulated is not bound to a specific goal. Instead, the formation of a vision is held to depend on sensemaking (Weick, 1995) or the construction of a mental model that allows people to understand performance requirements in complex, novel, dynamic situations (Rouse & Morris, 1986). Sensemaking in the case of leaders is, in turn, held to arise as people attempt to respond to crisis situations.

Some support for the importance of crises, either personal or organizational, in vision formation has been provided in a study by Bligh, Kohles, and Meindl (2004), who analyzed rhetorical language evident in President George W. Bush's speeches before and after the 9/11 attack on the World Trade Center. They found that charisma, and presumably vision, increased following this crisis event. In another study, Hunt, Boal, and Dodge (1999) asked undergraduates to work on a university strategic planning task. As students worked on this task, a sense of crisis was induced by unexpectedly reducing time to complete the task or by adding material to the task. It was found that under crisis conditions, confidence in the leader, follower performance, and attributed charisma were greater when leaders articulated a viable vision.

Crises induce a need for sensemaking because a crisis situation presents a novel, complex, high-risk/high-reward problem. High stakes change events, require leaders to make sense of, or attain an understanding of, the origins of the crisis to provide a framework for guiding subsequent action. The leaders' articulation of their understanding of the crisis provides a structure for followers' understanding of the crisis, thereby reducing stress, clarifying the origins of the crisis, identifying the goals applying to the crisis situation, and providing a framework in which followers coordinate actions. In keeping with this observation, Drazin, Glynn, and Kazanjian (1999), in a study of various crises arising in the development of a new airplane, found that leader sensemaking was a critical influence on both crisis resolution and the success of this new product development effort. The basis for sensemaking, and thus the formation of viable visions by leaders, is held to lie in the mental models leaders use to understand crises (Johnson-Laird, 1999).

This observation, in turn, provided the basis for Mumford's (Strange & Mumford, 2002; Mumford, Friedrich, Caughron, & Byrne, 2007) model of leader vision formation. This model holds that crisis events are identified through scanning of the internal and external environment (Ford & Gioia, 2000) with respect to key diagnostics of change embedded in monitoring models (Isenberg, 1986). With identification of a potential change event, leaders will begin gathering information to determine the nature and significance of this change (Gioia & Thomas, 1996). The nature of the information sought, and interpretation of the significance of this information, is held to be based on the descriptive mental models employed by leaders (Isenberg, 1986). These descriptive mental models serve to identify causes affecting relevant goals as they operate in a complex system of relationships (Rouse & Morris, 1986).

This descriptive mental model, along with the causes and goals implied by it, serve to activate relevant cases or available incidents of experiential knowledge. Activation of these cases is noteworthy, in part, because the available evidence indicates that plan formation is typically founded in analysis of available case-based or experiential knowledge (Mumford, Schultz, & Van Doorn, 2001). Cases are commonly held to be stored in a library structure indexed to critical diagnostics, or to tags with prototypic cases, which are activated along with major exceptions to these case prototypes. Cases, however, are complex knowledge structures incorporating information about actors, actions, causes, resources, restrictions, contingencies, goals, actor affect, and systems outcomes. As a result, analysis of a limited number of cases, typically the most highly activated cases, is used to formulate a prescriptive mental model or a model for acting with respect to the crisis at hand.

The prescriptive mental model formulated by a leader is noteworthy because it provides a basis for forecasting or predicting the downstream effects of various actions that might be taken to address the crisis. Evaluation of the forecasted effects of various actions is influenced by the leaders' reflection on their past lives and reflection on the demands made by the social system with respect to their actions. Indeed, self-reflection and systems reflection have been found to be significant influences on leader evaluation, including presumably evaluation of forecasts, in a number of studies (Yukl, 2012). Based on evaluation, leaders then formulate a plan of action along with backup plans needed to take into account various contingencies (Isenberg, 1986). These plans and backup plans are integrated into a vision prescribing how the leader understands the crisis situation (Strange & Mumford, 2005). With articulation of this vision, and social feedback, the vision held to underlie charismatic or transformational leadership emerges (Strange & Mumford, 2002).

This model of the leader vision formation process suggests that leader visions are based on plans. However, leaders' visions can be, and should be, viewed as overarching frameworks guiding the formation of more specific plans, either plans formulated by the leader or plans formulated by the followers. These plans, or global understanding of crises, that provide a basis for vision formation, however, depend on attributes not commonly of concern in other discussions of planning – for example, crises, self-reflection, and systems reflection. Moreover, the effectiveness of a plan and the resulting vision will depend on dissemination of that vision among followers and followers' identification with and investment in it. Nonetheless, the fact that visions arise from plans, and normative components of planning, for example forecasting, analysis of experience, and analysis of causes and goals (Mumford, Schultz, & Osburn, 2002; Mumford, Schultz, & Van Doorn, 2001), suggests that leader vision formation may be viewed as a special case of planning, where plans provide a basis for vision formation – visions which structure, motivate, and integrate followers' responses to crises.

Support for the Model

In an initial attempt to test this model of leader vision formation, Strange and Mumford (2005) asked 202 undergraduates to assume the role of principal of a new experimental secondary school. They were to prepare a plan for leading this school and write a speech, a vision statement, to be given to students, parents, and teachers. Students, parents, and teachers evaluated these speeches for emotional impact, perceived utility, and quality and originality. Prior to preparing their speeches, manipulations were made through email requests sent by a consulting firm. One manipulation presented good or poor case models. Another manipulation asked participants to identify key goals, key causes, both key goals and key causes, or neither key goals nor key causes. The third manipulation asked participants to reflect, or not reflect, on their personal experiences in high school. The findings obtained indicated that reflection on goals when poor models were presented or reflection on causes when good models were presented resulted in production of stronger vision statements. Moreover, these effects became more pronounced when participants were asked to reflect on their prior experiences. Thus, the Strange and Mumford (2005) study indicates that vision formation depends on analysis of goals and causes as well as self-reflection.

Another implication of this model of leader formation is that vision formation is founded in case-based or experiential knowledge. A recent study by Barrett, Vessey, and Mumford (2011), again employing Strange and Mumford's (2005) educational leadership task, examined the use of case-based knowledge in vision formation. In this study, participants' (193 undergraduates) use of associational, schematic or conceptual, and case-based knowledge was assessed by judges as reflected in their written plans and vision statements. It was found that the strongest plans and vision statements, as reflected in their affective impact, perceived utility, quality, originality, and elegance, were produced by those who used case-based, or experiential, knowledge in plan formation and visioning, as reflected in speech preparation. Thus, in accordance with this model, it does appear that leader vision formation is founded in the use of case-based knowledge. Other work by Scott, Lonergan, and Mumford (2005) and Vessey, Barrett, and Mumford (2011) points to a similar conclusion.

Still another implication of this model of leader planning and vision formation is that forecasting would prove critical to leader planning and vision formation. To assess the impact of forecasting on leader planning and vision formation, Shipman et al. (2010) again presented the Strange and Mumford (2005) vision formation task and obtained ratings of affective impact, perceived utility, and the quality, originality, and elegance of the visions provided in speeches. As participants (252 undergraduates) worked on this task, they received emails from the consulting firm asking them to forecast, think about what would happen after they had formulated their plan. These forecasts were evaluated by judges with respect to 21 potential attributes of forecasts (e.g. number of positive outcomes, resources forecast, timeframe of forecasts). Factor analysis yielded four dimensions: (1) forecasting resources, (2) extensiveness of forecasting, (3) forecasting negative outcomes, and (4) timeframe of forecasts. It was found that the quality, originality, and elegance of vision statements, as well as their perceived utility and affective impact, was positively related to forecasting extensiveness ($\bar{r} = 0.35$) and use of longer timeframes ($\bar{r} = 0.20$). Moreover, these relationships were stronger than those obtained from traditional individual difference measures such as intelligence and divergent thinking.

A final key proposition of Mumford and colleagues' (e.g. Mumford, Friedrich, Caughron, & Byrne, 2007) model of vision formation is that the formation of viable visions and plans will be based on the prescriptive and descriptive mental models used by leaders. The effects of mental models on leader performance have been examined in a study by Marcy and Mumford (2010). In this study, participants were asked to assume the role of a university president and work on a simulation exercise with the goal of improving educational quality. Prior to working on this task, however, participants were exposed to an instructional program intended to provide training in how to illustrate their mental models of the university. The quality of these mental models was assessed vis-à-vis a comparison to underlying system structure. It was found that mental model quality was positively related to both game performance and adaptability of game performance.

The impact of mental models on leader planning and vision formation is noteworthy for another reason. Mumford (2006) has argued that mental models may be formulated in a variety of ways. For example, one might frame mental models based on the future (charismatic leaders), the present (pragmatic leaders), or the past (ideological leaders). Alternatively, mental models may stress people as causes (charismatic leaders), situations as causes (ideological leaders), or interactions among people and situations (pragmatic leaders). In a series of studies (Bedell-Avers, Hunter, and Mumford, 2008; Bedell-Avers, Hunter, Angie, Eubanks, and Mumford, 2009; Hunter, Bedell-Avers, and Mumford, 2009; Hunter et al., 2011; Ligon et al., 2008; Mumford, 2006), it was shown that charismatic, ideological, and pragmatic leadership styles exist, styles based on leaders' mental models, and that these stylistic differences give rise to differential problem-solving performance, differential patterns of leader interactions, and differential patterns of leader performance.

When the findings obtained in these studies are considered in light of the findings emerging in other studies of scanning (Ford & Gioia, 2000), information gathering (Isenberg, 1986), and crises (e.g. Hunt, Boal, & Dodge, 1999), it seems reasonable to conclude that Mumford and colleagues' (e.g. Mumford, Friedrich, Caughron, & Byrne, 2007; Mumford & Mecca, in press; Strange & Mumford, 2002) model of the vision formation process and the basis of vision formation in planning or the mental simulation of future actions, is, in fact, plausible. Of course, not all variables, or variable linkages, implied by this model have, at this juncture, been explicitly tested. Nonetheless, the evidence available at this point does suggest this model is plausible. Moreover, the model indicates that the critical attribute of leader performance visioning is ultimately based on a form of planning – non-goal-specific planning where leaders envision a potential future. This model, however, is noteworthy because it also points to some of the variables that might influence leaders' planning and vision formation.

Influences on Vision Formation

Individual Influences

Given the nature of Mumford and colleagues' model (e.g. Mumford, Friedrich, Caughron, & Byrne, 2007; Mumford & Mecca, in press; Strange & Mumford, 2002) of vision formation and the nature of the cognitive processing operations underlying planning and vision formation, one would expect that cognitive abilities would influence performance. In fact, Barrett, Vessey, and Mumford (2011) and Vessey, Barrett, and Mumford (2011) have provided evidence indicating that effective execution of these processes is positively related to intelligence and divergent thinking. Although intelligence and divergent thinking influence planning and vision formation, the magnitude of these relationships ($\bar{r} = 0.35$) indicates that other attributes will also influence planning and vision formation.

One variable that appears to be of some importance in this regard is leaders' skill in working with various types of information in planning and vision formation. In an initial study along these lines, Marcy and Mumford (2007, 2010) developed a set of self-paced instructional modules for improving peoples' skills in causal analysis. These instructional modules described a set of seven skills contributing to causal analysis – for example, think about causes that have large effects, think about causes that have direct effects, and think about causes that affect multiple outcomes. After describing each strategy in the form of one block of instruction followed by feedback, another block of instruction described its impact on performance. Two later blocks then provided people with practice applying this strategy. Marcy and Mumford (2007, 2010) found that this training resulted in the formation of stronger mental models underlying leader sensemaking and vision formation, which proved particularly useful when the performance task was complex. Moreover, training in causal analysis strategies contributed to overall game performance on the leadership simulation exercise used in the Marcy and Mumford (2010) study.

Of course, causes are not the only material people must analyze when executing these processing operations. For example, people must analyze goals. They must also analyze the cases activated as a basis for plan construction and vision formation. Accordingly, Vessey, Barrett, and Mumford (2011) employed Marcy and Mumford's (2010) approach to strategy training. In this study, however, in addition to training people in strategies for working with causes, they were also trained in strategies for working with contingencies (e.g. can this contingency be manipulated?), resources (e.g. how important is this resource?), restrictions (e.g. can the effects of this restriction be minimized?), actors (e.g. how large an effect will this actor have?), goals (e.g. how are goals interrelated?), and systems (e.g. what aspects of the social system might be changed?). Following training, participants (170 undergraduates) were asked to provide solutions to leadership problems where judges assessed attributes of vision (e.g. reputation) and solution quality, originality, and elegance. It was found that training in strategies for working with various aspects of case-based knowledge resulted in the production of better problem solutions and stronger visions. Thus the strategies people employ in working with different aspects of case-based knowledge, and their skill in employing these strategies, contributes to planning and vision formation.

In addition to strategies tied to working with specific aspects of case-based knowledge, one might also ask whether metacognitive strategies might contribute to planning and vision formation. Some initial clues about relevant metacognitive strategies have been provided in a recent study by Antes and Mumford (2012). In this study, 200 undergraduate participants were asked to assume the role of leader of an educational technology firm and prepare a plan and vision statement. The plans and vision statements were evaluated by judges for quality, originality, elegance, affective impact, and perceived utility. Prior to preparing their plans and vision statements, however, participants were given instructions to think about either positive or negative outcomes and to think about steps either to achieve success or to avoid failure. It was found the strongest plans and vision statements were obtained either when people thought about negative outcomes and steps for attaining success or when people thought about positive outcomes and steps for avoiding failure. Thus metacognitive strategies, in this case a balanced approach to planning and vision formation, can apparently contribute to leader performance. By the same token, however, the findings obtained by Antes and Mumford (2012) raise the question as to what other metacognitive strategies might contribute to leader planning and vision formation.

Another implication of Mumford and colleagues' (e.g. Mumford, Friedrich, Caughron, & Byrne, 2007; Mumford & Mecca, in press; Strange & Mumford, 2002) model of planning and leader vision formation, is that planning and vision formation are resource intensive. Thus Antes and Mumford (2012) found that when people exhibited cognitive fatigue, the viability of plans and leader visions declined. In this regard, however, it should be recognized that a variety of other variables might also cause people to fail to invest sufficient resources in process execution – for example, interest and motivation (Kanfer, 1994).

Shipman and Mumford (2011) examined one variable that might be of some importance with regard to leaders' planning and vision formation. In this study, participants (159 undergraduates) were asked to work on Strange and Mumford's (2005) vision formation task. The resulting plans, and speeches reflecting the participants' vision for leading this experimental secondary school, were appraised by judges for affective impact, perceived utility, quality, originality, and elegance. In a consultant's email, participants were presented with a set of prompt questions bearing on their confidence in their plans. Responses to these prompts were coded by judges and judges' ratings were factored. Two dimensions of overconfidence emerged – failing to see deficiencies and expecting positive outcomes. More centrally, it was found that failure to see deficiencies was negatively related to vision quality and the quality of leaders' plans. These relationships, of course, reflect the negative effects of overconfidence on people's willingness to invest resources in complex cognitive operations such as those required of leaders in planning and vision formation.

The impact of resource investment on planning and vision formation by leaders also raises the question as to whether personality might also prove to be a noteworthy influence. Although personality has not been found to be a strong, or consistent, predictor of planning performance in general (Mumford, Schultz, & Van Doorn, 2001), the Shipman and Mumford (2011) study indicated that certain personality variables may prove of greater importance when *leader* planning and vision formation are of concern. Although the plans and vision statements formulated by people in this leadership role were not strongly influenced by the standard, Big Five, personality characteristics (conscientiousness, openness, agreeableness, neuroticism, and extraversion), two more specific variables, self-esteem and narcissism, were found to exert stronger effects. Of course, self-esteem encourages people to invest resources in complex demanding activities (Bandura, 1976) such as those involved in leader planning and vision formation. Notably, narcissism may result in both overconfidence and failure to formulate plans taking into account the needs and actions of others. Accordingly, select, task-specific, personality characteristics may prove of greater value in accounting for leader planning and vision formation than has proven to be the case in other studies of planning.

Personality is often of interest because it is assumed to at least partially, along with heredity, reflect action preferences arising as a function of past experience. Past experience, however, can be expected to exert a stronger effect on leader planning and vision formation for three reasons. First, prior experience provides people with case-based knowledge – knowledge which provides the basis for planning and vision formation. Second, prior experience provides the background underlying the formation of the descriptive mental models used as a basis for planning. Third, prior experience influences the diagnostics considered in appraising change. As a result, there is reason to suspect that concrete life experience may represent a significant influence on leaders' planning and vision formation (Mumford, Marks, Connelly, Zaccaro, & Reiter-Palmon, 2000).

The impact of life experience on leader planning activities and vision formation has been investigated in a study by Ligon, Hunter, and Mumford (2008). In this study, the actions of 120 historically notable leaders, all of whom had formulated viable visions and plans, were examined. Based on their behavior during their period at the pinnacle of power, these leaders were classified as charismatic, ideological, or pragmatic and personalized or socialized. Subsequently, valid academic biographies were obtained for these leaders. The early career chapters included in these biographies were coded with respect to key developmental event type (McAdams, 2001): (1) originating events, (2) anchoring events, (3) analogous events, (4) turning point events, (5) redemptive events, and (6) contaminating events. Moreover, judges rated these events with respect to attributes of thematic content – injustice, power motives, negative view of others, exposure to diversity, and spirituality, among other dimensions. Moreover, performance criteria, for example social contributions, institutions established, and initiation of mass movements, were drawn from summary chapters. It was found that exposure to certain types of life events distinguished charismatic (e.g. turning point events more common), ideological (e.g. anchoring events more common), and pragmatic (e.g. originating events more common) leaders. More centrally, it was found that subsequent leader performance, based on the vision being articulated by the leader, was tied to events which inculcated a concern for others. Thus leaders must learn, and learn by experience, the value of thinking for and about others as they formulate plans and visions.

Situational Influences

Mumford and colleagues' (e.g. Mumford, Friedrich, Caughron, & Byrne, 2007; Mumford & Mecca, in press; Strange & Mumford, 2002) model of leader vision formation and planning is inherently an interactional model. Thus, it is assumed that visions emerge from plans based, in part, on social feedback from followers. Although studies examining how follower feedback influences leader planning and vision formation are not available, a number of studies have examined situational influences on leader planning and vision formation. These situational influences might be described broadly as demand-relevant influences and task-relevant influences.

Demand Influences

The description of leader planning and vision formation provided above leads to a straightforward conclusion: leader planning and vision formation are cognitively demanding. Cognitive demand arises from both the number of processes involved in leader planning and the processing demands made by these processes. Although leaders might seek to minimize demand by employing various simplification heuristics (for example, forming plans based on only one readily accessible case; Nutt, 1984), the demands made by leader planning processes suggest that situational variables which "enable processing" will influence planning performance.

Some rather direct evidence bearing on this point has been provided by Barrett, Vessey, and Mumford (2011). As noted earlier, participants in this study were asked to work on Strange and Mumford's (2005) secondary school leadership task. The resulting plans and vision statements were evaluated by judges for affective impact, perceived utility, quality, originality, and elegance. In this study, however, manipulations were made in time pressure by giving fixed completion times 30 percent below typical completion times versus allowing students to work at their own pace. Additionally, threat, or potential risk, was manipulated by adjusting, or not adjusting, the scenario to describe potential negative consequences for students, the school, and the community if the leader's plans did not prove effective.

The findings obtained by Barrett et al. (2011) indicated that time pressure resulted in production of weaker plans and vision statements. Thus, by reducing leader investment in process execution, time pressure resulted in poorer planning performance and vision statements. Threat, however, did not disrupt performance but instead caused people to focus on social information bearing on the constituencies under threat. Thus, the focus of leader planning and vision formation is influenced by threat, although planning performance is not disrupted. Similar conclusions emerged in another study by Vessey et al. (2011), where it was found that threat encouraged leaders to focus on the facts in planning and vision formation. However, if leaders do not have the time or resources required for process execution, planning performance and vision formation suffers.

A similar conclusion emerged from a study conducted by Antes and Mumford (2012), who developed a seven-item self-report questionnaire to measure cognitive fatigue under the assumption that fatigue, like time pressure, would reduce the resources invested in process execution. They administered this measure in their study in which participants were to provide plans and vision statements to be evaluated for affective impact, perceived utility, quality, originality, and elegance by judges. It was found that cognitive fatigue was negatively related ($r = -0.20$) to the production of viable plans and vision statements. Thus, fatigue, like time pressure, by reducing resource investment, acts to undermine leader planning and vision formation. Accordingly, it appears that tired, stressed, and pressured leaders are unlikely to produce viable plans and effective vision statements.

Of course, one way to manage the effects of pressure and fatigue is to give leaders time away from normal job demands when they are engaged in planning and vision formation. Another strategy that might prove of some value in this regard is suggested in a study conducted by Shipman et al. (2010). In this study, again employing Strange and Mumford's (2005) vision formation task, undergraduates were asked to formulate a plan and vision statement for leading an experimental secondary school with these being evaluated for affective impact, perceived utility, quality, originality, and elegance. Crucially, prior to preparing their plans and vision statements, participants were presented with three cases where they were asked to think about either the facts of the case or the implications of the case. Moreover, in working though this material, they were instructed to think about either goals or causes of goal attainment. It was found that the strongest plans and vision statements were obtained when people thought about the implications of cases. Thus, actions which encourage leaders to focus on more critical aspects of process execution may reduce demand and improve leader planning and vision formation.

Task Influences

Although the availability of cognitive resources, and effective use of available cognitive resources, apparently contributes to leader planning and vision formation, the nature of the task on which leaders are working also appears to be a noteworthy influence. Prior studies (e.g. Dean & Sharfman, 1996; O'Hara & Payne, 1998) have indicated that people are willing to invest resources in planning only when the task at hand is relatively demanding. In organizations, two key conditions act to increase the demands imposed by planning – complexity of the planning task and the amount of turbulence.

The impact of task complexity and turbulence on leader planning has been examined in a study by Marta et al. (2005). In this study, participants were asked to work in three- or four-person teams to formulate plans for turning around a failing automotive company. These plans were evaluated by judges for quality and originality. As noted earlier, it was found that leaders' planning skills were the critical influences on team performance. Notably, however, the complexity of the planning task was increased by providing additional information about the automotive company. Turbulence, or change, was induced later by providing, or by not providing, additional information about competitors after teams had worked on the planning task for 10 to 15 minutes. Idea diversity was assessed by appraising the range of preferred plans within groups. It was found that better quality and more original plans were produced when the planning task was more complex and more ideas were available for producing a viable plan. Thus, complexity of the task, or complexity of the work group, apparently contributes to effective planning by leaders, presumably because complexity encourages leaders to invest resources in planning.

Complexity of the work task and work team, however, are not the only variables that cause leaders to invest in planning. Caughron and Mumford (2012) asked undergraduate participants to work on a middle management leadership task involving formulating a plan for improving sales in a mid-size manufacturing firm. Notably, however, as individuals formed their plans, material was presented in which participants were told that personal contingencies (e.g. demotion) were likely to result from the success of their plan or, alternatively, that they were simply expected to spend time working on their plan. It was found that when the planning task had negative individual consequences attached, sensemaking, or vision formation, as evident in their plans, declined. Thus, leader planning performance appears to decline when negative contingencies are attached to their work. Thus, overly tight, negative evaluations of plans may result in a decline in investment of resources in planning processes as leaders spend more time contemplating personal contingencies.

A final task contingency that appears to influence the intensity and effectiveness of planning and vision formation is based on the role ascribed to a person. As noted earlier, the available evidence indicates that planning is considered critical for people in leadership roles (e.g. Globerson & Zwikael, 2002). Thus, one would expect that when people see themselves as adopting a leadership role, greater attention would be given to planning. Some support for this observation has been provided in a study by Bedell-Avers, Hunter, and Mumford (2008). In this study, participants were asked to formulate plans for solving various leadership problems, where judges appraised the plans provided for quality and originality. Notably, however, prior to starting work on this task, participants were either instructed, or not instructed, to adopt a leadership role. It was found that activation of a leadership role diminished performance on some types of problems (e.g. participation problems) but increased performance on other types of problems (e.g. initiating structure problems) where planning is seen as critical. Thus, these findings suggest that adoption of a leadership role may encourage more planning, albeit potentially at the cost of other aspects of leadership, such as encouraging participation (Fleishman et al., 1992).

Conclusions

Our foregoing observations point to a noteworthy limitation with respect to the present effort. Leadership performance is a complex phenomenon involving a variety of behaviors (Yukl, 2012). We have not, in the present effort, sought to examine the impact of planning on every aspect of leadership. Rather, we have here focused on the effectiveness of leader planning with respect to one critical leadership behavior – vision formation (Bass, 1985; Conger & Kanungo, 1998; Mumford, 2006). Accordingly, caution is called for in generalizing our conclusions to other critical leadership behaviors such as relationship formation (Graen & Uhl-Bien, 1998) or participation (Friedrich, Vessey, Schuelke, Ruark, & Mumford, 2009).

Along related lines, it should be recognized that the value of planning for those occupying organizational leadership positions has been questioned (Finkelstein, 2002; Mintzberg, 1991). At times, it may, in fact, become more important for leaders to act than to think or think about plans that may never be realized. Specifically, it has been suggested that because of the role demands and unrelenting pace required of managers, planning may actually act to inhibit performance and information flow (Mintzberg, 1990). However, Mintzberg's (1990, 1991) arguments regarding the negatives of planning tend to focus on interruptions to plans representing derailment and subsequent failure, a problem which can be ameliorated through proper backup planning (Giorgini & Mumford, in press; Xiao, Milgram, Doyle, 1997). By the same token, there are also times leaders must think and plan, and planning appears critical when leaders must make sense of complex organizational crises, formulate plans for addressing these crises, and articulate their vision to followers (Mumford, Schultz, & Osburn, 2002; Weick, 1995). Indeed, given the impact of vision on leader performance, there is reason to suspect that, as a basis for vision formation, planning may prove critical to performance in leadership roles.

Aside from these two general limitations, it should also be noted that virtually all of the studies examined in the present chapter were based on experimental methods. As a result, an obvious question arises as to the generality of our conclusions to leaders in non-experimental settings. By the same token, however, it must also be recognized that followers often do not see, and are unable to report, planning activities of leaders (Marta et al., 2005). As a result, using the survey methods commonly employed in leadership research, statements can be made only about the visions articulated by leaders (Yukl, 2012).

Equally, leader visions do not arise in a vacuum – they come from somewhere (Strange & Mumford, 2005). In the present chapter, we have argued that the basis for leader vision formation is planning (Mumford, Friedrich, Caughron, & Byrne, 2007). However, the significance of planning in vision formation is not the identification of a set of efficient actions. Rather, vision formation is linked to planning through the generative nature of plans. Mumford, Schultz, and Van Doorn (2001) and Noice (1991) have argued that planning requires envisioning, on mentally simulating, the impact of future actions on the entities of concern. Thus, the basis of vision, as an image of the future (Conger & Kanungo, 1998), is held to lie in planning or the mental simulation of the future effects of potential actions.

This observation led Mumford, Friedrich, Caughron, and Byrne (2007) to propose a model of the cognitive processes underlying leader planning and vision formation. This model assumes leader vision formation occurs under conditions of crisis (Hunt et al., 1999). To formulate a vision, leaders must scan their environments to gather critical information with respect to descriptive mental models reflecting their understanding of the sociotechnical system. This descriptive mental model, along with information bearing on relevant cases and goals, activates case-based, or experiential, knowledge. Analysis of the activated cases provides a basis for formulation of a prescriptive mental model (Strange & Mumford, 2002). This prescriptive mental model provides a basis for forecasting (Shipman et al., 2010). Forecasts, through self-reflection and systems-reflection, are evaluated and provide the basis for planning, backup plan formation, and, with articulation of these plans to followers, the articulation of a leader's vision. This vision, in turn, seems to both direct and motivate followers through mechanisms such as identification, role modeling, and peer feedback (Yukl, 2012).

Broadly speaking, the results obtained in the various experimental studies described in this chapter provide rather compelling support for the two key sets of propositions implied by Mumford and colleagues' model of leader planning and vision formation (Mumford, Friedrich, Caughron, & Byrne, 2007; Mumford & Mecca, in press; Strange & Mumford, 2002). The first critical set of propositions involves leaders' use of case-based knowledge in planning and vision formation. In fact, a series of studies by Barrett et al. (2011), Strange and Mumford, (2005), and Vessey et al. (2011) have all shown that case-based knowledge influences the viability of the plans people formulate when they are working on leadership tasks. Moreover, case-based knowledge, along with the resulting plans, was shown to impact the vision statements subsequently articulated by people working in these leadership roles.

The second set of key propositions flowing from this model concerns the critical cognitive processing operations involved in working with case-based knowledge to formulate viable vision statements. Prior studies have provided evidence, compelling evidence, for the importance of descriptive and prescriptive mental models (Marcy & Mumford, 2010), analysis of causes and goals (Marcy & Mumford, 2007, 2010; Strange & Mumford, 2005), forecasting (Shipman et al.,

2010), and self-reflection (Strange & Mumford, 2005). Although not all processes involved in this model have been explicitly examined, and neither have process interdependencies been investigated (Friedrich & Mumford, 2009), these studies taken as a whole do provide some evidence – in fact, substantial evidence – for the plausibility of the processes that Mumford and colleagues have argued to underlie leader planning and vision formation.

This model is noteworthy, in fact, because it suggests a variety of variables which might influence the success of leaders' plans and their ability to articulate viable visions. One key set of variables in this regard may be found in the demands imposed by leadership roles. Broadly speaking, leaders appear more likely to plan and formulate viable visions when the task they are presented with, either the task per se or followers' ideas about how to approach the task, are complex. This complexity does not decrease but rather it increases the need for planning in vision formation. And, indeed, people in leadership roles appear to invest resources in planning when they believe they are structuring a complex task.

The investment of resources in planning and vision formation is critical, in fact, because planning and vision formation are cognitively demanding, resource intensive, activities. In this regard, it is not surprising that time pressure and cognitive fatigue act to undermine planning and vision formation when people are working in leadership roles. Thus, if organizations want plans and viable visions, they must give leaders time to think. Indeed, they must give them time to think where they believe they will not be penalized for their thoughts (Caughron & Mumford, 2012).

Of course, the resource investment required for planning and vision formation will decrease when people employ more effective strategies in process execution (Shipman et al., 2010). This finding is of some importance because it suggests that the practical significance of Mumford and colleagues' model of leader planning and vision formation.

Future Directions

Isolating critical processes may provide a basis for identifying both more effective and less effective strategies for process execution and for the eventual development of training interventions intended to encourage application of more effective strategies for process execution. Training interventions that should, in turn, improve leader planning and vision formation. In fact, studies by Barrett et al. (2011), Marcy and Mumford (2007, 2010), and Vessey et al. (2011) have shown that instructional interventions along these lines results in improved leader planning and vision formation.

Another potential avenue for future research may be to examine how other individual attributes contribute to leader planning and vision formation, for example personality, leadership style, individual problem-solving ability, and self-regulation and emotion management. Specifically, self-regulation and emotion management have been shown to facilitate leader performance (Palmer, Walls, Burgess, & Stough, 2001; Sosik, Potosky, & Jung, 2002). Self-regulation and emotion management may negate the importance of planning for leaders possessing these skills. This could, in turn, lead to further research providing more information regarding when and under what conditions planning may be detrimental to performance. It would also be of value for future research to examine the impact of planning on other aspects of leadership besides vision formation, such as formation and maintenance of relationships with followers. Finally, research along the lines of Dörner and Schaub's (1994) work is needed to examine how execution of planning processes (e.g. environmental scanning, identification of applicable cases) varies across types of leader or leaders of different types of organizations. We hope the present effort will serve as an impetus for further work along these lines, work that will help leaders envision a better future through planning.

Acknowledgments

We would like to thank Tamara Friedrich, Jay Caughron, Cristina Byrne, Suzie Marta, and Jill Strange for their contributions to the present effort.

References

Antes, A. L., & Mumford, M. D. (2012). Strategies for leader cognition: Viewing the glass "half full" and "half empty." *The Leadership Quarterly, 23*, 425–442.

Anzai, Y. (1984). Cognitive control of real-time event driven systems. *Cognitive Science, 8*, 221–254.

Avolio, B. J., & Gardner, W. L. (2005). Authentic leadership development: Getting to the root of positive forms of leadership. *The Leadership Quarterly, 16*, 315–338.

Bandura, A. (1976). Self-reinforcement: Theoretical and methodological considerations. *Behaviorism, 135*–155.

Barrett, J. D., Vessey, W. B., & Mumford, M. D. (2011). Getting leaders to think: Effects of training, threat, and pressure on performance. *The Leadership Quarterly, 22*, 729–750.

Bass, B. M. (1985). *Leadership and performance beyond expectations.* New York: Free Press.

Bass, B. M., & Avolio, B. J. (1990). *Multifactor leadership questionnaire.* Palo Alto, CA: Consulting Psychologists Press.

Bass, B. M., & Bass, R. (2008). *The Bass handbook of leadership: Theory, research, and managerial applications.* New York: Free Press.

Bass, B. M., & Steidlmeier, P. (1999). Ethics, character, and authentic transformational leadership behavior. *The Leadership Quarterly, 10*, 181–217.

Bedell-Avers, K. E., Hunter, S. T., & Mumford, M. D. (2008). Conditions of problem-solving and the performance of charismatic, ideological, and pragmatic leaders: A comparative experimental study. *The Leadership Quarterly, 19*, 89–106.

Bedell-Avers, K., Hunter, S. T., Angie, A. D., Eubanks, D. L., & Mumford, M. D. (2009). Charismatic, ideological, and pragmatic leaders: An examination of leader–leader interactions. *The Leadership Quarterly, 20*, 299–315.

Bennis, W., & Nanus, B. (1985). *Leadership: The strategies for taking charge.* New York: Harper & Row.

Bligh, M. C., Kohles, J. C., & Meindl, J. R. (2004). Charting the language of leadership: a methodological investigation of President Bush and the crisis of 9/11. *Journal of Applied Psychology, 89*, 562.

Bono, J. E., & Illies, R. (2006). Charisma, positive emotions and mood contagion. *The Leadership Quarterly, 17*, 317–334.

Caughron, J. J., & Mumford, M. D. (2012). Embedded leadership: How do a leader's superiors impact middle-management performance? *The Leadership Quarterly, 23*, 342–353.

Conger, J., & Kanungo, R. N. (1998). *Charismatic leadership in organizations.* Thousand Oaks, CA: Sage.

Dean, J. W., & Sharfman, M. P. (1996). Does decision process matter? A study of strategic decision-making effectiveness. *Academy of Management Journal, 39*, 368–396.

Dörner, D., & Schaub, H. (1994). Errors in planning and decision-making and the nature of human information processing. *Applied Psychology: An International Review, 43*, 433–453.

Drazin, R., Glynn, M. A., & Kazanjian, R. K. (1999). Multilevel theorizing about creativity in organizations: A sensemaking perspective. *Academy of Management Review, 24*, 286–307.

Ellis, J. J. (2001). *Founding brothers: The revolutionary generation.* New York: Alfred Knopf.

Finkelstein, S. (2002). Planning in organizations: One vote for complexity. In F. J. Yammarino & F. Dansereau (Eds.), *Research in multi-level issues: The many faces of multi-level issues* (pp. 73–80). New York: Elsevier.

Fleishman, E. A. (1953). Leadership climate, human relations training, and supervisory behavior. *Personnel Psychology, 6*, 205–222.

Fleishman, E. A., Mumford, M. D., Zaccaro, S. J., Levin, K. Y., Korotkin, A. L., & Hein, M. B. (1992). Taxonomic efforts in the description of leader behavior: A synthesis and functional interpretation. *The Leadership Quarterly, 2*, 245–287.

Ford, C. M., & Gioia, D. A. (2000). Factors influencing creativity in the domain of managerial decision making. *Journal of Management, 26*, 705–732.

Friedrich, T. L., & Mumford, M. D. (2009). The effects of conflicting information on creative thought: A source of performance improvements or decrements? *Creativity Research Journal, 21*, 265–281.

Friedrich, T. L., Vessey, W. B., Schuelke, M. J., Ruark, G. A., & Mumford, M. D. (2009). A framework for understanding collective leadership: The selective utilization of leader and team expertise within networks. *The Leadership Quarterly*, 20, 933–958.

Gardner, W. L., Avolio, B. J., Luthans, F., May, D. R., & Walumbwa, F. (2005). "Can you see the real me?" A self-based model of authentic leader and follower development. *The Leadership Quarterly*, 16, 343–372.

Gioia, D. A., & Thomas, J. B. (1996). Identity, image, and issue interpretation: Sensemaking during strategic change in academia. *Administrative Science Quarterly*, 41, 370–403.

Giorgini, V., & Mumford, M. D. (in press). Backup plans and creative problem solving: Effects of causal, error, and resource planning. *International Journal of Creative Problem Solving*.

Globerson, S., & Zwikael, O. (2002). The impact of the project manager on project management planning processes. *Project Management Journal*, 33, 58–64.

Graen, G. B., & Uhl-Bien, M. (1995). Relationship-based approach to leadership: Development of leader–member exchange (LMX) theory of leadership over 25 years: Applying a multilevel multi-domain perspective. *Leadership Quarterly*, 6, 219–247.

Graen, G. B., & Uhl-Bien, M. (1998). Relationship-based approach to leadership: Development of Leader–Member Exchange (LMX) theory of leadership over 25 years: Applying a multi-level multi-domain perspective. In F. Dansereau & F. J. Yammarino (Eds.), *Leadership: The multiple-level approaches*, Part B (pp. 103–133). Stamford, CT: JAI Press.

Graen, G., Novak, M. A., & Sommerkamp, P. (1982). The effects of leader–member exchange and job design on productivity and satisfaction: Testing a dual attachment model. *Organizational Behavior and Human Performance*, 30, 109–131.

Hemlin, S. (2009). Creative knowledge environments: An interview study with group members and group leaders of university and industry R&D groups in biotechnology★. *Creativity and Innovation Management*, 18, 278–285.

House, R. J. (1977). A 1976 theory of charismatic leadership. In J. G. Hunt & L. L. Larson (Eds.), *Leadership: The cutting edge* (pp. 189–207). Carbondale, IL: Southern Illinois University Press.

House, R. J. (1996). Path-goal theory of leadership: Lessons, legacy, and a reformulated theory. *The Leadership Quarterly*, 7, 323–352.

Hunt, J. G., Boal, K. B., & Dodge, G. E. (1999). The effects of visionary and crisis-responsive charisma on followers: An experimental examination of two kinds of charismatic leadership. *The Leadership Quarterly*, 10, 423–448.

Hunter, S. T., Bedell-Avers, K. E., & Mumford, M. D. (2009). Impact of situational framing and complexity on charismatic, ideological and pragmatic leaders: Investigation using a computer simulation. *The Leadership Quarterly*, 20, 383–404.

Hunter, S. T., Cushenbery, L., Thoroughgood, C., Johnson, J. E., & Ligon, G. S. (2011). First and ten leadership: A historiometric investigation of the CIP leadership model. *The Leadership Quarterly*, 22, 70–91.

Isenberg, D. J. (1986). Thinking and managing: A verbal protocol analysis of managerial problem solving. *Academy of Management Journal*, 29, 775–788.

Johnson-Laird, P. N. (1999). Deductive reasoning. *Annual Review of Psychology*, 50, 109–135.

Kanfer, R. (1994). *Work motivation: New directions in theory and research*. San Francisco, CA: Jossey-Bass.

Katz, D., & Kahn, R. L. (1978). *The social psychology of organizations*. New York: Wiley.

Kirkpatrick, S. A., & Locke, E. A. (1996). Direct and indirect effects of three core charismatic leadership components on performance and attitudes. *Journal of Applied Psychology*, 81, 36.

Ligon, G. S., Hunter, S. T., & Mumford, M. D. (2008). Development of outstanding leadership: A life narrative approach. *The Leadership Quarterly*, 19, 312–334.

Lowe, K. B., Kroeck, K. G., & Sivasubramaniam, N. (1996). Effectiveness correlates of transformational and transactional leadership: A meta-analytic review of the MLQ literature. *The Leadership Quarterly*, 7, 385–425.

McAdams, D. P. (2001). The psychology of life stories. *Review of General Psychology*, 5, 100.

Marcy, R. T., & Mumford, M. D. (2007). Social innovation: Enhancing creative performance through causal analysis. *Creativity Research Journal*, 19, 123–140.

Marcy, R. T., & Mumford, M. D. (2010). Leader cognition: Improving leader performance through causal analysis. *The Leadership Quarterly*, 21, 1–19.

Marta, S., Leritz, L. E., & Mumford, M. D. (2005). Leadership skills and the group performance: Situational demands, behavioral requirements, and planning. *The Leadership Quarterly*, 16, 97–120.

Mehta, A., Feild, H., Armenakis, A., & Mehta, N. (2009). Team goal orientation and team performance: The mediating role of team planning. *Journal of Management*, 35, 1026–1046.

Mintzberg, H. (1990). The manager's job: Folklore and fact. *Harvard Business Review*, 68, 163–176.

Mintzberg, H. (1991). Planning on the left side and managing on the right. In J. Henry (Ed.), *Creative management* (pp. 58–71). Thousand Oaks, CA: Sage.

Mumford, M. D. (2006). *Pathways to outstanding leadership: A comparative analysis of charismatic, ideological, and pragmatic leaders*. Mahwah, NJ: Lawrence Erlbaum Associates.

Mumford, M. D., & Mecca, J. (in press). Vision and mental models: A decade later. In B. J. Avolio & F. J. Yammarino (Eds.), *Charismatic and transformational leadership: the road ahead*. Oxford, UK: Elsevier.

Mumford, M. D., Marks, M. A., Connelly, M. S., Zaccaro, S. J., & Reiter-Palmon, R. (2000). Development of leadership skills: Experience and timing. *The Leadership Quarterly*, 11, 87–114.

Mumford, M. D., Schultz, R. A., & Van Doorn, J. R. (2001). Performance in planning: Processes, requirements, and errors. *Review of General Psychology*, 5, 213.

Mumford, M. D., Schultz, R. A., & Osburn, H. K. (2002). Planning in organizations: Performance as a multi-level phenomenon. In F. J. Yammarino & F. Dansereau (Eds.), *The many faces of multi-level issues* (pp. 3–65). New York: Elsevier Science/JAI Press.

Mumford, M. D., Friedrich, T. L., Caughron, J. J., & Byrne, C. L. (2007). Leader cognition in real-world settings: How do leaders think about crises? *The Leadership Quarterly*, 18, 515–543.

Noice, H. (1991). The role of explanations and plan recognition in the learning of theatrical scripts. *Cognitive Science*, 15, 425–460.

Nutt, P. C. (1984). Types of organizational decision processes. *Administrative Science Quarterly*, 29, 414–450.

O'Hara, K. P., & Payne, S. J. (1998). The effects of operator implementation cost on planfulness of problem-solving and learning. *Cognitive Psychology*, 35, 34–70.

Palmer, B., Walls, M., Burgess, Z., & Stough, C. (2001). Emotional intelligence and effective leadership. *Leadership & Organization Development Journal*, 22(1), 5–10.

Piccolo, R. F., Bono, J. E., Heinitz, K., Rowold, J., Duehr, E., & Judge, T. A. (2012). The relative impact of complementary leader behaviors: Which matter most? *The Leadership Quarterly*, 23, 567–581.

Roberts, N. C. (1985). Transforming leadership: A process of collective action. *Human Relations*, 38, 1023–1046.

Rosing, K., Frese, M., & Bausch, A. (2011). Explaining the heterogeneity of the leadership–innovation relationship: Ambidextrous leadership. *The Leadership Quarterly*, 22, 956–974.

Rouse, W. B., & Morris, N. M. (1986). On looking into the black box: Prospects and limits in the search for mental models. *Psychological Bulletin*, 100, 349.

Scholnick, E. K., & Friedman, S. L. (1993). Planning in context: Developmental and situational considerations. *International Journal of Behavioral Development*, 16, 145–167.

Scott, G. M., Lonergan, D. C., & Mumford, M. D. (2005). Conceptual combination: Alternative knowledge structures, alternative heuristics. *Creativity Research Journal*, 17, 79–98.

Shamir, B., House, R. J., & Arthur, M. B. (1993). The motivational effects of charismatic leadership: A self-concept based theory. *Organization Science*, 4, 577–594.

Shipman, A. S., & Mumford, M. D. (2011). When confidence is detrimental: Influence of overconfidence on leadership effectiveness. *The Leadership Quarterly*, 22, 649–665.

Shipman, A. S., Byrne, C. L., & Mumford, M. D. (2010). Leader vision formation and forecasting: The effects of forecasting extent, resources, and timeframe. *The Leadership Quarterly*, 21, 439–456.

Sosik, J. J., Kahai, S. S., & Avolio, B. J. (1999). Leadership style, anonymity, and creativity in group decision support systems: The mediating role of optimal flow. *The Journal of Creative Behavior*, 33, 227–256.

Sosik, J. J., Potosky, D., & Jung, D. I. (2002). Adaptive self-regulation: Meeting others' expectations of leadership and performance. *The Journal of Social Psychology*, 142(2), 211–232.

Sternberg, R. J. (2007). A systems model of leadership: WICS. *American Psychologist*, 62, 34.

Strange, J. M., & Mumford, M. D. (2002). The origins of vision: Charismatic versus ideological leadership. *The Leadership Quarterly*, 13, 343–377.

Strange, J. M., & Mumford, M. D. (2005). The origins of vision: Effects of reflection, models, and analysis. *The Leadership Quarterly*, 16, 121–148.

Vessey, W. B., Barrett, J., & Mumford, M. D. (2011). Leader cognition under threat: "Just the Facts." *The Leadership Quarterly, 22,* 710–728.

Weick, K. (1995). *Sensemaking in organizations.* Thousand Oaks, CA: Sage.

Weingart, L. R. (1992). Impact of group goals, task component complexity, effort, and planning on group performance. *Journal of Applied Psychology, 77,* 682.

Weldon, E., Jehn, K. A., & Pradhan, P. (1991). Processes that mediate the relationship between a group goal and improved group performance. *Journal of Personality and Social Psychology, 61,* 555–569.

Xiao, Y., Milgram, P., & Doyle, D. J. (1997). Planning behavior and its functional role in interactions with complex systems. *IEEE Transactions on Systems, Man and Cybernetics, Part A: Systems and Humans, 27,* 313–324.

Yukl, G. (2012). *Leadership in organizations* (8th ed.). Upper Saddle River, NJ: Prentice Hall.

Yukl, G., & Tracey, J. B. (1992). Consequences of influence tactics used with subordinates, peers, and the boss. *Journal of Applied Psychology, 77,* 525.

14

STRATEGIC PLANNING AND FIRM PERFORMANCE

Towards a Better Understanding of a Controversial Relationship

Laura B. Cardinal, C. Chet Miller, Markus Kreutzer, and Candace TenBrink

From an intuitive standpoint, strategic planning would seem to be a useful practice for senior managers. First, planning serves an integrative function whereby various units of the firm contribute to the joint planning exercise (Kohtamäki, Kraus, Mäkelä, & Rönkkö, 2012; Vancil & Lorange, 1975). Second, planning serves an adaptation function whereby individuals in the firm systematically examine their industrial environments for possible future changes in technology trajectories, strategic postures of competitors, and government regulations (Rogers & Bamford, 2002; van Gelderen, Frese, & Thurik, 2000). Scenario planning has been a key tool for this second function of strategic planning (Stokke, Ralston, Boyce, & Wilson, 1990). Third, planning serves a legitimizing function. In most parts of the world, the institutional environment carries implicit, if not explicit, expectations for systematic study of the future. Absent concerted efforts to better understand unfolding trends and possible discontinuous changes, legitimacy can be compromised, resulting in a reduced flow of resources from environmental actors (Feldman & March, 1981).

In contrast to the positive view of planning presented above, a strong thread of dissent has existed for a number of decades. From this perspective, planning causes damage through errors in forecasting and a general tendency to create the wrong impressions and conclusions about the future (Mintzberg, 1994). These concerns can be grounded in classical decision theory, where decision makers are deemed unable to discern (1) the future consequences of actions taken today and (2) the preferences that will be held in the future (March, 2006). In response to such issues, day-to-day experiential learning has been positioned as a preferred substitute for strategic planning by a number of contributors to research on organizational adaptation and survival (March, 2006; Mintzberg, 1994).

The existence of these two broad perspectives on planning has led to exciting research debates but it also has been symptomatic of an inconsistent evidence base. Empirical findings have been difficult to reconcile with one another, and a coherent cumulative body of knowledge has been slow to develop. From the standpoint of evidence-based management (Rousseau, 2006; Rynes, 2007), the planning domain could be seen as quite troubled. One problem has been the inconsistent and sometimes loose conceptual and operational definitions. Previous contributors to planning research have had broad leeway in conceptualizing strategic planning. Some have defined it in terms of standardized processes and written plans (e.g. Gershefski & Harvey, 1970). Others have defined it as a comprehensive process encompassing both standardized and non-standardized elements (e.g. Gibson & Cassar, 2005). Still others have seen planning as a flexible process that provides the foundation for a wide variety of people to contribute to the planning process as they see fit (e.g. Rogers & Bamford, 2002). Without a clear, accepted definition of strategic planning and with a large number of studies making up the evidence base, comparing and interpreting myriad empirical results presents a challenge.

A second problem has been ungrounded conceptualizations and assessments of performance. While this problem exists in all strategy research streams (Miller, Washburn, & Glick, 2013), it seems to be particularly influential in the planning domain. Based on loose conceptualizations, performance has been assessed using dozens of metrics with differing timeframes and lag structures, adding to the complexity of comparing analyses. Studies have been based on a variety of self-reported perceptions as well as a variety of archival assessments. Measures based on self-reported comparisons are understandable when access to financial data is severely limited, such as in studies of emerging-market firms, start-ups, privately owned firms, and non-profits. Nonetheless, perceptual data used in the analyses may suffer from judgment error, inconsistency across raters, and naïve modeling. Archival data, while easier in some ways to compare across studies, also suffers from several issues, including manipulation by firms. Further, a tendency for reverse lags was observed in studies based on archival data when performance was assessed for the time period that preceded the assessment of planning (Miller & Cardinal, 1994). Assessing performance may seem to be a simple task, but in reality it is quite difficult (Miller et al., 2013).

A third problem has corresponded to a somewhat myopic search for linear effects between planning and performance. In the typical study, investigator expectations and analyses have been focused on the idea that higher levels of planning result in higher levels of performance. Planning, however, could exhibit an inverted U-shaped relationship with performance. It may be positive in its low to moderate range, but negative in its moderate to high range. For the low to moderate range, strategic planning may create the integration, adaptation, and legitimacy benefits described earlier. For the moderate to high range, it may create the problems associated with overstepping the bounds of human cognition, which may result in, for example, paralysis by analysis.

A fourth problem has involved the use of very different types of firms in studies of planning and performance. Small firms and large firms have been examined for decades, with variance in firm size appearing both across and within studies (Brews & Hunt, 1999; Reid & Smith, 2000). Start-ups and established firms constitute a newer point of comparison, with most of this variance appearing across rather than within studies (Frese, van Gelderen, & Ombach, 2000; Liao & Gartner, 2006). Firms from non-US settings and firms from the US also constitute a newer point of comparison. Once again, most of the variance in country setting appears across studies rather than within them (Andersen & Nielsen, 2009; Gibson & Cassar, 2005; Shane & Delmar, 2004). Overall, with this degree of variance in the types of firms studied, findings can be difficult to compare and reconcile.

In spite of the divergent research contexts and other issues that pervade this field, the idea that strategic planning can aid in achieving an enhanced competitive position remains appealing. Previous broad-based meta-analyses (Boyd, 1991; Brinckmann, Grichnik, & Kapsa, 2010; Miller & Cardinal, 1994; Schwenk & Shrader, 1993) suggest that, in the aggregate, strategic planning does contribute positively to performance, at least to some degree. The planning–performance relationship, however, seems to vary widely across studies and substantive contexts (Wolf & Floyd, 2013).

In light of the above, the purpose of our current work is fourfold. First, after presenting a brief historical overview, we intend to critically assess existing research in order to determine the degree to which the problems described above have been causing difficulties in establishing the positive effects of planning. The existence of these problems is not disputed, but the degree to which each is causing difficulty is less clear and agreed upon. Their relative impact is an important issue for both scholarly and practical purposes. Second, we intend to identify emerging trends within each problem area. The underlying nature of each problem has not been static. Third, we intend to suggest a roadmap for future research. Based on our findings in assessing past work, we will offer suggestions for how the planning–performance domain could evolve effectively in the future. Fourth, we will offer prescriptions for practice in light of current evidence and our critical assessment of that evidence.

Historical Context

In the first half of the twentieth century, firms expanded into new territories and broadened their product lines in unprecedented ways (Chandler, 1962). Consequently, organizational and technological complexity increased, and firms grew to the point where day-to-day oversight and communication became problematic. In his well-regarded book on the history of corporate strategy and structure, Chandler (1962) posits that firms broadly followed a pattern of growth in products and geographies that eventually led to the reconfiguration of managerial resources from a functional form to a multidivisional form (i.e. the M-form structure). Strategic planning and the other primary functions of management (Fayol, 1949) – controlling, coordinating, and organizing – took on increased importance as the M-form of management spread during post-World War II industrialization and also as economic growth increased significantly. Systematic research on planning also began around this same time.

Research in the 1970s generally focused on the relationship between formal strategic planning and firm performance in large US firms (Denning & Lehr, 1972; Karger & Malik, 1975; Thune & House, 1970; Wood & LaForge, 1979). Subsequent decades brought a proliferation of new emphases and contexts to the study of strategic planning. As research progressed, however, comparisons across studies often revealed contradictory findings. With two decades of research during the 1970s and 1980s and no clear agreement as to the economic value of strategic planning, Pearce, Freeman, and Robinson (1987a) reviewed 18 empirical studies focused on formal planning and reported several concerns. Their investigation revealed that prior research suffered from methodological inconsistencies and ambiguity concerning the meaning of contextual variables tested in contingency hypotheses. Shortly after Pearce et al.'s (1987a) review, three different meta-analyses (see Boyd, 1991; Schwenk & Shrader, 1993; Miller & Cardinal, 1994) demonstrated that strategic planning was positively associated with firm performance, despite the methodological differences and problems across studies. Even so, those differences and problems were making interpretations of empirical findings difficult.

Looking beyond the three meta-analyses from the 1990s, research in this domain seems to have changed little. Specifically, research on strategic planning and performance has exhibited substantial heterogeneity and ongoing methodological issues. Moreover, it has been subjected to minimal theoretical and cumulative empirical study.[1]

Challenges in Planning-Performance Research

In terms of a general conceptual sketch, we define strategic planning as the process of setting goals and determining an organizational path to goal attainment that takes into account external environmental and internal organizational factors, constraints, and opportunities. Research that was focused on the value of strategic planning was sought for our critical review, with a multifaceted approach being used in the process of identifying past work. First, the studies included in the comprehensive reviews by Boyd (1991), Miller and Cardinal (1994), and Schwenk and Shrader (1993) were identified and collected. Second, an issue-by-issue journal search was used for the years 1993–2012 in the following journals: *Academy of Management Journal, Administrative Science Quarterly, British Journal*

TABLE 14.1 Studies of strategic planning and firm performance[1]

Author(s)	Year
Ansoff et al.	1970
Gershefski & Harvey	1970
Thune & House	1970
Denning & Lehr	1972
Herold	1972
Fulmer & Rue	1974
Grinyer & Norburn	1974
Karger & Malik	1975
Burt	1978
Kallman & Shapiro	1978
Wood & LaForge	1979
Kudla	1980
Leontiades & Tezel	1980
Klein	1981
Robinson & Littlejohn	1981
Sapp & Seiler	1981
Jones	1982
Kudla & Cesta	1982
Robinson	1982
Robinson & Pearce	1983
Fredrickson	1984
Fredrickson & Mitchell	1984
Robinson et al.	1984
Welch	1984
Ackelsberg & Arlow	1985
Orpen	1985
Sexton & Van Auken	1985
Whitehead & Gup	1985
Bracker & Pearson	1986
Rhyne	1986
Robinson et al.	1986
Gable & Topol	1987
Pearce et al.	1987
Bracker et al.	1988
Odom & Boxx	1988
Wood et al.	1988
Shrader et al.	1989
Jenster & Overstreet	1990
Kukalis	1991
Powell	1992
Baker et al.	1993
Lyles et al.	1993
Walters	1993
Capon et al.	1994
McKiernan & Morris	1994
Orpen	1994
Powell	1994
Risseeuw & Masurel	1994
Olson & Bokor	1995
Priem et al.	1995

TABLE 14.1 (*cont.*)

Author(s)	Year
Glen & Weerawardena	1996
Kargar	1996
Berman et al.	1997
Goll & Rasheed	1997
Hopkins & Hopkins	1997
Slevin & Covin	1997
Lumpkin et al.	1998
Peel & Bridge	1998
Rauch & Frese	1998
Rue & Ibrahim	1998
Smith	1998
Brews & Hunt	1999
Rogers et al.	1999
Andersen	2000
Desai	2000
Frese et al.	2000
Masurel & Smit	2000
Orser et al.	2000
Rauch et al.	2000
Reid & Smith.	2000
van Gelderen et al.	2000
Baker & Leidecker	2001
Perry	2001
Griggs	2002
Love et al.	2002
Baker	2003
Delmar & Shane	2003
Sarason & Tegarden	2003
Andersen	2004
French et al.	2004
Honig & Karlsson	2004
O'Regan & Ghobadian	2004
Shrader et al.	2004
Shane & Delmar	2004
Barringer et al.	2005
Gibson & Cassar	2005
Yusuf & Saffu	2005
Falshaw et al.	2006
Kraus et al.	2006
Liao & Gartner	2006
Al-Shammari & Hussein	2007
Frese et al.	2007
Haber & Reichel	2007
Hoffman	2007
Lange et al.	2007
Elbanna	2008
Flores et al.	2008
Ghobadian et al.	2008
Glaister et al.	2008
Rudd et al.	2008

TABLE 14.1 (*cont.*)

Author(s)	Year
Andersen & Nielsen	2009
Kirsch et al.	2009
Aldehayyat & Anchor	2010
Cassar	2010
Efendioglu & Karabulut	2010
Hahn & Powers	2010
Aldehayyat & Twaissi	2011
Song et al.	2011
Elbanna	2012
Honig & Samuelsson	2012
Kohtamaki et al.	2012
Suklev & Debarliev	2012

of Management, Entrepreneurship: Theory & Practice, Journal of Business, Journal of Business Research, Journal of Management, Journal of Management Studies, Journal of Small Business Management, Long Range Planning, Management Science, Organization Studies, Organization Science, and *Strategic Management Journal.* Third, a keyword search was applied to ABI Complete, EBSCO, Emerald Net, and Science Direct for all journals. Fourth, the reference lists of articles identified through the above steps were examined for any studies that had been missed. The 112 studies identified through these steps are listed in Table 14.1.[2] The data drawn upon in our analysis appears in the Appendix.

Issues Related to Operational Definitions

Operational Definitions of Planning

Today, research in the strategic planning field is even more prevalent than it was four decades ago when researchers were curious about what was to them a relatively new concept and relationship (see Ansoff, Avner, Brandenburg, Portner, & Radosevich, 1970). In some studies, a broad concept of planning is often used (e.g. Desai, 2000; O'Regan & Ghobadian, 2002), yet a narrow concept connected to degree of formalized planning seems to remain strong for many (Falshaw, Glaister, & Tatoglu, 2006; O'Regan & Ghobadian, 2002). We define the narrow conceptualization of planning as focused on formal, explicit, and codified aspects of planning and the broad conceptualization as focused on a wide-ranging array of activities associated with planning that may include, but go beyond, the formal aspects.

In terms of the empirical operationalization of strategic planning, many researchers have focused on standardization of planning steps, provision of concrete planning guidelines, and/or existence of written plans (Efendioglu & Karabulut, 2010; Herold, 1972; Honig & Karlsson, 2004; Orpen, 1994). These elements underlie the narrow formal approach for examining relevant phenomena. Other researchers have focused their measures on a more encompassing set of activities not exclusively targeting explicit, standardized, or written aspects of planning. Still others have incorporated a component that emphasizes flexibility in terms of a wide variety of people contributing to the planning process as they see fit. The focus of these encompassing and flexible operational definitions has been broad, taking into account more of the relevant phenomena.[3] Those adopting narrow and those adopting broad approaches tend to do so in an exclusive way. Only a handful of researchers have examined within the same study both narrow and broad operationalizations (see Ackelsberg & Arlow, 1985; Efendioglu & Karabulut, 2010; Shrader, Chacko, Hermann, & Mulford,

TABLE 14.2 Outcomes of planning studies

	Non-positive effects	Positive effects
Operationalization of planning		
Broad	32%	68%
Narrow	40%	60%
Source of performance data		
Archival	35%	65%
Key-informant	38%	62%
Curvilinear testing		
Yes	NA	NA
No	NA	NA
Firm size		
Small	34%	66%
Large	40%	60%
Stage of firm development		
Established	38%	62%
Start-up	50%	50%
Country of origin		
US	40%	60%
Non-US	38%	62%

2004; Kraus, Harms, & Schwartz, 2006). More interestingly, the proportion of studies based on a narrow versus broad assessment of strategic planning has remained constant from the 1970s through today.

Comparing the studies with a narrow operationalization to those with a broader operationalization, there appears to be a slightly higher likelihood of positive effects for broader approaches (68 percent of broad studies report positive effects while 60 percent of narrow studies report positive effects) as shown in Table 14.2.[4] In essence, strategic planning and firm performance are somewhat more likely to exhibit a positive linkage with less restrictive operationalizations. This is consistent with the meta-analytic findings of Miller and Cardinal (1994).

The focus on narrow formality of planning has been pervasive throughout the history of research on strategic planning and firm performance. This seems to be somewhat problematic based on our assessment and those of previous analysts. As a next methodological step, researchers might want to compare and contrast the narrow and broad operationalizations within the same studies. That would be the best way to showcase the differences. Moreover, it is also important for researchers to begin unpacking the underlying processes represented by the different operationalizations and incorporate these deeper, more detailed processes in their theories of planning and performance. For practitioners, the key idea would be to design planning systems that incorporate not only systematic SWOT (strengths, weaknesses, opportunities, and threats) and scenario analyses executed by a select few, but also informal brainstorming sessions by various groups, informal yet rich benchmarking by interested parties, and wide-ranging debates across levels of the firm regarding preferred goals, to name just a few examples.

Sources of Data for Planning and Performance

Researchers have used different sources of data in their examinations of the planning–performance linkage. For planning, most have relied on key informants to provide perceptual data while a few have obtained data through archival sources. Most researchers have gathered data on firms' planning practices from CEOs and other senior managers, with archival sources having been used in only four studies. Two of these studies were conducted in the early 1980s (Robinson, 1982; Robinson, Pearce, Vozikis, & Mescon, 1984) and two were conducted in more recent years (Desai, 2000; Kirsch, Goldfarb, & Gera, 2009). The very limited use of the archival approach is interesting given the significant focus for many on written plans and guidelines. These materials could be acquired and evaluated directly, rather than evaluated through surveys. Detailed analyses could reveal nuanced differences not captured in pre-constructed surveys.

For performance, the situation is similar but not quite as stark. Most researchers have obtained data from key informants, but, to date, a non-trivial number have obtained their performance data through archival means. Approximately 70 percent of available studies have been built on key-informant information, and the trend since 2000 has been in the direction of greater and greater reliance on this source of data.

In some cases, arguments have been made in favor of using archival measures because of the reduced potential for bias from key informants. Informants could engage in naïve modeling whereby they assume that planning and performance should covary and then report data accordingly. Informants also could be driven by impression management and report generally inflated performance data. On the other side, arguments have been made in favor of informants because accounting-based archival data can be easily manipulated by firms in their financial reporting and market-based archival data can be affected by an enormous set of extraneous factors. Further, some highlight the simple fact that archival data are not available for many types of firms (e.g. small firms, private firms).

Several prior empirical reviews have reported that the relationship between strategic planning and performance is weaker when archival data are used to assess performance (e.g. Miller & Cardinal, 1994). Brinckmann et al. (2010), however, found that use of archival data led to stronger results in a quantitative review of small-firm studies. Based on our qualitative review, studies using archival performance data provided evidence for a positive linkage at about the same rate as studies based on key-informant data (65 percent vs. 62 percent), as displayed in Table 14.2. The four studies that combined archival planning data and archival performance data provided the highest rate (75 percent), but with only four studies, this is not a conclusive finding. Overall, it seems that archival and key-informant data are equally valuable in establishing the effects of planning. This is an important conclusion for both scholars and practitioners. For scholars, it provides a foundation for flexibility in empirical assessments of performance. For practitioners, it lends credibility to informal assessments connecting planning to firm outcomes.

Issues Related to Theoretical Models

There is a very real possibility that planning exhibits a curvilinear linkage with performance. Theoretically, planning's effects could be characterized by a function that increases at a decreasing rate. Efforts at planning could be positive but with diminishing returns. Alternatively, planning's effects could be characterized by a function that resembles an inverted-U. Here, planning would be positive up to a point, but after that maximum point it would become negative due to information overload and paralysis by analysis. Further, with more and more investigatory activity being applied to the planning exercise, trivial and redundant information is likely to be generated. Trivial information lacks diagnostic value and is potentially harmful because it can create a dilution effect. This effect is associated with useless information interfering with cognitive processes in subtle and dysfunctional ways, such that useful information is not effectively processed (Hoffman & Patton, 1997; Iselin, 1993; Nisbett, Zukier, & Lemley, 1981; Whitecotton, Sanders, & Norris, 1998). Redundant information is valid and relevant but can cause decision makers to ignore earlier information while also not fully processing the newer overlapping reports and data (Davis, Lohse, & Kottemann, 1994; Hwang & Lin, 1999).

Surprisingly, there have been no theoretical explorations of the above possibilities and only one reported empirical test, with that test suggesting an intriguing inverted U-shaped linkage (Love, Priem, & Lumpkin, 2002). Either a number of curvilinear tests have gone unreported or there has been too little interest in such tests. Going forward, a strong need exists for theoretical and empirical explorations of curvilinearity. Without this research, both scholars and practitioners will remain blind to intriguing possibilities.[5]

Beyond curvilinear effects, there is the possibility that planning and performance exhibit a non-monotonic relationship, where positive planning effects exist in one context but negative planning effects exist in another context. Only ten studies thus far have been based on this theoretical possibility, which is a very, very small number. In six cases, evidence supporting a non-monotonic relationship has been produced, which is very intriguing but not enough to establish a major pattern, particularly in light of divergent contingency factors having been used across studies (e.g. dynamic vs. stable external environments, organic vs. mechanistic structures, prospector vs. defender strategies). As an example of non-monotonic findings, Slevin and Covin (1997) found that planning had positive effects for firms with mechanistic structures and hostile external environments, but negative effects for firms with organic structures and benign environments. Theoretical and empirical follow-ups on their findings have not been forthcoming. Again, there is a need for research on non-monotonic models to ensure that scholars and practitioners do not remind blind to important possibilities.[6]

Issues Related to Contextual Factors

Firm Size

Planning research was predominantly focused on large firms until the close of the 1970s, consistent with the novelty of strategic planning as a phenomenon that surfaced with the evolution of industrialization and growth in the USA (Chandler, 1990). Beginning in the 1980s, strong interest developed for the study of planning in small firms. Interest in small-firm planning quickly moved to the forefront, with a decided majority of planning-performance studies in the 1990s and twenty-first century having been focused on smaller firms (approximately two-thirds of the studies). Many of these studies stressed the importance of small size as an important contextual factor (Rauch & Frese, 1998; Rauch, Frese, & Sonnentag, 2000). In almost all cases, the standard US Small Business Administration definition of small has been adhered to.

In early studies, research centered on whether small firms (up to 500 employees) planned, how they planned in comparison to medium (500 to 1,499 employees) and large firms (1,500 or more employees), and whether a planning-performance relationship existed at all (Ackelsberg & Arlow, 1985; Jones, 1982; Robinson & Littlejohn, 1981). One of the recurrent questions has been whether, due to their limited size, small firms have the capacity to employ strategic planning (Robinson & Littlejohn, 1981; Robinson, 1982). They often do not have dedicated human resources for planning.

Studies across multiple samples and contexts indicate that small firms on average do plan to some degree. Some firms engage in formalized planning (Baker, Addams, & Davis, 1993; Smith, 1998), while others eschew formality for more informal plans that perhaps reside only in the minds of senior managers (Glen & Weerawardena, 1996). Still other firms do not plan and do not have a strategic plan of any type (Rue & Ibrahim, 1998). This leads to the second query related to whether planning in small firms is associated with performance.

Many studies have suggested positive effects for planning in small firms (Orser, Hogarth-Scott, & Riding, 2000; Smith, 1998), but some have suggested no effects (French, Kelly, & Harrison, 2004; Kargar, 1996) and a few have even suggested negative effects (Reid & Smith, 2000). Quantitative syntheses, however, have shed light on the overall planning–performance linkage among small firms. A meta-analysis of 14 small-firm planning studies (Schwenk & Shrader, 1993) reported that there is a positive and significant overall relationship between planning and performance. A later meta-analysis of 47 small-firm studies reported similar results (Brinckmann et al., 2010). A third meta-analysis, this one incorporating both small-firm and large-firm studies, revealed positive effects for small firms and large firms that were similar in magnitude (Miller & Cardinal, 1994). Our qualitative review supports the idea that small firms derive benefits from planning, with studies of small firms delivering a slightly higher rate of positive results compared to large firms (66 percent vs. roughly 60 percent), as can be seen in Table 14.2. This is interesting, given that researchers have generally argued that planning should be more beneficial for large firms since integration is needed to handle the high levels of complexity these firms face (Armstrong, 1982; Grinyer, Al-Bazzaz, & Yasai-Ardekani, 1986).

Beyond the data and findings presented above, research suggests that planning in small firms differs from that of larger firms in terms of duration and style. The small firm tends to plan less frequently (Orser et al., 2000), for a shorter duration, and with a more informal style (Robinson & Littlejohn, 1981). Facing limited complexity in smaller firms, managers are able to make most of the decisions and execute direct control over implementation. Further, there are particular considerations that suggest in some cases actual effect sizes could be somewhat smaller or perhaps could exhibit greater variance. Founders and senior managers of some small firms may have found micro niches or geographic foci that are not under threat. Thus, there might be less need for strategic planning. Additionally, the founders and senior managers of some small firms may wish the firm to remain small and may face little pressure to grow if participation in the equity markets has not occurred. This would also lower the need for planning somewhat. Finally, the goal of achieving high levels of performance may not be applicable, as some small business owners may work for pleasure, a cause, or other non-monetarist reasons (March & Simon, 1958; Nelson & Winter, 1982). Conceivably, future research could take into account the aspirations of small-firm principals.

In a very interesting and welcome contribution, Frese et al. (2007) brought cognition directly into small-firm research. In their study of African micro firms, they examined the impact of cognitive resources on the degree of proactive and elaborate planning, and also the impact of planning on firm outcomes. Cognitive resources did have substantial effects on planning, and thus indirectly on outcomes. Further research that includes cognitive aspects would be interesting (Wolf & Floyd, 2013).

Overall, the benefits of planning for both small and large firms seem to have been reasonably well established. For researchers, the study of other contextual factors may generate more value. For practitioners, the knowledge that size does not matter can be put to effective use.

Stage of Firm Development

Planning research has predominantly been focused on established firms rather than start-ups. Start-ups, however, have received some attention, with 93 percent of all start-up studies conducted since the close of the 1990s. Start-up firms are those that are less than five years old and they tend to be small (conversely, not all small firms are start-ups). Some research conceptualizes start-up firms as those that are entrepreneurial, but that approach has shortcomings as a firm can be entrepreneurial at any age.

Start-up-oriented studies were uncommon before the year 1998; however, after that point, interest in understanding important relationships among new firms began to accelerate. Similar to other planning streams, early studies analyzed whether start-ups planned and if there was a simple relation with performance. Compared to prior research on established firms, investigations in this sector moved into contextual variables more quickly, with monotonic interaction hypotheses being common. Perhaps this was a result of the later development of research in the start-up area.

Research does indicate that start-up ventures plan. In a study of 94 US-based firms, Lumpkin, Shrader, and Hills (1998) found that 41 percent of start-ups had a formal business plan. In a Scotland-based study of 150 firms, Smith (1998) reported a much higher rate of 79 percent. Analyzing the period prior to start-up, Olson and Bokor (1995) found that 50 percent of 90 high-growth US firms planned prior to the official start-up point.

In terms of performance outcomes, once again, studies have delivered varied results. Delmar and Shane (2003) conducted a longitudinal study of 223 start-ups in Sweden and found that business planning reduced the firm hazard rate. Similarly, Liao and Gartner (2006), in a study of 817 US firms, found that nascent entrepreneurs with a business plan were 2.6 times more likely to persist with the start-up. On the other hand, some studies have pointed to null and even negative effects. In a Swedish sample of 396 entrepreneurial firms, Honig and Karlsson (2004) found that writing a business plan affected neither profit nor survival. A few years later, Lange, Mollov, Pearlmutter, Singh, and Bygrave (2007), in a study of 116 US-centric entrepreneurs, also failed to find a significant relationship between writing a business plan and receiving capital. Reid and Smith (2000) found in a sample of 150 Scottish firms that writing a business plan provided a negative return on performance. They also found, however, that forward planning had a positive impact on firm survival. As a result of their findings, the authors suggested that writing a formal business plan might be an overly simple or constrained ritual and as such did not offer substantial value. This is consistent with our previous observation that a narrow formal focus produces less value.

Although not definitive because of the small number of start-up studies, a recent meta-analysis that incorporated start-ups in addition to other types of small firms (Brinckmann et al., 2010) found a positive relationship between planning and new firm success. This relationship, however, was substantially smaller than for more established small firms. This is an interesting finding as it suggests limited benefits for nascent firms. Consistent with the above research, our qualitative review revealed that studies of established firms produced positive results at a higher rate than studies of start-up firms (62 percent vs. 50 percent) (see Table 14.2).

In summary, the impact of strategic planning on performance in start-up firms seems to be weak and varied. Planning may or may not help these firms. With only 14 studies focused on start-ups and entrepreneurs, the evidence, however, is a bit shallow for drawing firm conclusions (for a more detailed treatment of the advantages and disadvantages of planning for entrepreneurial firms, see Gielnik, Frese, & Stark, Chapter 16). Additional research is required. It may be that senior managers in start-ups have much narrower perspectives on strategic planning than do managers in more established firms, and this could limit the benefits of planning. Start-ups often struggle with survival, capital, market introductions, and legal requirements (Milliman, von Glinow, & Nathan, 1991; Shane & Delmar, 2004), and the constant crises associated with these areas may cause cognitive constriction.

Country of Origin

During the first two decades of research on planning and performance, studies were heavily US-centric, with only 4 of 37 having been based on samples from outside of the USA (i.e. Burt, 1978; Denning & Lehr, 1972; Grinyer & Norburn, 1974; Orpen, 1985). Even those four studies remained within the confines of Anglo culture (Australia and the UK). In the 1990s, a dramatic increase in research outside of the USA was seen, but the studies were predominately focused on Australia and Europe, with no studies in the Far East, Middle East, or the Subcontinent. Exceptions to this general pattern include a study focused on South African firms in the late 1990s (Brews & Hunt, 1999) and a study of African micro firms (Frese et al., 2007).

By the twenty-first century, research conducted on firms outside of the USA had increased significantly, with 61 percent of studies taking place elsewhere. The growth in the study of non-US firms in strategic management generally and in planning research specifically coincided with a tremendous increase in the internationalization of businesses (Cardinal, Miller, & Palich, 2011).

Researchers have offered many reasons for why it is important to expand planning research beyond the USA and Western Europe to contexts that vary across a range of cultural and national differences (Al-Shammari & Hussein, 2007; Hoffman, 2007), such as a national culture's characteristic of uncertainty avoidance (Herbert, 1999). Perhaps the most fundamental reason is that western research on planning and planning–performance relationships may not be applicable to firms in other parts of the world, including emerging markets. Resource constraints are vastly different for firms in emerging and transition economies. Many have argued that it is important to test the application of western strategic management theory in other contexts and cultures (e.g. Glaister, et al., 2008), and this has begun to take place. Firms have been studied, for example, in the Middle East (e.g. Israel, Jordan, Turkey, Egypt, UAE) and Sub-Saharan Africa (i.e. Ghana, Namibia, Zimbabwe).

Based on our qualitative review, studies focused on US samples demonstrate a positive linkage at the same basic rate as studies focused on non-US samples (60 percent vs. 62 percent), as presented in Table 14.2. This belies, however, differences that may be more robustly detected after additional studies accumulate in non-western countries. For example, to date, only 12 of 43 non-US studies have been focused on emerging markets. Overall, researchers need to (1) extend existing research on emerging economies and (2) conduct additional comparative analyses within studies rather than only across studies.

Discussion and Implications

The purpose of our qualitative review has been to take stock of over 40 years of empirical research on strategic planning and its relationship with firm performance. With opposing camps advocating positive versus negative arguments for and against planning and with disparate findings appearing across studies, an evaluation and interpretation of where this critical area of study stands is an important task. At face value, strategic planning is an activity that is intuitively appealing to practitioners and often promoted to managers as a way to achieve sustainable competitive advantage (Bryson, 2011). Providing a strong evidence base that supports or does not support this view is the responsibility of academic researchers. Research on planning and performance can be considered an old-line topic in strategic management, but its allure has not diminished. Since the three original meta-analyses in the early 1990s (Boyd, 1991; Miller & Cardinal, 1994; Schwenk & Shrader, 1993), the pace of research in this domain has accelerated. During the 1980s and the 1990s, for each decade, 26 empirical studies were conducted examining the planning and performance relationship. In just the past 13 years, however, 49 new empirical studies have appeared.

While one can become confused and disheartened with the different conceptual and operational definitions of planning and performance, the different types of firms (small, large, nascent, mature), and the different countries of origin, we have been able to sift through the chaff and highlight some key features of the substantive landscape. First, both broader and narrower operationalizations of strategic planning reveal positive linear effects on firm performance, but broader definitions that are less restrictive seem more likely to generate the positive connection. Second, both archival and key-informant sources of data for firm performance reliably and similarly capture the positive effects of planning. Third, both small and large firms engage in and benefit from planning. Fourth, established firms benefit from planning, but start-ups may not see strong returns on the investment. Fifth, both US and non-US firms seem to benefit to the same degree from planning, but additional studies in emerging economies could alter that conclusion. Last but certainly not least, the absence of theorizing and empirical work on more complex models is a major problem. Scholarship and actionable advice to senior managers is being held back by this deficiency.

Our review helps to delineate future paths researchers should take in the study of strategic planning and performance. First, researchers should consider incorporating many of the contrasts presented in our work in within-study tests. To date, most comparisons, whether methodological or substantive, have been accomplished across studies rather than within them, which results in loss of control and also creates ecological fallacies for many substantive factors. Also, the across-study approach has drawn out the process and prolonged many of the debates in the planning–performance domain. For example, comparisons of broad versus narrow planning conceptualizations and operationalizations have almost never been examined in a within-study context, and this has obscured the importance of the issue and delayed full recognition of it. A cumulative body of knowledge could be created in a more efficient and effective manner with more within-study examinations of potentially important methodological and substantive contingency factors. In some cases, these examinations may reveal the "tyranny of the either–or." To put this another way, some examinations may show the futility of a methods debate focused on the superiority of either this approach or that approach because both approaches work equally well. This seems to be the case for archival vs. key-informant assessments of firm performance.

Second, researchers must drill down more deeply on the underlying mechanisms that support and enhance the benefits of planning. Similar to the need for theorizing related to curvilinearity and non-monotonic relationships, there is a major need for increased attention to the mechanisms through which planning works. At a macro level, planning seems to work through integration inside the firm and adaptation outside of it. At a micro level, less is known. What are the key cognitive, affective, and behavioral mechanisms (see, for example, Sitkin, See, Miller, Lawless, & Carton, 2011)? Which features of planning create vigilance versus dysfunctional hypervigilence in information acquisition and processing? Which features of planning tend to promote opportunity frames versus threat frames? Which features of planning tend to create optimism versus helplessness? How can these mechanisms be better managed through the design of planning systems? These are critical questions that have not been addressed in the strategic management literature and must be addressed to a greater degree in the future. Interestingly, a rich research stream on the micro processes underlying planning exists in the psychology literature, but has not been incorporated by strategic management scholars (for a discussion of how micro mechanisms work in planning, see Gielnik et al., Chapter 16 and Mumford, Mecca, & Watts, Chapter 4).

Turning to practitioners, our overarching message is that strategic planning is a good-news story. It is clear that engaging in strategic planning is generally better than not engaging in such planning. While there is a great deal that academics do not yet know, practitioners can move forward effectively. Being sure to follow more encompassing practices rather than highly stylized formal ones would be positive. Being aware of the elements of high-involvement management and applying those to the planning process would also be positive as a way to make a good preliminary bet on effectively managing the mechanisms through which planning probably works. Those elements include broad provision of not only operational information but also strategic information, training in how to apply that information, egalitarianism, and delegation (Pfeffer, 2005). With the value of these practices firmly established in the general case, managers would be following evidence-based management by implementing them in the special case of planning practices.

While our qualitative review lends credence to the idea that strategic planning has substantial benefits for firms, we have not completely settled the age-old debate between proponents of learning versus proponents of planning (c.f. Ansoff, 1991, 1994; Mintzberg, 1990). Planning has proven itself to be a viable management process over and over and has much to offer senior managers in charting strategies for their firms. Even so, the question that needs to be addressed is this: is day-to-day experiential learning a partial substitute for planning or is it a complement? If it is a partial substitute, then when does it function in this capacity? If it is a complement to planning, then under what conditions is the complementary role more pronounced, and how exactly do learning and planning processes reinforce each other? Revisiting this debate would afford the strategy community the opportunity to develop rich, insightful theory and possibly change the direction of the conversation.

Strategic planning is a complex and important phenomenon for academics and managers alike. In our qualitative review, we have attempted to unmask some of the key mysteries and needs that have confounded planning-performance research for quite some time. If future empirical research is to be executed in a cumulative way, it is critical that researchers recognize these mysteries and needs. We hope that our qualitative review will provide the infrastructure and scaffolding for future research that is more cumulative and grounded.

Appendix

Strategic Planning and Performance Empirical Studies

Study	Primary findings	Planning categorization	Source of planning data	Source of performance data	Firm size	Established	Country of origin
Ansoff, Avner, Brandenburg, Portner, & Radosevich (1970)	Some mixed; generally positive linear	Narrow	Informant	Archival	Large	Established	US
Gershefski & Harvey (1970)	Positive linear; negative linear for three of five performance measures	Narrow	Informant	Informant	Large	Established	US
Thune & House (1970)	Positive linear	Narrow	Informant	Informant	Large	Established	US
Denning & Lehr (1972)	No linkage	Narrow	Informant	Informant	Large	Established	non-US
Herold (1972)	Positive linear	Narrow	Informant	Informant	Large	Established	US
Fulmer & Rue (1974)	No linkage	Narrow	Informant	Archival	Small, Large	Established	US
Grinyer & Norburn (1974)	No linkage	Narrow	Informant	Informant	Large	Established	non-US
Karger & Malik (1975)	Positive linear	Narrow	Informant	Archival	Large	Established	US
Burt (1978)	Positive linear	Broad	Informant	Archival	Medium	Established	non-US
Kallman & Shapiro (1978)	No linkage	Broad	Informant	Archival	Medium	Established	US
Wood & LaForge (1979)	Positive linear	Narrow	Informant	Informant	Large	Established	US
Kudla (1980)	No linkage	Narrow	Informant	Archival	Large	Established	US
Leontiades & Tezel (1980)	No linkage	Narrow	Informant	Archival	Medium	Established	US
Klein (1981)	No linkage	Broad	Informant	Informant	Small, Medium, Large	Established	US
Robinson & Littlejohn (1981)	Positive linear for three of three tests	Broad	Informant	Informant	Small	Established	US
Sapp & Seiler (1981)	Positive linear for three of four linkages; no linkage for one test	Narrow	Informant	Archival	Medium	Established	US
Jones (1982)	Positive linear	Broad	Informant	Informant	Small	Established	US
Kudla & Cesta (1982)	No linkage	Narrow	Informant	Archival	Large	Established	US
Robinson (1982)	Positive linear for profitability and change and effectiveness	Broad	Archival	Archival	Small	Established	US

Robinson & Pearce (1983)	No linkage	Narrow	Informant	Archival	Small	Established	US
Fredrickson (1984)	One (average ROA) of two positive linear in stable industry	Broad	Informant	Archival	Medium	Established	US
Fredrickson & Mitchell (1984)	Two of two negative linear in unstable industry	Broad	Informant	Archival	Large	Established	US
Robinson, Pearce, Vozikis, & Mescon (1984)	Positive linear, no interaction; positive linear; positive interaction by centralization (i.e. corporate-instead of division-level)	Narrow	Archival	Archival	Small	Established	US
Welch (1984)	Positive linear for broad planning regardless of industry; no linkage for non-manufacturing and negative linkage for manufacturing for narrow planning	Narrow	Informant	Archival	Medium	Established	US
Ackelsberg & Arlow (1985)		Broad / Narrow	Informant	Informant	Small	Established	US
Orpen (1985)	No linkage	Broad	Informant	Informant	Small	Established	non-US
Sexton & Van Auken (1985)	Positive linear	Broad	Informant	Informant	Small	Established	US
Whitehead & Gup (1985)	Two of three negative linear and one no linkage	Narrow	Informant	Informant	Large	Established	US
Bracker & Pearson (1986)	Two (revenue growth, entrepreneurial compensation growth) of three positive linear	Narrow	Informant	Informant	Small	Established	US
Rhyne (1986)	Partially positive linear	Broad	Informant	Archival	Large	Established	US
Robinson, Logan, & Salem (1986)	Three of four positive linear	Broad	Informant	Informant	Small	Established	US
Gable & Topol (1987)	No linkage	Broad	Informant	Informant	Small	Established	US
Pearce, Robbins, & Robinson, Jr. (1987b)	No linkage	Broad	Informant	Informant	Small	Established	US
Bracker, Keats, & Pearson (1988)	Positive linear	Narrow	Informant	Archival	Small	Established	US

Study	Primary findings	Planning categorization	Source of planning data	Source of performance data	Firm size	Established	Country of origin
Odom & Boxx (1988)	Three of four positive linear	Narrow	Informant	Archival	Small	Established	US
Wood, Johnston, & DeGenaro (1988)	Two of three positive linear	Narrow	Informant	Informant	Small	Established	US
Shrader, Mulford, & Blackburn (1989)	Support for null hypothesis: planning not consistently related to performance	Narrow	Informant	Informant	Small	Established	US
Jenster & Overstreet (1990)	Four (market penetration, growth in membership, growth in deposits, growth in loans) of ten linear positive	Narrow	Informant	Informant	Small	Established	US
Kukalis (1991)	Positive linear monotonic interaction by environmental complexity, firm size, capital intensity, structure, firm life cycle	Narrow	Informant	Archival	Large	Established	US
Powell (1992)	Positive linear interaction in "planning disequilibrium industries"	Broad	Informant	Informant	Small	Established	US
Baker, Addams, & Davis (1993)	No linkage	Narrow	Informant	Informant	Small	Established	US
Lyles, Baird, Orris, & Kuratko (1993)	Positive linear for one out of three tests	Narrow	Informant	Informant	Small	Established	US
Walters (1993)	Positive linear; no linkage	Broad	Informant	Informant	Small, Medium	Established	US
Capon, Farley, & Hulbert (1994)	Positive linear; no interaction effects	Narrow	Informant	Archival	Large	Established	US
McKiernan & Morris (1994)	No linkage; only one of 20 positive linear and no relationship for the other 19 tests	Narrow	Informant	Archival	Small	Established	non-US

Study	Findings						
Orpen (1994)	Limited positive linear; limited positive mediation effect by the "acquisition and utilization of information about the firm and its environment"	Narrow	Informant	Informant	Small	Established	non-US
Powell (1994)	One (sales growth but not profitability) of two positive linear; positive interaction by firm size, stability of industry, and business strategy (for one of two performance measures) no linkage;	Broad	Informant	Informant	Small	Established	US
Risseeuw & Masurel (1994)	Non-monotonic interaction with environmental dynamism	Narrow	Informant	Informant	Small	Established	non-US
Olson & Bokor (1995)	Positive interaction between degree of formal planning and degree of innovativeness in strategy	Narrow	Informant	Archival	Small	Established	US
Priem, Rasheed, & Kotulic (1995)	Degree of planning is positive in dynamic environments and no effect in stable environments	Broad	Informant	Informant	Small	Established	US
Glen & Weerawardena (1996)	Limited positive linear: two out of four industries for employment growth and return, on sales; one out of four for sales and after tax profit	Narrow	Informant	Informant	Small	Established	non-US
Kargar (1996)	Two of three positive linear	Broad	Informant	Informant	Small	Established	US
Berman, Gordon, & Sussman (1997)	Positive linear	Broad	Informant	Informant	Small	Established	US
Goll & Rasheed (1997)	No positive linear main effects; positive in munificent environments; no linkage in non-munificient environments; no main or interaction with dynamism	Broad	Informant	Archival	Large	Established	US
Hopkins & Hopkins (1997)	Positive linear	Broad	Informant	Archival	Large	Established	US

Study	Primary findings	Planning categorization	Source of planning data	Source of performance data	Firm size	Established	Country of origin
Slevin & Covin (1997)	Planning is more positively related with a mechanistic structure and with a hostile environment; planning is more negatively related with an organic structure and with a benign environment	Narrow	Informant	Informant	Medium	Established	US
Lumpkin, Shrader, & Hills (1998)	Two of four positive linear for start-ups; No linkage for established firms	Broad	Informant	Informant	Small	Start-up, Established	US
Peel & Bridge (1998)	Two of two positive linear	Broad	Informant	Informant	Small	Established	non-US
Rauch & Frese (1998)	Positive direct short-term; no direct long-term; four of nine cross-sectional and two of six longitudinal positive interaction by environmental hostility and uncertainty	Narrow	Informant	Informant	Small	Start-up (first wave); Established (second-wave)	non-US
Rue & Ibrahim (1998)	Two (growth in sales and perceived performance compared to industry; not ROI) of three positive linear	Broad	Informant	Informant	Small	Established	US
Smith (1998)	Positive linear to both means planning and ends planning;	Narrow	Informant	Informant	Small	Start-up	non-US
Brews & Hunt (1999)	Planning and performance are not moderated by environmental stability	Narrow	Informant	Informant	Large	Established	US, non-US

Study	Finding	Scope			Size	Stage	Location
Rogers, Miller, & Judge (1999)	As three indicators of planning increase, ROA and ROE increase for prospectors and decrease for defenders; loan growth has no effect for prospectors, but negative for defenders	Broad	Informant	Archival	Medium	Established	US
Andersen (2000)	Positive linear; no interaction by industry or autonomous action	Broad	Informant	Informant	Medium	Established	US
Desai (2000)	Positive linear	Narrow	Archival	Archival	Medium	Established	US
Frese, van Gelderen, & Ombach (2000)	No linkage	Broad	Informant	Informant	Small	Start-up	non-US
Masurel & Smit (2000)	Positive linear	Narrow	Informant	Archival	Small	Established	non-US
Orser, Hogarth-Scott, & Riding (2000)	Positive linear	Narrow	Informant	Archival	Small	Established	non-US
Rauch, Frese, & Sonnentag (2000)	Positive linear (Germany); negative linear (Ireland)	Narrow	Informant	Informant	Small	Start-up	non-US
Reid & Smith (2000)	Negative linear (having a business plan); positive linear (forward planning)	Narrow	Informant	Archival	Small	Start-up	non-US
van Gelderen, Frese, & Thurik (2000)	Positive linear	Narrow	Informant	Informant	Small	Start-up	non-US
Baker & Leidecker (2001)	Positive linear for planning tool composite; no linkage for six planning process characteristics	Broad	Informant	Informant	Small	Established	US
Perry (2001)	Positive linear	Narrow	Informant	Archival	Small	Established	US
Griggs (2002)	Positive linear	Broad	Informant	Informant	Small	Established	non-US
Love, Priem, & Lumpkin (2002)	U-shaped; linear interaction with centralization not robust when squared terms included	Narrow	Informant	Informant	Small	Established	US
Baker (2003)	Positive linear	Broad	Informant	Informant	Small	Established	US
Delmar & Shane (2003)	Positive linear	Broad	Informant	Informant	Small	Start-up	non-US
Sarason & Tegarden (2003)	Positive linear monotonic interaction involving firm stage	Narrow	Informant	Informant	Small	Established	US

Study	Primary findings	Planning categorization	Source of planning data	Source of performance data	Firm size	Established	Country of origin
Andersen (2004)	Positive linear; Positive linear interaction with (1) environmental dynamism and (2) distributed decision authority; Negative linear interaction with (3) participation in decisions	Broad	Informant	Informant	Medium	Established	U.S.
French, Kelly, & Harrison (2004)	No linkage	Narrow	Informant	Informant	Small	Established	non-U.S.
Honig & Karlsson (2004)	Positive linear in survival; No finding in profitability	Narrow	Informant	Informant	Small	Start-up	non-U.S.
O'Regan & Ghobadian (2004)	Partly positive linear (e.g., learning/growth); No finding for financial performance	Broad	Informant	Informant	Small	Established	non-U.S.
Shrader, Chacko, Herrmann, & Mulford (2004)	Positive linear for both broad and narrow planning (i.e., sales growth, market share); linkage (i.e., income growth, ROI); Very limited interaction effects (i.e., no interaction between formal and informal planning)	Broad/Narrow	Informant	Informant	Small	Established	U.S.
Shane & Delmar (2004)	Positive linear	Narrow	Informant	Informant	Small	Start-up	non-U.S.
Barringer, Jones, & Neubaum (2005)	No linkage	Broad	Informant	Archival	Small	Established	U.S.
Gibson & Cassar (2005)	Positive linear	Narrow	Informant	Informant	Small	Established	non-U.S.
Yusuf & Saffu (2005)	Positive linear in one relationship; No finding in two relationships	Broad	Informant	Informant	Small	Established	non-U.S.
Falshaw, Glaister, & Tatoglu (2006)	No linkage	Narrow	Informant	Informant	Large	Established	non-U.S.

Study	Findings	Operationalization			Size	Stage	Location
		Two Narrow Categories; One Broad Category					
Kraus, Harms, & Schwarz (2006)	Positive linear for one out of two narrow tests; No relationship for broad category	Two Narrow Categories; One Broad Category	Informant	Informant	Small	Established	non-U.S.
Liao & Gartner (2006)	Positive linear	Narrow	Informant	Informant	Small	Start-up	U.S.
Al-Shammari & Hussein (2007)	Positive linear	Narrow	Informant	Informant	Small	Established	non-U.S.
Frese, Krauss, Keith, Escher, Grabarkiewicz, Luneng, Heers, Unger, & Friedrich (2007)	Positive linear	Broad	Informant	Informant	Small	Established	non-U.S.
Haber & Reichel (2007)	Partial positive linear	Narrow	Informant	Informant	Small	Start-up	non-U.S.
Hoffman (2007)	Positive linear interaction for culture; Positive linear interaction for three of four cultural values	Broad	Informant	Informant	Large	Established	U.S., non-U.S.
Lange, Mollov, Pearlmutter, Singh, & Bygrave (2007)	No linkage	Narrow	Informant	Informant	Small	Start-up	U.S.
Elbanna (2008)	Limited positive linear; Positive interaction between practice of SP and management participation	Broad	Informant	Informant	Medium	Established	non-U.S.
Flores, Catalanello, Rau, & Saxena (2008)	Negative interaction between planning and learning; Planning had a positive effect when learning was low and no effect when learning was high	Broad	Informant	Informant	Medium	Established	U.S.
Ghobadian, O'Regan, Thomas & Liu (2008)	Positive linear (on all performance measures; No interaction effects	Narrow	Informant	Informant	Small	Established	non-U.S.
Glaister, Dincer, Tatoglu, Demirbag & Zaim (2008)	Positive linear; Positive interaction between planning and (1) environmental turbulence, (2) organizational structure, and (3) firm size	Narrow	Informant	Informant	Medium	Established	non-U.S.

Study	Primary findings	Planning categorization	Source of planning data	Source of performance data	Firm size	Established	Country of origin
Rudd, Greenley, Beats on & Lings (2008)	Four of four positive linear mediation	Broad	Informant	Informant	Medium	Established	non-U.S.
Andersen & Nielsen (2009)	Positive linear	Broad	Informant	Informant	Medium	Established	U.S.
Kirsch, Goldfarb & Gera (2009)	No linkage	Narrow	Archival	Archival	Small	Start-up	U.S.
Aldehayyat & Anchor (2010)	Positive linear	Broad	Informant	Informant	Small	Established	non-U.S.
Cassar (2010)	Positive linear	Narrow	Informant	Informant	Small	Start-up	U.S.
Efendioglu & Karabulut (2010)	Limited positive linear; Majority no linkage	Three Narrow/Four Broad	Informant	Informant	Medium	Established	non-U.S.
Hahn & Powers (2010)	Positive linear	Broad	Informant	Informant	Small, Medium, Large	Established	U.S.
Aldehayyat & Twaissi (2011)	Positive linear	Broad	Informant	Informant	Small	Established	non-U.S.
Song, Im, van der Bij, & Song (2011)	Positive linear	Narrow	Informant	Informant	Small	Established	U.S.
Elbanna (2012)	No linkage	Narrow	Informant	Informant	Medium	Established	non-U.S.
Honig & Samuelsson (2012)	No linkage	Narrow	Informant	Informant	Small	Start-up	non-U.S.
Kohtamaki, Kraus, Makela, & Ronkko (2012)	Positive linear	Broad	Informant	Informant	Small	Established	non-U.S.
Suklev & Debarliev (2012)	Positive linear	Narrow	Informant	Informant	Medium	Established	non-U.S.

Notes

1 This is true in other domains in the broader management literature (e.g. Sitkin, Cardinal, & Bijlsma-Frankema, 2010).
2 This list contains all empirical studies we identified for our qualitative review and are designated with an asterisk* in the references.
3 We recognize that the characteristics that comprise planning conceptualizations may co-vary, offering the potential for a strategic planning typology.
4 In calculating these and other outcome percentages, the few non-monotonic findings reported in the research domain have been netted out.
5 It should be noted that asymmetric inverted-U functions are compatible with the generally modest positive linear effect sizes reported in most previous planning-performance studies. Given those positive effects, any inverted U would likely have a shorter and perhaps less steep negative slope on its right-hand side. Absent concrete empirical work, these ideas are, however, only theoretical speculations.
6 It should be noted that asymmetric non-monotonic relationships are compatible with the generally modest, non-interactive, positive effects reported in most previous planning-performance studies. Given those positive effects, the slope for the positive aspect is likely to be greater than the slope for the negative aspect of any non-monotonic function that is empirically sustained across rigorous, repeated testing. Absent concrete empirical work, these ideas are, however, only theoretical speculations.

References

*Ackelsberg, R., & Arlow, P. (1985). Small businesses do plan and it does pay off. *Long Range Planning*, 18(5), 61–67.

*Aldehayyat, J. S., & Anchor, J. R. (2010). Strategic planning implementation and creation of value in the firm. *Strategic Change*, 19(3/4), 163–176.

*Aldehayyat, J. S., & Twaissi, N. (2011). Strategic planning and corporate performance relationship in small business firms: Evidence from a Middle East country context. *International Journal of Business & Management*, 6(8), 255–263.

*Al-Shammari, H., & Hussein, R. T. (2007). Strategic planning-firm performance linkage: Empirical investigation from an emergent market perspective. *Advances in Competitiveness Research*, 15(1), 15–26.

*Andersen, T. J. (2000). Strategic planning, autonomous actions and corporate performance. *Long Range Planning*, 33(2), 184–200.

*Andersen, T. J. (2004). Integrating decentralized strategy making and strategic planning processes in dynamic environments. *The Journal of Management Studies*, 41(8), 1271–1299.

*Andersen, T. J., & Nielsen, B. B. (2009). Adaptive strategy making: The effects of emergent and intended strategy modes. *European Management Review*, 6(2), 94–106.

Ansoff, H. I. (1991). Critique of Henry Mintzberg's "The design school: Reconsidering the basic premises of strategic planning." *Strategic Management Journal*, 12(6), 449–461.

Ansoff, H. I. (1994). Comment on Henry Mintzberg's rethinking strategic planning. *Long Range Planning*, 27(3), 31–31.

*Ansoff, H. I., Avner, J., Brandenburg, R. C., Portner, F. E., & Radosevich, R. (1970). Does planning pay? The effects of planning on success of acquisition. *Long Range Planning*, 3(2), 2–7.

Armstrong, J. S. (1982). The value of formal planning for strategic decisions: Review of empirical research. *Strategic Management Journal*, 3(3), 197–211.

*Baker, G. A. (2003). Strategic planning and financial performance in the food processing sector. *Review of Agricultural Economics*, 25(2), 470–482.

*Baker, W. H., Addams, H. L., & Davis, B. (1993). Business planning in successful small firms. *Long Range Planning*, 26(6), 82–88.

*Baker, G. A., & Leidecker, J. K. (2001). Does it pay to plan?: Strategic planning and financial performance. *Agribusiness*, 17(3), 355–364.

*Barringer, B. R., Jones, F. F., & Neubaum, D. O. (2005). A quantitative content analysis of the characteristics of rapid-growth firms and their founders. *Journal of Business Venturing*, 20(5), 663–687.

*Berman, J., Gordon, D., & Sussman, G. (1997). A study to determine the benefits small business firms derive from sophisticated planning versus less sophisticated types of planning. *Journal of Business and Economic Studies*, 3(3), 1–11.

Boyd, B. K. (1991). Strategic planning and financial performance: A meta-analysis review. *Journal of Management Studies, 28*(4), 353–374.

*Bracker, J. S., & Pearson, J. N. (1986). Planning and financial performance of small, mature firms. *Strategic Management Journal, 7*(6), 503–522.

*Bracker, J. S., Keats, B. W., & Pearson, J. N. (1988). Planning and financial performance among small firms in a growth industry. *Strategic Management Journal, 9*(6), 591–603.

*Brews, P. J., & Hunt, M. R. (1999). Learning to plan and planning to learn: Resolving the planning school/learning school debate. *Strategic Management Journal, 20*(10), 889–889.

Brinckmann, J., Grichnik, D., & Kapsa, D. (2010). Should entrepreneurs plan or just storm the castle? A meta-analysis on contextual factors impacting the business planning-performance relationship in small firms. *Journal of Business Venturing, 25*(1), 24–40.

Bryson, J. M. (2011). *Strategic planning for public and nonprofit organizations: A guide to strengthening and sustaining organizational achievement.* San Francisco, CA: Jossey-Bass.

*Burt, D. N. (1978). Planning and performance in Australian retailing. *Long Range Planning, 11*(3), 62–66.

Cardinal, L. B., Miller, C. C., & Palich, L. P. (2011). Breaking the cycle of iteration: Forensic failures of international diversification and firm performance research. *Global Strategy Journal, 1*(1), 175–186.

*Capon, N., Farley, J. U., & Hulbert, J. M. (1994). Strategic planning and financial performance: More evidence. *The Journal of Management Studies, 31*(1), 105–105.

*Cassar, G. (2010). Are individuals entering self-employment overly optimistic? An empirical test of plans and projections on nascent entrepreneur expectations. *Strategic Management Journal, 31*(8), 822–840.

Chandler, A. D. (1962). *Strategy and structure: Chapters in the history of the American industrial enterprise.* Cambridge, MA: MIT Press.

Chandler, A. D. (1990). *Scale and scope: The dynamics of industrial capitalism.* Cambridge, MA: Harvard University Press.

Davis, F. D., Lohse, G. L., & Kottemann, J. E. (1994). Harmful effects of seemingly helpful information on forecasts of stock earnings. *Journal of Economic Psychology, 15*(2), 253–267.

*Delmar, F., & Shane, S. (2003). Does business planning facilitate the development of new ventures? *Strategic Management Journal, 24*(12), 1165–1165.

*Denning, B. W., & Lehr, M. E. (1972). The extent and nature of corporate long-range planning in the United Kingdom – II. *Journal of Management Studies, 9*(1), 1–18.

*Desai, A. B. (2000). Does strategic planning create value? The stock market's belief. *Management Decision, 38*(10), 685–693.

*Dess, G. G., & Priem, R. L. (1995). Consensus-performance research: Theoretical and empirical extensions. *The Journal of Management Studies, 32*(4), 401–417.

*Efendioglu, A. M., & Karabulut, A. T. (2010). Impact of strategic planning on financial performance of companies in Turkey. *International Journal of Business and Management, 5*(4), 3–12.

*Elbanna, S. (2008). Planning and participation as determinants of strategic planning effectiveness. *Management Decision, 46*(5), 779–96.

*Elbanna, S. (2012). Slack, planning and organizational performance: Evidence from the Arab Middle East. *European Management Review, 9*(2), 99–115.

*Falshaw, J., Glaister, K., & Tatoglu, E. (2006). Evidence on formal strategic planning and company performance. *Management Decision, 44*(1), 9–30.

Fayol, H. (1949). *General and industrial management.* C. Storrs (trans.) London: Pitman.

Feldman, M., & March, J. (1981). Information in organizations as a signal and symbol. *Administrative Science Quarterly, 26*(2), 171–86.

*Flores, L. G., Catalanello, R. F., Rau, D., & Saxena, N. (2008). Organizational learning as a moderator of the effect of strategic planning on company performance. *International Journal of Management, 25*(3), 569–577, 594.

*Fredrickson, J. W. (1984). The comprehensiveness of strategic decision processes: Extension, observations, future directions. *Academy of Management Journal, 27*(3), 445–466.

*Fredrickson, J. W., & Mitchell, T. R. (1984). Strategic decision processes: Comprehensiveness and performance in an industry with an unstable environment. *Academy of Management Journal, 27*(2), 399–423.

*French, S. J., Kelly, S. J., & Harrison, J. L. (2004). The role of strategic planning in the performance of small, professional service firms: A research note. *The Journal of Management Development, 23*(8), 765–76.

*Frese, M., Kraus, S. I., Keith, N., Escher, S., Grabarkiewicz, R., Luneng, S. T., Heers, C., Unger, J., & Friedrich, C. (2007). Business owners' action planning and its relationship to business success in three African countries. *Journal of Applied Psychology, 92*(6), 1481–1498.

★Frese, M., van Gelderen, M., & Ombach, M. (2000). How to plan as a small scale business owner: Psychological process characteristics of action strategies and success. *Journal of Small Business Management*, 38(2), 1–18.

★Fulmer, R. M., & Rue, L. W. (1974). The practice and profitability of long-range planning. *Managerial Planning*, 22(6), 1–7.

★Gable, M., & Topol, M. T. (1987). Planning practices of small-scale retailers. *American Journal of Small Business*, 12(2), 19–32.

★Gershefski, C. W., & Harvey, A. (1970). Corporate models – The state of the art. *Management Science*, 16(6), B-303–312.

★Ghobadian, A., O'Regan, N., Thomas, H., & Liu, J. (2008). Formal strategic planning, operating environment, size, sector and performance. *Journal of General Management*, 34(2), 1–20.

★Gibson, B., & Cassar, G. (2005). Longitudinal analysis of relationships between planning and performance in small firms. *Small Business Economics*, 25(3), 207–222.

Gielnik, M. M., Frese, M., & Stark, M. S. (2015). Planning and entrepreneurship. In M. D. Mumford & M. Frese (Eds.), *The Psychology of planning in organizations: Research and Applications*. New York: Routledge.

★Glaister, K., Dincer, O., Tatoglu, E., Demirbag, M., & Zaim, S. (2008). A causal analysis of formal strategic planning and firm performance evidence from an emerging country. *Management Decision*, 46(3), 365–91.

★Glen, W., & Weerawardena, J. (1996). Strategic planning practices in small enterprises in Queensland, *Small Enterprise Research*, 4(3), 5–16.

★Goll, I., & Rasheed, A. M. A. (1997). Rational decision-making and firm performance: The moderating role of environment. *Strategic Management Journal*, 18(7), 583–591.

★Griggs, H. E. (2002). Strategic planning system characteristics and organisational effectiveness in Australian small-scale firms. *Irish Journal of Management*, 23(1), 23–51.

Grinyer, P. H., & Norburn, D. (1974). Strategic planning in 21 UK companies. *Long Range Planning*, 7(4), 80–88.

★Grinyer, P. H., Al-Bazzaz, S., & Yasai-Ardekani, M. (1986). Towards a contingency theory of corporate planning: Findings in 48 UK companies. *Strategic Management Journal*, 7(1), 3–28.

★Haber, S., & Reichel, A. (2007). The cumulative nature of the entrepreneurial process: The contribution of human capital, planning and environment resources to small venture performance. *Journal of Business Venturing*, 22(1), 119–45.

★Hahn, W., & Powers, T. L. (2010). Strategic plan quality, implementation capability, and firm performance. *Academy of Strategic Management Journal*, 9(1), 63–81.

Herbert, T. T. (1999). Multinational strategic planning: Matching central expectations to local realities. *Long Range Planning*, 32(1), 81–87.

★Herold, D. M. (1972). Long-range planning and organizational performance: A cross-valuation study. *Academy of Management Journal*, 15(1), 91–102.

★Hoffman, R. C. (2007). The strategic planning process and performance relationship: Does culture matter? *Journal of Business Strategies*, 24(1):27–48.

Hoffman, V. B., & Patton, J. M. (1997). Accountability, the dilution effect, and conservatism in auditors' fraud judgments. *Journal of Accounting Research*, 35(2), 227–237.

Honig, B., & Karlsson, T. (2004). Institutional forces and the written business plan. *Journal of Management*, 30(1), 29–48.

★Honig, B., & Samuelsson, M. (2012). Planning and the entrepreneur: A longitudinal examination of nascent entrepreneurs in Sweden. *Journal of Small Business Management*, 50(3), 365–388

★Hopkins, W. E., & Hopkins, S. A. (1997). Strategic planning-financial performance relationships in banks: A causal examination. *Strategic Management Journal*, 18(8), 635–52.

Hwang, M. I., & Lin, J. W. (1999). Information dimension, information overload and decision quality. *Journal of Information Science*, 25(3), 213–218.

Iselin, E. R. (1993). The effects of the information and data properties of financial ratios and statements on managerial decision quality. *Journal of Business Finance and Accounting*, 20(2), 249–266.

★Jenster, P. V., & Overstreet, G. A., Jr. (1990). Planning for a non-profit service: A study of U.S. credit unions. *Long Range Planning*, 23(2), 103–111.

★Jones, W. D. (1982). Characteristics of planning in small firms. *Journal of Small Business Management*, 20(3), 15–19.

★Kallman, E. A., & Shapiro, H. J. (1978). The motor freight industry: A case against planning. *Long Range Planning*, 11(1), 81–86.

★Kargar, J. (1996). Strategic planning system characteristics and planning effectiveness in small mature firms. *The Mid-Atlantic Journal of Business*, 32(1), 19–19.

*Karger, D. W., & Malik, Z. A. (1975). Long-range planning and organizational performance. *Long Range Planning*, 8(6), 60–64.

*Kirsch, D., Goldfarb, B., & Gera, A. (2009). Form or substance: The role of business plans in venture capital decision making. *Strategic Management Journal*, 30(5), 487.

*Klein, H. E. (1981). The impact of planning on growth and profit. *Journal of Bank Research*, 12(2), 105–105.

*Kohtamäki, M., Kraus, S., Mäkelä, M., & Rönkkö, M. (2012). The role of personnel commitment to strategy implementation and organisational learning within the relationship between strategic planning and company performance. *International Journal of Entrepreneurial Behaviour & Research*, 18(2), 159–178.

*Kraus, S., Harms, R., & Schwarz, E. J. (2006). Strategic planning in smaller enterprises: New empirical findings. *Management Research News*, 29(6), 334–344.

*Kudla, R. J. (1980). The effects of strategic planning on common stock returns. *Academy of Management Journal*, 23(1), 5–20.

*Kudla, R. J., & Cesta, J. R. (1982). Planning and financial performance: A discriminant analysis. *Akron Business and Economic Review*, 13(1), 30–30.

*Kukalis, S. (1991). Determinants of strategic planning systems in large organizations: A contingency approach. *Journal of Management Studies*, 28(2), 143–160.

*Lange, J. E., Mollov, A., Pearlmutter, M., Singh, S., & Bygrave, W. D. (2007). Pre-start-up formal business plans and post-start-up performance: A study of 116 new ventures. *Venture Capital*, 9(4), 237–256.

*Leontiades, M., & Tezel, A. (1980). Planning perceptions and planning results. *Strategic Management Journal*, 7(1), 503–522.

*Liao, J., & Gartner, W. B. (2006). The effects of pre-venture plan timing and perceived environmental uncertainty on the persistence of emerging firms. *Small Business Economics*, 27(1), 23–23.

*Love, L. G., Priem, R. L., & Lumpkin, G. T. (2002). Explicitly articulated strategy and firm performance under alternative levels of centralization. *Journal of Management*, 28(5), 611–627.

*Lumpkin, G. T., Shrader, R. C., & Hills, G. E. (1998). Does formal business planning enhance the performance of new ventures? In P. D. Reynolds, W. D. Bygrave, N. M. Carter, S. Manigart, & C. M. Mason (Eds.), *Frontiers of entrepreneurship research* (pp. 180–189). Wellesley, MA: Babson College.

*Lyles, M. A., Baird, I. S., Orris, J. B., & Kuratko, D. F. (1993). Formalized planning in small business: Increasing strategic choices. *Journal of Small Business Management*, 31(2), 38–38.

*McKiernan, P., & Morris, C. (1994). Strategic planning and financial performance in UK SMEs: Does formality matter? *British Journal of Management*, 5(1), 11–S31.

March, J., & Simon, H. (1958). *Organizations*. New York: Wiley.

March, J. G. (2006). Rationality, foolishness, and adaptive intelligence. *Strategic Management Journal*, 27(3), 201–214.

*Masurel, E., & Smit, H. P. (2000). Planning behavior of small firms in central Vietnam. *Journal of Small Business Management*, 38(2), 95–102.

Miller, C. C., & Cardinal, L. B. (1994). Strategic planning and firm performance: A synthesis of more than two decades of research. *Academy of Management Journal*, 37(6), 1649–1665.

Miller, C. C., Washburn, N. T., & Glick, W. H. (2013). The myth of firm performance. *Organization Science*, 24(3), 948–964.

Milliman, J., Von Glinow, M., & Nathan, M. (1991). Organizational life cycles and strategic international human resource management in multinational companies: Implications for congruence theory. *Academy of Management Review*, 16(2), 318–339.

Mintzberg, H. (1990). The design school: Reconsidering the basic premises of strategic management. *Strategic Management Journal*, 11(3), 171–195.

Mintzberg, H. (1994). *The rise and fall of strategic planning*. New York: The Free Press.

Mumford, M. D., Mecca, J. T., & Watts, L. L. (2015). Planning processes: Relevant cognitive operations. In M. D. Mumford & M. Frese (Eds.), *The psychology of planning in organizations: Research and applications*. New York: Routledge.

Nelson, R. R., & Winter, S. G. (1982). *An evolutionary theory of economic change*. Boston, MA: Harvard University Press.

Nisbett, R. E., Zukier, H., & Lemley, R. E. (1981). The dilution effect: Nondiagnostic information weakens the implications of diagnostic information. *Cognitive Psychology*, 13(2), 248–277.

*Odom, R. Y., & Boxx, W. R. (1988). Environment, planning processes, and organizational performance of churches. *Strategic Management Journal*, 9(2), 197–205.

*Olson, P. D., & Bokor, D. W. (1995). Strategy process–content interaction: Effects on growth performance in small, start-up firms. *Journal of Small Business Management*, 33(1), 34–44.

*O'Regan, N., & Ghobadian, A. (2002). Effective strategic planning in small and medium sized firms. *Management Decision*, 40(7), 663–671.

*Orpen, C. (1985). The effects of long-range planning on small business performance: A further examination. *Journal of Small Business Management*, 23(1), 16–23.

*Orpen, C. (1994). Strategic planning, scanning activities and the financial performance of small firms. *Journal of Strategic Change*, 3(1), 45–55.

*Orser, B. J., Hogarth-Scott, S., & Riding, A. L. (2000). Performance, firm size, and management problem solving. *Journal of Small Business Management*, 38(4), 42–58.

Pearce, J. A., Freeman, E. B., & Robinson, R. B. (1987a). The tenuous link between formal strategic planning and financial performance. *Academy of Management Review*, 12(4), 658–675.

*Pearce, J. A., Robbins, D. K., & Robinson, R. B. (1987b). The impact of grand strategy and planning formality on financial performance. *Strategic Management Journal*, 8(2), 125–134.

*Peel, M. J., & Bridge, J. (1998), How planning and capital budgeting improve SME performance. *Long Range Planning*, 31(6), 848–56.

*Perry, S. C. (2001). The relationship between written business plans and the failure of small businesses in the *Journal of Small Business Management*, 39(3), 201–208.

Pfeffer, J. (2005). Producing sustainable competitive advantage through the effective management of people. *Academy of Management Executive*, 19(4), 95–106.

*Powell, T. C. (1992). Strategic planning as competitive advantage. *Strategic Management Journal*, 13(7), 551–558.

*Powell, T. C. (1994). Untangling the relationship between strategic planning and performance: The role of contingency factors. *Revue Canadienne Des Sciences De l'Administration*, 11(2), 124–138.

*Priem, R. L., Rasheed, A. M. A., & Kotulic, A. G. (1995). Rationality in strategic decision processes, environmental dynamism and firm performance. *Journal of Management*, 21(5), 913–929.

*Rauch, A., & Frese, M. (1998). A contingency approach to small scale business success: A longitudinal study on the effects of environmental hostility and uncertainty on the relationship of planning and success. In P. D. Reynolds, W. D. Bygrave, N. M. Carter, S. Manigart, & C. M. Mason (Eds.), *Frontiers of entrepreneurship research* (pp. 190–200). Wellesley, MA: Babson College.

*Rauch, A., Frese, M., & Sonnentag, S. (2000). Cultural differences in planning-success relationship: A comparison of small enterprises in Ireland, West Germany, and East Germany. *Journal of Small Business Management*, 38(4), 28–41.

*Reid, G. C., & Smith, J. A. (2000). What makes a new business start-up successful? *Small Business Economics*, 14(3), 165–182.

*Rhyne, L. C. (1986). The relationship of strategic planning to financial performance. *Strategic Management Journal*, 7(5), 423–436.

*Risseeuw, P., & Masurel, E. (1994). The role of planning in small firms: Empirical evidence from a service industry. *Small Business Economics*, 6(4), 313–22.

*Robinson, R. B. (1982). The importance of outsiders in small firm strategic planning. *Academy of Management Journal*, 25(1), 80–93.

*Robinson, R. B., & Littlejohn, W. F. (1981). Important contingencies in small firm planning. *Journal of Small Business Management*, 19(3), 45–48.

*Robinson, R. B., & Pearce, J. A. (1983). The impact of formalized strategic planning on financial performance in small organizations. *Strategic Management Journal*, 4(3), 197–207.

*Robinson, R. B., Pearce, J. A., Vozikis, C. S., & Mescon, T. S. (1984). The relationship between stage of development and small firm planning and performance. *Journal of Small Business Management*, 22(2), 45–52.

*Robinson, R. B., Logan, J. E., & Salem, M. Y. (1986). Strategic versus operational planning in small retail firms. *American Journal of Small Business*, 10(3), 7–16.

Rogers, P. R., & Bamford, C. E. (2002). Information planning process and strategic orientation: The importance of fit in high-performing organizations. *Journal of Business Research*, 55(3), 205–215.

*Rogers, P. R., Miller, A., & Judge, W. Q. (1999). Using information-processing theory to understand planning/performance relationships in the context of strategy. *Strategic Management Journal*, 20(6), 567–567.

Rousseau, D. M. (2006). Is there such a thing as "evidence based management"? *Academy of Management Review*, 31(2), 256–269.

★Rudd, J., Greenley, G., Beatson, A., & Lings, I., (2008). Strategic planning and performance: Extending the debate. *Journal of Business Research*, 61(2), 99–108.

★Rue, L. W., & Ibrahim, N. A. (1998). The relationship between planning sophistication and performance in small businesses. *Journal of Small Business Management*, 36(4), 24–32.

Rynes, S. L. (2007). Tackling the "great divide" between research production and dissemination in human resource management. *Academy of Management Journal*, 50(5), 985–986.

★Sapp, R. W., & Seiler, R. E. (1981). The relationship between long-range planning and financial performance of U.S. commercial banks. *Managerial Planning*, 30(2), 32–36.

★Sarason, Y., & Tegarden, L. F. (2003). The erosion of the competitive advantage of strategic planning: A configuration theory and resource based view. *Journal of Business and Management*, 9(1), 1–20.

Schwenk, C. B., & Shrader, C. B. (1993). Effects of formal strategic planning on financial performance in small firms: A meta-analysis. *Entrepreneurship Theory and Practice*, 17(3), 53–64.

★Sexton, D. L., & Van Auken, P. (1985). A longitudinal study of small business strategic planning. *Journal of Small Business Management*, 23(1), 7–15.

★Shane, S., & Delmar, F. (2004). Planning for the market: business planning before marketing and the continuation of organizing efforts. *Journal of Business Venturing*, 19(6), 767–785.

★Shrader, C. B., Mulford, C. L., & Blackburn, V. L. (1989). Strategic and operational planning, uncertainty, and performance in small firms. *Journal of Small Business Management*, 27(4), 45–45.

★Shrader, C. B., Chacko, T. I., Herrmann, P., & Mulford, C. (2004). Planning and firm performance: Effects of multiple planning activities and technology policy. *International Journal of Management & Decision Making*, 5(2/3), 171–195.

Sitkin, S. B., Cardinal, L. B., & Bijlsma-Frankema, K. M. (Eds.) (2010). *Organizational control*. Cambridge, UK: Cambridge University Press.

Sitkin, S. B., See, K. E., Miller, C. C., Lawless, M. W., & Carton, A. M. (2011). The paradox of stretch goals: Organizations in the pursuit of the seemingly impossible. *Academy of Management Review*, 36(3), 544–566.

★Slevin, D. P., & Covin, J. G. (1997). Strategy formation patterns, performance, and the significance of context. *Journal of Management*, 23(2), 189–209.

★Smith, J. A. (1998). Strategies for start-ups. *Long Range Planning*, 31(6), 857–872.

★Song, M., Im, S., van der Bij, H., & Song, L. Z. (2011). Does strategic planning enhance or impede innovation and firm performance? *The Journal of Product Innovation Management*, 28(4), 503–520.

Stokke, P. R., Ralston, W. K., Boyce, T. A., & Wilson, I. H. (1990). Scenario planning for Norwegian oil and gas. *Long Range Planning*, 23(2), 17–26.

★Suklev, B., & Debarliev, S. (2012). Strategic planning effectiveness comparative analysis of the Macedonian context. *Economic and Business Review*, 14(1), 63–93.

★Thune, S. S., & House, R. J. (1970). Where long-range planning pays off. *Business Horizons*, 13(4), 81–87.

Vancil, R. F., & Lorange, P. (1975). Strategic planning in diversified companies. *Harvard Business Review*, 53(1), 81–90.

★van Gelderen, M., Frese, M., & Thurik, R. (2000). Strategies, uncertainty and performance of small business startups. *Small Business Economics*, 15(3), 164–181.

★Walters, P. G. P. (1993). Patterns of formal planning and performance in U.S. exporting firms. *Management International Review*, 33(1), 43–43.

★Welch, J. B. (1984). Strategic planning could improve your share price. *Long Range Planning*, 17(2), 144–147.

Whitecotton, S. M., Sanders, D. E., & Norris, K. B. (1998). Improving predictive accuracy with a combination of human intuition and mechanical decision aids. *Organizational Behavior and Human Decision Processes*, 76(3), 325–348.

★Whitehead, D. D., & Gup, B. E. (1985). Bank and thrift profitability: Does strategic planning really pay? *Economic Review* (Federal Reserve Bank of Atlanta), 70(9), 14–25.

Wolf, C., & Floyd, S. W. (2013). Strategic planning research: Toward a theory-driven agenda. *Journal of Management*, 0149206313478185, first published on March 26, 2013 as doi:10.1177/0149206313478185.

★Wood, D. R., & LaForge, R. L. (1979). The impact of comprehensive planning on financial performance. *Academy of Management Journal*, 7(22), 516–526.

★Wood, D. R., Johnston, R. A., & DeGenaro, G. J. (1988). The impact of formal planning on the financial performance of real estate firms. *Journal of Business Strategies*, 5(1), 44–51.

★Yusuf, A., & Saffu, K. (2005). Planning and performance of small and medium enterprise operators in a country in transition. *Journal of Small Business Management*, 43(4), 480–497.

15

PLANNING AND ENTREPRENEURSHIP

Michael M. Gielnik, Michael Frese, and Miriam S. Stark

Entrepreneurship is defined as detecting and pursuing future opportunities (Shane & Venkataraman, 2000). Future opportunities are usually developed in the context of high uncertainty and complexity. Because of the uncertainty and complexity inherent in entrepreneurship, there has been great skepticism towards planning in entrepreneurship. As a matter of fact, one could even talk of a common stereotype that both researchers of entrepreneurship and entrepreneurs themselves perceive that planning is not helpful for entrepreneurs and that it may even backfire (Baker, Miner, & Eesley, 2003; Honig & Karlsson, 2004; Sarasvathy, 2001). We think that this stereotype exists because it is easy to misunderstand the multifactorial functions of planning for entrepreneurship. Planning has multifactorial functions because planning can be done at different levels (i.e. the individual, the team, or the organization) and planning can be formal or informal. Formal planning may be in the form of a business plan (often done by one entrepreneur) or in the form of a strategic plan (often developed as a longer exercise of bottom-up and top-down planning by a strategic department as a staff function for the CEO). Informal plans are usually in the head of the planner(s) and they are usually more concerned with detailing specific actions relevant for goal accomplishment. The various functions of planning may have advantages and disadvantages for entrepreneurship. Therefore, a comprehensive perspective on planning in entrepreneurship is necessary. In this chapter, we seek to present such a comprehensive perspective. We first discuss the potential disadvantages and advantages of planning. We emphasize that it is important to consider the different levels and the different degrees of formality to better understand the positive and negative effects of planning discussed in the literature. We then present a theory of planning that helps us to better understand planning in entrepreneurship. In our discussion, we focus on the individual entrepreneur (or a small group of entrepreneurs) because entrepreneurial firms are often highly affected by an individual and the process of starting a firm and growing it is highly dependent upon the lead entrepreneur. Thus, the following discussion is centered mainly around the entrepreneur or a small group of founders or top managers of a firm (if not otherwise noted).

Disadvantages of Planning

Mintzberg (2000) sees three problems in planning: (a) the planner has insufficient knowledge of how to do business planning, (b) the future is unpredictable, and (c) there may be negative side effects of planning. Although Mintzberg (2000) was referring to organizations, we think that his framework also helps to structure the discussion about the disadvantages of planning in entrepreneurship on the individual level.

Insufficient Knowledge of Business Planning

Many entrepreneurs lack basic knowledge and skills in developing a business plan (Bewayo, 2010). In fact, lack of knowledge and lack of skills to prepare business plans are the main reasons for not writing one (along with not needing a business plan and the inconvenience of preparing one) (Bewayo, 2010). Entrepreneurs are usually not experts in business administration or business planning but in the domain in which they intend to start their business. For example, Baker et al. (2003) have described several cases of entrepreneurs deciding to start a business in their job domain but with no or only a little knowledge on how to do formal business planning. Some scholars have argued that this approach may be functional. Learning to write a business plan and preparing a business plan may be too time consuming. Instead, entrepreneurs should jump into the entrepreneurial process and engage in the necessary start-up activities to establish business structures (Carter, Gartner, & Reynolds, 1996).

In addition to lack of knowledge specifically related to business planning, Dörner and Schaub (1994, p. 448) identified four general cognitive problems in people's planning: "(1) the restricted capacity of human conscious thinking, (2) the tendency of humans to guard their feeling of competence and efficacy, (3) the weight of the actual problem, and (4) forgetting." All four factors lead to frequent mistakes in planning, or at least they tie up resources, thus restricting attention to important things outside the planning process. Even more problems in planning occur when people display low cognitive effort in planning (Josephs & Hahn, 1995) or when general mental ability or general schooling is low (Frese et al., 2007). Errors in planning can also be based on the wrong choice of information. Once plans are based on inappropriate information and knowledge, corrections take time and can create additional costs (Mumford, Schultz, & Van Doorn, 2001).

The above arguments against planning tell us that inexperienced young entrepreneurs may not be able to write a good business plan. Moreover, writing a business plan may take too much cognitive capacity and thus be a distraction from entrepreneurial actions and creative thinking. However, business plans often have to be written for banks and for reasons of legitimacy, and a certain amount of learning may take place in developing a plan. Business schools (and other learning institutions) should therefore teach how to do good business planning. So, there remains the problem about the inability to predict the future and the negative side effects of planning.

Lack of Knowledge about the Future

Planning implies making forecasts based on assumptions about the future. Both Sarasvathy (2001) and Mintzberg (1994) have criticized the theoretical foundation of planning because, in most entrepreneurial situations, it is not possible to predict the future. Accordingly, Sarasvathy (2001) has suggested using effectuation instead of planning. *Effectuation* is defined as taking the existing means as a starting point for one's actions and then selecting between possible effects that can be achieved with those available means (Sarasvathy, 2001). Effectuation is thus means oriented (Sarasvathy, 2001). Effectuation is conceptualized to contrast with causation (which implies planning). *Causation* is defined as taking a particular effect as the starting point and selecting between different means to create this effect (Sarasvathy, 2001). This means that in causation, people form a goal (e.g. to start a new venture) and then do the planning in assembling the necessary resources (the means) to accomplish the goal. Causation is thus a goal- and plan-oriented approach. According to Sarasvathy, Dew, Stuart, and Wiltbank (2008), causation corresponds to the planned strategy approaches towards entrepreneurship. Entrepreneurs using causation envision their business, define the goals and plans to implement the vision, and direct their efforts at achieving the pre-envisioned venture (Chandler, DeTienne, McKelvie, & Mumford, 2011). They thus follow a systematic plan that has been determined up front.

Sarasvathy and colleagues (2008, 2001) have noted that planning and effectuation are two opposing approaches because the logic underlying the two approaches is fundamentally different. In planning (or causation), the logic is to predict the future (what will happen and how can I prepare for it?). Typical predictive tools are market surveys, financial projections with calculations of risk-adjusted expected returns, or competitors' retaliation strategies (Wiltbank, Stuart, Dew, & Sarasvathy, 2009). Causation is most commonly used in approaches towards entrepreneurship that are built around the development of formal business plans (e.g. entrepreneurship courses). In contrast, the effectuation logic is to control the future (what can I make happen?). Sarasvathy et al. (2008) have argued that the future is uncertain (probabilities for future consequences cannot be calculated), there is ambiguity regarding the preferences of other stakeholders, and there is ambiguity regarding relevant information. This means that effectuation (i.e. non-planning) is the more promising approach because it does not rely on predicting or adapting to the future environment. The "future is contingent upon actions by willful agents intersubjectively seeking to reshape the world and fabricate new ones" (Sarasvathy et al., 2008, p. 339). According to the logic of effectuation, we do not have to predict the future (which is impossible to predict anyway) if we can control the future by our own actions. Entrepreneurs should thus consider making more use of non-predictive strategies, such as focusing on the available means, and seek to control the future (Wiltbank et al., 2009).

Similar to effectuation, the concepts of *improvisation* and *bricolage* also do not rely on prediction of the future. Improvisation and bricolage are two different concepts and we therefore discuss them separately (Baker et al., 2003). Improvisation means that the design and execution of actions converge (Baker et al., 2003). When entrepreneurs improvise, it is not necessary that they know a lot about the future because they design and execute their actions at the same time. In contrast, in the design-precedes-execution approach, entrepreneurs plan their activities and then work on their entrepreneurial tasks according to this plan. Baker et al. (2003) found empirically both types of entrepreneurs – improvising and planning entrepreneurs. Planning entrepreneurs used a design-precedes-execution approach, which means that new venture creation was preceded by a plan. In this approach, the creation of a new venture was a planned and well-structured process. Improvising entrepreneurs usually started with a rough idea (e.g. a preliminary testing device) and the process of creating the new venture unfolded during ongoing interactions with other stakeholders. In this case, design or planning did not precede action but the entrepreneurs "just started moving" and designed their actions along the process of creating the new venture (Baker et al., 2003).

Bricolage is a related but conceptually a slightly different construct. Bricolage means that entrepreneurs 'make do' by recombining readily available resources for new purposes (Baker et al., 2003; Baker & Nelson, 2005). 'Making do' means that entrepreneurs exploit opportunities or solve problems. 'Recombining resources for new purposes' means that entrepreneurs creatively use resources for new purposes that have not been originally associated with these resources. 'Readily available' means that entrepreneurs use resources which are available in their direct environment or are cheap and easy to get. Bricolage can be used in all areas, such as financing, supply, premises, equipment, and customers (Baker & Nelson, 2005). Bricolage may be particularly useful in environments which require entrepreneurs to take action quickly to exploit opportunities and in environments which provide only few resources (Baker & Nelson, 2005). When entrepreneurs use bricolage, they draw on the resources that are readily available, which means that they usually do not plan in advance for specific resources. Furthermore, when entrepreneurs use improvisation, it is not possible for them to plan for the resources they need but they have to make do with the resources that are at hand at the moment of execution. Any form of improvisation thus implies bricolage. However, bricolage does not always imply improvisation. Bricolage can also occur in the implementation of pre-determined plans (Baker et al., 2003). It is possible that entrepreneurs have a pre-existing plan which specifies the use of bricolage to accomplish the goal. In this case, behavior following a design-precedes-execution (planning) approach includes the strategy of bricolage. Baker et al. (2003) provides the example of planning to go on a hiking trip and intending to make a campfire with whatever materials are at hand at the camp.

In summary, scholars have argued that planning implies some knowledge of the future, but because it is impossible to predict the future, planning may be a waste of effort and resources (e.g. Sarasvathy, 2001). Instead, other approaches, such as effectuation (Sarasvathy, 2001), improvisation, or bricolage (Baker et al., 2003; Baker & Nelson, 2005) might be better for entrepreneurs. We note that this perspective might not give full consideration to the complexity of people's ability to make forecasts. There is some evidence that in more uncertain environments (and thus environments that are more difficult to predict), entrepreneurs put less emphasis on the development of sophisticated plans (Matthews & Scott, 1995). However, there is also research showing that people are accurate in their forecasts if they have expertise and a mindset of wanting to implement the idea (Dailey & Mumford, 2006). This means that entrepreneurs who have better knowledge of the business environment (expert or repeat entrepreneurs) will probably be better able to plan because they can predict future trends more accurately. In contrast, because of their lower knowledge about the turbulences of the environment, novice entrepreneurs are less likely to be served well by extensive planning (Brinckmann, Grichnik, & Kapsa, 2010; Miller & Cardinal, 1994). In conclusion, not being able to forecast may only hold for some entrepreneurs (e.g. novice entrepreneurs in uncertain environments) but not for others (e.g. expert entrepreneurs).

The Negative Side Effects of Planning: Lack of Time and Stickiness of Plans

Scholars have argued that planning is time consuming and leads to rigidity and escalation of commitment (Dörner & Schaub, 1994). Instead of working on business plans, the time could be invested in practical actions (Carter et al., 1996). Furthermore, entrepreneurs may perceive the entrepreneurial process as more difficult when they plan too much. Pascha, Schöppe, and Hacker (2001) showed an increase in perceived task difficulty when the planning scope was increased. The more activities people had to plan for, the more time they needed to complete a given task and the more they perceived the task as difficult. Also, greater difficulties in planning lead people to use not just mental processes but also external planning tools (e.g. notes, drafts), which may consume even more time (Pascha et al., 2001). Additionally, planning may not only consume time but also lead to more time pressure afterwards. People often underestimate the time to complete tasks in planning processes (Hayes-Roth & Hayes-Roth, 1979). Possibly, they model their timing on idealized cases that simplify the tasks (Mumford et al., 2001).

Planning may lead to rigidity and inflexibility. Mintzberg (1994) has argued that the concept of strategic planning actually blocks the manager from strategic thinking. Referring to the structure of planning as a fixed destination of the joint entrepreneurship journey of management and employees, he criticizes that planning stands for a "calculating style of management" and not for a committed style (Mintzberg, 1994, p. 109). In this debate, Jack Welch, former CEO of General Electric, is often cited because he saw in the strategic planning departments of large companies tendencies towards top-down authoritarianism and bureaucracy. Rigid organizational planning creates a bureaucratic atmosphere that hinders the cultivation of a nimble entrepreneurial atmosphere. Moreover, Welch saw the strategic planning departments as nitpickers who would destroy good ideas by worrying about potential failures (Welch & Welch, 2005). Both Mintzberg and Welch regarded centralized strategic planning departments as counterforces towards becoming learning organizations. Honig (2004) has argued that planning is often the opposite of creative approaches to entrepreneurs' problems. Planning limits the range of creative activities in a dynamic environment. A resulting disadvantage is the inability of firms to react flexibly to shifts in the market. They seem to adhere too often to a given plan. Planning can inhibit the entrepreneur from reacting quickly and spontaneously to meet business opportunities (Bewayo, 2010). Findings by Slotegraaf and Dickson (2004) further underline this line of reasoning. Although marketing plans were positively related to firm performance, strong marketing plans were related to a lower degree of improvisation (Slotegraaf & Dickson, 2004). Moreover, there was a curvilinear relationship with performance. Companies with very high marketing planning actually showed lower performance than those with average marketing planning.

Another form of the stickiness of plans is escalation of commitment (Staw & Ross, 1987). Escalation of commitment is related to the investments made (and planning is obviously such an investment) and to the feeling of responsibility (Staw & Ross, 1987). Planning is a psychological investment of time and effort, and such investments often contribute to sticking to a plan. The reluctance to deviate from a plan can be an example of escalation of commitment, which can increase inflexibility (Rauch, Frese, & Sonnentag, 2000; Wiltbank, Dew, Read, & Sarasvathy, 2006). Entrepreneurs make investment in plans, they receive negative feedback (because of some error in their plan, which invariably happens) and they feel personally responsible for the course of action. Escalation of commitment results in pressure to continue and to justify the investments. To counter escalation of commitment and rigidity, Wiltbank et al. (2006) have suggested adaptive planning approaches that do not invest time in detection or prediction of future events but train organizations in situational flexibility to be able to adapt quickly to changes in the environment and learn from environmental feedback. However, it is important to note that escalation of commitment also has positive consequences – entrepreneurs do not give up too easily and, therefore, they resist and are even motivated by negative events (Gollwitzer, 1996).

What follows from the above: the higher the investment, the stronger may be the negative effects of planning. This speaks for a low degree of planning. Moreover, it may pay off to teach a planning style that increases flexibility within the planning process (Frese, van Gelderen, & Ombach, 2000; Wiltbank et al., 2006). We do not know yet when escalation of commitment has positive or negative consequences in entrepreneurship. Not giving up in spite of a difficult environment may be a prerequisite of any form of entrepreneurship; throwing good money after bad in a losing course of action is certainly a negative consequence of escalation of commitment. However, it is unclear whether a strategy is part of a losing course of action. Four de-escalation strategies may be useful: "(a) making negative outcomes less threatening, (b) setting minimum target levels that, if not achieved, would lead to a change in policy, (c) evaluating decision makers on the basis of their decision process rather than outcome" (Simonson & Staw, 1992, p. 419), and (d) setting milestones.

Disadvantages of Planning: Conclusions

We think of the issues discussed above as *potential* problems related to planning, such as lack of knowledge and skills in business planning, lack of knowledge about the future, too time consuming, inhibiting other actions, and rigidity. Furthermore, Honig and Karlsson (2004) criticized the function of the business plan as being only an instrument to satisfy the pressure of the business environment to produce written business plans. The authors furthermore see the danger that entrepreneurs are forced by business planning into imitating other successful businesses (Honig & Karlsson, 2004). Given this discussion of the potential negative effects of planning, why is there an overall positive effect of planning on performance in entrepreneurship (Brinckmann et al., 2010)? In the next section, we answer this question by turning to the positive aspects of planning.

The Advantages of Planning

Empirical Answer: Meta-Analyses of Planning Show Positive Relationship with Success

In a way, an easy response to some of these common stereotypes would be to refer to the meta-analyses that demonstrated planning to have positive consequences: the more entrepreneurs (Brinckmann et al., 2010) and organizations (Schwenk & Shrader, 1993) plan, the greater is their success. However, there are two problems with such an answer. First, there are contradictions in these meta-analyses (and unfortunately the authors do not comment on them or resolve them, although there is an overlap of authors). Brinckmann et al.'s (2010) effect size was based on a "d" and the average effect size was 0.20. In another study with overlapping authors (Mayer-Haug, Read, Brinckmann, Dew, & Grichnik, 2013) the effect size for planning was about $r = 0.19$. These two effects sizes look alike but they are not – when r is converted into d, the d is most likely to be about twice as large as the r (Hunter & Schmidt, 2004). Calculating the d for the r of 0.19 of Mayer-Haug et al. (2013) leads to $d = 0.39$, which is about double the effect size reported in Brinckmann et al. (2010). The meta-analysis by Schwenk and Shrader (1993) was done much earlier and concentrated on formal planning in small firms; it is based on fewer studies with an effect size of $d = 0.40$, which is roughly the same as in Mayer-Haug et al. (2013) and double of the effect size reported by Brinckmann et al. (2010). Thus, at the very least, there are incompatible results and unresolved issues in these published meta-analyses (cf. also the chapter by Cardinal, Miller, Kreutzer, and TenBrink in this book).

Second, the effects of the studies analyzed in the meta-analyses are not homogeneous. This means that effect sizes differ widely between studies. This is not a problem of these meta-analyses – as a matter of fact, it is precisely one of the advantages of meta-analyses that they can give an empirical answer to the issue of whether the reported relationships are hetero- or homogeneous. Thus, in the case of planning, there are positive relationships between planning and entrepreneurial success; however, some studies find only weak relationships, and some even a negative relationship (Carland, Carland, & Abhy, 1989; Honig & Karlsson, 2004; Robinson & Pearce, 1983; Sexton & Auken, 1985). The above-mentioned meta-analyses found some moderators of the relationships between planning and entrepreneurial success. They found that the relationships are moderated by firm factors (such as newness) or by cultural environment. This means that planning is beneficial for some firms or environments but less so for others. For example, planning at an early stage of business formation may lead to negative outcomes for business performance (Boyd, 1991; Carter et al., 1996; Honig & Karlsson, 2004; Keeley & Kapp, 1994; Lumpkin, Schrader, & Hills, 1998; Robinson & Pearce, 1983). However, given the empirical literature on planning in entrepreneurship, the meta-analyses were not able to fully determine which moderators lead to homogeneous relationships. Again, this is not surprising and it is true of most meta-analyses in the area of entrepreneurship (Frese, Bausch, Schmidt, Rauch, & Kabst, 2012). We assume that many studies up to this point have not been differentiated enough for a full understanding of the processes and outcomes of planning. Our next part attempts to provide a comprehensive overview of the processes and outcomes relevant to the positive functions of planning.

Action-Regulatory Function of Planning

Planning regulates action and entrepreneurship requires entrepreneurial action (Baron, 2007; Frese, 2009; McMullen & Shepherd, 2006). Entrepreneurs have to take action to develop an initial business idea into a viable and feasible business concept, they have to take action to assemble the necessary resources and equipment to establish business structures, and they have to take action to manage the business and ensure its sustainability (Delmar & Shane, 2004; Dimov, 2007; Gartner, 1985). According to action regulation theory (Frese & Zapf, 1994; Frese, 2009), entrepreneurs have to form some sort of action plans to successfully initiate and maintain action. As long as there is no goal and as long as one does not know how to achieve the goal, there is no action. From this perspective, Sarasvathy's (2001) concept of effectuation in its radical form without goals and without any plans, leads to lack of action and, at best, to some form of reaction.[1] If there is one consistent finding in entrepreneurship, it is the fact that reactive forms of behavior – the opposite of proactive planning – are highly correlated with failure and predictive of entrepreneurial bankruptcy (Frese et al., 2000; Hiemstra, van der Kooy, & Frese, 2006; van Gelderen, Frese, & Thurik, 2000; Keyser, De Kruif, & Frese, 2000; van Steekelenburg, Lauw, & Frese, 2000). Moreover, when confronted with errors and problem situations, a reactive form of trial and error leads to negative effects in performance (Rooks, Sserwanga, & Frese, in press; van der Linden, Sonnentag, Frese, & van Dyck, 2001; van Gelder, de Vries, Frese, & Goutbeek, 2007). In contrast, psychological action planning measured as elaborated and proactive informal planning is, indeed, related to entrepreneurial success, even in difficult environments (Frese et al., 2007).

One of the best theories to explain the function of planning is the theory by Gollwitzer (1996). Gollwitzer (1996) differentiates between goal intentions – intentions in the sense of Ajzen (1991), which have only small relationships to actions – and implementation intentions, which combine a goal intention with a plan of action. Gollwitzer (1999) defines plans as simple if–then programs ("if it is Dec 25th, I shall do the following … " or "if I see person X, I am going to ask him to invest some money in my firm"). Gollwitzer (1999) states that goal intentions alone are not sufficient to initiate action. Goal intentions only capture the motivation and amount of effort people are willing to invest (Ajzen, 1991). Goal intentions must be complemented with action plans (Gielnik et al., 2014a). Once a plan of action is in place, the implementation intentions regulate actions (Gielnik et al., 2014a). Action plans thus bridge the gap between goal intentions and actions by specifying the operational steps that lead to goal accomplishment (Brandstätter, Heimbeck, Malzacher, & Frese, 2003). Specifying the operational steps in the form of what, how, when, and where to do something increases the likelihood of initiating goal-oriented behavior (Brandstätter, Lengfelder, & Gollwitzer, 2001; Gollwitzer & Sheeran, 2006; Gollwitzer, 1999; Johnson, Chang, & Lord, 2006). Moreover, there is a certain degree of automaticity once an implementation intention is formed on the basis of an if–then plan. People automatically pay attention to the situation specified in this plan (Brandstätter et al., 2001). Plans thus help to focus the attention on relevant information cues for taking action. This is particularly important in entrepreneurship where information cues may be a signal for taking action to exploit business opportunities (Gielnik et al., 2014b). This is in line with research showing that forming action plans increases the likelihood of recognizing an opportunity to take action at a later point in time (Patalano & Seifert, 1997).

Action plans function to initiate and direct entrepreneurs' efforts. Furthermore, action plans increase persistence and structure the process of goal accomplishment, which contributes to maintaining action once it has been initiated (Frese & Zapf, 1994; Locke & Latham, 2002; Tripoli, 1998). Action plans provide markers people can use to stay on track when they are facing distractions. These markers are also useful to monitor the process of goal accomplishment and evaluate progress. Monitoring and evaluating progress is an important regulatory factor to make necessary corrections or to speed up the process (Frese & Zapf, 1994; Locke & Latham, 2002) Action plans also help people to focus their efforts on key activities. Prioritizing activities helps to avoid spending time on unnecessary activities or completing activities in an ineffective sequence (Castrogiovanni, 1996; Delmar & Shane, 2003). Research provides evidence for the regulatory function of plans showing that nascent entrepreneurs are more likely to implement their entrepreneurial goal intentions (Gielnik et al., 2014a) and to be more persistent in pursuing their goal of starting a new venture (Delmar & Shane, 2003; Liao & Gartner, 2006; Shane & Delmar, 2004).

Legitimacy Function of Planning

Several scholars argue that an important function of planning is to provide and demonstrate legitimacy (Honig & Karlsson, 2004; Honig & Samuelsson, 2012; Honig, 2004). Legitimacy of a new venture is defined as the extent to which people perceive that it "adheres to accepted principles, rules, norms, standards, and ways of doing things" (Delmar & Shane, 2004, p. 388). Getting legitimacy is important for new ventures to signal that the business is reliable and accountable and that it has been accepted and validated by other stakeholders (Honig & Samuelsson, 2012). Legitimacy thus facilitates social endorsement and support by stakeholders as it helps to overcome other stakeholders' resistance to dealing with the new venture (Delmar & Shane, 2004; Honig & Samuelsson, 2012). According to Delmar and Shane (2004), there are two ways to get legitimacy: establishing a legal entity and developing a business plan. Business plans are written documents which present the entrepreneurs' visions (for the new venture) and concepts of how to implement the vision. The simplest mechanism through which business plans provide legitimacy is that many people think and expect that this is how it should be done (Castrogiovanni, 1996). More elaborate mechanisms are that by describing in detail what they will do and how they will do it, entrepreneurs can demonstrate that their ideas are internally consistent (Delmar & Shane, 2004). In this way, a business plan also demonstrates that the entrepreneur has a certain understanding and know-how of the business, the industry, and the process of creating a new venture. Furthermore, by completing a business plan, entrepreneurs show that they are committed to the new venture because they voluntarily and openly invest effort into it (Delmar & Shane, 2004). Business plans thus have a symbolic function signaling quality (through consistency), capability, and/or commitment, which contributes to a new venture's legitimacy independent of forming a legal entity (Castrogiovanni, 1996). This legitimacy can have very concrete positive outcomes for the entrepreneurs, such as suppliers charging a lower price and a lower likelihood of disbanding a new venture (Delmar & Shane, 2004).

Planning as Communication

There is no question that any organization and team requires some degree of alignment of goals to be effective (Katz & Kahn, 1978). Goals, sub-goal setting, and planning facilitate the process of alignment because there is an explicit communication of what needs to be achieved and which methods are or are not legitimate. Strategic plans often have the function of communicating these issues. Therefore, most firms have some kind of strategic plan and most firms draw goals for individuals from this plan and provide guidance with a sub-goal process. Developing sub-goals and planning are related. Therefore, there is little question in theory and practice that goal setting helps, and that these goals need to be connected in some way (which constitutes a plan). It is obvious that for this purpose there is no need for extremely specific plans. Moreover, there is good reason to assume that people should be involved in such planning. Team research has shown that shared leadership in terms of shared planning helps in the process of efficient teams (Hackman, 1990). Indeed, formal planning does not just help with such common goal specification and individual strategy formulation, but also reduces conflict, helps teams to agree with one another, and increases motivation to pursue common goals (Mathieu & Schulze, 2006).

Learning Function of Planning

Castrogiovanni (1996) describes planning as a method of learning. Developing plans may include practices, such as environmental scanning, business feasibility analyses, and/or computer simulations. Through these practices, entrepreneurs get new information and they can acquire knowledge about the environment and the causal relationships in that environment. Having more knowledge about the environment and its causal relationships should reduce the uncertainty entrepreneurs may experience when they make decisions (Castrogiovanni, 1996). Furthermore, by forming plans, entrepreneurs develop a set of ideas and expectations of what will happen and what the future will look like. When entrepreneurs have pre-set expectations or criteria, they can conduct a realistic analysis to compare the projected with the actual state. This analysis allows entrepreneurs to understand where the actual environment is different from the expected environment. By figuring out reasons why the projected and actual states are different, entrepreneurs develop a better understanding of causal mechanisms and factors that have an influence in their business environment. Plans allow the development of criteria to better interpret the feedback entrepreneurs receive. As a matter of fact, a number of theories assume and have shown that, without goals and some type of plan, feedback cannot be interpreted (goals are criteria and planning helps in the development of such criteria) (Ashford & Tsui, 1991; Carver & Scheier, 1982; Frese & Zapf, 1994; Locke & Latham, 2002).

The Function of Planning in Non-Planning Approaches: Towards an Integration of Foes and Friends of Planning

In this section, we describe the important function of planning in effectuation and improvisation/ bricolage. As described above, Sarasvathy (2001) and Baker et al. (2003) have suggested using the approaches of effectuation or improvisation and bricolage as alternatives to planning. Effectuation and improvisation/bricolage seem to place planning at the opposite end of effectuation and improvisation/bricolage. It appears to be difficult to integrate these seemingly opposing concepts. With a somewhat martial touch, Chandler et al. (2011) have noted that there is a "dichotomous war between the need to 'develop a full-blown business and marketing plan' and the need to 'just get started'" (p. 376). We argue that the concepts of effectuation and improvisation/bricolage are not opposite to planning and, moreover, that even these concepts require some degree of planning. To better understand the role of planning in effectuation and improvisation/bricolage, it is important to have a more fine-grained perspective on planning.

There are at least two different conceptual approaches towards planning. First, a strategic approach which describes planning as a formal process of establishing goals and developing operational plans to achieve those goals; strategic planning includes collecting data, forecasting, and modeling future scenarios (Boyd, 1991). In entrepreneurship, strategic planning usually manifests itself in a business plan. The second approach is a psychological perspective on planning. The psychological perspective defines planning as mental simulations of actions specifying the sub-steps and operational details leading to goal accomplishment (Frese & Zapf, 1994; Mumford et al., 2001); see also Mumford, Mecca, & Watts in this book). Planning may be a long time prior to action or it may be intertwined with action – as in the case of improvisation. It may also become formal and be written down, but most likely it is not recorded in writing.

So far, the entrepreneurship literature has not made a clear distinction between these two perspectives on planning (see Brinckmann et al., 2010). These two different approaches may have different functions in entrepreneurship. For example, strategic planning (i.e. business planning) may primarily have a strong legitimating and communication function and only a limited action-regulatory function. In contrast, psychological planning (i.e. action planning) may have a strong action-regulatory function, helping to initiate and maintain action, but only a limited legitimating function (Gielnik et al., 2014a; Frese, 2009; Frese et al., 2007). The learning function may be important for both types of plans. This advantage of planning may be more salient in chaotic environments for which it is essential to have alternative plans in case a specific plan does not work out.

When effectuation and improvisation/bricolage were introduced as being opposite to planning, the authors most likely had the strategic perspective of planning in mind. With regard to the strategic perspective on planning, it is possible that planning can easily be overdone. Thus, the potentially detrimental effects of planning might be valid with regard to strategic planning (Sarasvathy et al., 2008; Sarasvathy, 2001). It is important to note, however, that the overall relationship with success is positive and significant, as described by Schwenk and Shrader (1993).

With regard to the psychological and action-regulatory perspective on planning, it is important to have a more integrative view. The action-regulatory function of planning is relevant in all approaches to action: causation, effectuation, and improvisation/bricolage. For example, Dew, Read, Sarasvathy, and Wiltbank (2009) note that expert entrepreneurs are more likely to use an effectuation approach compared to novice entrepreneurs, and the authors then describe what the effectuation approach among expert entrepreneurs looks like. They describe how the expert entrepreneurs planned to sell their products/services to various segments, for example through personal contacts or through a sales force (Dew et al., 2009). This shows that whatever the strategic approach (effectuation or causation), some form of (action) planning is necessary. Similarly, although Sarasvathy notes that planning is antithetical to effectuation, she provides the following example of Gillette when discussing effectuation: the founder "had to develop a cheap, effective removable-blade razor, generate an adequate initial market, and so on, always modifying his plans as he gained new knowledge and new stakeholders from his initial efforts" (Sarasvathy, 2003, p. 207). This means that the founder had (action) plans for how to proceed. These action plans were clearly variable as he constantly changed them according to the feedback he received from the environment. This corresponds to the learning function of planning. Planning provides a starting point for interpreting new information and for modifying and improving the business concept (Castrogiovanni, 1996). Finally, Read, Song, and Smit (2009) have discussed leveraging contingencies as an important aspect of effectuation and they noted that having a business plan does not mean that entrepreneurs cannot leverage contingency – the important point is to change flexibly or modify the plan when receiving new information about the business environment. Thus, planning can work alongside an effectual approach instead of being antithetical to it (Read et al., 2009).

The same is true for improvisation/bricolage. As noted above, in improvisation, planning and execution converge, which means that long-term (strategic) planning is absent but not a short-term (action) planning that specifies how, when, and where to execute the actions. Improvisation is described as the temporal overlap between planning and acting. Nonetheless, plans are still necessary to put goals into action – albeit that these action plans are developed during the action process. Similarly, for bricolage, action planning is needed as well. Bricolage implies 'making do,' which means that people take action (Baker & Nelson, 2005). The actions may not have a long-term, strategic orientation (thus, there is a lack of strategic planning) but to initiate and maintain the actions to 'make do,' action planning is necessary (Frese, 2009). Particularly in entrepreneurship, which involves complex tasks comprising many different steps and sub-steps, (action) planning should be important because in the case of complex and non-routine tasks, the positive effects of plans are even stronger (Gollwitzer & Brandstätter, 1997). Furthermore, both bricolage and effectuation imply some degree of experimenting. If one does not think of the potential outcomes of an experiment, an experiment is not useful. Thinking about these potential outcomes is, of course, planning. Moreover, any experimenting without thought and metacognitive thinking is pure trial and error – and that is clearly a non-efficient way of learning, as shown in experimental studies (Keith & Frese, 2005; van der Linden et al., 2001).

Advantages of Planning: Conclusions

While there are slightly different results in the meta-analyses on planning and entrepreneurship, all of them agree that there is a positive relationship between planning and performance (Brinckmann et al., 2010). Planning has several positive functions: planning regulates actions, provides legitimacy, increases communication, and promotes learning. The positive effects of planning hold for formal business plans (Delmar & Shane, 2003; Liao & Gartner, 2006; Shane & Delmar, 2004) and for action plans (Frese et al., 2007, 2000; Gielnik et al., 2014a). There are studies providing evidence that the proposed negative effects of planning, such as rigidity or reduced creativity, may not hold across all situations. Osburn and Mumford (2006) have shown that creative problem-solving and divergent thinking were improved as a consequence of planning. Furthermore, planning may compensate for low cognitive abilities. Escher et al. (2002) have found that entrepreneurs with low general mental ability could achieve great success by developing detailed plans. Nevertheless, we acknowledge that the positive effects of planning are not homogeneous across studies. There are factors moderating the effect (Brinckmann et al., 2010). Scholars have argued that planning is more beneficial in some contexts than in others (Miller & Cardinal, 1994). In the following section, we illustrate this by discussing culture as a contextual factor moderating the positive effect of planning on performance.

Cultural Differences of Planning Requirements

Some cultures may reinforce and demand planning more than others. The most important variable here is most likely the cultural dimension of uncertainty avoidance. A high degree of uncertainty avoidance implies that the culture is uncomfortable with unclear and uncertain situations. The best way to reduce these feelings of discomfort is to plan well because it decreases uncertainty (Hofstede, 2001). It is useful to think of culture to constitute norms of behavior. Thus, uncertainty avoidance demands that members of this culture plan well to cope with the worries that uncertainty produces. Such a normative view is useful because it produces an understanding that cultures with a high degree of uncertainty avoidance should demand more planning while cultures with a low degree of uncertainty avoidance demand more flexibility and would not demand planning. Indeed, Rauch et al. (2000) have shown that entrepreneurial planning was positively related to success only in a culture with a high degree of uncertainty avoidance. They present the argument that customers of small businesses in Ireland (a low uncertainty avoidance culture) demand flexibility even if this means that one arrives too late for a customer planned later in the day. This stands in contrast to Germany (a high uncertainty avoidance culture), where customers demand that small business does things on time.

At first sight, surprisingly, Brinckmann et al. (2010) appear to get the opposite results. In their meta-analysis, a high degree of uncertainty avoidance leads to a lower relationship between planning and entrepreneurial success. A more precise discussion of cross-cultural measurement issues may explain these results. Brinckmann et al. (2010) used the old and imprecise measure of uncertainty avoidance by Hofstede (2001), instead of the more precise measurement of the GLOBE study (House, Hanges, Javidan, Dorfman, & Gupta, 2004). While there is no doubt that Hofstede has been the most important cross-cultural psychologist and developed this area in the first place, his measures were not specifically developed for cross-cultural purposes. Therefore, the more recent developments of scales by GLOBE render better measures of cultural dimensions (Hanges & Dickson, 2004, 2006) and they are also more specifically related to norms (Shteynberg, Gelfand, & Kim, 2009). It happens that uncertainty avoidance as measured by Hofstede (2001) is highly but *negatively* correlated with the norm (practice) measure of uncertainty avoidance by GLOBE. In other words, Hofstede has inadvertently measured only an individual trait without actually examining a cultural dimension (Hanges & Dickson, 2006). Thus, in reality, high and low need to be reversed in the meta-analysis by Brinckmann et al. (2010) and, thus, the correlation is most likely higher for high uncertainty avoidance countries. The articles by Rauch et al. (2000) and Brinckmann et al. (2010) therefore agree.[2]

Towards a Theory of Entrepreneurial Planning

Table 15.1 presents a first cut of a theory of entrepreneurial planning. We are well aware that this theoretical sketch is a first approximation. The major thrust of our model is that planning can have positive *and* negative consequences and that it depends on how the planning is done whether or not it leads to positive *or* negative consequences. Moreover, it is important to differentiate formal planning (e.g. in the sense of business planning) from informal planning. It is the latter that we concentrate on in this chapter and which relates to the rest of Table 15.1. The major point of our table is that the various functions of planning may well counter each other, and whether the positive or the negative functions prevail depends on the specifics of the planning process and the specifics of the environment. Thus, we suggest that science should search for moderator functions for the effect of planning, as well as curvilinear relationships with success.

We now walk through Area A in Table 15.1 discussing the positive and negative functions of planning. Developing formal plans (business plans) can lead to learning. However, this learning function is comparatively weak if the plan is developed by outside consultants or if outsiders have a large impact on the plan. While some learning may take place even under these circumstances, more learning occurs when one is actively involved in developing a business plan. On the other hand, the legitimacy is high in either case. Whether or not legitimacy itself is important is another question – usually it is important for investment and credit decisions. Business plans might be important for banks or venture capitalists but investments by friends and relatives may be little affected by the legitimacy derived from having a business plan.

The positive function of formal planning for communication exists in all those situations where there is little face-to-face communication, for example, in somewhat larger companies or in virtual groups or organizations. Thus, the larger and more virtual an organization, the more important it is to have formal business plans. Note, however, that communication advantages were shown even in small groups (Brodbeck, 2001; Mathieu & Schulze, 2006).

We postulate a very small effect of formal strategies or business planning for implementation intentions. As a matter fact, if anything, we see a slight disadvantage in this area. As small plans are important for putting intentions into actions (by producing an implementation intention) and as this is primarily a within-person cognitive process, the extra effort and extra time of making the plan formal may actually hinder other goal intentions from being translated into implementation intentions (an issue that figures high in Sarasvathy's work).

TABLE 15.1 Framework for a theory of entrepreneurial planning

Positive and negative functions of planning

Type of planning	Learning	Legitimacy	Communication	Implementation intention – action initiation	Over-motivation (escalation of commitment)	Stickiness, inflexibility	Prerequisites of planning: predictability & knowledge
A. Formal planning (business plans)	Only if done by entrepreneur or by top management team	Positive effect even if done by outside consultants; moderator: how important is legitimacy for this kind of business?	Positive function; the larger the organization, the more important this function is	– (no effect, if this is not translated into individual or small-group plans)	Can lead to inflexible use; the more inflexible, the less escalation of commitment because no perception of responsibility for plan in organization	Stickiness to plan is low and plan will be flexibly adjusted but goal will likely not be given up	Problem of plan's misfit with reality; in bureaucratized structures, negative effects; negative effects in unpredictable environment
B. Informal planning	High learning, but see B1, B2, B3, B4	Low legitimacy because no document can be shown	Communication effect can be high if informal planning done in discussion groups or work-groups of larger units	Highly important function – a small if–then plan helps entrepreneurs to become active	Escalation of commitment can have positive or negative effects; but see B2, B3, B4	People committed to the plan; thus stickiness may be high; but see B2, B3, B4	Less problem of non-predictability of environment; knowledge issues important
B1. Long- vs. short-term planning	Learning with long-term planning	Informal legitimacy is answer to long-term questions	Stronger effect for long term than short term	Equal	Long-term plans, more over-commitment	Equal stickiness and inflexibility to short-and long-term plans	Long-term plans more affected by unpredictability and lack of knowledge than short-term plans

TABLE 15.1 (cont.)

Positive and negative functions of planning

Type of planning	Learning	Legitimacy	Communication	Implementation intention – action initiation	Over-motivation (escalation of commitment)	Stickiness, inflexibility	Prerequisites of planning: predictability & knowledge
B2. Comprehensiveness of planning	More learning with more comprehensive plan because more thoughtful and mindful	Informal legitimacy when things have been thought through because better answers to questions	Stronger effect for more comprehensive	Equal	Highly comprehensive plans, more over-commitment	More stickiness and inflexibility with highly comprehensive plans	Comprehensive plans are more affected by unpredictability and lack of knowledge than non-comprehensive plans
B3. Planning for flexibility	More learning with more flexibility, because of Plan B	–	–	Equal	Planning for flexibility reduces wrong over-commitment	Less stickiness and inflexibility with critical point planning and option planning	Explicit acknowledgment of lack of predictability and high attention to feedback
B4. Pre-planning vs. planning while acting (improvisation)	More learning with more pre-planning	Informal legitimacy when things have been thought through in pre-planning	Stronger effect for pre-planning	Pre-planning allows better implementation intention than improvisation – however, curvilinear effects possible	Over-commitment only a problem when pre-planning	Stickiness and inflexibility only a problem for pre-planning	Improvisation reduces the need for predictability and knowledge – therefore, often a preferred mode of planning for entrepreneurs
C. Milestones developed as sub-goals	–	–	–	Important to stop being over-committed	Milestones every few months important to stop being over-committed	Milestones every few months important to stop being over-committed	Entrepreneurs are better able to deal with low predictability and knowledge when they set milestones

Escalation of commitment and inflexibility can result from a formal plan. There may be two different reasons for being over-motivated to stick to a plan. First, entrepreneurs (or a team of entrepreneurs) invest effort and develop a feeling of responsibility, which may result in an escalation of commitment. Entrepreneurial units may escalate their commitment because they most likely participated in the development of the strategy. Second, larger organizations with a top-down plan may persist in pursuing a certain goal. However, this is probably less due to over-commitment than to power issues and dysfunctional routines and too little overall commitment due to lack of feelings of responsibility. Formal plans may imply a formal application process in which things are not thought through and in which they are not adapted to changing circumstances. Therefore, there may be a high recourse to formal strategic plans in highly bureaucratic organizations. This was the point that Welch made at General Electrics. We also want to discuss two things which may reduce the likelihood of escalation of commitment and inflexibility: first, whenever something is seen as a bureaucratic outside plan that is presented to the organization members without any input from the organization, escalation of commitment is less of a problem. Second, in organizations in which decision making is distributed, people may not stick to the plan but will change it if it seems necessary. People will stick to the goal and adjust the plan to changing circumstances.

Whenever a plan is formalized, it becomes exterior. Thus, it is not internalized but seen as an external power over the processes in an organization. This may allow a high degree of misfit with reality (because nobody assumes responsibility to adapt the plan). Furthermore, it may be very difficult to change the plan (because of power and habit issues) once it is formalized (e.g. in the form of a three-year plan), particularly in highly bureaucratic organizations. However, this is again less of a problem in non-bureaucratic entrepreneurial environments.

Informal planning (the next row B in Table 15.1) allows participating people to learn. Therefore, it is a good instrument to develop more knowledge for entrepreneurs. However, this effect is stronger if the plan is long term, because then entrepreneurs take a more proactive stance which allows them to develop a better knowledge of long-term opportunities and problems (Frese, 2009). This, in turn, allows them to develop preparatory plans for taking advantage of those opportunities (Shane, 2000) and to develop coping strategies for potential future problems. A similar argument holds for the comprehensiveness of planning. As it turns out, the time horizons and comprehensiveness of plans are highly correlated, so they were collapsed in some studies (Frese et al., 2007).

Legitimacy is higher for formal planning than for informal planning. However, a certain degree of legitimacy also follows from people who have better ideas about what can occur as potential outcomes and who foresee the problems better. This is a result of stronger informal planning, particularly long-term planning and high comprehensiveness of planning. Thus, legitimacy may follow from these factors.

The communication function is probably stronger for formal plans and the communication function of formal plans is more important in larger organizations. Informal plans can be used in smaller organizations. However, the communication function is probably more important for long-term plans, more comprehensive plans, and pre-planning than for short-term plans, low comprehensiveness of plans, and improvisation.

Implementation intention is most likely affected by any kind of plan. However, it is enough to have some small plans, and therefore, as far as getting people to act is concerned, it does not matter whether one has a long- or a short-term plan, a comprehensive or non-comprehensive plan. The only difference appears for pre-planning vs. improvisation. Improvisation does not help to get people to start acting to achieve a goal. If improvisation is included in a general plan of action, then it is unproblematic, because the action has already started. As a matter of fact, Gollwitzer (1996, 1999) shows that once people have started to act, then problems (such as insufficient resources, bad tools, or insufficient skills and knowledge) will actually enhance the motivation to still achieve the goal. Thus, improvisation tendencies will be enhanced. But to produce an action as a result of an intention requires pre-planning of some sort (this may be a highly abstract kind of pre-planning of the type "whenever I can make a fast buck, I do it").

Over-motivation to the plan (escalation) is a function of when problems occur. When they occur at the stage of developing an intention, problems are usually dealt with in a straightforward and realistic fashion, and they may well lead to giving up an intention. In contrast, when the difficulties appear at a later stage of the action process, that is, after an action plan has led to an implementation intention, then problems in action actually lead to higher motivation (Gollwitzer, 1993; Gollwitzer, Heckhausen, & Ratajczak, 1990; Gollwitzer, Heckhausen, & Steller, 1990). Thus, at this later stage, the problem of over-motivation through escalation of commitment is particularly high. However, it needs to be recognized that there are many case studies of entrepreneurs who were actually over-motivated and who persisted in an idea that was originally seen to be unrealistic but turned out to be highly useful. Escalation of commitment can be explained by Gollwitzer's theory. Escalation is highest when people feel responsible for a negative outcome – this is precisely the situation described above of an entrepreneur who is in the midst of difficulties but still does not give up. A greater degree of investment increases escalation of commitment. Therefore, more investment in planning (such as long-term planning and high comprehensiveness) also leads to higher escalation of commitment. One important consequence is to build milestones into the system. Gollwitzer explains that people become open to rationally processing feedback again (in the sense of being able to give up a course of action) when they have achieved a goal. Milestones have the function of mimicking in-between achievements of goals. If a milestone is achieved, then a (sub-)goal is achieved and it is easier to ask the question whether one should stop a course of action.

Dealing with stickiness and inflexibility can be built into a plan. One of the problems of articles on planning in entrepreneurship is that they do not take notice of different forms of plans, for example, an approach to planning that explicitly builds flexibility into plans. Flexible plans make it easier to change the plan once negative feedback suggests that the original plan is not working out. The most obvious example for flexibility in plans is to have another plan available if one plan does not work out. This is the example of having a 'Plan B'. Another example is critical point planning which "concentrates on the most difficult, most unclear and most important point first (Zempel, 1994). Only after solving the first critical point are further steps planned. This approach constitutes an iterative problem solving strategy" (Frese et al, 2000, p. 2). And, indeed, critical point planning has clear relationships with entrepreneurial success, as shown in some studies (Frese, 2000; van Steekelenburg, Lauw, & Frese, 2000). A second form of planning that builds flexibility into the plan is planning for actions that optimize future options. The argument is that because the future is not completely predictable, optimal plans attempt first to find action paths that leave the greatest number of options open for future actions; however, the general direction is one of achieving one's goals. Thus, in-between goals are optimized to allow the greatest number of options to advance in the future and at the same time to improve the chances of getting nearer to the goal (Resch & Oesterreich, 1987).

Informal planning is, by its very nature, less binding and allows more input from feedback than formal planning – which tends to have a life of its own after it has been written down. Thus, there is less of a problem when unpredictable events occur. When there is less stickiness of the plan, there is also a higher reactiveness towards changing circumstances. However, learning and knowledge is as important a prerequisite as it is for formal plans. Thus, the plans may be wrong or misapplied to the situation, or follow the wrong idea or model of reality, or may not be well enough adapted to the important issues of the environment. Lack of knowledge/expertise may be a particular problem for novice entrepreneurs (Baron & Ensley, 2006) because they may concentrate on the wrong issues. Informal planning can be more adaptive to unpredictable events and less of a problem if there is lack of knowledge. Long-term and comprehensive planning have a particularly strong negative effect in case of low predictability and lack of knowledge. Therefore, novice entrepreneurs may well have lower performance when they plan too far into the future or in too much detail. In contrast, those entrepreneurs can deal with the problem of low predictability and lack of knowledge if they set milestones and develop flexible plans – all forms of flexible planning can deal with the problem of low predictability and lack of knowledge. Of course, improvisation is least affected by these issues.

In short, what this conceptual framework of entrepreneurial planning suggests is that there are, indeed, negative as well as positive effects of planning. However, this theory also suggests that, without a plan, there is no action – thus, planning in one form or another is necessary to be able to put ideas and intentions into actions.

Future Research

We think there are several interesting avenues for future research on planning in entrepreneurship. Future research could use the theoretical framework developed in this chapter to investigate and integrate the positive and negative functions of planning for entrepreneurship. Future research could also integrate the strategic and psychological approaches towards planning in entrepreneurship. We discussed the different functions of formal and action planning. Formal business planning might have a stronger legitimating function (Honig & Karlsson, 2004), while action planning might have a stronger action-regulatory function (Frese, 2009). Previous research assumed that business plans also have a regulatory function (Delmar & Shane, 2003; Shane & Delmar, 2004), while other scholars argued that writing a business plan is only an academic exercise with no positive effects on initiating and maintaining action (Honig, 2004). Integrating the strategic and psychological approach towards planning would help to better understand whether and under which conditions formal business plans have a (stronger) action-regulatory function. Research on the strength of the action-regulatory function of formal business plans would also complement existing research that attempted to examine whether business plans have a stronger learning or legitimating function. In their meta-analysis, Brinckmann et al. (2010) examined whether the process versus the outcome of business planning was a moderating factor influencing the strength of the relationship between planning and performance. They argued that a sophisticated process of writing a business plan should lead to learning, while a sophisticated outcome should provide legitimacy (it is not necessarily the case that a sophisticated process leads to a sophisticated outcome). They did not find a significant difference, indicating that both functions are equally important for performance. Similarly, Mayer-Haug et al. (2013) have examined the effect of planning on different performance measures (e.g. growth, size, sales, profit, and other more qualitative performance measures). They found that planning is more strongly related to growth, size, and sales than to profit. However, they did not differentiate between the different functions of planning. Future research could disentangle the different strategic and psychological functions of planning and relate them to different performance measures. Such research would provide a more comprehensive and fine-grained theoretical model of the planning–performance relationship with multiple mediating mechanisms and performance outcomes.

We also hope that Table 15.1 might help to develop hypotheses on differentiated positive and negative effects of planning and how the more negative issues can be avoided and the more positive ones enhanced. Future research could investigate contextual factors moderating the effect of planning on performance. Previous research provided some insights into moderating factors, such as culture (Brinckmann et al., 2010; Rauch et al., 2000) and stage of firm development (Brinckmann et al., 2010), which showed that planning has stronger effects in uncertainty avoidance cultures and for older firms. It is further possible to argue that strategic planning plays a less important role in resource-constrained environments (in contrast to environments providing plenty of resources). Scholars have argued that effectuation and bricolage may be particularly useful in environments presenting constantly new opportunities but only few resources (Baker & Nelson, 2005; Sarasvathy, 2001). Entrepreneurs may use bricolage or effectuation instead of causation to successfully deal with adverse business environments by recombining and using the resources which serendipitously occur (Edelman & Yli-Renko, 2010; Mair & Marti, 2009). Research investigating moderators of the planning–performance relationship, such as availability of resources, could further contribute to a comprehensive theoretical model of planning in entrepreneurship by revealing boundary conditions and curvilinear effects (see also Miller & Cardinal, 1994) (cf. also the chapter on strategic planning by Cardinal, Miller, Kreutzer, and TenBrink in this volume).

We believe that future research should adopt a more dynamic perspective on planning. With regard to the strategic approach, Honig (2004) suggested the adoption of a contingency-based approach towards business planning. Business planning should not be a convergent process leading to a pre-determined solution, but it should be regarded as a divergent process in which the outcomes are more open. In this divergent process, plans change not only quantitatively but also qualitatively. Based on the changing requirements of the environment, entrepreneurs may modify and adjust their plans in real time. Entrepreneurs repeatedly and incrementally acquire new information and knowledge and they should adapt their plans accordingly. Business planning should thus become an iterative process of integrating new information (Honig, 2004). Future research could investigate whether entrepreneurs who dynamically adapt their business plans according to the information they receive from the environment are more successful in starting and managing a new venture.

Similarly, with regard to the psychological approach, future research could investigate how entrepreneurs dynamically change or maintain their action plans. Entrepreneurs may update their action plans as a result of changing aspects in the environment or because of successes and setbacks. Recently, scholars have emphasized that much of the variability in motivational and action-regulatory factors is within-person variance (Lord, Diefendorff, Schmidt, & Hall, 2010). We assume that action planning is also a dynamic concept that changes within entrepreneurs over time. There is some preliminary evidence of a virtuous cycle with recursive effects of planning and success in entrepreneurship: more planning leads to more success, and more success, in turn, leads to more planning (van Gelderen, Frese, & Thurik, 2000). Frese (2009) suggests that action plans should be flexibly adapted based on the feedback entrepreneurs receive from the environment when they start implementing their plans. In this case, changing the action plans is based on a process of acquiring and reflecting on information; entrepreneurs thus avoid engaging in a habitual or rigid implementation of their plans. However, research on this topic is not yet conclusive and it is necessary to develop theoretical models which explain why and under which conditions entrepreneurs may adapt, maintain, or increase their action planning.

Conclusions

In this chapter, we discussed the advantages and disadvantages of planning to develop a theoretical framework of entrepreneurial planning. Although meta-analytic evidence suggests that planning has a positive effect on performance (Brinckmann et al., 2010), this chapter shows that the planning–performance relationship is more complex than a purely linear relationship. For example, as discussed in this chapter, the cultural context in terms of uncertainty avoidance may be an important moderating factor reversing the positive effect of planning into a negative effect (Rauch et al., 2000). Our theoretical framework suggests disentangling the positive and negative effects of formal (strategic) and action planning to better understand why and under which conditions planning promotes and/or hinders entrepreneurship.

Acknowledgments

This research was supported by a grant from MOE/National University of Singapore.

Notes

1 Of course, Sarasvathy (2001) does not really advocate such a radical position, although at times her writings may sound like this (e.g. when she contrasts strongly two logics – one being goal oriented, the other being means oriented). Rather, she argues that people should be open to feedback from the environment, should experiment, be flexible, and take careful affordable loss positions, and that they should not just follow blindly one idea but change ideas depending upon the reaction of stakeholders – a position we agree with (Cha, Ruan, & Frese, 2013).

2 As it turns out, Rauch et al. also refer to Hofstede and his measure of uncertainty avoidance. These authors were lucky. Their study was done before the data of GLOBE were published and, therefore, they relied on Hofstede's (1991) reports of uncertainty avoidance differences for Ireland and Germany when they chose the participating countries. In this particular (and exceptional) case, Hofstede and GLOBE agree that Ireland is lower on uncertainty avoidance than Germany.

References

Ajzen, I. (1991). The theory of planned behavior. *Organizational Behavior and Human Decision Processes*, 50, 179–211.

Ashford, S. J., & Tsui, A. S. (1991). Self-regulation for managerial effectiveness: The role of active feedback seeking. *Academy of Management Journal*, 34, 251–280.

Baker, T., & Nelson, R. E. (2005). Creating something from nothing: Resource construction through entrepreneurial bricolage. *Administrative Science Quarterly*, 50, 329–366.

Baker, T., Miner, A. S., & Eesley, D. T. (2003). Improvising firms: bricolage, account giving and improvisational competencies in the founding process. *Research Policy*, 32, 255–276.

Baron, R. A. (2007). Behavioral and cognitive factors in entrepreneurship: Entrepreneurs as the active element in new venture creation. *Strategic Entrepreneurship Journal*, 1, 167–182.

Baron, R. A., & Ensley, M. D. (2006). Opportunity recognition as the detection of meaningful patterns: Evidence from comparisons of novice and experienced entrepreneurs. *Management Science*, 52, 1331–1344.

Bewayo, E. D. (2010). Pre-start-up preparations: Why the business plan isn't always written. *The Entrepreneurial Executive*, 15, 9–23.

Boyd, B. K. (1991). Strategic planning and financial performance: A meta-analytic review. *Journal of Management Studies*, 28, 353–374.

Brandstäatter, V., Lengfelder, A., & Gollwitzer, P. M. (2001). Implementation intentions and efficient action initiation. *Journal of Personality and Social Psychology*, 81, 946–960.

Brandstätter, V., Heimbeck, D., Malzacher, J. T., & Frese, M. (2003). Goals need implementation intentions: The model of action phases tested in the applied setting of continuing education. *European Journal of Work and Organizational Psychology*, 12, 37–59.

Brinckmann, J., Grichnik, D., & Kapsa, D. (2010). Should entrepreneurs plan or just storm the castle? A meta-analysis on contextual factors impacting the business planning-performance relationship in small firms. *Journal of Business Venturing*, 25, 24–40.

Brodbeck, F. C. (2001). Communication and performance in software development projects. *European Journal of Work and Organizational Psychology*, 10, 73–94.

Carland, J. W., Carland, J. A., & Abhy, C. (1989). An assessment of the psychological determinants of planning in small businesses. *International Small Business Journal*, 7, 23–34.

Carter, N. M., Gartner, W. B., & Reynolds, P. D. (1996). Exploring start-up event sequences. *Journal of Business Venturing*, 11, 151–166.

Carver, C. S., & Scheier, M. F. (1982). Control theory: A useful conceptual framework for personality-social, clinical, and health psychology. *Psychological Bulletin*, 92, 111–135.

Castrogiovanni, G. J. (1996). Pre-startup planning and the survival of new small businesses: Theoretical linkages. *Journal of Management*, 22, 801–822.

Cha, V., Ruan, A. Y., & Frese, M. (2013). *Is effectuation really enough? An examination on the relationship of logic, experience, and innovativeness in entrepreneurial decision making*. NUS Business School, Singapore: Manuscript.

Chandler, G. N., DeTienne, D. R., McKelvie, A., & Mumford, T. V. (2011). Causation and effectuation processes: A validation study. *Journal of Business Venturing*, 26, 375–390.

Dailey, L., & Mumford, M. D. (2006). Evaluative aspects of creative thought: Errors in appraising the implications of new ideas. *Creativity Research Journal*, 18, 385–390.

Delmar, F., & Shane, S. (2003). Does business planning facilitate the development of new ventures? *Strategic Management Journal*, 24, 1165–1185.

Delmar, F., & Shane, S. (2004). Legitimating first: Organizing activities and the survival of new ventures. *Journal of Business Venturing*, 19, 385–410.

Dew, N., Read, S., Sarasvathy, S. D., & Wiltbank, R. (2009). Effectual versus predictive logics in entrepreneurial decision-making: Differences between experts and novices. *Journal of Business Venturing*, 24, 287–309.

Dimov, D. (2007). Beyond the single-person, single-insight attribution in understanding entrepreneurial opportunities. *Entrepreneurship Theory and Practice*, 31, 713–731.

Dörner, D., & Schaub, H. (1994). Errors in planning and decision-making and the nature of human information processing. *Applied Psychology: An International Review*, 43, 433–454.

Edelman, L. F., & Yli-Renko, H. (2010). The impact of environment and entrepreneurial perceptions on venture-creation efforts: Bridging the discovery and creation views of entrepreneurship. *Entrepreneurship Theory and Practice*, 34, 833–856.

Escher, S., Grabarkiewicz, R., Frese, M., van Steekelenburg, G., Lauw, M., & Friedrich, C. (2002). The moderator effect of cognitive ability on the relation between planning strategies and business success of small scale business owners in South Africa: A longitudinal study. *Journal of Developmental Entrepreneurship*, 7, 305–318.

Frese, M. (2000). Executive summary, conclusions, and policy implications. In M. Frese (Ed.), *Success and failure of microbusiness owners in Africa: A psychological approach*. Westport, CT: Greenwood.

Frese, M. (2009). Toward a psychology of entrepreneurship: An action theory perspective. *Foundations and Trends in Entrepreneurship*, 5, 437–496.

Frese, M., & Zapf, D. (1994). Action as the core of work psychology: A German approach. In H. C. Triandis, M. D. Dunnette, & L. M. Hough (Eds.), *Handbook of industrial and organizational psychology* (Vol. 4, pp. 271–340). Palo Alto, CA: Consulting Psychologists Press.

Frese, M., van Gelderen, M., & Ombach, M. (2000). How to plan as a small scale business owner: Psychological process characteristics of action strategies and success. *Journal of Small Business Management*, 38, 1–18.

Frese, M., Krauss, S. I., Keith, N., Escher, S., Grabarkiewicz, R., Luneng, S. T., … Friedrich, C. (2007). Business owners' action planning and its relationship to business success in three African countries. *Journal of Applied Psychology*, 92, 1481–1498.

Frese, M., Bausch, A., Schmidt, P., Rauch, A., & Kabst, R. (2012). Evidence-based entrepreneurship: Cumulative science, action principles, and bridging the gap between science and practice. *Foundations and Trends in Entrepreneurship*, 8, 1–62.

Gartner, W. B. (1985). A conceptual framework for describing the phenomenon of new venture creation. *Academy of Management Review*, 10, 696–706.

Gielnik, M. M., Barabas, S., Frese, M., Namatovu-Dawa, R., Scholz, F. A., Metzger, J. R., & Walter, T. (2014a). A temporal analysis of how entrepreneurial goal intentions, positive fantasies, and action planning affect starting a new venture and when the effects wear off. *Journal of Business Venturing*, 29(6), 755–772.

Gielnik, M. M., Krämer, A.-C., Kappel, B., & Frese, M. (2014b). Antecedents of business opportunity identification and innovation: Investigating the interplay of information processing and information acquisition. *Applied Psychology: An International Review*, 63(2), 344–381.

Gollwitzer, P. M. (1993). Goal achievement: The role of intentions. In W. Stroebe & M. Hewstone (Eds.), *European review of social psychology* (Vol. 4, pp. 141–185). London: Wiley.

Gollwitzer, P. M. (1996). The volitional benefits of planning. In P. M. Gollwitzer & J. A. Bargh (Eds.), *The psychology of action* (pp. 287–312). New York: The Guilford Press.

Gollwitzer, P. M. (1999). Implementation intentions: Strong effects of simple plans. *American Psychologist*, 54, 493–503.

Gollwitzer, P. M., & Brandstätter, V. (1997). Implementation intentions and effective goal pursuit. *Journal of Personality and Social Psychology*, 73, 186–199.

Gollwitzer, P. M., & Sheeran, P. (2006). Implementation intentions and goal achievement: A meta-analysis of effects and processes. *Advances in Experimental Social Psychology*, 38, 69–119.

Gollwitzer, P. M., Heckhausen, H., & Ratajczak, H. (1990). From weighing to willing: Approaching a change decision through pre- and postdecisional mentation. *Organizational Behavior and Human Decision Making Processes*, 45, 41–65.

Gollwitzer, P. M., Heckhausen, H., & Steller, B. (1990). Deliberative and implemental mind-sets: Cognitive tuning towards congruous thoughts and information. *Journal of Personality and Social Psychology*, 59(6), 1119–1127.

Hackman, R. (1990). *Groups that work (and those that don't): Creating conditions for effective teamwork*. San Francisco, CA: Jossey-Bass.

Hanges, P. J., & Dickson, M. W. (2004). The development and validation of the GLOBE culture and leadership scales. In R. J. House, P. J. Hanges, M. Javidan, P. W. Dorfman, & V. Gupta (Eds.), *Cultures, leadership and organizations: A 62 nation GLOBE study* (pp. 122–151). Thousand Oaks, CA: Sage.

Hanges, P. J., & Dickson, M. W. (2006). Agitation over aggregation: Clarifying the development of and the nature of the GLOBE scales. *Leadership Quarterly*, 17, 522–536.

Hayes-Roth, B., & Hayes-Roth, F. (1979). A cognitive model of planning. *Cognitive Science*, 3, 275–310.

Hiemstra, A. M. F., van der Kooy, K. G., & Frese, M. (2006). Entrepreneurship in the street food sector of Vietnam – Assessment of psychological success and failure factors. *Journal of Small Business Management*, 44, 474–481.

Hofstede, G. (1991). *Cultures and organizations. Software of the mind*. London: McGraw-Hill.

Hofstede, G. (2001). *Culture's consequences* (2nd ed.). Thousand Oaks, CA: Sage.

Honig, B. (2004). Entrepreneurship education: Toward a model of contingency-based business planning. *Academy of Management Learning & Education*, 3, 258–273.

Honig, B., & Karlsson, T. (2004). Institutional forces and the written business plan. *Journal of Management*, 30, 29–48.

Honig, B., & Samuelsson, M. (2012). Planning and the entrepreneur: A longitudinal examination of nascent entrepreneurs in Sweden. *Journal of Small Business Management*, 50, 365–388.

House, R. J., Hanges, P. J., Javidan, M., Dorfman, P. W., & Gupta, V. (Eds.) (2004). *Cultures, leadership and organizations: A 62 nation GLOBE study*. Thousand Oaks, CA: Sage.

Hunter, J. E., & Schmidt, F. L. (2004). *Methods of meta-analysis: Correcting error and bias in research findings* (2nd ed.). Thousand Oaks, CA: Sage.

Johnson, R. E., Chang, C. H., & Lord, R. G. (2006). Moving from cognition to behavior: What the research says. *Psychological Bulletin*, 132, 381–415.

Josephs, R. A., & Hahn, E. D. (1995). Bias and accuracy in estimates of task duration. *Organizational Behavior and Human Decision Processes*, 61, 202–213.

Katz, D., & Kahn, R. L. (1978). *Social psychology of organizations* (2nd ed.). New York: Wiley.

Keeley, R. H., & Kapp, R. (1994). Founding conditions and business performance: "High performers" vs. small venture-capital-backed start- ups. In W. D. Bygrave, S. Birley, N. C. Churchill, E. Gatewood, F. Hoy, R. H. Keeley, & W. E. Wetzel, Jr. (Eds.), *Frontiers of entrepreneurship research* (pp. 236–238). Wellesley, MA: Babson College.

Keith, N., & Frese, M. (2005). Self-regulation in error management training: Emotion control and metacognition as mediators of performance effects. *Journal of Applied Psychology*, 90, 677–691.

Keyser, M., De Kruif, M., & Frese, M. (2000). The psychological strategy process and socio-demographic variables as predictors of success in micro- and small-scale business owners in Zambia. In M. Frese (Ed.), *Success and failure of microbusiness owners in Africa: A psychological approach*. Westport, CT: Greenwood.

Liao, J. W., & Gartner, W. B. (2006). The effects of pre-venture plan timing and perceived environmental uncertainty on the persistence of emerging firms. *Small Business Economics*, 27, 23–40.

Locke, E. A., & Latham, G. P. (2002). Building a practically useful theory of goal setting and task motivation: A 35-year odyssey. *American Psychologist*, 57, 705–717.

Lord, R. G., Diefendorff, J. M., Schmidt, A. M., & Hall, R. J. (2010). Self-regulation at work. *Annual Review of Psychology*, 61, 543–568.

Lumpkin, G. T., Shrader, R. C., & Hills, G. E. (1998). Does formal business planning enhance the performance of new ventures? In P. D. Reynolds, W. D. Bygrave, N. M. Carter, S. Manigart, & C. M. Mason (Eds.), *Frontiers of entrepreneurship research* (pp. 180–189). Wellesley, MA: Babson College.

McMullen, J. S., & Shepherd, D. A. (2006). Entrepreneurial action and the role of uncertainty in the theory of the entrepreneur. *Academy of Management Review*, 31, 132–152.

Mair, J., & Marti, I. (2009). Entrepreneurship in and around institutional voids: A case study from Bangladesh. *Journal of Business Venturing*, 24, 419–435.

Mathieu, J. E., & Schulze, W. (2006). The influence of team knowledge and formal plans on episodic team process-performance relationships. *Academy of Management Journal*, 49, 605–619.

Matthews, C. H. and Scott, S. G. (1995). Uncertainty and planning in small and entrepreneurial firms: an empirical assessment. *Journal of Small Business Management*, 33(4), 34–48.

Mayer-Haug, K., Read, S., Brinckmann, J., Dew, N., & Grichnik, D. (2013). Entrepreneurial talent and venture performance: A meta-analytic investigation of SMEs. *Research Policy*, 42, 1251–1273.

Miller, C. C., & Cardinal, L. B. (1994). Strategic planning and firm performance: A synthesis of more than two decades of research. *Academy of Management Journal*, 37, 1649–1665.

Mintzberg, H. (1994). The fall and rise of strategic planning. *Harvard Business Review*, 72, 107–114.

Mintzberg, H. (2000). *Mintzberg on management: Inside our strange world of organizations*. New York: The Free Press.

Mumford, M. D., Schultz, R. A., & Van Doorn, J. R. (2001). Performance in planning: Processes, requirements, and errors. *Review of General Psychology*, 5, 213–240.

Osburn, H. K., & Mumford, M. D. (2006). Creativity and planning: Training interventions to develop creative problem-solving skills. *Creativity Research Journal*, 18, 173–190.

Pascha, A., Schöppe, B., & Hacker, W. (2001). Was macht Planen kompliziert? – Zum Einfluß von Aufgabenmerkmalen auf die Schwierigkeit von Abfolgeplanung. [What makes planning complicated? – On the influence of task characteristics on the difficulty of planning]. *Zeitschrift für Psychologie*, 209, 245–276.

Patalano, A. L., & Seifert, C. M. (1997). Opportunistic planning: Being reminded of pending goals. *Cognitive Psychology*, 34, 1–36.

Rauch, A., Frese, M., & Sonnentag, S. (2000). Cultural differences in planning/success relationships: A comparison of small enterprises in Ireland, West Germany, and East Germany. *Journal of Small Business Management*, 38, 28–41.

Read, S., Song, M., & Smit, W. (2009). A meta-analytic review of effectuation and venture performance. *Journal of Business Venturing*, 24, 573–587.

Resch, M., & Oesterreich, R. (1987). Bildung von Zwischenzielen in Entscheidungsnetzen. [Formulation of intermediate goals in decision networks]. *Zeitschrift für Experimentelle und Angewandte Psychologie*, 34, 301–317.

Robinson, R. B., & Pearce, II, J. A. (1983). The impact of formalized strategic planning on financial performance in small organizations. *Strategic Management Journal*, 4, 197–207.

Rooks, G., Sserwanga, A., & Frese, M. (in press). Unpacking the personal initiative–performance relationship: A multi-group analysis of innovation by Ugandan rural and urban entrepreneurs. *Applied Psychology: An International Review*. doi: 10.1111/apps.12033

Sarasvathy, S. D. (2001). Causation and effectuation: Toward a theoretical shift from economic inevitability to entrepreneurial contingency. *Academy of Management Review*, 26, 243–263.

Sarasvathy, S. D. (2003). Entrepreneurship as a science of the artificial. *Journal of Economic Psychology*, 24, 203–220.

Sarasvathy, S. D., Dew, N., Stuart, R., & Wiltbank, R. (2008). Designing organizations that design environments: Lessons from entrepreneurial expertise. *Organization Studies*, 29, 331–350.

Schwenk, C. R., & Shrader, C. B. (1993). Effects of formal strategic planning on financial performance in small firms: A meta-analysis. *Entrepreneurship Theory and Practice*, 17, 53–64.

Sexton, D. L., Auken, P. V. (1985). A longitudinal study of small business strategic planning. *Journal of Small Business Management*, 23, 7–15.

Shane, S. (2000). Prior knowledge and the discovery of entrepreneurial opportunities. *Organization Science*, 11, 448–469.

Shane, S., & Delmar, F. (2004). Planning for the market: business planning before marketing and the continuation of organizing efforts. *Journal of Business Venturing*, 19, 767–785.

Shane, S., & Venkataraman, S. (2000). The promise of entrepreneurship as a field of research. *Academy of Management Review*, 25, 217–226.

Shteynberg, G., Gelfand, M. J., & Kim, K. (2009). Peering into the "magnum mysterium" of culture. *Journal of Cross-Cultural Psychology*, 40, 46–69.

Simonson, I., & Staw, B. M. (1992). Deescalation strategies: A comparison of techniques for reducing commitment to losing courses of action. *Journal of Applied Psychology*, 77, 419–426.

Slotegraaf, R. J., & Dickson, P. R. (2004). The paradox of a marketing planning capability. *Journal of the Academy of Marketing Science*, 32, 371–385.

Staw, B. M., & Ross, J. (1987). Behavior in escalation situations: Antecedents, prototypes and solutions. *Research in Organizational Behavior*, 9, 39–78.

Tripoli, A. M. (1998). Planning and allocating: Strategies for managing priorities in complex jobs. *European Journal of Work and Organizational Psychology*, 7, 455–476.

van der Linden, D., Sonnentag, S., Frese, M., & van Dyck, C. (2001). Exploration strategies, performance, and error consequences when learning a complex computer task. *Behaviour and Information Technology*, 20, 189–198.

van Gelder, J.-L., de Vries, R. E., Frese, M., & Goutbeek, J.-P. (2007). Differences in psychological strategies of failed and operational business owners in the Fiji Islands. *Journal of Small Business Management*, 45, 388–400.

Van Gelderen, M., Frese, M., & Thurik, A. R. (2000). Strategies, uncertainty and performance of small business startups. *Small Business Economics*, 15, 165–181.

van Steekelenburg, W., Lauw, A. M., & Frese, M. (2000). Problems and coping, strategies and initiative in microbusiness owners in South Africa. In M. Frese (Ed.), *Success and failure of microbusiness owners in Africa* (pp. 77–102). Westport, CT: Quorum Books.

Welch, J., & Welch, S. (2005). *Winning*. New York: Harper Collins.

Wiltbank, R., Dew, N., Read, S., & Sarasvathy, S. D. (2006). What to do next? The case for non-predictive strategy. *Strategic Management Journal*, 27, 981–998.

Wiltbank, R., Stuart, R., Dew, N., & Sarasvathy, S. D. (2009). Prediction and control under uncertainty: Outcomes in angel investing. *Journal of Business Venturing*, 24, 116–133.

Zempel, J. (1994). Psychologische Strategien der Handlungsplanung. [Psychological strategies of action planning]. Univ. of Giessen, unpublished paper, Giessen.

16

TIME MANAGEMENT AND PROCRASTINATION

Wendelien van Eerde

Introduction

Time management and procrastination would appear to be logically related, in the sense that time management may be a way to overcome procrastination. The research in the two areas, however, has been relatively separate. Perhaps because some procrastination researchers, such as Ferrari (2010), find that "Time management skills do not help chronic procrastinators. Time management is nothing more than a Band-Aid." (p.6). In this chapter, I aim to answer the question to what extent planning, the core of time management, helps to overcome procrastination. The recent developments in both research fields will be reviewed, first time management and then procrastination. Most studies on both topics have been conducted among students, and only a handful of studies have combined the topics. I will then discuss which interventions have been shown to reduce procrastination, whether these have been subsumed under the term time management or not. Throughout the chapter, I will focus on studies that are work related.

Theoretical Framework

Time management (TM) can be seen as a container concept that includes several tools to organize work and life in order to accomplish tasks effectively and efficiently. The concept of managing time is awkward, as if anyone might influence time in some way, while in fact only activities are organized and managed over time. TM has been a popular term ever since behaviors of successful managers were systematically assessed and translated into advice (McCay, 1959) and were popularized (Drucker, 1967). It is important to realize that a wise time manager in these books is an executive, who has the discretion to make autonomous decisions. This person is allowed to delegate or can choose not to attend to certain tasks altogether.

As TM was derived from practice, it remained without a theoretical basis for a long time. Yet, its principles can be incorporated into self-regulation theory (van Eerde, 2007). Behavior is regarded in a dynamic cycle in which a person adapts to changing circumstances. The behavior includes cognition, affect, and volition (Lord, Diefendorff, Schmidt, & Hall, 2010). Self-regulation is also referred to as self-management, and TM is a specific case of it, focused on the use of time.

Figure 16.1 shows TM as the dynamic cycle in the center: planning, implementation, and evaluation are the three phases that may be distinguished in the dynamic adaptation of behaviors.

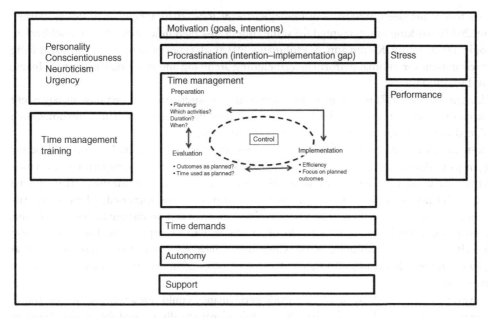

FIGURE 16.1   A model of time management

Note that in this figure procrastination is pictured as separate from this cycle, because authors consider procrastination as an intention–implementation gap, rather than part of a planning cycle. In the cycle, feedback mechanisms allow adaptation: in each phase, a continuation or change of the behavior may be considered, depending on how well the outcomes are achieved. In each phase, strategies can be used to achieve outcomes. Examples of strategies are planning, heuristics for decision making, or combining actions to increase efficiency. Achieving the outcomes implies an increase in the control of time, which would lead to less effort needed and, parallel to this, less stress, as it is less likely that things will go wrong and more likely that they will be achieved on time.

In Figure 16.1, the boxes surrounding the dynamic cycle are based upon Burt, Weststrate, Brown, and Champion's (2010) model of TM. It contains antecedents and moderators of TM, particularly those present in the organizational context. The model assumes a person–environment fit approach to TM, where characteristics of the environment necessitate certain behaviors or vice versa (cf. Greenberg, 2002 who compared emergency nurses to librarians on time urgency). In the following, I will address the antecedents and the moderators, but first I consider TM in relation to outcomes: does it lead to less stress and higher performance, as it claims?

Effects of Time Management

Many different behaviors and techniques have been subsumed under TM. Claessens, van Eerde, Rutte, and Roe (2007) defined time management as "behaviors that aim at achieving an effective use of time while performing certain goal-directed activities" (p. 36). Thus, TM is a somewhat broader concept than planning. Behaviors under the heading of TM include the increased awareness of time use, goal setting, prioritizing, planning, monitoring, and organizing. The techniques and tools used in TM aim at making smart decisions on how to allocate time wisely, that is, to spend as little time as possible on unimportant tasks and to spend the time thus gained on important tasks. Also, an increased awareness of how time is wasted is encouraged, and how certain activities can be combined within the same timeframe. Some tools used in

TM are to-do lists (see Claessens, van Eerde, Rutte, & Roe, 2010; Grawitch, Maloney, Barber, & Yost, 2011); working uninterrupted for some time, a so-called quiet hour (Käser, Fischbacher, & König, 2013; König, Kleinmann, & Höhmann, 2013); all types of reminders; and organizing the environment for optimal performance, including archiving and email management (Huang, Lin, & Lin, 2011).

Claessens et al.'s (2007) review provided an overview of studies that assessed time management as behavior that differs between individuals, and focused on the relation of TM and outcomes, such as reduced stress, feelings of control, and increased performance.

Most studies on TM provide evidence for a positive relation between TM and well-being, being organized, and feelings of control (e.g. Chang & Nguyen, 2011). An experiment in which students were trained in TM for two hours (Häfner, Stock, Pinneker, & Ströhle, 2013) showed that stress did not increase over the semester, and control of time increased, whereas the students in the control group showed an increased level of stress and no change in control of time. This result is in accordance with the results of a meta-analysis on experimental stress-reduction studies (Richardson & Rothstein, 2008). Cognitive-behavioral types of interventions, such as TM, had considerably greater effect sizes than other types of interventions, such as relaxation interventions.

However, the direct effects of TM on work performance could not always be demonstrated. Despite the popularity of TM, only a handful of studies have actually assessed the relation between TM and work performance (see Rapp, Bachrach, & Rapp, 2013). Some of these studies included objective performance (Hoff Macan, 1994), and more specifically, sales performance (Barling, Cheung, & Kelloway, 1996; Nonis & Sager, 2003; Rapp et al., 2013); others included self-rated performance (Claessens, van Eerde, Rutte, & Roe, 2004; Nonis, Fenner, & Sager, 2011). Some studies were (quasi-)experimental in design. These have used supervisor ratings of employees attending TM training (Häfner & Stock, 2010; Macan, 1996; Orpen, 1994; Slaven & Totterdell, 1993; Woolfolk & Woolfolk, 1986), or made use of self-rated performance (King, Winett, & Lovett, 1986; van Eerde, 2003b; Woolfolk & Woolfolk 1986). In most of these studies, self-reported performance was related to TM, but only one of them could demonstrate performance improvements detected by others (Orpen, 1994). The strongest test, an experiment in which Häfner and Stock (2010) compared participants of a one-day TM training with a control group, controlling for workload, did not show an improvement in performance (supervisor ratings, time spent on an important task). The training helped to decrease stress and to increase feelings of control, however.

TM affected outcomes that were more specific, such as handling email. Huang et al. (2011) conducted a quasi-experiment using a three-hour instruction on the TM of email in the experimental condition. Major functions of email were covered: filtering and searching, folder management, archiving, address book management, schedule management, and message management. The participants in the experimental condition spent less time on email after the instruction. Also, their self-efficacy and feelings of control increased.

Thus, overall, the studies showed that perceived control improved, and TM training may benefit performance in the longer term by means of stress reduction, but a direct effect of TM on work performance was not demonstrated. This would seem to be in contradiction to the positive effects of planning at work, for example in entrepreneurship (Gielnik, Frese, & Stark, this volume) or when performing complex tasks (Mumford, Mecca, & Watts, this volume). However, it would be consistent with the idea that planning and TM strategies can only be of additional value in interaction with motivation and goals. In other words, both goal intentions (motivation) and implementation intentions (planning) are needed, in interaction, to affect performance (Gollwitzer, 1999). In the following, TM will be considered as a variable that influences performance in interaction with other variables.

Time Management: A Skill?

From a resource allocation theory perspective, TM as a skill would help people to perform better at work because resources needed for high performance are allocated to those activities that help to deliver high performance, rather than being allocated to activities that do not lead to such output. Within this perspective, TM skills moderate the relation between motivation and performance. Barling et al. (1996) conducted a study on high versus average performers in car sales. Years of sales and achievement striving were direct predictors of sales. Additionally, the interaction between achievement striving and daily planning was predictive of sales. Interestingly, while it may be expected that the interaction with long-term planning would be beneficial, too, the results did not show this. More recent research (Gielnik et al., 2013), however, clearly demonstrated the interaction between intentions and planning. Also, Rapp et al. (2013) showed that TM skills moderate the relation between organizational citizenship behavior (OCB) – specifically helping others at work – and work performance. Those who had high TM skills benefited from helping others over time, whereas for those who had low TM skills, an inverted U-relationship was found between OCB and performance: both low and high helping behavior detracted from performance (call activity), whereas an intermediate level of helping was best for those with low TM skills. Peeters and Rutte (2005) also established that TM was a moderator between job demands and emotional exhaustion: those teachers who had high demands and low control and who engaged in TM felt less exhausted than those who used less TM. TM skills were also found to moderate between boredom and distraction (Van der Heijden, Schepers, & Nijssen, 2012), such that TM helped people to remain focused even though they were bored. Sitzmann and Johnson (2012) showed in their experiment on self-regulated learning that planning was helpful for learning following a training, and that attrition from the training was diminished. However, planning in combination with another intervention that targeted self-regulatory processes that occur subsequent to planning such as monitoring, concentration, and learning strategies, was even more effective. They concluded that a dynamic perspective helps planning: not only making a plan, but also keeping the plan alive as time progresses.

Thus, TM has been established as a moderating factor of importance to performance. However, there may be doubt as to whether TM is actually a skill or is rather a stable personality factor. Many of the research designs do not allow this distinction to be made. Macan (1994) showed that there was no difference in TM behaviors between those who had gone to TM training and those who had not. Conscientiousness incorporates TM, as it includes organization and discipline. Thus, it may be worthwhile to find a way to distinguish personality from skill, for example, in terms of temperament and knowledge applied, in future research on TM.

Claessens et al.'s review also concluded that much was still unknown about "how people plan and prioritize their work activities, whether and how they perform their planned actions, and how they implement time management techniques" (2007, pp. 270–271). It may be relevant to devote more attention to what the techniques mean to people. For example, consider an item in a questionnaire (cf. Paul, Baker, & Cochran, 2012) "I make a list of things to do every day." Is this a sign of good time management? Or is it a list with the same things on it every day? Or is it a list that serves to get things off one's mind and not to be bothered about? (cf. Masicampo & Baumeister, 2011). TM may be criticized for its emphasis on tools, as the planning process may also be seen as behavior that does not require the use of specific tools but of cognitive processes. The mental simulation of actions, specifying the sub-steps and operational details leading to goal accomplishment, may not always be explicit (Mumford et al., this volume).

In an experimental study (Fernandes & Lynch, 2012), those who were low on propensity to plan actually delayed tasks when they were instructed to make reminders for these tasks. Once the reminders came up, they did not engage in the tasks they were reminded of. If, however, they were instructed to elaborate on the reminder and to decompose it into different sub-tasks, they were more likely to engage in the reminded behavior.

In addition, Townsend and Liu (2012) established this differential effect: for those who considered themselves poor planners, making a plan actually led them to engage less in these behaviors (spending, eating a snack) than those who did not plan. In these experiments, considering a concrete plan for goal implementation created emotional distress, thereby undermining their motivation for self-regulation. These last two studies appear to contradict the findings of other studies on planning. The difference appears to lie in the extent to which a person is confident and has the self-regulatory strength to actually implement the plan. Another explanation that Buehler and colleagues (this volume) report may be found in the type of task. In so-called "open" tasks in which assignments or other types of task may be distributed over time rather than in one session, actual completion times were not affected by planning. In the following, I extend the overview from TM of certain tasks to the wider context of an organization.

Time Management and Context

One of the issues that Claessens et al. (2007) addressed in their review, was that TM cannot be separated from the context in which it takes place. Burt et al. (2010) incorporated variables relevant to the context into their TM-model. Figure 16.1 also displays these variables, i.e. time demands, autonomy, and support, as moderators of the effects that TM may have on outcomes.

Time Demands

With regard to time demands, not all jobs may require planning. Service-oriented or highly standardized jobs may require mostly reactions, rather than planning and evaluation. Also, the assumption that persons are allowed quiet time, or at least some time undisturbed for tasks that need concentration, can be called into question given the studies on work fragmentation that only leaves time for individual work in slots of a few minutes (e.g. Tengblad, 2006). Frequent interruptions by others, for example, for spontaneous meetings (Rogelberg, Leach, Warr, & Burnfield, 2006), can create vicious cycles of time pressure (Perlow, 1999). Also, technological advances and working on the internet may make uninterrupted work more difficult. Research on resisting the temptation to be distracted showed that, particularly in the work setting, much can be gained. Respondents indicated that (social) media in particular was highly distracting and most difficult not to attend to (Hofmann, Baumeister, Förster, & Vohs, 2012). Thus, it is important to consider where TM takes place and to what extent the time demands of the task actually allow the person to self-regulate and gain control.

Autonomy

Not every employee can delegate tasks, for example, as is assumed in the original approach to TM for executives. The autonomy for personal TM allowed by a supervisor, or "supervisor-related time control," defined as "the perceived level of time control as a result of the synchronization of employees' own rhythms with demands and requests from supervisors" was also examined in an Asian context (Chen, Zhang, Leung, & Zhou, 2010, p. 183). Particularly in cultural settings that do not allow autonomous decisions even when the work is complex, and where a paternalistic style of leadership may be used, this appears to be highly relevant. The measurement scale assesses the perceived lack of time control caused by supervisors' disruption and uses the reverse score to indicate control of time. Understandably, the scale was related to job satisfaction, and the relation between control of time and job satisfaction was found to be moderated by perceptions of justice. Summarizing, autonomy is important to consider; people may not be given the discretion to decide on their own actions to increase effectiveness.

Support

Does an organization provide the conditions in which employees can actually manage their time well? Is there sufficient structure and clarity to act upon priorities? And how do others react to individual TM behaviors? Peers may view TM as socially unacceptable when they are confronted with messages from individuals managing their time, such as "do not disturb" or "say no to low priority tasks." Interestingly, lists have appeared that provide strategies for declining requests that would diminish scholarship productivity while maintaining a good relationship (Chase et al., 2013). Examples of these strategies are: do not say yes to a request unless you have a clear view of its priority; diminish your role; plan it at a later moment; or negotiate on what the person will do for you in return. People appear to have problems with this trade-off between individual TM and social expectations. They would like to do both to please everyone concerned, but a trade-off decision needs to be made. Summarizing, support is a precondition to manage time. Even if an individual attempts to manage time it will impossible in an organizational climate that is not supportive to TM because it does not provide opportunities for shielding the time for focused work of individuals.

Burt et al. (2010) developed a measurement instrument of factors deemed to be supportive to TM: supervision, peers, task structure, support for TM practices, and time values in the organization. Of these five factors, the supervisory role was most highly (negatively) related to stress, and support for TM in general was related most strongly (negatively) to turnover intentions. This supervisory role in relation to time was also investigated in two recent studies (Gevers & Demerouti, 2013; Mohammed & Nadkarni, 2011). The first study showed that supervisors' reminders may be useful for some employees but may actually be superfluous for others. The second showed that strong temporal leadership is positively related to performance, especially when teams are diverse in their styles in working towards deadlines.

As this overview shows, there are many dimensions to consider when studying TM. Within a self-regulatory framework, individual differences and context matter. Recent research has addressed these issues in more detail, but much is still unknown. The self-management of distractions at work will become an issue that needs more attention, in light of the growing use of the internet at work. In addition, the wider context that incorporates sociocultural factors (Levine, 2005; White, Valk, & Dialmy, 2011) plays a role in TM. Overall, the context may play a larger role than TM would state, as it focuses on the individual and not necessarily on the social and organizational context.

In the next section, I will discuss TM in relation to procrastination, starting with what procrastination entails.

Procrastination

Van Eerde (2000, p. 375) defined procrastination as the delay due to "the avoidance of the implementation of an intention." Mostly, the avoidance concerns an aversive task, or at least something less attractive than an alternative that can be acted upon. This delay is often seen as irrational. Why would anyone delay doing something that they should do and do something less important instead? Clearly, this behavior has a moral connotation, associated with the idea that only lazy or unreliable people engage in this behavior. In most contexts, it is not considered a serious offense, but there are many jokes about the weakness of a person who procrastinates. Something that looks appealing in the future does not always look that way once it is in the present. Thus, procrastination has been termed preference reversal or time discounting within behavioral economics (cf. Steel & König, 2006). The aversiveness of the postponed action may be highly personal. Examples range from doing a difficult and effortful piece of work to calling a friend or buying a present.

Why do people engage in this irrational behavior? The research suggests that avoidance serves a function: a temporary relief from the aversive task. In the short term, it provides distraction, relief, perhaps also relaxation, and it enhances well-being, but in the longer term, delay may cause problems (Tice & Baumeister, 1997). The distraction is often something effortless or relaxing, something that may be easily interrupted, supposedly to resume the avoided task soon, even though this interval may be stretched for a very long time (Sabini & Silver, 1982). In this light, the omnipresence of quick fun distraction on the internet makes distraction much easier than before. The avoidance leads to delay and this delay may be dysfunctional. Whether delay actually results in negative consequences may depend on the nature of the postponed action, and the reactions of others, for example, whether it affects meeting a deadline, or whether it influences the perception of how dependable someone is. For many, procrastination is associated with internal consequences: guilt, shame, anxiety, or stress in general, possibly leading to psychosomatic complaints. Not doing something that you should do is often self-defeating, and the moral connotation of being like this may be an important part of the experience. People are often disappointed in themselves when they have postponed an obligation towards themselves or others.

The definition of procrastination has been debated by different authors. The least controversial in the definition is that a person delays. Also, not much discussion involves the voluntary nature: nobody forces a procrastinator to delay. Procrastinators often have enough possibilities not to delay, yet they do. This is seen as irrational as people may even engage in delay while experiencing discomfort. Should this discomfort be incorporated into the definition? Another issue in the debate is intentionality: do procrastinators really intend to delay, or is it something that happens to them without them intending it? To what extent do they feel control over the delay?

Procrastination is most often studied as a trait or disposition. Trait (or chronic) procrastination is considered to be the tendency to delay intended actions. This tendency appears to be stable, and some personality traits, such as conscientiousness, are highly (negatively) related to procrastination. Procrastination may also be seen as a state or a process. A definition of this phenomenon is complicated due to its subjective nature; what may seem delay to one person may be right on time to someone else. It can only be defined depending on the intention of the person. If a person plans or intends a delay, it is not procrastination but may be referred to as strategic delay (cf. Klingsieck, 2013).

Studying procrastination as a trait has the disadvantage that the process by which behavior may be changed may not be apparent (cf. Van Eerde, 2000). A dynamic within-person approach takes into account that everyone may procrastinate yet also leaves room for the idea that some procrastinate more than others. When it is considered a process, the avoidance that can be highly personal may become more easily identified – people differ in what they find aversive. In the following, I will provide an overview of some of the important issues in the research on procrastination.

Overview of the Research Field

I will discuss reasons and antecedents, incidence, theoretical notions, and measurement issues, and finally I focus more closely on procrastination in work settings.

It is important to know why people postpone actions, it is debatable whether self-attributed reasons are meaningful, as they may be rationalizations of the behavior. That is why some argue that it is better to measure procrastination and other constructs separately and then establish what the relation is between them without asking directly for the reasons. I will therefore present the reasons people give for their procrastination separately from the antecedents.

Reasons

Students who delay their academic work have been researched in quite some detail. Grunschel, Patrzek, and Fries (2013a) found four distinct types based upon an analysis of 14 self-attributed reasons, including the lack of time management. They termed these types inconspicuous, successful pressure-seeking, worried/anxious, and discontented with studies. Only the last two types would be considered procrastinators, as the first two types use purposeful delay, with the second type adding stimulation by creating pressure. The third type clearly shows that the delay is paired with negative emotions, and with low confidence and high perfectionism, while the fourth indicates an unmotivated and dissatisfied type, without anxiety. At any rate, the students who indicated they engaged in purposeful delay, inconspicuous or stimulated by pressure, obtained better grades, felt more satisfied, did not feel a need to change their study behaviors, and felt less strain than the other two types. The inconspicuous type in particular was found to be more conscientious than the other types. This shows that delay should be carefully examined and cannot be called procrastination if no further assessment is made of the reasons for it. There is not much empirical support for so-called active procrastination (Chu & Choi, 2005) that might indicate that procrastination may be functional. As previously mentioned, if delay is strategic and planned, it might be better not to call it procrastination.

Antecedents

In meta-analyses on procrastination (Steel, 2007; van Eerde, 2003a), the relations between procrastination and its antecedents and outcomes have been combined. Most effect sizes were retrieved from cross-sectional studies, and it may be better to think of a nomological network of procrastination in relation to several concepts, because empirically it is not clear whether procrastination is an antecedent, co-occurring phenomenon, or consequence. One of the surprising findings was that fear of failure and perfectionism were not related, or only very slightly, to procrastination. However, when people are asked why they procrastinate they often refer to fear of failure or perfectionism. How may the differences be reconciled? Most likely because in the meta-analyses all studies are combined. An important moderator might explain why there is no overall effect: the relation between fear of failure and procrastination for students with high competence is negative, while for those low on competence, the relation is positive, resulting in a null effect when studies are combined (Haghbin, McCaffrey, & Pychyl, 2012). The same goes for the relation between perfectionism and procrastination; perfectionism can be maladaptive, at least in clinical practice, as procrastinators appear to struggle with the idea that they need to be perfect (Pychyl & Flett, 2012). However, perfectionism can also lead to exerting more effort and achieving more because of it. Again, combining all studies on perfectionism is likely to cause a null effect when no distinction is made. These findings show that it is important to consider that procrastination is indeed often paired with fear of failure and perfectionism, but it does not automatically imply that everyone who is a perfectionist or fears failure actually procrastinates.

Incidence

Many articles state that procrastination is widespread, problematic, and on the increase (e.g. Steel & Ferrari, 2013). However, a closer look at the numbers that would support this makes them susceptible to different interpretations. First, looking at students, incidence rates of 70 to 95 percent are mentioned. These percentages come from surveys. The average score lies around 3 on a 5-point scale, which would mean a neutral score with a normal distribution. One of the issues in this type of research is to consider what the range of normal behavior is. When is someone considered a chronic procrastinator, and when is the behavior dysfunctional? Although it is clear that the extreme cases are clearly dysfunctional in terms of mental and physical well-being (Steel & Ferrari, 2013), no clear answers arise from the research regarding the cut-off values that need to be considered.

Theory

The field of procrastination research has diversified over the last 40 years. Many different perspectives have been taken, mainly based upon traits, but motivational/volitional, clinical, and situational factors have also been considered (cf. Klingsieck, 2013). These perspectives have not been clearly separated, and they overlap in many instances. It is important to acknowledge that the different perspectives complement rather than contradict each other.

Some recent research also addressed the possibility that there are neurophysiological roots of procrastination, examining executive functions (Rabin, Fogel, & Nutter-Upham, 2011). However, two aspects of the study make the results inconclusive: first, the functioning is self-reported rather than tested, and second, some of these functions overlap with conscientiousness. For example, conscientiousness overrode the significance of some of the components of executive functioning, such as the ability to shift from one situation or activity to another and to modulate emotional responses.

Measurement

Several instruments have been developed to measure procrastination, and sometimes distinctions were made between decisional or behavioral procrastination, or avoidance or arousal procrastination (for an overview of scales, see Negra & Mzoughi, 2012). Steel (2010) combined the items from several procrastination scales in a factor analysis. This study supported a one-factor model of procrastination rather than one of different types. The analysis revealed that many items in longer scales do not actually measure procrastination. This scale is termed the pure procrastination scale and it contains 12 items. An alternative is to measure avoidance reactions to a deadline using eight items, also a one-factor scale without any redundant items (van Eerde, 2003b).

Procrastination in Work Settings

Research on procrastination in work settings is relatively rare. Nguyen, Steel, and Ferrari (2013) conducted a study using a very large internet sample that assessed procrastination at work. They concluded, among other things, that men procrastinate more than women, procrastination is associated with unemployment, part-time work, shorter employment duration, and lower salaries. Overall, a bleak picture is painted of the variables associated with the behavior. Regarding types of jobs, procrastination appears to be less prevalent in investigative and enterprising professions. The value of the study lies in the large scale of the study. It is nevertheless difficult to interpret the results because in such an epidemiological approach, alternative explanations may be given based upon omitted variables, such as depression or physical health.

Notwithstanding the scarcity of research on procrastination at work, it may have more negative consequences in the workplace than it has for students, as not only the procrastinator may
be affected by the behavior, but also others who are in some way dependent upon him or her.
However, this has only been addressed in about four studies, as far as could be established.

Procrastination can be rather well observed by others. This was demonstrated in a study among
skilled Indian men ($n = 200$); supervisors were asked to categorize workers as procrastinators
or non-procrastinators, and these scores corresponded well with self-ratings (Sharma, 1997). Van
Eerde (2003b) also showed that peers confirm their self-ratings. Ferrari (1992) showed that procrastinators judged scenarios of a co-worker procrastinating more harshly than non-procrastinators.
They attributed the behavior of the person in the scenario more internally and were more likely
to agree with the statement that the person should be fired. Procrastinators were also harsh in rating others who delay academic tasks or tasks in daily life (Ferrari & Patel, 2004), possibly reflecting
their own dislike for the behavior.

In studying procrastination at work, it may be useful to consider procrastination in terms of
"empty labor," "the part of our working hours that we spend on other things than work" (Paulsen,
2013), depending on whether the distractions that replace the intended actions are work-related
or not. Paulsen developed a tentative typology based upon the employee's sense of work obligation
and how much work the job actually entails:

> *Soldiering* is the active withdrawal of the employee despite high potential output; *slacking* is
> a combination of little to do and weak sense of work obligation in the employee; *coping* is
> when the employee wants to perform and there is much to do, but when empty labor is used
> as stress relief; *enduring* is when the employee is motivated to work, but work tasks are lacking.
>
> *(p. 1)*

Procrastination at work could be occurring in the first three instances. D'Abate and Eddy (2007)
studied this under the term "presenteeism," being at work but working below capacity, and found
that personal business on the job, both on family matters and on leisure activities, is associated
with procrastination. Personal business on the job was not associated with being dissatisfied, being
uncommitted, or intending to leave the organization, nor was it related to self-reported measures
of performance or efficiency, only to procrastination. Wan, Downey, and Stough (2014) also established this relation. Their findings were in contrast to a study on email use conducted by Phillips
and Reddie (2007). These authors found that procrastination was not a predictor of personal email
use, only of work-related email use. As mentioned before, studies on procrastination in a work
setting are relatively rare, but it is expected that distraction and self-regulation will become more
urgent topics to study in the near future.

Overcoming Procrastination

Many people use some kind of strategy to help them through the difficulty of initiating necessary but unpleasant activities, for example, cleaning a toilet or reading a boring text to prepare
for a meeting. Sokolowski (1994) asked respondents what their strategies were. He distinguished
the following strategies: making specific plans, increasing time pressure, thinking of positive consequences, thinking of negative consequences of not doing it, removing distractions, suppressing
negative emotions, anticipating goal attainment, and focusing on the responsibility of having to
do the activity. These categories are not definitive, but they appear in many articles that address
overcoming procrastination. There are large individual differences in procrastination and the ability
to overcome it (Steel, 2007; van Eerde, 2003a). At the same time, there are many who wish they

could change their procrastination habit. Many popular books are devoted to this wish, and there is a clear demand for some type of solution. However, in terms of an evidence base on what is actually helpful, the research does not provide a clear answer. There are at least three explanations as to why procrastination is hard to change: (1) there are strong indications that it is part of generalized behavior patterns and can be considered a trait; (2) avoidance may be experienced as "addictive," and the distractions to engage in may be too tempting. As such, avoidance learning may take place, leading to vicious cycles over time. Finally, (3) there are emotional barriers to deal with that often cannot be tackled because the person does not feel confident enough.

This section reviews some of the studies on interventions to reduce procrastination.

Schouwenburg (2004, ch. 14) provides an overview of the three components used in interventions aimed at helping students overcome procrastination: (1) training self-regulatory skills; (2) building emotional strength; and (3) using social support to sustain desirable behavior.

First, training self-regulatory skills to reduce the gap between intentions and behavior mainly involves planning, but also includes other strategies that overlap with TM. Similar to what was stated in the chapter on planning and entrepreneurship (Gielnik, Frese, & Stark, this volume), planning may be problematic because there is a lack of knowledge about the future. Procrastinators seem to overestimate their control of the implementation of their plans. As was discussed in connection to overcoming the planning fallacy (Buehler & Griffin, this volume), the strategies include creating an overview of tasks, setting realistic goals, subdividing and specifying large and vaguely formulated goals, specifying deadlines for these goals, allocating time, training to overcome tempting distractions, monitoring progress, and stimulus–control techniques that help to ensure that the environment is distraction-free.

Second, and different from TM, procrastination interventions are focused on ways to enhance self-efficacy, by, for example, building on principles in rational-emotive behavioral therapy to emphasize that thoughts, behaviors, and feelings are interrelated, so that changing thoughts and feelings may lead to changing the behavior. Emphasis is placed on replacing irrational beliefs with more realistic and positive thoughts.

Third, the support of peers is used to help to recognize, support, or disapprove of certain behaviors. Overall, the three components could be seen as TM with extras: the interventions not only include the cognitive, behavioral, and contextual structuring that helps in organizing, but also devote attention to the emotional aspects of procrastination and to invoking social support to sustain efforts in overcoming it. Most interventions have addressed academic and health-related behaviors. In the following, the interventions will be reviewed according to the three components mentioned above: cognitive-motivational structuring, building emotional strength, and invoking social support.

Cognitive-Motivational Structuring

Planning is a cognitive-motivational intervention. Making goals more concrete by elaborating on them in more detail helps to implement them, as action theory asserts (Frese & Zapf, 1994). Procrastination researchers do not call their interventions TM, and may be more inclined to call them self-regulation, even though the content overlaps. Often, some kind of cognitive restructuring of irrational beliefs may be included in procrastination interventions. In the following, however, I will specifically consider the actions that deal with planning. These include TM, implementation intentions, and additional strategies as forms of planning conducive to the reduction of procrastination.

Time Management

Van Eerde (2003b) assessed procrastination after a commercial TM training and found a significant decrease of procrastination compared to a waiting control group. Renn, Allen, and Huning (2011) investigated procrastination as a self-defeating strategy within the broader term self-management. These authors tested a model in which the relation between self-defeating behaviors (inability to delay gratification, procrastination, and emotional self-absorption) and self-management (goal setting, monitoring, and operating) was investigated. Self-defeating behaviors were proposed as mediators in the relation between personality traits (neuroticism and conscientiousness) and self-management. They concluded that the relationship between neuroticism and self-management was accounted for by the inability to delay gratification and emotional absorption. On the other hand, conscientiousness and self-management practices were partially accounted for by self-defeating behaviors; conscientiousness was also directly related to taking action.

Green and Skinner (2005) provide some indication that procrastination decreased to a lesser extent than the other behaviors predicted to decrease after TM training, such as learning not to forget things or email management.

Michinov, Brunot, Le Bohec, Juhel, and Delaval (2011) also combined TM and procrastination in their study on online learning. Their analyses show that motivation was high at the start of the project for both low and high procrastinators. However, this level dropped off during the project for high procrastinators, whereas it remained relatively high for the low procrastinators. Only right before the end of the project did high procrastinators indicate they were motivated again. Also, the effect of procrastination on performance was partly mediated by participation in online forums. However, those scoring high on procrastination participated less in online forums than those who scored low on it.

Another example is a detailed case study of seven students going through several sessions of cognitive behavioral coaching (Karas & Spada, 2009). The coaching program may be considered an intensive one-on-one TM training, and it also included some behavioral restructuring exercises to deal with irrational beliefs. It consisted of: (1) enhancing motivation to change; (2) goal setting; (3) monitoring progress; (4) time management; (5) disputing unrealistic beliefs; and (6) relapse prevention. It was effective in reducing procrastination after six months. Thus, only a few studies combined TM and procrastination. In these, TM helps to decrease procrastination.

Implementation Intentions

Here, I focus on the type of planning particularly relevant to procrastination: forming implementation intentions (Gollwitzer, 1999). From an action-theoretical perspective, a motivational phase results in the intention to enact behaviors, but a volitional phase is needed to implement them, and so-called action plans, or implementation intentions, are needed. People often have good intentions but fail to act upon them, either because the required behavior is not initiated or because they are unable to maintain the required behavior to reach a goal. Formulating behavior as specifically as possible ("if x happens, I will do y") makes it more likely that the behavior will be performed (Thürmer, Wieber, & Gollwitzer, this volume). Although some moderators of this effect seem to be present (e.g. goal difficulty, Prestwich & Kellar, 2010), the research shows positive effects of implementation intentions on the implementation of many behaviors that need self-control, such as dieting and exercising. People who spontaneously form implementation intentions procrastinate less (Howell, Watson, Powell, & Buro, 2006). Also, in research in which implementation intentions were assessed in a field study, support was found for the proposed mediating role of implementation intentions in the relation between job search intention and job search behavior (van Hooft, Born, Taris, van der Flier, & Blonk, 2005). The proposed moderating roles of action–state orientation and trait procrastination, however, were not supported. This would imply that implementation intentions are equally useful for everyone, whether they are procrastinators or not.

However, the spontaneous formation of implementation intentions may be attributed to individual differences in being organized in general and should thus be distinguished from using it as an intervention to reduce procrastination. In one experiment, people who were instructed to form implementation intentions were much more likely to keep their appointments (71 percent) than people who were asked not to do so (only 17 percent). It could be expected that this type of action plan would be even more beneficial for procrastinators, but no moderation effect was found, only a direct effect (Owens, Bowman, & Dill, 2008). Summarizing, both studies support the idea that implementation intentions are useful for implementation, independent of one's tendency to procrastinate.

With regard to implementation intentions, some moderators have been studied that have not been applied to procrastination research. Two of them are particularly interesting: future time perspective and self-efficacy.

Future time perspective is the tendency to consider the future rather than the past or the present (Zimbardo & Boyd, 1999). Procrastination is negatively associated with future time orientation (Ferrari & Díaz-Morales, 2007). The more people perceive their future as being constrained, the stronger becomes the relationship between planning and behavior. As such, planning seems to operate as a compensatory strategy for a lack of future time perspective (Gellert, Ziegelmann, Lippke, & Schwarzer, 2012). Similarly, plans are more likely to be implemented if people feel more self-efficacious about the behaviors needed to implement them (Lippke, Wiedemann, Ziegelmann, Reuter, & Schwarzer, 2009).

This would imply that somehow broadening the future time perspective and the confidence of procrastinators would help them to decrease the delay. And if the time perspective remains very restricted, a good strategy is to engage in thorough planning.

Additional Planning Strategies

There are many new developments in the field of action plans that have not been incorporated into procrastination research. A detailed critique and suggestions for the future of the field of action plans was presented by Sniehotta (2009). Some of his ideas are related to additional planning for implementation intentions, such as barrier-focused strategies, which involve coping plans for high-risk situations. Another important issue in relation to procrastination is that there is a need to study how plans develop in real situations as opposed to plans provided by researchers in many of the implementation intention studies. In other words, both the formation of spontaneous implementation intentions and the researcher-instructed way of forming implementation intentions may have limitations. For procrastination, it would be useful to know whether it is possible to train people in using these strategies if they are not inclined to do so spontaneously.

Adriaanse et al. (2010) suggested mental contrasting as one of the additional strategies helpful for implementation of actions. Mental contrasting involves formulating a wish for a certain behavior, and imagining the positive future in the event of successful behavior change versus a negative reality that stands in the way of reaching this desired future. In using mental contrasting, both the positive future and the negative reality become mentally accessible. This may help a person to make the right decision: choosing a positive future reality. Related to this approach, and emphasizing the dynamics over time in relation to procrastination, Krause and Freund (2013) developed a model that emphasizes a focus on the process rather than the outcomes during goal pursuit for overcoming procrastination.

Another new development is training prospective memory to reduce the steepness of time discounting and to change the meaning of a future action to learn. These memory training sessions involved intensive memorization of digits and words. The (yoked) control group went through the same training, except for having to use their working memory. So far, these interventions have been successful in changing drug addicts' perceptions and reducing their drug habit considerably

(Bickel, Yi, Landes, Hill, & Baxter, 2011; Radu, Yi, Bickel, Gross, & McClure, 2011). It may be worthwhile to attempt to use this type of training among procrastinators.

Overall, planning is a useful strategy to overcome procrastination because it helps to implement actions, but it is not yet clear how people can be encouraged to plan in real life if they do not do so spontaneously – after all, time discounting may also be considered a trait (Odum, 2011). Automated tools that help planning and that provide cues to the person over time to sustain self-control (Alias, 2012; Kamphorst, 2011) may help these people in particular. Many interventions to overcome procrastination have targeted other behaviors than planning, and in the following, the emphasis is on the emotional side of procrastination.

Building Emotional Strength

As described earlier, TM helps to increase feelings of control and self-efficacy. Studies on procrastination show similar results. In an experimental set-up with measurements over time (Schmitz & Wiese, 2006), a self-regulation training for self-regulated learning was evaluated. The training involved goal setting, planning and time management, and volitional strategies, such as avoidance of procrastination, attention control, self-motivation, and dealing with distraction. Using a diary as a measurement tool, self-efficacy went up and procrastination went down. Another study on self-regulated learning with a longitudinal design showed that after goal achievement during a semester, self-efficacy increased and procrastination decreased. The authors of this study refer to the time paths as vicious and virtuous cycles (Wäschle, Allgaier, Lachner, Fink, & Nückles, 2014).

Some interventions to overcome procrastination target self-efficacy and emotional strength directly. Increasing confidence to implement actions and reducing the anxiety associated with them may also be helpful in overcoming procrastination. An example of such a study (Ramsay, 2002, p. 89) used a 10-minute rule to stay on a task, even if the task was experienced as overwhelming. This is a way to get started on a task and to gain experience, rather than making a decision to avoid it because of negative thoughts or images of what might go wrong. After completing the initial commitment, the participant is then encouraged to reassess the task with regard to how he or she had anticipated it beforehand. The exercise can be varied from a time increment to a certain number of tasks that a person can commit to, such as to listen to five voicemails. Another intervention that looks similar to this works on the basis of time restriction, which leads to successful implementation and therefore to higher self-efficacy – although it may also be categorized as a planning intervention. Participants are instructed to work for no more than the time planned, starting with small time intervals. In sessions with others, feedback is provided, and only if the planning has been met is the person is allowed to spend more time on the subsequent tasks (Höcker, Engberding, Haferkamp, & Rist, 2012). The authors claim that this is the most successful intervention for procrastination so far. Perhaps this kind of intervention leads to successful implementation because it is based upon reference forecasting (see Buehler & Griffin, this volume); the planning is based upon the success of previous experiences – which were very limited up to that point – rather than upon an optimistic view of the future. It would be interesting to find out whether the severe cases benefit as much as the less severe, as the average of the sample had procrastination scores lower than 3 on a 5-point scale to start with.

Besides enhancing self-efficacy, some interventions target reduction of stress and learning how to cope with the stress related to difficult or aversive tasks. A strategy that appears to be helpful in reducing procrastination is to be more forgiving about one's own behavior (Wohl, Pychyl, & Bennett, 2010). The effect was found to be mediated by the reduction of negative affect. Thus, although this sounds contradictory, being nice, rather than harsh, about one's own procrastination may actually help. Similarly, self-compassion (Sirois, 2014) and mindfulness (Sirois & Tosti, 2012) mediated the relation between procrastination and stress. These studies demonstrate that at least part of the stress caused by procrastination is related to being strict with oneself and may perhaps be alleviated by learning more self-compassion. Mindfulness training might be another way to deal with the difficulties experienced in procrastination. Focusing on the here and now, as is instructed in mindfulness training, would appear to be contradictory to planning and focusing on a future goal. However, both appear to be useful in the case of procrastination. Distancing oneself emotionally from what is unpleasant and replacing avoidance by accepting the here and now of the situation may be the part of mindfulness that helps (Howell & Buro, 2011). Perhaps it is the balance between living in the here and now and a future focus that is optimal. A web-based mindfulness training of 13 ten-minute sessions over a period of four weeks also found that the intervention reduced stress via increased mindfulness and decreased procrastination (Drozd, Raeder, Kraft, & Bjørkli, 2013).

An example of a more clinical approach, or therapeutic change, to overcome procrastination (Rice, Neimeyer, & Taylor, 2011) is coherence therapy, designed to help clients through deeper understanding of the emotional truth of a symptom. The idea behind this therapy is that it is good to follow the procrastinator's reasoning and not to counteract the procrastination. The client is encouraged to reach a more complete understanding of the symptom through a process of experiential discovery, and to discover which adaptive function the behavior fulfills. Rice et al.'s (2011) study evaluated coherence therapy in comparison to an active bibliotherapy intervention based upon *The Now Habit* by Fiore (2007) as a self-help instruction. Fiori reintroduced Burka and Yuen's (1983) "unscheduling," that is, first eliminating time slots in a schedule that are busy to see what time is left, rather than planning all activities as consuming time. The outcomes of the study revealed that neither coherence therapy in which the number of sessions with a therapist varied according to the needs of the patient nor reading the self-help book helped to reduce procrastination.

Thus, building emotional strength and self-efficacy appears to be useful in dealing with the stressful aspects of procrastination, for example, using experiential learning and time restriction. But, as mentioned before, planning and TM also help to reduce stress. In addition, being compassionate with oneself and mindful appeared to be helpful. In contrast, coherence therapy was not as useful as expected. In the following, the support from peers in dealing with procrastination is examined.

Peer Support

Peer groups can be very influential in many different areas of life, and the same appears to be the case for the treatment of procrastination. Tuckman (2007) established in an experiment among distance-learning students that procrastinators specifically benefited from what he termed "motivational scaffolding." This intervention resembles a group–TM intervention. It uses online chats and a study skills support group, in which students serve as another student's supporter. The supporter's task is to help the student manage his/her time by reviewing weekly to-do checklists prepared by the partner and comparing them to the partner's report of subsequent task accomplishment (i.e. successes and failures). This approach can be compared to having a person help with planning from an outside perspective (see Buehler & Griffin, this volume). The checklists contain weekly study tasks, broken down into small steps, and listed as specific and measurable concrete activities. After discussing the prior week's accomplishments, the checklist for the coming week is discussed. The students send their checklists in and these are discussed in larger groups. Overall, increased monitoring by others had an effect on procrastination, and the grades of the procrastinators improved. Interestingly, those who were low on procrastination did not profit from the intervention in terms of better grades. The study points out that it may be useful to consider type-specific interventions for those who find they need to change their dilatory behaviors.

This was also stated in a recent overview of procrastination (Klingsieck, 2013, p. 29): "to meet the multifaceted phenomenon of procrastination, procrastination research needs to develop custom-tailored interventions." This would be wise to keep in mind for the future. Peer support, tackling irrational cognitions, and improving planning and self-regulation skills would appear to be useful for all procrastinators. Dealing with negative emotions may only be needed for the worried/anxious types, and they would need more help in building self-efficacy. For those who procrastinate because of discontent and lack of motivation, interest enhancement interventions may be used, such as reconsidering activities in the light of goals and exploring their own interests, as well as finding other ways of making activities less boring, such as creating a good atmosphere while performing them, and the support of others.

At work, other issues may play a role, of course, as lack of interest in the content of a job may not always be easily solved unless a job change is possible. When it is clear that workers cannot keep their jobs if they do not meet deadlines, the external pressure may be much higher and may lead the procrastinator to function adequately. Thus, the procrastinator at work is under more social pressure than the academic procrastinator (cf. Van Eerde, 2000) and can be found more often in constrained, rather than autonomous, jobs (Nguyen et al., 2013). Whereas some of the research on students' procrastination may apply to how to help employees, another intervention that could be considered is for managers to take care of other people's TM by setting goals and deadlines, and enforcing certain procedures.

Concluding, there have been many interventions, but not all have used a research design that allows strong conclusions regarding the causality of a particular part of the intervention. Nevertheless, the more controlled studies usually show positive effects. All three types of intervention discussed appear to contribute to the reduction of procrastination.

Conclusion

Does planning help to overcome procrastination? Many procrastination interventions have incorporated some kind of planning and it does at least appear to be an important precondition for overcoming it. However, to answer this question in more detail, two issues need to be considered: (1) the intervention studies have not been rigorous in many cases, leaving open alternative explanations; and (2) some interventions may not transfer to real life. That is, we do not know in detail how people procrastinate, plan, and implement as time goes by and as situations change. Some studies show that if people think of themselves as poor planners, they do not follow up on their plans (Townsend & Liu, 2012), and this may even lead to a lower likelihood of implementation. Considering the types of jobs that procrastinators occupy, these appear to be constrained and not of an investigative or enterprising nature (Nguyen et al., 2013). This may imply that a structured context helps procrastinators to function adequately. In other words, self-initiated planning may not be needed in these jobs, and procrastinators may select those jobs in which others control them to some extent.

Some types of intervention are related to planning but do not involve setting goals and plans as such. Instead, they involve time restriction, 10-minute time-on-task intervention, or memory training. These may be other ways to enhance cognitive structuring and they are worthwhile investigating further.

The emotional, and particularly the social-emotional, implications of procrastination are not dealt with if only planning is used as an intervention. Emotional and social issues have been neglected in TM, and the studies on procrastination show that social control, at least in student groups, is actually a very good way to help procrastinators.

The studies conducted on TM have not revealed direct positive influences on work performance. The contradiction with studies on planning may be resolved by considering the emphasis on tool use in TM, and the possibly limited type of planning associated with it. These may be insufficient when regulating one's own behavior over time – self-control is neglected in TM and it is likely that a more flexible approach to planning is needed than what TM usually offers.

Future Research Directions

It is important that we understand how planning affects procrastination, or, for that matter, how TM affects performance. Is it through increased control and confidence, the reduction of stress, and the organization of tasks in itself, or is it due to a reduction of the steepness of the discounting function, or are these all affected at the same time?

Moderators in terms of individual differences and context can be identified. In future studies, these should be carefully examined. Also, it would be useful to unravel the effects of particular variables rather than combining them, particularly in the intervention studies. Almost any intervention used a combination of different elements and the separate effects are difficult to distinguish. Particularly in these studies, multiple measurement moments and the use of control groups would help to understand what might help to overcome procrastination.

As can be seen from this overview, there are still many questions open regarding TM and procrastination. One of the topics that needs more attention is the lack of energy or fatigue in relation to procrastination (cf. Gröpel & Steel, 2008), which is highly relevant given the studies on depletion and self-regulation. Students mention mental and physical states less often as reasons for procrastination than, for example, motivation (Grunschel, Patrzek, & Fries, 2013b), but these states may nevertheless be important. Some research on fatigue has concluded that people tend to use familiar options when they are tired. They also increase demands on others, imitate others, and pursue risky options. Lost sleep might also result in using easier options, not necessarily risky, such as cyberloafing (Wagner, Barnes, Lim, & Ferris, 2012), behavior that is strongly linked to a lack of self-control (e.g. Restubog et al., 2011). The personal use of the internet at work may also be used as a way to recover from fatigue, boredom, or stress (Ivarsson & Larsson, 2011). An integration of TM and workload management strategies (cf. Barnes & Van Dyne, 2009) may be promising in managing fatigue.

In addition, if the training used for drug addicts (Bickel et al., 2011; Radu et al., 2011) may be generalized to the addictive nature of temptations, prospective memory training may be part of changing attitudes towards the future and time discounting.

Is TM only a bandage for chronic procrastinators? Yes, but it is a very important bandage that serves as a precondition. If it is left out of an intervention, it is unlikely that the stress will be alleviated. Even though relaxation may take place, the problems associated with procrastination will not be solved. Confidence may be built, but the disorganization and delay will remain without planning. Procrastination is an important problem in many people's lives. Planning and other interventions should be evidence-based and custom-tailored. This would increase the likelihood that they will help those who suffer from procrastination to overcome it.

References

Adriaanse, M. A., Oettingen, G., Gollwitzer, P. M., Hennes, E. P., De Ridder, D. T., & De Wit, J. B. (2010). When planning is not enough: Fighting unhealthy snacking habits by mental contrasting with implementation intentions (MCII). *European Journal of Social Psychology, 40*(7), 1277–1293.

Alias, N. A. (2012). Design of a motivational scaffold for the Malaysian e-learning environment. *Educational Technology and Society, 15*(1), 137–151.

Barling, J., Cheung, D., & Kelloway, E. K. (1996). Time management and achievement striving interact to predict car sales performance. *Journal of Applied Psychology, 81*(6), 821.

Barnes, C. M., & Van Dyne, L. (2009). `I'm tired': Differential effects of physical and emotional fatigue on workload management strategies. *Human Relations, 62*(1), 59–92. doi:10.1177/0018726708099518

Bickel, W. K., Yi, R., Landes, R. D., Hill, P. F., & Baxter, C. (2011). Remember the future: Working memory training decreases delay discounting among stimulant addicts. *Biological Psychiatry, 69*(3), 260–265.

Burka, J. N., & Yuen, L. M. (1983). *Procrastination: Why you do it, what to do about it.* Reading, MA: Addison-Wesley.

Burt, C. D. B., Weststrate, A., Brown, C., & Champion, F. (2010). Development of the time management environment (TiME) scale. *Journal of Managerial Psychology, 25*(6), 649–668.

Chang, A., & Nguyen, L. T. (2011). The mediating effects of time structure on the relationships between time management behaviour, job satisfaction, and psychological well-being. *Australian Journal of Psychology, 63*(4), 187–197. doi:10.1111/j.1742-9536.2011.00008.x

Chase, J. D., Topp, R., Smith, C. E., Cohen, M. Z., Fahrenwald, N., Zerwic, J. J., ... Conn, V. S. (2013). Time management strategies for research productivity. *Western Journal of Nursing Research, 35*(2), 155–176.

Chen, Z., Zhang, X., Leung, K., & Zhou, F. (2010). Exploring the interactive effect of time control and justice perception on job attitudes. *The Journal of Social Psychology, 150*(2), 181–197.

Chu, C. A. H., & Choi, J. N. (2005). Rethinking procrastination: Positive effects of "active" procrastination behavior on attitudes and performance. *The Journal of Social Psychology, 145*(3), 245–264.

Claessens, B. J. C., Van Eerde, W., Rutte, C. G., & Roe, R. A. (2004). Planning behavior and perceived control of time at work. *Journal of Organizational Behavior, 25*(8), 937–950.

Claessens, B. J. C., Van Eerde, W., Rutte, C. G., & Roe, R. A. (2007). A review of the time management literature. *Personnel Review, 36*(2), 255–276.

Claessens, B. J. C., Van Eerde, W., Rutte, C. G., & Roe, R. A. (2010). Things to do today ... : A daily diary study on task completion at work. *Applied Psychology: An International Review, 59*(2), 273–295.

D'Abate, C. P., & Eddy, E. R. (2007). Engaging in personal business on the job: Extending the presenteeism construct. *Human Resource Development Quarterly, 18*(3), 361–383. doi:10.1002/hrdq.1209

Drozd, F., Raeder, S., Kraft, P., & Bjørkli, C. A. (2013). Multilevel growth curve analyses of treatment effects of a web-based intervention for stress reduction: Randomized controlled trial. *Journal of Medical Internet Research, 15*(4), e84.

Drucker, P. F. (1967). *The effective executive.* New York: Harper & Row.

Fernandes, D., & Lynch, J. (2012). Mañana: Motivational effects of reminders on accelerating or delaying task completion. *European Marketing Academy Doctoral Colloquium,* Lisbon, Portugal.

Ferrari, J. R. (1992). Procrastination in the workplace: Attributions for failure among individuals with similar behavioral tendencies. *Personality and Individual Differences, 13*(3), 315–319.

Ferrari, J. R. (2010). *Still procrastinating: The no-regrets guide to getting it done.* New York: Wiley.

Ferrari, J. R., & Díaz-Morales, J. F. (2007). Procrastination: Different time orientations reflect different motives. *Journal of Research in Personality, 41*(3), 707–714.

Ferrari, J. R., & Patel, T. (2004). Social comparisons by procrastinators: Rating peers with similar or dissimilar delay tendencies. *Personality and Individual Differences, 37*(7), 1493–1501.

Fiore, N. A. (2007). *The now habit: A strategic program for overcoming procrastination and enjoying guilt-free play.* New York: Penguin.

Frese, M., & Zapf, D. (1994). Action as the core of work psychology: A German approach. *Handbook of Industrial and Organizational Psychology, 4,* 271–340.

Gellert, P., Ziegelmann, J. P., Lippke, S., & Schwarzer, R. (2012). Future time perspective and health behaviors: Temporal framing of self-regulatory processes in physical exercise and dietary behaviors. *Annals of Behavioral Medicine, 43*(2), 208–218.

Gevers, J. M. P., & Demerouti, E. (2013). How supervisors' reminders relate to subordinates' absorption and creativity. *Journal of Managerial Psychology*, 28(6), 677–698.

Gielnik, M. M., Frese, M., Kahara-Kawuki, A., Katono, I., Kyejjusa, S., Munene, J., … Dlugosch, T. J. (2013). Action and action-regulation in entrepreneurship: Evaluating a student training for promoting entrepreneurship. *Academy of Management Learning & Education*. Online before print, doi: 10.5465/amle.2012.0107

Gollwitzer, P. M. (1999). Implementation intentions: Strong effects of simple plans. *American Psychologist*, 54, 493–503.

Grawitch, M. J., Maloney, P. W., Barber, L. K., & Yost, C. (2011). Moving toward a better understanding of the work and nonwork interface. *Industrial and Organizational Psychology*, 4(3), 385–388.

Green, P., & Skinner, D. (2005). Does time management training work? An evaluation. *International Journal of Training and Development*, 9(2), 124–139.

Greenberg, J. (2002). Time urgency and job performance: Field evidence of an interactionist Perspective1. *Journal of Applied Social Psychology*, 32(9), 1964–1973. doi:10.1111/j.1559-1816.2002.tb00267.x

Gröpel, P., & Steel, P. (2008). A mega-trial investigation of goal setting, interest enhancement, and energy on procrastination. *Personality and Individual Differences*, 45(5), 406–411.

Grunschel, C., Patrzek, J., & Fries, S. (2013a). Exploring different types of academic delayers: A latent profile analysis. *Learning and Individual Differences*, 23, 225–233. doi: http://dx.doi.org/10.1016/j.lindif.2012.09.014

Grunschel, C., Patrzek, J., & Fries, S. (2013b). Exploring reasons and consequences of academic procrastination: An interview study. *European Journal of Psychology of Education*, 28, 841–861.

Häfner, A., & Stock, A. (2010). Time management training and perceived control of time at work. *The Journal of Psychology*, 144(5), 429–447.

Häfner, A., Stock, A., Pinneker, L., & Ströhle, S. (2013). Stress prevention through a time management training intervention: An experimental study. *Educational Psychology*, (ahead-of-print), 1–14.

Haghbin, M., McCaffrey, A., & Pychyl, T. A. (2012). The complexity of the relation between fear of failure and procrastination. *Journal of Rational-Emotive & Cognitive-Behavior Therapy*, 30(4), 249–263.

Höcker, A., Engberding, M., Haferkamp, R., & Rist, F. (2012). Wirksamkeit von arbeitszeitrestriktion in der prokrastinationsbehandlung [Effectiveness of working time restriction in the treatment of procrastination]. *Verhaltenstherapie*, 22(1), 9–16.

Hofmann, W., Baumeister, R. F., Förster, G., & Vohs, K. D. (2012). Everyday temptations: An experience sampling study of desire, conflict, and self-control. *Journal of Personality and Social Psychology*, 102(6), 1318.

Howell, A. J., & Buro, K. (2011). Relations among mindfulness, achievement-related self-regulation, and achievement emotions. *Journal of Happiness Studies*, 12(6), 1007–1022.

Howell, A. J., Watson, D. C., Powell, R. A., & Buro, K. (2006). Academic procrastination: The pattern and correlates of behavioural postponement. *Personality and Individual Differences*, 40(8), 1519–1530.

Huang, E. Y., Lin, S. W., & Lin, S. (2011). A quasi-experiment approach to study the effect of e-mail management training. *Computers in Human Behavior*, 27(1), 522–531. doi:10.1016/j.chb.2010.09.021

Ivarsson, L., & Larsson, P. (2011). Personal internet usage at work: A source of recovery. *Journal of Workplace Rights*, 16(1), 63–81.

Kamphorst, B. A. (2011). *Reducing procrastination by scaffolding the formation of implementation intentions.* Unpublished Master's thesis, Utrecht University.

Karas, D., & Spada, M. M. (2009). Brief cognitive-behavioural coaching for procrastination: A case series. *Coaching: An International Journal of Theory, Research and Practice*, 2(1), 44–53. doi:10.1080/17521880802379700

Käser, P. A. W., Fischbacher, U., & König, C. J. (2013). Helping and quiet hours: Interruption-Free time spans can harm performance. *Applied Psychology: An International Review*, 62(2), 286–307.

King, A. C., Winett, R. A., & Lovett, S. B. (1986). Enhancing coping behaviors in at-risk populations: The effects of time-management instruction and social support in women from dual-earner families. *Behavior Therapy*, 17(1), 57–66.

Klingsieck, K. B. (2013). Procrastination: When good things don't come to those who wait. *European Psychologist*, 18(1), 24–34.

König, C. J., Kleinmann, M., & Höhmann, W. (2013). A field test of the quiet hour as a time management technique. *Revue Européenne De Psychologie Appliquée/European Review of Applied Psychology*, 63(3), 137–145.

Krause, K., & Freund, A. M. (2013). How to beat procrastination: The role of goal focus. *European Psychologist*, 19(2), 132–144.

Levine, R. (2005). A geography of busyness. *Social Research: An International Quarterly*, 72(2), 355–370.

Lippke, S., Wiedemann, A. U., Ziegelmann, J. P., Reuter, T., & Schwarzer, R. (2009). Self-efficacy moderates the mediation of intentions into behavior via plans. *American Journal of Health Behavior*, 33(5), 521–529.

Lord, R. G., Diefendorff, J. M., Schmidt, A. C., & Hall, R. J. (2010). Self-regulation at work. *Annual Review of Psychology*, 61(3),1–3.26.

Macan, T. H. (1994). Time management: Test of a process model. *Journal of Applied Psychology*, 79(3), 381–391.

Macan, T. H. (1996). Time-management training: Effects on time behaviors, attitudes, and job performance. *The Journal of Psychology*, 130(3), 229–236.

McCay, J. T. (1959). *The management of time*. Englewood Cliffs, NJ: Prentice Hall.

Masicampo, E., & Baumeister, R. F. (2011). Consider it done! Plan making can eliminate the cognitive effects of unfulfilled goals. *Journal of Personality and Social Psychology*, 101(4), 667.

Michinov, N., Brunot, S., Le Bohec, O., Juhel, J., & Delaval, M. (2011). Procrastination, participation, and performance in online learning environments. *Computers & Education*, 56(1), 243–252.

Mohammed, S., & Nadkarni, S. (2011). Temporal diversity and team performance: The moderating role of team temporal leadership. *The Academy of Management Journal*, 54(3), 489–508.

Negra, A., & Mzoughi, N. (2012). How wise are online procrastinators? A scale development. *Internet Research*, 22(4), 2–2.

Nguyen, B., Steel, P., & Ferrari, J. R. (2013). Procrastination's impact in the workplace and the workplace's impact on procrastination. *International Journal of Selection and Assessment*, 21(4), 388–399. doi:10.1111/ijsa.12048

Nonis, S. A., & Sager, J. K. (2003). Coping strategy profiles used by salespeople: Their relationships with personal characteristics and work outcomes. *Journal of Personal Selling and Sales Management*, 23(2), 139–150.

Nonis, S. A., Fenner, G. H., & Sager, J. K. (2011). Revisiting the relationship between time management and job performance. *World Journal of Management*, 3(2), 153–171.

Odum, A. L. (2011). Delay discounting: Trait variable? *Behavioural Processes*, 87(1), 1–9.

Orpen, C. (1994). The effect of time-management training on employee attitudes and behavior: A field experiment. *The Journal of Psychology*, 128(4), 393–396.

Owens, S. G., Bowman, C. G., & Dill, C. A. (2008). Overcoming procrastination: The effect of implementation Intentions1. *Journal of Applied Social Psychology*, 38(2), 366–384.

Paul, J. A., Baker, H. M., & Cochran, J. D. (2012). Effect of online social networking on student academic performance. *Computers in Human Behavior*, 28(6), 2117–2127. doi:10.1016/j.chb.2012.06.016

Paulsen, R. (2013). *Empty labor: Subjectivity and idleness at work*. Unpublished Ph.D., Uppsala University.

Peeters, M. A., & Rutte, C. G. (2005). Time management behavior as a moderator for the job demand-control interaction. *Journal of Occupational Health Psychology*, 10(1), 64.

Perlow, L. A. (1999). The time famine: Toward a sociology of work time. *Administrative Science Quarterly*, 44(1), 57–81.

Phillips, J. G., & Reddie, L. (2007). Decisional style and self-reported email use in the workplace. *Computers in Human Behavior*, 23(5), 2414–2428. doi:10.1016/j.chb.2006.03.016

Prestwich, A., & Kellar, I. (2010). How can the impact of implementation intentions as a behaviour change intervention be improved? *Revue Européenne De Psychologie Appliquée/European Review of Applied Psychology*. doi:10.1016/j.erap.2010.03.003

Pychyl, T. A., & Flett, G. L. (2012). Procrastination and self-regulatory failure: An introduction to the special issue. *Journal of Rational-Emotive & Cognitive-Behavior Therapy*, 30(4), 203–212.

Rabin, L. A., Fogel, J., & Nutter-Upham, K. E. (2011). Academic procrastination in college students: The role of self-reported executive function. *Journal of Clinical and Experimental Neuropsychology*, 33(3), 344–357.

Radu, P. T., Yi, R., Bickel, W. K., Gross, J. J., & McClure, S. M. (2011). A mechanism for reducing delay discounting by altering temporal attention. *Journal of the Experimental Analysis of Behavior*, 96(3), 363–385.

Ramsay, J. R. (2002). A cognitive therapy approach for treating chronic procrastination and avoidance: Behavioral activation interventions. *Journal of Group Psychotherapy, Psychodrama, & Sociometry*, 55(2), 79–92.

Rapp, A. A., Bachrach, D. G., & Rapp, T. L. (2013). The influence of time management skill on the curvilinear relationship between organizational citizenship behavior and task performance. *Journal of Applied Psychology*, 98(4), 668–677. doi: 10.1037/a0031733

Renn, R. W., Allen, D. G., & Huning, T. M. (2011). Empirical examination of the individual-level personality-based theory of self-management failure. *Journal of Organizational Behavior*, 32(1), 25–43. doi:10.1002/job.667

Restubog, S. L. D., Garcia, P. R. J. M.,Toledano, L. S.,Amarnani, R. K.,Tolentino, L. R., &Tang, R. L. (2011). Yielding to (cyber)-temptation: Exploring the buffering role of self-control in the relationship between organizational justice and cyberloafing behavior in the workplace. *Journal of Research in Personality*, 45(2), 247–251.

Rice, K. G., Neimeyer, G. J., &Taylor, J. M. (2011). Efficacy of coherence therapy in the treatment of procrastination and perfectionism. *Counseling Outcome Research and Evaluation*, 2, 126–136.

Richardson, K. M., & Rothstein, H. R. (2008). Effects of occupational stress management intervention programs: A meta-analysis. *Journal of Occupational Health Psychology*, 13(1), 69.

Rogelberg, S. G., Leach, D. J.,Warr, P. B., & Burnfield, J. L. (2006)."Not another meeting!" Are meeting time demands related to employee well-being? *Journal of Applied Psychology*, 91(1), 83–89.

Sabini, J., & Silver, M. (1982). *Moralities of everyday life*. Oxford, UK: Oxford University Press.

Schmitz, B., & Wiese, B. S. (2006). New perspectives for the evaluation of training sessions in self-regulated learning: Time-series analyses of diary data. *Contemporary Educational Psychology*, 31(1), 64–96. doi:10.1016/j. cedpsych.2005.02.002

Schouwenburg, H. C. (2004). Perspectives on counseling the procrastinator. In H. C. Schouwenburg, C. H. Lay, T. A. Pychyl, & J. R. Ferrari (Eds.), *Counseling the procrastinator in academic settings* (pp. 197–208). Washington, DC: American Psychological Association.

Sharma, M. P. (1997).Task procrastination and its determinants. *Indian Journal of Industrial Relations*, 33(1), 17–33.

Sirois, F. M. (2014). Procrastination and stress: Exploring the role of self-compassion. *Self and Identity*, 13(2), 128–145.

Sirois, F. M., & Tosti, N. (2012). Lost in the moment? An investigation of procrastination, mindfulness, and well-being. *Journal of Rational-Emotive & Cognitive-Behavior Therapy*, 30(4), 237–248.

Sitzmann, T., & Johnson, S. K. (2012).The best laid plans: Examining the conditions under which a planning intervention improves learning and reduces attrition. *Journal of Applied Psychology*, 97(5), 967.

Slaven, G., & Totterdell, P. (1993). Time management training: Does it transfer to the workplace? *Journal of Managerial Psychology*, 8(1), 20–28.

Sniehotta, F. F. (2009).Towards a theory of intentional behaviour change: Plans, planning, and self-regulation. *British Journal of Health Psychology*, 14(2), 261–273.

Sokolowski, K. (1994).The role of action and state orientation in affiliative situations. In J. Kuhl & J. Beckmann (Eds.), *Volition and personality: Action versus state orientation* (pp. 417–425). Seattle, WA: Hogrefe & Huber.

Steel, P. (2007). The nature of procrastination: A meta-analytic and theoretical review of quintessential self-regulatory failure. *Psychological Bulletin*, 133(1), 65.

Steel, P. (2010). Arousal, avoidant and decisional procrastinators: Do they exist? *Personality and Individual Differences*, 48(8), 926–934.

Steel, P., & Ferrari, J. (2013). Sex, education and procrastination: An epidemiological study of procrastinators' characteristics from a global sample. *European Journal of Personality*, 27(1), 51–58. doi:10.1002/per.1851

Steel, P., & König, C. J. (2006). Integrating theories of motivation. *Academy of Management Review*, 31(4), 889–913.

Tengblad, S. (2006). Is there a "New managerial work"? A comparison with Henry Mintzberg's classic study 30 years later. *Journal of Management Studies*, 43(7), 1437–1461.

Tice, D. M., & Baumeister, R. F. (1997). Longitudinal study of procrastination, performance, stress, and health: The costs and benefits of dawdling. *Psychological Science*, 454–458.

Townsend, C., & Liu, W. (2012). Is planning good for you? The differential impact of planning on self-regulation. *Journal of Consumer Research*, 39(4), 688–703.

Tuckman, B. W. (2007).The effect of motivational scaffolding on procrastinators' distance learning outcomes. *Computers & Education*, 49(2), 414–422.

Van der Heijden, G. A. H., Schepers, J. J., & Nijssen, E. J. (2012). Understanding workplace boredom among white collar employees: Temporary reactions and individual differences. *European Journal of Work and Organizational Psychology*, 21(3), 349–375.

Van Eerde, W. (2000). Procrastination: Self-regulation in initiating aversive goals. *Applied Psychology: An International Review*, 49(3), 372–389.

Van Eerde, W. (2003a). A meta-analytically derived nomological network of procrastination. *Personality and Individual Differences*, 35, 1401–1418.

Van Eerde, W. (2003b). Procrastination at work and time management training. *The Journal of Psychology*, 137(5), 421–434.

Van Eerde, W. (2007). Time management. In S. G. Rogelberg (Ed.), *Encyclopedia of industrial/organization psychology* (pp. 812–813). Los Angeles, CA: Sage.

Van Hooft, E. A. J., Born, M. P., Taris, T. W., van der Flier, H., & Blonk, R. W. B. (2005). Bridging the gap between intentions and behavior: Implementation intentions, action control, and procrastination. *Journal of Vocational Behavior*, 66(2), 238–256. doi:10.1016/j.jvb.2004.10.003

Wagner, D. T., Barnes, C. M., Lim, V. K. G., & Ferris, D. L. (2012). Lost sleep and cyberloafing: Evidence from the laboratory and a daylight saving time quasi-experiment. *Journal of Applied Psychology*, 97(5), 1068.

Wan, H. C., Downey, L. A., & Stough, C. (2014). Understanding non-work presenteeism: Relationships between emotional intelligence, boredom, procrastination and job stress. *Personality and Individual Differences*, 65, 86–90.

Wäschle, K., Allgaier, A., Lachner, A., Fink, S., & Nückles, M. (2014). Procrastination and self-efficacy: Tracing vicious and virtuous circles in self-regulated learning. *Learning and Instruction*, 29, 103–114.

White, L. T., Valk, R., & Dialmy, A. (2011). What is the meaning of "On time"? The sociocultural nature of punctuality. *Journal of Cross-Cultural Psychology*, 42(3), 482–493.

Wohl, M. J. A., Pychyl, T. A., & Bennett, S. H. (2010). I forgive myself, now I can study: How self-forgiveness for procrastinating can reduce future procrastination. *Personality and Individual Differences*, 48(7), 803–808.

Woolfolk, A. E., & Woolfolk, R. L. (1986). Time management: An experimental investigation. *Journal of School Psychology*, 24(3), 267–275.

Zimbardo, P. G., & Boyd, J. N. (1999). Putting time in perspective: A valid, reliable individual-differences metric. *Journal of Personality and Social Psychology*, 77(6), 1271–1288.

17

TRAINING AND DEVELOPMENT FOR ORGANIZATIONAL PLANNING SKILLS

Holly K. Osburn, Jenifer M. Hatcher, and Bianca M. Zongrone

Introduction

Effective planning allows organizations to manage the rapid change occurring in today's business environment (Dervitsiotis, 1998), where companies must either learn to adapt quickly or die (Miles, Snow, Myer, & Coleman, 1978). Planning helps businesses to better navigate through their dynamic work environments. It offers companies a competitive advantage that propels a business forward, rather than taking a stagnant or defensive stance.

Planning is instrumental to an organization realizing its vision. Plans create organizations that are purposeful in their decision making. As a result, organizations that engage in extensive planning are likely to be more efficient and to avoid common pitfalls than those organizations that do not plan (Blair, 2010; Brinckmann, Grichnik, & Kapsa, 2010). In short, plans allow businesses to anticipate possible demands that are on the horizon and avoid being caught unprepared (Delmar & Shane, 2003).

Because plans have such positive benefits for organizations, the competency of planning is considered an important skill set to have in the workplace. In fact, both academic and popular literature emphasize that managers should be spending even more time than they do in this important quadrant of work duties (Cater & Pucko, 2010; Drucker, 1954, Mintzberg, 1987). In addition, planning is considered a critical component to entrepreneurial start-up success and long-term organization survival (Brinckmann et al., 2010; Henricks, 2008), and some suggest that the benefits of the planning process even outweigh the plan itself (Brinckmann et al., 2010).

Although planning is considered essential to organizational success, scholars have yet to provide a comprehensive strategy concerning how to develop planning skills. There are at least two possible explanations for this omission. First, it could be due to the sheer amount and variety of information available on the topic. The volume of research dedicated to this topic may be too vast and diverse to condense in order to extrapolate common principles. An alternative explanation is that the vast majority of the literature dedicated to planning focuses on the definitive skills required for effective planning to occur, rather than examining the process one would take to acquire those skills. For example, many articles discuss that good planners must be good goal setters, decision makers, and time managers but they do not address how one would acquire those specific skills. Either way, practitioners seeking to develop planning skills in their workforce are left to fend for themselves as they seek a development strategy for planning skills. Hence, a comprehensive approach to develop planning skills is needed.

In order to produce a developmental strategy for planning skills, it is necessary to define planning and identify the central components that must be trained. Traditionally, proposed training methods for planning have been behaviorally based. The behavioral approach identifies the superficial tasks that need to be undertaken and the tools that can be used to accomplish those tasks. A behavioral perspective of planning will concentrate on the action steps of planning rather than the internal cognitive mechanisms that enable those steps. An example of the behavioral perspective of development in environmental scanning would be to create a series of lists. These lists would include a list of all the relevant factors that could affect your internal organizational goals and a similar list of factors that could affect your external goals, as well as a list of opportunities you could pursue, and a list of obstacles you would like to avoid. Business strategists would recognize this environmental examination as a SWOT (strengths, weaknesses, opportunities, and threats) analysis.

Alternatively, a process approach would examine the underlying cognitive heuristics required to complete these steps. The process approach considers what mental models are accessed, the decision-making rules that are followed, and the common cognitive errors that may be in play when creating these lists. In our example of environmental scanning, the behavioral approach fails to address how one determines relevance, how one defines internal and external factors, or how one prioritizes received information when creating lists of relevant factors.

There is good deal of evidence to support the notion that cognitive training is necessary and important to improve the quality of the planning process. One important argument for including the process approach in training is Mintzberg's findings that planning in business is often an emerging process rather than a deliberate one (1979). If this is the case, we have to assume that much of planning is being done on an intellectual level rather than through outward visible steps.

Building on the idea that planning often occurs more at a psychological level, a survey of entrepreneurial businesses found that over half of them did not start with formal plans, and close to half of those who indicated they had a plan had created it mainly for funding purposes (Shuman & Seeger, 1986). Based on these arguments, it seems that people often plan in their heads without ever moving to the formal plan process. This makes the training of the mental planning process of utmost importance since, realistically, people often avoid the formal or behavioral planning process. Finally, we can argue that the cognitive aspects of planning are important because the behavioral steps of the planning process depend on underlying mental processes (Mumford, Schultz, & Van Doorn, 2001). For example, identifying several goals to pursue is a behavioral step. But the quality of those goals largely depends on the cognition that occurred prior to identification of the goals, such as being able to identify the level of difficulty needed to spur growth but not overwhelm the pursuit.

In addition, cognition creates a good foundation on which to build behavioral components. Behavioral steps build on the cognitive capacities that support them. There is evidence that more basic cognitive skills can enhance planning skills (Eubanks, Murphy, & Mumford, 2010). Examining the effects of instruction on divergent thinking, creative problem-solving, and creative achievement have provided evidence indicating that training interventions typically prove effective, often highly effective, in enhancing creativity in planning (Robledo et al., 2012). Stronger mental models produced through experiencing errors in planning can increase knowledge of a system, which helps in planning (Robledo et al., 2012). Thus, these arguments provide a compelling case that cognition should be emphasized when training individual-level planning skills.

Definition of Planning

While both cognitive and behavioral practices occur simultaneously during the planning process, the two methods are quite different from one another. There are many definitions of planning, but not all are suitable to use as a foundation for building planning skills. Since our focus is on developing planning processes, the definition of planning we will use is: *planning is the mental simulation of future actions used to organize efforts towards goal attainment* (Mumford, Schultz, & Osburn, 2000).

The emphasis placed on the cognitive aspects of the planning process is important here. The process approach explains planning as a mental simulation of events (Hayes-Roth & Hayes-Roth, 1979) and focuses on the internal processes that occur as an individual attempts to create a plan. This approach is distinctly different from the alternative of an applied approach, which focuses on the behavioral steps involved in planning (Caughron & Mumford, 2008). The process approach is most often covered in the psychological literature, while the applied approach tends to be included in the business literature (Caughron & Mumford, 2008).

Core Elements of Planning

In the present chapter, we will examine one model of planning processes to draw some conclusions in training development. Although independent studies of the planning process date back to the 1950s, a comprehensive model of the psychology of planning was not developed until somewhat more recently. In the business literature, there is no shortage of planning models. However, process models of planning are much less common.

In 2001, Mumford, Schultz, and Van Doorn reviewed 14 previous theories of the cognitive planning process. Many of these theories were based on a qualitative examination of the planning process. The focus of these studies was to identify the underlying mental processes that occurred while a person planned. Methods included conducting think-aloud protocols during recipe preparation, planning how to run errands, ship maneuvering, or other performance tests. Although the tasks varied greatly, consistencies were found in the way people went about creating their plans. Mumford and his colleagues examined these studies to identify consistent mental steps that occur during the planning process (2001).

Based on the review of the literature, three major divisions of the planning process were identified. These include: (1) generation, (2) projection and revision, and (3) implementation. Each category is broken down further into more specific steps. In total, this model identifies 14 steps that a planner would engage in while planning his or her event. With such a large number of mental processes identified, it makes sense that this task cannot be trained using one approach, tool, or methodology.

For the purpose of logical coherence and organization, we will group our ideas for planning training according to the steps of this model. We will focus on seven of the 14 steps given: (1) environmental scanning, (2) goal identification, (3) case-based reasoning, (4) identification of key causes, constraints, and resources, (5) plan generation, (6) forecasting, and (7) plan refinement and implementation.

As we examine each step, we will briefly describe it, discuss its merits, and present thoughts on how best to train it. Within the developmental considerations, three major concerns will be addressed. First, we will consider the explicit knowledge needed to perform this process step. Second, we will explore what tacit knowledge is required to effectively carry out the process step. Third, we will suggest several ways to develop this knowledge.

Expertise as a Boundary Condition

Prior to focusing on the development of underlying process skills associated with planning, it is critical that we address the acquisition of domain, organizational, and field-level expertise that frequently serve as a foundation to skill implementation. Each of these skills is somewhat dependent on domain and organizational expertise, and any effort to develop the underlying cognitive skills associated with planning must simultaneously include a plan to develop domain and organizational expertise. In some senior positions, field-level expertise is also a requisite. Without this, the heuristics taught will not be supported by the necessary knowledge structures.

To gain the requisite expertise, learners must dedicate themselves to large amounts of daily deliberate practice (Ericsson & Charness, 1994). Deliberate practice must be separate from regular work activities. It involves the learner working on a goal that stretches his or her current capabilities. After the learner's attempts to achieve the goal, direct, detailed, and immediate feedback should be given (Bransford & Schwartz, 2009; Day, 2010; Ericsson, 2009).

Training Planning Skills

Due to the complex nature of the planning process, there is no one singular method or approach to take when developing planning skills. The training and development needed to produce a solid planner calls for an intricate combination of objectives, methodologies, and assessments. Our model of planning as described above will be used to organize the training needs and subsequent suggested development activities. Table 17.1 outlines planning skills and the related development strategies.

Environmental Scanning

Environmental scanning can be defined as the activity of acquiring information from both internal and external sources that assists in determining future courses of action (Aguilar, 1967). This assessment may include an evaluation of relevant strengths and weaknesses or significant past accomplishments and failures (Wang & Tai, 2003). Other points of interest that might be involved in an environmental assessment include the analysis of economic, political, and social trends, considerations of relevant regulatory factors, or the current state of the technological sectors (Wang & Tai, 2003). Sources of information may include customer and supplier feedback, market research, competition monitoring, technology monitoring, and international contacts (Mumford, Eubanks, & Murphy, 2007).

Because environments change rapidly, the information gathered must be current and accurate. This step helps discover possible threats or opportunities and determine the relative significance of each (Barrett, Vessey, & Mumford, 2011; Ford & Gioia, 2000; Rodan, 2002). Gathering relevant information helps to clarify vision, focus energies, and define reality more objectively (Dervitsiotis, 1998).

Developmental Considerations for Environmental Scanning

Planners must learn two main objectives when completing an environmental scan. The first objective is to ensure that all pertinent information that would affect plan completion is retrieved and assessed (Salancik & Pfeffer, 1978). Explicitly, planners should be taught what sources should be accessed while scanning the environment. This may differ depending on plan goals and

TABLE 17.1 Planning skills and expertise development strategy

Relevant planning skills	Description	Developmental strategies
Environmental scanning	Identifying appropriate sources and avoiding information overload	Reading manuals or past planning documents that list ways to gather information Receiving training regarding informational distractors Experiential learning through project assignments, attending or presenting at profession conferences, and internal or external training Deliberate practice Receiving immediate, detailed, directed feedback
Goal identification	Identifying challenging and specific "growth" and "fix-it" goals	Training in problem identification, establishing goals that can obtain feedback, and creating commitment from team members Comparing relevant past goals to set difficulty levels accurately Creating new goals based on limitations, constraints, and compatibility with existing goals
Case-based reasoning	Using past experiences to create new plans	Focusing on retrieval of matching cases/ experiences and subsequent features within the case that are relevant to effective planning Engaging in problem construction Identifying potential biases and methods to avoid bias
Identification of key causes, constraints, and resources	Identifying the key causes of the situation, the constraints that are present, and the resources that will be needed based on knowledge of prior situations	Looking for and focusing on controllable components that have a large impact on the situation Being aware that perception of the complexity of the situation will affect the ability to recall and search previous cases Looking for atypical features within a case or anomalies found when comparing multiple cases Elaborating on each recalled case so that they may better identify particular features within it Identifying the important features within past cases
Plan generation	Creating, merging, and organizing ideas into concrete, executable strategies while making sure to be aware of the scope of the work and flexibility	Training and exercises in critical thinking Engaging in creative thinking when creating a plan Developing writing and organizational skills

TABLE 17.1 (*cont.*)

Relevant planning skills	Description	Developmental strategies
Forecasting	Making predictions of possible future events that have a relation to the present situation	Increasing flexibility of ideas Considering potential failures that may occur in plan implementation Training to specifically consider how effects will interact as they progress over time Limiting self-reflection
Plan refinement and implementation	Reflecting on the initially generated plan and the forecasted outcomes and assessing what advantages and harm will come from separate features of the plan	Training on what deliberations should be made with regard to the plan's impact, popularity, and workability within the setting, domain, or field where it will be employed Considering sound change-management strategies Being aware of the organization's culture and power or leadership structures Avoiding escalation of commitment

organizational strategy (Hambrick, 1982). This skill can be learned simply by reading manuals or past planning documents that list the formal ways that were used to gather information. Planners must also be taught to access information implicitly through informal lines of communication. Understanding an organization's politics, culture, and history will help in this type of information gathering.

Second, an environmental scan must avoid collecting too much information, either redundant or superfluous, to the point where it confuses or stalls the planning process. Analysts have long argued that managers have access to more information than they can process (Mintzberg, 1975). Being able to make good decisions with the information one has is a constant balancing act between getting enough information from all facets and getting too much information that overpowers the thinker (Dörner & Schaub, 1994). In essence, planners must be able to gain access to all pieces of crucial information while simultaneously sifting the information that is received. This is necessary to prevent them from experiencing information overload.

Information overload occurs when the amount of input to a system exceeds its capacity to process that information (Speier, Valacich, & Vessey, 1999). Information overload has become a growing problem as the advances of the digital age have exponentially increased availability and accessibility of information and information sources (Berghel, 1997; Mintzberg, 1975; Speier et al., 1999). The expansion of global and virtual environments has increased the number of ecosystems one must consider when gathering information. The use of texting, social media, and portable electronic devices keep us inundated with new information to the point that information gathering often becomes a form of constant interruption. These continual interruptions can reduce decision-making quality, particularly when dealing with complex plans (Speier et al., 1999). Thus, planners must be trained to avoid informational overload.

To develop planners who can effectively scan their environments, scanners must be taught how to determine what information is relevant and distinguish between pertinent information and distractors. There is a great deal of evidence that this skill comes with domain expertise. Those who have a great deal of expertise in a field are less distracted by irrelevant information (Anzai, 1984; Dörner & Schaub, 1994). One way to help planners become better at environmental scanning is to increase their knowledge base in the area in which they will be planning. Growing one's domain expertise can be done through project assignments, attending or presenting at professional conferences, and internal or external training (Ligon, Wallace, & Osburn, 2011).

Another possible way to teach people to identify relevant information is through deliberate practice. Planners should be given case studies or samples of likely informational sources. They could then be asked to identify distractors and non-relevant information from these sources. Research supports the idea that experiential learning can greatly improve discernment of relevant information (Bonwell & Eison, 1991; Downs, 1992).

Following Ericsson's recommendations for gaining expertise, learners need to receive feedback as they attempt to identify relevant information in a process of trial and error (Ericsson, Prietula, & Cokely, 2007). This is an exercise that would allow the learner to look at an information source and identify what parts are relevant and what information is superfluous to the issues. Feedback should be immediate, detailed, and directive. This process of trial and error helps the learner to quickly make small adjustments as he or she learns to home in on the target.

Goal Identification

Goals are defined as the objectives that create standards to be reached through actions (Saavedra, Earley, & Van Dyne, 1993). For plans, goals usually satisfy one of two purposes. First, goals aspire to obtain new objectives based on personal or organizational vision. These are commonly referred to as growth goals that focus on future development. Next, goals may be aimed at correcting problems that are identified during the environmental scanning phase. These "fix-it" goals are focused on recovery of past states rather than development of new ones.

Once current opportunities have been identified and risks have been assessed, the planner will start to identify the goals of a plan. Most research supports the idea that goals result in a higher level of individual performance because they are the key drivers of intensity and persistence of effort (Locke & Latham, 1990). At the group level, goals provide a shared vision, resulting in a higher interdependency among group members (Saavedra et al., 1993; Wong, Tjosvold, & Yu, 2005). Research further indicates that goals increase levels of motivation and adaptation planning during the task (Latham, 2004; Locke, Shaw, Saari, & Latham, 1981). These benefits makes goal setting an important part of the planning process.

Developmental Considerations for Goal Identification

Because goals have two very different purposes, there are two distinct pathways to train goal setting. Growth-oriented goals identify new areas to pursue or enhance current pursuits in a bigger and better way. Training this type of goal setting involves knowing how to identify new standards that encourage growth that is attainable. Goals designed to address problems must identify the key causes in the situation. Therefore, those who are setting goals geared toward problem resolution need to be trained in problem identification. Problem identification is intermingled with case-based reasoning and identification of key causes, constraints, and resources. Therefore, training techniques for this will be covered in the following sections.

Considering the tacit knowledge required to create goals, we consider Locke and Latham's (1990) goal-setting theory. According to this theory, planners must be trained to create specific goals that are challenging enough to increase performance but not so challenging that they demotivate. Drawing from the research that surrounds this theory, we also know that planners must know how to create goals that can obtain feedback and secure goal commitment from those following the plan. Creating a specific goal may require reducing the complexity of the task at hand. This may include breaking the task into smaller portions or reducing the interdependency required to accomplish a task. The main purpose of increasing goal specificity is to eliminate the different perceptions that can arise in interpreting a plan.

Goal-setting theorists emphasize that special attention must be given to setting the level of goal difficulty (Locke & Latham, 1990). If the goal is too easy it will not challenge the individual or team and no increase in performance will be gained. However, if the goal is set too high or is too difficult, the individual or team will lose hope and give up their efforts, resulting in low performance. Experts may often set goals too high and novices will likely set the goals too low. Relevant past goals are needed to set new goal-difficulty levels accurately. A percentage of growth is usually encouraged. This percentage varies based on the type of goal. For example, if raising funds is the goal, a 10 percent increase might be appropriate. To develop the skill of finding the right level of difficulty is challenging and often learned through practice.

Planners should be trained to establish goals that can obtain feedback. If a planner cannot obtain feedback on whether or not a goal is being reached at some point in the process, he or she will not be able to evaluate the effectiveness of the plan. If the planner cannot tell whether the plan is working, it will be impossible to adapt the plan accordingly.

Ways to achieve feedback can vary greatly. For some, money raised or made can be a good indicator of success. For others, customer satisfaction, efficiency markers, product quality markers, or still other measures may be key indicators of success or failure. While some feedback indicators are obvious, others may not be.

Often goal accomplishment cannot be assessed through objective measurements. Sometimes, goal success can only be evaluated using intuitive evaluations. For example, the outward appearances of a piece of art, a magazine advertisement, or a finished building cannot be as objectively measured as generated revenue or reduction in safety errors. The ability to assess performance intuitively comes from expertise. If the results of a plan are more subjective in nature, planners must create goals that can obtain the appropriate feedback. Learners can obtain this skill by assessing existing goals – they can be given simple multiple-choice quizzes that ask "Which goals will obtain useful feedback in this situation?" Planning students should receive immediate feedback that explains the correct answers.

Finally, planners must be trained to set goals that will create commitment from team members. Goal commitment is defined as the degree to which someone has accepted a goal and is determined to work to reach it (Locke & Latham, 1990). Goals that attract little or no commitment from team members will probably not be accomplished. To increase goal commitment, planners may decide to have those affected by the plan participate in part of the goal-setting process (Hollenbeck & Klein, 1987; Locke & Latham, 2002). Planners must also consider whether the resources needed to achieve the determined goals are available or team members may not commit to those goals (Hollenbeck & Klein, 1987).

The type of goals discussed thus far include those that attempt to fix things and those that exist to achieve new things. However, both of these goals assume that goals drive plans. An alternative possibility is that plans determine goals (Hambrick & Snow, 1977; Mahon & Murray, 1981). For example, if the plan is to go to the store, then we start to scan our memory for needed items so we can determine what our goals should be once we arrive there.

With this third option, goals must be chosen based on limitations, constraints, and compatibility with existing goals. For goals that are derived from plans, training is very different. The issue is no longer what should be fixed or what new achievements should be made. Rather, planners must focus on how they will take advantage of the opportunities present to maximize their resources within the framework they are given (Mahon & Murray, 1981). A viable option for training in this context is case studies or simulated activities where multiple constraints are present and perhaps increase during the exercise. Learning to set viable goals within the confines of multiple constraints should expand people's creativity and ability to reason under pressure.

Case-Based Reasoning

Once goals have been identified, the planner must identify what strategies he or she should employ to accomplish them. The model suggests that planners reference experiential cases to find these strategies. Case-based reasoning occurs when planners use their own past experiences to create new plans (Hammond, 1990). Rather than use a set of rules, this theory argues that planners refer to past experiences to develop plans. The planner selects relevant cases from memory that align with the current plan. To do this, the planner matches goals from past experiences with the current goals they wish to pursue. Identified cases are then used to locate effective versus ineffective strategies. Strategies that were successful in the past are pursued, while strategies from past cases that led to failure are avoided.

A cadre of research supports the idea that highly skilled planners use experiential cases in knowledge retrieval rather than relying solely on schematic or principle-based knowledge structures (Berger & Jordan, 1992; Hammond, 1990; Hershey, Walsh, Read, & Chulef, 1990; Kolodner, 1993). Hershey and colleagues (1990) found that expert planners were more likely to retrieve cases from memory than novice planners. Using this approach, the key to creating good plans lies in the matching of past cases and the subsequent altering of the case.

Developmental Considerations for Case-Based Reasoning

A case-based approach is a viable training method that can enhance the development of an individual's planning skills, as demonstrated with training in the ethics and leadership literature (Connelly, Allen, & Waples, 2007; Harkrider et al., 2012), and has been shown to be more effective than a standard lecture approach (Antes et al., 2009). By providing viable, relevant cases for learners to review and analyze, individuals may learn appropriate techniques for the task at hand (Mumford, Connelly, Brown, et al., 2008). Further, when combined with cooperative learning, development of planning skills is strengthened through shared experiences and social reinforcement (Mumford, Connelly, Brown et al., 2008).

Case-based learning is a highly researched area (Connelly et al., 2007; Nutt, 1984; Osburn & Mumford, 2006; Scott, Lonergan, & Mumford, 2005). Research has found that variables such as the type of case presented (Nutt, 1984), the content of the case (Harkrider et al., 2012), how the case is presented (Osburn & Mumford, 2006), and the strategies that are given along with the case (Scott et al., 2005) play a part in the effectiveness of case-based training. Thus, multiple considerations will be presented here that should be taken into consideration when working with case-based learning here or elsewhere in the planning stages.

A case-based approach should not be used alone, however. Along with cooperative learning, strategies for working with these relevant cases must also be provided (Scott et al., 2005). When solutions, not processes, are the focus, fewer quality alternatives are generated or considered and novel tactics are less likely to be employed (Nutt, 1984). When strategies are offered with a case, individuals are more likely to be successful when tackling complex, ill-defined problems, including those that call for creative thought (Mumford et al., 2008; Scott, Leritz, & Mumford, 2004).

Nutt (1984) identified five different types of case-processing models: evaluative, historical model, off-the-shelf, search, and nova process types. It should be noted that while case-based learning can improve performance in the intended skill development, individuals tend to prefer working with only one or two case models at once (Nutt, 1984; Scott et al., 2005). To combat this, individuals seeking planning skill development should be presented with only one or two types of these process types in their case-based learning.

To train for case-based reasoning, the focus must be on retrieval of matching cases. Cases are typically derived from experiences. However, this presents quite a problem for novices because they have few cases to draw from. There is some evidence that case knowledge can be trained (Osburn & Mumford, 2006). To do this, individuals are given real cases to read, examine, and draw from in a planning practice exercise. These cases, if salient enough, will expand the planner's library of cases. Thus, having new planners listen to stories of past successes and failures may be helpful. However, the most frequently accessed cases will be those one has personally experienced.

Even if we expand the new planner's library of relevant cases, retrieving the best match for the current situation is not easy. The planner's challenge is to remember all cases that match the current case well, narrow that down to the best two or three cases, and then remember them accurately enough to copy and alter the cases appropriately for the current circumstance. This takes a considerable amount of cognitive processing resources. To cut down on this processing demand, conceptual combination would be a useful training to employ (Baughman & Mumford, 1995; Scott et al., 2005; Kohn, Paulus, & Korde, 2011). Although no clear guidelines for conceptual combination currently exist, one interesting and novel idea might be to allow learners to explore combining concepts using available software (Hammond, 1990). Software would allow one to pull out ideas from cases and combine them in a physical capacity that might help the planner to make cognitive connections.

There is some evidence that it is possible to train the process of identifying key features within a case to find the most relevant cases. Osburn and Mumford (2006) conducted a study where planners were trained and then asked to identify key features within a case they were given. The experiment used two different training methodologies. The first group was asked to identify key features from the case and then given the case-based scenario only. The second group was given the same instructions but provided with the case as well as a set of key knowledge principles to remember while scanning the case. Those who were given both the case and the principles outperformed those who were just given case-based scenarios. Thus, in training, planners should not be given a set of relevant cases alone. Rather planners should be given relevant cases accompanied by key planning principles extracted from that case.

Since the model of planning we are using was published, subsequent research has both supported and challenged the focus of training on case-based planning. Although there is a good amount of evidence to suggest that case-based reasoning is a key component of effective planning, more recent research indicates that the utility of case-based knowledge may be limited in certain areas. Along the lines of Reeves and Weisberg's (1994) argument, the existence of principle-based knowledge is needed to extract relevant experiences. Osburn and Mumford (2006) found that when training penetration planning skills, cases should be used in conjunction with principles to enhance planning quality, but cases were not beneficial alone. Most recently, Caughron and Mumford (2008) found that recalling and reusing cases during planning reduced the level of creativity in their chosen problem-solving strategies. Thus, training case retrieval alone or apart from principle-based knowledge may be unhelpful.

Evidence from these two lines of research suggests that planners should learn how to use both case-based and principle-based knowledge searches in planning. The argument is that new planners cannot simply be presented with past cases and hope to gain an inventory of workable strategies. Rather, planners must be asked to identify and pull out certain features of cases that address principles that are relevant to good planning. This means planners will be trained to identify features within the case that are relevant to effective planning. Learning to do this can be done through guided practice using case studies.

There is also research to suggest that those planners who take a more active role in problem construction will produce higher quality plans. Planners should be trained to actively process as they look for cases rather than pull an immediate case match to the state problem. In a study conducted by Redmond and his colleagues (1993), marketing students were asked to create advertising campaigns for a new product. Individuals who were instructed to restate the problem before solving the problem generated better-quality solutions than those who were instructed to read the problem and immediately solve it.

Identification of Key Causes, Constraints, and Resources

Planners must be able to identify the key elements of any situation to be successful. These elements include the key causes of the situation, the constraints that are present, and the resources that will be needed. Each of these elements is often found by looking at a complex and convoluted scenario and pulling out relevant pieces of information.

Identification of key causes occurs when one determines the origins of key factors that are in a given scenario. Each individual factor within a case was caused by a previous one. After planners extract important factors they must be able to trace backward to determine what caused the ultimate effect. Once the causes have been determined, planners are better equipped to create strategies that would enact further change (Marcy & Mumford, 2007; Anzai, 1984; Baughman & Mumford, 1995).

Constraints, or restrictions or limitations in past or current cases that will keep the planner from being able to fully implement the plan can come in both tangible and intangible forms. For example, physical restraints include budget limitations, space or logistical concerns, increased or limited technology, and lack of qualified personnel. Intangible restrictions may include culture or diversity issues (Hofstede, 1993), limited cognitive capacities (Florian & Klein, 1971), language, and ethical concerns. Planners who identify as many constraints as possible can then circumvent the barriers that these constraints present (Porac & Thomas, 1990; Thomas & McDaniel 1990).

Identification of needed resources involves discovering the assets one has available to accomplish the objectives of the plan. Resources consist of all components that are necessary for the plan to succeed. Resources are often scarce, and most often individuals will need to plan on competing for key resources. Because key resources are often an uncertain entity and a highly volatile piece of the plan, differentiating between critical resources and non-critical resources is imperative.

Developmental Considerations for Identification of Key Causes, Constraints, and Resources

Based on what we know of the separate components of this step within the model, it seems reasonable that we would be able to train these as a whole. Although each component focuses on identifying a separate feature, the skills needed for each are the same. The planner must be able to search prior cases, analyze the case components, and identify the most relevant elements. To do this, planners should be trained in five areas.

First, planners should know to look for and focus on controllable components that have a large impact on the situation (Osburn & Mumford, 2006). Identifying causes, constraints, and resources that are uncontrollable is wasteful of the time and resources dedicated to project completion. In addition, focusing on minutiae instead of large-impact components spends unnecessary energy.

Second, planners should be made aware that their perception of the complexity of the situation will affect their ability to recall and search previous cases. Studies have found that planners will often not exert the effort necessary to search for causes, constraints, and needed resources in simple or seemingly straightforward situations, likely due to the time-demanding nature of these searches (Marta, Leritz, & Mumford, 2005). Thus, planners should be warned that, when dealing with circumstances that seem common or easy to handle, they need to consciously force themselves to search previous cases for these important features.

Third, planners should be trained to look for atypical features within a case or anomalies found when comparing multiple cases. This search for inconsistencies tends to improve information gathering. This targeted search tends to trigger searches for more relevant cases, while searches that produce cues consistent with prior knowledge might only bring to mind one case from the planner's case repertoire (Baughman & Mumford, 1995; Mumford, Medeiros, & Partlow, 2012).

Fourth, planners should be taught to elaborate on each recalled case so that they may better identify particular features within it (Harkrider et al., 2012). The more expansive the knowledge of the case, the more features the planner has to investigate. To train this, planners could simply learn that they must evoke a requisite number of features of the recollected case before they continue.

Finally, researchers argue that planners who have expertise in their industry can more readily identify the important features within past cases. Thus, planners should be given developmental opportunities to create industry-relevant expertise. These experiences might include advanced education, conferences or seminars, hands-on practice, job shadowing or job sharing, and new project assignments.

Plan Generation

The purpose of plan generation is to create, merge, and organize ideas into concrete executable strategies (Mumford, Schultz, & Van Doorn, 2001). Before the planner enters this phase, his or her ideas are scattered and isolated from one another, held together loosely by common goals. During the plan-generation phase, the planner combines knowledge, goals, past cases, and current constraints to formulate a new plan that uniquely fits the current situation. The planner arranges these separate but relevant concepts into a framework so that the mental simulation of future events becomes coherent and works together to accomplish the targeted goals.

It is during this phase that the plan starts to emerge and become reality. In other words, it is during this phase that the generative process begins. Prior to this phase, most mental activity has been reflective in nature. Plan generation allows the planner to begin mental simulation of future events (Osburn & Mumford, 2006).

Plan generation is an important turning point in the planning process. At this point, the planner will begin to shift his or her focus from the past to the future. The planner will be less concerned with past knowledge and experiences and concentrate more on projecting future steps and likely outcomes. Although the initial plan produced in the generation phase will not be the final product, it will be the catalyst for all future considerations. Forecasting downstream consequences and plan refinement will be constructed from this initial plan. Thus, the quality of the initial plan is critical.

Developmental Considerations for Plan Generation

Research suggests planners engage in two distinct mental processes in order to accomplish the plan-generation phase. Hammond (1990) and others contend that planners recall past cases that are relevant to the current situation and combine aspects of these cases into a new plan that meets the current demands (Kuhn, 1970; Mumford, Mobley, Reiter-Palmon, Uhlman, & Doares, 1991). To do this, planners must identify relevant features from past experiences, map existing knowledge structures onto those frames, synthesize the relevant information, and then combine and reorganize the information to form a new plan that will meet the current needs (Baughman & Mumford, 1995; Kuhn, 1970; Mumford et al., 1991). In other words, one mental activity that occurs during plan generation is a process of evaluating existing ideas and reorganizing past concepts to meet present-day needs (Baughman & Mumford, 1995). Mumford (2000) referred to this as a synergistic process where the planner must look backward and forward simultaneously in order to form a viable solution.

To enhance the generation of plans using past cases, developmental activities should give planners practice in critical thinking. Planners must be able to take the information they have gathered and extract key pieces of information that will help them devise their plan. The ability to identify these important exemplars ties in heavily with plan quality (Berger, Guilford, & Christensen, 1957). Individuals in training might be asked to research other plans and summarize them. They may also be asked to create outlines or make lists of important things to consider.

Additionally, research indicates that being able to critically evaluate problems and find patterns within the cases depends on an individual's level of expertise and the nature of his or her knowledge structures (Anzai & Simon, 1979; Hunter, Bedell-Avers, Hunsicker, Mumford, & Ligon, 2008; Weisberg, 2006). Effort should therefore be given to developing industry-specific knowledge and expertise. Methods to develop this include traditional classes, self-guided study, or a range of applied experiences.

Likewise, we know planners use a great deal of case-based knowledge to find past features from cases that will work in current circumstances. Recall that case-based knowledge is finding key components of past experiences and combining them into new mental models (Hammond, 1990). Research indicates that case-based knowledge should be combined with principle-based knowledge or analogical reasoning principles (Osburn & Mumford, 2006), so practitioners should remember to include both while reviewing cases. Case planners in training should be prompted to combine schematic knowledge with associational knowledge (Hunter et al., 2008).

At times, case analysis and reuse of case features provide sufficient data to form a new effective plan. However, in some cases, the demands of the current environment cannot be met through the use of extracted features found in past cases. For example, there may be a new goal, circumstance, or constraint that does not match any of the past experiences the planner can reference. Planners must generate new tactics that will address these novel problems.

The second mental process that planners may engage in during the plan-generation process is creative thinking. Researchers have recognized a strong connection between planning and creativity (Berger et al., 1957; Mumford, Peterson, & Childs, 1999; Osburn & Mumford, 2006) and indicated that planning is an important component of the creative thinking process (Mumford, Bedell-Avers, & Hunter, 2008; Mumford et al., 2012). Although plans do not always need to be creative to be effective, in unfamiliar situations, plans that must deal with novel problems require creative components.

To develop creative thinking, trainers should alter their strategy. There is a good deal of evidence that indicates training can enhance creative performance (Scott et al., 2004). In a meta-analysis of creativity training, Scott and her colleagues (2004) found that the most effective training techniques provide learners with cognitive strategies and heuristics to work with their available knowledge structures. These strategies focus on problem finding, conceptual combination, and idea generation, which is an advantageous finding for the current effort, since many of these strategies are addressed in other areas of planning as well.

To produce new ideas, task instructors should try to encourage and enhance the ability to think divergently and come up with multiple answers. This may be a challenge for new planners because our education system does not traditionally ask for students to think in this fashion (Folsom, 2007). Typically, students are directed toward convergent thinking, which collects information for the purpose of finding one answer. Planning students must learn to question assumptions. They must build self-efficacy for idea development (Ford & Gioia, 2000; Eubanks et al., 2010). They should be encouraged to actively think and problem-solve while in training rather than have information delivered to them (Scott et al., 2004).

A final consideration of development for planners entering the plan-generation phase is the development of writing and organizational skills. Potential written components of plans include a project narrative or description, a schedule of major events, a list of needed resources, a division of labor, and a timeline. The written plan should provide guidance during plan implementation. Writing skills are needed to clearly communicate the plan to others. Thus, one critical component of training a person to generate plans is training them to write.

Writing skills can vary widely. It is important to assess a planner's writing skills before determining what training is required (Goldstein & Ford, 2002). Examples of possible items to train include the correct use of grammar, the ability to write clear and uncluttered task statements, or to offer plans that are easy to read and execute. New writers have a tendency to write too little, more experienced writers have a tendency to write too much. Taking out redundant statements, superfluous information, and flowery language is an example of what planners need at this stage of development. Practice in making outlines of the essential factors and developing those factors in a logical and ordered manner is necessary at this point. The ideal training format for this skill set is guided practice. Potential planners should be given small plans to create. Constant feedback from an experienced planner is a critical element in the learning process.

Forecasting

Forecasting is when a planner makes predictions of possible future events that have a relation to the present situation (Berger et al., 1957; Kettner, Guilford, & Christensen, 1959; Pant & Starbuck, 1990). Forecasting is an active process where multiple predictions are made based on various potential actions and where neither predictors nor outcomes are fixed (Byrne, Shipman, & Mumford, 2010; Patnaik, 2012). In addition, forecasting involves combining potential actions to predict paths as well as combining potential paths to analyze an even larger number of possible conclusions (Caughron & Mumford, 2008). This results in forecasting being a highly complex process of predicting multiple outcomes that could occur based on a list of alternative actions and action combinations that change based on a dynamic and interactive relationship.

Researchers have identified a number of robust benefits of forecasting for planners. First, forecasting engages higher cognitive strategies while planning. Forecasting has been recognized as a creative mental process where multiple cognitive processes merge (Mumford, Medeiros, & Partlow, 2012). This is especially true when planners are told to focus on possible or likely failures (Caughron & Mumford, 2008). Second, good forecasting leads to the formation of viable alternative plans. Third, forecasting leads to better overall quality of plans and solutions by enhancing vision formation, creative thinking, creative problem-solving, and accuracy (Forster, Higgins, & Bianco, 2003; Lonergan, Scott, & Mumford, 2004; Osburn & Mumford, 2006; Shipman et al., 2010).

Developmental Considerations for Forecasting

Based on a review of the literature, there are several ways to enhance forecasting skills in planners. Guilford (1968) suggested that forecasting could be enhanced through an increase in flexibility of ideas, which would help the examiner conceptualize different needs that might be present in the same situation. Trainers would be wise to employ divergent-thinking exercises to improve basic forecasting skills.

Second, as was mentioned above, planners should be encouraged to purposefully consider potential failures that may occur in plan implementation (Caughron & Mumford, 2008; Forster et al., 2003). This might be accomplished by giving the planner instructions to come up with a minimum number of possible future failures. Dedicating a certain amount of time to finding likely pitfalls or assigning an individual to the devil's advocate role can accomplish this task.

Third, planners should be trained to specifically consider how effects will interact as they progress over time. Dörner and Schaub (1994) found that a common error that occurs during forecasting is the failure to consider interactions of effects. Planners should contemplate how two seemingly separate actions may intersect and affect one another downstream.

A study completed by Shipman, Byrne, and Mumford (2010) on leader vision formation and forecasting identified several recommendations for training forecasting skills that would likely be helpful for planners as well. The authors suggest that those engaging in forecasting are given time to have focused thought. This time of reflection should focus on an array of conceivable organizational problems such as potential losses, potential gains, and contingencies. In addition, authors recommend that training interventions should encourage forecasters to "analyze the implications of their observations through exercises, coaching and peer feedback" (Shipman et al., 2010, p. 453). Finally, the authors of this study propose that individuals who forecast should be trained to limit the amount of self-reflection they engage in. Because of the extensive cognitive capacity that is required in forecasting, self-reflection would only impede a person's forecasting abilities (Dörner & Schaub, 1994).

Plan Refinement and Implementation

Plan refinement occurs when planners reflect on the initially generated plan and the forecasted outcomes and assess what advantages and harm will come from separate features of the plan (Dörner & Schaub, 1994; Mumford, Schultz, & Van Doorn, 2001; Xiao, Milgram, & Doyle, 1997). In the past, plan refinement was considered a passive process in which ideas are evaluated. Recently, this stage has been characterized not as a time when ideas are judged as good or bad, but as an active process in which idea revisions are made. Plan refinement is a processing activity that occurs late in the planning cycle but has large implications for the end result (Byrne et al., 2010). "Plan refinements will result in the formation of a fully situated plan that provides a basis for action" (Mumford, Schultz, & Van Doorn, 2001, p. 221). Adjustments that come as a result of plan refinement should create alternative strategies, add available options, and generate necessary backup plans.

The late-cycle process of plan refinement and implementation has been found to be instrumental in creating high-quality plans. Basadur and his colleagues (2000) found that evaluating ideas was strongly linked to producing ideas. Other researchers associate the practice of evaluation and plan refinement with building creative problem solutions and innovative tactics. (Castrogiovanni, 1996; Dailey & Mumford, 2006). Caughron and Mumford (2008) argue that switching one's mindset to that of implementation induces cognitive processing that improves forecasting and backup plan generation.

Developmental Considerations for Plan Refinement and Implementation

In both plan refinement and implementation, planners should be given instruction as to what deliberations they should be making. In other words, planners need to know what questions they should ask to maximize the evaluation and implementation process. For evaluating and refining the plan, one major area of evaluation should be the contextual factors present at the time of plan implementation (Lonergan et al., 2004). Planners should contemplate the plan's impact, popularity, and workability within the setting, domain, or field where it will be employed (Csikszentmihalyi, 1999). In a similar fashion, planners must also consider organizational settings that will influence acceptance of the plan. For example, will the plan gain popularity (Runco & Chand, 1994)? If the plan is not popular and doesn't promise to become so, then successful implementation may be unattainable.

When developing implementation planning skills, Hrebiniak (2005) provides a useful outline for training. He identifies four contextual conditions that often make implementation of plans challenging and argues that special attention should be given to change management. We realize that all plans are created to evoke change. However, change is often unwelcome and challenged. Considering change-management strategies such as employing procedural justice tactics may be needed. Second, Hrebiniak points out that culture must be considered (2005). As far as possible, the plan should be implemented in a way that fits within that organization's culture. The organization's values, norms, and rules should be honored. Third, planners must pay attention to the power structure within the organization. The proposed plan must fit within this structure if it is to be successfully implemented and supported. Finally, planners should reference and attend to the leadership structure in place within the organization. One of the greatest difficulties with planning implementation is leadership (Cater & Pucko, 2010).

Finally, planners in these late-cycle processes should be trained to avoid escalation of commitment. Escalation of commitment refers to the tendency for a decision maker to continue on a particular course of action even if that course of action shows signs of failure or a high potential for failure (Brockner, 1992). This common error involves making multiple decisions in one direction even though that direction has repeatedly shown to have negative consequences (Brockner, 1992; Teger, 1980). Within the context of planning, escalation of commitment would occur when a planner who had invested a great deal of time and resources into creating the initial plan chooses not to make necessary changes to the plan because of that investment. A common reason for this erroneous decision making is the individual's desire to make choices that justify previous behaviors (Staw, 1981). One possible training intervention is to simulate scenarios that encourage escalation of commitment but lead to poor results. Ku (2008) found that when people experienced escalation of commitment followed by failure they experienced regret and thus were less likely to escalate commitment in future cases.

Conclusion

On June 6, 1944, 160,000 allied troops attacked the Nazi army on a 50-mile stretch of the French coastline to accomplish one of the best-known military feats of the modern era (D-Day, http://www.army.mil/d-day/; Leighton, 1963). In 1988, the Global Polio Eradication Initiative, funded by over eight billion dollars, in cooperation with over 200 countries and 20 million volunteers, set out to vaccinate more than 2.5 million children and reduce the polio virus worldwide by 99 percent (Global Polio Eradication Initiative, http://www.polioeradication.org/). In 2007, Apple Inc. introduced its first version of the iPhone, a piece of technology that combined cellular phone capabilities with personal digital assistant computer capacities using a multi-touch interface to revolutionize the technology industry and allow the general public constant access to information (Agar, 2013). Although these events vary in purpose, they are all examples of great accomplishments that had profound influence on the world today.

It is important to remember that before any great accomplishment is made, effective plans must be created (Smith & Locke, 1990). No successful military campaign, no global health initiative, no great technological advancement was developed without a plan. Why, then, do we have managers who tell us they do not plan? The disconnect can be explained when we consider the traditional view of planning. The traditional view says that planning is a formal process that consists of behavioral steps completed in a set order and resulting in a document akin to an instructional manual that spells out play-by-play actions to follow. However, as we have discussed earlier in this chapter, the behavioral steps in the planning process may or may not occur. Plans may or may not produce a mission statement, SWOT analysis report, or any document, for that matter.

In fact, regardless of whether formal planning is completed, the cognitive processes are most certain to occur. Common sense would dictate that before one acts one will first consider one's surroundings (environmental scanning), decide what one wants to do (goal setting), determine how to do it (plan generation), and predict the end result (forecasting). And yet these essential internal steps are often ignored and replaced by behavioral steps that add little value.

Perhaps we have done students of planning a disservice by giving them the impression that planning is a long, painstaking series of steps that only occurs when you have the luxury of time to do so. In fact, one of the main reasons often cited for not "planning" is because there is too little time (Kinicki & Williams, 2013). Because we have presented planning as a behavioral practice, it is often seen as an academic ideal that has very little "real-world" application. But, this couldn't be further from the truth. When we consider that planning is a cognitive process that occurs before steps are taken, it would seem that everyone participates in this activity. With this understanding, the issue becomes whether or not we can introduce developmental activities to improve this process. That is, can we improve upon the cognitive process that occurs naturally but is often incomplete or distorted? We believe the answer is yes.

The current effort strives to produce a sequence of essential developmental activities that target this more natural cognitive process of planning. The proposed developmental activities create a more thorough approach to the planning process. Grounding our recommendations on a comprehensive planning model allows us to create developmental techniques that address the planning process from initial observations to plan refinement.

Further, using this model as a foundation enables us to propose training steps that fit and work together. Rather than segmented parts, the steps complement each other and build from each other in such a way that they interactively refine one another. The end result is a more fluid approach to planning. For example, identification of a key cause may trigger a case retrieval, or vice versa. Thus, using this training approach, development of one area increases capabilities in all other areas of the training process. For these reasons, although further research is still needed, the authors believe this training approach to be superior to the more traditional developmental approaches to planning.

Although we argue that the current effort is worthwhile, we must also advise readers of some notable limitations. First, this literature review and the consequent recommendations are based on the premise that planning is primarily a cognitive function (Hammond, 1990; Mumford et al., 2000; Xiao et al., 1997). Although this assumption is backed with substantial evidence, some planning researchers and practitioners may choose to focus on the applied aspects of planning (Caughron & Mumford, 2008). For those individuals who focus on applied behavioral steps, the training interventions proposed here may not be suitable for their needs. The training and developmental interventions offered in this chapter recommend new cognitive schemes rather than tactical behavioral changes.

Second, due to the limitations of the available literature, it should be noted that many of the recommendations listed here have not been tested with regard to developing planning skills. Many of the conclusions that were drawn are theoretically sound but are yet to be substantiated by experimental research. In addition, some of the experimental data that has been used to support the recommendations given in this work came from experimental studies that were completed for other cognitive processes, such as creativity. While we do not believe that this means our recommendations are invalid, we do ask the reader to use caution when implementing interventions that have not been validated.

Third, because we have chosen to follow a model of cognitive planning (Mumford et al., 2001) in order to structure our findings and recommendations, our review could give the reader the impression that planning is an entirely linear progression of mental processes. This leaves the false impression that one phase must be complete before the next begins. Some could interpret this to mean that once the next stages have been entered, the planner does not go backward or revisit completed steps. Some trainers may think that training must also be presented in a linear fashion, where one skill must be mastered before the next skill set can be pursued. There is no evidence to support that this strict interpretation is warranted. In fact, it appears that the mental processes that take place are dynamic, interactive, and cyclical. For example, planners may reach conclusions from their forecasting that takes them back to the goal-setting phase for revisions, or a referenced case may bring to light a new area in which environmental scanning is needed.

We can draw several implications from this review. First, there is much work to be done in designing a comprehensive stratagem for the development of cognitive planning skills. Most of the studies that examine the development of cognitive planning skills focus on one or two mental processes. This separation of processes is to be expected because each psychological step within planning is complex and multifaceted. Moreover, the typical empirical study of cognition does not lend itself to training that needs to be administered in stages over a period of time. Still, research suggests that the cognitive underpinnings of the planning process work in tandem with each other, build off one another, and should integrate in such a way that training the distinct parts of the process independently may be limiting the amount that could be accomplished in training sessions. Further effort should be given to designing training and development systems that will help new planners to see connections between the steps, integrate the knowledge that comes from each process, and produce seamless transitions between each cognitive evolution. Not only will this give us a more complete picture of the benefits of this process but it will also help us to understand what mental models and mental shortcuts may occur naturally when the information is presented simultaneously.

Second, we see a real need for further testing that can expand our knowledge and understanding in several domains dealing with the development of planning skills. The later cycles of planning including plan refinement and plan implementation have the greatest need for more study (Lonergan et al., 2004). Goal setting, case-based reasoning and forecasting seem to have more empirical support. Still, there is a lack of scholarly research that strictly centers on the development of cognitive planning skills. This lack of research leaves practitioners with many questions. For example, should planning steps be trained in order or would it be better to train all planning skills concurrently? Does training in creativity apply to training in planning? Is experiential training more effective than traditional training methods? Answering these types of questions would give us more confidence as we decide what training methods to employ.

Another opportunity for future work is to develop assessment tools for planning. Currently, there are very few validated, easy-to-use measurements of planning skills. Although some measurements exist, many assess plans for overall quality and originality. These give us a general indication of an individual's planning abilities. However, most often we are not able to pinpoint what specific cognitive strategy is improving. Perhaps tests that measure skill outcomes more specifically could provide us with a better understanding of how the training is working. For example, if we train individuals in environmental scanning, we would measure their incremental growth in environmental scanning abilities more specifically.

Finally, we would be remiss if we did not recognize that this review does not take into account how the training model of Goldstein and Ford (2002) would integrate into the current training recommendations. Clearly, the future development of this research agenda would benefit from the thoroughness of such a model. However, it is our opinion that many of the issues presented in this review must be addressed first before this type of structure could be employed. We anticipate the expansion of this and many more streams of research will continue to further our abilities to develop planning skills within individuals.

References

Agar, J. (2013). *Constant touch: A global history of the mobile phone*. London: Icon Books.

Aguilar, F. J. (1967). *Scanning the business environment*. New York: Macmillan.

Antes, A. L., Murphy, S. T., Waples, E. P., Mumford, M. D., Brown, R. P., Connelly, S., & Devenport, L. D. (2009). A meta-analysis of ethics instruction effectiveness in the sciences. *Ethics & Behavior*, 19(5), 379–402.

Anzai, Y. (1984). Cognitive control of real-time event driven systems. *Cognitive Science*, 8, 221–254.

Anzai, Y., & Simon, H. A. (1979). The theory of learning by doing. *Psychological Review*, 86, 124–140.

Barrett, J. D., Vessey, W. B., & Mumford, M. D. (2011). Getting leaders to think: Effects of training, threat, and pressure on performance. *The Leadership Quarterly*, 22, 729–750.

Basadur, M., Runco, M. A., & Vega, L. A. (2000). Understanding how creative thinking skills, attitudes, and behaviors work together: A causal process model. *Journal of Creative Behavior*, 34, 77–100.

Baughman, W. A., & Mumford, M. D. (1995). Process-analytic models of creative capacities: Operations influencing the combination-and-reorganization process. *Creativity Research Journal*, 8, 37–62.

Berger, C. R., & Jordan, J. M. (1992). Planning sources, planning difficulty, and verbal fluency. *Communication Monographs*, 59, 130–148.

Berger, R. M., Guilford, J. P., & Christensen, P. R. (1957). A factor-analytic study of planning abilities. *Psychological Monographs*, 71, 1–29.

Berghel, H. (1997). Cyberspace 2000: Dealing with information overload. *Communications of The ACM*, 40, 19–24.

Blair, C. (2010). The importance of planning processes: Impact on financial and innovation outcomes. *Dissertation Abstracts International*, 70.

Bonwell, C., & Eison, J. (1991). *Active learning: Creating excitement in the classroom*, AEHE- ERIC higher education report no. 1. Washington, DC: Jossey-Bass.

Bransford, J. D., & Schwartz, D. L. (2009). It takes expertise to make expertise. In K. A. Ericsson (Ed.), *Development of professional expertise: Toward measurement of expert performance and design of optimal learning environments* (pp. 432–448). Cambridge, UK: Cambridge University Press.

Brinckmann, J., Grichnik, D., & Kapsa, D. (2010). Should entrepreneurs plan or just storm the castle? A meta-analysis on contextual factors impacting the business planning–performance relationship in small firms. *Journal of Business Venturing*, 25(1), 24–40.

Brockner, J. (1992). The escalation of commitment to a failing course of action: Toward theoretical progress. *The Academy of Management Review*, 17, 39–61.

Byrne, C. L., Shipman, A. L., & Mumford, M. D. (2010). The effects of forecasting on creative problem-solving: An experimental study. *Creativity Research Journal*, 22, 119–138.

Castrogiovanni, G. J. (1996). Pre-startup planning and the survival of new small businesses: Theoretical linkages. *Journal of Management*, 22, 801–822.

Cater, T., & Pucko, D. (2010). Factors of effective strategy implementation: Empirical evidence from Slovenian business practice. *Journal for European Management Studies*, 15, 207–236.

Caughron, J. J., & Mumford, M. D. (2008). Project planning: The effects of using formal planning techniques on creative problem-solving. *Creativity and Innovation Management*, 17, 204–215.

Connelly, S., Allen, M. T., & Waples, E. (2007). The impact of content and structure on a case-based approach to developing leadership skills. *International Journal of Learning and Change*, 2, 218–249.

Csikszentmihalyi, M. (1999). Implications of a systems perspective for the study of creativity. In R. J. Sternberg (Ed.), *Handbook of creativity* (pp. 313–335). Cambridge: Cambridge University Press.

Dailey, L., & Mumford, M. D. (2006). Evaluative aspects of creative thought: Errors in appraising the implications of new ideas. *Creativity Research Journal*, 18, 367–384.

Day, D. (2010). The difficulties of learning from experience and the need for deliberate practice. *Industrial and Organizational Psychology*, 3, 41–44.

Delmar, F., & Shane, S. (2003). Does business planning facilitate the development of new ventures? *Strategic Management Journal*, 24, 1165–1185.

Dervitsiotis, K. N. (1998). The challenge of managing organizational change: Exploring the relationship of re-engineering, developing learning organizations and total quality management. *Total Quality Management*, 9, 109–122.

Dörner, D., & Schaub, H. (1994). Errors in planning and decision-making and the nature of human information processing. *Applied Psychology: An International Review*, 43, 433–453.

Downs, T. M. (1992). Superior and subordinate perceptions of communication during performance appraisal interviews. *Communication Research Reports*, 9, 153–159.

Drucker, P. F. (1954). *The practice of management*. New York: Harper & Row.

Ericsson, K. A., (2009). *Development of professional expertise: Toward measurement of expert performance and design of optimal learning environments*. New York: Cambridge University Press.

Ericsson, K. A., & Charness, N. (1994). Expert performance: Its structure and acquisition. *American Psychologist*, 49, 725–747.

Ericsson, K. A., Prietula, M. J., & Cokely, E. T. (2007). The making of an expert. *Harvard Business Review*, 85, 1–8.

Eubanks, D. L., Murphy, S. T., & Mumford, M. D. (2010). Intuition as an influence on creative problem-solving: The effects of intuition, positive affect, and training. *Creativity Research Journal*, 22, 170–184.

Florian, M., & Klein, M. (1971). Deterministic production planning with concave costs and capacity constraints. *Management Science*, 18, 12–20.

Folsom, C. (2007). Moving teacher education forward: A model for a new pedagogy. *Teacher Education and Practice*, 20(3), 320–333.

Ford, C. M., & Gioia, D. A. (2000). Factors influencing creativity in the domain of managerial decision making. *Journal of Management*, 26, 705–732.

Forster, J., Higgins, E. T., & Bianco, A. T. (2003). Speed/accuracy decisions in task performance: Built-in trade-off or separate strategic concerns? *Organizational Behavior and Human Decision Processes*, 90, 148–164.

Goldstein, I. L., & Ford, J. K. (2002). *Training in organizations: Needs assessment, development, and evaluation* (4th ed.). Canada: Wadsworth.

Guilford, J. P. (1968). *Creativity, intelligence, and their educational implications*. San Diego, CA: EDITS/Knapp.

Hambrick, D. C. (1982). Environmental scanning and organizational strategy. *Strategic Management Journal*, 3, 159–174.

Hambrick, D. C., & Snow, C. (1977). A contextual model of strategic decision making in organizations. *Academy of Management Proceedings*, 109–112.

Hammond, K. J. (1990). Case-based planning: A framework for planning from experience. *Cognitive Science*, 14, 385–443.

Harkrider, L. N., Thiel, C. E., Bagdasarov, Z., Mumford, M. D., Johnson, J. F., Connelly, S., & Devenport, L. D. (2012). Improving case-based ethics training with codes of conduct and forecasting content. *Ethics & Behavior*, 22(4), 258–280.

Hayes-Roth, B., & Hayes-Roth, F. (1979). A cognitive model of planning. *Cognitive Science*, 3, 275–310.

Henricks, M. (2008). Do you really need a business plan? *Entrepreneur*, 36(12), 92–95.

Hershey, D. A., Walsh, D. A., Read, S. J., & Chulef, A. S. (1990). The effects of expertise on financial problem-solving: Evidence for goal-directed problem solving scripts. *Organizational Behavior and Human Decision Processes*, 46, 77–101.

Hofstede, G. (1993). Cultural constraints in management theories. *The Academy of Management Executive*, 7(1), 81–94.

Hollenbeck, J. R., & Klein, H. J. (1987). Goal commitment and the goal-setting process: Problems, prospects, and proposals for future research. *Journal of Applied Psychology*, 72, 212–220.

Hrebiniak, L. G. (2005). *Making strategy work: Leading effective execution and change*. Upper Saddle River, NJ: Pearson Education.

Hunter, S. T., Bedell-Avers, K. E., Hunsicker, C. M., Mumford, M. D., & Ligon, G. S. (2008). Applying multiple knowledge structures in creative thought: Effects on idea generation and problem-solving. *Creativity Research Journal*, 20(2), 137–154.

Kettner, N. W., Guilford, J. P., & Christensen, P. R. (1959). A factor-analytic study across the domains of reasoning, creativity, and evaluation. *Psychological Monographs: General and Applied*, 73, 1–31.

Kinicki, A., & Williams, B. (2013). *Management: A practical introduction* (6th ed.). New York: McGraw Hill/Irwin.

Kohn, N. W., Paulus, P. B., & Korde, R. M. (2011). Conceptual combinations and subsequent creativity. *Creativity Research Journal*, 23(3), 203–210.

Kolodner, J. L. (Ed.) (1993). *Case-based learning*. Dordrecht, Netherlands: Kluwer Academic.

Ku, G. (2008). Before escalation: Behavioral and effective forecasting in escalation of commitment. *Personality and Social Psychology Bulletin*, 1477–1491.

Kuhn, T. S. (1970). *The structure of scientific revolutions*. Chicago, IL: The Chicago Press.

Latham, G. (2004). The motivational benefits of goal-setting. *Academy of Management Executive*, 18, 126–129.

Leighton, R. M. (1963). Overlord revisited: An interpretation of American strategy in the European War, 1942–1944. *The American Historical Review*, 68, 919–937.

Ligon, G. S., Wallace, J. H., & Osburn, H. K. (2011). Experiential development and mentoring processes for leaders for innovation. *Advances in Developing Human Resources*, 13(3), 297–317.

Locke, E. A., & Latham, G. P. (1990). Work motivation and satisfaction: Light at the end of the tunnel. *Psychological Science*, 1, 240–246.

Locke, E. A., & Latham, G. P. (2002). Building a practically useful theory of goal setting and task motivation: A 35-year odyssey. *American Psychologist*, 57, 705–717.

Locke, E. A., Shaw, K. N., Saari, L. M., & Latham, G. P. (1981). Goal setting and task performance, 1969–1980. *Psychological Bulletin*, 90, 125–152.

Lonergan, D. C., Scott, G. M., & Mumford, M. D. (2004). Evaluative aspects of creative thought: Effects of appraisal and revision standards. *Creativity Research Journal*, 16, 231–246.

Mahon, J. F., & Murray, E. A. (1981). Strategic planning for regulated companies. *Strategic Management Journal*, 2(3), 251–262.

Marcy, R. T., & Mumford, M. D. (2007). Social innovation: Enhancing creative performance through causal analysis. *Creativity Research Journal*, 19, 123–140.

Marta, S., Leritz, L. E., & Mumford, M. D. (2005). Leadership skills and the group performance: Situational demands, behavioral requirements, and planning. *Leadership Quarterly*, 16, 97–120.

Miles, R. E., Snow, C. C., Meyer, A. D., & Coleman, H. J., Jr. (1978). Organizational strategy, structure, and process. *Academy of Management Review*, 3, 546–562.

Mintzberg, H. (1975). Making management information useful. *Management Review*, 64, 30–42.

Mintzberg, H. (1979). An emerging strategy of "direct" research. *Administrative Science Quarterly*, 24(4), 582–589.

Mintzberg, H. (1987). *Crafting strategy*. Boston, MA: Harvard Business School Press.

Mumford, M. D. (2000). Managing creative people: Strategies and tactics for innovation. *Human Resources Management Review*, 10, 313–351.

Mumford, M. D., Mobley, M. I., Reiter-Palmon, R., Uhlman, C. E., & Doares, L. M. (1991). Process analytic models of creative capacities. *Creativity Research Journal*, 4, 91–122.

Mumford, M. D., Peterson, N. G., & Childs, R. A. (1999). Basic and cross-functional skills. In N. G. Peterson, M. D. Mumford, W. C. Borman, P. R. Jeanneret, & E. A. Fleishman (Eds.), *An occupational information system for the 21st century: The development of O*NET* (pp. 49–69). Washington, DC: American Psychological Association.

Mumford, M. D., Schultz, R. A., & Osburn, H. K. (2000). Planning in organizations: Performance as a multi-level phenomenon. *Research in Multi Level Issues*, 1, 3–65.

Mumford, M. D., Schultz, R., & Van Doorn, J. A. (2001). Performance in planning: Processes, requirements, and errors. *Review of General Psychology*, 5, 213–240.

Mumford, M. D., Eubanks, D. L., & Murphy, S. T. (2007). Creating the conditions for success: Best practices in leading for innovation. In J. A. Conger & R. E. Riggio (Eds.), *The practice of leadership: Developing the next generation of leaders* (pp. 129–149). San Francisco, CA: Jossey-Bass.

Mumford, M. D., Bedell-Avers, K. E., & Hunter, S. T. (2008). Planning for innovation: A multi-level perspective. *Research in Multi Level Issues*, 7, 107–154.

Mumford, M. D., Connelly, S., Brown, R. P., Murphy, S. T., Hill, J. H., Antes, A. L., Waples, E. P., & Devenport, L. D. (2008). A sensemaking approach to ethics training for scientists: Preliminary evidence of training effectiveness. *Ethics & Behavior*, 18(4), 315–339.

Mumford, M. D., Medeiros, K. E., & Partlow, P. J. (2012). Creative thinking: Processes, strategies, and knowledge. *The Journal of Creative Behavior*, 36, 30–47.

Nutt, P. C. (1984). Types of organizational decision processes. *Administrative Science Quarterly*, 29(3), 414–450.

Osburn, H. K., & Mumford, M. D. (2006). Creativity and planning: Training interventions to develop creative problem-solving skills. *Creativity Research Journal*, 18, 173–190.

Pant, P. N., & Starbuck, W. H. (1990). Innocents in the forest: Forecasting and research methods. *Journal of Management*, 16, 433–460.

Patnaik, R. (2012). Strategic planning through complexity: Overcoming impediments to forecast and schedule. *The IUP Journal of Business Strategy*, 9(1), 27–36.

Porac, J. F., & Thomas, H. (1990). Taxonomic mental models in competitor definition. *The Academy of Management Review*, 15, 224–240.

Redmond, M. R., Mumford, M. D., & Teach, R. (1993). Putting creativity to work: Effects of leader behavior on subordinate creativity. *Organizational Behavior and Human Decision Processes*, 55(1), 120–151.

Reeves, L., & Weisberg, R. W. (1994). The role of content and abstract information in analogical transfer. *Psychological Bulletin*, 115, 381–400.

Robledo, I. C., Hester, K. S., Peterson, D. R., Barrett, J. D., Day, E. A., Hougen, D. P., Mumford, M. D. (2012). Errors and understanding: The effects of error-management training on creative problem-solving. *Creativity Research Journal*, 24, 220–234.

Rodan, S. (2002). Innovation and heterogeneous knowledge in managerial contact networks. *Journal of Knowledge Management*, 6, 152–163.

Runco, M. A., & Chand, I. (1994). Problem finding, evaluative thinking, and creativity. In M. A. Runco (Ed.), *Problem finding, problem solving, and creativity* (pp. 40–76). New York: Ablex.

Saavedra, R., Earley, P. C., & Van Dyne, L. (1993). Complex interdependence in task-performing groups. *Journal of Applied Psychology*, 78, 61–72.

Salancik, G. R., & Pfeffer, J. (1978). A social information processing approach to job attitudes and task design. *Administrative Science Quarterly*, 23, 224–253.

Scott, G. M., Leritz, L. E., & Mumford, M. D. (2004). The effectiveness of creativity training: A meta-analysis. *Creativity Research Journal*, 16, 361–388.

Scott, G. M., Lonergan, D. C., & Mumford, M. D. (2005). Contractual combination: Alternative knowledge structures, alternative heuristics. *Creativity Research Journal*, 17, 21–36.

Shipman, A. S., Byrne, C. L., & Mumford, M. D. (2010). Leader vision formation and forecasting: The effects of forecasting extent, resources, and timeframe. *The Leadership Quarterly*, 21, 439–456.

Shuman, J., & Seeger, J. (1986). The theory and practice of strategic management in smaller rapid growth firms. *American Journal of Small Business*, 11, 7–18.

Smith, K., & Locke, E. A. (1990). Goal setting, planning and organizational performance: An experimental simulation. *Organizational Behavior and Human Decision Processes*, 46, 118–134.

Speier, C., Valacich, J. S., & Vessey, I. (1999). The influence of task interruption on individual decision making: An information overload perspective. *Decision Sciences*, 30, 337–360.

Staw, B. M. (1981). Escalation of commitment. *PsyCritiques*, 26, 21–22.

Teger, A. I. (1980). *Too much invested to quit: The psychology of the escalation of conflict*. New York: Pergamon Press.

Thomas, J. B., & McDaniel, R. R. (1990). Interpreting strategic issues: Effects of strategy and the information-processing structure of top management teams. *Academy of Management Journal*, 33, 286–306.

Wang, E. T. G., & Tai, J. C. F. (2003). Factors affecting information systems planning effectiveness: Organizational contexts and planning. *Information Systems Planning*, 40(4), 287–303.

Weisberg, R. W. (2006). *Creativity: Understanding innovation in problem solving, science, invention, and the arts*. Hoboken, NJ: John Wiley.

Wong, A., Tjosvold, D., & Yu, Z. (2005). Organizational partnerships in China: Self-interest, goal interdependence, and opportunism. *Journal of Applied Psychology*, 90, 782–791.

Xiao, Y., Milgram, P., & Doyle, D. J. (1997). Planning behavior and its functional role in interactions with complex systems, *IEEE Transactions on Systems, Man and Cybernetics, Part A: Systems and Humans*, 27(3), 313–325.

INDEX